WEBSTER'S REFERENCE LIBRARY

STUDENTS' COMPANION

GEDDES &
GROSSET

Published 2005 by Geddes & Grosset,
David Dale House, New Lanark, ML11 9DJ, Scotland

Editorial consultant: Betty Kirkpatrick

© 2002 Geddes & Grosset

First printed 2002
Reprinted 2002, 2003, 2004 (twice), 2005

This book is not published by the original publishers
of *Webster's Dictionary* or by their successors

ISBN 10: 1 84205 167 9
ISBN 13: 978 1 84205 167 2

Printed and bound in Poland

POLSKABOOK

Contents

APPENDIX

GRAMMAR AND USAGE

Grammar

abstract noun a noun which is the name of a thing that cannot be touched but refers to a quality, concept or idea. Examples of abstract nouns include 'anger', 'beauty', 'courage', 'Christianity', 'danger', 'fear', 'greed', 'hospitality', 'ignorance', 'jealousy', 'kudos', 'loyalty', 'Marxism', 'need', 'obstinacy', 'pain', 'quality', 'resistance', 'safety', 'truth', 'unworthiness', 'vanity', 'wisdom', 'xenophobia', 'youth', 'zeal'. *See also* **concrete noun.**

active voice one of the two voices that verbs are divided into, the other being passive voice. In verbs in the active voice, commonly called **active verbs**, the subject of the verb performs the action described by the verb. Thus, in the sentence 'The boy threw the ball', 'throw' is in the active voice since the subject of the verb (the boy) is doing the throwing. Similarly, in the sentence 'Her mother was driving the car', 'driving' is in the active voice since it is the subject of the sentence (her mother) that is doing the driving. Similarly, in the sentence 'We saw the cows in the field', 'saw' is the active voice since it is the subject of the sentence (we) that is doing the seeing.

adjectival clause a kind of subordinate clause that describes or modifies a noun or pronoun. It is better known by the name relative clause.

adjective a word that describes or gives information about a noun or pronoun. It is said to qualify a noun or pronoun since it limits the word it describes in some way, by making it more specific. Thus, adding the adjective 'red' to 'book' limits 'book', since it means we can forget about books of any other colour. Similarly, adding 'large' to 'book' limits it, since it means we can forget about books of any other size.

Adjectives tell us something about the colour, size, number, quality or classification of a noun or pronoun, as in 'purple curtains', 'jet-black hair', 'bluish eyes'; 'tiny baby', 'large houses', 'biggish gardens', 'massive estates'; five children', 'twenty questions', 'seventy-five books'; 'sad people', 'joyful occasions', 'delicious food', 'civil engineering', 'nuclear physics', 'modern languages', 'Elizabethan drama'.

adverb a word that adds to our information about a verb, as in 'work rapidly'; about an adjective, as in 'an extremely beautiful young woman'; or about another adverb, as in 'sleeping very soundly'. Adverbs are said to modify the words to which they apply since they limit the words in some way and make them more specific. Thus, adding 'slowly' to 'walk', as in 'They walked slowly down the hill', limits the verb 'walk' since all other forms of 'walk', such as 'quickly', 'lazily', etc, have been discarded.

adverbial clause a subordinate clause that modifies the main or principal clause by adding information about time, place, concession, condition, manner, purpose and result, as in 'He left after the meal was over', 'They left it where they found it', 'Wherever I went I saw signs of poverty', 'I have to admire his speech, although I disagree with what he said', 'He does his best at school work even though he is not very good at it', 'Whilst I myself do not like him, I can understand why he is popular', 'We cannot go unless we get permission', 'He looked at her as if he hated her', 'They will have to work long hours in order to make that amount of money', 'They started to run so as to get home before it rained'; and 'He fell awkwardly so that he broke his leg.' Adverbial clauses usually follow the main clause but most of them can be put in front of the main clause for reasons of emphasis or style.

agent noun a noun that refers to someone who is the 'doer' of the action of a verb. It is usually spelt ending in either *-er*, as 'enquirer', or in *-or*, as in 'investigator' and 'supervisor', but frequently either of these endings is acceptable, as 'adviser/advisor'.

agreement or **concord** the agreeing of two or more elements in a clause or sentence, i.e. they take the same number, person or gender. In English the most common form of agreement is that between subject and verb, and this usually involves **number agreement**. This means that singular nouns are usually accompanied by singular verbs, as in 'She looks well', 'He is working late' and 'The boy has passed the exam', and that plural nouns are usually accompanied by plural verbs, as in 'They look well', 'They are working late' and 'The boys have passed the exam'.

Problems arise when the noun in question can be either singular or plural, for example, 'audience', 'committee', 'crowd', 'family', 'government', 'group'. Such nouns take a singular verb if the user is regarding the people or items referred to by the noun as a group, as in 'The family is moving house', or as individuals, as in 'The family are quarrelling over where to go on holiday'.

Compound subjects, that is two or more nouns acting as the subject, whether singular or plural, joined with 'and', are used with a plural noun, as in 'My friend and I are going to the cinema tonight' and 'James and John are leaving today', unless the two nouns together represent a single concept, as 'brandy and soda', in which case the verb is in the singular, as in 'Brandy and soda is his favourite drink' and 'cheese and pickle' in 'Cheese and pickle is the only sandwich filling available'.

Indefinite pronouns such as 'anyone', 'everyone', 'no one', 'someone', 'either', 'neither' are singular and should be followed by a singular verb, as in 'Each of the flats is self-contained', 'Everyone is welcome', 'No one is allowed in without a ticket' and 'Neither is quite what I am looking for'.

Agreement with reference to both number and gender affects pronouns, as in 'She blames herself', 'He could have kicked himself' and 'They asked themselves why they had got involved'. Problems arise when the pronoun is indefinite and so the sex of the person is unspecified. Formerly in such cases the masculine pronouns were assumed to be neutral and so 'Each of the pupils was asked to hand in his work' was considered quite acceptable. The rise of feminism has led to a questioning of this assumption and alternatives have been put forward. These include 'Each of the pupils was asked to hand in his/her (or his or her) work', but some people feel that this is clumsy. Another alternative is 'Each of the pupils was asked to hand in their work'. Although it is ungrammatical, this convention is becoming quite acceptable in modern usage. To avoid both the clumsiness of the former and the ungrammatical nature of the latter, it is possible to cast the whole sentence in the plural, as in 'All the pupils were asked to hand in their work'.

also an adverb that should not be used as a conjunction instead of 'and'. Thus sentences such as 'Please send me some apples, also some pears' are grammatically incorrect.

although a conjunction that is used to introduce a subordinate adverbial clause of concession, as in 'They are very happy although they are poor', meaning 'Despite the fact they are poor they are happy'. 'Though' or 'even though' can be substituted for 'although', as in 'they are very happy even though they are poor'. *See* **adverbial clause** and **conjunction**.

and a conjunction that is called a coordinating conjunction because it joins elements of language that are of equal status. The elements may be words, as in 'cows and horses', 'John and James', 'provide wine and beer'; phrases, as in 'working hard and playing hard' and 'trying to look after her children and her elderly parents'; clauses, as in 'John has decided to emigrate and his brother has decided to join him' and 'He has lost his job and he now has no money'. When a coordinating conjunction is used, the subject of the second clause can sometimes be omitted if it is the same as the subject of the first clause, as in 'They have been forced to sell the house and are very sad about it'.

The use of and at the beginning of a sentence is disliked by many people. It should be used only for deliberate effect, as in 'And then he saw the monster', or in informal contexts.

Other coordinating conjunctions include 'but', 'or', 'yet', 'both... and', 'either... or', and 'neither.... nor', as in 'poor but honest' and 'the blue dress or the green one'.

antecedent a term that refers to the noun or noun phrase in a main clause to which a relative pronoun in a relative clause refers back. Thus in the sentence 'People who live dangerously frequently get hurt', 'people' is an antecedent. Similarly, in the sentence 'The child identified the old man who attacked her', 'the old man' is the antecedent. *See* **relative clause**.

any a pronoun that may take either a singular or plural verb, depending on the context. When a singular noun is used, a singular verb is used, as in 'Is any of the cloth still usable?' 'Are any of the children coming?' When a plural noun is used, either a plural or a singular verb can be used, the singular verb being more formal, as in 'Did you ask if any of his friends were/was there?'.

anyone a pronoun that should be used with a singular verb, as in 'Has anyone seen my book?' and 'Is anyone coming to the lecture?' To be grammatically correct, anyone should be followed, where relevant, by a singular, not plural, personal pronoun or possessive adjective, but, in order to avoid the sexist 'his', this involves sentences such as 'Has anyone left his/her book?' Because this construction is rather clumsy, there is a growing tendency to use 'their' and be ungrammatical.

apposition a term for a noun or a phrase that provides further information about another noun or phrase. Both nouns and phrases refer to the same person or thing. In the phrase 'Peter Jones, our managing director', ' Peter Jones' and 'our managing director' are said to be in apposition. Similarly, in the phrase 'his cousin, the chairman of the firm', 'his cousin' and 'the chairman of the firm' are in apposition.

as a conjunction that can introduce either a subordinate adverbial clause of time, as in 'I caught sight of him as I was leaving', a subordinate adverbial clause of manner, as in 'He acted as he promised', and a subordinate adverbial clause of reason, as in 'As it's Saturday he doesn't have to work'. it is also used in the as....as construction, as in 'She doesn't play as well as her sister does'.

The construction may be followed by a subject pronoun or an object pronoun, according to sense. In the sentence 'He plays as well as she', which is a slightly shortened form of 'She plays as well as he does', 'he' is a subject pronoun. In informal English the subject pronoun often becomes an object pronoun, as in 'She plays as well as him'. In the sentence 'They hate their father as much as her', 'her' is an object and the sentence means 'They hate their father as much as they hate her', but in the sentence 'They hate their father as much as she', 'she' is a subject and the sentence means 'They hate their father as much as she does'. *See* **adverbial clause** and **conjunction**.

attributive adjective a term for an adjective that is placed immediately before the noun that it qualifies. In the phrases 'a red dress', 'the big house' and 'an enjoyable evening', 'red', 'big' and 'enjoyable' are attributive adjectives.

auxiliary verb a verb that is used in forming tenses, moods and voices of other verbs. These include 'be', 'do' and 'have'.

The verb 'to be' is used as an auxiliary verb with the *-ing* form of the main verb to form the continuous present tense, as in 'They are living abroad just now' and 'We were thinking of going on holiday but we changed our minds'.

The verb 'to be' is used as an auxiliary verb with the past participle of the main verb to form the passive voice, as in 'Her hands were covered in blood' and 'These toys are manufactured in China'.

The verb 'to have' is used as an auxiliary verb along with the past participle of the main verb to form the perfect tenses, as in 'They have filled the post', 'She had realized her mistake' and 'They wished that they had gone earlier'.

The verb 'to be' is used as an auxiliary verb along with the main verb to form negative sentences, as in 'She is not accepting the job'. The verb 'to do' is used as an auxiliary verb along with the main verb to form negative sentences, as in 'he does not believe her'. It is also used along with the main verb to form questions, as in 'Does he know that she's gone?' and to form sentences in which the verb is emphasized, as in 'She *does* want to go'. *See* **modal verb**.

base the basic uninflected form of a verb. It is found as the infinitive form, as in 'to go' and 'to take', and as the imperative form, as in 'Go away!' and 'Take it!' It is also the form that the verb in the present indicative tense takes, except for the third person singular, as in 'I always go there on a Sunday' and 'They go there regularly.'

be *see* **auxiliary verb**.

because a conjunction that introduces a subordinate adverbial clause of reason, as in 'They sold the house because they are going abroad' and 'Because she is shy she never goes to parties'. It is often used incorrectly in such constructions as 'The reason they went away is because they were bored'. This should be rephrased as either 'The reason that they went away is that they were bored' or 'They went away because they were bored'. *See* **adverbial clause**.

before a word that can either be a preposition, an adverb or a conjunction. As a preposition it means either 'coming or going in front of in time', as in 'He was the chairman before this one', or coming or going in front of in place, as in 'She went before him into the restaurant'. As an adverb it means 'at a time previously', as in 'I told you before' and 'He has been married before'. As a conjunction it introduces a subordinate adverbial clause of time, as in 'The guests arrived before she was ready for them' and 'Before I knew it they had arrived'. *See* **adverbial clause**.

both a word that can be used in several ways: as a determiner, as in 'He broke both his arms' and 'He lost both his sons in the war'; as a pronoun, as in 'I don't mind which house we rent, I like them both' and 'Neither of them work here. The boss sacked them both'; as a conjunction, as in 'He both likes and admires her' and 'She is both talented and honest'. Both can sometimes be followed by 'of'. 'Both their children are grown up' and 'Both of their children are grown up' are both acceptable. Care should be taken to avoid using both unnecessarily. In the sentence 'The two items are both identical', 'both' is redundant.

but a conjunction that connects two opposing ideas. It is a coordinating conjunction in that it connects two elements of equal status. The elements may be words, as in 'not James but John'; phrases, as in 'working hard but not getting anywhere' and 'trying to earn a living but not succeeding'; clauses, as in 'He has arrived but his sister is late', 'I know her but I have never met him' and 'He likes reading but she prefers to watch TV'. It should not be used when no element of contrast is present. Thus the following sentence should be rephrased, at least in formal English—'She is not professionally trained but taught herself'. The two clauses are in fact agreeing, not disagreeing, with each other and so, strictly speaking, but should not be used.

The use of but at the beginning of a sentence is disliked by many people. It should be used only for deliberate effect or in informal contexts.

case one of the forms in the declension of a noun, pronoun or adjective in a sentence.

clause a group of words containing a finite verb which forms part of a compound or complex sentence. See main clause, subordinate clauses, adverbial clause, noun clause and relative clause.

commands these are expressed in the imperative mood, as in 'Be quiet!', 'Stop crying!', 'Go away!'

common noun simply the name of an ordinary, everyday non-specific thing or person, as opposed to proper nouns, which refer to the names of particular individuals or specific places. Common nouns include 'baby', 'cat', 'girl', 'hat', 'park', 'sofa' and 'table'.

comparison of adjectives this is achieved in two different ways. Some adjectives form their comparative by adding *-er* to the positive or absolute form, as in 'braver', 'louder', 'madder', 'shorter' and 'taller'. Other adjectives form their comparative by using 'more' in conjunction with them, as in 'more beautiful', 'more realistic', 'more suitable' and 'more tactful'. Which is the correct form is largely a matter of length. One-syllable adjectives, such as 'loud', add *-er*, as 'louder'. Two-syllable adjectives sometimes have both forms as a possibility, as in 'gentler/more gentle', and 'cleverest/most clever'. Adjectives with three or more syllables usually form their comparatives with 'more', as in 'more comfortable', 'more gracious', 'more regular' and 'more understanding'. Some adjectives are irregular in their comparative forms, as in 'good/better', 'bad/worse', 'many/more'. Only if they begin with *un-* are they likely to end in *-er*, as in 'untrustworthier'.

Some adjectives by their very definitions do not normally have a comparative form, for example 'unique'.

complement the equivalent of the object in a clause with a linking verb. In the sentence 'Jack is a policeman', 'a policeman' is the complement. In the sentence 'Jane is a good mother', 'a good mother' is the complement', and in the sentence 'His son is an excellent football player', 'an excellent football player' is the complement.

complex sentence a type of sentence in which there is a main clause and one or more subordinate clauses. The sentence 'We went to visit him although he had been unfriendly to us' is a complex sentence since it is composed of a main clause and one subordinate clause ('although he had been unfriendly to us'). The sentence 'We wondered where he had gone and why he was upset' is a complex sentence since it has a main clause and two subordinate clauses ('where he had gone' and 'why he was upset').

compound sentence a type of sentence with more than one clause and linked by a co-ordinating conjunction, such as 'and' or 'but', as in 'He applied for a new job and got it' and 'I went to the cinema but I didn't enjoy the film'.

concord *see* **number agreement**.

concrete noun the name of something that one can touch, as opposed to an abstract noun, which one cannot. Concrete nouns include 'bag', 'glass', 'plate', 'pot', 'clothes', 'field', 'garden', 'flower', 'potato', 'foot' and 'shoe'. *See* **abstract noun**.

conjunction a word that connects words, clauses or sentences. Conjunctions are of two types. A **coordinating conjunction** joins units of equal status, as in 'bread and butter', 'We asked for some food and we got it'. A **subordinating conjunction** joins a dependent or subordinating clause to main verbs: in 'We asked him why he was

there', 'why he was there' is a subordinate clause and thus 'why' is a subordinating conjunction.

content words *see* **function word**.

continuous tenses *see* **tense**.

contraction *see* **abbreviation** in **Style** section.

copula *see* **linking verb**.

copular verb *see* **equative** and **linking verb**.

count noun is the same as countable noun.

countable noun is one which can be preceded by 'a' and can take a plural, as in 'hat/hats', 'flower/flowers'. *See also* **uncountable noun**.

dangling participle a participle that has been misplaced in a sentence. A participle is often used to introduce a phrase that is attached to a subject mentioned later in a sentence, as in 'Worn out by the long walk, she fell to the ground in a faint'. 'Worn out' is the participle and 'she' the subject. Another example is 'Laughing in glee at having won, she ordered some champagne'. In this sentence 'laughing' is the participle and 'she' is the subject. It is a common error for such a participle not to be related to any subject, as in 'Imprisoned in the dark basement, it seemed a long time since she had seen the sun'. This participle is said to be 'dangling'. Another example of a dangling participle is contained in 'Living alone, the days seemed long'.

It is also a common error for a participle to be related to the wrong subject in a sentence, as in 'Painting the ceiling, some of the plaster fell on his head', 'Painting' is the participle and should go with a subject 'he'. Instead it goes with 'some of the plaster'. Participles in this situation are more correctly known as **misrelated participles**, although they are also called dangling participles.

declarative mood the same as **indicative mood**.

declarative sentence a sentence that conveys information. The subject precedes the verb in it. Examples include 'They won the battle', 'He has moved to another town', 'Lots of people go there' and 'There is a new person in charge'.

declension the variation of the form of a noun, adjective or pronoun to show different cases, such as nominative and accusa-

degree   **distributive pronoun**

tive. It also refers to the class into which such words are placed, as in first declension, second declension, etc. The term applies to languages such as Latin but is not applicable to English.

degree a level of comparison of gradable adjectives. The degrees of comparison comprise **absolute** or **positive**, as in 'big', 'calm', 'dark', 'fair', 'hot', 'late', 'short' and 'tall'; **comparative**, as in 'bigger', 'calmer', 'darker', 'fairest', 'hotter', 'late', 'shorter' and 'taller'; **superlative**, as in 'biggest', 'calmest', 'darkest', 'fairest', 'hottest', 'latest', 'shortest' and 'tallest'.

Degree can also refer to adverbs. Adverbs of degree include 'extremely', 'very', 'greatly', 'rather', 'really', 'remarkably', 'terribly', as in 'an extremely rare case', 'a very old man', 'He's remarkably brave' and 'We're terribly pleased'.

demonstrative determiner a determiner that is used to indicate things or people in relationship to the speaker or writer in space or time. 'This' and 'these' indicate nearness to the speaker, as in 'Will you take this book home?' and 'These flowers are for you'. 'That' and 'those' indicate distance from the speaker, as in 'Get that creature out of here!' and 'Aren't those flowers over there beautiful!'

demonstrative pronoun a pronoun that is similar to a demonstrative determiner except that it stands alone in place of a noun rather than preceding a noun, as in 'I'd like to give you this', 'What is that?', 'These are interesting books' and 'Those are not his shoes'.

dependent clause a clause that cannot stand alone and make sense, unlike an independent or main clause. Dependent clauses depend on the main clause. The term is the same as subordinate clause.

determiner a word that is used in front of a noun or pronoun to tell us something about it. Unlike an adjective, it does not, strictly speaking, 'describe' a noun or pronoun. Determiners are divided into the following categories: **articles** (a, an, the) as in 'a cat', 'an eagle', 'the book'; **demonstrative determiners** (this, that, these, those), as in 'this girl', 'that boy' and 'those people'; **possessive determiners** (my, your, his/

her/its, our, their), as in 'my dog', 'her house', 'its colour', 'their responsibility'; **numbers** (one, two, three, four, etc, first, second, third, fourth, etc), as in 'two reasons', 'five ways', 'ten children'; and **indefinite** or **general determiners** (all, another, any, both, each, either, enough, every, few, fewer, less, little, many, most, much, neither, no, other, several, some), as in 'both parents', 'enough food', 'several issues'. Many words used as determiners are also pronouns. *See* **adjective**; **demonstrative determiner**; **number**.

direct object the noun, noun phrase, noun or nominal clause or pronoun that is acted upon by the action of a transitive verb. In the sentence 'She bought milk', 'bought' is a transitive verb and 'milk' is a noun which is the direct object. In the sentence 'She bought loads of clothes', 'bought' is a transitive verb and 'loads of clothes' is the direct object. In the sentence 'He knows what happened', 'knows' is a transitive verb and 'what happened' is a 'noun clause' or 'nominal clause'. A direct object is frequently known just as object *See* **indirect object**.

direct speech the reporting of speech by repeating exactly the actual words used by the speaker, as in 'Peter said, "I am tired of this." ' *See* **quotation marks** in **Punctuation** section.

distributive pronoun a pronoun that refers to individual members of a class or group. These include 'each', 'either', 'neither', 'none', 'everyone', 'no one'. Such pronouns, where relevant, should be accompanied by singular verbs and singular personal pronouns, as in 'All the men are to be considered for the new posts. Each is to send in his application'. Problems arise when the sex of the noun to which the distributive pronoun refers back is either unknown or unspecified. Formerly it was the convention to treat such nouns as masculine and so to make the distributive pronoun masculine, as in 'All pupils must obey the rule.. Nowadays this convention is frequently considered to be unacceptably sexist and attempts have been made to get round this. One solution is to use 'him/her' (or 'him or her'), etc, as in 'The students have received a directive from the professor. Each is to produce his/her essay by tomorrow.' This convention is considered by many people to be clumsy. They prefer to be ungrammatical and use a plural personal pronoun, as in 'The pupils are being punished. Each is to inform their parents'. This use Is becomong increasingly common, even in textbooks. Where possible, it is preferable to rephrase sentences to avoid being either sexist or ungrammatical, as in 'All of the pupils must tell their parents.'

Each, either, etc, in such contexts is fairly formal. In less formal situations 'each of', 'either of', etc, is more usual, as in 'Each of the boys will have to train really hard to win' and 'Either of the dresses is perfectly suitable'.

do an auxiliary verb that is used to form negative forms, as in, 'I do not agree with you', 'They do not always win', 'He does not wish to go' and 'She did not approve of their behaviour'. It is also used to form interrogative forms, as in 'Do you agree?', 'Does she know about it?', 'Did you see that?' and 'I prefer to go by train. Don't you?' Do is also used for emphasis, as in 'I do believe you're right' and 'They do know, don't they?'

double passive a clause that contains two verbs in the passive, the second of which is an infinitive, as in 'The goods are expected to be despatched some time this week'. Some examples of double passives are clumsy or ungrammatical and should be avoided, as in 'Redundancy notices are proposed to be issued next week'.

dual gender a category of nouns in which there is no indication of gender. The nouns referred to include a range of words used for people, and occasionally animals, which can be of either gender. Unless the gender is specified we do not know the sex of the person referred to. Such words include 'artist', 'author', 'poet', 'singer', 'child', 'pupil', 'student', 'baby', 'parent', 'teacher', 'dog'. Such words give rise to problems with accompanying singular pronouns. *See* **each**.

dummy subject a subject that has no intrinsic meaning but is inserted to maintain a balanced grammatical structure. In the sentences 'It has started to rain' and 'It is

nearly midnight', 'it' is a dummy subject. In the sentences 'There is nothing else to say' and 'There is no reason for his behaviour', 'there' is a dummy subject.

dynamic verb a verb with a meaning that indicates action, as 'work' in 'They work hard', 'play' in 'The boys play football at the weekend' and 'come' in 'The girls come here every Sunday'.

each a word that can be either a determiner or a distributive pronoun. Each as a determiner is used before a singular noun and is accompanied by a singular verb, as in 'Each candidate is to reapply', 'Each athlete has a place in the final', 'Each country is represented by a head of state' and 'Each chair was covered in chintz'.

Each of can sometimes be used instead of each, as in 'each of the candidates'. Again a singular verb is used. If the user wishes to emphasize the fact that something is true about every member of a group, **each one of** should be used and not 'every', as in 'Each one of them feels guilty', 'Each one of us has a part to play.

As a pronoun, each also takes a singular verb, as in 'They hate each other. Each is plotting revenge', 'These exercises are not a waste of time. Each provides valuable experience'.

Each, where relevant, should be accompanied by a singular personal pronoun, as in 'Each girl has to provide her own sports equipment', 'Each of the men is to take a turn at working night shift', 'The boys are all well off and each can afford the cost of the holiday' and 'There are to be no exceptions among the women staff. Each one has to work full time'.

Problems arise when the noun that each refers back to is of unknown or unspecified sex. Formerly nouns in such situations were assumed to be masculine, as in 'Each pupil was required to bring his own tennis racket' and 'Each of the students has to provide himself with a tape recorder'. Nowadays such a convention is regarded as being sexist and the use of 'he/her', 'his/her', etc, is proposed, as in 'Each pupil was required to bring his/her (or 'his or her') own tennis racket' and 'Each student has to provide himself/herself (or 'himself or herself') with a tape recorder'. Even in written English such a convention can be clumsy and it is even more so in spoken English. For this reason many people decide to be ungrammatical and opt for 'Each pupil was required to bring their own tennis racket' and 'Each student has to provide themselves with a tape recorder'. This Is becoming Increasingly acceptable, even In textbooks.

Both sexism and grammatical error can be avoided by rephrasing such sentences, as in 'All pupils are required to bring their own tennis rackets' and 'All students have to provide themselves with tape recorders'.

either a word that can be used as either a determiner or distributive pronoun. As a determiner it is used with a singular verb, as in 'Either hotel is expensive' and 'In principle they are both against the plan but is either likely to vote for it?'

Either of can be used instead of either. It is used before a plural noun, as in 'either of the applicants' and 'either of the houses'. It is accompanied by a singular verb, as in 'Either of the applicants is suitable' and 'Either of the houses is big enough for their family'.

Either can be used as a distributive pronoun and takes a singular verb, as in 'We have looked at both houses and either is suitable' and 'She cannot decide between the two dresses but either is appropriate for the occasion'. This use is rather formal.

In the **either .... or** construction, a singular verb is used if both subjects are singular, as in 'Either Mary or Jane knows what to do' and 'Either my mother or my father plans to be present'. A plural verb is used if both nouns involved are plural, as in 'Either men or women can play' and 'Either houses or flats are available'.

When a combination of singular and plural subjects is involved, the verb traditionally agrees with the subject that is nearer to it, as in 'Either his parents or his sister is going to come' and 'Either his grandmother or his parents are going to come'.

As a pronoun, either should be used only of two possibilities.

emphasizing adjective an adjective that is used for emphasis. 'Very' is an emphasizing

adjective in the sentence 'His very mother dislikes him' and 'own' is an emphasizing adjective in 'He likes to think that he is his own master'.

emphasizing adverb an adverb used for emphasis. 'Really' is an emphasizing adverb in the sentence 'She really doesn't care whether she lives or dies', and 'positively' is an emphasizing adverb in the sentence 'He positively does not want to know anything about it'.

emphatic pronoun a reflexive pronoun that is used for emphasis, as in 'He knows himself that he is wrong', 'She admitted herself that she had made a mistake' and 'The teachers themselves say that the headmaster is too strict'.

ending the final part of a word consisting of an inflection that is added to a base or root word. The '-ren' part of 'children' is an ending, the '-er' of 'poorer' is an ending and the '-ing' of 'falling' is an ending.

equative a term that indicates that one thing is equal to, or the same as, another. The verb 'to be' is sometimes known as an **equative verb** because it links a subject and complement that are equal to each other, as in 'He is a rogue' ('he' and 'rogue' refer to the same person) and 'His wife is a journalist' ('his wife' and 'journalist' refer to the same person). Other equative verbs include 'appear', 'become', 'look', 'remain' and 'seem', as in 'She looks a nasty person' and 'He became a rich man'. Such verbs are more usually known as **copular verbs**.

every a word used with a singular noun to indicate that all the members of a group are being referred to. It takes a singular verb, as in 'Every soldier must report for duty', 'Every machine is to be inspected' and 'Every house has a different view'. Every should also be accompanied, where relevant, by a singular pronoun, as in 'Every boy has his job to do', 'Every girl is to wear a dress' and 'Every machine is to be replaced'. Problems arise when the sex of the noun to which every refers is unknown or unspecified. Formerly it was the custom to assume such a noun to be masculine and to use masculine pronouns, as in 'Every pupil is to behave himself properly'. This assumption is now regarded as sexist, and

everyone   **future tense**

to avoid this 'he/she', 'him/her' and 'his/her' can be used. Many people feel that this convention can become clumsy and prefer to be ungrammatical by using 'they', 'them' and 'their', as in 'Every pupil is to behave themselves properly.' This use is becoming Increasingly common, even In textbooks. Many sentences of this kind can be rephrased to avoid being either sexist or ungrammatical, as in 'All pupils are to behave themselves properly'. *See* **each**.

everyone a pronoun that takes a singular verb, as in 'Everyone is welcome' and 'Everyone has the right to a decent standard of living'. In order to be grammatically correct, it should be accompanied, where relevant, by a singular personal pronoun but it is subject to the same kind of treatment as every.

feminine the term for the gender that indicates female persons or animals. It is the opposite of 'masculine'. The feminine gender demands the use of the appropriate pronoun, including 'she', 'her', 'hers' and 'herself', as in 'The girl tried to save the dog but *she* was unable to do so', 'The woman hurt *her* leg', 'Mary said that the book is *hers*', and 'The waitress cut *herself*'.

The feminine forms of words, formed by adding —*ess*, used to be common but many such forms are now thought to be sexist. Words such as 'author', 'sculptor', 'poet' are now considered to be neutral terms that can be used to refer to a man or a woman. Some -*ess* words are either still being used or are in a state of flux, as in 'actress'. *See* -**ess** in **Affixes** section.

finite clause a clause that contains a finite verb, as in 'when she sees him', 'after she had defeated him', and 'as they were sitting there'.

finite verb a verb that has a tense and has a subject with which it agrees in number and person. For example 'cries' is finite in the sentence 'The child cries most of the time', and 'looks' is finite in the sentence 'The old man looks ill'. However 'go' in the sentence 'He wants to go' is non-finite since it has no variation of tense and does not have a subject. Similarly in the sentence 'Sitting on the river-bank, he was lost in thought', 'sitting' is non-finite.

first person this refers to the person who is speaking or writing when referring to himself or herself. The **first person pronouns** are 'I', 'me', 'myself' and 'mine', with the plural forms being 'we', 'us', 'ourselves' and 'ours'. Examples include 'She said, "*I* am going home" ', ' "*I* am going shopping," he said', ' "*We* have very little money left," she said to her husband' and 'He said, "*We* shall have to leave now if we are to get there on time" '.

The **first person determiners** are 'my' and 'our', as in 'I have forgotten to bring *my* notebook' and 'We must remember to bring *our* books home.'

form word *see* **function word**.

fragmentary sentence *see* **major sentence**.

frequentative a term referring to a verb that expresses frequent repetition of an action. In English the verb endings -*le* and -*el* sometimes indicate the frequentative form, as in 'waddle' from 'wade', 'sparkle' from 'spark', 'crackle' from 'crack' and 'dazzle' from 'daze'. The ending -*er* can also indicate the frequentative form, as in 'stutter', 'spatter' and 'batter'.

function word a word that has very little meaning but is primarily of grammatical significance but merely performs a 'function' in a sentence. Function words include determiners, and prepositions such as in, on and up. Words that are not function words are sometimes known as **content words**.

Function word is also known as **form word** or **structure word**.

future perfect tense the tense of a verb that is formed by 'will' or 'shall' together with the perfect tense, as in 'They will have been married ten years next week', 'You will have finished work by this time tomorrow' and 'By the time Jane arrives here she will have been travelling non-stop for forty-eight hours'.

future tense the tense of a verb that describes actions or states that will occur at some future time. It is marked by 'will' and 'shall'. Traditionally 'shall' was used with subjects in the first person, as in 'I shall see you tomorrow' and 'We shall go there next week', and 'will' was used with subjects in the second and third person, as in 'You will find out next week', 'He will recognize her when he sees her' and 'They will be on the next train'. Formerly 'will' was used with the first person and 'shall' with the second and third person to indicate emphasis or insistence, as in 'I *will* go on my own' and 'We *will* be able to afford it'; 'You *shall* pay what you owe' and 'The children *shall* get a holiday'. In modern usage 'shall' is usually used only for emphasis or insistence, whether with the first, second or third person, except in formal contexts. Otherwise 'will' is used, as in 'I will go tomorrow', 'We will have to see', 'You will be surprised', and 'They will be on their way by now'.

The future tense can also be marked by 'be about to' plus the infinitive of the relevant verb or 'be going to' plus the infinitive of the relevant verb. Examples include 'We are about to leave for work', 'They are about to go on holiday', 'She is going to be late' and 'They are going to demolish the building'.

gemination the doubling of consonants before a suffix.

gender in the English language this usually refers to the natural distinctions of sex (or absence of sex) that exist, and nouns are classified according to these distinctions—masculine, feminine and neuter. Thus, 'man', 'boy', 'king', 'prince', 'emperor', 'duke', 'heir', 'son', 'brother', 'father', 'nephew', 'husband', 'bridegroom', 'widower', 'hero', 'cock', 'drake', 'fox' and 'lion' are masculine nouns. Similarly, 'girl', 'woman', 'queen', 'princess', 'empress', 'duchess', 'heiress', 'daughter', 'sister', 'mother', 'niece', 'wife', 'bride', 'widow', 'heroine', 'hen', 'duck', 'vixen' and 'lioness' are feminine nouns. Similarly, 'table', 'chair', 'desk', 'carpet', 'window', 'lamp', 'car', 'shop', 'dress', 'tie', 'newspaper', 'book', 'building' and 'town' are all neuter.

Some nouns in English can refer either to a man or a woman, unless the sex is indicated in the context. Such neutral nouns are sometimes said to have dual gender. Examples include 'author', 'singer', 'poet', 'sculptor', 'proprietor', 'teacher', 'parent', 'cousin', 'adult' and 'child'. Some words in this category were formerly automatically assumed to be masculine and several of them had feminine forms, such as 'authoress',

'poetess', 'sculptress' and 'proprietrix'. In modern times this was felt to be sexist and many of these feminine forms are now rarely used, for example, 'authoress' and 'poetess'. However some, such as actress and waitress, are still in common use.

genitive case a case that indicates possession or ownership. It is usually marked by s and an apostrophe. Many spelling errors centre on the position of the s in relation to the apostrophe. *See* **apostrophe** in **Spelling** section

gerund the *-ing* form of a verb when it functions as a noun. It is sometimes known as a **verbal noun**. It has the same form as the present participle but has a different function. For example, in the sentence 'He was jogging down the road', 'jogging' is the present participle in the verb phrase 'was jogging', but in the sentence 'Running is his idea of relaxation', 'running' is a gerund because it acts as a noun as the subject of the sentence. Similarly, in the sentence 'We were smoking when the teacher found us', 'smoking' is the present participle in the verb phrase 'were smoking', but in the sentence 'We were told that smoking is bad for our health', 'smoking' is a gerund since it acts as a noun as the subject of the clause.

get this verb is sometimes used to form the passive voice instead of the verb 'to be'. The use of the verb 'to get' to form the passive, as in 'They get married tomorrow', 'Our team got beaten today' and 'We got swindled by the con man' is sometimes considered to be more informal than the use of 'be'. Often there is more action involved when the get construction is used than when be is used, since get is a more dynamic verb, as in 'She was late leaving the pub because she got involved in an argument' and in 'It was her own fault that she got arrested by the police. She hit one of the constables'.

Get is frequently overused. Such overuse should be avoided, particularly in formal contexts. Get can often be replaced by a synonym such as 'obtain', 'acquire', 'receive', 'get hold of', etc. Thus, 'If you are getting into money difficulties you should get some financial advice. Perhaps you

goal   **have**

could get a bank loan' could be rephrased as 'If you are in financial difficulty you should obtain some financial help. Perhaps you could receive a bank loan'.

Got, the past tense of get, is often used unnecessarily, as in 'She has got red hair and freckles' and 'We have got enough food to last us the week'. In these sentences 'has' and 'have' are sufficient on their own.

goal this can be used to describe the recipient of the action of a verb, the opposite of 'agent' or 'actor'. Thus, in the sentence 'The boy hit the girl', 'boy' is the 'agent' or 'actor' and 'girl' is the goal. Similarly, in the sentence 'The dog bit the postman', 'dog' is the 'agent' or 'actor' and 'postman' is the goal.

govern a term that is used of a verb or preposition in relation to a noun or pronoun to indicate that the verb or preposition has a noun or pronoun depending on it. Thus, in the phrase 'on the table', 'on' is said to govern 'table'.

gradable a term that is used of adjectives and adverbs to mean that they can take degrees of comparison. Thus 'clean' is a gradable adjective since it has a comparative form (cleaner) and a superlative form (cleanest). 'Soon' is a gradable adverb since it has a comparative form (sooner) and a superlative form (soonest). Such words as 'supreme', which cannot normally have a comparative or superlative form, are called **non-gradable**.

habitual a term used to refer to the action of a verb that occurs regularly and repeatedly. The **habitual present** is found in such sentences as 'He goes to bed at ten every night', 'She always walks to work' and 'The old man sleeps all day'. This is in contrast to the **stative present**, which indicates the action of the verb that occurs at all times, as in 'Cows chew the cud', 'Water becomes ice when it freezes', 'Children grow up' and 'We all die'. Examples of the **habitual past** tense include; 'They travelled by train to work all their lives', 'We worked twelve hours a day on that project' and 'She studied night and day for the exams'.

hanging participle *see* **dangling participle**.

have a verb that has several functions. A major use is its part in forming the 'perfect

tense' and 'past perfect tense', or 'pluperfect tense', of other verb tenses. It does this in conjunction with the 'past participle' of the verb in question.

The perfect tense of a verb is formed by the present tense of the verb have and the past participle of the verb. Examples include 'We have acted wisely', 'They have beaten the opposition', 'The police have caught the thieves', 'The old man has died', 'The child has eaten all the food', 'The baby has fallen downstairs', 'They have grabbed all the bargains', 'You have hated him for years' and 'He has indicated that he is going to retire'. The past perfect or pluperfect is formed by the past tense of the verb have and the past participle of the verb in question, as in 'He had jumped over the fence', 'They had kicked in the door', 'The boy had led the other children to safety', 'His mother had made the cake', 'The headmaster had punished the pupils' and 'They had rushed into buying a new house'. Both perfect tenses and past perfect or pluperfect tenses are often contracted in speech or in informal written English, as in 'We've had enough for today', 'You've damaged the suitcase', 'You've missed the bus', 'He's lost his wallet', 'She's arrived too late', 'They'd left before the news came through', 'She'd married without telling her parents', 'He'd packed the goods himself' and 'You'd locked the door without realizing it'.

Have is often used in the phrase **have to** in the sense that something must be done. In the present tense have to can be used instead of 'must', as in 'You have to leave now', 'We have to clear this mess up', 'He has to get the next train' and 'The goods have to be sold today'. If the 'something that must be done' refers to the future the verb **will have to** is used', as in 'He will have to leave now to get there on time', 'The old man will have to go to hospital' and 'They'll have to move out of the house when her parents return'. If the 'something that must be done' refers to the past, **had to** is used, as in 'We had to take the injured man to hospital', 'They had to endure freezing conditions on the mountain', 'They'd to take a reduction in salary' and 'We'd to wait all day for the workman to appear'.

Have is also used in the sense of 'possess' or 'own', as in 'He has a swimming pool behind his house ', 'She has a huge wardrobe', 'We have enough food' and 'They have four cars'. In spoken or in informal English 'have got' is often used, as in 'They've got the largest house in the street', 'We've got problems now', 'They haven't got time'. This use should be avoided in formal English.

Have is also used to indicate suffering from an illness or disease, as in 'The child has measles', 'Her father has flu' and 'She has heart disease'. Have can also indicate that an activity is taking place, as in 'She's having a shower', 'We're having a party', 'She is having a baby' and 'They are having a dinner party'.

he a personal pronoun that is used as the subject of a sentence or clause to refer to a man, boy, etc. It is thus said to be a 'masculine' personal pronoun. Since he refers to a third party and does not refer to the speaker or the person being addressed, it is a third-person pronoun. Examples include 'James is quite nice but he can be boring', 'Bob has got a new job and he is very pleased' and 'He is rich now but his parents are still very poor'.

He traditionally was used not only to refer to nouns relating to the masculine sex but also to nouns that are now regarded as being neutral or of dual gender. Such nouns include 'architect', 'artist', 'athlete', 'doctor', 'passenger', 'parent', 'pupil', 'singer', 'student'. Without further information from the context it is impossible to know to which sex such nouns are referring. In modern usage it is regarded as sexist to assume such words to be masculine by using he to refer to one of them unless the context indicates that the noun in question refers to a man or boy. Formerly it was considered acceptable to write or say 'Send a message to the architect who designed the building that he is to attend the meeting' whether or not the writer or speaker knew that the architect was a man. Similarly it was considered acceptable to write or say 'Please tell the doctor that he is to come straight away' whether or not the speaker or writer knew that the doctor was in fact a

man. Nowadays this convention is considered sexist. In order to avoid sexism it is possible to use the convention 'he/she', as in 'Every pupil was told that he/she was to be smartly dressed for the occasion', 'Each passenger was informed that he/she was to arrive ten minutes before the coach was due to leave' and 'Tell the doctor that he/she is required urgently'. However this convention is regarded by some people as being clumsy, particularly in spoken English or in informal written English. Some people prefer to be ungrammatical and use the plural personal pronoun 'they' instead of 'he/she' in certain situations, as in 'Every passenger was told that they had to arrive ten minutes before the coach was due to leave' and 'Every student was advised that they should apply for a college place by March' and this use is becoming increasingly common, even in textbooks. In some cases it may be possible to rephrase sentences and avoid being either sexist or ungrammatical, as in 'All the passengers were told that they should arrive ten minutes before the coach was due to leave' and 'All students were advised that they should apply for a college place by March'.

helping verb another name for **auxiliary verb**.

hendiadys a figure of speech in which two nouns joined by 'and' are used to express an idea that would normally be expressed by the use of an adjective and a noun, as in 'through storm and weather' instead of 'through stormy weather'.

her a personal pronoun. It is the third person singular, is feminine in gender and acts as the object in a sentence, as in 'We saw her yesterday', 'I don't know her', 'He hardly ever sees her', 'Please give this book to her', 'Our daughter sometimes plays with her' and 'We do not want her to come to the meeting'. *See* **he**; **she**.

hers a personal pronoun. It is the third person singular, feminine in gender and is in the poassessive case. 'The car is not hers', 'I have forgotten my book but I don't want to borrow hers', 'This is my seat and that is hers', and 'These clothes are hers'. *See* **his**; **her** and **possessive**.

him the third person masculine personal pronoun when used as the object of a sentence or clause, as in 'She shot him', 'When the police caught the thief they arrested him' and 'His parents punished him after the boy stole the money'. Traditionally him was used to apply not only to masculine nouns, such as 'man' and 'boy', but also to nouns that are said to be 'of dual gender'. These include 'architect', 'artist', 'parent', 'passenger', 'pupil' and 'student'. Without further information from the context, it is not possible for the speaker or writer to know the sex of the person referred to by one of these words. Formerly it was acceptable to write or say 'The artist must bring an easel with him' and 'Each pupil must bring food with him'. In modern usage this convention is considered sexist and there is a modern convention that 'him/her' should be used instead to avoid sexism, as in 'The artist must bring an easel with him/her' and 'Each pupil must bring food with 'him/her'. This convention is felt by some people to be clumsy, particularly in and in , and some people prefer to be ungrammatical and use the plural personal pronoun 'them' instead, as in 'The artist must bring an easel with them' and 'Each pupil must bring food with them'. This use has become increasingly, even in textbooks. In some situations it is possible to avoid being either sexist or ungrammatical by rephrasing the sentence, as in 'All artists must bring easels with them' and 'All pupils must bring food with them'. *See* **he**.

him/her *see* **him**.

his the third personal masculine pronoun when used to indicate possession, as in 'He has hurt his leg', 'The boy has taken his books home' and 'Where has your father left his tools?' Traditionally his was used to refer not only to masculine nouns, such as 'man', 'boy', etc, but to what are known as nouns 'of dual gender'. These include 'architect', 'artist', 'parent', 'passenger', 'pupil' and 'student'. Without further information from the context it is not possible for the speaker or the writer to know the sex of the person referred to by one of these words. Formerly it was considered acceptable to use his in such situations, as in 'Every pupil has to supply his own sports equipment' and 'Every passenger is responsible

for his own luggage'. In modern usage this is now considered sexist and there is a modern convention that 'his/her' should be used instead to avoid sexism, as in 'Every pupil has to supply his/her own sports equipment' and 'Every passenger is responsible for his/her own luggage'. This convention is felt by some people to be clumsy, particularly when used in spoken or informal written English. Some people prefer to be ungrammatical and use the plural personal pronoun 'their', as in 'Every pupil must supply their own sports equipment' and 'Every passenger is to be responsible for their own luggage' and this use has become increasingly common, even in textbooks. In some situations it is possible to avoid being sexist, clumsy and ungrammatical by rephrasing the sentence, as in 'All pupils must supply their own sports equipment' and 'All passengers are to be responsible for their own luggage.

his/her *see* **his**.

hybrid a word that is ᵒᵐᵉd from words or elements derived fᵒᵐ different languages, such as 'television

if a conjunction that is often used to introduce a subordinate adverbial clause of condition, as in 'If he is talking of leaving he must be unhappy', 'If you tease the dog it will bite you', 'If he had realized that the weather was going to be so bad he would not have gone on the expedition', 'If I had been in charge I would have sacked him' and 'If it were a better organized firm things like that would not happen'.

If can also introduce a 'nominal' or 'noun clause', as in 'He asked if we objected' and 'She inquired if we wanted to go'.

imperative mood the verb mood that expresses commands. The verbs in the following sentences are in the imperative mood: 'Go away!', 'Run faster!', 'Answer me!', 'Sit down!', 'Please get out of here!'. All of these expressions with verbs in the imperative mood sound rather imperious or dictatorial and usually end with an exclamation mark, but this is not true of all expressions with verbs in the imperative mood. For example, the following sentences all have verbs in the imperative mood: 'Have another helping of ice cream',

'Help yourself to more wine', 'Just follow the yellow arrows to the X-ray department', and 'Turn right at the roundabout'. Sentences with verbs in the imperative mood are known as **imperative sentences**.

imperfect a tense that denotes an action in progress but not complete. The term derives from the classification in Latin grammar and was traditionally applied to the 'past imperfect', as in 'They were standing there'. The imperfect has now been largely superseded by the progressive/continuous tense, which is marked by the use of 'be' plus the present participle. Continuous tenses are used when talking about temporary situations at a particular point in time, as in 'They were waiting for the bus'.

impersonal a verb that is used with a formal subject, usually 'it', as in 'It is raining' and 'They say it will snow tomorrow'.

indefinite pronouns these are used refer to people or things without being specific as to exactly who or what they are. They include 'everyone', 'everybody', 'everything', 'anyone', 'anybody', 'anything', 'somebody', 'someone', 'something' and 'nobody', 'no one', 'nothing', as in 'Everyone is to make a contribution', 'Anyone can enter', 'Something will turn up' and 'Nobody cares'.

independent clause a clause that can stand alone and make sense without being dependent on another clause, as in 'The children are safe'. Main clauses are independent clauses. Thus in the sentence 'She is tired and she wants to go home', there are two independent clauses joined by 'and'. In the sentence 'She will be able to rest when she gets home', 'She will be able to rest' is an independent clause and 'when she gets home' is a dependent clause. In the sentence 'Because she is intelligent she thinks for herself', 'she thinks for herself' is an independent clause and 'because she is intelligent' is a dependent clause.

indicative mood the mood of a verb which denotes making a statement. The following sentences have verbs in the indicative mood: 'We go on holiday tomorrow', 'He was waiting for her husband', 'They have lost the match' and 'She will arrive this afternoon'. The indicative mood is sometimes known as the **declarative mood**. The other moods are the imperative mood and subjunctive mood.

indirect object an object that can be preceded by 'to' or 'for'. The indirect object usually refers to the person who benefits from an action or receives something as the result of it. In the sentence 'Her father gave the boy food', 'boy' is the indirect object and 'food' is the direct object. The sentence could be rephrased as 'Her father gave food to the boy'. In the sentence 'He bought his mother flowers', 'his mother' is the indirect object and 'flowers' is the direct object. The sentence could have been rephrased as 'He bought flowers for his mother'. In the sentence 'They offered him a reward', 'him' is the indirect object and 'reward' is the direct object. The sentence could be rephrased as 'They offered a reward to him'.

indirect question a question that is reported in indirect speech, as in 'We asked them where they were going', 'They inquired why we had come' and 'They looked at us curiously and asked where we had come from'. Note that a question mark is not used.

indirect speech also known as **reported speech** a way of reporting what someone has said without using the actual words used by the speaker. There is usually an introductory verb and a subordinate 'that' clause, as in 'He said that he was going away', 'They announced that they were leaving next day' and 'She declared that she had seen him there before'. In direct speech these sentences would become 'He said, "I am going away" ', 'They announced, "We are leaving tomorrow" ' and 'She declared, "I have seen him there before" '. When the change is made from direct speech to indirect speech, the pronouns, adverbs of time and place and tenses are changed to accord with the viewpoint of the person doing the reporting.

infinitive the base form of a verb when used without any indication of person, number or tense. There are two forms of the infinitive. One is the **to infinitive** form, as in 'They wished to leave', 'I plan to go tomorrow', 'We aim to please' and 'They want to emigrate', 'To know all is to forgive all', 'To err is human', 'Pull the lever to open', 'You should bring a book to read', 'The child has nothing to do', 'She is not very nice to know' and 'It is hard to believe that it happened'. The other form of the infinitive is called the **bare infinitive**. This form consists of the base form of the verb without 'to', as in 'We saw him fall', 'She watched him go', 'They noticed him enter', 'She heard him sigh', 'They let him go', 'I had better leave' and 'Need we return' and 'we dare not go back'. *See* **split infinitive**.

inflect when applied to a word, this means to change form in order to indicate differences of tense, number, gender, case, etc. Nouns inflect for plural, as in 'ships', 'chairs', 'houses' and 'oxen'; nouns inflect for possessive, as in 'boys', 'woman's', 'teachers'', and 'parents''; some adjectives inflect for the comparative form, as in 'brighter', 'clearer', 'shorter' and 'taller'; verbs inflect for the third person singular present tense, as in 'hears', 'joins', 'touches' and 'kicks'; verbs inflect for the present participle, as in 'hearing', 'joining', 'touching' and 'kicking'; verbs inflect for the past participle, as in 'heard', 'joined', 'touched' and 'kicked'.

inflection the act of inflecting—*see* **inflect**. It also refers to an inflected form of a word or a suffix or other element used to inflect a word.

-ing form this form of a verb can be either a present participle or a gerund. Present participles are used in the formation of the progressive or continuous tenses, as in 'We were looking at the pictures', 'Children were playing in the snow', 'They are waiting for the bus', 'Parents were showing their anger', 'He has been sitting there for hours'. Present participles can also be used in non-finite clauses or phrases, as in 'Walking along, she did not have a care in the world', 'Lying there, he thought about his life', 'Sighing, he left the room' and 'Smiling broadly he congratulated his friend'.

A large number of adjectives end in -ing. Many of these have the same form as the present participle of a transitive verb and are similar in meaning. Examples include 'an amazing spectacle', 'a boring show', 'an interesting idea', 'a tiring day', 'an exhausting

climb' and 'aching limbs'. Some -ing adjectives are related to intransitive verbs, as 'existing problems', 'increasing responsibilities', 'dwindling resources', 'an ageing work force' and 'prevailing circumstances'. Some -ing adjectives are related to the forms of verbs but have different meanings from the verbs, as in 'becoming dress', 'an engaging personality', 'a dashing young man' and 'a retiring disposition'. Some -ing adjectives are not related to verbs at all. These include 'appetizing', 'enterprising', 'impending' and 'balding'. Some -ing adjectives are used informally for emphasis, as in 'a blithering idiot', 'a stinking cold' and 'a flaming cheek'.

Gerunds act as nouns and are sometimes known as **verbal nouns**. Examples include 'Smoking is bad for one's health', 'Cycling is forbidden in the park' and 'Swimming is his favourite sport'.

intensifier the term for an adverb that affects the degree of intensity of another word. Intensifiers include 'thoroughly' in 'We were thoroughly shocked by the news', 'scarcely' in 'We scarcely recognized them' and 'totally' in 'She was totally amazed'.

interjection a kind of exclamation. Sometimes they are formed by actual words and sometimes they simply consist of sounds indicating emotional noises. Examples of interjections include 'Oh! I am quite shocked', 'Gosh! I'm surprised to hear that!', 'Phew! It's hot!', 'Ouch! That was my foot!', 'Tut-tut! He shouldn't have done that!' and 'Alas! She is dead.'

interrogative adjective or **determiner** an adjective or determiner that asks for information in relation to the nouns which it qualifies, as in 'What dress did you choose in the end?', 'What kind of book are you looking for?', 'Which house do you like best?', 'Which pupil won the prize?', 'Whose bike was stolen?' and 'Whose dog is that?'

interrogative adverb an adverb that asks a question, as in 'When did they leave?', 'When does the meeting start?', 'Where do they live?', 'Where was the stolen car found?', 'Where did you last see her?', 'Why was she crying?', 'Why have they been asked to leave?', 'How is the invalid?', 'How do you know that she has gone?' and 'Wherever did you find that?'

interrogative pronoun a pronoun that asks a question, as in 'Who asked you to do that?', 'Who broke the vase?', 'What did he say?', 'What happened next?', 'Whose are those books?', 'Whose is that old car?', 'To whom was that remark addressed?' and 'To whom did you address the package?'

interrogative sentence a sentence that asks a question, as in 'Who is that?', 'Where is he?', 'Why have they appeared?', 'What did they take away?, 'Which do you prefer?' and 'Whose baby is that?'. Sentences that take the form of an interrogative question do not always seek information. Sometimes they are exclamations, as in 'Did you ever see anything so beautiful?', 'Isn't she sweet?' and 'Aren't they lovely?'. Sentences that take the form of questions may really be commands or directives, as in 'Could you turn down that radio?', 'Would you make less noise?' and 'Could you get her a chair?'. Sentences that take the form of questions may function as statements, as in 'Isn't there always a reason?' and 'Haven't we all experienced disappointment?'. Some interrogative sentences are what are known as rhetorical questions, which are asked purely for effect and require no answer, as in 'Do you think I am a fool?', 'What is the point of life?' and 'What is the world coming to?'.

intransitive verb a verb that does not take a direct object, as in 'Snow fell yesterday', 'The children played in the sand', 'The path climbed steeply', 'Time will tell', 'The situation worsened', 'Things improved' and 'Prices increased'. Many verbs can be either transitive or intransitive, according to the context. Thus 'play' is intransitive in the sentence 'The children played in the sand' but transitive in the sentence 'The boy plays the piano'. Similarly 'climb' is intransitive in the sentence 'The path climbs steeply' but transitive in the sentence 'The mountaineers climbed Everest'. Similarly 'tell' is intransitive in the sentence 'Time will tell' but transitive in the sentence 'He will tell his life story'.

introductory it the use of 'it' as the subject of a sentence in the absence of a meaningful

subject. It is used particularly in sentences about time and the weather, as in 'It is midnight', 'It is dawn', 'It is five o'clock', 'It is twelve noon', 'It is raining', 'It was snowing', 'It was windy' and 'It was blowing a gale'.

invariable a word whose form does not vary by inflection. Such words include 'sheep' and 'but'.

inversion the reversal of the usual word order. It particularly refers to subjects and verbs. Inversion is used in questions, in some negative sentences, and for literary effect. In questions, an auxiliary verb is usually put in front of the subject and the rest of the verb group is put after the subject, as in 'Are you going to see her?' and 'Have they inspected the goods yet?'. The verb 'to do' is frequently used in inversion, as in 'Did he commit the crime?' and 'Do they still believe that?'. Examples of the use of inversion in negative sentences include 'Seldom have I witnessed such an act of selfishness', 'Never had she experienced such pain' and 'Rarely do we have time to admire the beauty of the countryside'. This use in negative sentences is rather formal.

Inversion frequently involves adverbial phrases of place, as in 'Beyond the town stretched field after field', 'Above them soared the eagle' and 'Along the driveway grew multitudes of daffodils'.

Inversion is also found in conditional clauses that are not introduced by conjunction, as in 'Had you arrived earlier you would have got a meal' and 'Had we some more money we could do more for the refugees'.

irregular adjective an adjective that does not conform to the usual rules of forming the comparative and superlative (*see* **comparison of adjectives**). Many adjectives either add *-er* for the comparative and *-est* for the superlative, as in 'taller', 'shorter' and 'tallest', 'shortest' from 'tall' and 'short'. Some adjectives form their comparatives with 'more' and their superlatives with 'most', as in 'more beautiful', 'more practical' and 'most beautiful', 'most practical'. Irregular adjectives do not form their comparatives and superlatives in either of these ways. Irregular adjectives include:

some coffee'. The **subjunctive** was originally a term in Latin grammar and expressed a wish, supposition, doubt, improbability or other non-factual statement. It is used in English for hypothetical statements and certain formal 'that' clauses, as in 'If I were you I would have nothing to do with it', 'If you were to go now you would arrive on time', 'Someone suggested that we ask for more money' and 'It was his solicitor who suggested that he sue the firm'. The word 'mood' arose because it was said to indicate the verb's attitude or viewpoint.

more an adverb that is added to some adjectives to make the comparative form (*see* **comparison of adjectives**). In general it is the longer adjectives that have more as part of their comparative form, as in 'more abundant', 'more beautiful', 'more catastrophic', 'more dangerous', 'more elegant', 'more frantic', 'more graceful', 'more handsome', 'more intelligent', 'more luxurious', 'more manageable', 'more opulent', 'more precious', 'more ravishing', 'more satisfactory', 'more talented', 'more unusual', 'more valuable'. Examples of adverbs with more in their comparative form include 'more elegantly', 'more gracefully', 'more energetically', 'more dangerously' and 'more determinedly'.

most an adverb added to some adjectives and adverbs to make the superlative form. In general it is the longer adjectives that have most as part of their superlative form, as in 'most abundant', 'most beautiful', 'most catastrophic', 'most dangerous', 'most elegant', 'most frantic', 'most graceful', 'most handsome', 'most intelligent', 'most luxurious', 'most manageable', 'most noteworthy', 'most opulent', 'most precious', most ravishing', 'most satisfactory', 'most talented', 'most unusual', 'most valuable'. Examples of adverbs with most in their superlative form include 'most elegantly', 'most gracefully', 'most energetically', 'most dangerously' and 'most determinedly'.

multi-sentence a sentence with more than one clause, as in 'She tripped over a rock and broke her ankle' and 'She was afraid when she saw the strange man'.

negative sentence a sentence that is the opposite of a **positive sentence**. 'She has a dog' is an example of a positive sentence. 'She does not have a dog' is an example of a negative sentence. The negative concept is expressed by an auxiliary verb accompanied by 'not' or 'n't'. Other words used in negative sentences include 'never', 'nothing' and 'by no means', as in 'She has never been here' and 'We heard nothing'.

neither an adjective or a pronoun that takes a singular verb, as in 'Neither parent will come' and 'Neither of them wishes to come'. In the **neither ... nor** construction, a singular verb is used if both parts of the construction are singular, as in 'Neither Jane nor Mary was present'. If both parts are plural the verb is plural, as in 'Neither their parents nor their grandparents are willing to look after them'. If the construction involves a mixture of singular and plural, the verb traditionally agrees with the subject that is nearest it, as in 'Neither her mother nor her grandparents are going to come' and 'Neither her grandparents nor her mother is going to come'. If pronouns are used, the nearer one governs the verb as in 'Neither they nor he is at fault' and 'Neither he nor they are at fault'.

neuter one of the grammatical genders. The other two grammatical genders are masculine and feminine. Inanimate objects are members of the neuter gender. Examples include 'table', 'desk', 'garden', 'spade', 'flower' and 'bottle'.

nominal clause *see* **noun clause**.

non-finite clause a clause which contains a non-finite verb. Thus in the sentence 'He works hard to earn a living', 'to earn a living' is a non-finite clause since 'to earn' is an infinitive and so a non-finite verb. Similarly in the sentence 'Getting there was a problem', 'getting there' is a non-finite clause, 'getting' being a present participle and so a non-finite verb.

non-finite verb a verb that shows no variation in tense and has no subject. The non-finite verb forms include the infinitive form, as in 'go', the present participle and gerund, as in 'going', and the past participle, as in 'gone'.

non-gradable *see* **gradable**.

noun the name of something or someone. Thus 'anchor', 'baker', 'cat', 'elephant', 'foot', 'gate', 'lake', 'pear', 'shoe', 'trunk' and 'wallet' are all nouns. There are various categories of nouns. *See* **abstract noun, common noun, concrete noun, countable noun, proper noun** and **uncountable noun**.

noun clause a subordinate clause that performs a function in a sentence similar to a noun or noun phrase. It can act as the subject, object or complement of a main clause. In the sentence 'Where he goes is his own business', 'where he goes' is a noun clause. In the sentence 'They asked why he objected', 'why he objected' is a noun clause. A noun clause is also known as a **nominal clause**.

noun phrase a group of words containing a noun as its main word and functioning like a noun in a sentence. Thus it can function as the subject, object or complement of a sentence. In the sentence 'The large black dog bit him', 'the large black dog' is a noun phrase, and in the sentence 'They bought a house with a garden', 'with a garden' is a noun phrase. In the sentence 'She is a complete fool', 'a complete fool' is a noun phrase.

noun, plurals *see* **Spelling** section.

number in grammar this is a classification consisting of 'singular' and 'plural'. Thus the number of the pronoun 'they' is 'plural' and the number of the verb 'carries' is singular. *See* **number agreement**.

number agreement or **concord** the agreement of grammatical units in terms of number. Thus a singular subject is followed by a singular verb, as in 'The girl likes flowers', 'He hates work' and 'She was carrying a suitcase'. Similarly a plural subject should be followed by a plural verb, as in 'They have many problems', 'The men work hard' and 'The girls are training hard'.

object the part of a sentence that is acted upon or is affected by the verb. It usually follows the verb to which it relates. There are two forms of object—the direct object and indirect object. A direct object can be a noun, and in the sentence 'The girl hit the ball', 'ball' is a noun and the object. In the sentence 'They bought a house', 'house' is a noun and the object. In the sentence

'They made an error', 'error' is a noun and the object. A direct object can be a noun phrase, and in the sentence 'He has bought a large house', 'a large house' is a noun phrase and the object. In the sentence 'She loves the little girl', 'the little girl' is a noun phrase and the object. In the sentence 'They both wear black clothes', 'black clothes' is a noun phrase and the object'. A direct object can be a noun clause, and in the sentence 'I know what he means', 'what he means' is a noun phrase and the object. In the sentence 'He denied that he had been involved', 'that he had been involved' is a noun phrase and the object. In the sentence 'I asked when he would return', 'when he would return' is a noun phrase and the object. A direct object can also be a pronoun, and in the sentence 'She hit him', 'him' is a pronoun and the object. In the sentence 'They had a car but they sold it', 'it' is a pronoun and the object. In the sentence 'She loves them', 'them' is a pronoun and the object.

objective case the case expressing the object. In Latin it is known as the accusative case.

parenthesis *see* **brackets** in **Punctuation**.

part of speech each of the categories (e.g. verb, noun, adjective, etc) into which words are divided according to their grammatical and semantic functions.

participle a part of speech, so called because, although a verb, it has the character both of verb and adjective and is also used in the formation of some compound tenses. *See also* **-ing form** and **past participle**.

passive voice the voice of a verb whereby the subject is the recipient of the action of the verb. Thus, in the sentence 'Mary was kicked by her brother', 'Mary' is the receiver of the 'kick' and so 'kick' is in the passive voice. Had it been in the active voice it would have been 'Her brother kicked Mary'. Thus 'the brother' is the subject and not the receiver of the action.

past participle this is formed by adding -ed or -d to the base words of regular verbs, as in 'acted', ' alluded', 'boarded', 'dashed', 'flouted', 'handed', 'loathed', 'tended' and 'wanted', or in various other ways for irregular verbs.

past tense this tense of a verb is formed by adding -ed or -d to the base form of the verb in regular verbs, as in 'added', 'crashed', 'graded', 'smiled', 'rested' and 'yielded', and in various ways for irregular verbs.

perfect tense see **tense**.

personal pronoun a pronoun that is used to refer back to someone or something that has already been mentioned. The personal pronouns are divided into subject pronouns, object pronouns and possessive pronouns. They are also categorized according to 'person'. See **first person**, **second person** and **third person**.

phrasal verb a usually simple verb that combines with a preposition or adverb, or both, to convey a meaning more than the sum of its parts, e.g. to phase out, to come out, to look forward to.

phrase two or more words, usually not containing a finite verb, that form a complete expression by themselves or constitute a portion of a sentence.

positive sentence see **negative sentence**.

possessive see **genitive**.

possessive pronoun see **personal pronoun**; **first person**; **second person** and **third person**.

postmodifier a modifier that comes after the main word of a noun phrase, as in 'of stone' in 'tablets of stone'.

predicate all the parts of a clause or sentence that are not contained in the subject. Thus in the sentence 'The little girl was exhausted and hungry', 'exhausted and hungry' is the predicate. Similarly, in the sentence 'The tired old man slept like a top', 'slept like a top' is the predicate.

predicative adjective an adjective that helps to form the predicate and so comes after the verb, as 'tired' in 'She was very tired' and 'mournful' in 'The music was very mournful'.

premodifier a modifier that comes before the main word of a noun phrase, as 'green' in 'green dress' and 'pretty' in 'pretty houses'.

preposition a word that relates two elements of a sentence, clause or phrase together. Prepositions show how the elements relate in time or space and generally precede the words that they 'govern'. Words governed

by prepositions are nouns or pronouns. Prepositions are often very short words, as 'at', 'in', 'on', 'to', 'before' and 'after'. Some complex prepositions consist of two words, as 'ahead of', 'instead of', 'apart from', and some consist of three, as 'with reference to', 'in accordance with' and 'in addition to'. Examples of prepositions in sentences include 'The cat sat on the mat', 'We were at a concert', 'They are in shock', 'We are going to France', 'She arrived before me', 'Apart from you she has no friends' and 'We acted in accordance with your instructions'.

present continuous see **tense**.

present participle see **-ing words**.

present tense see **tense**.

principal clause see **main clause**.

progressive present see **tense**.

pronoun a word that takes the place of a noun or a noun phrase. See **personal pronouns**, **he**, **her**, **him** and **his**, **reciprocal pronouns**, **reflexive pronouns**, **demonstrative pronouns**, **relative pronouns**, **distributive pronouns**, **indefinite pronouns** and **interrogative pronouns**.

proper noun a noun that refers to a particular individual or a specific thing. It is the 'name' of someone or something', as in Australia, Vesuvius, John Brown, River Thames, Rome and Atlantic Ocean. See **capital letters** in **Spelling** section.

question tag a phrase that is interrogative in form but is not really asking a question. It is added to a statement to seek agreement, etc. Examples include 'That was a lovely meal, wasn't it?', 'You will be able to go, won't you?', 'He's not going to move house, is he?' and 'She doesn't drive, does she?' Sentences containing question tags have question marks at the end.

reciprocal pronoun a pronoun used to convey the idea of reciprocity or a two-way relationship. The reciprocal pronouns are 'each other' and 'one another'. Examples include 'They don't love each other any more', 'They seem to hate each other', 'We must try to help each other', 'The children were calling one another names', 'The two families were always criticizing one another' and 'The members of the family blame one another for their mother's death'.

reciprocal verb a verb such as 'consult', 'embrace', 'marry', 'meet', etc, that expresses a mutual relationship, as in 'They met at the conference', 'She married him in June'.

reflexive pronoun a pronoun that ends in '-self' or '-selves' and refers back to a noun or pronoun that has occurred earlier in the same sentence. The reflexive pronouns include 'myself', 'ourselves'; 'yourself', 'yourselves'; 'himself', 'herself', 'itself', 'themselves'. Examples include 'The children washed themselves', 'He cut himself shaving', 'Have you hurt yourself?' and 'She has cured herself of the habit'.

Reflexive pronouns are sometimes used for emphasis, as in 'The town itself was not very interesting' and 'The headmaster himself punished the boys'. They can also be used to indicate that something has been done by somebody by his/her own efforts without any help, as in 'He built the house himself', 'We converted the attic ourselves'. They can also indicate that someone or something is alone, as in 'She lives by herself' and 'The house stands by itself'.

reflexive verb a verb that has as its direct object a reflexive pronoun, e.g. 'They pride themselves on their skill as a team'.

regular sentence *see* **major sentence**.

regular verb *see* **irregular verb**.

relative clause a subordinate clause that has the function of an adjective. It is introduced by a relative pronoun.

relative pronoun a pronoun that introduces a relative clause. The relative pronouns are 'who', 'whom', 'whose', 'which' and 'that'. Examples of relative clauses introduced by relative pronouns include 'There is the man who stole the money', 'She is the person to whom I gave the money', 'This is the man whose wife won the prize', 'They criticized the work which he had done' and 'That's the house that I would like to buy'. Relative pronouns refer back to a noun or noun phrase in the main clause. These nouns and noun phrases are known as antecedents. The antecedents in the example sentences are respectively 'man', 'person', 'man', 'work' and 'house'.

Sometimes the relative clause divides the parts of the main clause, as in 'The woman whose daughter is ill is very upset', 'The people whom we met on holiday were

French' and 'The house that we liked best was too expensive'.

reported speech *same as* **indirect speech**

rhetorical question a question that is asked to achieve some kind of effect and requires no answer. Examples include 'What's this country coming to?', 'Did you ever see the like', 'Why do these things happen to me?', 'Where did youth go?', 'Death, where is thy sting?' and 'Where does time go?'. *See also* **interrogative sentence**.

second person the term used for the person or thing to whom one is talking. The term is applied to personal pronouns. The second person singular whether acting as the subject of a sentence is 'you', as in 'I told you so', 'We informed you of our decision' and 'They might have asked you sooner'. The second person personal pronoun does not alter its form in the plural in English, unlike in some languages. The possessive form of the second person pronoun is 'yours' whether singular or plural, as in 'These books are not yours'and 'This pen must be yours'.

sentence is at the head of the hierarchy of grammar. All the other elements, such as words, phrases and clauses, go to make up sentences. It is difficult to define a sentence. In terms of recognizing a sentence visually it can be described as beginning with a capital letter and ending with a full stop, or with an equivalent to the full stop, such as an exclamation mark. It is a unit of grammar that can stand alone and make sense and obeys certain grammatical rules, such as usually having a subject and a predicate, as in 'The girl banged the door', where 'the girl' is the subject and 'the door' is the predicate. *See* **major sentence**, **simple sentence**, **complex sentence**.

simple sentence a sentence that cannot be broken down into other clauses. It generally contains a finite verb. Simple sentences include 'The man stole the car', 'She nudged him' and 'He kicked the ball'. *See* **complex sentence** and **compound sentence**.

singular noun a noun that refers to 'one' rather than 'more than one', which is the plural form. *See also* **irregular plural**.

split infinitive an infinitive that has had an-

stative present | **tense**

other word in the form of an adverb placed between itself and 'to', as in 'to rudely push' and 'to quietly leave'. This was once considered a great grammatical sin but the split infinitive is becoming acceptable in modern usage. In any case it sometimes makes for a clumsy sentence if one slavishly adheres to the correct form.

stative present *see* **habitual** and **tense**.

strong verb the more common term for **irregular verb**.

structure word *see* **function word**.

subject that which is spoken of in a sentence or clause and is usually either a noun, as in 'Birds fly' (birds is the noun as subject); a noun phrase, as in 'The people in the town dislike him' (the people in the town' is the subject); a pronoun, as in 'She hit the child' (she is the pronoun as subject); a proper noun, as in 'Paris is the capital of France'. *See* **dummy subject**.

subjunctive *see* **mood**.

subordinate clause a clause that is dependent on another clause, namely the main clause. Unlike the main clause, it cannot stand alone and make sense. Subordinate clauses are introduced by conjunctions. Examples of conjunctions that introduce subordinate clauses include 'after', 'before', 'when', 'if', 'because' and 'since'. *See* **adverbial clause**; **noun clause**.

subordinating conjunction *see* **conjunction**.

suffix *see* **Affix** section.

superlative form the form of an adjective or adverb that expresses the highest or utmost degree of the quality or manner of the word. The superlative forms follow the same rules as comparative forms except that they end in *-est* instead of *-er* and the longer ones use 'most' instead of 'more'. *See also* **comparison of adjectives**.

tense the form of a verb that is used to show the time at which the action of the verb takes place. One of the tenses in English is the **present tense**. It is used to indicate an action now going on or a state now existing. A distinction can be made between the **habitual present**, which marks habitual or repeated actions or recurring events, and the **stative present**, which indicates something that is true at all times. Examples of habitual present include 'He works long

hours' and 'She walks to work'. Examples of the stative tense include 'The world is round' and 'Everyone must die eventually'.

The **progressive present** or **continuous present** is formed with the verb 'to be' and the present participle, as in, 'He is walking to the next village', 'She was driving along the road when she saw him' and 'They were worrying about the state of the economy'.

The **past tense** refers to an action or state that has taken place before the present time. In the case of regular verbs it is formed by adding -*ed* to the base form of the verb, as in 'fear/feared', 'look/looked', and 'turn/turned'. *See also* **irregular verbs**.

The **future tense** refers to an action or state that will take place at some time in the future. It is formed with 'will' and 'shall'. Traditionally 'will' was used with the second and third person pronouns ('you', 'he/she/it', 'they') and 'shall' with the first person ('I' and 'we'), as in 'You will be bored', 'He will soon be home', 'They will leave tomorrow', 'I shall buy some bread' and 'We shall go by train'. Also traditionally 'shall' was used with the second and third persons to indicate emphasis, insistence, determination, refusal, etc, as in 'You shall go to the ball' and 'He shall not be admitted'. 'Will' was used with the first person in the same way, as in 'I will get even with him'.

In modern usage 'will' is generally used for the first person as well as for second and third, as in 'I will see you tomorrow' and 'We will be there soon' and 'shall' is used for emphasis, insistence, etc, for first, second and third persons.

The future tense can also be formed with the use of 'be about to' or 'be going to', as in 'We were about to leave' and 'They were going to look for a house'.

Other tenses include the **perfect tense**, which is formed using the verb 'to have' and the past participle. In the case of regular verbs the past participle is formed by adding *ed* to the base form of the verb. *See also* **irregular verbs**. Examples of the perfect tense include 'He has played his last match', 'We have travelled all day' and 'They have thought a lot about it'.

The **past perfect tense** or **pluperfect tense** is formed using the verb 'to have' and the past participle, as in 'She had no idea that he was dead' and 'They had felt unhappy about the situation'.

The **future perfect** is formed using the verb 'to have' and the past participle, as in 'He will have arrived by now'.

they *see* **him** and **third person**.

third person a third party, not the speaker or the person or thing being spoken to. Note that 'person' in this context can refer to things as well as people. 'Person' in this sense applies to personal pronouns. The third person singular forms are 'he', 'she' and 'it' when the subject of a sentence or clause, as in 'She will win' and 'It will be fine'. The third person singular forms are 'him', 'her','it' when the object, as in 'His behaviour hurt her' and 'She meant it'. The third person plural is 'they' when the subject, as in 'They have left' and 'They were angry' and 'them' when the object, as in 'His words made them angry' and 'We accompanied them'.

The possessive forms of the singular are 'his', 'hers' and 'its', as in 'he played his guitar' and 'The dog hurt its leg', and the possessive form of the plural is theirs, as in 'That car is theirs' and 'They say that the book is theirs'. *See* **he**.

to-infinitive the infinitive form of the verb when it is accompanied by 'to' rather than when it is the bare infinitive without 'to'. Examples of the to-infinitive include 'We were told to go', 'I didn't want to stay' and 'To get there on time we'll have to leave now'.

transitive verb a verb that takes a direct object. In the sentence 'The boy broke the window', 'window' is a direct object and so 'broke' (past tense of break) is a transitive verb. In the sentence 'She eats fruit', 'fruit' is a direct object and so 'eat' is a transitive verb. In the sentence 'They kill enemy soldiers' 'enemy soldiers' is a direct object and so 'kill' is a transitive verb. *See* **intransitive verb**.

uncountable noun or **uncount noun** a noun that is not usually pluralized or 'counted'. Such a noun is usually preceded by 'some', rather than 'a'. Uncountable nouns often refer to substances or commodities or qualities, processes and states. Examples of uncountable nouns include butter, china, luggage, petrol, sugar, heat, information, poverty, richness and warmth. In some situations it is possible to have a countable version of what is usually an uncountable noun. Thus 'sugar' is usually considered to be an uncountable noun but it can be used in a countable form in contexts such as 'I take two sugars in my coffee please'. Some nouns exist in an uncountable and countable form. Examples include 'cake', as in 'Have some cake' and 'She ate three cakes' and 'She could not paint for lack of light' and 'the lights went out'.

verb the part of speech often known as a 'doing' word. Although this is rather restrictive, since it tends to preclude auxiliary verbs, modal verbs, etc, the verb is the word in a sentence that is most concerned with the action and is usually essential to the structure of the sentence. Verbs 'inflect' and indicate tense, voice, mood, number, number and person. Most of the information on verbs has been placed under related entries. *See* **active voice, auxiliary verb, finite verb, -ing form, intransitive verb, irregular verbs, linking verb, modal verb, mood, non-finite verb, passive voice** and **transitive verb**.

verb phrase a group of verb forms that have the same function as a single verb. Examples include 'have been raining', 'must have been lying', 'should not have been doing' and 'has been seen doing'.

verbal noun *see* **gerund** and **-ing form**.

vocative case a case that is relevant mainly to languages such as Latin which are based on cases and inflections. In English the vocative is expressed by addressing someone, as in 'John, could I see you for a minute', or by some form of greeting, endearment or exclamation.

voice one of the categories that describes verbs. It involves two ways of looking at the action of verbs. It is divided into active voice and passive voice.

weak verb a less common term for a regular verb, in which inflection is effected by adding a letter or syllable (dawn, dawned) rather than a change of vowel (rise, rose). *See* **irregular verb**.

Usage

a, an the indefinite article. *See* **Spelling.**

-abled is a suffix meaning 'able-bodied'. It is most usually found in such phrases as 'differently abled', a 'politically correct', more positive way of referring to people with some form of disability, as in 'provide access to the club building for differently abled members'.

ableism or **ablism** means discrimination in favour of able-bodied people as in 'people in wheelchairs unable to get jobs because of ableism'. Note that the suffix '-ism' is often used to indicate discrimination against the group to which it refers, as in 'ageism'.

Aboriginal rather than **Aborigine** is now the preferred term for an original inhabitant of Australia, especially where the word is in the singular.

abuse and **misuse** both mean wrong or improper use or treatment. However, **abuse** tends to be a more condemnatory term, suggesting that the wrong use or treatment is morally wrong or illegal. Thus we find 'misuse of the equipment' or 'misuse of one's talents', but 'abuse of a privileged position' or 'abuse of children'. 'Child abuse' is usually used to indicate physical violence or sexual assault. **Abuse** is also frequently applied to the use of substances that are dangerous or injurious to health, as 'drug abuse', or 'alcohol abuse'. In addition, it is used to describe insulting or offensive language, as in 'shout abuse at the referee'.

academic is used to describe scholarly or educational matters, as 'a child with academic rather than sporting interests'. From this use it has come to mean theoretical rather than actual or practical, as in 'wasting time discussing matters of purely academic concern'. In modern use it is frequently used to mean irrelevant, as in 'Whether you vote for him or not is academic. He is certain of a majority of votes'.

access is usually a noun meaning 'entry or admission', as in 'try to gain access to the building', or 'the opportunity to use something', as in 'have access to confidential information'. It is also used to refer to the right of a parent to spend time with his or her children, as in 'Father was allowed access to the children at weekends'.

However **access** can also be used as a verb. It is most commonly found in computing, meaning obtaining information from, as in 'accessing details from the computer file relating to the accounts'. In modern usage many technical words become used, and indeed overused, in the general language. Thus the verb **access** can now be found meaning to obtain information not on a computer, as in 'access the information in the filing cabinet'. It can also be found in the sense of gaining entry to a building, as in 'Their attempts to access the building at night were unsuccessful'.

accessory and **accessary** are interchangeable as regards only one meaning of **accessory**. A person who helps another person to commit a crime is known either as an **accessory** or an **accessary**, although the former is the more modern term. However, only **accessory** is used to describe a useful or decorative extra that is not strictly necessary, as in 'Seat covers are accessories that are included in the price of the car' and 'She wore a red dress with black accessories' ('accessories' in the second example being handbag, shoes and gloves).

accompany can be followed either by the preposition 'with' or 'by'. When it means 'to go somewhere with someone', 'by' is used, as in 'She was accompanied by her parents to church' Similarly, 'by' is used when **accompany** is used in a musical context, as in 'The singer was accompanied on the piano by her brother'. When **accompany** means 'to go along with something' or 'supplement something', either 'by' or 'with' may be used, as in 'The roast turkey was accompanied by all the trimmings', 'His words were accompanied by/with a gesture of dismissal', and 'The speaker accompanied his words with expressive gestures'.

acoustics can take either a singular or

plural verb. When it is being thought of as a branch of science it is treated as being singular, as in 'Acoustics deals with the study of sound', but when it is used to describe the qualities of a hall, etc, with regard to its sound-carrying properties, it is treated as being plural, as in 'The acoustics in the school hall are very poor'.

activate and **actuate** both mean 'make active' but are commonly used in different senses. **Activate** refers to physical or chemical action, as in 'The terrorists activated the explosive device'. **Actuate** means 'to move to action' and 'to serve as a motive', as in 'The murderer was actuated by jealousy'.

actress is still widely used as a term for a woman who acts in plays or films, although many people prefer the term 'actor', regarding this as a neutral term rather than simply the masculine form. The **-ess** suffix, used to indicate the feminine form of a word, is generally becoming less common as these forms are regarded as sexist or belittling.

acute and **chronic** both refer to disease. **Acute** is used of a disease that is sudden in onset and lasts a relatively short time, as in 'flu is an acute illness'. **Chronic** is used of a disease that may be slow to develop and lasts a long time, possibly over several years, as in 'Asthma is a chronic condition'.

AD and **BC** are abbreviations that accompany year numbers. **AD** stands for 'Anno Domini', meaning 'in the year of our Lord' and indicates that the year concerned is one occurring after Jesus Christ was born. Traditionally **AD** is placed before the year number concerned, as in 'Their great-grandfather was born in AD 1801', but in modern usage it sometimes follows the year number, as in 'The house was built in 1780 AD.' **BC** stands for 'Before Christ' and indicates that the year concerned is one occurring before Jesus Christ was born. It follows the year number, as in 'The event took place in Rome in 55 BC'.

adapter and **adaptor** can be used interchangeably, but commonly **adapter** is used to refer to a person who adapts, as in 'the adapter of the stage play for television and **adaptor** is used to refer to a thing that adapts, specifically a type of electrical plug.

admission and **admittance** both mean 'permission or right to enter'. **Admission** is the more common term, as in 'They refused him admission to their house', and, unlike **admittance**, it can also mean 'the price or fee charged for entry' as in 'Admission to the football match is £3'. **Admittance** is largely used in formal or official situations, as in 'They ignored the notice saying "No Admittance" '. **Admission** also means 'confession' or 'acknowledgement of responsibility', as in 'On her own admission she was the thief'.

admit may be followed either by the preposition 'to' or the preposition 'of', depending on the sense. In the sense of 'to confess', **admit** is usually not followed by a preposition at all, as in 'He admitted his mistake' and 'She admitted stealing the brooch'. However, in this sense **admit** is sometimes followed by 'to', as in 'They have admitted to their error' and 'They have admitted to their part in the theft'.

In the sense of 'to allow to enter', **admit** is followed by 'to', as in 'The doorman admitted the guest to the club'. Also in the rather formal sense of 'give access or entrance to', **admit** is followed by 'to', as in 'the rear door admits straight to the garden'. In the sense of 'to be open to' or 'leave room for', **admit** is followed by 'of', as in 'The situation admits of no other explanation'.

admittance *see* **admission**.

adopted and **adoptive** are liable to be confused. **Adopted** is applied to children who have been adopted, as in 'The couple have two adopted daughters'. **Adoptive** is applied to a person or people who adopt a child, as in 'Her biological parents tried to get the girl back from her adoptive parents'.

aeroplane is commonly abbreviated to **plane** in modern usage. In American English **aeroplane** becomes **airplane.**

affinity may be followed by the preposition 'with' or 'between', and means 'close relationship', 'mutual attraction' or similarity, as in 'the affinity which twins have with each other' and 'There was an affinity between the two families who had lost children'. In modern usage it is sometimes followed by 'for' or 'towards', and means 'liking', as in 'She has an affinity for fair-haired men'.

ageism means discrimination on the grounds of age, as in 'By giving an age range in their job advert the firm were guilty of ageism'. Usually it refers to discrimination against older or elderly people, but it also refers to discrimination against young people.

agenda in modern usage is a singular noun having the plural **agendas**. It means 'a list of things to be attended to', as in 'The financial situation was the first item on the committee's agenda'. Originally it was a plural noun, derived from Latin, meaning 'things to be done'.

aggravate literally means 'to make worse', as in 'Her remarks simply aggravated the situation'. In modern usage it is frequently found meaning 'to irritate or annoy', as in 'The children were aggravating their mother when she was trying to read'. It is often labelled as 'informal' in dictionaries and is best avoided in formal situations.

agnostic and **atheist** are both words meaning 'disbeliever in God', but there are differences in sense between the two words. **Agnostics** believe that it is not possible to know whether God exists or not. **Atheists** believe that there is no God.

alcohol abuse is a modern term for alcoholism. *See* **abuse**.

alibi is derived from the Latin word for 'elsewhere'. It is used to refer to a legal plea that a person accused or under suspicion was somewhere other than the scene of the crime at the time the crime was committed. In modern usage **alibi** is frequently used to mean simply 'excuse' or 'pretext', as in 'He had the perfect alibi for not going to the party—he was ill in hospital'.

all together and **altogether** are not interchangeable. **All together** means 'at the same time' or 'in the same place', as in 'The guests arrived all together' and 'They kept their personal papers all together in a filing cabinet'. **Altogether** means 'in all, in total' or 'completely', as in "We collected £500 altogether' and 'The work was altogether too much for him'.

alternate and **alternative** are liable to be confused. **Alternate** means 'every other' or 'occurring by turns', as in 'They visit her mother on alternate weekends' and 'between alternate layers of meat and cheese sauce'. **Alternative** means 'offering a choice' or 'being an alternative', as in 'If the motorway is busy there is an alternative route'. **Alternative** is found in some cases in modern usage to mean 'not conventional, not traditional', as in 'alternative medicine' and 'alternative comedy'.

Alternative as a noun refers to the choice between two possibilities, as in 'The alternatives are to go by train or by plane'. In modern usage, however, it is becoming common to use it to refer also to the choice among two or more possibilities, as in 'He has to use a college from five alternatives'.

although and **though** are largely interchangeable but **though** is slightly less formal, as in 'We arrived on time although/though we left late'.

amiable and **amicable** both refer to friendliness and goodwill. **Amiable** means 'friendly' or 'agreeable and pleasant', and is mostly used of people or their moods, as in 'amiable neighbours', 'amiable travelling companions', 'of an amiable temperament' and 'be in an amiable mood'. **Amicable** means 'characterized by friendliness and goodwill' and is applied mainly to relationships, agreements, documents, etc, as in 'an amicable working relationship', 'reach an amicable settlement at the end of the war' and 'send an amicable letter to his former rival'.

among and **amongst** are interchangeable, as in 'We searched among/amongst the bushes for the ball,' 'Divide the chocolate among/amongst you', and 'You must choose among/amongst the various possibilities'.

among and **between** may be used interchangeably in most contexts. Formerly **between** was used only when referring to the relationship of two things, as in 'Share the chocolate between you and your brother', and **among** was used when referring to the relationship of three or more things, as in 'Share the chocolate among all your friends'. In modern usage **between** may be used when referring to more than two things, as in 'There is agreement between all the countries of the EU' and 'Share the chocolate between all of you'. However,

among is still used only to describe more than two things.

amoral and **immoral** are not interchangeable. **Amoral** means 'lacking moral standards, devoid of moral sense', indicating that the person so described has no concern with morals, as in 'The child was completely amoral and did not know the difference between right and wrong'. **Immoral** means 'against or breaking moral standards, bad'. 'He knows he's doing wrong but he goes on being completely immoral' and 'commit immoral acts'. Note the spelling of both words. **Amoral** has only one *m* but **immoral** has double *m*.

anaesthetic and **analgesic** are liable to be confused. As an adjective, **anaesthetic** means 'producing a loss of feeling', as in 'inject the patient with an anaesthetic substance', and as a noun it means 'a substance that produces a loss of feeling', as in 'administer an anaesthetic to the patient on the operating table'. A local anaesthetic produces a loss of feeling in only part of the body, as in 'remove the rotten tooth under local anaesthetic'. A **general anaesthetic** produces loss of feeling in the whole body and induces unconsciousness, as in 'The operation on his leg will have to be performed under general anaesthetic'. As an adjective **analgesic** means 'producing a lack of or reduction in, sensitivity to pain, pain-killing', as in 'aspirin has an analgesic effect'. As a noun **analgesic** means 'a substance that produces a lack of, or reduction in, sensitivity to pain', as in 'aspirin, paracetamol, and other analgesics'.

arbiter and **arbitrator**, although similar in meaning, are not totally interchangeable. **Arbiter** means 'a person who has absolute power to judge or make decisions', as in 'Parisian designers used to be total arbiters of fashion'. **Arbitrator** is 'a person appointed to settle differences in a dispute', as in 'act as arbitrator between management and workers in the wages dispute'. **Arbiter** is occasionally used with the latter meaning also.

artist and **artiste** are liable to be confused. **Artist** refers to 'a person who paints or draws,' as in 'Renoir was a great artist'. The word may also refer to 'a person who is skilled in something', as in 'The mechanic is a real artist with an engine'. **Artiste** refers to 'an entertainer, such as a singer or a dancer', as in 'a list of the artistes in the musical performances'. The word is becoming a little old-fashioned.

at this moment in time is an overused phrase meaning simply 'now'. In modern usage there is a tendency to use what are thought to be grander-sounding alternatives for simple words. It is best to avoid such overworked phrases and use the simpler form.

atheist *see* **agnostic**.

au fait is French in origin but it is commonly used in English to mean 'familiar with' or 'informed about', as in 'not completely au fait with the new office system'. It is pronounced *o* fay.

authoress is not used in modern usage since it is considered sexist. **Author** is regarded as a neutral term to describe both male and female authors.

avoid *see* **evade**.

avoidance *see* **evasion**.

baited *see* **bated.**

barmaid is disliked by many people on the grounds that it sounds a belittling term and is thus sexist. It is also disliked by people who are interested in political correctness. However the word continues to be quite common, along with **barman**, and efforts to insist on **bar assistant** or **barperson** have not yet succeeded.

basically means literally 'referring to a base or basis, fundamentally', as in 'The scientist's theory is basically unsound', but it is frequently used almost meaninglessly as a fill-up word at the beginning of a sentence, as in 'Basically he just wants more money'. Overuse of this word should be avoided.

basis, meaning 'something on which something is founded', as in 'The cost of the project was the basis of his argument against it', has the plural form **bases** although it is not commonly used. It would be more usual to say 'arguments without a firm basis' than 'arguments without firm bases'.

bated as in 'with bated breath' meaning 'tense and anxious with excitement', is frequently misspelt **baited**. Care should be taken not to confuse the two words.

bathroom *see* **toilet**.

BC *see* **AD**.

because means 'for the reason that', as in 'He left because he was bored', and is sometimes misused. It is wrong to use it in a sentence that also contains 'the reason that', as in 'The reason she doesn't say much is that she is shy'. The correct form of this is 'She doesn't say much because she is shy' or 'The reason she doesn't say much is that she is shy'.

because of *see* **due to**.

beg the question is often used wrongly. It means 'to take for granted the very point that has to be proved', as in 'To say that God must exist because we can see all his wonderful creations in the world around us begs the question'. The statement assumes that these creations have been made by God although this has not been proved and yet this fact is being used as evidence that there is a God. **Beg the question** is often used wrongly to mean 'to evade the question', as in 'The police tried to get him to say where he had been but he begged the question and changed the subject'.

benign means 'kindly, well-disposed' when applied to people, as in 'fortunate enough to have a benign ruler'. This meaning may also be used of things, as in 'give a benign smile' and 'live in a benign climate'. As a medical term **benign** means 'nonmalignant, non-cancerous'. **Innocent** is another word for **benign** in this sense.

bête noire refers to 'something that one detests or fears', as in 'Loud pop music is her father's bête noire, although she sings with a pop group'. Note the spelling, particularly the accent (circumflex) on **bête** and the *e* at the end of **noire**. The phrase is French in origin and the plural form is **bêtes noires**, as in 'A bearded man is one of her many bêtes noires'.

better should be preceded by 'had' when it means 'ought to' or 'should', as in 'You had better leave now if you want to arrive there by nightfall' and 'We had better apologize for upsetting her'. In informal contexts, especially in informal speech as in 'Hey Joe, Mum says you better come now', the 'had' is often omitted but it should be retained in formal contexts. The negative form is 'had better not', as in 'He had better not try to deceive her'.

between is often found in the phrase 'between you and me' as in 'Between you and me I think he stole the money'. Note that 'me' is correct and that 'I' is wrong. This is because prepositions like 'between' are followed by an object, not a subject. 'I' acts as the subject of a sentence, as in 'I know her', and 'me' as the object, as in 'She knows me'.

between *see* **among**.

bi- of the words beginning with the prefix bi-, biannual and biennial are liable to be confused. **Biannual** means 'twice a year' and **biennial** means 'every two years'.

    Bicentenary and **bicentennial** both mean 'a 200th anniversary', as in 'celebrating the bicentenary/bicentennial of the firm'. **Bicentenary** is, however, the more common expression in British English, although **bicentennial** is more common in American English.

    Biweekly is a confusing word as it has two different meanings. It means both 'twice a week' and 'once every two weeks'. Thus there is no means of knowing without other information whether 'a bi-weekly publication' comes out once a week or every two weeks. The confusion arises because the prefix 'bi-', which means 'two', can refer both to doubling, as in 'bicycle', and halving, as in 'bisection'.

biannual *see* **bi-**.

bicentenary and **bicentennial** *see* **bi-**.

biennial *see* **bi-**.

billion traditionally meant 'one million million' in British English, but in modern usage it has increasingly taken on the American English meaning of 'one thousand million'. When the number of million pounds, etc, is specified, the number immediately precedes the word 'million' without the word 'of', as in 'The firm is worth five billion dollars', but if no number is present then 'of' precedes 'dollars, etc', ' as in 'The research project cost the country millions of dollars'. The word **billion** may also be used loosely to mean 'a great but unspecified number', as in 'Billions of people in the world live in poverty'.

birth name is a suggested alternative for

maiden name, a woman's surname before she married and took the name of her husband. **Maiden name** is considered by some to be inappropriate since maiden in one of its senses is another name for 'virgin' and it is now not at all usual for women to be virgins when they marry. Another possible name alternative is **family name**.

biweekly *see* **bi-**.

black is the word now usually applied to dark-skinned people of Afro-Caribbean origins and is the term preferred by most black-skinned people themselves. **Coloured** is considered by many to be offensive since it groups all non-Caucasians together. In America, African-American is becoming increasingly common as a substitute for **black**.

blond and **blonde** are both used to mean 'a fair-haired person', but they are not interchangeable. **Blond** is used to describe a man or boy, **blonde** is used to describe a woman or girl. They are derived from the French adjective, which changes endings according to the gender of the noun.

boat and **ship** are often used interchangeably, but usually **boat** refers to a smaller vessel than a ship.

bona fide is an expression of Latin origin meaning literally 'of good faith'. It means 'genuine, sincere' or 'authentic', as in 'a bona fide member of the group', 'a bona fide excuse for not going', or 'a bona fide agreement'.

bottom line is an expression from accountancy that has become commonly used in the general language. In accountancy it refers to the final line of a set of company accounts, which indicates whether the company has made a profit or a loss, obviously a very important line. In general English, **bottom line** has a range of meanings, from 'the final outcome or result', as in 'The bottom line of their discussion was that they decided to sell the company', through 'the most important point of something', as in 'The bottom line was whether they could get there on time or not', to 'the last straw', as in 'His affair with another woman was the bottom line of their stormy relationship and she left him'.

can and **may** both mean in one of their senses 'to be permitted'. In this sense **can** is much less formal than **may** and is best restricted to informal contexts, as in ' "Can I go to the park now?" asked the child.' **May** is used in more formal contexts, as in 'May I please have your name?' Both **can** and **may** have other meanings. **Can** has the meaning 'to be able', as in 'They thought his legs were permanently damaged but he can still walk'. **May** has the additional meaning 'to be likely', as in 'You may well be right'.

The past tense of **can** is **could**, as in 'The children asked if they could (= be permitted to) go to the park'. 'The old man could (= be unable to) not walk upstairs'. The past tense of **may** is **might**, as in 'The child asked if he might have a piece of cake (= be permitted to)'. 'They might (= be likely to) well get here tonight'.

cannot, can not, and **can't** all mean the same thing but they are used in different contexts. **Cannot** is the most usual form, as in 'The children have been told that they cannot go' and 'We cannot get there by public transport'. **Cannot** is written as two words only for emphasis, as in 'No, you can not have any more' and 'The invalid certainly can not walk to the ambulance'. **Can't** is used in less formal contexts and often in speech, as in 'I can't be bothered going out' and 'They can't bear to be apart'.

cardigan, jersey, jumper and **sweater** all refer to knitted garments for the top part of the body. **Cardigan** refers to a jacket-like garment with buttons down the front. **Jersey, jumper** and **sweater** refer to a knitted garment pulled over the head to get it on and off.

cardinal and **ordinal** numbers refer to different aspects of numbers. **Cardinal** is applied to those numbers that refer to quantity or value without referring to their place in the set, as in 'one', 'two', 'fifty' 'one hundred'. **Ordinal** is applied to numbers that refer to their order in a series, as in 'first', 'second', 'fortieth', 'hundredth'.

carer has recently taken on the meaning of 'a person who looks after a sick, handicapped or old relative or friend', as in 'carers requiring a break from their responsibilities'.

carpet and **rug** both refer to forms of floor covering. Generally a rug is smaller than a carpet, and the fitted variety of fabric floor covering is always known as carpet.

caster and **castor** are mainly interchangeable. Both forms can be applied to 'a swivelling wheel attached to the base of a piece of furniture to enable it to be moved easily' and 'a container with a perforated top from which sugar is sprinkled'. The kind of sugar known as **caster** can also be called **castor**, although this is less usual. The lubricating or medicinal oil known as **castor oil** is never spelt **caster**.

Catholic and **catholic** have different meanings. **Catholic** as an adjective refers to the Roman Catholic Church, as in 'The Pope is head of the Catholic Church', or to the universal body of Christians. As a noun it means 'a member of the Catholic Church', as in 'She is a Catholic but he is a Protestant'. Catholic with a lower-case initial letter means 'general, wide-ranging', as in 'a catholic selection of essays', and ' broadminded, liberal', as in 'a catholic attitude to the tastes of others'.

celibate means 'unmarried' or 'remaining unmarried and chaste, especially for religious reasons', as in 'Roman Catholic priests have to be celibate'. In modern usage, because of its connection with chastity, **celibate** has come to mean 'abstaining from sexual intercourse', as in 'The threat of Aids has made many people celibate'. The word is frequently misspelt. Note the *i* after *l*.

Celsius, centigrade and **Fahrenheit** are all scales of temperature. **Celsius** and **centigrade** mean the same and refer to a scale on which water freezes at 0° and boils at 100°. This scale is now the principal unit of temperature. **Celsius** is now the more acceptable term. **Fahrenheit** refers to a scale on which water freezes at 32° and boils at 212°. It is still used, informally at least, of the weather, and statements such as 'The temperature reached the nineties today' are still common.

Note the initial capital letters in **Celsius** and **Fahrenheit**. This is because they are named after people, namely the scientists who devised them.

centenary and **centennial** are both used to refer to a 'one-hundredth anniversary'.

Centenary is the more common term in British English, as in 'celebrate the town's centenary', whereas **centennial** is more common in American English. **Centennial** may be used as an adjective, as in 'organize the town's centennial celebrations'.

centigrade *see* **Celsius**.

centre and **middle** mean much the same, but **centre** is used more precisely than **middle** in some cases, as in 'a line through the centre of the circle' and 'She felt faint in the middle of the crowd'.

centre on and **centre around** are often used interchangeably, as in 'Her world centres on/around her children'. **Centre around** is objected to by some people on the grounds that **centre** is too specific to be used with something as vague as **around**. When it is used as a verb with place names, **centre** is used with 'at', as in 'Their business operation is centred at London'.

centuries are calculated from 1001, 1501, 1901, etc, not 1000, 1500, 1900, etc. This is because the years are counted from AD 1, there being no year 0.

chair is often used to mean 'a person in charge of a meeting, committee, etc', as in 'The committee has a new chair this year'. Formerly **chairman** was always used in this context, as in 'He was appointed chairman of the fund-raising committee' but this is disapproved of on the grounds that it is sexist. Formerly, **chairman** was sometimes used even if the person in charge of the meeting or committee was a woman, and sometimes **chairwoman** was used in this situation. **Chairperson**, which also avoids sexism, is frequently used instead of **chair**. **Chair** is also a verb meaning 'to be in charge of a meeting, committee, etc'.

-challenged is a modern suffix that is very much part of politically correct language. It is used to convey a disadvantage, problem or disorder in a more positive light. For example, 'visually challenged' is used in politically correct language instead of 'blind' or 'partially sighted', and 'aurally challenged' is used instead of 'deaf' or 'hard of hearing'. **-Challenged** is often used in humorous coinages, as in 'financially challenged', meaning 'penniless', and 'intellectually challenged', meaning 'stupid'.

charisma was formerly a theological word used to mean 'a spiritual gift', such as the gift of healing, etc. In modern usage it is used to describe 'a special quality or power that influences, inspires or stimulates other people, personal magnetism', as in 'The president was elected because of his charisma'. The adjective from **charisma** is **charismatic**, as in 'his charismatic style of leadership'.

chauvinism originally meant 'excessive patriotism', being derived from the name of Nicolas Chauvin, a soldier in the army of Napoleon Bonaparte, who was noted for his excessive patriotism. In modern usage **chauvinism** has come to mean 'excessive enthusiasm or devotion to a cause' or, more particularly, 'an irrational and prejudiced belief in the superiority of one's own cause'. When preceded by 'male', it refers specifically to attitudes and actions that assume the superiority of the male sex and thus the inferiority of women, as in 'accused of not giving her the job because of male chauvinism'. **Chauvinism** is frequently used to mean **male chauvinism**, as in 'He shows his chauvinism towards his female staff by never giving any of them senior jobs'. The adjective formed from **chauvinism** is **chauvinistic**.

chemist and **pharmacist** have the same meaning in one sense of **chemist** only. **Chemist** and **pharmacist** are both words for 'one who prepares drugs ordered by medical prescription'. **Chemist** has the additional meaning of 'a scientist who works in the field of chemistry', as in 'He works as an industrial chemist'.

childish and **childlike** both refer to someone being like a child but they are used in completely different contexts. **Childish** is used in a derogatory way about someone to indicate that he or she is acting like a child in an immature way, as in 'Even though she is 20 years old she has·childish tantrums when she does not get her own way' and 'childish handwriting for an adult'. **Childlike** is a term of approval or a complimentary term used to describe something that has some of the attractive qualities of childhood, as in 'She has a childlike enthusiasm for picnics' and 'He has a childlike trust in others'.

Christian name is used to mean someone's first name as opposed to someone's **surname**. It is increasingly being replaced by **first name** or **forename** since Britain has become a multicultural society where there are several religions as well as Christianity.

chronic *see* **acute**.

city and **town** in modern usage are usually distinguished on grounds of size and status, a city being larger and more important than a town. Originally in Britain a **city** was a town which had special rights conferred on it by royal charter and which usually had a cathedral.

clean and **cleanse** as verbs both mean 'to clean', as in 'clean the house' and 'cleanse the wound'. However, **cleanse** tends to indicate a more thorough cleaning than **clean** and sometimes carries the suggestion of 'to purify', as in 'prayer cleansing the soul'.

client and **customer**, although closely related in meaning, are not interchangeable. **Client** refers to 'a person who pays for the advice or services of a professional person', as in 'They are both clients of the same lawyer', 'a client waiting to see the bank manager' and 'hairdressers who keep their clients waiting'. **Customer** refers to 'a person who purchases goods from a shop, etc', as in 'customers complaining to shopkeepers about faulty goods' and 'a regular customer at the local supermarket'. **Client** is used in the sense of 'customer' by shops who regard it as a more superior word, as in ' clients of an exclusive dress boutique'.

climate no longer refers just to weather, as in 'go to live in a hot climate', 'Britain has a temperate climate'. It has extended its meaning to refer to 'atmosphere', as in 'live in a climate of despair' and to 'the present situation', as in 'businessmen nervous about the financial climate'.

clone originally was a technical word meaning 'one of a group of offspring that are asexually produced and which are genetically identical to the parent and to other members of the group'. In modern usage **clone** is frequently used loosely to mean 'something that is very similar to something else', as in 'In the sixties there were many

Beatles' clones', and 'grey-suited business-men looking like clones of each other'.

collaborate and **cooperate** are not interchangeable in all contexts. They both mean 'to work together for a common purpose', as in 'The two scientists are collaborating/cooperating on cancer research' and 'The rival building firms are collaborating/cooperating on the new shopping complex'. When the work concerned is of an artistic or creative nature **collaborate** is the more commonly used word, as in 'The two directors are collaborating on the film' and 'The composers collaborated on the theme music'. **Collaborate** also has the meaning of 'to work with an enemy, especially an enemy that is occupying one's country', as in 'a Frenchman who collaborated with the Germans when they installed a German government in France'.

coloured *see* **black**.

commence, begin, and **start** mean the same, but **commence** is used in a more formal context than the other two words, as in 'The legal proceedings will commence tomorrow' and 'The memorial service will commence with a hymn'. **Begin** and **start** are used less formally, as 'The match begins at 2 p.m.' and 'The film has already started'.

commensurate is followed by 'with' to form a phrase meaning 'proportionate to, appropriate to', as in 'a salary commensurate with her qualifications' and 'a price commensurate with the quality of the goods'.

comparatively means 'relatively, in comparison with a standard', as in 'The house was comparatively inexpensive for that area of the city' and 'In an area of extreme poverty they are comparatively well off'. In modern usage it is often used loosely to mean 'rather' or 'fairly' without any suggestion of reference to a standard, as in 'She has comparatively few friends' and 'It is a comparatively quiet resort'.

compare may take either the preposition 'to' or 'with'. 'To' is used when two things or people are being likened to each other or being declared similar, as in 'He compared her hair to silk' and 'He compared his wife to Helen of Troy'. 'With' is used when two things or people are being considered from the point of view of both similarities and differences, as in 'If you compare the new pupil's work with that of the present class you will find it brilliant', and 'If you compare the prices in the two stores you will find that the local one is the cheaper'. In modern usage the distinction is becoming blurred because the difference is rather subtle.

comparison is usually followed by the preposition 'with', as in 'In comparison with hers his work is brilliant'. However, when it means 'the action of likening something or someone to something or someone else', it is followed by 'to', as in 'the comparison of her beauty to that of Garbo'.

complementary medicine is a term applied to the treatment of illness or disorders by techniques other than conventional medicine. These include homoeopathy, osteopathy, acupuncture, acupressure, iridology, etc. The word **complementary** suggests that the said techniques complement and work alongside conventional medical techniques. **Alternative medicine** means the same as **complementary medicine**, but the term suggests that they are used instead of the techniques of conventional medicine rather than alongside them.

complex in one of its senses is used rather loosely in modern usage. It refers technically to 'an abnormal state caused by unconscious repressed desires or past experiences', as in 'an inferiority complex'. In modern usage it is used loosely to describe 'any obsessive concern or fear', as in 'She has a complex about her weight', 'He has a complex about his poor background'. **Complex** is also used to refer to 'a group of connected or similar things'. It is now used mainly of a group of buildings or units connected in some way, as in 'a shopping complex' or 'a sports complex'.

    Complex is also an adjective meaning 'complicated', as in 'His motives in carrying out the crime were complex' and 'The argument was too complex for most people to understand'.

compose, comprise and **constitute** are all similar in meaning but are used differently. **Compose** means 'to come together to make a whole, to make up'. It is most commonly found in the passive, as in 'The team was composed of young players' and 'The group was composed largely of elderly people'. It can be used in the active voice, as in 'the tribes which composed the nation' and 'the members which composed the committee', but this use is rarer. **Constitute** means the same as **compose** but it is usually used in the active voice, as in 'the foodstuffs that constitute a healthy diet' and 'the factors that constitute a healthy environment'. **Comprise** means 'to consist of, to be made up of'.

concave and **convex** are liable to be confused. **Concave** means 'curved inwards', as in 'The inside of a spoon would be described as concave'. **Convex** means 'curved outwards, bulging', as in 'The outside or bottom of a spoon would be described as convex'.

conducive, meaning 'leading to, contributing to', is followed by the preposition 'to', as in 'conditions conducive to health growth'.

conform may be followed by the preposition 'to' or the preposition 'with'. It is followed by 'to' when it means 'to keep to or comply with', as in 'conform to the conventions' and 'refuse to conform to the company regulations', and with 'with' when it means 'to agree with, to go along with', as in 'His ideas do not conform with those of the rest of the committee'.

connection and **connexion** are different forms of the same word, meaning 'a relationship between two things'. In modern usage **connection** is much the commoner spelling, as in 'no connection between the events' and 'a fire caused by a faulty connection'.

connote and **denote** are liable to be confused. **Connote** means 'to suggest something in addition to the main, basic meaning of something', as in 'the fear that the word cancer connotes' and 'The word 'home' connotes security and love'. **Denote** means 'to mean or indicate', as in 'The word cancer denotes a malignant illness' and 'The word "home" denotes the place where one lives'.

consist can be followed either by the preposition 'of' or by the preposition 'in', depending on the meaning. **Consist of** means

'to be made up of, to comprise', as in 'The team consists of eleven players and two reserve players'. **Consist in** means 'to have as the chief or only element or feature, to lie in', as in 'The charm of the village consists in its isolation' and 'The effectiveness of the plan consisted in its simplicity'.

constitute *see* **compose**.

contagious and **infectious** both refer to diseases that can be passed on to other people but they do not mean the same. **Contagious** means 'passed on by physical contact', as in 'He caught a contagious skin disease while working in the clinic' and 'Venereal diseases are contagious'. **Infectious** means 'caused by airborne or waterborne microorganisms', as in 'The common cold is highly infectious and is spread by people sneezing and coughing'.

contemporary originally meant 'living or happening at the same time', as in 'Shakespeare and Marlowe were contemporary playwrights' and 'Marlowe was contemporary with Shakespeare'. Later it came to mean also 'happening at the present time, current', as in 'What is your impression of the contemporary literary scene?' and 'Contemporary moral values are often compared unfavourably with those of the past'. These two uses of **contemporary** can cause ambiguity. In modern usage it is also used to mean 'modern, up-to-date', as in 'extremely contemporary designs'.

convex *see* **concave**.

cooperate *see* **collaborate**.

co-respondent *see* **correspondent**.

correspondent and **co-respondent** are liable to be confused. **Correspondent** refers either to 'a person who communicates by letter', as in 'They were correspondents for years but had never met', or to 'a person who contributes news items to a newspaper or radio or television programme', as in 'the foreign correspondent of the *Times*'. A **co-respondent** is 'a person who has been cited in a divorce case as having committed adultery with one of the partners'.

cousin can cause confusion. The children of brothers and sisters are **first cousins** to each other. The children of **first cousins** are **second cousins** to each other. The child of one's **first cousin** and the **first**

cousin of one's parents is one's **first cousin first removed**. The grandchild of one's **first cousin** or the **first cousin** of one's grandparent is one's **second cousin twice removed**.

crisis literally means 'turning point' and should be used to refer to 'a turning point in an illness', as in 'The fever reached a crisis and she survived' and 'a decisive or crucial moment in a situation, whose outcome will make a definite difference or change for better or worse', as in 'The financial situation has reached a crisis—the firm will either survive or go bankrupt'. In modern usage **crisis** is becoming increasingly used loosely for 'any worrying or troublesome situation', as in 'There's a crisis in the kitchen. The cooker's broken down'. The plural is **crises**.

criterion, meaning 'a standard by which something or someone is judged or evaluated', as 'What criterion is used for deciding which pupils will gain entrance to the school?' and 'The standard of play was the only criterion for entrance to the golf club'. It is a singular noun of which **criteria** is the plural, as in 'They must satisfy all the criteria for entrance to the club or they will be refused'.

critical has two main meanings. It means 'finding fault', as in 'His report on her work was very critical'. It also means 'at a crisis, at a decisive moment, crucial', as in 'It was a critical point in their relationship'. This meaning is often applied to the decisive stage of an illness, as in 'the critical hours after a serious operation', and is used also to describe an ill person who is at a crucial stage of an illness or dangerously ill. **Critical** also means 'involved in making judgements or assessments of artistic or creative works', as in 'give a critical evaluation of the author's latest novel'.

crucial means 'decisive, critical', as in 'His vote is crucial since the rest of the committee is split down the middle'. In modern usage it is used loosely to mean 'very important', as in 'It is crucial that you leave now'. **Crucial** is derived from crux, meaning 'a decisive point', as in 'the crux of the situation'.

curriculum is derived from Latin and origi-

nally took the plural form **curricula**, but in modern usage the plural form **curriculums** is becoming common.

curriculum vitae refers to 'a brief account of a person's qualifications and career to date'. It is often requested by an employer when a candidate is applying for a job. **Vitae** is pronounced *vee*-ti, the second syllable rhyming with my.

data was formerly used mainly in a scientific or technical context and was always treated as a plural noun, taking a plural verb, as in 'compare the data which were provided by the two research projects'. The singular form was **datum**, which is now rare. In modern usage the word **data** became used in computing as a collective noun meaning 'body of information' and is frequently used with a singular verb, as in 'The data is essential for our research'. This use has spread into the general language.

dates these are usually written in figures, as in 1956, rather than in words, as in nineteen fifty-six, except in formal contexts, such as legal documents. There are various ways of writing dates. The standard form in Britain is becoming day followed by month followed by year, as in '24 February 1970'. In North America the standard form of this is 'February 24, 1970', and that is a possibility in Britain also. Alternatively, some people write '24th February 1970'. Care should be taken with the writing of dates entirely in numbers, especially if one is corresponding with someone in North America. In Britain the day of the month is put first, the month second and the year third, as in '2/3/50', '2 March 1950'. In North America the month is put first, followed by the day of the month and the year. Thus in North America '2/3/50' would be '3 February 1950'.

Centuries may be written either in figures, as in 'the 19th century', or in words, as in 'the nineteenth century'

Decades and centuries are now usually written without apostrophes. as in '1980s' and '1990s'.

datum *see* **data**.

deadly and **deathly** both refer to death but they have different meanings. **Deadly** means 'likely to cause death, fatal', as in

'His enemy dealt him a deadly blow with his sword' and 'He contracted a deadly disease in the jungle'. **Deathly** means 'referring to death, resembling death', as in 'She was deathly pale with fear'.

decimate literally means 'to kill one in ten' and is derived from the practice in ancient Rome of killing every tenth soldier as a punishment for mutiny. In modern usage it has come to mean 'to kill or destroy a large part of', as in 'Disease has decimated the population'. It has also come to mean 'to reduce considerably', as in 'the recession has decimated the jobs in the area'.

defective and **deficient** are similar in meaning but are not interchangeable. **Defective** means 'having a fault, not working properly', as in 'return the defective vacuum cleaner to the shop', 'The second-hand car proved to be defective' and 'He cannot be a pilot as his eyesight is defective'. **Deficient** means 'having a lack, lacking in', as in 'The athlete is very fast but he is deficient in strength' and 'Her diet is deficient in vitamin C'.

deficient *see* **defective**.

definite article *see* **the**.

delusion and **illusion** in modern usage are often used interchangeably but they are not quite the same. **Delusion** means 'a false or mistaken idea or belief', as in 'He is under the delusion that he is brilliant' and 'suffer from delusions of grandeur'. It can be part of a mental disorder, as in 'He suffers from the delusion that he is Napoleon'. **Illusion** means 'a false or misleading impression', as in 'There was no well in the desert—it was an optical illusion', 'The conjurer's tricks were based on illusion' and 'the happy childhood illusions that everyone lived happy ever after'.

demise is a formal word for death, as in 'He never recovered from the demise of his wife'. In modern usage it applies to the ending of an activity, as in 'The last decade saw the demise of coal-mining in the area'. In modern usage it has come to mean also 'the decline or failure of an activity', as in 'the gradual demise of his business'.

dénouement means 'the final outcome', as in 'The novel had a unexpected denouement'. It is pronounced day-*noo*-mon.

derisive and **derisory** are both adjectives connected with the noun 'derision' but they have different meanings. **Derisive** means 'expressing derision, scornful, mocking' as in 'give a derisive smile' and 'His efforts were met with derisive laughter'. Derisory means 'deserving derision, ridiculous' as in 'Their attempts at playing the game were derisory'. **Derisory** is frequently used to mean 'ridiculously small or inadequate', as in 'The salary offered was derisory'.

despatch and **dispatch** are interchangeable. It is most common as a verb meaning 'to send', as in 'despatch/dispatch an invitation'. It is rarer as a noun. It means 'a message or report, often official', as in 'receive a despatch/dispatch that the soldiers were to move on'. It also means 'rapidity, speed', as in 'carry out the orders with despatch/dispatch'.

dessert, pudding, sweet and **afters** all mean the same thing. They refer to the last and sweet course of a meal. **Dessert** has relatively recently become the most widespread of these terms. **Pudding** was previously regarded by the upper and middle classes as the most acceptable word of these, but it is now thought of by many as being rather old-fashioned or as being more suited to certain types of dessert than others—thus syrup sponge would be a pudding, but not fresh fruit salad. **Sweet** is a less formal word and is regarded by some people as being lower-class or regional. **Afters** is common only in very informal English.

devil's advocate is a phrase that is often misunderstood. It means 'someone who points out the possible flaws or faults in an argument etc', as in 'He played the devil's advocate and showed her the weakness in her argument so that she was able to perfect it before presenting it to the committee'. The phrase is sometimes wrongly thought of as meaning 'someone who defends an unpopular point of view or person'.

diagnosis and **prognosis** are liable to be confused. Both are used with reference to disease but have different meanings. **Diagnosis** refers to 'the identification of a disease or disorder', as in 'She had cancer but the doctor failed to make the correct diagnosis until it was too late'. **Prognosis** refers to 'the prediction of the likely course of a disease or disorder', as in 'According to the doctor's prognosis, the patient will be dead in six months'.

dice was originally the plural form of the singular noun **die**, but **die** is now rarely used. Instead, **dice** is used as both a singular and a plural noun, as in 'throw a wooden dice' and 'use three different dice in the same game'.

different is most usually followed by the preposition 'from', as in 'Their style of living is different from ours'. **Different from** is considered to be the most correct construction, particularly in formal English. **Different to** is used in informal situations, as in 'His idea of a good time is different to ours'. **Different than** is used in American English.

dilemma is frequently used wrongly. It refers to 'a situation in which one is faced with two or more equally undesirable possibilities', as in 'I can't decide which of the offers to accept. It's a real dilemma'.

dinner, lunch, supper and **tea** are terms that can cause confusion. Their use can vary according to class, region of the country and personal preference. Generally speaking, people who have their main meal in the evening call it **dinner**. However, people who have their main meal in the middle of the day frequently call this meal **dinner**. People who have **dinner** in the evening usually refer to their midday meal, usually a lighter meal, as **lunch**. A more formal version of this word is **luncheon**, which is now quite a rare word. **Supper** has two meanings, again partly dependent on class and region. It can refer either to the main meal of the day if it is eaten in the evening—when it is virtually a synonym for **dinner**. Alternatively, it can refer to a light snack, such as cocoa and toasted cheese, eaten late in the evening before going to bed. **Tea** again has two meanings when applied to a meal. It either means a light snack-type meal of tea, sandwiches and cakes eaten in the late afternoon. Alternatively, it can refer to a cooked meal, sometimes taken with tea, and also referred to

as **high tea**, eaten in the early evening, rather than **dinner** later in the evening.

disabled is objected to by some people on the grounds that it is a negative term, but it is difficult to find an acceptable alternative. In politically correct language **physically challenged** has been suggested as has **differently abled**, but neither of these has gained widespread use. It should be noted that the use of 'the disabled' should be avoided. 'Disabled people' should be used instead.

disablism and **disableism** mean 'discrimination against disabled people', as in 'He felt his failure to get a job was because of disablism'. **Disablist** and **disableist** are adjectives meaning 'showing or practising disablism', as in 'guilty of disablist attitudes'. They also refer to 'a person who discriminates on the grounds of disability', as in 'That employer is a disablist'.

disassociate and **dissociate** are used interchangeably, as in 'She wished to disassociate/dissociate herself from the statement issued by her colleagues', but **dissociate** is the more usual.

discover and **invent** are not interchangeable. **Discover** means 'to find something that is already in existence but is generally unknown', as in 'discover a new route to China' and 'discover the perfect place for a holiday'. **Invent** means 'to create something that has never before existed', as in 'invent the telephone' and 'invent a new form of heating system'.

disempowered in modern usage does not mean only 'having one's power removed', as in 'The king was disempowered by the invading general', but also means the same as 'powerless', as in 'We are disempowered to give you any more money'. **Disempowered** is seen in politically correct language as a more positive way of saying **powerless**.

disinterested and **uninterested** are often used interchangeably in modern usage to mean 'not interested, indifferent', as in 'pupils totally disinterested/uninterested in school work'. Many people dislike **disinterested** being used in this way and regard it as a wrong use, but it is becoming increasingly common. **Disinterested** also means 'impartial, unbiased', as in 'ask a disinterested party to settle the dispute between them'.

disorient and **disorientate** are used interchangeably. 'The town had changed so much since his last visit that he was completely disoriented/disorientated' and 'After the blow to her head she was slightly disoriented/disorientated'.

divorcee refers to 'a divorced person', as in 'a club for divorcees'. **Divorcé** refers to 'a divorced man', and **divorcée** to 'a divorced woman'.

double negative the occurrence of two negative words in a single sentence or clause, as in 'He didn't say nothing' and 'We never had no quarrel'. This is usually considered incorrect in standard English, although it is a feature of some social or regional dialects. The use of the double negative, if taken literally, often has the opposite meaning to the one intended. Thus 'He didn't say nothing' conveys the idea that 'He said something'.

Some double negatives are considered acceptable, as in 'I wouldn't be surprised if they don't turn up', although it is better to restrict such constructions to informal contexts. The sentence quoted conveys the impression that the speaker will be quite surprised if 'they' do 'turn up'. Another example of an acceptable double negative is 'I can't not worry about the children. Anything could have happened to them'. Again this type of construction is best restricted to informal contexts.

It is the semi-negative forms, such as 'hardly' and 'scarcely', that cause most problems with regard to double negatives, as in 'We didn't have hardly any money to buy food' and 'They didn't have barely enough time to catch the bus'. Such sentences are incorrect.

doubtful and **dubious** can be used interchangeably in the sense of 'giving rise to doubt, uncertain', as in 'The future of the project is dubious/doubtful', and in the sense of 'having doubts, unsure', as in 'I am doubtful/dubious about the wisdom of going'. **Dubious** also means 'possibly dishonest or bad', as in 'of dubious morals'.

draughtsman/woman and **draftsman/woman** are not the same. **Draughtsman/woman** refers to 'a person who draws detailed plans of a building, etc', as in 'study the plans of the bridge prepared by the draughtsman'. **Draftsman/woman** refers to 'a person who prepares a preliminary version of plans, etc', as in 'several draftswomen working on the draft parliamentary bills'.

drawing room *see* **sitting room**.

dreamed and **dreamt** are interchangeable both as the past tense and the past participle of the verb 'dream', as in 'She dreamed/dreamt about living in the country' and in 'He has dreamed/dreamt the same dream for several nights'.

drier and **dryer** can both be used to describe 'a machine or appliance that dries', as in 'hair-drier/hair-dryer' and 'tumbler drier/dryer'. As an adjective meaning 'more dry', **drier** is the usual word, as in 'a drier summer than last year'.

dubious *see* **doubtful**.

due to, owing to and **because of** should not be used interchangeably. Strictly speaking, **due to** should be used only adjectivally, as in 'His poor memory is due to brain damage' and 'cancellations due to bad weather'. When a prepositional use is required **owing to** and **because of** should be used, as in 'the firm was forced to close owing to a lack of capital' and 'The train was cancelled because of snow on the line'. In modern usage it is quite common for **due to** to be used instead of **owing to** or **because of** because the distinction is rather difficult to comprehend.

e.g. means 'for example' and is an abbreviation of the Latin phrase *exempli gratia*. It is used before examples of something just previously mentioned, as in 'He cannot eat dairy products, e.g. milk, butter and cream'. A comma is usually placed just before it and, unlike some abbreviations, it has full stops.

each other and **one another** used not to be used interchangeably. It was taught that **each other** should be used when only two people are involved and that **one another** should be used when more than two people are involved, as in 'John and Mary really love each other' and 'All the members of the family love one another'. In modern use this restriction is often ignored.

EC and **EEC** both refer to the same thing, but **EC**, the abbreviation for **Economic Community** replaced **EEC**, the abbreviation for **European Economic Community**.

Both have now been replaced by **EU**, for **European Union**.

effeminate *see* **female**.

egoist and **egotist** are frequently used interchangeably in modern usage. Although they are not, strictly speaking, the same, the differences between them are rather subtle. **Egoist** refers to 'a person intent on self-interest, a selfish person', as in 'an egoist who never gave a thought to the needs of others'. **Egotist** refers to 'a person who is totally self-centred and obsessed with his/her own concerns', as in 'a real egotist who was always talking about herself'.

eke out originally meant 'to make something more adequate by adding to it or supplementing it', as in 'The poor mother eked out the small amount of meat with a lot of vegetables to feed her large family'. It can now also mean 'to make something last longer by using it sparingly', as in 'try to eke out our water supply until we reach a town', and 'to succeed or make with a great deal of effort', as in 'eke out a meagre living from their small farm'.

elder and **older** are not interchangeable. **Elder** is used only of people, as in 'The smaller boy is the elder of the two'. It is frequently used of family relationships, as in 'His elder brother died before him'. **Older** can be used of things as well as people, as in 'The church looks ancient but the castle is the older of the buildings' and 'The smaller girl is the older of the two'. It also can be used of family relationships, as in 'It was his older brother who helped him'. **Elder** used as a noun suggests experience or worthiness as well as age, as in 'Important issues used to be decided by the village elders' and 'Children should respect their elders and betters'.

elderly, as well as meaning 'quite or rather old', as in 'a town full of middle-aged and elderly people', is a more polite term than 'old', no matter how old the person referred to is, as in 'a residential home for elderly people'. **Elderly** is used only of people, except when used humorously, as in 'this cheese is getting rather elderly'.

eldest and **oldest** follow the same pattern as **elder** and **older**, as in 'The smallest boy is the eldest of the three', 'His eldest brother lived longer than any of them', 'The castle is the oldest building in the town' and 'He has four brothers but the oldest one is dead'.

empathy and **sympathy** are liable to be confused although they are not interchangeable. **Empathy** means 'the ability to imagine and share another's feelings, experiences, etc', as in 'As a single parent herself, the journalist has a real empathy with women bringing up children on their own' and 'The writer felt a certain empathy with the subject of his biography since they both came from a poverty-stricken childhood'. **Sympathy** means 'a feeling of compassion, pity or sorrow towards someone', as in 'feel sympathy for homeless children' and 'show sympathy towards the widow'.

endemic is usually used to describe a disease and means 'occurring in a particular area', as in 'a disease endemic to the coastal areas of the country' and 'difficult to clear the area of endemic disease'.

enervate is a word that is frequently misused. It means 'to weaken, to lessen in vitality', as in 'she was enervated by the extreme heat' and 'Absence of funding had totally enervated the society'. It is often wrongly used as though it meant the opposite.

enquiry and **inquiry** are frequently used interchangeably, as in 'make enquiries/inquiries about her health'. However some people see a distinction between them and use **enquiry** for ordinary requests for information, as in 'make enquiries about the times of trains'. They use **inquiry** only for 'investigation', as in 'The police have begun a murder inquiry' and 'launch an inquiry into the hygiene standards of the food firm'.

equal can be followed either by the preposition 'with' or the preposition 'to', but the two constructions are not interchangeable. **Equal to** is used in such sentences as 'He wished to climb the hill but his strength was not equal to the task'. **Equal with** is used in such sentences as 'After many hours of playing the two players remained equal with each other' and 'The women in the factory are seeking a pay scale equal with that of men'.

equally should not be followed by 'as'. Examples of it used correctly include 'Her brother is an expert player but she is equally talented' and 'He is trying hard but his competitors are trying equally hard'. These should not read 'but she is equally as talented' nor 'but his competitors are trying equally as hard'.

Esq. a word that can be used instead of 'Mr' when addressing an envelope to a man, as in 'John Jones, Esq.'. It is mostly used in formal contexts. Note that Esq. is used instead of 'Mr', not as well as it. It is usually spelt with a full stop.

etc the abbreviation of a Latin phrase *et cetera*, meaning 'and the rest, and other things'. It is used at the end of lists to indicate that there exist other examples of the kind of thing that has just been named, as in 'He grows potatoes, carrots, turnips, etc', 'The girls can play tennis, hockey, squash, etc', 'The main branch of the bank can supply francs, marks, lire, kroner, etc'. Etc is preceded by a comma and can be spelt with or without a full stop.

ethnic is a word that causes some confusion. It means 'of a group of people classified according to race, nationality, culture, etc', as in 'a cosmopolitan country with a wide variety of ethnic groups'. It is frequently used loosely to mean 'relating to race', as in 'violent clashes thought to be ethnic in origin', or 'foreign' as in 'prefer ethnic foods to British foods'.

EU the abbreviation for European Union, the term which has replaced European Community and European Economic Community.

evade and **avoid** are similar in meaning but not identical. **Evade** means 'to keep away from by cunning or deceit', as in 'The criminal evaded the police by getting his friend to impersonate him'. **Avoid** means simply 'to keep away from', as in 'Women avoid that area of town at night'.

evasion and **avoidance** are frequently applied to the non-payment of income tax but they are not interchangeable. Tax **avoidance** refers to 'the legal nonpayment of tax by clever means'. Tax **evasion** refers to 'the illegal means of avoiding tax by cunning and dishonest means'.

even should be placed carefully in a sentence since its position can influence the meaning. Compare 'He didn't even acknowledge her' and 'He didn't acknowledge even her'. and 'He doesn't even like Jane , let alone love her' and 'He hates the whole family—he doesn't like even Jane'. This shows that **even** should be placed immediately before the word it refers to in order to avoid ambiguity. In spoken English people often place it where it feels most natural, before the verb as in 'He even finds it difficult to relax on holiday'. To be absolutely correct this should be 'He finds it difficult to relax even on holiday' or 'Even on holiday he finds it difficult to relax'.

except is commoner than **except for**. **Except** is used in such sentences as 'They are all dead except his father', 'He goes every day except Sunday'. **Except for** is used at the beginning of sentences, as in 'Except for Fred, all the workers were present', and where **except** applies to a longish phrase, as in 'There was no one present except for the maid cleaning the stairs' and 'The house was silent except for the occasional purring of the cat'. When followed by a pronoun, this should be in the accusative or objective, as in 'There was no one there except *him*' and 'Everyone stayed late except *me*'.

explicit and **implicit** are liable to be confused although they are virtually opposites. **Explicit** means 'direct, clear', as in 'The instructions were not explicit enough' and 'Give explicit reasons for your decision'. **Explicit** is often used in modern usage to mean 'with nothing hidden or implied', as in 'explicit sex scenes'. **Implicit** means 'implied, not directly expressed', as in 'There was an implicit threat in their warning' and 'an implicit criticism in his comments on their actions'. **Implicit** also means 'absolute and unquestioning', as in 'an implicit faith in his ability to succeed' and 'an implicit confidence in her talents'.

extrovert and **introvert** are liable to be confused although they are opposites. **Extrovert** refers to 'a person who is more interested in what is going on around him/her than in his/her own thoughts and feelings, such a person usually being outgoing and sociable', as in 'She is a real extrovert who loves to entertain the guests at parties'. **Introvert** refers to 'a person who is more concerned with his/her own thoughts and feelings than with what is going around him/her, such a person usually being shy and reserved', as in 'an introvert who hates having to speak in public' and 'introverts who prefer to stay at home than go to parties'. Both **extrovert** and **introvert** can be adjectives as well as nouns, as in 'extrovert behaviour' and 'introvert personality'. Note the spelling of **extrovert**. It was formerly spelt with an *a* instead of an *o*.

fahrenheit *see* **Celsius**.

family name is used in politically correct language instead of **maiden name** since this is thought to imply that all women are virgins before they are married. Thus 'Her family name was Jones' would be used instead of 'Her maiden name was Jones'. Another politically correct term is **birth name**, as in 'Her birth name was Jones'.

fantastic literally means 'relating to fantasy, fanciful, strange', as in 'fantastic dreams' and 'tales of fantastic events'. In modern usage it is often used informally to mean 'exceptionally good, excellent', as in 'have a fantastic holiday' and 'be a fantastic piano player'. It can also mean in informal usage 'very large', as in 'pay a fantastic sum of money'.

farther and **further** are not used interchangeably in all situations in modern usage. **Farther** is mainly restricted to sentences where physical distance is involved, as in 'It is farther to Glasgow from here than it is to Edinburgh'. **Further** can also be used in this sense, as in 'It is further to the sea than I thought'. When referring to time or extent, **further** is used, as in 'Further time is required to complete the task' and 'The police have ordered further investigations'. It can also mean 'additional', as in 'We shall require further supplies'. **Further**, unlike **farther**, can be used as a verb to mean 'to help the progress or development about', as in 'further the cause of freedom'.

faux pas is a French phrase that has been adopted into the English language. It means 'a social blunder, an indiscreet or embarrassing remark or deed', as in 'The hostess made a faux pas when she asked after her guest's wife, not knowing that they had divorced last year'. **Faux** is pronounced to rhyme with *foe*, and **pas** is pronounced *pa*.

fax is an abbreviation of 'facsimile' and refers to 'an electronic system for transmitting documents using telephone lines'. As a noun **fax** can refer to the machine transmitting the documents, as in 'the fax has broken down again'; to the system used in the transmission, as in 'send the report by fax'; and the document or documents so transmitted, as in 'He replied to my fax at once'.

female, feminine and **feminist** all relate to women but they are by no means interchangeable. **Female** refers to the sex of a person, animal or plant, as in 'the female members of the group', 'the female wolf and her cubs' and 'the female reproductive cells'. It refers to the childbearing sex and contrasts with 'male'. **Feminine** means 'having qualities that are considered typical of women or are traditionally associated with women', as in 'wear feminine clothes', 'take part in supposedly feminine pursuits, such as cooking and sewing' and 'feminine hairstyles'. It is the opposite of 'masculine'. It can be used of men as well as women, when it is usually derogatory, as in 'He has a very feminine voice' and 'He walks in a very feminine way'. When applied in a derogatory way to a man, **feminine** means much the same as **effeminate**. **Feminine** also applies to the gender of words, as in 'Lioness is the feminine form of lion'. **Feminist** means 'referring to feminism', 'feminism' being 'a movement based on the belief that women should have the same rights, opportunities, etc', as in 'management trying to avoid appointing anyone with feminist ideas' and 'Equal opportunities is one of the aims of the feminist movement'.

ferment and **foment** can both mean 'to excite,

to stir up', as in 'Troublemakers out to ferment discontent' and 'People out to foment trouble in the crowd'. Both words have other meanings that do not relate to each other. **Ferment** means 'to undergo the chemical process known as fermentation', as in 'home-made wine fermenting in the basement'. **Foment** means 'to apply warmth and moisture to in order to lessen pain or discomfort', as in 'foment the old man's injured hip'.

few and **a few** do not convey exactly the same meaning. **Few** is used to mean the opposite of 'many', as in 'We expected a good many people to come but few did' and 'Many people entered the competition but few won a prize'. The phrase **a few** is used to mean the opposite of 'none', as in 'We didn't expect anyone to turn up but a few did' and 'We thought that none of the students would get a job but a few did'.

fewer see **less**.

fictional and **fictitious** are both derived from the noun 'fiction' and are interchangeable in the sense of 'imagined, invented', as in 'a fictional character based on an old man whom he used to know' and 'The events in the novel are entirely fictitious'. However, **fictitious** only is used in the sense of 'invented, false', as in 'an entirely fictitious account of the accident' and 'think up fictitious reasons for being late'.

fill in and **fill out** are both used to mean 'to complete a form, etc by adding the required details', as in 'fill in/fill out an application form for a passport'. In British English **fill in** is the more common term, although **fill out** is the accepted term in American English.

first and **firstly** are now both considered acceptable in lists, although formerly **firstly** was considered unacceptable. Originally the acceptable form of such a list was as in 'There are several reasons for staying here. First, we like the house, secondly we have pleasant neighbours, thirdly we hate moving house'. Some users now prefer to use the adjectival forms of 'second' and 'third' when using **first**, as in 'He has stated his reasons for going to another job. First, he has been offered a higher salary, second, he has more opportunities for promotion,

third, he will have a company car'. As indicated, **firstly** is now quite acceptable and is the form preferred by many people, as in 'They have several reasons for not having a car. Firstly they have very little money, secondly, they live right next to the busstop, thirdly, they feel cars are not environmentally friendly'.

first name see **Christian name**.

fish and **fishes** are both found as plural forms of 'fish', but **fish** is by far the more widely used form, as in 'He keeps tropical fish', 'Some fish live in fresh water and some in the sea' and 'there are now only three fish in the tank'. **Fishes** is rarely used but when it is, it is usually used to refer to different species of fish, as in 'He is comparing the fishes of the Pacific Ocean with those of the Indian Ocean'. **Fish** can also be used in this case.

flak originally referred to 'gunfire aimed at enemy aircraft', as in 'Pilots returning across the English Channel encountered heavy flak'. In modern usage it is also applied to 'severe criticism', as in 'the government receiving flak for raising taxes'.

flammable and **inflammable** both mean 'easily set on fire, burning easily', as in 'Children's nightclothes should not be made of flammable/inflammable material' and 'The chemical is highly flammable/inflammable'. **Inflammable** is frequently misused because some people wrongly regard it as meaning 'not burning easily', thinking that it is like such words as 'incredible', 'inconceivable' and 'intolerant' where the prefix 'in' means 'not'.

flotsam and **jetsam** are often used together to refer to 'miscellaneous objects, odds and ends', as in 'We have moved most of the furniture to the new house—there's just the flotsam and jetsam left', and 'vagrants, tramps', as in 'people with no pity in their hearts for the flotsam and jetsam of society'. In the phrase **flotsam and jetsam** they are used as though they meant the same thing but this is not the case. Both words relate to the remains of a wrecked ship, but **flotsam** refers to 'the wreckage of the ship found floating in the water', as in 'The coastguards knew the ship must have broken up when they saw bits of flotsam near the rocks', while **jetsam** refers to 'goods and equipment thrown overboard from a ship in distress in order to lighten it', as in 'The coastguards were unable to find the ship although they found the jetsam'.

forbear and **forebear** are interchangeable in one meaning of **forbear** only. **Forbear** is a verb meaning 'to refrain from', as in 'I hope she can forbear from pointing out that she was right' and this cannot be spelt **forebear**. However, **forebear** meaning 'ancestor' can also be spelt **forbear**, as in 'One of his *forebears/forbears* received a gift of land from Henry VIII'.

The verb **forbear** is pronounced with the emphasis on the second syllable as for-*bair*. The nouns **forbear** and **forebear** are pronounced alike with the emphasis on the first syllable as *for*-bair. The past tense of the verb **forbear** is **forbore**, as in 'He forbore to mention that he was responsible for the mistake'.

forever can be spelt as two words when it means 'eternally, for all time', as in 'doomed to separate forever/for ever' and 'have faith in the fact that they would dwell forever/for ever with Christ'. In the sense of 'constantly or persistently', only **forever** is used, as in 'His wife was forever nagging' and 'the child was forever asking for sweets'.

former and **latter** are opposites. **Former** refers to 'the first of two people or things mentioned' while **latter** refers to 'the second of two people or things mentioned', as in 'He was given two options, either to stay in his present post but accept less money or to be transferred to another branch of the company. He decided to accept the former/latter option'. **Former** also means 'previous, at an earlier time', as in 'He is a former chairman of the company' and 'She is a former holder of the championship title'.

further *see* **farther**.

gaol *see* **jail**.

gay originally meant 'merry, light-hearted', as in 'the gay laughter of children playing' and 'everyone feeling gay at the sight of the sunshine'. Although this meaning still exists in modern usage, it is rarely used since **gay** has come to be an accepted word

for 'homosexual', as in 'gay rights' and 'gay bars'. Although the term can be applied to men or women it is most commonly applied to men, the corresponding word for women being **lesbian**. There is a growing tendency among homosexuals to describe themselves as **queer**, a term that was formerly regarded as being offensive.

geriatric is frequently found in medical contexts to mean 'elderly' or 'old', as in 'an ever-increasing number of geriatric patients' and 'a shortage of geriatric wards'. In such contexts **geriatric** is not used in a belittling or derogatory way, **geriatrics** being the name given to the branch of medicine concerned with the health and diseases of elderly people. However, **geriatric** is often used in the general language to refer to old people in a derogatory or scornful way, as in 'geriatric shoppers getting in the way' or 'geriatric drivers holding up the traffic'.

gibe and **jibe** both mean 'to jeer at, mock, make fun of', as in 'rich children gibing/jibing at the poor children for wearing out-of-date clothes'. **Gibe** and **jibe** are nouns as well as verbs as in 'politicians tired of the gibes/jibes of the press'.

Gipsy and **Gypsy** are both acceptable spellings, as in 'Gipsies/Gypsies travelling through the country in their caravans'. Some people object to the word **Gipsy** or **Gypsy**, preferring the word traveller, as in 'councils being asked to build sites for travellers'. The term **traveller** is used to apply to a wider range of people who travel the country, as in 'New Age travellers', and not just to Gipsies, who are Romany in origin.

girl means 'a female child or adolescent', as in 'separate schools for girls and boys' and 'Girls tend to mature more quickly than boys'. However it is often applied to a young woman, or indeed to a woman of any age, as in 'He asked his wife if she was going to have a night out with the girls from the office'. Many women object to this use, regarding it as patronizing, although the user of the term does not always intend to convey this impression.

gourmand and **gourmet** and **glutton** all have reference to food but they do not mean quite the same thing. **Gourmand** refers to 'a person who likes food and eats a lot of it', as in 'Gourmands tucking into huge helpings of the local food'. It means much the same as **glutton**, but **glutton** is a more condemnatory term, as in 'gluttons stuffing food into their mouths'. **Gourmet** is a more refined term, being used to refer to 'a person who enjoys food and who is discriminating and knowledgeable about it', as in 'gourmets who spend their holidays seeking out good local restaurants and produce'. In modern usage **gourmet** is often used as an adjective to mean 'high-class, elaborate, expensive', as in 'gourmet restaurants' and 'gourmet foods'.

graffiti Italian in origin and actually the plural form of **graffito**, meaning a single piece of writing or drawing, but this is now hardly ever used in English.

green is used to mean 'concerned with the conservation of the environment', as in 'a political party concerned with green issues' and 'buy as many green products as possible'. The word is derived from German *grün*, the political environmental lobby having started in West Germany, as it was then called.

grey and **gray** are both acceptable spellings. In British English, however, **grey** is the more common, as in 'different shades of grey' and 'grey hair', but **gray** is the standard form in American English.

gypsy *see* **gipsy**.

handicapped is disliked by some people because they feel it is too negative a term. There is as yet no widespread alternative apart from **disabled**, although various suggestions have been made as part of the politically correct language movement, such as **physically challenged** and **differently abled**.

hard and **soft** are both terms applied to drugs. **Hard drugs** refer to 'strong drugs that are likely to be addictive', as in 'Heroin and cocaine are hard drugs'. **Soft drugs** refer to 'drugs that are considered unlikely to cause addiction', as in 'cannabis and other soft drugs'.

hardly is used to indicate a negative idea. Therefore a sentence or clause containing it does not require another negative. Sentences, such as 'I couldn't hardly see him'

and 'He left without hardly a word' are *wrong*. They should read 'I could hardly see him' and 'He left with hardly a word'. **Hardly** is followed by 'when', not 'than', as in 'Hardly had he entered the house when he collapsed', although the 'than' construction is very common.

he/she is a convention used to avoid sexism. Before the rise of feminism anyone referred to, whose sex was not specified, was assumed to be male, as in 'Each pupil must take his book home' and 'Every driver there parked his car illegally'. The only exception to this occurred in situations that were thought to be particularly appropriate to women, as in 'The cook should make her own stock' and 'The nurse has left her book behind'. In modern usage where attempts are made to avoid sexism either **he/she** or 'he or she' is frequently used, as in 'Each manager is responsible for his/her department' or 'It is a doctor's duty to explain the nature of the treatment to his or her patient'. People who regard this convention as being clumsy should consider restructuring the sentence or putting it in the plural, as in 'All managers are responsible for their departments'. Some users prefer to be ungrammatical and use a plural pronoun with a singular noun, as in 'Every pupil should take their books home' and this use is becoming increasingly common, even in textbooks.

heterosexism refers to discrimination and prejudice by a heterosexual person against a homosexual one, as in 'He was convinced that he had not got the job because he was gay—that the employer had been guilty of heterosexism'.

historic and **historical** are both adjectives formed from the noun 'history' but they are not interchangeable. **Historic** refers to events that are important enough to earn, or have earned, a place in history, as in 'Nelson's historic victory at Trafalgar' and 'the astronaut's historic landing on the moon'. It can be used loosely to mean 'extremely memorable', as in 'attend a historic party'. **Historical** means 'concerning past events', as in 'historical studies', or 'based on the study of history'.

hopefully has two meanings. The older

meaning is 'with hope', as in 'The child looked hopefully at the sweet shop window' and 'It is better to travel hopefully than to arrive'. A more recent meaning, which is disliked by some people, means 'it is to be hoped that', as in 'Hopefully we shall soon be there'.

humanism and **humanitarianism** are liable to be confused. **Humanism** is a philosophy that values greatly human beings and their rôle, and rejects the need for religion, as in 'She was brought up as a Christian but she decided to embrace humanism in later life'. **Humanitarianism** refers to the philosophy and actions of people who wish to improve the lot of their fellow human beings and help them, as in 'humanitarians trying to help the refugees by taking them food and clothes'.

hyper- and **hypo-** are liable to be confused. They sound rather similar but they are opposites. **Hyper-** means 'above, excessively', as in 'hyperactive', 'hyperexcitable'. **Hypo-** means 'under, beneath', as in 'hypothermia'.

I and **me** are liable to be confused. I should be used as the subject of a sentence, as in 'You and I have both been invited', 'May Jane and I play?' and me as the object, as in 'The cake was made by Mary and me' and 'My brother and father played against my mother and me'. People often assume wrongly that me is less 'polite' than I. This is probably because they have been taught that in answer to such questions as 'Who is there?' the grammatically correct reply is 'It is I'. In fact, except in formal contexts, 'It is me' is frequently found in modern usage, especially in spoken contexts. Confusion arises as to whether to use I or me after 'between'. Since 'between' is followed by an object, me is the correct form. Thus it is correct to say 'Just between you and me, I think he is dishonest'.

i.e. is the abbreviation of a Latin phrase *id est*, meaning 'that is', as in 'He is a lexicographer, i.e. a person who edits dictionaries'. It is mostly used in written, rather than formal contexts.

identical in modern usage can be followed by either 'with' or 'to'. Formerly only 'with' was considered correct, as in 'His new suit is identical with the one he bought last year'. Now 'to' is also considered acceptable, as in 'a brooch identical to one which he bought for his wife'.

illegible and **unreadable** are not totally interchangeable. **Illegible** refers to something that is impossible to make out or decipher, as in 'her handwriting is practically illegible'. **Unreadable** can also mean this, as in 'unreadable handwriting', but it can also mean 'unable to be read with understanding or enjoyment', as in 'His writing is so full of jargon that it is unreadable'.

imbroglio means 'a confused, complicated or embarrassing situation', as in 'politicians getting involved in an international imbroglio during the summit conference'. It is liable to be misspelt and mispronounced. Note the *g* which is liable to be omitted erroneously as it is not pronounced. It is pronounced im-*bro*-lio with emphasis on the second syllable which rhymes with 'foe'. **Imbroglio** is used only in formal or literary contexts.

impasse causes problems with reference to meaning, spelling and pronunciation. It means 'a difficult position or situation from which there is no way out, deadlock', as in 'The negotiations between management and workers have reached an impasse with neither side being willing to compromise'. Note the final *e* in the spelling. The first syllable can be pronounced 'am', or 'om' in an attempt at following the original French pronunciation, although in modern usage it is frequently totally anglicized as 'im'.

implicit *see* **explicit**.

imply and **infer** are often used interchangeably but they in fact are different in meaning. **Imply** means 'to suggest, to hint at', as in 'We felt that she was implying that he was lying' and 'She did not actually say that there was going to be a delay but she implied it'. **Infer** means 'to deduce, to conclude', as in 'From what the employer said we inferred that there would be some redundancies' and 'From the annual financial reports observers inferred the company was about to go bankrupt'. Note that **infer** doubles the *r* when adding '-ed' or '-ing' to form the past tense, past participle or present participle as **inferred** and **inferring**.

impracticable and **impractical** are liable to be confused. **Impracticable** means 'impossible to put into practice, not workable', as in 'In theory the plan is fine but it is impracticable in terms of costs'. **Impractical** means 'not sensible or realistic', as in 'It is impractical to think that you will get there and back in a day'; 'not skilled at doing or making things', as in 'He is a brilliant academic but he is hopelessly impractical'.

indefinite article *see* **a**, **an**.

in lieu, which means 'instead of', as in 'receive extra pay in lieu of holidays', causes problems with pronunciation. It may be pronounced in lew or in loo.

indexes and **indices** are both plural forms of 'index'. In modern usage **indexes** is the more common form in general language, as in 'Indexes are essential in large reference books'. An **index** in this sense is 'an alphabetical list given at the back of a book as a guide to its contents'. The form **indices** is mostly restricted to technical contexts, such as mathematical information. **Indices** is pronounced in-dis-is and is the Latin form of the plural.

individual refers to 'a single person as opposed to a group', as in 'The rights of the community matter but so do the rights of the individual'. **Individual** is also sometimes used instead of 'person', but in such cases it is often used in a disapproving or belittling way, as in 'What an unpleasant individual she is!' and 'The individual who designed that building should be shot'.

indoor and **indoors** are not interchangeable. **Indoor** is an adjective, as in 'have an indoor match' and 'indoor games'. **Indoors** is an adverb, as in 'children playing outdoors instead of watching television indoors' and 'sleep outdoors on warm evenings instead of indoors'.

infer *see* **imply**.

infinite and **infinitesimal** are similar in meaning but are not interchangeable. **Infinite** means 'without limit', as in 'infinite space', or 'very great', as in 'have infinite patience' and 'He seems to have an infinite capacity for hard work'. **Infinitesimal** means 'very small, negligible', as in 'an infinitesimal difference in size' and 'an infinitesimal increase'. **Infinitesimal** is pronounced with the emphasis on the fourth syllable in-fin-it-*es*-im-il.

informer and **informant** both refer to 'a person who provides information' but they are used in different contexts. **Informer** is used to refer to 'a person who gives information to the police or authorities about a criminal, fugitive, etc', as in 'The local police have a group of informers who tell them what is going on in the criminal underworld' and 'The resistance worker was caught by the enemy soldier when an informer told them about his activities'. An **informant** provides more general information, as in 'My informant keeps me up-to-date with changes in personnel'.

in-law is usually found in compounds such as 'mother-in-law' and 'father-in-law'. When these compounds are in the plural the *s* should be added to the first word of the compound, not to **in-law**, as in 'mothers-in-law' and 'fathers-in-law'.

input used to be a technical term with particular application to computers. This meaning still exists and **input** can refer to the data, power, etc, put into a computer. As a verb it means 'to enter data into a computer', as in 'input the details of all the travel resorts in the area'. In modern usage it is frequently used in general language to mean 'contribution', as in 'Everyone is expected to provide some input for tomorrow's conference'. It is even found in this sense as a verb, as in 'input a great deal to the meeting'.

inquiry *see* **enquiry**.

install and **instal** are now both considered acceptable spellings. **Install** was formerly considered to be the only correct spelling and it is still the more common. The *l* is doubled in **instal** in the past participle, past tense and present participle as **installed**, **installing**. It means 'to put in', as in 'he installed a new television set'. The noun is spelt **instalment**.

instantaneously and **instantly** are interchangeable. Both mean 'immediately, at once', as in 'They obeyed instantaneously/instantly' and 'The accident victims were killed instantly/instantaneously'.

intense and **intensive** are not interchangeable. Intense means 'very strong, extreme', as in 'an intense desire to scream' and 'unable to tolerate the intense cold on the icy slopes'. **Intensive** means 'thorough', as in 'conduct an intensive search', and 'concentrated', as in 'an intensive course in first aid' and 'intensive bombing'.

invalid refers to two different words. If it is pronounced with the emphasis on the second syllable, as in-*val*-id it means 'not valid, no longer valid', as in 'This visa becomes invalid after six months'. If it is pronounced with the emphasis on the first syllable, as *in*-val-id, it means 'a person who is ill', as in 'The doctor has arrived to see the invalid'.

invent *see* **discover**.

inward and **inwards** are not used interchangeably. **Inward** is an adjective, as in 'an inward curve' and 'No one could guess her inward feelings'. **Inwards** is an adverb, as in 'toes turning inwards' and 'thoughts turning inwards'. **Inward** can be used as an adverb in the same way as **inwards.**

IQ is the abbreviation of 'intelligence quotient', as in 'He has a high IQ'. It is always written in capital letters and is sometimes written with full stops and sometimes not, according to preference.

irrespective is followed by the preposition 'of'. The phrase means 'not taking account of, not taking into consideration', as in 'All can go on the trip, irrespective of age'.

irrevocable is frequently misspelt and mispronounced. Note the double *r* and the -*able* ending. It is pronounced with the emphasis on the second syllable, as ir-*rev*-ok-ibl. When applied to legal judgements, etc, it is sometimes pronounced with the emphasis on the third syllable, as ir-rev-*ok*-ibl. The word means 'unable to be changed or revoked', as in 'Their decision to get divorced is irrevocable' and 'The jury's decision is irrevocable'.

its and **it's** are liable to be confused. **Its** is an adjective meaning 'belonging to it', as in 'The house has lost its charm' and 'The dog does not like its kennel'. **It's** means 'it is', as in 'Do you know if it's raining?' and 'It's not fair to expect her to do all the chores'.

jail and **gaol** are both acceptable spellings although jail is the more common. They mean 'prison' and can be both nouns and

verbs, as in 'sent to jail/gaol for killing his wife' and 'jail/gaol him for his part in the bank robbery'.

jersey *see* **cardigan**.

jetsam *see* **flotsam**.

just is liable to be put in the wrong place in a sentence. It should be placed before the word it refers to, as in 'He has just one book left to sell', not 'He just has one book left to sell'. **Just** in the sense of 'in the very recent past' is used with the perfect tense, as in 'They have just finished the job', not 'They just finished the job'.

kind should be used with a singular noun, as 'This kind of accident can be avoided'. This should not read 'These kind of accidents can be avoided'. Similarly 'The children do not like that kind of film' is correct, not 'The children do not like those kind of films'. A plural noun can be used if the sentence is rephrased as 'Films of that kind are not liked by children'.

kindly can be either an adjective or adverb. The adjective means 'kind, friendly, sympathetic', as in 'A kindly lady took pity on the children and lent them some money to get home' and 'She gave them a kindly smile'. The adverb means 'in a kind manner', as in 'We were treated kindly by the local people' and 'They will not look kindly on his actions'.

kind of, meaning 'rather', as in 'That restaurant's kind of dear' and 'She's kind of tired of him', is informal and should be avoided in formal contexts.

knit in modern usage is becoming increasingly used as a noun to mean 'a knitted garment', as in 'a shop selling beautifully coloured knits'.

lady and **woman** cause controversy. **Lady** is objected to by many people when it is used instead of **woman**. Formerly, and still in some circles, it was regarded as a polite form of **woman**, as in '"Please get up and give that lady a seat", said the mother to her son'. Indeed, **woman** was thought to be rather insulting. For many people **woman** is now the preferred term and **lady** is seen as classist, because it is associated with nobility, privilege, etc, or condescending. However, **lady** is still quite commonly used, particularly when women are being addressed in a group, as in '"Ladies, I hope we can reach our sales target", said the manager' and 'Come along, ladies the bus is about to leave'. Phrases, such as **dinner lady** and **cleaning lady** are thought by some to be condescending but others still find **woman** rather insulting.

last is liable to cause confusion because it is not always clear which meaning is meant. **Last** as an adjective has several meanings. It can mean 'final', as in 'That was the musician's last public appearance—he died shortly after'; 'coming after all others in time or order', as in 'December is the last month in the year', 'The last of the runners reached the finishing tape'; 'latest, most recent', as in 'Her last novel is not as good as her earlier ones'; 'previous, preceding', as in 'This chapter is interesting but the last one was boring'. In order to avoid confusion it is best to use a word other than **last** where ambiguity is likely to arise. An example of a sentence which could cause confusion is 'I cannot remember the title of his last book', which could mean either 'his latest book' or 'his final book'.

latter *see* **former**.

lavatory *see* **toilet**.

lay and **lie** are liable to be confused. They are related but are used in different contexts. **Lay** means 'to put or place' and is a transitive verb, i.e. it takes an object. It is found in such sentences as 'Ask them to lay the books carefully on the table' and 'They are going to lay a new carpet in the bedroom'. **Lie**, meaning 'to rest in a horizontal position', is an intransitive verb, i.e. it does not take an object. It is found in such sentences as 'They were told to lie on the ground' and 'Snow is apt to lie on the mountain tops for a long time'. The confusion between the two words arises from the fact that **lay** is also the past tense of **lie**, as in 'He lay still on the ground' and 'Snow lay on the mountain tops'. The past tense of **lay** is **laid**, as in 'They laid the books on the table'. There is another verb **lie**, meaning 'to tell falsehoods, not to tell the truth', as in 'He was told to lie to the police'. The past tense of **lie** in this sense is **lied**, as in 'We suspect that he lied but we cannot prove it'.

leading question is often used wrongly. It should be used to mean 'a question that is so worded as to invite (or lead to) a particular answer desired by the questioner', as in 'The judge refused to allow the barrister to ask the witness the question on the grounds that it was a leading question'. However, it is often used wrongly to mean 'a question that is difficult, unfair or embarrassing'.

learn and **teach** are liable to be confused. **Learn** means 'to gain information or knowledge about', as in 'She learnt Spanish as a child', or 'to gain the skill of', as in 'She is learning to drive'. **Teach** means 'to give instruction in, to cause to know something or be able to do something', as in 'She taught her son French' and 'She taught her son to swim'. **Learn** is frequently used wrongly instead of **teach**, as in 'She learnt us to drive'.

learned and **learnt** are both acceptable forms of the past participle and past tense of the verb 'to learn', as in 'She has now learned/ learnt to drive' and 'They learned/learnt French at school'. **Learned** in this sense can be pronounced either lernd or leant. However, **learned** can also be an adjective, meaning 'having much knowledge, erudite', as in 'an learned professor', or 'academic', as in 'learned journals'. It is pronounced *ler*-ned.

leave and **let** are not interchangeable. **Leave go** should not be substituted for **let go** in such sentences as 'Do not let go of the rope'. 'Do not leave go of the rope' is considered to be incorrect. However both **leave alone** and **let alone** can be used in the sense of 'to stop disturbing or interfering with', as in 'Leave/let the dog alone or it will bite you' and 'leave/let your mother alone—she is not feeling well'. **Leave alone** can also mean 'leave on one's own, cause to be alone', as in 'Her husband went away and left her alone', but **let alone** cannot be used in this sense. **Let alone** can also mean 'not to mention, without considering', as in 'They cannot afford proper food, let alone a holiday', but **leave alone** should not be used in this sense.

legible and **readable** are not interchangeable. **Legible** means 'able to be deciphered or made out', as in 'His writing is scarcely legible'. **Readable** can also be used in this sense, as in 'His handwriting is just not readable'. However **readable** is also used to mean 'able to be read with interest or enjoyment', as in 'He is an expert on the subject but I think his books are simply not readable' and 'I find her novels very readable but my friend does not like her style'.

lend and **loan** can cause confusion. **Lend** is used as a verb in British English to mean 'to allow someone the use of temporarily', as in 'Can you lend me a pen?' and 'His father refused to lend him any money'. **Loan** is a noun meaning 'something lent, the temporary use of', as in 'They thanked her for the loan of her car'. In American English **loan** is used as a verb to mean **lend**, and this use is becoming common in Britain although it is still regarded as not quite acceptable.

lengthways and **lengthwise** are used interchangeably, as in 'fold the tablecloth lengthways/lengthwise' and 'measure the room lengthwise/lengthways'.

lengthy and **long** are not interchangeable. **Lengthy** means 'excessively long', as in 'We had a lengthy wait before we saw the doctor' and 'It was such a lengthy speech that most of the audience got bored'. **Lengthy** is frequently misspelt. Note the *g*.

less and **fewer** are often confused. Less means 'a smaller amount or quantity of' and is the comparative form of 'little'. It is found in sentences such as 'less milk', 'less responsibility' and 'less noise'. **Fewer** means 'a smaller number of' and is the comparative of 'few'. It is found in sentences such as 'buy fewer bottles of milk', 'have fewer responsibilities', 'have fewer opportunities' and 'hear fewer noises'. **Less** is commonly wrongly used where **fewer** is correct. It is common but ungrammatical to say or write 'less bottles of milk' and 'less queues in the shops during the week'.

liable to and **likely to** both express probability. They mean much the same except that **liable to** suggests that the probability is based on past experience or habit. 'He is liable to lose his temper' suggests that he has been in the habit of doing so in the past.

'He is likely to lose his temper' suggests that he will probably lose his temper, given the situation, but that the probability is not based on how he has reacted in the past. This distinction is not always adhered to, and some people use the terms interchangeably.

libel and **slander** both refer to defamatory statements against someone but they are not interchangeable. **Libel** refers to defamation that is written down, printed or drawn, as in 'The politician sued the newspaper for libel when it falsely accused him of fraud'. **Slander** refers to defamation in spoken form, as in 'She heard that one of her neighbours was spreading slander about her'. Both **libel** and **slander** can act as verbs, as in 'bring a suit against the newspaper for libelling him' and 'think that one of her neighbours was slandering her'. Note that the verb **libel** doubles the *l* in the past participle, past tense and present participle, as **libelled** and **libelling**.

licence and **license** are liable to cause confusion in British English. **Licence** is a noun meaning 'an official document showing that permission has been given to do, use or own something', as in 'require a licence to have a stall in the market', 'have a licence to drive a car', and 'apply for a pilot's licence'. **License** is a verb meaning 'to provide someone with a licence', as in 'The council have licensed him as a street trader', 'The restaurant has been licensed to sell alcohol'. Note **licensed grocer** and **licensing laws** but **off-licence**. In American English both the noun and verb are spelt **license**.

lie *see* **lay**.

light years are a measure of distance, not time. A **light year** is the distance travelled by light in one year (about six million, million miles) and is a term used in astronomy. **Light years** are often referred to in an informal context when time, not distance, is involved, as in 'Owning their own house seemed light years away' and 'It seems light years since we had a holiday'.

like tends to cause confusion. It is a preposition meaning 'resembling, similar to', as in 'houses like castles', gardens like jungles', 'actors like Olivier', 'She looks like her mother', 'She plays like an expert', 'The child swims like a fish' and 'Like you, he cannot stand cruelty to animals'. To be grammatically correct **like** should not be used as a conjunction. Thus 'The house looks like it has been deserted' is incorrect. It should read 'The house looks as though/ if it has been deserted'. Similarly, 'Like his mother said, he has had to go to hospital' should read 'As his mother said, he has had to go to hospital'.

likeable and **likable** are both acceptable spellings. The word means 'pleasant, agreeable, friendly', as in 'He is a likeable/likable young man'.

likely to *see* **liable to**.

literally is frequently used simply to add emphasis to an idea rather than to indicate that the word, phrase, etc, used is to be interpreted word for word. Thus, 'She was literally tearing her hair out' does not mean that she was pulling her hair out by the handful but that she was very angry, anxious, frustrated, etc.

livid and **lurid** are liable to be confused although they mean different things. **Livid** means 'discoloured, of a greyish tinge', as in 'a livid bruise on her face', and 'furious', as in 'When he saw his damaged car he was livid'. **Lurid** means 'sensational, shocking', as in 'give the lurid details about finding the body', and 'garish, glaringly bright', as in 'wear a lurid shade of green'.

living room *see* **sitting room**.

loo *see* **toilet**.

lots of and **a lot of**, meaning 'many' and 'much', should be used only in informal contexts, as in '"I've got lots of toys," said the child' and 'You're talking a lot of rubbish'. They should be avoided in formal prose.

lounge *see* **sitting room**.

low and **lowly** are not interchangeable. **Low** means 'not high', as in 'a low fence', 'a low level of income', 'speak in a low voice' and 'her low status in the firm'. It can also mean 'despicable, contemptible', as in 'That was a low trick' or 'He's a low creature'. **Lowly** means 'humble', as in 'of lowly birth' and 'the peasant's lowly abode'.

lunch and **luncheon** both refer to a meal eaten in the middle of the day. **Lunch**, as

in 'a business lunch' and 'have just a snack for lunch', is by far the more usual term. **Luncheon**, as in 'give a luncheon party for the visiting celebrity', is a very formal word and is becoming increasingly uncommon. *See also* **dinner**.

lurid *see* **livid**.

madam and **madame** are liable to be confused. **Madam** is the English-language form of the French **madame**. It is a form of formal of address for a woman, as in 'Please come this way, madam'. It is used in formal letters when the name of the woman being written to is not known, as in 'Dear Madam'. **Madam** can be written either with a capital letter or a lower-case letter. **Madam** is pronounced *mad*-am, with the emphasis on the first syllable. **Madame**, which is the French equivalent of 'Mrs', is occasionally found in English, as in Madame Tussaud's, and is pronounced in the same way as **madam**. In French **madame** is pronounced ma-*dam*.

majority and **minority** are opposites. **Majority** means 'more than half the total number of', as in 'The majority of the pupils live locally' and 'the younger candidate received the majority of the votes'. **Minority** means less than half the total number of', as in 'A small minority of the football fans caused trouble' and 'Only a minority of the committee voted against the motion'. **Majority** and **minority** should not be used to describe the greater or lesser part of a single thing. Thus it is wrong to say 'The majority of the book is uninteresting'.

male, masculine and **mannish** all refer to the sex that is not female but the words are used in different ways. **Male** is the opposite of 'female' and refers to the sex of a person or animal, as in 'no male person may enter', 'a male nurse', 'a male elephant' and 'the male reproductive system'. **Masculine** is the opposite of 'feminine' and refers to people or their characteristics. It refers to characteristics, etc, that are traditionally considered to be typically **male**. Examples of its use include 'a very masculine young man', 'a deep, masculine voice'. It can be used of women, as in 'She has a masculine walk' and 'She wears masculine clothes'. When used of women it is often derogatory and is sometimes replaced with **mannish**, which is derogatory, as in 'women with mannish haircuts'. **Male** can also be used as a noun, as in 'the male of the species' 'of the robins, the male is more colourful' and 'the title can be held only by males'.

man causes a great deal of controversy. To avoid being sexist it should be avoided when it really means 'person'. 'We must find the right man for the job' should read 'We must find the right person for the job'. Similarly, 'All men have a right to a reasonable standard of living' should read 'All people have a right to a reasonable standard of living' or 'Everyone has a right to a reasonable standard of living'. Problems also arise with compounds, such as 'chairman'. In such situations 'person' is often used, as in 'chairperson'. Man is also used to mean 'mankind, humankind', as in 'Man is mortal' and 'Man has the power of thought'. Some people also object to this usage and consider it sexist. They advocate using 'humankind' or 'the human race'.

many is used in more formal contexts rather than 'a lot of' or 'lots of', as in 'The judge said the accused had had many previous convictions'. **Many** is often used in the negative in both formal and informal contexts, as in 'They don't have many friends' and 'She won't find many apples on the trees now'.

masculine *see* **male**.

may *see* **can**.

maybe and **may be** are liable to be confused although they have different meanings. **Maybe** means 'perhaps', as in 'Maybe they lost their way' and 'He said, "Maybe" when I asked him if he was going'. It is used in more informal contexts than 'perhaps'. **May be** is used in such sentences as 'He may be poor but he is very generous' and 'They may be a little late'.

mayoress means 'the wife or partner of a male mayor', as in 'an official dinner for the mayor and mayoress'. A mayor who is a woman is called either 'mayor' or 'lady mayor'.

me *see* **I**.

meaningful originally meant 'full of meaning', as in 'make very few meaningful state-

ments' and 'There was a meaningful silence'. In modern usage it has come to mean 'important, significant, serious', as in 'not interested in a meaningful relationship' and 'seeking a meaningful career'. The word now tends to be very much overused.

means in the sense of 'way, method' can be either a singular or plural noun, as in 'The means of defeating them is in our hands' and 'Many different means of financing the project have been investigated'. **Means** in the sense of 'wealth' and 'resources' is plural, as in 'His means are not sufficient to support two families'.

media gives rise to confusion. In the form of **the media** it is commonly applied to the press, to newspapers, television and radio, as in 'The politician claimed that he was being harassed by the media'. **Media** is a plural form of 'medium', meaning 'means of communication', as in 'television is a powerful medium'. In modern usage **media** is beginning to be used as a singular noun, as in 'The politician blamed a hostile media for his misfortunes', but this is still regarded as being an incorrect use.

middle *see* **centre**.

mileage and **milage** are both acceptable spellings for 'the distance travelled or measured in miles', as in 'The car is a bargain, given the low mileage'. However **mileage** is much more common than **milage**. The word also means informally 'benefit, advantage', as in 'The politician got a lot of mileage from the scandal surrounding his opponent' and 'There's not much mileage in pursuing that particular line of inquiry'.

militate and **mitigate** are liable to be confused. **Militate** means 'to have or serve as a strong influence against', as in 'Their lack of facts militated against the success of their application' and 'His previous record will militate against his chances of going free'. **Mitigate** means 'to alleviate', as in 'try to mitigate the suffering of the refugees', or 'moderate', as in 'mitigate the severity of the punishment'.

millennium is liable to be misspelt. Note the double *n* which is frequently omitted in error. The plural form is **millennia**.

Millennium refers to 'a period of 1000 years', as in 'rock changes taking place over several millennia'. In religious terms it refers to 'the thousand-year reign of Christ prophesied in the Bible'.

minority *see* **majority**.

Miss *see* **Ms**.

misuse *see* **abuse**.

mitigate *see* **militate**.

mnemonic refers to 'something that aids the memory'. For example, some people use a **mnemonic** in the form of a verse to remind them how to spell a word or to recall a date. The word is liable to be misspelt and mispronounced. Note the initial *m*, which is silent. **Mnemonic** is pronounced nim-*on*-ik, with the emphasis on the second syllable.

modern and **modernistic** are not quite the same. **Modern** means 'referring to the present time or recent times', as in 'the politics of modern times' and 'a production of Shakespeare's *Twelfth Night* in modern dress'. It also means 'using the newest techniques, equipment, buildings, etc, as in 'a modern shopping centre' and 'a modern office complex'. **Modernistic** means 'characteristic of modern ideas, fashions, etc', and is often used in a derogatory way, as in 'She says she hates that modernistic furniture'.

modus vivendi refers to 'a practical, sometimes temporary, arrangement or compromise by which people who are in conflict can live or work together', as in 'The two opposing parties on the committee will have to reach a modus vivendi if any progress is to be made'. It is a Latin phrase that literally means 'a way of living' and is pronounced *mo*-dus viv-*en*-di.

more is used to form the comparative of adjectives and adverbs that do not form the comparative by adding *-er*. This usually applies to longer adjectives, as in 'more beautiful', 'more gracious', 'more useful', and 'more flattering'. **More** should not be used with adjectives that have a comparative ending already. Thus it is wrong to write 'more happier'. **Most** is used in the same way to form the superlative of adjectives and adverbs, as in 'most beautiful', 'most gracious' etc.

Moslem *see* **Muslim**.

most *see* **more**.

movable and **moveable** are both possible spellings but **movable** is the more common, as in 'movable possessions' and 'machines with movable parts'.

Ms, Mrs and **Miss** are all used before the names of women in addressing them and in letter-writing. Formerly **Mrs** was used before the name of a married woman and **Miss** before the name of an unmarried woman or girl. In modern usage **Ms** is often used instead of **Miss** or **Mrs**. This is sometimes because the marital status of the woman is not known and sometimes from a personal preference. Many people feel that since no distinction is made between married and unmarried men when they are being addressed, no distinction should be made between married and unmarried women. On the other hand some people, particularly older women, object to the use of **Ms**.

much, except in negative sentences, is used mainly in rather formal contexts, as in 'They own much property'. 'A great deal of' is often used instead, as in 'They own a great deal of property'. In informal contexts 'a lot of' is often used instead of **much**, as in 'a lot of rubbish' not 'much rubbish'. **Much** is used in negative sentences, as in 'They do not have much money'.

Muslim and **Moslem** refer to 'a follower of the Islamic faith'. In modern usage **Muslim** is the preferred term rather than the older spelling **Moslem**.

naught and **nought** are not totally interchangeable. **Naught** means 'nothing', as in 'All his projects came to naught', and is rather a formal or literary word in this sense. **Naught** is also a less usual spelling of **nought**, which means 'zero' when it is regarded as a number, as in 'nought point one (0.1)'.

nearby and **near by** can cause problems. **Nearby** can be either an adjective, as in 'the nearby village', or an adverb, as in 'Her mother lives nearby'. **Near by** is an adverb, as in 'He doesn't have far to go—he lives near by'. In other words, the adverbial sense can be spelt either **nearby** or **near by**.

née is used to indicate the maiden or family name of a married woman, as in 'Jane Jones, née Smith'. It is derived from French, being the feminine form of the French word for 'born'. It can be spelt either with an acute accent or not—**née** or **nee**.

never in the sense of 'did not', as in 'He never saw the other car before he hit it', should be used in only very informal contexts. **Never** means 'at no time, on no occasion', as in 'He will never agree to their demands' and 'She has never been poor'. It is also used as a negative for the sake of emphasis, as in 'He never so much as smiled'.

nevertheless and **none the less** mean the same thing, as in 'He has very little money. Nevertheless/none the less he gives generously to charity'. **None the less** is usually written as three words but **nevertheless** is spelt as one word. In modern usage **none the less** is sometimes written as one word, as **nonetheless**.

next and **this** can cause confusion. **Next** in one of its senses is used to mean the day of the week, month of the year, season of the year, etc, that will follow next, as in 'They are coming next Tuesday', 'We are going on holiday next June' and 'They are to be married next summer'. **This** can also be used in this sense and so ambiguity can occur. Some people use **this** to refer to the very next Tuesday, June, summer, etc, and use **next** for the one after that. Thus someone might say on Sunday, 'I'll see you next Friday', meaning the first Friday to come, but someone else might take that to mean a week on from that because they would refer to the first Friday to come as 'this Friday'. The only solution is to make sure exactly which day, week, season, etc, the other person is referring to.

nice originally meant 'fine, subtle, requiring precision', as in 'There is rather a nice distinction between the two words', but it is widely used in the sense of 'pleasant, agreeable, etc', as in 'She is a nice person' and 'We had a nice time at the picnic'. It is overused and alternative adjectives should be found to avoid this, as in 'She is an amiable person' and 'We had an enjoyable time at the picnic'.

no one and **no-one** are interchangeable but the word is never written 'noone', unlike 'everyone'. **No one** and **no-one** are used with a singular verb, as in 'No one is allowed to leave' and 'No one is anxious to leave'. They are used by some people with a plural personal pronoun or possessive case when attempts are being made to avoid sexism, as in 'No one is expected to take their child away'. The singular form is grammatically correct, as in 'No one is expected to take his/her child away', but it is clumsy. 'No one is expected to take his child away' is sexist. Nobody is interchangeable with no one, as in 'You must tell no one/nobody about this'.

nobody *see* **no one**.

none can be used with either a singular verb or plural verb. Examples of sentences using a singular verb include 'There is none of the food left' and 'None of the work is good enough' and 'None of the coal is to be used today'. In sentences where none is used with a plural noun the verb was traditionally still singular, as in 'None of the books is suitable' and 'None of the parcels is undamaged'. This is still the case in formal contexts but, in the case of informal contexts, a plural verb is often used in modern usage, as in 'None of these things are any good'.

none the less *see* **nevertheless**.

not only is frequently used in a construction with 'but also', as in 'We have not only the best candidate but also the most efficient organization' and 'The organizers of the fête not only made a great deal of money for charity but also gave a great many people a great deal of pleasure'.

nought *see* **naught**.

noxious and **obnoxious** are liable to be confused. They both refer to unpleasantness or harmfulness but they are used in different contexts. **Noxious** is used of a substance, fumes, etc, and means 'harmful, poisonous', as in 'firemen overcome by noxious fumes' and 'delinquent children having a noxious influence on the rest of the class'. **Obnoxious** means 'unpleasant, nasty, offensive', as in 'He has the most obnoxious neighbours' and 'The child's parents let him off with the most obnoxious behaviour'. **Noxious** is used in formal and technical contexts rather than **obnoxious**.

nubile originally meant 'old enough to marry, marriageable' as in 'he has five nubile daughters'. In modern usage **nubile** is frequently used in the sense of 'sexually attractive', as in 'admiring the nubile girls sunbathing on the beach' and 'nubile models posing for magazine illustrations'.

numbers can be written in either figures or words. It is largely a matter of taste which method is adopted. As long as the method is consistent it does not really matter. Some establishments, such as a publishing house or a newspaper office, will have a house style. For example, some of them prefer to have numbers up to 10 written in words, as in 'They have two boys and three girls'. If this system is adopted, guidance should be sought as to whether a mixture of figures and words in the same sentence is acceptable, as in 'We have 12 cups but only six saucers', or whether the rule should be broken in such situations as 'We have twelve cups but only six saucers'.

nutritional and **nutritious** are liable to be confused. They both refer to 'nutrition, the process of giving and receiving nourishment' but mean different things. **Nutritional** means 'referring to nutrition', as in 'doubts about the nutritional value of some fast foods' and 'people who do not receive the minimum nutritional requirements'. **Nutritious** means 'nourishing, of high value as a food', as in 'nutritious homemade soups' and 'something slightly more nutrtious than a plate of chips'.

O and **Oh** are both forms of an exclamation made at the beginning of a sentence. **Oh** is the usual spelling, as in 'Oh well. It's Friday tomorrow' and 'Oh dear, the baby's crying again'.

loan *see* **lend**.

objective and **subjective** are opposites. **Objective** means 'not influenced by personal feelings, attitudes, or prejudices', as in 'She is related to the person accused and so she cannot give an objective view of the situation' and 'It is important that all members of a jury are completely objective'. **Subjective** means 'influenced by personal feelings,

attitudes and prejudices', as in 'It is only natural to be subjective in situations regarding one's children' and 'She wrote a very subjective report on the conference and did not stick to the facts'. **Objective** can also be a noun in the sense of 'aim, goal', as in 'Our objective was to make as much money as possible'. **Object** can also be used in this sense, as in 'Their main object is to have a good time'.

oblivious means 'unaware of, unconscious of, not noticing'. Traditionally it is followed by the preposition 'of', as in 'The lovers were oblivious of the rain' and 'When he is reading he is completely oblivious of his surroundings'. In modern usage its use with the preposition 'to' is also considered acceptable, as in 'They were oblivious to the fact that he was cheating them' and 'sleep soundly, oblivious to the noise'.

obnoxious *see* **noxious**.

obscene and **pornographic** are not interchangeable. **Obscene** means 'indecent, especially in a sexual way, offending against the accepted standards of decency', as in 'obscene drawings on the walls of the public toilet' and 'When his car was damaged he let out a stream of obscene language'. **Pornographic** means 'intended to arouse sexual excitement', as in 'pornographic videos' and 'magazines with women shown in pornographic poses'. **Obscene** is frequently misspelt. Note the *c* after the *s*.

oculist *see* **optician**.

of is sometimes wrongly used instead of the verb 'to have', as in 'He must of known she was lying' instead of 'He must have known she was lying'. The error arises because the two constructions sound alike when not emphasized.

Oh *see* **O**.

OK and **okay** are both acceptable spellings of an informal word indicating agreement or approval, as in 'OK/okay, I'll come with you', 'We've at last been given the OK/okay to begin building'. When the word is used as a verb it is more usually spelt **okay** because of the problem in adding endings, as in 'They've okayed our plans at last'. **OK** is sometimes written with full stops as **O.K.**

older *see* **elder**.

one is used in formal situations to indicate

an indefinite person where 'you' would be used in informal situations, as in 'One should not believe all one hears' and 'One should be kind to animals'. This construction can sound rather affected. Examples of the informal 'you' include 'You would've thought he would've had more sense' and 'You wouldn't think anyone could be so stupid'. **One** when followed by 'of the' and a plural noun takes a singular verb, as in 'One of the soldiers was killed' and 'One of the three witnesses has died'. However, the constructions 'one of those ... who' and 'one of the ... that' take a plural verb, as in 'He is one of those people who will not take advice' and 'It is one of those houses that are impossible to heat'.

only must be carefully positioned in written sentences to avoid confusion. It should be placed before, or as close as possible before, the word to which it refers. Compare 'She drinks only wine at the weekend', 'She drinks wine only at the weekend' and 'Only she drinks wine at the weekend'. In spoken English, where the intonation of the voice will indicate which word **only** applies to it may be placed in whichever position sounds most natural, usually between the subject and the verb, as in 'She only drinks wine at the weekend'.

onto and **on to** are both acceptable forms in sentences such as 'The cat leapt onto/on to the table' and 'He jumped from the plane onto/on to the ground'. However, in sentences such as 'It is time to move on to another city' **onto** is not a possible alternative.

onward and **onwards** are not interchangeable. **Onward** is an adjective, as in 'onward motion' and 'onward progress'. **Onwards** is an adverb, as in 'march onwards' and 'proceed onwards'.

optician, ophthalmologist, optometrist and **oculist** all refer to 'a person who is concerned with disorders of the eyes' but they are not interchangeable. **Dispensing optician** refers to 'a person who makes and sells spectacles or contact lenses'. **Ophthalmic optician** refers to 'a person who tests eyesight and prescribes lenses'. **Optometrist** is another term for this. **Ophthalmologist** refers to 'a doctor who specializes in disorders of the eyes' and **oculist** is another name for this.

optimum means 'the most favourable or advantageous condition, situation, amount, degree, etc', as in 'A temperature of 20° is optimum for these plants'. It is mostly used as an adjective meaning 'most favourable or advantageous', as in 'the optimum speed to run the car at', 'the optimum time at which to pick the fruit' and 'the optimum amount of water to give the plants'. It should not be used simply as a synonym for 'best'.

optometrist see **optician**.

orientate and **orient** are both acceptable forms of the same word. **Orientate** is the more common in British English but the shorter form, **orient**, is preferred by some people and is the standard form in American English. They are verbs meaning 'to get one's bearings', as in 'difficult to orientate/orient themselves in the mist on the mountain'; 'to adjust to new surroundings', as in 'It takes some time to orientate/orient oneself in a new job'; 'to direct at', as in 'The course is orientated/oriented at older students'; 'to direct the interest of to', as in 'try to orientate/orient students towards the sciences'.

orthopaedic and **paediatric** are liable to be confused. They both apply to medical specialties but they are different. **Orthopaedic** means 'referring to the treatment of disorders of the bones', as in 'attend the orthopaedic clinic with an injured back'. **Paediatric** means 'referring to the treatment of disorders associated with children', as in 'Her little boy is receiving treatment from a paediatric consultant'. In American English these are respectively spelt **orthopedic** and **pediatric**.

other than can be used when **other** is an adjective or pronoun, as in 'There was no means of entry other than through a trap door' and 'He disapproves of the actions of anyone other than himself'. Traditionally, it should not be used as an adverbial phrase, as in 'It was impossible to get there other than by private car'. In such constructions **otherwise than** should be used, as in 'It is impossible to get there otherwise than by private car'. However, **other than** used adverbially is common in modern usage.

otherwise traditionally should not be used as an adjective or pronoun, as in 'Pack your clothes, clean or otherwise' and 'We are not discussing the advantages, or otherwise, of the scheme at this meeting'. It is an adverb, as in 'We are in favour of the project but he obviously thinks otherwise' and 'The hours are rather long but otherwise the job is fine'. *See* **other than**.

owing to *see* **due to**.

p *see* **pence**.

paediatric *see* **orthopaedic**.

panacea and **placebo** are liable to be confused. **Panacea** means 'a universal remedy for all ills and troubles', as in 'The new government does not have a panacea for the country's problems'. It is often used loosely to mean any remedy for any problem, as in 'She thinks that a holiday will be a panacea for his unhappiness'. **Panacea** is pronounced pan-a-*see*-a. **Placebo** refers to 'a supposed medication that is just a harmless substance given to a patient as part of a drugs trial etc', as in 'She was convinced the pills were curing her headaches but the doctor has prescribed her a placebo'. It is pronounced pla-*see*-bo.

parameter is a mathematical term that is very loosely used in modern usage to mean 'limit, boundary, framework' or 'limiting feature or characteristic', as in 'work within the parameters of our budget and resources'. The word is over-used and should be avoided where possible. The emphasis is on the second syllable as par-*am*-it-er.

paranoid is an adjective meaning 'referring to a mental disorder, called **paranoia**, characterized by delusions of persecution and grandeur', as in 'a paranoid personality'. In modern usage it is used loosely to mean 'distrustful, suspicious of others, anxious etc', as in 'It is difficult to get to know him—he's so paranoid' and 'paranoid about people trying to get his job', when there is no question of actual mental disorder. **Paranoia** is pronounced par-a-*noy*-a.

paraphernalia means 'all the bits and pieces of equipment required for something', as in 'all the paraphernalia needed to take a baby on holiday', 'put his angling paraphernalia in the car'. Strictly speaking it is a plural noun but it is now frequently used with a singular verb, as in 'The artist's paraphernalia was lying all over the studio'. **Paraphernalia** is liable to be misspelt. Note the *er* before the *n*.

parlour *see* **sitting room**.

particular means 'special, exceptional', as in 'a matter of particular importance', or 'individual', as in 'Have you a particular person in mind?', and 'concerned over details, fastidious', as in 'very particular about personal hygiene'. **Particular** is often used almost meaninglessly, as in 'this particular dress' and 'this particular car', when **particular** does not add much to the meaning.

partner can be used to indicate one half of an established couple, whether the couple are married or living together, as in 'Her partner was present at the birth of the child'.

passed and **past** are liable to be confused. **Passed** is the past participle and past tense of the verb 'to pass', as in 'She has already passed the exam' and 'They passed an old man on the way'. **Past** is used as a noun, as in 'He was a difficult teenager but that is all in the past now' and 'He has a murky past'. It is also used as an adjective, as in 'I haven't seen him in the past few weeks' and 'Her past experiences affected her opinion of men'. **Past** can also be a preposition, as in 'We drove past their new house', 'It's past three o'clock' and 'He's past caring'. It can also be an adverb, as in 'He watched the athletes running past' and 'The boat drifted past'.

patent, in British English, is usually pronounced *pay*-tent, as in 'patent leather dancing shoes'. **Patent** in the sense of 'obvious', as in 'his patent dislike of the situation' and 'It was quite patent that she loved him' is also pronounced in that way. **Patent** in the sense of 'a legal document giving the holder the sole right to make or sell something and preventing others from imitating it', as in 'take out a patent for his new invention', can be pronounced either *pay*-tent or *pat*-ent. **Patent** in this last sense can also be a verb, as in 'He should patent his invention as soon as possible'.

peddler and **pedlar** are not interchangeable in British English. **Peddler** refers particularly to 'a person who peddles drugs', as in

pence

person

'drug-peddlers convicted and sent to prison'. **Pedlar** refers to 'a person who sells small articles from house to house or from place to place', as in 'pedlars selling ribbons at the fair'.

pence, p and **pennies** are liable to be confused. **Pence** is the plural form of 'penny', as in 'There are a hundred pence in the pound'. It is commonly found in prices, as in 'apples costing 10 pence each'. **Pence** has become much more common than 'pennies', which tends to be associated with pre-decimalization money (the British currency was decimalized in 1972), as in 'There were twelve pennies in one shilling'. **Pence** is sometimes used as though it were singular, as in 'have no one-pence pieces'. In informal contexts it is often used, as in 'Have you got a 10p (pronounced ten pee) piece' and 'Those chocolate bars are fifteen p'. **Pence** in compounds is not pronounced in the same way as pence was pronounced in compounds before decimalization. Such words as 'ten pence' are now pronounced *ten pens*, with equal emphasis on each word. In pre-decimalization days it was pronounced *ten*-pens, with the emphasis on the first word.

pennies *see* **pence**.

people is usually a plural noun and so takes a plural verb, as in 'The local people were annoyed at the stranger's behaviour' and 'People were being asked to leave'. In the sense of 'nation', 'race' or 'tribe' it is sometimes treated as a singular noun, as in 'the nomadic peoples of the world'. **People** acts as the plural of 'person', as in 'There's room for only one more person in that car but there's room for three people in this one'. In formal or legal contexts **persons** is sometimes used as the plural of 'person', as in 'The lift had a notice saying "Room for six persons only"'.

per capita is a formal expression meaning 'for each person', as in 'The cost of the trip will be £300 per capita'. It is a Latin phrase which has been adopted into English and literally means 'by heads'. It is pronounced per *ka*-pi-ta.

per cent is usually written as two words. It is used adverbially in combination with a number in the sense of 'in or for each

hundred', as in 'thirty per cent of the people are living below the poverty line'. The number is sometimes written in figures, as in '50 per cent of the staff are married'. The symbol % is often used instead of the words 'per cent', especially in technical contexts, as in 'make savings of up to 30%'. **Per cent** in modern usage is sometimes used as a noun, as in 'They have agreed to lower the price by half a per cent'.

per means 'for each' and is used to express rates, prices, etc, as in 'driving at 60 miles per hour', 'cloth costing £5 per square metre', 'The cost of the trip is £20 per person' and 'The fees are £1000 a term per child'. It can also mean 'in each', as in 'The factory is inspected three times per year'.

per se is a Latin phrase that has been adapted into English and means 'in itself', as in 'The substance is not per se harmful but it might be so if it interacts with other substances' and 'Television is not per se bad for children'. It should be used only in formal contexts.

percentage refers to 'the rate, number or amount in each hundred', as in 'the number of unemployed people expressed as a percentage of the adult population' and 'What percentage of his salary is free?'. It is also used to mean proportion, as in 'Only a small percentage of last year's students have found jobs' and 'A large percentage of the workers are in favour of a strike'. In modern usage it is sometimes used to mean 'a small amount' or 'a small part', as in 'Only a percentage of the students will find work'.

perquisite *see* **prerequisite**.

person is now used in situations where 'man' was formerly used to avoid sexism in language. It is used when the sex of the person being referred to is either unknown or not specified, as in 'They are advertising for another person for the warehouse'. It often sounds more natural to use 'someone', as in 'They are looking for someone to help out in the warehouse'. **Person** is often used in compounds, as in **chairperson**, **spokesperson** and **salesperson**, although some people dislike this convention and some compounds, such as **craftsperson**, have not really caught on.

Person has two possible plurals. *See* **people**. **Person with** and **people with** are phrases advocated in 'politically correct' language to avoid negative terms such as 'victim', 'sufferer', as in 'person with Aids'.

phenomenal means 'referring to a phenomenon'. It is often used to mean 'remarkable, extraordinary', as in 'a phenomenal atmospheric occurrence', and in modern usage it is also used loosely to mean 'very great', as in 'a phenomenal increase in the crime rate' and 'a phenomenal achievement'. This use is usually restricted to informal contexts.

phenomenon is a singular noun meaning 'a fact, object, occurrence, experience, etc, that can be perceived by the senses rather than by thought or intuition', as in 'She saw something coming out of the lake but it remained an unexplained phenomenon', and 'a strange, unusual or remarkable fact, event or person of some particular significance', as in 'Single parenthood is one of the phenomena of the 1990s'. The plural is **phenomena**, as in 'natural phenomena'. It is a common error to treat **phenomena** as a singular noun. Note the spelling of **phenomenon** as it is liable to be misspelt.

phone, which is a short form of 'telephone', is not regarded as being as informal as it once was. It is quite acceptable in sentences such as 'He is going to buy a mobile phone'. Note that **phone** is now spelt without an apostrophe.

phoney and **phony** are both acceptable spellings but **phoney** is the more common in British English. The word means 'pretending or claiming to be what one is not, fake', as in 'He has a phoney American accent' and 'There's something phoney about him'.

placebo *see* **panacea**.

plane and **aeroplane** mean the same thing, both referring to a 'a machine that can fly and is used to carry people and goods'. In modern usage **plane** is the usual term, as in 'The plane took off on time' and 'nearly miss the plane'. **Aeroplane** is slightly old-fashioned or unduly formal, as in 'Her elderly parents say that they refuse to travel by aeroplane'. The American English spelling is **airplane**. Note that **plane** is not spelt with an apostrophe although it is a shortened form.

pleaded and **pled** mean the same thing, both being the past tense and past participle of the verb 'to plead'. **Pleaded** is the usual form in British English, as in 'They pleaded with the tyrant to spare the child's life' and 'The accused pleaded guilty'. **Pled** is the usual American spelling.

plenty is used only informally in some contexts. It is acceptable in formal and informal contexts when it is followed by the preposition 'of', as in 'We have plenty of food', or when it is used as a pronoun without the 'of' construction, as in 'You can borrow some food from us—we have plenty'. Some people think its use as an adjective, as in 'Don't hurry—we have plenty time' and 'There's plenty food for all in the fridge', should be restricted to informal contexts. As an adverb it is a acceptable in both formal and informal contexts in such sentences as 'Help yourself—we have plenty more'. However, such sentences as 'The house is plenty big enough for them' is suitable only for very informal or slang contexts.

political correctness is a modern movement aiming to remove all forms of prejudice in language, such as sexism, racism and discrimination against disabled people. Its aims are admirable but in practice many of the words and phrases suggested by advocates of political correctness are rather contrived or, indeed, ludicrous. The adjective is **politically correct**.

practicable and **practical** should not be used interchangeably. **Practicable** means 'able to be done or carried out, able to be put into practice', as in 'His schemes seem fine in theory but they are never practicable'. **Practical** has several meanings, such as 'concerned with action and practice rather than with theory', as in 'He has studied the theory but has no practical experience of the job'; 'suitable for the purpose for which it was made', as in 'practical shoes for walking'; 'useful', as in 'a practical device with a wide range of uses'; 'clever at doing and making things', as in 'She's very practical when it comes to dealing with an emergency'; 'virtual', as in 'He's not the owner but he's in practical control of the firm'.

practically can mean 'in a practical way', as

in 'Practically, the scheme is not really possible', but in modern usage it is usually used to mean 'virtually', as in 'He practically runs the firm although he is not the manager', and 'almost', as in 'The driver of that car practically ran me over'.

prefer is followed by the preposition 'to' not 'than', as in 'She prefers dogs to cats', 'They prefer Paris to London' and 'They prefer driving to walking'.

prerequisite and **perquisite** are liable to be confused although they are completely different in meaning. **Perquisite** means 'money or goods given as a right in addition to one's pay', as in 'various perquisites such as a company car'. It is frequently abbreviated to 'perks', as in 'The pay's not very much but the perks are good'. **Prerequisite** refers to 'something required as a condition for something to happen or exist', as in 'Passing the exam is a prerequisite for his getting the job' and 'A certain amount of studying is a prerequisite of passing the exam'.

prevaricate and **procrastinate** are liable to be confused although they have completely different meanings. **Prevaricate** means 'to try to avoid telling the truth by speaking in an evasive or misleading way', as in 'She prevaricated when the police asked her where she had been the previous evening'. **Procrastinate** means 'to delay or postpone action', as in 'The student has been procrastinating all term but now he has to get to grips with his essay'.

preventative and **preventive** both mean 'preventing or intended to prevent, precautionary', as in 'If you think the staff are stealing from the factory you should take preventative/preventive measures' and 'Preventative/preventive medicine seeks to prevent disease and disorders rather than cure them'. **Preventive** is the more frequently used of the two terms.

prima facie is a Latin phrase that has been adopted into English. It means 'at first sight, based on what seems to be so' and is mainly used in legal or very formal contexts, as in 'The police say they have prima facie evidence for arresting him but more investigation is required'. The phrase is pronounced *pri*-ma *fay*-shee.

prognosis *see* **diagnosis**.

programme and **program** are liable to cause confusion. In British English **programme** is the acceptable spelling in such senses as in 'a television programme', 'put on a varied programme of entertainment' 'buy a theatre programme' and 'launch an ambitious programme of expansion'. However, in the computing sense **program** is used. **Programme** can also be a verb meaning 'to plan, to schedule', as in 'programme the trip for tomorrow'; 'to cause something to conform to a particular set of instructions', as in 'programme the central heating system'; or 'to cause someone to behave in a particular way, especially to conform to particular instructions', as in 'Her parents have programmed her to obey them implicitly'. In the computing sense of 'to provide with a series of coded instructions', the verb is spelt **program** and the *m* is doubled to form the past participle, past tense and present participle, as **programmed** and **programming**. In American English **program** is the accepted spelling for all senses of both noun and verb.

protagonist was originally a term for 'the chief character in a drama', as in 'Hamlet is the protagonist in the play that bears his name'. It then came to mean also 'the leading person or paticipant in an event, dispute, etc', as in 'The protagonists on each side of the dispute had a meeting'. In modern usage it can now also mean 'a leading or notable supporter of a cause, movement, etc,' as in 'She was one of the protagonists of the feminist movement'.

provided and **providing** are used interchangeably, as in 'You may go, provided/providing that you have finished your work' and 'He can borrow the car provided/providing he pays for the petrol'. 'That' is optional. The phrases mean 'on the condition that'.

pudding *see* **dessert**.

pupil and **student** are not interchangeable. **Pupil** refers to 'a child or young person who is at school', as in 'primary school pupils and secondary school pupils'. **Student** refers to 'a person who is studying at a place of further education, at a university or college', as in 'students trying to find work during the vacations'. In modern usage senior **pupils** at secondary school are sometimes known as **students**. In American English student refers to people at school as well as to people in further education. **Pupil** can also refer to 'a person who is receiving instruction in something from an expert' as in 'The piano teacher has several adult pupils'. **Student** can also refer to 'a person who is studying a particular thing', as in 'In his leisure time he is a student of local history'.

quasi- is Latin in origin and means 'as if, as it were'. In English it is combined with adjectives in the sense of 'seemingly, apparently, but not really', as in 'He gave a quasi-scientific explanation of the occurrence which convinced many people but did not fool his colleagues', or 'partly, to a certain extent but not completely', as in 'It is a quasi-official body which does not have full powers'. **Quasi-** can also be combined with nouns to mean 'seeming, but not really', as in 'a quasi-socialist who is really a capitalist' and 'a quasi-Christian who will not give donations to charity'. **Quasi-** has several possible pronunciations. It can be pronounced *kway*-zi, *kway*-si or *kwah*-si

queer in the sense of 'homosexual' was formerly used only in a slang and derogatory or offensive way. However, it is now used in a non-offensive way by homosexual people to describe themselves, as an alternative to 'gay'.

question *see* **beg the question**; **leading question**.

quick is an adjective meaning 'fast, rapid', as in 'a quick method', 'a quick route' and 'a quick walker'. It should not be used as an adverb, as in 'Come quick', in formal contexts since this is grammatically wrong.

quite has two possible meanings when used with adjectives. It can mean 'fairly, rather, somewhat', as in 'She's quite good at tennis but not good enough to play in the team' and 'The house is quite nice but it's not what we're looking for'. Where the indefinite article is used, **quite** precedes it, as in 'quite a good player' and 'quite a nice house'. '**Quite** can also mean 'completely, totally', as in 'We were quite overwhelmed by their generosity' and 'It is quite impossible for him to attend the meeting'.

raison d'être is French in origin and is used in English to mean 'a reason, a justification for the existence of', as in 'Her children are her raison d'être' and 'His only raison d'être is his work'. The phrase is liable to be misspelt. Note the accent (^) on the first *e*. It is pronounced *ray*-zon detr.

rara avis is French in origin and means literally 'rare bird'. In English it is used to refer to 'a rare or unusual person or thing', as in 'a person with such dedication to a company is a rara avis'. It is pronounced *ray*-ra *ayv*-is or *ra*-ra *ay*-vis.

ravage and **ravish** are liable to be confused. They sound rather similar although they have different meanings. **Ravage** means 'to cause great damage to, to devastate', as in 'low-lying areas ravaged by floods' and 'a population ravaged by disease', or 'to plunder, to rob', as in 'neighbouring tribes ravaging their territory'. **Ravish** means either 'to delight greatly, to enchant', as in 'The audience were ravished by the singer's performance'. It also means 'to rape', as in 'The girl was ravished by her kidnappers', but this meaning is rather old-fashioned and is found only in formal or literary contexts.

re- is a common prefix, meaning 'again', in verbs. In most cases it is not followed by a hyphen, as in 'retrace one's footsteps', 'a retrial ordered by the judge' and 'reconsider his decision'. However, it should be followed by a hyphen if its absence is likely to lead to confusion with another word, as in 're-cover a chair'/'recover from an illness', 're-count the votes'/'recount a tale of woe', 'the re-creation of a 17th-century village for a film set'/'play tennis for recreation' and 're-form the group'/'reform the prison system'. In cases where the second element of a word begins with *e*, **re-** is traditionally followed by a hyphen, as in 're-educate', re-entry' and 're-echo', but in modern usage the hyphen is frequently omitted.

re, meaning 'concerning, with reference to', as in 'Re your correspondence of 26 November', should be restricted to business or formal contexts.

readable *see* **legible**.

re-cover, recover *see* **re-**.

re-creation, recreation *see* **re-**.

referendum causes problems with regard to its plural form. It has two possible plural forms, **referendums** or **referenda**. In modern usage **referendums** is the more usual plural. **Referendum** means 'the referring of an issue of public importance to a general vote by all the people of a country', as in 'hold a referendum on whether to join the EC'.

re-form, reform *see* **re-**.

registry office and **register office** are interchangeable, although **registry office** is the more common term in general usage. The words refer to 'an office where civil marriage ceremonies are performed and where births, marriages and deaths are recorded', as in 'She wanted to be married in church but he preferred a registry office ceremony' and 'register the child's birth at the local registry office'.

rigour and **rigor** are liable to be confused. They look similar but they have completely different meanings. **Rigour** means 'severity, strictness', as in 'the rigour of the punishment', and 'harshness, unpleasantness', as in 'the rigour of the climate' (in this sense it is often in the plural, **rigours**), and 'strictness, detailedness', as in 'the rigour of the editing'. **Rigor** is a medical term meaning 'rigidity', as in 'muscles affected by rigor', or 'a feeling of chilliness often accompanied by feverishness', as in 'infectious diseases of which rigor is one of the symptoms'. **Rigor** is also short for **rigor mortis**, meaning 'the stiffening of the body that occurs after death'. The first syllable of **rigour** is pronounced to rhyme with 'big', but **rigor** can be pronounced either in this way or with the *i* pronounced as in 'ride'.

roof causes problems with regard to its plural form. The usual plural is **roofs**, which can be pronounced either as it is spelt, to rhyme with 'hoofs', or to rhyme with 'hooves'.

rout and **route** are liable to be confused. They look similar but are pronounced differently and have completely different meanings'. **Rout** as a noun means 'overwhelming defeat', as in 'the rout of the opposing army', and as a verb 'to defeat utterly', as in 'Their team routed ours last time'. **Route** refers to 'a way of getting somewhere', as in 'the quickest route' and 'the scenic route'. **Route** can also be a verb meaning 'to arrange a route for, to send by a certain route', as in 'route the visitors along the banks of the river'. **Rout** is pronounced to rhyme with 'shout'. **Route** is pronounced to rhyme with 'brute'.

scarfs and **scarves** are both acceptable spellings of the plural of 'scarf', meaning a piece of cloth worn around the neck or the head', as in 'a silk scarf at her neck' and 'wearing a head scarf'.

Scotch, Scots and **Scottish** are liable to be confused. **Scotch** is restricted to a few set phrases, such as 'Scotch whisky', 'Scotch broth' and 'Scotch mist'. As a noun **Scotch** refers to 'Scotch whisky', as in 'have a large Scotch with ice'. **Scots** as an adjective is used in such contexts as 'Scots accents', 'Scots people' and 'Scots attitudes'. As a noun **Scots** refers to the Scots language, as in 'He speaks standard English but he uses a few words of Scots.' The noun **Scot** is used to refer to 'a Scottish person', as in 'Scots living in London'. **Scottish** is found in such contexts as 'Scottish literature', 'Scottish history' and 'Scottish culture'.

sculpt and **sculpture** are interchangeable as verbs meaning 'to make sculptures, to practise sculpting', as in 'commissioned to sculpt/sculpture a bust of the chairman of the firm' and 'She both paints and sculpts/sculptures.

seize Note the *ei* combination, which is an exception to the '*i* before *e* except after *c*' rule.

sentiment and **sentimentality** are liable to be confused. They are related but have different shades of meaning. **Sentiment** means 'feeling, emotion', as in 'His actions were the result of sentiment not rationality'. It also means 'attitude, opinion', as in 'a speech full of anti-Christian sentiments'. **Sentimentality** is the noun from the adjective **sentimental** and means 'over-indulgence in tender feelings', as in 'dislike the sentimentality of the love songs' and 'She disliked her home town but now speaks about it with great sentimentality'.

sexism in language has been an issue for some time, and various attempts have been made to avoid it. For example, 'person' is often used where 'man' was traditionally used and 'he/she' substituted for 'he' in situations where the sex of the relevant person is unknown or unspecified.

ship *see* **boat**.

sine qua non is a Latin phrase that has been adopted into English and means 'essential condition, something that is absolutely necessary', as in 'It is a sine qua non of the agreement that the rent is paid on time'. It is used only in formal or legal contexts.

sitting room, living room, lounge and **drawing room** all refer to 'a room in a house used for relaxation and the receiving of guests'. Which word is used is largely a matter of choice. Some people object to the use of **lounge** as being pretentious but it is becoming increasingly common. **Drawing room** is a more formal word and applies to a room in rather a grand residence.

skilful, as in 'admire his skilful handling of the situation' is frequently misspelt. Note the single *l* before the *f*. In American English the word is spelt **skillful**.

slander *see* **libel**.

sometime and **some time** are liable to be confused. **Sometime** means 'at an unknown or unspecified time', as in 'We must get together sometime' and 'I saw her sometime last year'. There is a growing tendency in modern usage to spell this as **some time**. Originally **some time** was restricted to meaning 'a period of time', as in 'We need some time to think'.

spelled and **spelt** are both acceptable forms of the past tense and past participle of the verb 'to spell', as in 'They spelled/spelt the word wrongly' and 'He realized that he had spelled/spelt the word wrongly'.

stadium causes problems with regard to its plural form. **Stadiums** and **stadia** are both acceptable. **Stadium** is derived from Latin and the original plural form followed the Latin and was **stadia**. However, anglicized plural forms are becoming more and more common in foreign words adopted into English, and **stadiums** is now becoming the more usual form.

stanch and **staunch** are both acceptable spellings of the word meaning 'to stop the flow of', as in 'stanch/staunch the blood

from the wound in his head' and 'try to stanch/staunch the tide of violence'. **Staunch** also means 'loyal, firm', as in 'the team's staunch supporters'.

start *see* **commence**.

stationary and **stationery** are liable to be confused. They sound alike but have completely different meanings. **Stationary** means 'not moving, standing still', as in 'stationary vehicles'. **Stationery** refers to 'writing materials', as in 'office stationery'. An easy way to differentiate between them is to remember that **stationery** is bought from a 'stationer', which, like 'baker' and 'butcher', ends in -*er*.

staunch *see* **stanch**.

stimulant and **stimulus** are liable to be confused. Formerly the distinction between them was quite clear but now the distinction is becoming blurred. Traditionally **stimulant** refers to 'a substance, such as a drug, that makes a person more alert or more active', as in 'Caffeine is a stimulant'. **Stimulus** traditionally refers to 'something that rouses or encourages a person to action or greater effort', as in 'The promise of more money acted as a stimulus to the work force and they finished the job in record time'. In modern usage the words are beginning to be used interchangeably. In particular, **stimulus** is used in the sense of **stimulant** as well as being used in its own original sense.

straight away and **straightaway** are both acceptable ways of spelling the expression for 'without delay, at once', as in 'attend to the matter straight away/straightaway'.

strata *see* **stratum**.

stratagem and **strategy** are liable to be confused. They look and sound similar but they have different meanings. **Stratagem** means 'a scheme or trick', as in 'think of a stratagem to mislead the enemy' and 'devise a stratagem to gain entry to the building'. **Strategy** refers to 'the art of planning a campaign', as in 'generals meeting to put together a battle strategy', and 'a plan or policy, particularly a clever one, designed for a particular purpose', as in 'admire the strategy which he used to win the game'.

stratum and **strata** are liable to be confused. **Stratum** is the singular form and **strata** is the plural form of a word meaning 'a layer or level', as in 'a stratum of rock' and 'different strata of society'. It is a common error to use **strata** as a singular noun.

student *see* **pupil**.

subconscious and unconscious are used in different contexts. **Subconscious** means 'concerning those areas or activities of the mind of which one is not fully aware', as in 'a subconscious hatred of her parents' and 'a subconscious desire to hurt her sister'. **Unconscious** means 'unaware', as in 'She was unconscious of his presence' and 'unconscious of the damage which he had caused', and 'unintentional', as in 'unconscious humour' and 'an unconscious slight'. **Unconscious** also means 'having lost consciousness, insensible', as in 'knocked unconscious by the blow to his head'.

subjective *see* **objective**.

such and **like** are liable to be confused. **Such** is used to introduce examples, as in 'herbs, such as chervil and parsley' and 'citrus fruits, such as oranges and lemons'. **Like** introduces comparisons. 'She hates horror films like *Silence of the Lambs*', and 'Very young children, like very old people, have to be kept warm.'

supper *see* **dinner**.

syndrome in its original meaning refers to 'a set of symptoms and signs that together indicate the presence of a physical or mental disorder', as in 'Down's syndrome'. In modern usage it is used loosely to indicate 'any set of events, actions, characteristics, attitudes that together make up, or are typical of, a situation', as in 'He suffers from the "I'm all right Jack" syndrome and doesn't care what happens to anyone else' and 'They seem to be caring people but they are opposing the building of an Aids hospice in their street—a definite case of "the not in my back yard" syndrome'.

tea *see* **dinner**.

teach *see* **learn**.

telephone *see* **phone**.

terminal and **terminus** in some contexts are interchangeable. They both refer to 'the end of a bus route, the last stop on a bus route, the building at the end of a bus route', as in 'The bus doesn't go any further—this is the terminus/terminal', but

terminus is the more common term in this sense. They can also both mean 'the end of a railway line, the station at the end of a railway line', but **terminal** is the more common term in this sense. **Terminal** can refer to 'a building containing the arrival and departure areas for passengers at an airport' and 'a building in the centre of a town for the arrival and departure of air passengers'. **Terminal** also refers to 'a point of connection in an electric circuit', as in 'the positive and negative terminals', and 'apparatus, usually consisting of a keyboard and screen, for communicating with the central processor in a computing system', as in 'He has a dumb terminal so he can read information but not input it'. As an adjective **terminal** means 'of, or relating to, the last stage in a fatal illness', as in 'a terminal disease' and 'terminal patients'.

than is used to link two halves of comparisons or contrasts, as in 'Peter is considerably taller than John is', 'He is older than I am' and 'I am more informed about the situation than I was yesterday'. Problems arise when the relevant verb is omitted. In order to be grammatically correct, the word after 'than' should take the subject form if there is an implied verb, as in 'He is older than I (am)'. However this can sound stilted, as in 'She works harder than he (does)', and in informal contexts this usually becomes 'She works harder than him'. If there is no implied verb, the word after **than** is in the object form, as in 'rather you than me!'

the the definite article, which usually refers back to something already identified or to something specific, as in 'Where is the key?', 'What have you done with the book that I gave you?' and 'We have found the book that had we lost'. It is also used to denote someone or something as being the only one, as in 'the House of Lords', 'the King of Spain' and 'the President of Russia' and to indicate a class or group, as in 'the aristocracy', 'the cat family' and 'the teaching profession'. The is sometimes pronounced 'thee' when it is used to identify someone or something unique or important, as in 'Is that the John Frame over there?' and 'She is the fashion designer of the moment'.

their and **there** are liable to be confused because they sound similar. **There** means 'in, to or at that place', as in 'place it there' and 'send it there'. **Their** is the possessive of 'they', meaning 'of them, belonging to them', as in 'their books' and 'their mistakes'.

their and **they're** are liable to be confused because they sound similar. **Their** is the possessive of 'they', meaning 'of them, belonging to them', as in 'their cars' and 'their attitudes'. **They're** is a shortened form of 'they are', as in 'They're not very happy' and 'They're bound to lose'.

their used in conjunction with 'anyone', everyone', 'no one' and 'someone', is becoming increasingly common, even in textbooks, although this use is ungrammatical. The reason for this is to avoid the sexism of using 'his' when the sex of the person being referred to is either unknown or unspecified, and to avoid the clumsiness of 'his/her' or 'his or her'. Examples of **they** being so used include 'Everyone must do their best' and 'No one is to take their work home'.

this *see* **next**.

till and **until** are more or less interchangeable except that **until** is slightly more formal, as in 'They'll work till they drop' and 'Until we assess the damage we will not know how much the repairs will cost'.

toilet, lavatory, loo and **bathroom** all have the same meaning but the context in which they are used sometimes varies. **Toilet** is the most widely used of the words and is used on signs in public places. The informal **loo** is also very widely used. **Lavatory** is less common nowadays although it was formerly regarded by all but the working class and lower-middle class as the most acceptable term. **Bathroom** in British English usually refers to 'a room containing a bath', but in American English it is the usual word for **toilet**. **Ladies** and **gents** are terms for **toilet**, particularly in public places. **Powder room** also means this, as does the American English **rest room**.

town *see* **city**.

trade names should be written with a capital letter, as in 'Filofax' and 'Jacuzzi'. When trade names are used as verbs they are

written with a lower case letter, as in 'hoover the carpet'.

try to and **try and** are interchangeable in modern usage. Formerly **try and** was considered suitable only in spoken and very informal contexts, but it is now considered acceptable in all but the most formal contexts, as in 'Try to/and do better' and 'They must try to/and put the past behind them'.

ultra is used as a prefix meaning 'going beyond', as in 'ultraviolet' and 'ultrasound', or 'extreme, very', as in 'ultra-sophisticated', 'ultra-modern', and 'ultra-conservative'. Compounds using it may be spelt with or without a hyphen. Words such as 'ultrasound' and 'ultraviolet' are usually spelt as one word, but words with the second sense of **ultra**, such as 'ultra-sophisticated', are often hyphenated.

unconscious *see* **subconscious**.

under way, meaning 'in progress', is traditionally spelt as two words, as in 'Preparations for the conference are under way'. In modern usage it is frequently spelt as one word, as in 'The expansion project is now underway'. It is a common error to write 'under weigh'.

underhand and **underhanded** are interchangeable in the sense of 'sly, deceitful', as in 'He used underhand/underhanded methods to get the job' and 'It was underhand/underhanded of him to not to tell her that he was leaving'. **Underhand** is the more common of the two terms.

uninterested *see* **disinterested**.

unique traditionally means 'being the only one of its kind', as in 'a unique work of art' and 'everyone's fingerprints are unique' and so cannot be modified by such words as 'very', 'rather', 'more', etc, although it can be modified by 'almost' and 'nearly'. In modern usage **unique** is often used to mean 'unrivalled, unparalleled, outstanding', as in 'a unique opportunity' and 'a unique performance'.

unreadable *see* **illegible**.

until *see* **till**.

up and **upon** mean the same and are virtually interchangeable, except that **upon** is slightly more formal. Examples include 'sitting on a bench', 'the carpet on the floor', 'the stamp on the letter', caught with the stolen goods on him' and 'something on his mind'; and 'She threw herself upon her dying mother's bed', 'a carpet of snow upon the ground' and 'Upon his arrival he went straight upstairs'.

upward and **upwards** are not interchangeable. **Upward** is used as an adjective, as in 'on an upward slope' and 'an upward trend in prices'. **Upwards** is an adverb, as in 'look upwards to see the plane'.

vacation, meaning 'holiday', in British English is mostly restricted to a university or college situation, as in 'students seeking paid employment during their vacation'. In American English it is the usual word for 'holiday'.

verbal and **oral** are liable to be confused. **Oral** means 'expressed in speech', as in 'an oral, rather than a written examination'. **Verbal** means 'expressed in words', as in 'He asked for an instruction diagram but he was given verbal instructions' and 'They were going to stage a protest match but they settled for a verbal protest'. It is also used to mean 'referring to the spoken word, expressed in speech', as in 'a verbal agreement'. Because of these two possible meanings, the use of **verbal** can lead to ambiguity. In order to clarify the situation, **oral** should be used when 'expressed in speech' is meant. **Verbal** can also mean referring to verbs, as in 'verbal endings'.

vice versa means 'the other way round, with the order reversed', as in 'He will do his friend's shift and vice versa' and 'Mary dislikes John and vice versa'. It is pronounced vis-e ver-sa, vi-si ver-sa or vis ver-sa and is derived from Latin.

vis-à-vis means 'in relation to', as in 'their performance vis-à-vis their ability' and 'the company's policy vis-à-vis early retirement'. It is pronounced vee-za-vee and is derived from French. Note the accent on the *a*.

-ways *see* **-wise**.

what ever and **whatever** are not interchangeable. **What ever** is used when 'ever' is used for emphasis, as in 'What ever does he think he's doing?' and 'What ever is she wearing'. **Whatever** means 'anything, regardless of what, no matter what', as in 'Help yourself to whatever you want' and 'Whatever he says I don't believe him'.

which and **what** can cause problems. In questions **which** is used when a limited range of alternatives is suggested, as in 'Which book did you buy in the end?' and **what** is used in general situations, as in 'What book did you buy?'

whisky and **whiskey** both refer to a strong alcoholic drink distilled from grain. **Whisky** is made in Scotland and **whiskey** in Ireland and America. **Whisky** is the usual British English spelling.

who and **whom** cause problems. **Who** is the subject of a verb, as in 'Who told you?', 'It was you who told her' and 'the girls who took part in the play'. **Whom** is the object of a verb or preposition, as in 'Whom did he tell?', 'To whom did you speak?' and 'the people from whom he stole'. In modern usage **whom** is falling into disuse, especially in questions, except in formal contexts. **Who** is used instead even although it is ungrammatical, as in 'Who did you speak to?' **Whom** should be retained when it is a relative pronoun, as in 'the man whom you saw', 'the person to whom he spoke' and 'the girl to whom she gave the book'.

whose and **who's** are liable to be confused. They sound alike but have different meanings. **Whose** means 'of whom' or 'of which', as in 'the woman whose child won', 'the boy whose leg was broken', 'Whose bicycle is that?' and 'the firm whose staff went on strike'. **Who's** is a shortened form of 'who is', as in 'Who's that?', 'Who's first in the queue?' and 'Who's coming to the cinema?'

-wise and **-ways** cause problems. Added to nouns, **-wise** can form adverbs of manner indicating either 'in such a position or direction', as in 'lengthwise' and 'clockwise', and 'in the manner of', as in 'crabwise'. In modern usage **-wise** is frequently used to mean 'with reference to', as in 'Weatherwise it was fine', 'Workwise all is well' and 'Moneywise they're not doing too well'. The suffix **-ways** has a more limited use. It means 'in such a way, direction or manner of', as in 'lengthways' and 'sideways'.

woman *see* **lady**.

Xmas is sometimes used as an alternative and shorter form of 'Christmas'. It is common only in a written informal context and is used mainly in commercial situations, as in 'Xmas cards on sale here' and 'Get your Xmas tree here'. When pronounced it is the same as 'Christmas'. The X derives from the Greek *chi*, the first letter of *Christos*, the Greek word for Christ.

X-ray is usually written with an initial capital letter when it is a noun meaning 'a photograph made by means of X-rays showing the bones or organs of the body', as in 'take an X-ray of the patient's chest'. Another term for the noun **X-ray** is 'radiograph'. As a verb it is also usually spelt with an initial capital, as 'After the accident he had his leg X-rayed', but it is sometimes spelt with an initial lower-case letter, as in 'have his chest x-rayed'.

you is used in informal or less formal situations to indicate an indefinite person referred to as 'one' in formal situations. Examples include 'You learn a foreign language more quickly if you spend some time in the country where it is spoken', 'You would think that they would make sure that their staff are polite', 'You can get used to anything in time' and 'You have to experience the situation to believe it'. **You** in this sense must be distinguished from **you** meaning the second person singular', as in 'You have missed your bus', 'You must know where you left your bag' and 'You have to leave now'. *See* **one**.

your and **you're** are liable to be confused. **Your** is a possessive adjective meaning 'belonging to you, of you', as in 'That is your book and this is mine', 'Your attitude is surprising' and 'It is your own fault'. **You're** is a shortened form of 'you are', as in 'You're foolish to believe him', 'You're going to be sorry' and 'You're sure to do well'. Note the spelling of the pronoun **yours**, as in 'This book is yours' and 'Which car is yours?' It should not be spelt with an apostrophe as it is not a shortened form of anything.

Spelling

-able and -ible are both used to form adjectives. It is easy to confuse the spelling of words ending in these. *See* **Adjectives Liable to be Misspelt**

accent refers to certain symbols used on some foreign words adopted into English. In modern usage, which has a tendency to punctuate less than was formerly the case, accents are frequently omitted. For example, an actor's part in a play is now usually spelt 'role' but originally it was spelt 'rôle', the accent on *o* being called a circumflex.

The accent is most likely to be retained if it affects the pronunciation. Thus 'cliché' and 'divorcé' usually retain the acute accent, as it is called, on the *e*. On the other hand, the accent known as the cedilla is frequently omitted from beneath the *c* in words such as 'façade/facade', although it is there to indicate that the *c* is soft, pronounced like an *s*, rather than a hard sound pronounced like a *k*.

apostrophe *see* **Punctuation** section.

book titles these can cause problems as to spelling and style. How they are treated in publications, business reports, etc, depends largely on the house style of the firm concerned. However, they are generally written in documents, letters, etc, as they appear on their title pages, that is with the first letter of the first word and of the following main words of the title in capital letters, and those of words of lesser importance, such as the articles, prepositions and coordinate conjunctions, in lowercase letters, as in The Guide to Yoga, Hope for the Best and In the Middle of Life.

Some people, and some house-style manuals, prefer to put the titles in italic, as in *A Room with a View* and *A Guide to Dental Health*. Others prefer to put book titles in quotation marks, as in 'Gardening for Beginners'. Such a convention can make use of either single or double quotation marks. Thus either 'Desserts for the Summer' or "Desserts for the Summer" is possible provided that the writer is consistent throughout any one piece of writing.

If the title of a book is mentioned in a piece of direct speech in quotation marks it goes within the opposite style of quotation marks from the piece in direct speech. Thus if the direct speech is within single quotation marks, the book title goes within double quotation marks, as in 'Have you read "Wuthering Heights" or are you not a Bronte fan?' If the direct speech is within double quotation marks, the book title goes between single quotation marks, as in "Would you say that 'Animal Farm' was your favourite Orwell novel?"

It is even quite common for book titles to appear in documents both in italic type and with quotation marks. To some extent the punctuation of book titles is a matter of choice as long as they are consistent, but there is a growing tendency to have as little punctuation as possible and to have as uncluttered a page as possible.

buildings can cause problems with regard to capital letters. The proper noun attached to the name of the building should have an initial capital letter, as should have the common noun that may be part of the name, as in The White House and The National Portrait Gallery.

businesses and **organizations** often cause problems with regard to their names or titles. In general the initial letters of the main words of the title should be in capital letters and the words of lesser importance, such as the articles, coordinating conjunctions and prepositions, should be in lower case, except when they are the first word of the title, as in 'The Indian Carpet Company', 'Kitchens for All' and 'Capital Industrial Cleaners'. Obviously, when the names of people are involved these should have initial capital letters, as in 'Jones and Brown'.

capital letters are used in a number of different situations.

The first word of a sentence or a direct quotation begins with a **capital letter**, as in 'They left early', 'Why have they gone?' and 'He said weakly, "I don't feel very well".

The first letter of a name or proper noun is always a **capital letter**, as in 'Mary Brown', 'John Smith', 'South America', 'Rome', 'speak Italian', 'Buddhism', 'Marxism'.

Capital letters are also used in the titles of people, places or works of art, as in 'Uncle Fred', 'Professor Jones', 'Ely Cathedral', Edinburgh University', 'reading *Wuthering Heights*', 'watching *Guys and Dolls*', 'listen to Beethoven's Third Symphony' and 'a copy of *The Potato Eaters* by van Gogh'. They are also used in the titles of wars and historical, cultural and geological periods, as in 'the Wars of the Roses', 'the Renaissance', 'the Ice Age'.

Note that only the major words of titles, etc, are in capital letters, words, such as 'the', 'on', 'of', etc, being in lower-case letters.

A capital letter is used as the first letter of days of the week, months of the year, and religious festivals, as in 'Monday', 'October', 'Easter', 'Yom Kippur'. It is a matter of choice whether the seasons of the year are given capital letters or not, as in 'spring/Spring', 'autumn/Autumn'.

Apart from 'I', pronouns are lower-case except when they refer to God or Christ, when some people capitalize them, as in 'God asks us to trust in Him'.

Trade names should be spelt with an initial capital letter, as in 'Filofax', 'Jacuzzi', 'Xerox', 'Biro', 'Hoover'. When verbs are formed from these, they are spelt with an initial lower-case letter, as 'xerox the letter', 'hoover the carpet'.

doubling of consonants There are a few rules that can help you decide whether or not to double a consonant.

In words of one syllable ending in a single consonant preceded by a single vowel, the consonant is doubled when an ending starting with a vowel is added, as in 'drop' and 'dropped', 'pat' and 'patting' and 'rub' and 'rubbing'.

In words of more than one syllable that end in a single consonant preceded by a single vowel, the consonant is doubled if the stress is on the last syllable, as in 'begin' and 'beginning', 'occur' and 'occurring', 'prefer' and 'preferred', 'refer' and 'refer-

ring' and 'commit' and 'committed'. In similar words where the stress is not on the last syllable, the consonant does not double, as in 'bigot' and 'bigoted', 'develop' and 'developed'

Exceptions to this rule include words ending in 'l'. The 'l' doubles even in cases where the last syllable containing it is unstressed, as in 'travel' and 'travelled' and 'appal' and 'appalling'. 'Worship', in which the stress is on the first syllable, is also an exception, as in 'worshipped'.

geographical features these should be written with initial capital letters. They include the common nouns that are part of the name of the feature, as in Niagara Falls, Atlantic Ocean, River Thames, Mount Everest and Devil's Island.

hyphen *see* **Punctuation** section.

indefinite article a and an are the forms of the indefinite article.

The form a is used before words that begin with a consonant sound, as in *a* box, *a* garden, *a* road, *a* wall.

The form an is used before words that begin with a vowel sound, as in *an* apple, *an* easel, *an* ostrich, *an* uncle.

Note that it is the *sound* of the initial letter that matters and not the *spelling*. Thus a is used before words beginning with a *u* when they are pronounced with a *y* sound as though it were a consonant, as *a* unit, *a* usual occurrence. Similarly an is used, for example, before words beginning with the letter *h* where this is not pronounced, as in *an* heir, *an* hour, *an* honest man.

Formerly it was quite common to use an before words that begin with an *h* sound and also begin with an unstressed syllable, as *an* hotel, *an* historic occasion, but nowadays it is more usual to use *a* in such cases.

months of the year these are spelt with initial capital letters, as in January, February, March, April, May, June, July, August, September, October, November and December.

plural nouns singular nouns in English form plural forms in different ways.

Most in add *s* to form the plural, as in 'cats', 'machines' and 'boots'.

plural nouns

Words ending in -s, -x, -z, -ch and -sh add es, as in 'buses', 'masses', 'foxes', 'fezzes or fezes', 'churches' and 'sashes'.

Nouns ending in a consonant followed by y have -ies in the plural, as 'fairies' and 'ladies', but note 'monkey', where the y is preceded by a vowel and becomes 'monkeys'. Proper nouns ending in y add s, as in 'the two Germanys'.

Some words ending in f have ves in the plural, as 'wives' and 'halves', but some simply add s to the singular form, as 'beliefs'. Some words ending in f can either add s or change to ves, as 'hoofs or hooves'.

Words ending in o cause problems as some end in oes in the plural, as 'potatoes' and 'tomatoes', and some end in s, as in 'pianos', while some can be spelt either way and have to be learned or looked up in a dictionary etc. Shortened forms, such as

commonly misspelt words

'photo' and 'video', add simply s, as 'photos', 'videos'.

Some words have the same form in the plural as they do in the singular, such as 'sheep' and 'deer'. Some are plural in form already and so do not change. These include 'trousers' and 'scissors'.

Several words in English have irregular plural forms which just have to be learned or looked up in a dictionary, etc. These include 'men', 'mice' and 'feet'.

Some foreign words adopted into English used to retain the foreign plural form in English but this is becoming less common and, at the very least there is now often an English-formed alternative, as 'gateaux/gateaus', 'index/indices', 'formulae/formulas', 'appendixes/appendices'. However, several nouns of foreign extraction retain the foreign-style plural in English, such as 'criteria' and 'crises'.

Commonly misspelt words

All of us have problem words that cause spelling difficulties but there are some words that are generally misspelt. These include:

A

abbreviation	actual	agoraphobia	analyse
abscess	additional	agreeable	analysis
absence	address	agreed	anarchist
abysmal	adequate	aisle	ancestor
accelerator	adieu	alcohol	ancestry
accessible	adjacent	alfresco	anemone
accessories	admissible	alibis	angrily
accommodate	admittance	align	anguish
accompaniment	adolescence	alignment	annihilate
accumulate	adolescent	allege	annihilation
accurate	advantageous	allergic	anniversary
accustomed	advertisement	alleys	announcement
achieve	advice	alligator	annulled
aching	advise	allocate	annulment
acknowledge	aerate	allotment	anonymous
acknowledgement/	aerial	allotted	anorak
acknowledgment	aesthetic	almond	answered
acquaint	affect	alms	Antarctic
acquaintance	affiliation	alphabetically	antibiotic
acquiesce	afforestation	already	antithesis
acquiescence	aggravate	although	anxiety
acquire	aggravation	aluminium	apartheid
acquit	aggregate	ambiguous	apologize
acquittal	aggression	amethyst	appalling
acreage	aggressive	ammunition	apparently
across	aghast	anachronism	appearance
	agnosticism	anaesthetic	appendicitis

appreciate commission

appreciate
approval
aquarium
aquiline
arbiter
arbitrary
arbitration
archaeology
architectural
Arctic
arguably
arrangement
arrival
artichoke
ascend
ascent
asphalt
asphyxiate
asphyxiation
assassin
assassinate
assessment
assistance
associate
asthma
asthmatic
astrakhan
atheist
atrocious
attach
attendant
attitude
aubergine
auburn
auctioneer
audible
aural
automatic
autumn
awful
awkward

B

bachelor
bagatelle
baggage
bailiff
ballast
ballerina
banana
banister
bankruptcy
banquet

barbecue
barometer
barrister
basically
basis
bassoon
battalion
bazaar
beautiful
befriend
beguile
behaviour
beleaguer
belief
believe
belligerent
benefited
bequeath
berserk
besiege
bettered
bevelled
bewitch
bias
bicycle
biennial
bigamous
bigoted
bilingual
biscuit
bivouacked
blancmange
blasphemous
blasphemy
bleary
blitz
bodily
bonfire
bootee
borough
bouquet
bourgeois
boutique
bracketed
braille
brassiere
breadth
breathalyser
brief
broccoli
brochure
bronchitis

bruise
brusque
buccaneer
Buddhist
budding
budgerigar
budgeted
buffeted
bulletin
bumptious
bungalow
buoyancy
buoyant
bureau
bureaucracy
business
buttoned

C

cabbage
cafeteria
caffeine
camouflage
campaign
campaigned
cancelled
cancerous
candour
cannabis
cannibal
canvassing
capability
capillary
capitalist
caravan
carbohydrate
carburettor
career
caress
caries
carriage
cartoonist
cashier
cassette
castanets
casualty
catalogue
catarrh
catechism
catering
cauliflower
cautious
ceiling

cellophane
cemetery
centenary
centilitre
centimetre
certainty
champagne
championed
chancellor
changeable
channelled
characteristic
chasm
chauffeur
cheetah
cherish
chief
chilblain
chintz
chiropody
chisel
choreographer
choreography
chronically
chrysanthemum
cigarette
cinnamon
circuitous
cistern
civilian
claustrophobia
clientele
clique
coalesce
cocoa
coconut
coffee
cognac
coincidence
colander
collaborate
collapsible
colleague
colonel
colossal
comically
commandeer
commemorate
commentator
commercial
commiserate
commission

commissionaire
commitment
committal
committed
committee
communicate
commuter
companion
comparative
comparison
compatibility
compelled
competitive
computer
conceal
concealment
conceit
conceive
concession
concurrent
concussion
condemned
condescend
confectionery
conference
confetti
congeal
congratulations
conjunctivitis
conned
connoisseur
conscience
conscientious
conscious
consequently
consignment
consolation
conspicuous
constitute
consumer
contemptible
continent
continuous
contraception
contradictory
controlled
controller
controversial
convalesce
convenient
convertible
conveyed

convolvulus
coolly
cooperate
cooperative
coordinate
copying
coquette
corduroy
co-respondent
coronary
correspondence
correspondent
corridor
corroborate
corrugated
cosmopolitan
cosseted
councillor
counselling
counterfeit
courageous
courteous
crèche
credible
credited
crematorium
creosote
crescent
crisis
criterion
crocheted
crocodile
croupier
crucial
crucifixion
cruelly
cruise
cryptic
cubicle
cupful
curable
curiosity
curious
currency
curriculum vitae
customary
cynic
cynicism
cynosure
D
dachshund
daffodil

dahlia
dais
damage
dandruff
darkened
debatable
debauched
debility
deceased
deceit
deceive
deciduous
decipher
decoyed
decrease
decreed
defamatory
defeat
defendant
defied
definite
definitely
dehydrate
deign
deliberate
delicatessen
delicious
delinquent
delirious
demeanour
demonstrate
denouement
denunciation
dependence
depth
derailment
dermatitis
derogatory
descend
descendant
desiccate
desperate
detach
detachable
detergent
deterred
deterrent
deuce
develop
developed
development
diabetes

diagnosis
dialogue
diametrically
diaphragm
diarrhoea
difference
different
dilapidated
dilemma
dilettante
diminish
diminution
dinosaur
diphtheria
diphthong
disadvantageous
disagreeable
disagreed
disagreement
disappearance
disappeared
disappoint
disapproval
disastrous
disbelief
disbelieve
discipline
discotheque
discouraging
discourteous
discrepancy
discrimination
discussion
disease
disguise
dishevelled
dishonourable
disillusion
disinfectant
disinherited
dismissal
disobeyed
disparage
dispelled
disposal
dispossess
dissatisfaction
dissatisfy
dissect
disseminate
dissent
dissimilar

dissipated
dissipation
dissociate
dissolute
dissuade
distilled
distillery
distinguish
distraught
disuse
divisible
documentary
doggerel
domineering
donate
doubt
dragooned
drastically
draughty
drooled
drooped
drunkenness
dubious
dumbfounded
dungarees
duress
dutiful
dynamite
dysentery
dyspepsia
E
eccentric
ecclesiastic
ecologically
economically
ecstasy
eczema
effective
effervescence
efficacious
efficient
effrontery
eightieth
elaborate
electrician
elevenses
eligible
emancipate
embarrass
embarrassment
emergence
emergent

emolument
emotional
emphasize
employee
emptied
enable
encourage
encyclopedia
endeavour
endurance
energetically
enervate
engineer
enough
ensuing
entailed
enthusiasm
enumerate
epilepsy
equalize
equalled
equipped
erroneous
erudite
escalator
escapism
espionage
essence
essential
estranged
etiquette
euthanasia
eventually
evidently
exaggerate
exaggeration
exalt
exasperate
exceed
exceedingly
excellent
excessive
exchequer
excommunicate
exercise
exhaust
exhibit
exhilarate
exorcise
explanation
exquisite
extinguish

extraneous
extravagant
F
fabulous
facetious
faeces
Fahrenheit
fallacious
fanatic
farcical
fascinate
fatigue
fatuous
February
feeler
feign
ferocious
festooned
feud
feudal
fevered
fiasco
fibre
fictitious
fiend
fierce
fiery
filial
finesse
flabbergasted
flaccid
flammable
flannelette
fluent
fluoridate
fluoride
fluoridize
foliage
forcible
foreigner
forfeit
forthwith
fortieth
fortuitous
fortunately
frailty
frankincense
fraudulent
freedom
freight
frequency
friend

frolicked
fuchsia
fugitive
fulfil
fulfilled
fulfilment
fullness
fulsome
furious
furniture
furthered
G
gaiety
galloped
garrison
garrotted
gases
gateau
gauge
gazetteer
geisha
generator
genuine
gerbil
gesticulate
ghastly
ghetto
gigantic
gingham
giraffe
glamorous
glamour
glimpse
global
gluttonous
glycerine
gnarled
gnash
goitre
gossiped
government
graffiti
grammar
grandeur
gratefully
gratitude
gratuitous
greetings
gregarious
grief
grieve
grovelled

incontrovertible
incorrigible
incredulous
incriminate
incubator
incurred
indefatigable
indefinable
indefinite
independence
independent
indescribable
indict
indictment
indigenous
indigestible
indomitable
indubitable
ineligible
inescapable
inexcusable
inexhaustible
infallible
infatuated
inferred
infinitive
inflamed
inflammable
inflationary
ingratiate
ingredient
inhabitant
inheritance
inhibition
iniquitous
initiate
initiative
innate
innocuous
innumerable
innumerate
inoculate
insecticide
inseparable
insincere
insistence
instalment
instantaneous
intercept
interference
interior
intermediate

intermittent
interpret
interpretation
interrogate
interrupt
interview
intrigue
intrinsically
intuition
intuitive
invariably
inveigle
inveterate
involuntary
involvement
irascible
irrelevant
irreparable
irreplaceable
irresistible
irresponsible
irrevocable
irritable
italicize
itinerant
itinerary
J
jackal
Jacuzzi
jeopardize
jettisoned
jewellery
jodhpurs
juggernaut
jugular
K
kaleidoscopic
karate
keenness
khaki
kidnapped
kilometre
kiosk
kitchenette
kleptomania
knick-knack
knowledgeable
kowtow
L
labelled
laboratory
labyrinth

gruesome
guarantee
guarantor
guard
guardian
guest
guillotine
guinea
guise
guitar
gymkhana
gypsy/gipsy
H
haemoglobin
haemorrhage
halcyon
hallucination
hammered
handfuls
handicapped
handkerchief
happened
harangue
harass
harlequin
haughty
hazard
hearse
height
heightened
heinous
heir
herbaceous
hereditary
heroism
hesitate
hiccup, hiccough
hideous
hierarchy
hieroglyphics
hijack
hilarious
hindrance
hippopotamus
holiday
holocaust
homonym
honorary
honour
hooligan
horoscope
horrible

horticulture
hullabaloo
humorous
humour
hurricane
hurried
hygiene
hyphen
hypnosis
hypochondria
hypocrisy
hypotenuse
hypothesis
hypothetical
hysterical
I
icicle
ideological
idiosyncrasy
ignorance
illegible
illegitimate
illiberal
illiterate
imaginative
imitation
immaculate
immediate
immemorial
immoral
immovable
impasse
impeccable
imperative
imperceptible
imperious
impetuous
implacable
impresario
imprisoned
imprisonment
inaccessible
inadmissible
inappropriate
inaugural
incandescent
incessant
incipient
incognito
incommunicado
inconceivable
incongruous

lackadaisical   **paralyse**

lackadaisical
laddered
lager
language
languor
languorous
laryngitis
larynx
lassitude
latitude
laundered
launderette
layette
league
leanness
ledger
legendary
legible
legitimate
length
lengthened
leukaemia
levelled
liaise
liaison
lieu
lieutenant
lilac
limousine
lineage
linen
lingerie
linguist
liqueur
literature
litre
livelihood
loneliness
loosened
loquacious
lorgnette
lucrative
lucre
luggage
lugubrious
luminous
luscious
lustre
luxurious
lyric
M
macabre

maelstrom
magician
magnanimous
mahogany
maintenance
malaise
malaria
malignant
manageable
management
mannequin
manoeuvre
mantelpiece
manually
margarine
marijuana
marquee
martyr
marvellous
marzipan
masochist
massacre
matinee
mayonnaise
meagre
measurement
medallion
medieval
mediocre
melancholy
meningitis
meringue
messenger
meteorological
metropolitan
microphone
midday
migraine
mileage
milieu
millionaire
mimicked
mimicry
miniature
miraculous
mirrored
miscellaneous
mischief
mischievous
misogynist
misshapen
misspell

misspent
modelled
modelling
morgue
mortgage
mosquito
mountaineer
moustache
multitudinous
muscle
museum
mysterious
mythical
N
naive
narrative
naughty
nausea
nautical
necessary
necessity
negligence
negligible
negotiate
neighbourhood
neither
neurotic
neutral
niche
niece
ninetieth
ninth
nocturnal
nonentity
notably
noticeably
notoriety
nuance
numbered
numerate
numerous
nutrient
nutritious
O
obedient
obese
obituary
oblige
oblique
oblivious
obnoxious
obscene

obscenity
obsessive
obstetrician
occasion
occupancy
occupier
occupying
occurred
occurrence
octogenarian
odorous
odour
offence
offered
official
officious
ominous
omission
omitted
oneself
opaque
ophthalmic
opinion
opponent
opportunity
opposite
orchestra
ordinary
original
orthodox
orthopaedic
oscillate
ostracize
outlying
outrageous
overdraft
overrate
overreach
overwrought
oxygen
P
pacifist
pageant
pamphlet
panacea
panegyric
panicked
papered
parachute
paraffin
paragraph
paralyse

paralysis
paraphernalia
parcelled
parliament
paroxysm
parquet
partially
participant
particle
partner
passenger
passers-by
pastime
patterned
pavilion
peaceable
peculiar
pejorative
pencilled
penicillin
peppered
perceive
perennial
perilous
permissible
permitted
pernicious
perpetrate
persistence
personnel
persuasion
perusal
pessimism
pessimistically
pesticide
phantom
pharmacy
pharyngitis
pharynx
phenomenon
phial
phlegm
physician
physiotherapist
picketed
picnic
picnicked
picturesque
pioneered
pious
piteous
pitiful

plaintiff
plausible
pleurisy
pneumonia
poignant
politician
pollution
polythene
porridge
portrait
portray
positive
possession
possibility
posthumous
potatoes
precede
precedent
precinct
precipice
precocious
preference
preferred
prejudice
preliminary
prepossessing
prerequisite
prerogative
prescription
presence
preservative
prestige
prestigious
pretentious
prevalent
priest
primitive
procedure
proceed
procession
professional
profiteering
prohibit
promiscuous
pronunciation
propeller
proposal
proprietor
prosecute
protagonist
protein
provocation

prowess
psalm
psyche
psychiatric
psychic
publicly
pursuit
putative
pyjamas
Q
quarrelsome
questionnaire
queue
quintet
R
rabies
radioed
radios
railing
rancour
ransack
rapturous
reassurance
rebelled
rebellious
recalcitrant
receipt
receive
recommend
reconnaissance
reconnoitre
recruitment
recurrence
redundant
referee
reference
referred
regatta
regrettable
regretted
rehabilitation
reign
relevant
relief
relieve
reminisce
reminiscence
remuneration
rendezvous
repertoire
repetitive
reprieve

reprisal
requisite
rescind
resemblance
reservoir
resistance
resourceful
responsibility
restaurant
restaurateur
resurrection
resuscitate
retrieve
reunion
reveille
revelry
revenue
reversible
rhapsody
rheumatism
rhododendron
rhomboid
rhubarb
rhyme
rhythm
ricochet
righteous
rigorous
rigour
risotto
riveted
rogue
roughage
roulette
royalty
rucksack
ruinous
rummage
rumour
S
sabotage
sacrilege
saddened
salmon
salvage
sanctuary
sandwich
sanitary
sapphire
satellite
scaffolding
scandalous

scenic
sceptre
schedule
scheme
schizophrenic
schooner
sciatica
science
scissors
scruple
scrupulous
scurrilous
scythe
secretarial
secretary
sedative
sedentary
sensitive
separate
sergeant
serrated
serviceable
serviette
settee
shampooed
shattered
sheikh
sheriff
shield
shovelled
shuddered
siege
significant
silhouette
simply
simultaneous
sincerely
sixtieth
skeleton
skilful
slanderous
slaughter
sleigh
sleight of hand
sluice
smattering
smithereens
snivelled
soccer
solemn
solicitor
soliloquy

soloist
sombre
somersault
sophisticated
sovereign
spaghetti
spectre
spherical
sphinx
sponsor
spontaneity
spontaneous
squabble
squandered
squawk
staccato
staggered
stammered
statistics
statutory
stealth
stereophonic
stirrup
storage
strait-laced
straitjacket
strategic
strength
strenuous
stupor
suave
subpoena
subtle
succeed
successful
successor
succinct
succulent
succumb
suddenness
suede
sufficient
suffocate
suicide
sullenness
summoned
supercilious
superfluous
supersede
supervise
supervisor
supplementary

surgeon
surveillance
surveyor
susceptible
suspicious
sweetener
sycamore
symmetry
sympathize
symphony
synagogue
syndicate
synonym
syringe
T
tableau
taciturn
taffeta
tangerine
tangible
tattoo
technique
teenager
televise
temperature
tenuous
terrifically
terrifying
territory
terrorist
therapeutic
therefore
thief
thinness
thirtieth
thorough
thoroughfare
threshold
thrombosis
throughout
thwart
thyme
tightened
titivate
tobacconist
toboggan
toffee
tomatoes
tomorrow
tonsillitis
topsy turvy
tornadoes

torpedoes
torpor
tortoiseshell
tortuous
totalled
tourniquet
towelling
trafficked
tragedy
traitorous
tranquillity
tranquillizer
transcend
transferable
transferred
transparent
travelled
traveller
tremor
troublesome
trousseau
truism
trustee
tsetse
tuberculosis
tumour
tunnelled
tureen
turquoise
twelfth
typhoon
tyranny
U
unanimous
unconscios
undoubted
unduly
unequalled
unique
unnecessary
unremitting
unrequited
unrivalled
upheaval
uproarious
V
vaccinate
vacuum
vague
vanilla
variegate
vehement

vendetta
veneer
ventilator
verandah
vermilion
veterinary
vetoes
vice versa
vicissitude
vigorous
vigour
viscount
visibility
vivacious
vociferous

voluminous
volunteered
vulnerable
W
walkie-talkie
walloped
warrior
wastage
watered
weakened
wearisome
Wednesday
weight
weird
whereabouts

wherewithal
widened
width
wield
wintry
witticism
wizened
woebegone
wooden
woollen
worsened
worship
worshipped
wrapper

wrath
wreak
writhe
X
xylophone
Y
yield
yoghurt
Z
zealous
zigzagged

Adjectives liable to be misspelt

-able and -ible are both used to form adjectives. It is easy to confuse the spelling of words ending in these. The following adjectives are likely to be misspelt.

-able:
abominable
acceptable
adaptable
adorable
advisable
agreeable
amiable
approachable
available
bearable
beatable
believable
calculable
capable
changeable
comfortable
commendable
conceivable
definable
delectable
demonstrable
dependable
desirable
discreditable
disreputable
durable
enviable
excitable
excusable

expendable
foreseeable
forgettable
forgivable
healable
hearable
immovable
impassable
impeccable
implacable
impracticable
impressionable
indescribable
indispensable
inimitable
insufferable
lamentable
manageable
measurable
memorable
nameable
non-flammable
objectionable
operable
palpable
pleasurable
preferable
readable
recognizable
regrettable

renewable
reputable
sizeable
stoppable
tenable
tolerable
transferable
understandable
undoable
unmistakable
usable
variable
viable
washable
wearable
winnable
workable

ible:
accessible
admissible
audible
collapsible
combustible
compatible
comprehensible
contemptible
credible
defensible
destructible

digestible
discernible
divisible
edible
exhaustible
expressible
fallible
feasible
flexible
forcible
gullible
indelible
intelligible
irascible
negligible
perceptible
permissible
possible
repressible
reproducible
resistible
responsible
reversible
risible
sensible
susceptible
tangible
visible

Punctuation

Punctuation is the use of punctuation marks within a written text to enhance its meaning or fluency or to indicate aspects of pronunciation.

accent *see* **Spelling** section.

apostrophe a form of punctuation that is mainly used to indicate possession. Many spelling errors centre on the position of the apostrophe in relation to *s*.

Possessive nouns are usually formed by adding *'s* to the singular noun, as in 'the girl's mother', and 'Peter's car'; by adding an apostrophe to plural nouns that end in *s*, as in 'all the teachers' cars'; by adding *'s* to irregular plural nouns that do not end in *s*, as in 'women's shoes'.

In the possessive form of a name or singular noun that ends in *s*, *x* or *z*, the apostrophe may or may not be followed by *s*. In words of one syllable the final *s* is usually added, as in 'James's house', 'the fox's lair', 'Roz's dress'. The final *s* is most frequently omitted in names, particularly in names of three or more syllables, as in 'Euripides' plays'. In many cases the presence or absence of final *s* is a matter of convention.

The apostrophe is also used to indicate omitted letters in contracted forms of words, as in 'can't' and 'you've'. They are sometimes used to indicate missing century numbers in dates, as in 'the '60s and '70s', but are not used at the end of decades, etc, as in '1960s', not '1960's'

Generally apostrophes are no longer used to indicate omitted letters in shortened forms that are in common use, as in 'phone' and 'flu'.

Apostrophes are often omitted wrongly in modern usage, particularly in the media and by advertisers, as in 'womens hairdressers', 'childrens helpings'. In addition, apostrophes are frequently added erroneously (as in 'potato's for sale' and 'Beware of the dog's'). This is partly because people are unsure about when and when not to use them and partly because of a modern tendency to punctuate as little as possible.

brackets are used to enclose information that is in some way additional to a main statement. The information so enclosed is called **parenthesis** and the pair of brackets enclosing it can be known as **parentheses**. The information that is enclosed in the brackets is purely supplementary or explanatory in nature and could be removed without changing the overall basic meaning or grammatical completeness of the statement. Brackets, like commas and dashes, interrupt the flow of the main statement but brackets indicate a more definite or clear-cut interruption. The fact that they are more visually obvious emphasizes this.

Material within brackets can be one word, as in 'In a local wine bar we had some delicious crepes (pancakes)' and 'They didn't have the chutzpah (nerve) to challenge her'. It can also take the form of dates, as in 'Robert Louis Stevenson (1850–94) wrote *Treasure Island*' and '*Animal Farm* was written by George Orwell (1903–50)'.

The material within brackets can also take the form of a phrase, as in 'They served lasagne (a kind of pasta) and some delicious veal' and 'They were drinking Calvados (a kind of brandy made from apples)' or in the form of a clause, as in 'We were to have supper (or so they called it) later in the evening' and 'They went for a walk round the loch (as a lake is called in Scotland) before taking their departure'.

It can also take the form of a complete sentence, as in 'He was determined (we don't know why) to tackle the problem alone' and 'She made it clear (nothing could be more clear) that she was not interested in the offer'. Sentences that appear in brackets in the middle of a sentence are not usually given an initial capital letter or a full stop, as in 'They very much desired (she had no idea why) to purchase her house'. If the material within brackets comes at the end of a sentence the full stop comes outside the second bracket, as in 'For some reason we agreed to visit her at home (we had no idea where she lived).'

capital letters **comma**

If the material in the brackets is a sentence which comes between two other sentences it is treated like a normal sentence with an initial capital letter and a closing full stop, as in 'He never seems to do any studying. (He is always either asleep or watching television.) Yet he does brilliantly in his exams.' Punctuation of the main statement is unaffected by the presence of the brackets and their enclosed material except that any punctuation that would have followed the word before the first bracket follows the second bracket, as in 'He lives in a place (I am not sure exactly where), that is miles from anywhere.'

There are various shapes of brackets. Round brackets are the most common type. Square brackets are sometimes used to enclose information that is contained inside other information already in brackets, as in '(Christopher Marlowe [1564–93] was a contemporary of Shakespeare)' or in a piece of writing where round brackets have already been used for some other purpose. Thus in a dictionary if round brackets are used to separate off the pronunciation, square brackets are sometimes used to separate off the etymologies.

Square brackets are also used for editorial comments in a scholarly work where the material within brackets is more of an intrusion to the flow of the main statement than is normally the case with bracketed material. Angle brackets and brace brackets tend to be used in more scholarly or technical contexts.

capital letters *see* **Spelling** section.

colon a punctuation mark (:) that is used within a sentence to explain, interpret, clarify or amplify what has gone before it. 'The standard of school work here is extremely high: it is almost university standard', 'The fuel bills are giving cause for concern: they are almost double last year's'. 'We have some new information: the allies have landed'. A capital letter is not usually used after the colon in this context.

The colon is also used to introduce lists or long quotations, as in 'The recipe says we need: tomatoes, peppers, courgettes, garlic, oregano and basil', 'The boy has a huge list of things he needs for school:

blazer, trousers, shirts, sweater, ties, shoes, tennis shoes, rugby boots, sports clothes and leisure wear' and 'One of his favourite quotations was: "If music be the food of love play on".

The colon is sometimes used in numerals, as in '7:30 a.m.', '22:11:72' and 'a ratio of 7:3'. It is used in the titles of some books, for example where there is a subtitle or explanatory title, as in 'The Dark Years: the Economy in the 1930s'.

In informal writing, the dash is sometimes used instead of the colon, indeed the dash tends to be overused for this purpose.

comma a very common punctuation mark (,). In modern usage there is a tendency to adopt a system of minimal punctuation and the comma is one of the casualties of this new attitude. Most people use the comma considerably less frequently than was formerly the case.

However there are certain situations in which the comma is still commonly used. One of these concerns lists. The individual items in a series of three or more items are separated by commas. Whether a comma is put before the 'and' which follows the second-last item is now a matter of choice. Some people dislike the use of a comma before 'and' in this situation, and it was formerly considered wrong. Examples of lists include—'at the sports club we can play tennis, squash, badminton and table tennis', 'We need to buy bread, milk, fruit and sugar', and 'They are studying French, German, Spanish and Russian'. The individual items in a list can be quite long, as in 'We opened the door, let ourselves in, fed the cat and started to cook a meal' and 'They consulted the map, planned the trip, got some foreign currency and were gone before we realized it'. Confusion may arise if the last item in the list contains 'and' in its own right, as in 'In the pub they served ham salad, shepherd's pie, pie and chips and omelette'. In such cases it as well to put a comma before the final 'and'.

In cases where there is a list of adjectives before a noun, the use of commas is now optional although it was formerly standard practice. Thus both 'She wore a long, red, sequinned dress' and 'She wore a long red sequinned dress' are used. When the adjective immediately before the noun has a closer relationship with it than the other adjectives no comma should be used, as in 'a beautiful old Spanish village'.

The comma is used to separate clauses or phrases that are parenthetical or naturally cut off from the rest of a sentence, as in 'My mother, who was of Irish extraction, was very superstitious'. In such a sentence the clause within the commas can be removed without altering the basic meaning. Care should be taken to include both commas. Commas are not normally used to separate main clauses and relative clauses, as in 'The woman whom I met was my friend's sister'. Nor are they usually used to separate main clauses and subordinate clauses, as in 'He left when we arrived' and 'They came to the party although we didn't expect them to'. If the subordinate clause precedes the main clause, it is sometimes followed by a comma, especially if it is a reasonably long clause, as in 'Although we stopped and thought about it, we still made the wrong decision'. If the clause is quite short, or if it is a short phrase, a comma is not usually inserted, as in 'Although it rained we had a good holiday' and 'Although poor they were happy'. The use of commas to separate such words and expression from the rest of the sentence to which they are related is optional. Thus one can write 'However, he could be right' or 'However he could be right'. The longer the expression is, the more likely it is to have a comma after it, as in 'On the other hand, we may decide not to go'.

Commas are always used to separate terms of address, interjections or question tags from the rest of the sentence, as in 'Please come this way, Ms Brown, and make yourself at home', 'Now, ladies, what can I get you?' and 'It's cold today, isn't it?'

Commas may be used to separate main clauses joined by a coordinating conjunction, but this is not usual if the clauses have the same subject or object, as in 'She swept the floor and dusted the table'. In cases where the subjects are different and the clauses are fairly long, it is best to insert a

comma, as in 'They took all the furniture with them, and she was left with nothing'.

A comma can be inserted to avoid repeating a verb in the second of two clause, as in 'he plays golf and tennis, his brother rugby'.

dash a punctuation mark in the form of a short line that indicates a short break in the continuity of a sentence, as in 'He has never been any trouble at school—quite the reverse', 'I was amazed when he turned up—I thought he was still abroad'. In such situations it serves the same purpose as brackets, except that it is frequently considered more informal. The dash should be used sparingly. Depending on it too much can lead to careless writing with ideas set down at random rather than turned into a piece of coherent prose. The dash can be used to emphasize a word or phrase, as in 'They said goodbye then—forever'. It can also be used to add a remark to the end of a sentence, as in 'They had absolutely no money—a regular state of affairs towards the end of the month.'

The dash can also be used to introduce a statement that amplifies or explains what has been said, as in 'The burglars took everything of value—her jewellery, the silver, the TV set, her hi-fi and several hundred pounds.' It can be used to summarize what has gone before, as in 'Disease, poverty, ignorance—these are the problems facing us.

The dash is also used to introduce an afterthought, as in 'You can come with me—but you might not want to'. It can also introduce a sharp change of subject, as in 'I'm just making tea—what was that noise?' It can also be used to introduce some kind of balance in a sentence, as in 'It's going to take two of us to get this table out of here—one to move it and one to hold the door open.'

The dash is sometimes found in pairs. A pair of dashes acts in much the same way as a set of round brackets. A pair of dashes can be used to indicate a break in a sentence, as in 'We prayed—prayed as we had never prayed before—that the children would be safe', 'It was—on reflection—his best performance yet', and 'He introduced

direct speech   **hyphen**

me to his wife—an attractive pleasant woman—before he left'.

Dashes are used to indicate hesitant speech, as in 'I don't—well—maybe—you could be right'. They can be used to indicate the omission of part of a word or name, as in 'It's none of your b— business', 'He's having an affair with Mrs D—'.

They can also be used between points in time or space, as in 'Edinburgh–London' and '1750–1790.'

direct speech *see* **quotation marks**.

exclamation mark a punctuation mark **(!)** which occurs at the end of an exclamation, which is a word, phrase or sentence called out with strong feeling of some kind as in 'Get lost!', 'What a nerve!', 'Help!', 'Ouch!', 'Well I never!', 'What a disaster!', 'I'm tired of all this!' and 'Let me out of here!'

full stop a punctuation mark consisting of a small dot (.). Its principal use is to end a sentence that is not a question or an exclamation, as in 'They spent the money.', 'She is studying hard.', 'He has been declared redundant and is very upset.' and 'Because she is shy, she rarely goes to parties.'

The full stop is also used in decimal fractions, as in '4.5 metres', '6.3 miles' and '12.2 litres'. It can also be used in dates, as in '22.2.94', and in times, as in '3.15 tomorrow afternoon'.

In modern usage the tendency is to omit full stops from abbreviations. This is most true of abbreviations involving initial capital letters as in TUC, BBC, EEC and USA. In such cases full stops should definitely not be used if one or some of the initial letters do not belong to a full word. Thus, television is abbreviated to TV and educationally subnormal to ESN.

There are usually no full stops in abbreviations involving the first and last letters of a word (contractions) Dr, Mr, Rd, St, but this is a matter of taste.

Abbreviations involving the first few letters of a word, as in 'Prof' (Professor) are the most likely to have full stops, as in 'Feb.' (February), but again this is now a matter of taste.

For the use of the full stop in direct speech *see* **direct speech**. The full stop can also be called **point** or **period**.

hyphen a small stroke (-) that is used to join two words together or to indicate that a word has been broken at the end of a line because of lack of space. It is used in a variety of situations.

The hyphen is used as the prefixed element in a proper noun, as in 'pre-Christian', 'post-Renaissance', 'anti-British', 'anti-Semitic', 'pro-French' and 'pro-Marxism'. It is also used before dates or numbers, as in 'pre-1914', 'pre-1066', 'post-1920', 'post-1745'. It is also used before abbreviations, as in 'pro-BBC', 'anti-EEC' and 'anti-TUC'.

The hyphen is used for clarification. Some words are ambiguous without the presence of a hyphen. For example, 're-cover', as in 're-cover a chair', is spelt with a hyphen to differentiate it from 'recover', as in 'The accident victim is likely to recover'. Similarly, it is used in 're-form', meaning 'to form again', as in 'They have decided to re-form the society which closed last year', to differentiate the word from 'reform', meaning 'to improve, to become better behaved', as in 'He was wild as a young man but he has reformed now'. Similarly 're-count' in the sense of 'count again', as in 're-count the number of votes cast', is spelt with a hyphen to differentiate it from 'recount' in the sense of 'tell', as in 'recount what happened on the night of the accident'.

The hyphen was formerly used to separate a prefix from the main element of a word if the main element begins with a vowel, as in 'pre-eminent', but there is a growing tendency in modern usage to omit the hyphen in such cases. At the moment both 'pre-eminent' and 'preeminent' are found. However, if the omission of the hyphen results in double *i*, the hyphen is usually retained, as in 'anti-inflationary' and 'semi-insulated'.

The hyphen was formerly used in words formed with the prefix *non-*, as in 'nonfunctional', 'non-political', 'non-flammable' and 'non-pollutant'. However there is a growing tendency to omit the hyphen in such cases, as in 'nonfunctional' and 'nonpollutant'. At the moment both forms of such words are common.

The hyphen is usually used with 'ex-' in the sense of 'former', as in 'ex-wife' and 'ex-president'.

The hyphen is usually used when 'self-' is prefixed to words, as in 'self-styled', 'a self-starter' and 'self-evident'.

Use or non-use of the hyphen is often a matter of choice, house style or frequency of usage, as in 'drawing-room' or 'drawing room', and 'dining-room' or 'dining room'. There is a modern tendency to punctuate less frequently than was formerly the case and so in modern usage use of the hyphen in such expressions is less frequent. The length of compounds often affects the inclusion or omission of the hyphen. Compounds of two short elements that are well-established words tend not to be hyphenated, as in 'bedroom' and 'toothbrush'. Compound words with longer elements are more likely to be hyphenated, as in 'engine-driver' and 'carpet-layer'.

Some fixed compounds of two or three or more words are always hyphenated, as in 'son-in-law', 'good-for-nothing' and 'devil-may-care'

Some compounds formed from phrasal verbs are sometimes hyphenated and sometimes not. Thus both 'take-over' and 'takeover' are common, and 'run-down' and 'rundown' are both common. Again the use of the hyphen is a matter of choice. However some words formed from phrasal verbs are usually spelt without a hyphen, as in 'breakthrough'.

Compound adjectives consisting of two elements, the second of which ends in -ed, are usually hyphenated, as in 'heavy-hearted', 'fair-haired', 'fair-minded' and 'long-legged'.

Compound adjectives when they are used before nouns are usually hyphenated, as in 'gas-fired central heating', 'oil-based paints', 'solar-heated buildings' and 'chocolate-coated biscuits'.

Compounds containing some adverbs are usually hyphenated, sometimes to avoid ambiguity, as in 'his best-known opera', a 'well-known singer', 'an ill-considered venture' and 'a half-planned scheme'.

Generally adjectives and participles preceded by an adverb are not hyphenated if the adverb ends in -ly, as in 'a highly talented singer', 'neatly pressed clothes' and 'beautifully dressed young women'.

In the case of two or more compound hyphenated adjectives with the same second element qualifying the same noun, the common element need not be repeated but the hyphen should be, as in 'two- and three-bedroom houses' and 'long- and short-haired dogs'.

The hyphen is used in compound numerals from 21 to 99 when they are written in full, as in 'thirty-five gallons', 'forty-four years', 'sixty-seven miles' and 'two hundred and forty-five miles'. Compound numbers such as 'three hundred' and 'two thousand' are not hyphenated.

Hyphens are used in fractions, as in 'three-quarters', 'two-thirds', and 'seven-eighths'.

Hyphens are also used in such number phrases as 'a seventeenth-century play', 'a sixteenth-century church', 'a five-gallon pail', 'a five-year contract' and a 'third-year student'.

The other use of hyphens is to break words at the ends of lines. Formerly people were more careful about where they broke words. Previously, words were broken up according to etymological principles, but there is a growing tendency to break words according to how they are pronounced. Some dictionaries or spelling dictionaries give help with the division and hyphenation of individual words. General points are that one-syllable words should not be divided and words should not be broken after the first letter of a word or before the last letter. Care should be taken not to break up words, for example by forming elements that are words in their own right, in such a way as to mislead the reader. Thus divisions such as 'the-rapist' and 'mans-laughter' should be avoided.

inverted comma *see* **quotation marks.**

italic type a sloping typeface that is used for a variety of purposes. It is used to differentiate a piece of text from the main text, which is usually in Roman type. For example, it is used sometimes for the titles of books, newspapers, magazines, plays, films, musical works and works of art, as in 'he is

ligature   **quotation marks**

a regular reader of *The Times*', 'She reads *Private Eye*', 'Have you read *Animal Farm* by George Orwell', 'He has never seen a production of Shakespeare's *Othello*', 'We went to hear Handel's *Messiah*', '*Mona Lisa* is a famous painting'. Sometimes such titles are put in quotation marks rather than in italics.

Italic type is also sometimes used for the names of ships, trains, etc, as in 'the launch of *The Queen Elizabeth II*', 'She once sailed in *The Queen Mary*' and 'Their train was called *The Flying Scotsman*'.

Italic type is also used for the Latin names of plants and animals, as in 'of the genus *Lilium*', 'trees of the genus *Pyrus*', '*Panthera pardus*' and '*Canis lupus*'.

Italic type is sometimes used for foreign words that have been adopted into the English language but have never been fully integrated. Examples include *bête noire*, *raison d'être*, *inter alia* and *Weltschmerz*.

Italic type can also sometimes be used to draw attention to a particular word, phrase or passage, as in 'How do you pronounce *formidable*?', or to emphasize a word or phrase, as in 'Is he *still* in the same job?'

ligature a printed character combining two letters in one, as in æ and œ. It is sometimes called a digraph.

line-break the division of a word at the end of a line for space purposes. This is marked by a hyphen.

lower-case letter the opposite of capital letter. It is also known informally as 'small letter'. Lower-case letters are used for most words in the language. It is capital letters that are exceptional in their use.

oblique a diagonal mark (/) that has various uses. Its principal use is to show alternatives, as in 'he/she', 'Dear Sir/Madam', 'two/three-room flat' and 'the budget for 1993/4'. The oblique is used in some abbreviations, as in 'c/o Smith' (meaning 'care of Smith'). The word 'per' is usually shown by means of an oblique, as in 60km/h (60 kilometres per hour).

paragraph a subdivision of a piece of prose. Many people find it difficult to divide their work into paragraphs. Learning to do so can be difficult but it is an area of style that improves with practice.

A paragraph should deal with one particular theme or point of the writer's writing or argument. When that has been dealt with, a new paragraph should be started.

However, there are other considerations to be taken into account. If the paragraph is very long it can appear offputting visually to the would-be reader and can be difficult to make one's way through. In such cases it is best to subdivide themes and shorten paragraphs. On the other hand, it is best not to make all one's paragraphs too short as this can create a disjointed effect. It is best to try to aim for a mixture of lengths to create some variety.

Traditionally it was frowned upon to have a one-sentence paragraph but there are no hard and fast rules about this. Usually it takes more than one sentence to develop the theme of the paragraph, unless one is a tabloid journalist or copywriter for an advertising firm, and it is best to avoid long, complex sentences.

The opening paragraph of a piece of writing should introduce the topic about which one is writing. The closing paragraph should sum up what one has been writing about. New paragraphs begin on new lines and they are usually indented from the margin. In the case of dialogue in a work of fiction, each speaker's utterance usually begins on a new line for the clarification of the reader.

parentheses *see* **brackets**.

period *see* **full stop**.

point *see* **full stop**.

punctuation mark one of the standardized symbols used in punctuation, as the **full stop, comma, question mark**, etc.

question mark the punctuation mark (?) that is placed at the end of a question or interrogative sentence, as in 'Who is he?', 'Where are they?', 'Why have they gone?', 'Whereabouts are they?', 'When are you going?' and 'What did he say?'. The question mark is sometimes known as the **query**.

quotation marks or **inverted commas** are used to enclose material that is part of **direct speech**, which is the reporting of speech by repeating exactly the actual words used by the speaker. In the sentence:

Peter said, 'I am tired of this.'

'I am tired of this' is a piece of direct speech because it represents exactly what Peter said. Similarly, in the sentence:

Jane asked, 'Where are you going?'

'Where are you going' is a piece of direct speech since it represents what Jane said.

Quotation marks are used at the beginning and end of pieces of direct speech. Only the words actually spoken are placed within the quotation marks, as in:

'If I were you,' he said, 'I would refuse to go.'

The quotation marks involved can be either single or double, according to preference or house style.

If there is a statement such as 'he said' following the piece of direct speech, a comma is placed before the second inverted comma, as in:

'Come along,' he said.

If the piece of direct speech is a question or exclamation, a question mark or exclamation mark is put instead of the comma, as in:

'What are you doing?' asked John.
'Get away from me!' she screamed.

If a statement such as 'he said' is placed within a sentence in direct speech, a comma is placed after 'he said' and the second part of the piece of direct speech does not begin with a capital letter, as in:

'I know very well,' he said, 'that you do not like me.'

If the piece of direct speech includes a complete sentence, the sentence begins with a capital letter, as in:

'I am going away,' she said, 'and I am not coming back. I don't feel that I belong here anymore.'

Note that the full stop at the end of a piece of direct speech that is a sentence should go before the closing inverted comma.

If the piece of direct speech quoted takes up more than one paragraph, quotation marks are placed at the beginning of each

new paragraph. However, quotation marks are not placed at the end of each paragraph, just at the end of the final one.

When writing a story, etc, that includes dialogue or conversation, each new piece of direct speech should begin on a new line or sometimes in a new paragraph.

Quotation marks are not used only to indicate direct speech. For example, they are sometimes used to indicate the title of a book or newspaper.

The quotation marks used in this way can be either single or double, according to preference or house style. If a piece of direct speech contains the title of a poem, song, etc, it should be put in the opposite type of quotation marks to those used to enclose the piece of direct speech. Thus, if single quotation marks have been used in the direct speech, then double quotation marks should be used for the title within the direct speech, as in:

'Have you read "Ode to a Nightingale" by Keats?' the teacher asked.

If double quotation marks have been used for the direct speech, single quotation marks should be used for the title, as in:

"Have you read 'Ode to a Nightingale' by Keats?" the teacher asked.

Roman type the normal upright type used in printing, not bold or italic type.

semicolon (;) a rather formal form of punctuation. It is mainly used between clauses that are not joined by any form of conjunction, as in 'We had a wonderful holiday; sadly they did not', 'She was my sister; she was also my best friend' and 'He was a marvellous friend; he is much missed'. A dash is sometimes used instead of a semicolon but this more informal.

The semicolon is also used to form subsets in a long list or series of names so that the said list seems less complex, as in 'The young man who wants to be a journalist has applied everywhere. He has applied to *The Times* in London; *The Globe and Mail* in Toronto; *The Age* in Melbourne; *The Tribune* in Chicago'.

The semicolon is also sometimes used before 'however', 'nevertheless' 'hence', etc, as in 'We have extra seats for the concert; however you must not feel obliged to come'.

Style

abbreviation a shortened form of words, usually used as a space-saving technique and becoming increasingly common in modern usage. Abbreviations cause problems with regard to punctuation. The common question asked is whether the letters of an abbreviation should be separated by full stops. In modern usage the tendency is to omit full stops from abbreviations. This is most true of abbreviations involving initial capital letters, as in TUC, BBC, EC and USA. In such cases full stops should definitely not be used if one or some of the initial letters do not belong to a full word. Thus 'television' is abbreviated to TV and 'educationally subnormal' to ESN.

There are usually no full stops in abbreviations involving the first and last letters of a word (contractions)—Dr, Mr, Rd, St—but this is a matter of taste.

An abbreviation involving the first few letters of a word, as in 'Prof' (Professor), is the most likely to have full stop, as in 'Feb.' (February), but again this is now a matter of taste.

Plurals of abbreviations are mostly formed by adding lower-case s, as in Drs, JPs, TVs. Note the absence of apostrophes. *See also* **acronym**.

acronym a word that, like some abbreviations, is formed from the initial letters of several words. Unlike abbreviations, however, acronyms are pronounced as words rather than as just a series of letters. For example, OPEC (Organization of Petroleum Producing Countries) is pronounced *o-pek* and is thus an acronym, unlike USA (United States of America) which is pronounced as a series of letters and not as a word (*yoo-ess-ay,* not *yoo-say* or *oo-sa*) and is thus an abbreviation.

Acronyms are written without full stops, as in UNESCO (United Nations Educational, Scientific and Cultural Organization). Mostly acronyms are written in capital letters, as in NASA (National Aeronautics and Space Administration). However, very common acronyms, such as Aids (Acquired Immune Deficiency Syndrome), are written with just an initial capital, the rest of the letters being lower case

Acronyms that refer to a piece of scientific or technical equipment are written like ordinary words in lower-case letters, as laser (light amplification by simulated emission of radiation).

affix refers to an element that is added to the root or stem of a word to form another word. Affixes can be in the form of **prefixes** or **suffixes**. A prefix is added to the beginning of a word, as audio in audiovisual, an affix to the end, as -aholic in workaholic.

back formation the process of forming a new word by removing an element from an existing word. This is the reversal of the usual process since many words are formed by adding an element to a base or root word. Examples of back formation include 'burgle' from 'burglary'; 'caretake' from 'caretaker'; 'donate' from 'donation; 'eavesdrop' from 'eavesdropper'; 'enthuse' from 'enthusiasm'; 'intuit' from 'intuition'; 'liaise' from 'liaison'; 'reminisce' from 'reminiscence'; 'televise' from 'television'.

base the basic element in word formation, also known as **root** or **stem**, e.g. in the word 'infectious' 'infect' is the base.

blend a word that is formed by the merging of two other words or elements, as in 'brunch' from 'breakfast' and 'lunch'; 'camcorder' from 'camera' and 'recorder'; 'chocoholic' from 'chocolate' and 'alcoholic'; 'motel' from 'motor' and 'hotel'; 'smog' from 'smoke' and 'fog'; 'televangelist' from 'television' and 'evangelist'.

book titles *see* **Spelling** section and **italic type** in **Punctuation** section.

borrowing the taking over into English of a word from a foreign language and also to the word so borrowed. Many words are borrowed into English are totally assimilated as to spelling and pronunciation. Others remain obviously different and retain their own identity as to spelling or pronunciation, as *raison d'être*, borrowed from

French. Many of them have been so long part of the English language, such as since the Norman Conquest, that they are no longer thought of as being foreign words. However the process goes on, and recent borrowings include *glasnost* and *perestroika* from Russian.

French, Latin and Greek have been the main sources of our borrowings over the centuries. However, we have borrowed extensively from other languages as well. These include Italian, from which we have borrowed many terms relating to music, art and architecture. These include *piano*, *libretto*, *opera*, *soprano*, *tempo*, *corridor*, *fresco*, *niche*, *parapet* and *grotto*, as well as many food terms, such as *macaroni*, *pasta*, *semolina* and *spaghetti*.

From the Dutch we have acquired many words relating to the sea and ships since they were a great sea-faring nation. These include *cruise*, *deck*, *skipper* and *yacht*. Through the Dutch/Afrikaans connection we have borrowed *apartheid*, *boss* and *trek*.

From German we have borrowed *dachshund*, *hamster*, *frankfurter*, *kindergarten* and *waltz*, as well as some words relating to World War II, for example, *blitz*, *flak* and *strafe*.

From Norse and the Scandinavian languages have come a wide variety of common words, such as *egg*, *dirt*, *glitter*, *kick*, *law*, *odd*, *skill*, *take*, *they*, *though*, as well as some more modern sporting terms such as *ski* and *slalom*.

From the Celtic languages have come *bannock*, *bog*, *brogue*, *cairn*, *clan*, *crag*, *slogan* and *whisky*, and from Arabic have come *algebra*, *alkali*, *almanac*, *apricot*, *assassin*, *cypher*, *ghoul*, *hazard*, *mohair*, *safari*, *scarlet* and *talisman*.

The Indian languages have provided us with many words, originally from the significant British presence there in the days of the British Empire. They include *bungalow*, *chutney*, *dinghy*, *dungarees*, *gymkhana*, *jungle*, *pundit* and *shampoo*. In modern times there has been an increasing interest in Indian food and cookery, and words such as *pakora*, *poppadom*, *samosa*, etc, have come into the language.

From the South American languages have come *avocado*, *chocolate*, *chilli*, *potato*, *tobacco* and *tomato*. From Hebrew have come *alphabet*, *camel*, *cinnamon* and *maudlin*, as well as more modern borrowings from Yiddish such as *bagel*, *chutzpah*, *schmaltz* and *schmuck*.

From the native North American languages have come *anorak*, *kayak*, *raccoon* and *toboggan*, and from the Aboriginal language of Australia have come *boomerang* and *kangaroo*.

Judo, *bonsai* and *tycoon* have come from Japanese, *rattan* from Malay and *kung-fu*, *sampan* and *ginseng* from Chinese.

The borrowing process continues. With Britain becoming more of a cosmopolitan and multi-cultural nation the borrowing is increasing.

cliché *see* **Clichés** section.

coinage the invention of a new word or expression.

colloquialism a term used to describe an expression of the kind used in informal conversation.

derivative a word that has been formed from a simpler word or word element. For example, 'sweetly' is a derivative of 'sweet', 'peaceful' is a derivative from 'peace', 'clinging' is derived from 'cling' and 'shortest' is derived from 'short'.

dialect the language of a region or community with regard to vocabulary, structure, grammar and pronunciation.

doubles words that habitually go together, as in 'out and out', 'neck and neck', 'over and over', 'hale and hearty', 'rant and rave', 'fast and furious', 'hue and cry', 'stuff and nonsense', 'rough and ready', 'might and main', 'give and take', 'ups and downs', 'fair and square', 'high and dry' and 'wear and tear'. Doubles are also sometimes called **dyads**.

doublets pairs of words that have developed from the same original word but now differ somewhat in form and usually in meaning. Examples include 'human' and 'humane', 'shade' and 'shadow', 'hostel' and 'hotel', 'frail' and 'fragile', and 'fashion' and 'faction'.

dyads see **doubles**.

EFL English as a foreign language.

etymology the origin and history of a word; the study of the history of words.

euphemism *see* **Euphemism** section.

figurative a term that refers to words that are not used literally. For example, 'mine' in the sense of 'excavation in the earth from which coal, tin, etc, is taken' is a literal use of the word. 'Mine' in the sense of 'He is a mine of information' is a figurative use of the word.

first language *same as* **mother tongue**.

formal the term used to refer to speech and writing that is characterized by more complicated and more difficult language and by more complicated grammatical structures. Short forms and contractions are avoided in formal speech and writing.

gobbledygook a noun that is used informally to refer to pretentious and convoluted language of the type that is found in official documents and reports. It is extremely difficult to understand and should be avoided and 'plain English' used instead.

hybrid a word that is formed from words or elements derived from different languages, such as 'television'.

idiolect a person's own style of language with regard to vocabulary, structure, etc, is known as ideolect, as in 'He is the son of academic parents and has rather a formal idiolect'.

homograph *see* **Homograph** section.

homonym *see* **Homonym** section.

homophone *see* **Homophone** section.

idioms *see* **English Idioms** section.

jargon refers to the technical or specialized language used by a particular group, e.g. doctors, computer engineers, sociologists, etc, to communicate with each other within their specialty. It should be avoided in the general language as it will not be clear to the ordinary person exactly what is meant.

journalese a derogatory name for the style of writing and choice of vocabulary supposedly found in newspapers. It is usually the style of writing in tabloid newspapers, such as widespread use of clichés, sensational language and short sentences, that is meant by the term.

language the means by which human beings communicate using words. Language can refer either to spoken or written communication. It can also refer to the variety of communication used by a particular nation or state, as in 'the French language'.

The term can also be used to refer to the style and vocabulary of a piece of writing, as in 'The language of his novels is very poetic'. It can also be used to denote the particular style and variety of language that is used in a particular profession or among a particular group of people with some common interest, as in 'legal language', 'technical language', etc. Such specialist language is sometimes referred to rather pejoratively as legalese, 'computerese', etc. *See* **jargon**.

lexicography the art and practice of defining words, selecting them and arranging them In dictionaries or glossaries.

lingua franca a language adopted as a common language by speakers whose mother tongues are different from each other. This enables people to have a common medium of communication for various purposes, such as trading. Examples include Swahili in East Africa, Hausa in West Africa and Tok Pisin in Papua New Guinea. The term historically referred to a language that was a mixture of Italian, French, Greek, Spanish and Arabic, used for trading and military purposes.

linguistics the systematic, scientific study of language. It describes language and seeks to establish general principles rather than to prescribe rules of correctness.

loanword a word that has been taken into one language from another. From the point of view of the language taking the word in, the word is known as a borrowing. Some loanwords become naturalized or fully integrated into the language and have a pronunciation and spelling reflecting the conventions of the language which has borrowed them. Other loanwords retain the spelling and pronunciation of the language from which they have been borrowed. These include 'Gastarbeiter', borrowed from German and meaning 'a foreign worker'.

localism a word or expression the use of which is restricted to a particular place or area. The area in question can be quite small, unlike dialect words or 'regionalism'.

malapropism the incorrect use of a word, often through confusion with a similar-sounding word. It often arises from someone's attempt to impress someone else with a knowledge of long words or of technical language. *See* **Literature** section in the **Wordfinder**.

mother tongue the language that one first learns, the language of which one is a native speaker.

native speaker *see* **mother tongue**.

neologism a word that has been newly coined or newly introduced into the language, as 'camcorder', 'Jacuzzi' and 'karaoke'.

palindrome a word which reads the same backwards a forwards, such as 'level' or 'madam'. It can also apply to a phrase, as 'Able was I ere I saw Elba'.

pangram a phrase or sentence which contains all the letters of the alphabet. The ideal pangram contains each letter only once, but this is quite difficult to do, if the result is to be meaningful.

officialese a derogatory term for the vocabulary and style of writing often found in official reports and documents and thought of as being pretentious and difficult to understand. It is usually considered to be the prime example of gobbledegook.

orthography the study or science of how words are spelt.

philology the science, especially comparative, of languages and their history and structure.

prefix *see* **affix**.

redundancy *same as* **tautology**.

retronym a word or phrase that has had to be renamed slightly in the light of another invention, etc. For example, an ordinary guitar has become 'acoustic guitar' because of the existence of 'electric guitar'. Leather has sometimes become 'real leather' because of the existence of 'imitation leather'.

root *same as* **base**.

semantics the study of the historical development and change of word meaning

slang the name given to a set of highly colloquial words and phrases, often rapidly changing and ephemeral, which are regarded as being below the level of educated standard speech. The term is also used to refer to the language used by a particular group of people e.g. surfer's slang.

stem *same as* **base**.

stress emphasis placed on a particular sound or syllable of a word by pronouncing it with more force than those surrounding it.

suffix *see* **affix**.

synonym a word which has the same, or a similar, meaning to another word.

tautology unnecessary repetition, as in 'new innovations', 'a see-through transparent material' and 'one after the other in succession'. In these examples 'new', 'see-through' and 'in succession' are all unnecessary or **redundant** because the idea which they convey is conveyed by 'innovations', 'transparent' and 'one after the others respectively.

Pronunciation

accent commonly refers to a regional or individual way of speaking or pronouncing words, as in 'a Glasgow accent'.

cedilla the **diacritic** used in French to indicative a soft pronunciation, as 'façade'. *See also* **umlaut**.

consonant a speech sound which is produced by a closing movement, either partial or total, involving the vocal organs, such as the lips, teeth, tongue or the throat, which forms such a narrow constriction that the sound of air can be heard passing through. The term also applies to a letter of the alphabet sounded in this way. *See* **vowel**.

dental produced by the tip of the tongue positioned near the front teeth, as in the pronunciation of the letter 'd'.

diacritic a mark placed a either above or below a letter to indicate a certain emphasis or pronunciation.

diaeresis a mark that is placed over a vowel to indicate that it is sounded separately from a neighbouring vowel, as in 'naïve', 'Chloë'.

digraph a group of two letters representing one sound, as in 'ay' in 'hay', 'ey' in 'key', 'oy' in 'boy', 'ph' in 'phone' and 'th' in 'thin'. When the digraph consists of two letters physically joined together, as 'æ', it is called a 'ligature'.

diphthong a speech sound that changes its quality within the same single syllable. The sound begins as for one vowel and moves on as for another. Since the sound glides from one vowel into another, a diphthong is sometimes called a **gliding vowel**. Examples include the vowels sounds in 'rain', 'weigh', 'either', 'voice', 'height', 'aisle', 'road', 'soul', 'know', 'house', 'care', 'pure', 'during', 'here' and 'weird'.

disyllabic a term that describes a word with two syllables. For example, 'window' is disyllabic, since it consists of the syllable 'win' and the syllable 'dow'. Similarly 'curtain' is disyllabic since it consists of the syllable 'cur' and 'tain'.

elision the omission of a speech sound or syllable, as in the omission of 'd' in one of the possible pronunciations of 'Wednesday' and in the omission of 'ce' from the pronunciation of 'Gloucester'.

fricative a sound produced by forcing air through a partly closed passage, as in the pronunciation of 'th'.

gliding vowel same as **diphthong**.

hiatus a break in pronunciation between two vowels that come together in different syllables, as in 'Goyaesque' and 'cooperate'.

inflection a varying of tone or pitch.

International Phonetic Alphabet a system of written symbols designed to enable the speech sounds of any language to be consistently represented. Some of the symbols are the ordinary letters of the Roman alphabet but some have been specially invented. The alphabet was first published in 1889 and is commonly known as **IPA**.

intrusive r the pronunciation of the *r* sound between two words or syllables where the first of these ends in a vowel sound and the second begins with a vowel sound and where there is no 'r' in the spelling. It appears in such phrases as 'law and order', which is frequently pronounced as 'lawr and order'.

IPA *see* **International Phonetic Alphabet**.

labial formed by closing, or partially closing, the lips, as in the pronunciation of the letter 'm'.

labiodental produced by the lips and teeth together, as in the pronunciation of the letter 'v'.

length mark a mark used in phonetics in relation to a vowel to indicate that it is long. This can take the form of a 'macron', a small horizontal stroke placed above a letter, or a symbol resembling a colon placed after a vowel in the IPA pronunciation system.

macron *see* **length mark**.

phoneme the smallest unit of speech.

phonetics the science connected with pronunciation and the representation of speech sounds.

plosive denoting a burst of air, such as is produced when pronouncing the letter 'p'.

sibilant suggesting a hissing sound, as that produced when pronouncing the letter 's'.

umlaut the **diacritic** which indicates a change of vowel sound in German, as in *mädchen*.

spoonerism the accidental or deliberate transposition of the initial letters of two or more words when speaking, as in 'the queer old dean' instead of 'the dear old queen', 'a blushing crow' instead of a 'crushing blow' and 'a well-boiled icicle' instead of a 'well-oiled bicycle'. Spoonerisms are called after the Reverend William Archibald Spooner (1844–1930) of Oxford University.

velar produced by the back of the tongue on the soft palate, as in the pronunciation of the letter 'g' in the word 'grand', etc.

voiceless spoken without using the vocal cords, as in the pronunciation of the letter 'p'.

vowel a sound produced by the passage of air through the larynx, virtually unobstructed, no part of the mouth being closed and none of the vocal organs being so close together that the sound of air can be heard passing between them. The term is also applied to a letter of the alphabet sounded in this way. The vowels in the alphabet are a, e, i, o and u.

Words liable to be mispronounced

abdomen is now usually pronounced with the emphasis on the first syllable (*ab*-do-men).

acumen is now usually pronounced *ak*-yoo-men, with the emphasis on the first syllable, although formerly the stress was usually on the second syllable (yoo).

adult may be pronounced with the emphasis on either of the two syllables. Thus *a*-dult and a-*dult* are both acceptable although the pronunciation with the emphasis on the first syllable (*a*-dult) is the more common.

adversary is commonly pronounced with the emphasis on the first syllable (*ad*-ver-sar-i) although in modern usage it is also found with the emphasis on the second syllable (ad-*ver*-sar-i).

aged has two possible pronunciations depending on the sense. When it means 'very old', as in 'aged men with white beards', it is pronounced *ay*-jid. When it means 'years of age', as in 'a girl aged nine', it is pronounced with one syllable, ayjd.

banal should rhyme with 'canal', with the emphasis on the second syllable (ba-*nal*).

blackguard, meaning 'a scoundrel', has an unusual pronunciation. It is pronounced *blagg*-ard.

brochure is usually pronounced *bro*-sher, despite the *ch* spelling, rather than bro-*shoor*, which is French-sounding.

Celtic is usually pronounced kel-tik.

cervical has two possible pronunciations. Both *ser*-vik-al, with the emphasis on the first syllable, and ser-*vik*-al, with the emphasis on the second syllable which has the same sound as in *Vik*ing in 'cervical cancer'.

chamois in the sense of 'a kind of cloth (made from the skin of the chamois antelope) used for polishing or cleaning' is pronounced *sham*-mi. In the sense of 'a kind of antelope', it is pronounced *sham*-wa.

chiropodist is usually pronounced kir-*op*-od-ist with an initial *k* sound, but the pronunciation shir-*op*-od-ist with an initial *sh* sound is also possible.

clandestine usually has the emphasis on the second syllable, as klan-*des*-tin', but it is acceptable to pronounce it with the emphasis on the first syllable, as *klan*-des-tin.

comparable is liable to be mispronounced. The emphasis should be on the first syllable, as in *kom*-par-able. It is often mispronounced with the emphasis on the second syllable.

contrary has two possible pronunciations. When it means 'opposite', as in 'On the contrary, I would like to go very much', it is pronounced with the emphasis on the first syllable (*kon*-trar-i). When it means 'perverse, stubborn', as in 'contrary children' it is pronounced with the emphasis on the second syllable, which is pronounced to rhyme with 'Mary'.

controversy is usually pronounced with the emphasis on the first syllable (*kon*-tro-ver-si). In modern usage there is a growing tendency to place the emphasis on the second syllable (kon-*tro*-ver-si).

dais meaning 'platform' or 'stage', is now usually pronounced as two syllables, as day-is. Formerly it was pronounced as one syllable, as days.

decade   **naïve**

decade is pronounced with the emphasis on the first syllable as *dek*-ayd. An alternative but rare pronunciation is dek-*ayd*.

demonstrable is most commonly pronounced di-*mon*-strabl, with the emphasis on the second syllable, in modern usage. Previously the emphasis was on the first syllable as *dem*-on-strabl.

explicable is now usually pronounced with the emphasis on the second syllable (ex-*plik*-ibl). Formerly it was commonly pronounced with the emphasis on the first syllable (*ex*-plikibl).

exquisite has two possible pronunciations. It is most usually pronounced with the emphasis on the first syllable (*ex*-kwis-it) but some prefer to put the emphasis on the second syllable (iks-*kwis*-it).

finance can be pronounced in two ways. The commoner pronunciation has the emphasis on the second syllable and the first syllable pronounced like the fin of a fish (fin-*ans*). The alternative pronunciation has emphasis on the first syllable, which then is pronounced as fine (*fin*-ans).

formidable may be pronounced with the emphasis on the first syllable as *for*-mid-ibl or with the emphasis on the second syllable as for-*mid*-ibl.

forte the usual pronunciation is *for*-tay but it can also be pronounced as single syllable fort. The word means 'someone's strong point', as in 'Putting people at their ease is not her forte' and 'The chef's forte is desserts'. There is also a musical word **forte** meaning 'loud' or 'loudly'. It is of Italian origin and is pronounced either *for*-ti or *for*-tay.

foyer the most widely used pronunciation is foi-ay but it can also be pronounced fwah-yay following the original French pronunciation.

harass traditionally is pronounced with the stress on the first syllable, as *har*-as. However, in modern usage there is an increasing tendency to put the emphasis on the second syllable, as har-*as*, which is how the word is pronounced in America.

heinous is most commonly pronounced *hay*-nis, although *hee*-nis also exists.

hospitable can be pronounced in two ways. The more traditional pronunciation has the emphasis on the first syllable, as *hos*-pit-ibl. In modern usage it is sometimes pronounced with the emphasis on the second syllable, as hos-*pit*-ibl.

impious the emphasis should be on the first syllable as *im*-pi-us. This is unlike 'impiety' where the stress is on the second syllable.

incomparable the emphasis should be on the second syllable and not the third. It should be pronounced in-*kom*-pir-ibl.

inventory unlike the word 'invention', the emphasis is on the first syllable as *in*-ventri or *in*-ven-tor-i.

kilometre has two possible pronunciations in modern usage. It can be pronounced with the emphasis on the first syllable, as *kil*-o-meet-er, or with the emphasis on the second syllable, as kil-*om*-it-er. The first of these is the more traditional pronunciation but the second is becoming common.

laboratory should be pronounced with the emphasis on the second syllable, as lab-*or*-a-tor-i or lab-*or*-a-tri. In American English the emphasis is on the first syllable.

lamentable should be pronounced with the emphasis on the first syllable, as *lam*-en-tabl. However it is becoming common to place the emphasis on the second syllable in the same way that 'lament' does.

longevity should be pronounced lon-*jev*-iti. Some people pronounce it lon-*gev*-iti, but this is rarer.

machinations should be pronounced makin-*ay*-shunz but mash-in *ay*-shunz is becoming increasingly common in modern usage.

mandatory the emphasis should be on the first syllable, as *man*-da-tor-i.

margarine formerly the usual pronunciation was mar-ga-reen but now the most common pronunciation is mar-ja-reen.

migraine is pronounced *mee*-grayn in British English but the American pronunciation of *mi*-grayn, in which the first syllable rhymes with 'eye', is sometimes used in Britain.

motif is pronounced with the emphasis on the second syllable, as mo-*teef*.

naïve is pronounced ni-*eev*, with the emphasis on the second syllable, and the first syllable rhyming with 'my'. The accent on the *ï* (called a diaeresis) indicates that the two vowels *a* and *i* are to be pronounced separately.

necessarily is traditionally pronounced with the emphasis on the first syllable, but this is often very difficult to say except when one is speaking exceptionally carefully. Because of this difficulty it is often pronounced with the emphasis on the third syllable although this is considered by many people to be incorrect.

niche the most common pronunciation is *nitch*, but *neech*, following the French pronunciation, is also a possibility.

pejorative in modern usage it is pronounced with the emphasis on the second syllable, as in pi-*jor*-at-iv.

phlegm is pronounced *flem*.

prestige is pronounced prez-*teezh* .

primarily is traditionally pronounced with the emphasis on the first syllable, as *prim*-ar-el-i. Since this is difficult to say unless one is speaking very slowly and carefully, it is becoming increasingly common to pronounce it with the emphasis on the second syllable, as prim-*err*-el-i.

quay the spelling of the word does not suggest the pronunciation, which is *kee*.

questionnaire formerly the acceptable pronunciation was kes-tyon-*air*, but in modern usage kwes-chon-*air* is more common.

schedule is usually pronounced *shed*-yool in British English. However, the American English pronunciation *sked*-yool is now sometimes found in British usage.

subsidence has two acceptable pronunciations. It can be pronounced either sub-*sid*-ens, with the emphasis on the middle syllable which rhymes with 'hide', or *sub*-sid-ens, with the emphasis on the first syllable and with the middle syllable rhyming with 'hid'.

suit is pronounced *soot* or *syoot*.

suite is pronounced *sweet*.

swingeing is pronounced *swin*-jing, not like swinging.

trait is traditionally pronounced *tray* but *trayt* is also an acceptable pronunciation in modern usage

victuals is pronounced *vitlz*.

vitamin is pronounced vit-a-min, with the first syllable rhyming with 'lit' in British English. In American English the first syllable rhymes with 'light'.

Words Liable to be Confused

Some words with totally different meanings are liable to be confused, often, but not always, because they are pronounced in a similar way or have similar spellings. Below is a list of words which are often confused, together with short examples of usage to help you to differentiate them.

accept	accept a gift	**amend**	amend the law
except	everyone except Mary	**emend**	emend the text before printing
access	access to the building; access to computer data	**angel**	heavenly angels
excess	an excess of food at the picnic	**angle**	a triangle has three angles; a new angle to the story
adapter	the adapter of the novel for TV	**annex**	annex a neighbouring country
adaptor	an electrical adaptor	**annexe**	build an annexe to the house
addition	an addition to the family	**antiquated**	antiquated attitudes
edition	a new edition of the book	**antique**	valuable antique furniture
adverse	an adverse reaction to the drug	**arisen**	a problem has arisen
averse	not averse to the idea	**arose**	a problem arose today
		ascent	the ascent of Everest
advice	seek legal advice	**assent**	he gave his assent to the proposal
advise	We advise you to go		
affect	badly affected by the news	**astrology**	believers in astrology read horoscopes
effect	the effects of the drug	**astronomy**	astronomy involves the scientific study of the stars and the planets
alley	a bowling alley		
allay	allay the child's fears		
allusion	make no allusion to recent events	**ate**	we ate bread and cheese
delusion	under the delusion that he is immortal	**eaten**	we have eaten too much
illusion	an optical illusion	**aural**	an aural impairment requiring a hearing aid; an aural comprehension test
altar	praying at the altar	**oral**	both oral and written language exams; oral hygiene recommended by the dentist
alter	alter the dress		
alternately	feeling alternately hot and cold		
alternatively	we could drive there – alternatively we could walk	**bad**	bad men arrested by the police
		bade	We bade him farewell

bail	the accused was granted bail	**began**	the child began to cry
bale	a bale of cotton; bale out; bale out water; bale out of an aircraft	**begun**	it had begun to rain
		belief	have belief in his son's abilities
ballet	practising ballet steps	**believe**	believe that his son could succeed
ballot	voting by means of a secret ballot		
		beside	the bride stood beside the groom
bare	bare feet	**besides**	besides, he has no money; who, besides your mother, was there
bear	bear the pain; bear children; bears looking for food		
base	at the base of the pillar; base the argument on facts	**bit**	the dog bit the postman
		bitten	he was bitten by a rat
bass	sing bass; fishermen catching bass	**blew**	the wind blew; the hat blew away
bath	lie soaking in the bath; bath the baby	**blown**	the wind had blown fiercely; the papers have been blown away
bathe	bathe in the sea; bathe a wound		
		bloc	the African bloc of countries
baton	the conductor's baton; a relay baton	**block**	a block of flats; a block of wood; block a pipe
batten	secure the broken door with wooden battens; batten down the hatches	**boar**	shooting wild boar
		bore	the speaker is a bore
beach	building sand castles on the beach	**boast**	boast about his achievements
beech	beech and oak trees	**boost**	give a boost to the economy
been	having been famous	**bonny**	a bonny little girl with beautiful hair
being	being poor scared her		
		bony	the man's bony knees
beat	beat them at tennis; beat the dog with a stick	**born**	babies born in hospital
beet	sugar beet; soup made with beet	**borne**	I could not have borne the pain; water-borne diseases
beat	we should beat them	**bouquet**	a bouquet of roses
beaten	we should have beaten them	**bookie**	place a bet with a bookie
		bow	take a bow after the performance; bow to the queen
became	she became famous		
become	he wants to become a doctor	**bough**	the bow of a tree
beer	a pint of beer	**boy**	boys and girls
bier	a funeral bier	**buoy**	a mooring buoy in the bay

breach	a breach of the peace; breach the enemy's defences	**cannon**	soldiers firing cannons
		canon	the canons of the cathedral; the canons and principles of the Christian church
breech	the breech of a gun; a breech delivery of a baby		
bread	bread and butter	**canvas**	a bag made of canvas; the canvas painted by a local artist
bred	born and bred		
		canvass	canvass for votes
break	break an arm		
brake	failure of the car's brakes; brake suddenly on seeing the dog in the road	**carton**	a carton of milk
		cartoon	children laughing at TV cartoons
		cast	the whole cast came on stage; cast a quick glance; a cast in the eye
breath	take a deep breath		
breathe	breathe deeply		
		caste	the caste system in india
bridal	the bridal party going to the church	**censor**	appoint a film censor; censor letters
bridle	the horse's bridle		
		censure	censure the child's unruly behaviour
broke	the watch fell and broke		
broken	the watch was broken		
		cereal	cereal crops; breakfast cereal
brooch	wear a silver brooch		
broach	afraid to broach the subject	**serial**	a magazine serial
		chafe	tight shoes will chafe your heels; chafe at the delay
buffet	[buffit] heavy waves regularly buffet the cliffs		
buffet	[boofay] serve a cold buffet at the party; the station buffet	**chaff**	separate the wheat from the chaff
		chartered	a chartered surveyor; a chartered boat
but	he was dead, but his family did not know	**charted**	the charted areas of the region
butt	butt in rudely to the conversation; the goat will butt you; a cigarette butt	**cheap**	buy cheap clothes at the market
		cheep	birds beginning to cheep
calf	a cow and her calf; the calf of the leg	**check**	check the addition; check the tyre pressure; act as a check on her extravagance
calve	hoping the cow would calve soon		
callous	a cruel, callous tyrant	**cheque**	pay by cheque
callus	the callus on her finger		
		checked	a checked tablecloth
came	they came late	**chequered**	a chequered career
come	they promised to come		

choose	you may choose a cake	**conscience**	suffering from a guilty conscience
chose	she chose a peach from the fruit dish	**conscious**	he was knocked out but is conscious now; conscious that she was all alone; a conscious decision
chosen	you have chosen well; the chosen few		
chord	a musical chord; strike a chord	**conservative**	wear conservative clothes; a conservative, rather than radical, approach
cord	the cord of a dressing gown; spinal cord; vocal cord	**Conservative**	the Conservative Party in British politics
coarse	made of some coarse material; a coarse sense of humour	**consul**	he was British consul in Rome then
course	taking a French course; a golf course; in due course	**council**	she was elected to the town council
		counsel	counsel for the defence; seeking professional counsel
coma	the patient is still in a coma	**contemptible**	a contemptible act of cowardice; a contemptible fellow
comma	put a comma instead of the full stop		
commissionaire	the hotel commission-aire	**contemptuous**	contemptuous of the achievements of others; contemptuous of the law
commissioner	a police commissioner		
compliment	embarrassed at being paid a compliment	**continual**	disturbed by continual interruptions; in continual pain
complement	a full complement of staff; the complement of a verb	**continuous**	a continuous line of cars; a continuous roll of paper
complimentary	complimentary remarks; complimentary tickets	**coop**	a hencoop
		coup	a military coup
complementary	complementary medicine; a comple-mentary amount; complementary angles	**corps**	an army corps; the corps de ballet
		corpse	a corpse found in a shallow grave
compulsive	a compulsive gambler	**councillor**	a town councillor
compulsory	compulsory to wear school uniform	**counsellor**	a bereavement counsellor
concert	an orchestral concert	**courtesy**	treat the visitors with courtesy
consort	the queen's consort	**curtsy**	curtsy to the queen
confident	confident of success		
confidant	he was the king's trusted confidant	**credible**	a credible story
		creditable	a creditable performance
confidante	she was the queen's closest confidante	**credulous**	credulous enough to believe anything

crevasse	a crevasse in the glacier	**devolution**	the population voted for the devolution of power from the government to the assembly
crevice	a crevice in the rock		
cue	a billiards cue; an actor famous for missing his cue	**evolution**	the theory of evolution was first proposed by Charles Darwin
queue	the bus queue		
curb	curb their extravagance	**dew**	the morning dew
kerb	cars parked by the kerb	**due**	payment is due now; in due course
currant	a currant bun		
current	unable to swim against the strong current	**did**	you did enough; He did steal the money
		done	you have done enough
cygnet	a swan and her cygnets		
signet	a signet ring	**die**	very ill and likely to die
		dye	about to dye her fair hair black
cymbal	banging the cymbals		
symbol	a symbol of purity; a mathematical symbol	**died**	the poet died young
		dyed	he dyed his white shirt blue
dairy	milk from the dairy		
diary	writing in her diary every night	**dinghy**	a dinghy capsizing in the storm
		dingy	a dingy basement flat
dear	dear friends; clothes which are too dear	**disadvantageous**	disadvantageous to one of the teams; disadvantageous, rather than favourable, circumstances
deer	hunting deer		
dependant	trying to provide for his wife and other dependants		
dependent	dependent on her family for personal care	**disadvantaged**	disadvantaged people in society
deprecate	strongly deprecate the behaviour of the gang of youths	**discomfit**	the question seemed to discomfit her
depreciate	depreciate in value	**discomfort**	living in great discomfort
desert	camels in the desert; He deserted his wife and family	**discriminating**	discriminating in their choice of wines
		discriminatory	discriminatory against women
dessert	have chocolate cake for dessert		
		discus	throwing the discus
detract	detract from his reputation as an actor	**discuss**	discuss the matter
distract	try not to distract the driver	**distinct**	see a distinct improvement; a style quite distinct from others
device	a device designed to save water		
devise	devise a rescue plan	**distinctive**	the distinctive markings of the zebra

draft	a first draft of a report	**elude**	elude capture by the police
draught	there was a draught in the room from the open window; a draught of cold beer	**allude**	allude to facts which he had concealed
		emigrant	emigrants weeping for their native land
dragon	a dragon breathing fire	**immigrant**	illegal immigrants to the country
dragoon	the dragoon guards; We dragooned her into helping us		
		emigration	the poor standard of living led to mass emigration from the country
drank	we drank some white wine		
drunk	to have drunk too much; a drunk woman staggering down the street	**immigration**	anxious to reduce the extent of immigration into the country
drunken	a drunken, violent man; a drunken brawl		
		emission	the emission of poisonous gases
drew	the child drew a picture		
drawn	he has drawn a picture of a house	**omission**	the omission of her name from the invitation list
driven	we were driven home by my father	**emotional**	an emotional person; an emotional reaction
drove	we drove home after midnight	**emotive**	an emotive subject
		employee	hiring several new employees
dual	serve a dual purpose		
duel	fight a duel	**employer**	asking their employer for an increase in salary
economic	a country facing economic disaster; charging an economic rent for the flat	**enormity**	the enormity of the crime
		enormousness	the enormousness of the elephant
economical	the economical use of resources; an economical car to run; economical with the truth	**envelop**	she wanted to envelop the child in her arms; Mist began to envelop the mountains
eerie	in the eerie atmosphere of a thick mist	**envelope**	a brown envelope
eyrie	the eagle's eyrie	**enviable**	an enviable affluent lifestyle
elder	Mary has two brothers and James is the elder	**envious**	envious of other people's wealth
eldest	John has three sisters and Jill is the eldest	**epitaph**	carve an epitaph on a gravestone
elicit	elicit information	**epithet**	King Alfred was given the epithet 'great'
illicit	an illicit love affair		
eligible	eligible for promotion; an eligible bachelor	**equable**	an equable climate; an equable temperament
legible	scarcely legible handwriting	**equitable**	an equitable system

erotic			**flow**

erotic	erotic picture of naked women	**fair**	a fair result; fair hair; sideshows at a fair
erratic	an erratic driver; impulsive, erratic behaviour	**fare**	bus fare; How did you fare in the exam?
ewe	a ewe and her lambs	**fate**	suffer a terrible fate; by a strange twist of fate
yew	the yew tree in the graveyard	**fête**	a fête in aid of charity
exceedingly	exceedingly beautiful	**fearful**	fearful of being left behind; what a fearful smell
excessively	excessively fond of alcohol		
exceptional	a singer of exceptional talent; an exceptional amount of rain	**fearsome**	see a fearsome sight
exceptionable	find their behaviour exceptionable	**feat**	perform a brave feat
		feet	sore feet
executioner	bring the condemned man to the executioner	**fiancé**	Jill and her fiancé
		fiancée	Jim and his fiancée
executor	an executor of a will	**final**	a final warning
exercise	physical exercise; an English exercise	**finale**	all the cast took part in the final
exorcise	exorcise evil spirits	**flair**	have a flair for languages
exhausting	an exhausting climb	**flare**	send up a flare as a signal for help; make the fire flare up; a skirt with a slight flare
exhaustive	an exhaustive search		
expand	expand the business; metals expanding in the heat		
expend	expend a great deal of energy	**flammable**	clothes made of flammable material
		inflammable	highly inflammable substances such as petrol
expansive	his knowledge of literature was expansive	**flea**	bitten by a flea
expensive	spending a lot of money on expensive meals	**flee**	people beginning to flee from the burning houses
expedient	politically expedient	**fleshy**	fleshy upper arms; a fleshy fruit
expeditious	a parcel sent by the most expeditious method	**fleshly**	fleshly pleasures
extant	old customs which are still extant in some areas	**flu**	suffering from flu
		flue	cleaning the flue
extinct	an endangered species that is likely to be extinct soon; a volcano that has been extinct for centuries	**flew**	the bird flew away
		flown	the bird has flown away
faint	feel faint; a faint noise	**floe**	an ice floe
feint	a feint in fencing	**flow**	the flow of water

flour   **grizzly**

flour	flour to make bread	**gaff**	blow the gaff
flower	pick a flower from the garden	**gaffe**	a social gaffe
		gamble	decide to gamble on a horse in the next race
flout	flout the new school rule		
flaunt	flaunt her long legs	**gambol**	lambs beginning to gambol about
font	babies christened at the font		
fount	printed in a small size of fount	**gate**	shut the gate
		gait	a shuffling gait
forbade	she forbade them to leave	**gave**	he gave money to the poor
forbidden	she was forbidden to leave	**given**	we had been given some money
foresaw	we foresaw trouble	**gentle**	a gentle touch; a gentle breeze
foreseen	the problem could not have been foreseen		
		genteel	a genteel tea party
forgave	we forgave them	**glacier**	a glacier beginning to melt
forgiven	we have forgiven them	**glazier**	a glazier mending the window
forgot	we forgot about the party		
forgotten	I had forgotten the event	**goal**	score a goal
		gaol	escape from gaol
formally	formally dressed		
formerly	formerly the president of the club	**gone**	he has gone
		went	she went yesterday
fort	soldiers defending the fort	**gorilla**	a gorilla in the zoo
forte	tact is not his forte	**guerrilla**	guerrillas fighting in the mountains
foul	commit a foul on the football pitch; a foul smell		
		grate	a fire burning in the grate
fowl	a chicken is a type of fowl	**great**	a great improvement; a great man
found	they found the missing child		
founded	their grandfather founded the firm	**grew**	the plants grew well
		grown	the plant had grown tall
		grief	weeping from grief
freeze	freeze the vegetables; freeze to death	**grieve**	time to grieve for her dead husband
frieze	a decorative frieze		
		grill	put the meat under the grill
froze	we froze the meat immediately	**grille**	a metal grille on the window
frozen	frozen vegetables; have frozen to death		
		grisly	the grisly sight of a decaying body
funeral	mourners at the funeral		
funereal	solemn funereal music	**grizzly**	a grizzly bear

hail	a hail storm; a hail of bullets; hail a taxi	**imaginary**	the child's imaginary friend
hale	hale and hearty	**imaginative**	an imaginative story; an imaginative person
hair	cut off her hair		
hare	a running hare	**immoral**	wicked and immoral
		immortal	no one is immortal
half	a half of the apple		
halve	halve the apple	**inapt**	an inapt remark
		inept	an inept attempt
hangar	an aeroplane hangar		
hanger	a clothes hanger	**incredible**	find the story incredible
		incredulous	incredulous enough to believe anything
hanged	they hanged the murderer		
hung	they hung the pictures	**industrial**	an industrial estate
		industrious	studious and industrious
heal	the wound began to heal		
heel	a blister on the heel	**ingenious**	an ingenious plan
		ingenuous	an ingenuous young person
hear	hear the news		
here	here and there		
		its	a dog wagging its tail
hereditary	a hereditary title	**it's**	it's raining
heredity	part of his genetic heredity		
		jam	strawberry jam; a traffic jam; the machine seemed to jam
heron	a heron catching fish		
herring	fishermen catching herring	**jamb**	a door jamb
hid	we hid the treasure	**jib**	jib at the high price
hidden	they have hidden the treasure	**jibe**	ignore the nasty jibe
hoard	a hoard of treasure	**judicial**	a judicial enquiry into the accident
horde	a horde of invaders	**judicious**	a judicious choice of words
honorable	an honorable gentleman; honorable deeds	**junction**	a road junction
honorary	the honorary post of secretary	**juncture**	at this juncture we went home
hoop	jump through a hoop	**key**	a door key
whoop	a whoop of delight	**quay**	the boat tied to the quay
human	a human being	**knead**	knead the bread dough
humane	the humane killing of the injured animal	**kneed**	he kneed his attacker in the stomach
idle	too idle to work	**knew**	we knew him slightly
idol	the pop star as teenage idol; worshipping an idol	**know**	we did not know him
		known	if I had known

knight	a knight in shining armour	**loath/loth**	loath/loth to join in
night	a stormy night	**loathe**	I loathe him
laid	we laid the patient on the bed; they laid a new carpet	**local**	the local shops; drinking at his local
lain	he had lain injured for days	**locale**	a perfect locale for a rock concert
lair	the animal's lair	**loose**	loose clothing
layer	a layer of dust	**lose**	lose your luggage; lose weight
laterally	moving laterally; thinking laterally	**loot**	the thieves' loot
latterly	latterly she was very ill	**lute**	playing the lute
lath	a lath of wood	**lumbar**	lumbar pain
lathe	using a lathe in the factory	**lumber**	to lumber along awkwardly
lead	pipes made of lead	**luxuriant**	luxuriant vegetation
led	he led the group	**luxurious**	a luxurious lifestyle
leak	a leak in the pipe	**magnate**	a shipping magnate
leek	a leek to make soup	**magnet**	a fridge magnet
licence	have a driving licence	**mail**	deliver the mail
license	to license the sale of alcohol	**male**	male and female
		main	the main reason
lifelong	a lifelong ambition	**mane**	the lion's mane
livelong	the livelong day		
		maize	grow maize
lighted	a lighted match	**maze**	get lost in the maze
lit	we lit the fire; we have lit the fire	**manner**	a friendly manner
		manor	a manor surrounded by beautiful gardens
lightening	lightening the load		
lightning	struck by lightning; a lightning decision	**masterful**	she prefers masterful men
		masterly	a masterly performance
liqueur	an after-dinner liqueur	**mat**	a door mat
liquor	strong liquor such as whisky	**matt, matte**	matt/matte paint
liquidate	liquidate a debt; liquidate an asset; liquidate an enemy	**meat**	meat such as beef
		meet	meet a friend
liquidize	liquidize the soup	**medal**	a gold medal
		meddle	meddle in the affairs of others
literal	a literal translation		
literary	literary and artistic tastes	**mediate**	mediate between the rival groups
literate	people who are scarcely literate	**meditate**	meditate to relax

melted	the ice cream melted; melted chocolate	**negligent**	negligent parents
molten	molten lava	**negligible**	a negligible amount of money
metal	chairs made of metal	**net**	caught in a net
mettle	a test of the football team's mettle	**net, nett**	net, nett profit
		niceness	appreciate the old lady's niceness
meter	read the gas meter		
metre	a metre of silk	**nicety**	the nicety of the distinction
miner	a coal miner	**notable**	a notable figure in the town
minor	a minor incident; legally still a minor	**noticeable**	a noticeable improvement
missal	members of the congregation carrying missals	**nougat**	nougat is a sweet
missile	hit by a missile	**nugget**	a nugget of gold; a nugget of information
mistaken	a case of mistaken identity; we were mistaken	**oar**	the boat's oars
mistook	I mistook him for you in the dark	**ore**	iron oar
		observance	the observance of school rules
model	a model of a ship; a fashion module	**observation**	keep the patient under observation
module	a space module; a software module; a study module	**of**	made of gold; tired of working; a glass of wine
momentary	a momentary lapse of memory	**off**	run off; switch off; badly off
momentous	a momentous decision	**official**	an official report; official duties; council official
moral	the moral of the story; a person with no morals	**officious**	upset at the officious manner of the hotel receptionist
morale	morale was low in the firm		
motif	decorated with a motif of roses	**organism**	an organism found in the water supply
motive	a motive for murder	**orgasm**	to reach orgasm
muscle	strain a muscle	**outdoor**	an outdoor sport
mussel	eat fresh mussels	**outdoors**	playing outdoors
naturalist	a naturalist interested in local flowers	**overcame**	we overcame the enemy
naturist	naked people on a naturist beach	**overcome**	an enemy difficult to overcome
		overtaken	he had overtaken the other runners
naval	a naval cadet		
navel	your navel is in the middle of your abdomen	**overtook**	they overtook the car in front

pail	a pail of water	persecute	persecute members of other religions
pale	looking pale; a pale colour	prosecute	prosecute thieves
pain	suffering from pain		
pane	a pane of glass	personal	a personal letter; a personal assistant
pair	a pair of gloves	personnel	the person in charge of office personnel
pare	he began to pare his toenails		
pear	an apple and a pear	phase	the next phase of the development; phase in the changes
palate	the soft palate		
palette	an artist's palette		
pallet	a straw pallet	faze	nothing seems to faze her
passed	she passed the exam; we passed the other car; the feeling passed	pigeon	a pigeon looking for food
		pidgin	pidgin English
past	past times; in the past; walking past the church; a mile past the village	place	a sunny place; get a place at university
		plaice	plaice and chips
pastel	pastel colours	plain	a plain carpet; rather a plain girl; corn growing on the plain
pastille	sucking a throat pastille		
pâté	chicken liver pâté on toast	plane	a plane taking off; the plane used by the joiner; writing on a different plane from other crime writers
patty	a small meat patty		
peace	warring nations now at peace		
piece	a piece of cake		
peak	a mountain peak; talent at its peak	plaintiff	evidence on behalf of the plaintiff
peek	peek through the window	plaintive	a plaintive cry
peal	the bells began to peal	plate	the food on the plate
peel	peel an orange	plait	wearing her hair in a plait
pearl	a pearl necklace	plum	eating a plum
purl	knit two, purl two	plumb	plumb straight; plumb in the middle; plumb the depths; plumb-in the bath
pedal	pedal the bike		
peddle	peddle their wares		
		politic	not politic to ask any questions
pendant	wearing a silver pendant	political	political parties
pendent	pendent lights lighting up the room		
		pour	pour water
perceptible	a perceptible improvement	pore	pore over the book; a clogged pore
perceptive	a perceptive remark		
perpetrate	perpetrate a crime	practice	go to football practice
perpetuate	perpetuate the myth	practise	to practise dance steps

pray	pray to God	**purposely**	leave the book behind purposely
prey	the fox's prey; prey on one's mind	**purposefully**	walk purposefully into the room
precede	the leader who preceded the present one; precede them into the room	**quash**	quash a rebellion; quash a conviction
proceed	You may proceed; proceed to cause trouble	**squash**	squash the tomatoes; squash the insect with his foot
precipitate	rash, precipitate action; precipitate economic panic	**quiet**	a quiet child; a quiet time of day
precipitous	a precipitous slope	**quite**	quite good; quite right
premier	a meeting of European premiers; one of the country's premier actors	**racket**	the noisy children made quite a racket; a drugs racket; tennis racket
première	the premiere of the film	**racquet**	tennis racquet (variant spelling)
premises	seek new office premises	**rain**	get wet in the rain
premise	based on a mistaken premise	**reign**	in the reign of the last king
prescribe	prescribe antibiotics for the disease	**rein**	a horse's reins
proscribe	proscribe the carrying of dangerous weapons	**raise**	raise one's arm; raise a family
principal	the college principal	**raze**	raze the whole street to the ground
principle	a person of principle; the principle of the steam engine	**ran**	they ran away
		run	he started to run; She had run away
prise	prise open the lid of the tin	**rang**	they rang the bell
prize	win a prize	**rung**	they had rung the bell
program	a computer program	**rap**	rap at the window
programme	a theatre programme	**wrap**	wrap the presents
proof	no proof of his guilt	**rapt**	with rapt attention
prove	able to prove her innocence	**wrapped**	we wrapped the presents
prophecy	the gift of prophesy; her prophecy came true	**read**	I read the book last week
prophesy	prophesy that there would be a war	**red**	a red dress
prostate	the prostate gland	**real**	made of real leather; a real friend
prostrate	lying prostrate on the ground	**reel**	a reel of thread; dance a reel

refuge	seek refuge from the storm	**rough**	a rough material; rough weather
refugee	a political refugee	**ruff**	a lace ruff at the neck
regal	a regal wave of the hand	**rout**	rout the enemy
regale	regale them with his adventures	**route**	the shortest route to the town
relief	bring relief from pain	**rung**	the bottom rung of the ladder; we had rung the bell
relieve	relieve the pain		
rest	rest after work	**wrung**	she wrung her hands in grief
wrest	wrest the knife from his hand	**rye**	grow rye and barley
retch	feel sick and begin to retch	**wry**	a wry smile; a wry sense of humour
wretch	the poor wretch		
review	the review of the play; the annual salary review	**sail**	the sail of a boat; go for a sail
revue	a musical revue	**sale**	an end-of-season sale
rhyme	children reciting a rhyme; cook rhymes with book	**salon**	a hair-dressing salon
rime	rime on the grass on a cold morning	**saloon**	a saloon car; a saloon bar
		sang	they sang a song
ridden	she had ridden the horse home	**sung**	we had sung a song earlier
rode	he rode a fine stallion	**sank**	the ship sank
		sunk	the ship has sunk
right	the right person for the job; the right to be free; the right hand	**sunken**	a sunken wreck
rite	a religious rite	**saviour**	the saviour of the organization; Christ the saviour
write	write in pencil		
risen	the sun had risen	**savour**	savour the delicious food
rose	the sun rose	**saw**	we saw him go
		seen	I have seen the film before
road	the road through the town		
rode	the child rode her bicycle	**sawed**	we sawed the wood
		sawn	all the wood has been sawn
roe	cod roe	**scared**	scared of the dark
row	a row of green beans; row a boat	**scarred**	scarred for life in the accident
role	play the role of Hamlet; the parental role	**scene**	a scene in the play; the scene of the accident
roll	a roll of carpet; a ham roll; roll a ball	**seen**	have seen the play
rote	learn the answers by rote	**scent**	the scent of roses
wrote	he wrote a letter	**sent**	she sent a letter

sceptic	a sceptic arguing with the believers	**shear**	to shear sheep
septic	a septic wound; a septic tank	**sheer**	a sheer slope; sheer impertinence; sheer silk
scraped	he scraped the car on the gate	**shelf**	put the book on the shelf
scrapped	they scrapped their original plans	**shelve**	shelve the plan
		shoe	a high-heeled shoe
		shoo	shoo the dog away
sculptor	a statue by a famous sculptor	**showed**	we showed them the house
sculpture	carve a piece of sculpture	**shown**	he has shown me the book
seam	sew the seam of a dress; a seam of coal	**shrank**	the child shrank back in fear; the dress shrank in the wash
seem	they seem familiar	**shrunk**	the child had shrunk from the angry man; the dress had shrunk
seasonal	seasonal hotel work		
seasonable	seasonable weather for spring	**sight**	the sight of the woman crying
seasoned	a seasoned dish of stew; seasoned travellers	**site**	the battle site; a building site
secret	a secret hideout; their engagement was a secret	**singeing**	singeing a blouse with an iron
secrete	secrete the money under the floorboards	**singing**	singing a song
		slay	slay an enemy in battle
see	I see a light	**sleigh**	a sleigh ride in the snow
sea	boats sailing on the sea		
		slow	at a slow pace
sensual	a sensual mouth	**sloe**	a ripe sloe
sensuous	the sensuous feel of the silk sheets	**soar**	soar up high
		sore	a sore finger
series	a series of disasters; a TV series	**solder**	to solder metal
serious	a serious matter; looking serious	**soldier**	a soldier in the British army
sew	sew new curtains	**sole**	the sole reason; the sole of the foot; a dish of sole
sow	sow seeds	**soul**	body and soul; a poor old soul
sewed	she sewed tiny stitches		
sewn	the dress which she had sewn	**some**	some people
		sum	the sum total
shaken	she was shaken by the accident	**son**	a son and two daughters
shook	he shook the child angrily	**sun**	lie in the sun on the beach

soot	soot falling down the chimney	**storey**	the top storey of the house
suit	an evening suit	**story**	tell a story
sped	the car sped away into the night	**straight**	a straight road; a straight answer
speeded	we speeded up to pass the car in front	**strait**	the Bering Strait
		straightened	she had her teeth straightened
spoke	she spoke with feeling	**straitened**	in straitened circumstances
spoken	he has spoken to the parents	**strategy**	the team's winning strategy; devise a strategy to counteract bullying
sprang	he sprang to his feet		
sprung	the lion had sprung over the fence	**stratagem**	devise a stratagem to mislead the enemy
stair	a stone stair	**strewed**	they strewed flowers
stare	stare into space	**strewn**	flowers were strewn
stake	a stake missing from the fence; stake a claim	**strife**	quarrelling and strife
steak	eat a large steak	**strive**	strive to overcome the difficulty
stalk	the stalk of the flower	**striven**	we haven't striven to succeed
stock	a large stock of goods; stocks and shares	**strove**	they strove to win
stank	he stank of beer	**suede**	a jacket made of real suede
stunk	the room had stunk for days	**swede**	cutting up a swede for dinner
stationary	the car was stationary		
stationery	a shop stocking stationery	**suit**	wearing a smart suit; a law suit; a suit of cards
statue	stone statues in the grounds of the house	**suite**	a three-piece suite; a suite of rooms; a ballet suite
statute	pass a new statute	**summary**	a summary of the report; his summary dismissal
steal	steal the money from the till	**summery**	sunny, summery weather
steel	tools made of steel	**sundae**	an ice cream sundae
stile	climb over the stile	**Sunday**	have a rest on Sunday
style	dress with style; a style of writing	**surplice**	the priest's surplice
stimulant	athletes taking illegal stimulants	**surplus**	a surplus of food at the party
stimulus	the stimulus of a valuable prize	**swam**	we swam in the river
		swum	he has swum across the river

swingeing	a swingeing blow; swingeing cuts	**thrash**	thrash the youth with a belt
swinging	a swinging gate; the swinging sixties	**thresh**	thresh the corn
		threw	he threw the ball
swollen	her eye has swollen up; swollen glands	**through**	go through the door
swelled	her injured ankle swelled	**threw**	he threw the ball
		thrown	he had thrown the ball
swore	they swore they would find the killer	**throes**	in the throes of studying for exams
sworn	he has sworn to get revenge	**throws**	he throws the ball
		thyme	flavour the sauce with thyme
tail	the dog's tail	**time**	what time is it?; not enough time
tale	tell a tale		
taken	she has taken the book	**tic**	a nervous tic
took	she took the book	**tick**	the tick of the clock; the dog bitten by the tick; in a tick; a tick at a correct answer
taper	a lighted taper; The road seems to taper there		
tapir	a tapir is a pig-like animal	**timber**	a house made of timber
		timbre	the timbre of his voice
taught	he taught us maths	**tire**	runners beginning to tire
taut	a taut rope; a face taut with concentration	**tyre**	change a car tyre
tea	a cup of tea	**to**	go to town
tee	a golf tee	**too**	she wants to go too
		two	two or three times
team	a football team		
teem	the town will teem with tourists	**toe**	injure a toe
		tow	tow the broken-down car
tear	wipe away a tear	**tomb**	the tomb of the Egyptian king
tier	one tier of the wedding cake	**tome**	struggling to read a legal tome
teeth	have two teeth extracted	**topi**	wear a topi in the hot sun
teethe	the child has begun to teethe	**toupee**	a bald man wearing a toupee
temporal	temporal, not spiritual	**tore**	she tore her dress
temporary	a temporary post	**torn**	she has torn her dress; a torn dress
their	their home		
there	stay there	**trait**	dishonesty is an unpleasant trait
they're	they're quarrelling again		
thorough	a thorough cleaning	**tray**	tea served on a tray
through	pass through		

treaties	signing treaties to end the war	**vain**	a vain young woman; a vain attempt
treatise	write a treatise on company law	**vane**	a weather vane
		vein	inject the drug into a vein; a vein of pessimism in the novel
trod	she trod on the cat's tail		
trodden	she had trodden on some mud	**vale**	the Vale of Evesham
		veil	a hat with a veil; draw a veil over the incident
troop	a troop of soldiers; troop out of school		
troupe	a troupe of actors	**veracity**	doubt the veracity of the account
turban	hair hidden by a turban	**voracity**	the voracity of the youth's appetite
turbine	a turbine engine		
tycoon	a business tycoon	**vertex**	the vertex of a cone
typhoon	a ship damaged in a typhoon	**vortex**	the swimmer was caught in a vortex of water and drowned
unaware	unaware of what had happened	**vigilant**	be vigilant because of pickpockets
unawares	taken unawares by the attack	**vigilante**	the thief was caught by a vigilante
unconscionable	an unconscionable delay	**wafer**	an ice cream wafer; a Communion wafer
unconscious	knocked unconscious by the blow; unconscious of the recent event		
		waver	begin to waver about the decision
undid	they undid all the damage	**waif**	a starving waif
undone	the damage could not be undone	**waive**	waive the extra charges
		wave	wave to their departing guests
unexceptional	a disappointing, unexceptional performance	**waist**	a leather belt round the waist
unexceptionable	unnecessary complaints about unexceptionable behaviour	**waste**	liquid waste from the factory; a waste of food
		want	want more money; for want of enough money
unwanted	unwanted guests		
unwonted	speak with unwonted enthusiasm	**wont**	she was wont to arrive late
		warden	the warden of the hostel
urban	prefer urban to rural life	**warder**	a prison warder
urbane	an urbane young man		
		ware	kitchen ware; stallholders selling their wares
vacation	go on vacation to America		
vocation	have a vocation to be a priest	**wear**	wear a skirt; show signs of wear

way   **you're**

way	the quickest way home; the correct way to do it	**woe**	sadness and woe
weigh	weigh the apples	**woo**	woo her and marry her
weak	invalids too weak to get out of bed	**woke**	she woke early
		woken	she had woken early
week	go to the supermarket every week	**wore**	he wore the shoes
		worn	he had worn the shoes; an old, worn carpet
weakly	weakly children who did not survive	**would**	we knew she would go
weekly	look forward to their weekly visit	**wood**	a pine wood
		wove	he wove the material
went	they went quite suddenly; She went pale	**woven**	he has woven the material
gone	he has gone home; She had gone deaf	**weaved**	the cyclist weaved in and out of the line of traffic
wet	a wet day; wet the floor	**wreak**	wreak vengeance; wreak havoc
whet	whet the appetite	**wreck**	wreck the car; wreck their plans
whit	not care a whit		
wit	find his wit amusing; a person of wit and intelligence	**wreath**	a holly wreath
		wreathe	mist had begun to wreathe the mountain peaks
whole	the whole group		
hole	dig a hole	**wrote**	she wrote the letter
		written	she has written the letter
withdrawn	he has withdrawn from the election; a shy, withdrawn child	**yoke**	the yoke of a dress; the yoke of a plough
withdrew	he withdrew from the election	**yolk**	egg yolk
		yore	in days of yore
wittily	he spoke wittily after dinner	**your**	your house
wittingly	she wittingly told a lie	**you're**	you're wrong

117

Affixes

Affix refers to an element that is added to the root or stem of a word to form another word. Affixes can be in the form of **prefixes or suffixes**. A prefix is added to the beginning of a word, as audio in audiovisual, an affix to the end, as -aholic in workaholic. Some common affixes are listed below.

a-, an- a prefix meaning without or not, as amoral, anonymous and atypical.

-able, -ible a suffix meaning 'that can be', as laughable, washable, horrible and edible.

aero- a prefix meaning **1** air, as aerobics and aeroplane, **2** aeroplane, as aerodrome.

agro-, agri- a prefix meaning field, as agriculture and agrochemicals.

-aholic a suffix indicating an addiction, formed on analogy with alcoholic, as workaholic and shopaholic. It sometimes becomes **-oholic**, as chocoholic.

ambi- a prefix meaning two or both as ambivalent, having mixed or uncertain feelings about something and ambidextrous, able to use both the right and left hand with equal skill.

-ana a suffix meaning 'things associated with', as Americana.

ante- a prefix meaning before, as antenatal, before birth.

anti- a prefix meaning against. It is used in many words that have been established In English for a long time, as antipathy, a feeling of hostility or dislike, but it has also been used to form many modern words, as anti-freeze, anti-nuclear and anti-warfare.

arch- a prefix meaning chief, as archbishop, archduke and arch-enemy.

-arch a suffix meaning ruler or leader, as monarch and patriarch.

astro- a prefix meaning star, as in astrology, astronomy, astronaut, astrophysics.

-athon, -thon a suffix meaning large-scale or long-lasting contest or event, as sima thon. such words are formed on analogy with the word marathon.

audio- a prefix referring to hearing. It is found in several words that have been established in the language for some time, as audition, but it is also used to form many modern words, as audiotape and audiovisual.

auto- a prefix meaning of or by itself, as autobiography, autograph and automatic, meaming working by itself.

bi- a prefix meaning two, as in bicycle, bifocal, bilingual and bisect. Bi- forms words in English in which it means half, and other words in which it means twice. This can give rise to confusion in such words as biweekly and bimonthly, where there are two possible sets of meanings. Biweekly can mean either every two weeks or twice a week so that one would not be able to be certain about the frequency of a biweekly publication. Similarly, a bimonthly publication might appear either twice a month or once every two months.

biblio- a prefix meaning book, as bibliophile, a person who is fond of or collects books, and bibliography.

bio- a prefix meaning life or living material, as biography and biology.

-bound a suffix meaning **1** confined or restricted, as housebound and snowbound, **2** It can also mean obligated, as duty-bound.

by- a prefix **1** meaning subordinate, secondary, as by-product, **2** around, as in by-pass.

cardi- a prefix meaning heart, as cardiology and cardiac.

cent-, centi- a prefix meaning hundred, as centenary and centigrade.

chrono- a prefix meaning time, as chronology and chronicle.

-cide a suffix meaning killing, as infanticide, patricide and pesticide.

circum- a prefix meaning around, as circumnavigate and circumvent.

con-, com- a prefix meaning together with, as connect, compare and compound.

contra- a prefix meaning opposite or against, as contrary, contradict and contraflow.

deca- a prefix meaning ten, as decade and decathlon.

deci- a prefix meaning tenth, as decibel and decimal

demi- a prefix meaning half, as demigod.

di- a prefix meaning two or double, as in dioxide, dilemma, diphthong and disyllabic.

dia- a prefix meaning **1** through, as in diaphanous, **2** apart, as in diacritical, diaphragm and dialysis, **3** and across, as in diameter.

dis- a prefix indicating opposite or meaning not, as disappear, disapprove, dislike, disobey, dispossess, distrust and disunite.

-dom a suffix meaning state or condition, as in boredom, freedom, officialdom, martyrdom, **2** rank or status, as in earldom, dukedom, **3** domain or territory as in kingdom.

dys- a prefix meaning, bad, impaired or abnormal, as dysfunctional and dyslexia, dyspepsia

eco- a prefix indicating ecology. Following the increased awareness of the importance of the environment, there has been a growing interest in ecology and many words beginning with eco- have been added to the English language. Some of these are scientific terms such as ecotype, ecosystem or ecospecies. Others are more general terms, such as ecocatastrophe and ecopolitics, and some are even slang terms, such as ecofreak and econut.

-ectomy a suffix that indicates surgical removal, as hysterectomy (the surgical removal of the womb), mastectomy (the surgical removal of a breast) and appendicectomy (the surgical removal of the appendix).

-ed a suffix that forms the past tense and past participles of regular verbs, as in asked, caused, dropped and escaped.

-ee a suffix that is used as part of nouns that are the recipients of an action, as in deportee (a person who has been deported); employee, and interviewee. The prefix can also be used as part of a noun indicating a person who acts or behaves in a particular way, as absentee (a person who absents himself/herself) and escapee (a person who escapes).

electro- a prefix meaning electric, electrical as electromagnetic.

-en a suffix with several functions. In one sense it indicates causing to be, as broaden, darken, gladden, lighten and sweeten. It also indicates a diminutive or small version of something, as chicken and maiden. It also indicates what something is made of, as in silken and wooden. It is also used to form the past participle of many irregular verbs, such as broken and fallen.

en- a prefix indicating causing to be, as in enrich and enlarge, and putting into, as endanger and enrage. enslave.

equi- a prefix meaning equal, as equidistant and equivalent.

-er a suffix with several functions. It can indicate a person who does something, as in bearer, cleaner, employer, farmer, manager. Some words in this category can also end in '-or', as in adviser/advisor. It can also indicate a person who is engaged in something, as in lawyer. It also indicates a thing that does something, as in blender, cooker, mower, printer and strainer. It can also indicate the comparative form of an adjective, as in darker, fairer, older, shorter and younger. It can also indicate someone who comes from somewhere, as in Londoner.

-ese a suffix that indicates belonging to, coming from and is used of people and languages, as Chinese, Japanese and Portuguese. By extension it refers to words indicating some kind of jargon, as computerese, journalese and legalese.

-esque a suffix of French origin that means in the style or fashion of, as in Junoesque, statuesque, Picassoesque, Ramboesque.

-ess a suffix that was formerly widely used to indicate the feminine form of a word, as authoress from author, poetess from poet, editress from editor, and sculptress from sculptor. In many cases the supposed male form, such as author, is now considered a neutral form and so is used of both a woman and a man. Thus a woman as well as a man may be an author, a poet, an editor and a sculptor, etc. Some words ending in -ess remain, as princess, duchess, heiress and hostess. Actress and waitress are still also fairly widespread.

-est a suffix that indicates the superlative forms of adjectives, as biggest, smallest and ugliest.

-ette a suffix indicating **1** a diminutive or smaller version, as cigarette and kitchenette, **2** imitation, as in flannelette and leatherette, **3** a female version, as usherette, a female usher in a cinema. In this last sense it is sometimes used disparagingly, as in jockette (a derogatory word for a female jockey) and hackette a derogatory word for a female journalist.

Euro- a prefix meaning **1** referring to Europe, as in Eurovision, **2** (more commonly now) referring to the European Community, as in Euro-MP, Eurocrat and Eurocurrency.

ex- a prefix meaning former, as ex-chairman, ex-president, ex-wife.

extra- a prefix meaning beyond, outside as in extra-marital, meaning outside marriage and extra-curricular, meaning outside the curriculum.

-fold a suffix meaning 'times', multiplied by, as in fourfold, a hundredfold.

for- a prefix with several meanings. These include prohibition, as forbid; abstention as in forbear, forgo and forswear; neglect, as forsake; excess, intensity, as forlorn; and away, off, apart, as forgive.

fore- a prefix meaning **1** before, as forecast, foregoing and forefathers, **2** front as forehead, foreground.

-form a suffix meaning **1** having the form of, as cruciform, meaning in the form of a cross, **2** having such a number of, as uniform, multiform.

-ful a suffix indicating **1** the amount that fills something, as handful, spoonful and bagful, **2** full of, as beautiful, truthful and scornful, **3** having the qualities of, as masterful, **4** apt to, able to, as forgetful and useful.

-free a suffix used to form adjectives indicating absence of, freedom from as carefree, trouble-free, anxiety-free, tax-free, lead-free.

-friendly a modern suffix formed on analogy with user-friendly to mean helpful to, supporting, as child-friendly and environment-friendly.

-gate a modern suffix that is added to a noun to indicate something scandalous. Most of the words so formed are short-lived and forgotten about almost as soon as they are invented. In modern usage they are frequently used to apply to sexual scandals, but originally -gate was restricted to some form of political scandal. The suffix is derived from Watergate, and refers to a po-

litical scandal in the United States during President Richard Nixon's re-election campaign in 1972, when Republican agents were caught breaking into the headquarters of the Democratic Party in Washington, which were in a building called the Watergate Building. The uncovering of the attempts to cover up the break-in led to Richard Nixon's resignation.

geo- a prefix meaning earth, as geography and geology.

-gram a suffix meaning **1** writing or drawing, as telegram, electrocardiogram and diagram, **2** used in modern usage to indicate a greeting or message, as in kissogram.

-graph a suffix meaning **1** written or recorded, as autograph, monograph, photograph, **2** an instrument that records, as seismograph, tachograph and cardiograph.

gynaec-, gynaeco- a prefix meaning female, woman, as gynaecology.

-hand a suffix meaning **1** worker, as deckhand, farmhand and cowhand, **2** position, as right-hand and left-hand.

haem-, haemo- a prefix meaning blood, as haemorrhage and haematology.

hemi- a prefix meaning half, as hemisphere.

hetero- a prefix meaning other, another, different, as heterosexual.

holo- a prefix meaning complete, whole, as holistic

homo- a prefix meaning same, as in homogenous, homonym and homosexual.

-hood a suffix meaning state or condition, as babyhood, childhood, manhood, priesthood, womanhood and widowhood.

hydro- a prefix meaning water, as hydroelectric and hydrophobia. It also means 'hydrogen', as in hydrochloride.

hyper- a prefix meaning over, above, as hyperactive, hypercritical and hypersensitive.

hypo- a prefix meaning under, as hypothermia and hypodermic.

-ian a suffix indicating **1** a profession, job or pastime, as comedian, musician, optician, physician, **2** proper names, as Dickensian, Orwellian and Shakesperian.

-iana a suffix which is a form of form of -ana and indicates memorabilia or collections relating to people or places of note, as Churchilliana.

-ible see **-able.**

-ics a suffix indicating science or study, as electronics, genetics, and politics.

-ify a suffix indicating 'making or becoming', as clarify, purify, satisfy and simplify.

infra- a prefix meaning below or beneath, as infrared and infrastructure.

-in a suffix meaning **1** in or into, as income, inside and invade, **2** not, as incurable, incapable and inconvenient

-ine a suffix indicating 'belonging to', as canine, divine and feline.

-ing a suffix used to form the present participle of verbs, as living, going and running.

inter- a prefix meaning between, as in intercity, intercontinental and interstate.

intra- a prefix meaning within, as intravenous.

ise and **-ize** are both verb endings. In British English there are many verbs that can be spelt ending in either **-ise** or **-ize**, as 'computerise/ize', 'economise/ize', 'finalise/ize', 'hospitalise/ize', 'modernise/ize', 'organise/ize', 'realise/ize', 'theorise/ize'. There are a few verbs that cannot be spelt **-ize**. These include 'advertise', 'advise', 'comprise', 'despise', 'exercise', 'revise', 'supervise' and 'televise'.

-ish a suffix meaning **1** somewhat, as baldish, smallish and youngish, **2** nationality, as Spanish, Turkish and Polish.

-ism a suffix indicating **1** a state or condition, as conservatism, egotism and heroism, sometimes an abnormal state, as alcoholism. **2** doctrine, theory or system of beliefs, as Catholicism and Marxism. **3** discrimination or prejudice, as ageism, discrimination on the grounds of age, often against old or older people, classicism, discrimination on the grounds of social class, racism, discrimination on the grounds of race and sexism, discrimination on the grounds of sex or gender, often against women.

iso- a prefix meaning equal, as in isobar, isotherm and isosceles.

-ist a suffix indicating believer, supporter, practitioner, as in atheist, fascist, feminist and Methodist.

-ite a suffix indicating a believer, supporter, practitioner, as in Thatcherite and Trotskyite.

-itis a suffix indicating an illness or disease, as bronchitis, a disease of the chest and hepatitis, a disease of the liver.

-ize see **-ise**.

kilo- a prefix meaning a thousand, as in kilogram, kilohertz, kilolitre, kilometre and kilowatt.

-kin a suffix that indicates a diminutive or smaller version, as in lambkin and mannikin.

-kind a suffix indicating a group of people, as in humankind, mankind, womankind.

-less a suffix meaning **1** without or lacking added to nouns to form adjectives, as expressionless, fearless, harmless, homeless and hopeless, **2** without being able to be measured, as ageless, countless, priceless and timeless.

-let a suffix indicating a diminutive or smaller form of something, as in booklet, coverlet, droplet, islet, piglet, starlet and streamlet.

-like a suffix indicating similarity, as in childlike, dreamlike, lifelike and warlike.

-ling a suffix indicating a diminutive or smaller version of something, as duckling, gosling and nestling.

-logue a suffix meaning conversation or discussion, as dialogue, monologue, prologue and travelogue.

-ly a common adverbial ending, as hurriedly, sharply and tightly.

macro- a prefix meaning large in size or scope, as in macrobiotic, macrocosm and macrostructure.

-mania a suffix indicating abnormal or obsessive behaviour, as kleptomania and pyromania.

mal- a prefix meaning **1** bad, unpleasant, as malodorous, having an unpleasant smell, **2** imperfect, faulty, as malformation and malfunctioning.

-man a suffix used with nouns to form nouns indicating someone's job, as barman, chairman, clergyman, policeman and salesman. In modern usage, when attempts are being made to remove sexism from the language, alternatives have been sought for any words ending in -man. Formerly, words ending in -man were often used whether or not the person referred to was definitely known to be a man. Different ways have been found to avoid the sexism of -man. Salesman has been changed in many cases to salesperson, chairman often becomes chairperson or chair. Similarly, fireman has become fire-fighter and policeman frequently becomes police officer.

-mate a suffix referring to someone who shares something with someone, as classmate, room, schoolmate, team-mate and workmate.

mega- a prefix meaning very large, as megabucks and megastar. Many words using mega- in this way are modern and many are also informal or slang. In technical language mega- means a million times bigger than the unit to which it is attached, as in megabyte, megacycle, megahertz and megawatt.

meta- a prefix meaning alteration or transformation, as metamorphosis.

-meter a suffix meaning a measuring instrument, as altimeter, barometer, speedometer and thermometer.

-metre a suffix indicating meter, the unit of length, as centimetre, kilometre and millimetre.

micro- a prefix meaning very small, as microscope and microsurgery.

milli- a prefix meaning a thousand, as millisecond and millennium.

mini- a prefix meaning very small or least, as minimum, minimal, and miniature. Mini- is frequently used to form modern words, as minibus, minicab, mini-computer, minicruise and miniskirt. Modern words beginning with mini- can often be spelt either with a hyphen or without.

mis- a prefix meaning badly, wrongly, as in misbehave, miscalculate, mistreat and misunderstanding.

-monger a suffix meaning dealer, trader, as fishmonger and ironmonger. As well as being used for occupations in which people sell things, it is used for people who 'trade' in less tangible things, as in gossipmonger, rumourmonger, scaremonger and warmonger.

mono- a prefix meaning one or single, as monochrome, monologue, monoplane and monosyllabic.

multi- a prefix indicating many, as in multiply and multitude. Multi- is frequently used to form new modern words, as in multimedia, multi-purpose, multi-storey and multi-talented.

-naut a suffix meaning navigator, as in astronaut and cosmonaut.

neo- a prefix meaning new or recent, as neologism and neo-natal.

neuro- a prefix meaning nerve, as neurology, neuron and neurosurgery.

non- a prefix meaning not, as nonsense and nonconformist.

-ock a suffix indicating a diminutive form, as hillock and bullock.

-ocracy a suffix meaning a form of government, as democracy, bureaucracy and meritocracy.

-ology a suffix meaning study of, as biology and geology.

oholic *see* -aholic.

-ology a suffix meaning study of, as in biology, geology and technology.

omni- a prefix meaning all, as in omnipotent and omnivorous.

-osis a suffix meaning **1** a disease as tuberculosis. **2** a development or process , as metamorphosis, a complete or major change.

para- a prefix meaning **1** beside, as paramilitary, paramedic and paranormal. **2** (defence) against, as parasol and parapet.

pen- a prefix meaning almost, as peninsula and penultimate.

per- a prefix meaning through, as permit.

peri- a prefix meaning round, as perimeter and periphery.

-phile a suffix meaning someone who loves or likes someone or something very much, as Francophile, someone who loves France, bibliophile, someone who loves books.

-phobe a suffix meaning someone who hates or fears someone or something very much, as Europhobe and Francophobe. The condition has the suffix **-phobia**, as Europhobia, and there is a whole range of conditions of this kind, as claustrophobia, hatred or fear of enclosed spaces. *See* section in the **Wordfinder** on **Phobias**.

-phone a suffix meaning sound or voice, as megaphone, telephone and saxophone.

poly- a prefix meaning more than one, many, as polyandry, the practice of having more than one husband.

-person *see* -man.

post- a prefix meaning after, as postpone, postscript and post-war.

pre- a prefix meaning before, as precede, predict and preface.

pro- a prefix meaning **1** on or forth, as proceed and progress, **2** before, as prologue and prophet. **3** in favour of, as pro-British and pro-hunting.

pseudo- a prefix meaning false, spurious or sham, as pseudo-literary and pseudo-leather.

psych-, psycho- meaning mind, as psychiatry and psychology.

re- a prefix meaning **1** back, as return, resign and retract, **2** again, as reconsider and retrial.

retro- a prefix indicating back, backwards, as retrograde, retrospect and retrorocket.

semi- a prefix meaning half, as semicircle and semi-detached.

-ship a suffix indicating a state or quality, as friendship, hardship and leadership

sub- a prefix meaning under, as submarine, submerge and subconscious.

super- a prefix meaning over, as supervise, supernatural and superfluous.

syn- a prefix meaning together, as synthesis and synonym

techno- a prefix meaning craft or skill, as technical and technology.

tele- a prefix meaning distance, as telephone, telescope and television.

-tor a prefix indicating a person, especially a person who does something, as actor, sponsor and victor.

trans- a prefix meaning across, as transaction, translate and trans-Atlantic.

-trix a prefix indicating a female equivalent, as proprietrix of proprietor, now not very common.

un- a prefix indicating **1** not, as unclean, untrue and unwise, **2** back, reversal, as in undo, unfasten and untie.

uni- a prefix meaning one, as in unicycle, unilateral and unity.

vice- a prefix meaning in place of, as vice-president and vice-chancellor.

-ward, -wards a suffix indicating direction, as homeward, seaward and outwards.

-ware a suffix meaning manufactured goods, as glassware and silverware.

-ways a suffix indicating manner, way or direction, as sideways.

-wise a suffix indicating **1** manner, way, or direction as clockwise, lengthwise and otherwise, **2** with reference to, as careerwise, **3** clever, sensible, as streetwise.

-work a suffix indicating **1** material from which something is made, as ironwork and woodwork, **2** a job or activity, as farmwork, housework and needlework.

Eponyms

An **eponym** refers to a person after whom something is named. The name of the thing in question can also be referred to as an eponym, or it can be said to be **eponymous**, eponymous being the adjective from eponym. English has several eponymous words. Some examples are listed below together with their derivations:

Bailey bridge, a type of temporary military bridge that can be assembled very quickly, called after Sir Donald **Bailey** (1901–85), the English engineer who invented it.

Bowie knife, a type of hunting knife with a long curving blade, called after the American soldier and adventurer, James **Bowie** (1799–1836), who made it popular.

cardigan, a knitted jacket fastened with buttons called after the Earl of **Cardigan** (1797–1868) who was fond of wearing such a garment and was the British cavalry officer who led the unsuccessful Charge of the Light Brigade during the Crimean War (1854).

Celsius the temperature scale, called after the Swedish astronomer, Anders **Celsius** (1701–44).

freesia, a type of sweet-smelling flower, called after the German physician, Friedrich Heinrich Theodor **Freese** (died 1876).

garibaldi, a type of biscuit with a layer of currants in it, called after Giuseppe **Garibaldi** (1807–1882), an Italian soldier patriot who is said to have enjoyed such biscuits.

Granny Smith, a variety of hard green apple, called after the Australian gardener, Maria Ann Smith, known as **Granny Smith** (died 1870), who first grew the apple in Sydney in the 1860s.

greengage, a type of greenish plum, called after Sir William **Gage** who introduced it into Britain from France (1777–1864).

leotard, a one-piece, close-fitting garment worn by acrobats and dancers, called after the French acrobat, Jules **Leotard** (1842–70), who introduced the costume as a circus garment.

mackintosh, a type of raincoat, especially one made of rubberized cloth, called after the Scottish chemist, Charles **Mackintosh** (1766–1843), who patented it in the early 1820s.

praline, a type of confectionery made from nuts and sugar, is called after Count Plessis-**Praslin** (1598–1675), a French field marshal, whose chef is said to have been the first person to make the sweet.

plimsoll, a type of light rubber-soled canvas shoe, called after the English shipping reform leader, Samuel **Plimsoll** (1824–98). The shoe is so named because the upper edge of the rubber was thought to resemble the **Plimsoll** Line, the set of markings on the side of a ship which indicate the levels to which the ship may be safely loaded. The Plimsoll Line became law in 1876.

salmonella, the bacteria that causes some diseases such as food poisoning, called after Daniel Elmer **Salmon** (1850–1914), the American veterinary surgeon who identified it.

sandwich, a snack consisting of two pieces of buttered bread with a filling, called after the Earl of **Sandwich** (1718–92) who was such a compulsive gambler that he would not leave the gaming tables to eat, but had some cold beef between two slices of bread brought to him.

saxophone, a type of keyed brass instrument often used in jazz music, called after Adolphe **Sax** (1814–94), the Belgium instrument-maker who invented it.

shrapnel, an explosive projectile that contains bullets or fragments of metal and a charge that is exploded before impact, called after the British army officer, Henry **Shrapnel** (1761–1842), who invented it.

stetson, a type of wide-brimmed, high-crowned felt hat, called after its designer, the American hat-maker, John Batterson **Stetson** (1830–1906).

trilby

wellington

trilby, a type of soft felt hat with an indented crown, called after *Trilby*, the dramatized version of the novel by the English writer, George du Maurier. The heroine of the play, Trilby O'Ferrall, wore such a hat.

wellington, a waterproof rubber boot that extends to the knee, called after the Duke of **Wellington** (1769–1852), who defeated Napoleon at Waterloo (1815).

Homographs, Homonyms and Homophones

Homographs

A homograph is a word that is spelt the same as another word but has a different meaning and pronunciation. Some examples are:

bow, pronounced to rhyme with how, a verb meaning to bend the head or body as a sign of respect or in greeting, etc, as in 'The visitors bowed to the emperor' and 'The mourners bowed their heads as the coffin was lowered into the grave'.

bow, pronounced to rhyme with low, a noun meaning a looped knot, a ribbon tied in this way', as in 'She tied her hair in a bow and 'She wears blue bows in her hair'.

lead, pronounced leed, a verb meaning to show the way, as in 'The guide will lead you down the mountain'.

lead, pronounced led, a noun meaning a type of greyish metal, as in 'They are going to remove any water pipes made from lead'.

row, pronounced to rhyme with low, a noun meaning a number of people or things arranged in a line', as in 'The princess sat in the front row'.

row, pronounced to rhyme with how, a noun meaning a quarrel, a disagreement, as in 'He has had a row with his neighbour over repairs to the garden wall'.

slough, pronounced to rhyme with rough, a verb meaning to cast off, as in 'The snake had sloughed off its old skin'.

slough, pronounced to rhyme with how, a noun meaning a swamp, as in 'Get bogged down in a slough' and 'in the Slough of Despond'.

sow, pronounced to rhyme with low, a verb meaning to scatter seeds in the earth, as in 'In the spring the gardener sowed some flower seeds in the front garden'.

sow, pronounced to rhyme with how, a noun meaning a female pig, as in 'The sow is in the pigsty with her piglets'.

Homonyms

A homonym is a word that has the same spelling and the same pronunciation as another word but has a different meaning from it. Examples include:

bill, a noun meaning a written statement of money owed, as in 'You must pay the bill for the conversion work immediately', or a written or printed advertisement, as in 'We were asked to deliver handbills advertising the play'.

bill, a noun meaning a bird's beak, as in 'The seagull has injured its bill'.

fair, an adjective meaning attractive, as in 'fair young women'; light in colour, as in 'She has fair hair'; fine, not raining, as in 'I hope it keeps fair'; just, free from prejudice, as in 'We felt that the referee came to a fair decision'.

fair, a noun meaning a market held regularly in the same place, often with stalls, entertainments and rides (now often simply applying to an event with entertainments and rides without the market), as in 'He won a coconut at the fair'; a trade exhibition, as in 'the Frankfurt Book Fair'.

pulse, a noun meaning the throbbing caused by the contractions of the heart, as in 'The patient has a weak pulse'.

pulse, a noun meaning the edible seeds of any of various crops of the pea family, as lentils, peas and beans, as in 'Vegetarians eat a lot of food made with pulses'.

row, a verb, pronounced to rhyme with low, meaning to propel a boat by means of oars, as in 'He plans to row across the Atlantic single-handed'.

row, a noun, pronounced to rhyme with low, meaning a number of people or things arranged in a line, as in 'We tried to get into the front row to watch the procession'

Homophones

A homophone is a word that is pronounced in the same way as another but is spelt in a different way and has a different meaning. Examples include:

aisle, a noun meaning a passage between rows of seats in a church, theatre, cinema etc, as in 'The bride walked down the aisle on her father's arm'.

isle, a noun meaning an island, as in 'the Isle of Wight'.

alter, a verb meaning to change, as in 'They have had to alter their plans'.

altar, a noun meaning in the Christian church, the table on which the bread and wine are consecrated for Communion and which serves as the centre of worship, as in 'The priest moved to the altar, from where he dispensed Communion', 'There is a holy painting above the altar'; or 'a raised structure on which sacrifices are made or incense burned in worship', as in 'The Druids made human sacrifices on the altar of their gods'.

ail, a verb meaning to be ill, as in 'The old woman is ailing'; or to be the matter, to be wrong, as in 'What ails you?'

ale, a noun meaning a kind of beer, as in 'a pint of foaming ale'.

blew, a verb, the past tense of the verb to blow, as in 'They blew the trumpets loudly'.

blue, a noun and adjective meaning a colour of the shade of a clear sky, as in 'She wore a blue dress'.

boar, a noun meaning a male pig, as in 'a dish made with wild boar'.

bore, a verb meaning to make tired and uninterested, as in 'The audience was obviously bored by the rather academic lecture'.

bore, a verb, the past tense of the verb to bear, as in 'They bore their troubles lightly'.

cereal, a noun meaning a plant yielding grain suitable for food, as in 'countries which grow cereal crops' and a prepared food made with grain, as in 'We often have cereal for breakfast'.

serial, a noun meaning a story or television play which is published or appears in regular parts, as in 'the final instalment of the magazine serial which she was following'.

cite, a verb meaning to quote or mention by way of example or proof, as in 'The lawyer cited a previous case to try and get his client off'.

sight, a noun meaning the act of seeing, as in 'They recognized him at first sight'.

site, a noun meaning a location, place, as in 'They have found a site for the new factory'.

feat, a noun meaning a notable act or deed, as in 'The old man received an award for his courageous feat'.

feet, a noun, the plural form of foot, as in 'The child got her feet wet from wading in the puddle'.

none, a pronoun meaning not any, as in 'They are demanding money but we have none'.

nun, a noun meaning a woman who joins a religious order and takes vows of poverty, chastity and obedience, as in 'She gave up the world to become a nun'.

know, a verb meaning to have understanding or knowledge of, as in 'He is the only one who knows the true facts of the situation', and 'to be acquainted with', as in 'I met her once but I don't really know her'.

no, an adjective meaning not any, as in 'We have no food left'.

rite, a noun meaning a ceremonial act or words, as in 'rites involving witchcraft'.

right, an adjective meaning correct, as in 'Very few people gave the right answer to the question'.

write a verb meaning to form readable characters, as in 'He writes regularly for the newspapers'.

stare, a verb and noun meaning to look fixedly and a fixed gaze, as in 'She stared at him in disbelief when he told her the news' and 'He has the stare of a basilisk'.

stair, a noun meaning a series of flights of stairs, as in 'The old lady is too feeble to climb the stairs to her bedroom'.

Euphemism

Euphemism is a term given to an expression that is a milder, more pleasant, less direct way of saying something that might be thought to be too harsh or direct. English has a great many euphemisms, many of these referring to specific areas of life. Euphemisms range from the high-flown, to the coy, to slang. Some examples of euphemisms, and of the areas in which they tend to occurs, are listed below:

euphemisms for die or be dead: be in the arms of Jesus, be laid to rest, be with one's maker, be no longer with us, be with the Lord, be written out of the script, bite the dust, cash in one's chips, croak, depart this life, go to a better place, go the way of all flesh, go to one's long home, go to the happy hunting grounds, have been taken by the grim reaper, have bought it, have breathed one's last, have gone to a better place, kick the bucket, meet one's end, pass away, pay the supreme sacrifice, pop off, push up the daisies, rest in peace, shuffle off this mortal coil, slip one's rope, turn up one's toes.

euphemisms for old: getting on a bit, not as young as one was, not in the first flush of youth, in the sunset years, in the twilight years, of advanced years, so many years young (as in '90 years young').

euphemisms for suicide: do away with oneself, die by one's own hand, end it all, make away with oneself, take one's own life, take the easy way out, top oneself.

euphemisms for to dismiss: declare (someone) redundant, deselect, dispense with (someone's) services, give early retirement to, give (someone) a golden handshake, give (someone) his/her marching orders, let (someone) go, not to renew (someone's) contract, to rationalize staff.

euphemisms for drunk: blotto, feeling no pain, happy, half-cut, legless, merry, one over the eight, plastered, three sheets to the wind, tiddly, tipsy, tired and emotional, squiffy, well-oiled.

euphemisms for naked: in a state of nature, in one's birthday suit, in the buff, in the nuddy, in the raw, starkers, without a stitch, wearing only a smile.

euphemisms for pregnant: awaiting the patter of tiny feet, expecting, expecting a happy event, in a delicate condition, in an interesting condition, in the club, in the family way, in the pudding club, up the pole, up the spout, with a bun in the oven.

euphemisms for to have sexual intercourse: be intimate with, do it, get one's end away, go to bed with, have it off with, make love, make out, sleep with, score.

euphemisms for sexual intercourse: hanky panky, intimacy, nookie, roll in the hay, rumpy pumpy/rumpty pumpty.

euphemisms for to go to the toilet: answer the call of nature, freshen up, go somewhere, pay a visit, powder one's nose, spend a penny, take a slash, wash one's hands.

euphemisms for toilet: bathroom, bog, can, john, karzy, powder room, rest room, the facilities, the conveniences, the geography of the house, the little boys' room/the little girls' room, the littlest room, the smallest room, the plumbing, wash room.

euphemisms and political correctness: Many of the expressions advocated by the politically correct movement for viewing physical and mental disabilities in a more positive light are in fact euphemisms. These include 'aurally challenged' for 'deaf', 'optically challenged' for 'blind', and 'uniquely abled' for 'physically disabled'.

Irregular Verbs and Nouns

Irregular verbs

Irregular verbs are verbs that do not conform to the usual pattern of the addition of *-ed* to the past tense and past participle. They fall into several categories.

One category concerns those which have the same form in the past tense and past participle forms as the infinitive and do not end in *-ed*, like regular verbs. These include:

infinitive	past tense	past participle
bet	bet	bet
burst	burst	burst
cast	cast	cast
cost	cost	cost
cut	cut	cut
hit	hit	hit
hurt	hurt	hurt
let	let	let
put	put	put
set	set	set
shed	shed	shed
shut	shut	shut
slit	slit	slit
split	split	split
spread	spread	spread

Some irregular verbs have two past tenses and two past participles which are the same, as in:

infinitive	past tense	past participle
burn	burned, burnt	burned, burnt,
dream	dreamed, dreamt	dreamed, dreamt,
dwell	dwelled, dwelt	dwelled, dwelt,
hang	hanged, hung,	hanged, hung
kneel	kneeled, knelt,	kneeled, knelt
lean	leaned, leant	learned, learnt
leap	leaped, leapt,	leaped, leapt
learn	learned, learnt	learned, learnt
light	lighted, lit	lighted, lit
smell	smelled, smelt	smelled, smelt
speed	speeded, sped	speeded, sped
spill	spilled, spilt	spilled, spilt
spoil	spoiled, spoilt	spoiled, spoilt
weave	weaved, woven	weaved, woven
wet	wetted, wet	wetted, wet,

Some irregular verbs have past tenses that do not end in *-ed* and have the same form as the past participle. These include:

infinitive	past tense	past participle
bend	bent	bent

infinitive	past tense	past participle
bleed	bled	bled
breed	bred	bred
build	built	built
cling	clung	clung
dig	dug	dug
feel	felt	felt
fight	fought	fought
find	found	found
flee	fled	fled,
fling	flung	flung
get	got	got
grind	ground	ground
hear	heard	heard
hold	held	held
keep	kept	kept
lay	laid	laid
lead	led	led
leave	left	left
lend	lent	lent
lose	lost	lost
make	made	made
mean	meant	meant
meet	met	met
pay	paid	paid
rend	rent	rent
say	said	said
seek	sought	sought
sell	sold	sold
send	sent	sent
shine	shone	shone
shoe	shod	shod
sit	sat	sat
sleep	slept	slept
slide	slid	slid
sling	slung	slung
slink	slunk	slunk
spend	spent	spent
stand	stood	stood
stick	stuck	stuck
sting	stung	stung
strike	struck	struck
string	strung	strung
sweep	swept	swept
swing	swung	swung
teach	taught	taught
tell	told	told
think	thought	thought
understand	understood	understood
weep	wept	wept
win	won	won
wring	wrung	wrung

mow   **shrink**

Some irregular verbs have regular past tense forms but two possible past participles, one of which is regular. These include:

infinitive	past tense	past participle
mow	mowed	mowed, mown
prove	proved	proved, proven
sew	sewed	sewn, sewed
show	showed	showed, shown
sow	sowed	sowed, sown
swell	swelled	swelled, swollen

Some irregular verbs have past tenses and past participles that are different from each other and different from the infinitive. These include:

infinitive	past tense	past participle
arise	arose	arisen
awake	awoke	awoken
bear	bore	borne
begin	began	begun
bid	bade	bidden
bite	bit	bitten
blow	blew	blown
break	broke	broken
choose	chose	chosen
do	did	done
draw	drew	drawn
drink	drank	drunk
drive	drove	driven
eat	ate	eaten
fall	fell	fallen
fly	flew	flown
forbear	forbore	forborne
forbid	forbade	forbidden
forgive	forgave	forgiven
forget	forgot	forgotten
forsake	forsook	forsaken
freeze	froze	frozen
forswear	forswore	foresworn
give	gave	given
go	went	gone
grow	grew	grown
hew	hewed	hewn
hide	hid	hidden
know	knew	known
lie	lay	lain
ride	rode	ridden
ring	rang	rung
saw	sawed	sawn
see	saw	seen
rise	rose	risen
shake	shook	shaken
shrink	shrank	shrunk

infinitive	past tense	past participle
slay	slew	slain
speak	spoke	spoken
spring	sprang	sprung
steal	stole	stolen
stink	stank	stunk
strew	strewed	strewn
stride	strode	stridden
strive	strove	striven
swear	swore	sworn
swim	swam	swum
take	took	taken
tear	tore	torn
throw	threw	thrown
tread	trod	trodden
wake	woken	woke
wear	wore	worn
write	written	wrote

Irregular plural pouns

Irregular plurals refer to the plural form of nouns that do not form their plural in the regular way. Most nouns in English add -s to the singular form to form the plural form, as in *boy* to *boys*.

Some add -es to the singular form to form the plural, as in *church* to *churches*. Nouns ending in a consonant followed by -y have -ies as a regular plural ending. Thus *fairy* becomes *fairies* and *berry* becomes *berries*. The foregoing are all examples of *regular plurals*.

Irregular plurals include words that are different in form from the singular forms and do not simply add an ending. These include *men* from *man*, *women* from *woman* and *mice* from *mouse*.

Some irregular plurals are formed by changing the vowel of the singular forms, as in *feet* from *foot*, *geese* from *goose* and *teeth* from *tooth*.

Some irregular plural forms are formed by adding -en, as *oxen* from *ox* and *children* from *child*.

Some nouns ending in -f form plurals in -ves, as in *loaf* to *loaves*, *half* to *halves*, *wife* to *wives* and *wolf* to *wolves*, but some have alternative endings, as *hoof* to either *hoofs* or *hooves*, and some form regular plurals unchanged, as *roof* to *roofs*.

Some irregular plural forms are the original foreign plural forms of words adopted into English, for example *stimuli* from *stimulus*, *phenomena* from *phenomenon*, *criteria* from *criterion*, *larvae* from *larva*. In modern usage there is a growing tendency to anglicize the plural forms of foreign words. Many of these coexist with the plural form, for example *thesauruses* and *thesauri*, *formulas* and *formulae*, *gateaus* and *gateaux* and *indexes* and *indices*. Sometimes the anglicized plural formed according to the regular English rules differs slightly in meaning from the irregular foreign plural. Thus, *indexes* usually applies to guides in books and *indices* is usually used in mathematics.

Some nouns have irregular plurals in that the plural form and the singular form are the same. These include *sheep*, *grouse* (the game-bird) and *salmon*. Also, some nouns have a regular plural and an irregular plural form. Thus, *brother* has the plural forms *brothers* and *brethren*, although *brethren* is now mainly used in a religious context and is archaic in general English.

PHRASEFINDER

English Idioms

A

- **A1** first class, of the highest quality. <A1 is the highest rating given to the condition of ships for Lloyd's Register, Lloyds of London being a major insurance company>.
- **from A to Z** thoroughly, comprehensively.

above

- **above board** open, honest and without trickery. <Card cheats tend to keep their cards under the table, or board>.
- **above (someone's) head** too difficult to understand.
- **get a bit above oneself** to become very vain or conceited.

accident

- **accidents will happen** things go wrong at some time in everyone's life.
- **a chapter of accidents** a series of misfortunes.

account

- **give a good account of oneself** to do well.

ace

- **within an ace of** very close to. <From the game of dice, ace being the term for the side of a dice with one spot>.

Achilles

- **Achilles' heel** the one weak spot in a person. <Achilles, the legendary Greek hero, is said to have been dipped in the River Styx by his mother at birth to make him invulnerable but his heel, by which she was holding him, remained unprotected and he was killed by an arrow through his heel>.

acid

- **acid test** a test that will prove or disprove something conclusively. <From the use of nitric acid to ascertain whether a metal was gold or not. If it was not gold the acid decomposed it>.

across

- **across the board** applying to everyone or to all cases.

act

- **act of God** a happening, usually sudden and unexpected, for which no human can be held responsible.
- **get in on the act** to become involved in some profitable or advantageous activity, especially an activity related to someone else's success.
- **get one's act together** to get organized.

action

- **action stations** a state of preparedness for some activity. <From positions taken up by soldiers in readiness for battle>.
- **get a piece** *or* **slice of the action** to be involved in something, get a share of something.

ad

- **ad hoc** for a particular (usually exclusive) purpose. <Latin, 'to this'>.
- **ad-lib** to speak without preparation, to improvise. <Latin, 'according to pleasure'>.

Adam <Refers to the biblical Adam>.

- **Adam's ale** water.
- **not to know (someone) from Adam** not to recognize (someone).
- **the old Adam in us** the sin or evil that is in everyone.

add

- **add fuel to the fire** to make a difficult situation worse.
- **add insult to injury** to make matters worse.

Adonis

- **an Adonis** a very attractive young man. <In Greek legend Adonis was a beautiful young man who was loved by Aphrodite, the goddess of love, and who was killed by a boar while hunting>.

advantage

- **have the advantage of (someone)** to recognize (someone) without oneself being recognized by that person.

aegis

- **under the aegis of (someone)** with the support or backing of (someone). <In Greek legend Aegis was the shield of the god Zeus>.

after

- **after a fashion** in a manner that is barely adequate.
- **after (someone's) own heart** to one's liking; liked or admired by (someone).

against

- **against the clock** in a hurry to get something done before a certain time.
- **be up against it** to be in a difficult or dangerous situation.

age

- **a golden age** a time of great achievement.
- **a ripe old age** a very old age.
- **of a certain age** no longer young.

agony

- **agony aunt** *or* **uncle** a woman or man who gives advice on personal problems either in a newspaper or magazine column, or on television or radio.
- **agony column** a newspaper or magazine column in which readers write in with their problems, which are answered by the agony aunt or uncle. <Originally a newspaper column containing advertisements for missing relatives and friends>.

ahead

- **ahead of the game** in an advantageous position; in front of one's rivals.
- **streets ahead of (someone** *or* **something)** much better than (someone or something).

air

- **air** *or* **wash one's dirty linen in public** to discuss private or personal matters in public.
- **clear the air** to make a situation less tense by settling disagreements.
- **hot air** boasting; empty or meaningless words.
- **into thin air** seemingly into nowhere.
- **put on airs** to behave as though one were superior to others, to act in a conceited way.
- **up in the air** uncertain, undecided.
- **walk on air** to be very happy.

Aladdin

- **Aladdin's cave** a place full of valuable or desirable objects. <From the tale of Aladdin in the Arabian Nights who gained access to such a cave with the help of the genie from his magic lamp>.

alive

- **alive and kicking** in a good or healthy condition.

all

- **all and sundry** everybody, one and all.
- **all chiefs and no Indians** a surplus of people wishing to give orders or to administrate and a deficiency of people willing to carry orders out or to do the work.
- **all ears** listening intently.
- **all in** exhausted.
- **all in one piece** safely, undamaged.
- **all over bar the shouting** at an end to all intents and purposes.
- **all set** ready to go, prepared.
- **all-singing, all-dancing** of a machine, system, very advanced with a great many modern features, sometimes not all necessary. <Used originally of a stage show to indicate how lavish it was>.

alley

- **alley cat** a wild or promiscuous person.

alliance

- **an unholy alliance** used of an association or partnership between two people or organizations that have nothing in common and would not normally work together, especially when this association has a bad purpose.

alma mater

- one's old university, college or school. <Latin, 'bountiful mother'>.

alpha

- **alpha and omega** the beginning and the end. <The first and last letters of the Greek alphabet>.

also

- **also-ran** an unsuccessful person. <A horse-racing term for a horse that is not one of the first three horses in a race>.

altar

- **be sacrificed on the altar of (something)** to be destroyed or suffer harm or damage so that something can be achieved or prosper.

alter

- alter ego a person who is very close or dear to someone. <Latin, 'other self'>.

altogether

- **in the altogether** in the nude.

Amazon

- a very strong or well-built woman. <In Greek legend the Amazons were a race of female warriors who had their right breasts removed in order to draw their bows better>.

American

- **as American as apple pie** typical of the traditional American way of life or culture.
- **the American dream** the hope of achieving success and prosperity through hard work, from the dreams which immigrants had when they landed in America to start a new life.

angel

- **an angel of mercy** a person who gives help and comfort, especially one who appears unexpectedly.
- **a fallen angel** a person who had formerly a good reputation for being virtuous or successful but no longer does so.
- **on the side of the angels** supporting or agreeing with what is regarded as being the good or the right side.

angry

- **angry young man** a person who expresses angry dissatisfaction with established social, political and intellectual values. <A term applied to British dramatist, John Osborne, author of the *play Look Back in Anger*>.

answer

- **the answer to a maiden's prayer** exactly what one desires and is looking for. <The answer to a maiden's prayer was thought to be an eligible bachelor>.

ant

- **have ants in one's pants** to be restless or agitated.

any

- **any old how** in an untidy and careless way.
- **anything goes** any kind of behaviour, dress, etc, is acceptable.

apart

- **be poles** or **worlds apart** to be completely different.

ape

- **go ape** to become extremely angry or excited

appearance

- **keep up appearances** to behave in public in such a way as to hide what is going on in private.

apple

- **in apple-pie order** with everything tidy and correctly arranged. <From French *nappe pliée*, 'folded linen', linen neatly laid out>.
- **rotten apple** a person who is bad or unsatisfactory and will have a bad influence on others.
- **the apple of (someone's) eye** a favourite, a person who is greatly loved by (someone). <Apple refers to the pupil of the eye>.
- **upset the apple-cart** to spoil plans or arrangements. <From the practice of selling fruit from carts in street markets>.

apron

- **tied to (someone's) apron-strings** completely dependent on a woman, especially one's mother or wife.

ark

- **like something out of the ark** very old-fashioned looking. <From Noah's ark in the Bible>.

arm

- **armed to the hilt** or **teeth** provided with all the equipment that one could possibly need.
- **be up in arms** to protest angrily.
- **chance one's arm** to take a risk.
- **cost an arm and a leg** to cost a great deal of money.
- **give one's right arm for (something)** to be willing to go to any lengths to get something.
- **keep (someone) at arm's length** to avoid becoming too close to or too friendly with someone.
- **the long arm of the law** the power or authority of the police.
- **right arm** chief source of help and support.
- **twist (someone's) arm** to force (someone) to do (something), to persuade (someone) to do (something).
- **with one arm tied behind one's back** very easily.
- **with open arms** welcomingly.

armour

- **chink in (someone's) armour** a weak or vulnerable spot in someone who is otherwise very strong and difficult to get through to or attack. <A knight in armour could be injured only through a flaw or opening in his protective armour>.
- **knight in shining armour** a person who it is hoped will save a situation or come to one's aid. <From medieval legends in which knights in armour came to the aid of damsels in distress>.

ashes

- **rake over the ashes** to discuss things that are passed, especially things that are best forgotten.
- **rise from the ashes** to develop and flourish out of ruin and destruction. <In Greek legend the phoenix, a mythical bird, who after a certain number of years of life set fire to itself and was then reborn from the ashes>.

attendance

- **dance attendance on (someone)** to stay close to (someone) in order to carry out all his or her wishes and so gain favour.

aunt

- **Aunt Sally** a person or thing that is being subjected to general abuse, mockery and criticism. <An Aunt Sally at a fair was a wooden model of a woman's head, mounted on a pole, at which people threw sticks or balls in order to win a prize>.

awakening

- **get/have a rude awakening** suddenly to become aware that a situation is not as good or pleasant as one thinks it is.

away

- **get away from it all** to escape from the problems of daily life, usually by taking a holiday.
- **the one that got away** a chance of success which one either did not or could not take advantage of at the time but which one always remembers. <Refers to a supposedly large fish which an angler fails to catch but about which he tells many stories>.

axe

- **get the axe** to be dismissed.

- **have an axe to grind** to have a personal, often selfish, reason for being involved in something. <From a story told by Benjamin Franklin, the American politician, about how a man had once asked him in his boyhood to demonstrate the working of his father's grindstone and had sharpened his own axe on it while it was working>.

baby

- **be left holding the baby** to be left to cope with a difficult situation that has been abandoned by the person who is really responsible for it.
- **throw out the baby with the bath water** accidentally to get rid of something desirable or essential when trying to get rid of undesirable or unnecessary things.

back

- **backhanded compliment** a supposed compliment that sounds more like criticism.
- **back number** a person or thing that is no longer of importance or of use. <Refers to an out-of-date or back copy of a newspaper or magazine>.
- **backseat driver 1** a passenger in a car who gives unasked-for and unwanted advice. **2** a person who is not directly involved in some activity but who offers unwanted advice.
- **back to the drawing board** to have to start again on a project or activity. <Refers to the board on which plans of buildings, etc, are drawn before being built>.
- **back to the grindstone** back to work.
- **bend over backwards** to go to great trouble.
- **get off (someone's) back** to stop harassing or bothering (someone).
- **have one's back to the wall** to be in a very difficult or desperate situation. <Someone being pursued has to face his or her pursuers or be captured when a wall prevents retreat>.
- **know (something) backwards** or **like the back of one's hand** to know all there is to know about (something).
- **know (someone** or **something) like the back of one's hand** to know (someone or something) very well indeed.

bacon

- **put one's back into (something)** to put the greatest possible effort into (something).
- **put (someone's) back up** to annoy (someone). <A cat's back arches up when it is angry>.
- **see the back of (someone** *or* **something)** to get rid of (someone or something), not to see (someone or something) again.
- **take a back seat** to take an unimportant or minor role.
- **talk through the back of one's head** to talk nonsense.
- **the back of beyond** a very remote place.

bacon

- **bring home the bacon 1** to earn money to support one's family. **2** to succeed in doing (something). <Perhaps from the winning of a greased pig as a prize at a country fair>.
- **save (someone's) bacon** to save someone from a danger or difficulty.

bad

- **hit a bad patch** to encounter difficulties or a difficult period.
- **in (someone's) bad** *or* **black books** out of favour with (someone). <Refers to an account book where bad debts are noted>.
- **with a bad grace** in an unwilling and bad-tempered way.

bag

- **bag of bones** a person who is extremely thin.
- **bag of tricks** the equipment necessary to do something.
- **in the bag** certain to be obtained. <From the bag used in hunting to carry what one has shot or caught>.
- **mixed bag** a very varied mixture.

bait

- **rise to the bait** to do what someone has been trying to get one to do. <Refers to fish rising to the surface to get the bait on an angler's line>.
- **swallow the bait** to accept completely an offer, proposal, etc, that has been made purely to tempt one. <As above>.

baker

- **baker's dozen** thirteen. <From the former custom of bakers adding an extra bun or

loaf to a dozen in order to be sure of not giving short weight>.

balance

- **in the balance** undecided, uncertain. <A balance is a pair of hanging scales>.
- **strike a balance** to reach an acceptable compromise.
- **tip the balance** to exert an influence which, although slight, is enough to alter the outcome of something.

bald

- **bald as a coot** extremely bald. <A coot is a bird with a spot of white feathers on its head>.

ball[1]

- **have a ball** to have a very enjoyable time.

ball[2]

- **a whole new ball game** used to emphasize how much a situation has changed.
- **be in the right ballpark** to be reasonably close to the amount which is required or wanted.
- **have the ball at one's feet** to be in a position to be successful. <From football>.
- **on the ball** alert, quick-witted, attentive to what is going on around one. <Referring to a football player who watches the ball carefully in order to be prepared if it comes to him>.
- **play ball** to act in accordance with someone else's wishes.
- **set** *or* **start the ball rolling** to start off an activity of some kind, often a discussion.

balloon

- **go down like a lead balloon** of a suggestion, idea, joke, etc, to be very badly received.
- **when the balloon goes up** when something serious, usually something that is expected and feared, happens. <From balloons sent up to undertake military observation in World War I, signifying that action was about to start>.

banana

- **go bananas** to go mad, to get extremely angry.

band

- **jump on the bandwagon** to show an interest in, or become involved in, something

bang

bear

simply because it is fashionable or financially advantageous. <Refers to a brightly coloured wagon for carrying the band at the head of a procession>.

* **looking as though one has stepped out of a bandbox** looking very neat and elegant. <Refers to a lightweight box formerly used for holding small articles of clothing such as hats>.

bang

* **bang one's head against a brick wall** to do (something) in vain.
* **go with a bang** to be very successful.

bank

* **break the bank** to leave (oneself or someone) without any money. <In gambling terms, to win all the money that a casino is prepared to pay out in one night>.

baptism

* **baptism of fire** a first, usually difficult or unpleasant, experience of something. <From Christian baptism>.

bare

* **the bare bones of (something)** the essential and basic details of (something).

bargain

* **get more than one bargained for** to encounter more difficulty than one had expected or was prepared for.
* **drive a hard bargain** to try to get a deal that is very favourable to oneself.

barge

* **wouldn't touch (someone *or* something) with a bargepole** to wish to have absolutely no contact with (someone or something).

bark

* **bark up the wrong tree** to have the wrong idea or impression about (something), to approach (something) in the wrong way. <From raccoon-hunting, in which dogs were used to locate trees that had raccoons in them>.
* **(someone's) bark is worse than his *or* her bite** a person is not as dangerous or as harmful as he or she appears to be. <Refers to a barking dog that is often quite friendly>.

barrel

* **have (someone) over a barrel** to get (someone) into such a position that one can

get him or her to do anything that one wants. <From holding someone over a barrel of boiling oil, etc, where the alternatives for the victim are to agree to demands or be dropped in the barrel>.

* **scrape the (bottom of the) barrel** to have to use someone or something of poor or inferior quality because that is all that is available. <Referring to the fact that people will only scrape out the bottom of an empty barrel if they have no more full ones>.

bat¹

* **off one's own bat** by oneself, without the help or permission of any one else. <From the game of cricket>.

bat²

* **blind as a bat** having very poor eyesight. <Referring to the fact that bats live their lives in darkness>.
* **like a bat out of hell** very quickly.

battle

* **win the battle, but lose the war** to get some of the things which you wanted from an argument, discussion, etc, but to lose your most important goal.

bay

* **keep (someone *or* something) at bay** to keep (someone or something) from coming too close.

be

* **the be-all and end-all** the most important aim or purpose. <From Shakespeare's *Macbeth*, Act 1, scene VII>.

beam

* **off beam 1** on the wrong course. **2** inaccurate. <From the radio beam that is used to bring aircraft to land in poor visibility>.
* **on one's beam ends** very short of money. <Originally a nautical term used to describe a ship lying on its side and in danger of capsizing completely>.

bean

* **know how many beans make five** to be experienced in the ways of the world.
* **spill the beans** to reveal a secret or confidential information.

bear

* **bear garden** a noisy, rowdy place. <Originally referred to a public place used for

bear-baiting, in which dogs were made to attack bears and get them angry, for public amusement>.

* **like a bear with a sore head** extremely bad-tempered.

beard

* **beard the lion in its den** to confront or face (someone) openly and boldly.

beat

* **beat about the bush** to approach (something) in an indirect way. <In game-bird hunting, bushes are beaten to make the birds appear>.
* **beat a (hasty) retreat** to run away. <Military orders used to be conveyed by a series of different drum signals>.
* **beat the drum** to try to attract public attention. <The noise of a drum makes people stop and listen>.
* **if you can't beat them (**or **'em), join them (**or **'em)** if you cannot persuade other people to think and act like you, the most sensible course of action is for you to begin to think and act like them.
* **off the beaten track** in an isolated position, away from towns or cities.

beauty

* **beauty is in the eye of the beholder** different people have different ideas of what is beautiful.
* **beauty is only skin deep** people have more important qualities than how they look.

beaver

* **eager beaver** a very enthusiastic and hard-working person.
* **work like a beaver** to work very industriously and enthusiastically. <Beavers are small animals that build dams, etc, with great speed and skill>.

beck

* **at (someone's) beck and call** having to be always available to carry out (someone's) orders or wishes. <Beck is a form of 'beckon'>.

bed

* **bed of roses** an easy, comfortable or happy situation.
* **get out of bed on the wrong side** to start the day in a very bad-tempered mood.

bee

* **have a bee in one's bonnet** to have an idea that one cannot stop thinking or talking about, to have an obsession. <A bee trapped under one's hat cannot escape>.
* **make a beeline for (someone** or **something)** to go directly and quickly to (someone or something). <Bees are reputed to fly back to their hives in straight lines>.

beer

* **not all beer and skittles** not consisting just of pleasant or enjoyable things.
* **small beer** something unimportant.

before

* **before one can say Jack Robinson** very rapidly, in an instant.

beg

* **beggar description** to be such that words cannot describe it. <From Shakespeare's *Antony and Cleopatra*, Act 2, scene II>.
* **beg the question** in an argument, to take for granted the very point that requires to be proved; to fail to deal effectively with the point being discussed.
* **going a-begging** unclaimed or unsold.

bell

* **bell the cat** to be the person in a group who undertakes something dangerous for the good of the group. <Refers to a story about some mice who wanted to put a bell on the neck of the cat so that they would hear it coming and who needed a volunteer to do it>.
* **ring a bell** to bring back vague memories.
* **saved by the bell** rescued from an unpleasant situation by something suddenly bringing that situation to an end. <From the bell that marks the end of a round in boxing>.

belt

* **below the belt** unfair. <In boxing, a blow below the belt is against the rules>.
* **belt and braces** used to describe extra precautions taken to make sure that all is well.
* **tighten one's belt** to reduce one's expenditure. <Belts have to be tightened if one loses weight in this case from having less to spend on food>.

bend

* **on bended knee** very humbly or earnestly.
* **round the bend** mad.

berth

- **give (someone) a wide berth** to keep well away from (someone). <Refers to a ship that keeps a good distance away from others>.

best

- **have the best of both worlds** to benefit from the advantages of two sets of circumstances.
- **put one's best foot forward** to make the best attempt possible.

bet

- **hedge one's bets** to try to protect oneself from possible loss, failure, disappointment, etc. <From betting the same amount on each side to make sure of not losing>.

better

- **have seen better days** to be no longer new or fresh.
- **the better part of (something)** a large part of (something), most of (something).
- **think better of (something)** to reconsider (something), to change one's mind about (something).

beyond

- **beyond the pale** beyond normal or acceptable limits. <The pale was an area of English government in Ireland in the 16th century>.

big

- **a big fish in a small pond** a person who seems better, more important, etc, than he or she is because he or she operates in a small, limited area.
- **the Big Apple** New York.
- **big guns** the most important people in an organization.
- **hit the big time** to be become extremely successful and famous
- **the Big Smoke** London.

bill

- **a clean bill of health** verification that someone is well and fit.
  <Ships were given clean bills of health and allowed to sail when it was certified that no one aboard had an infectious disease>.
- **fir** or **fill the bill** to be exactly what is required. <Refers originally to a handbill or public notice>.

- **foot the bill** to pay for something, usually something expensive.

bird

- **a bird in the hand is worth two in the bush** something that one already has is much more valuable than things that one might or might not acquire. <A bird in the bush might fly away>.
- **a little bird told me** I found out by a means which I do not wish to reveal.
- **birds of a feather flock together** people who share the same interests, ideas, etc, usually form friendships.
- **give (someone) the bird** of an audience, to express its disapproval of a performer by hissing or booing so that he or she leaves the stage. <From the resemblance of the noise of the audience to the hissing of geese>.
- **kill two birds with one stone** to fulfil two purposes with one action.
- **the birds and the bees** the basic facts of human sexual behaviour and reproduction.
- **the early bird catches the worm** a person who arrives early or acts promptly is in a position to gain advantage over others.

biscuit

- **take the biscuit** to be much worse than anything that has happened so far.

bit

- **champing at the bit** very impatient. <A horse chews at its bit when it is impatient>.
- **take the bit between one's teeth** to act on one's own and cease to follow other people's instructions or advice. <Refers to a horse escaping from the control of its rider>.

bite

- **bite off more than one can chew** to try to do more than one can without too much difficulty.
- **bite the bullet** to do something unpleasant but unavoidable with courage.
- **bite the dust** to die or cease to operate or function.
- **bite the hand that feeds one** to treat badly someone who has helped one.
- **have more than one bite at the cherry** to have more than one opportunity to succeed at something.

bitter   **bolt**

- **the biter bit** used to indicate a situation in which someone who has tried to harm or do wrong to someone has suffered in some way as a consequence of this action.

bitter
- **a bitter pill to swallow** something unpleasant or difficult that one has to accept.

black
- **as black as one is painted** as bad as everyone says one is.
- **black sheep** a member of a family or group who is not up to the standard of the rest of the group.
- **in black and white** in writing or in print.
- **in (someone's) black books** *same as* **in (someone's) bad books** *see* **bad.**
- **in the black** showing a profit, not in debt. <From the use of black ink to make entries on the credit side of a ledger>.

blanket
- **on the wrong side of the blanket** illegitimate.
- **wet blanket** a dull person who makes other people feel depressed.

blessing
- **a blessing in disguise** something that turns out to advantage after first seeming unfortunate.

blind
- **the blind leading the blind** referring to a situation in which the person who is in charge of others knows as little as they do.

blood
- **in cold blood** deliberately and calmly.
- **like getting blood out of a stone** very difficult, almost impossible.

blow
- **blow hot and cold** to keep changing one's mind or attitude.
- **blow one's own trumpet** to boast about one's achievements.
- **blow the gaff** to tell something secret, often something illegal, to someone, often the police. <Perhaps from gaff, meaning mouth>.
- **blow the whistle on (someone)** to reveal or report someone's wrongdoing so that it will be stopped. <From the practice of

blowing a whistle to indicate a foul in some ball games>.
- **see which way the wind blows** to wait and find out how a situation is developing before making a decision. <From sailing>.

blue
- **blue-eyed boy** a person who is someone's favourite.
- **bluestocking** an educated, intellectual woman. <From a group of women in the 18th century who met in London to discuss intellectual and philosophical issues and some of whom wore blue worsted stockings>.
- **once in a blue moon** hardly ever.
- **out of the blue** without warning.

bluff
- **call (someone's) bluff** to make (someone) prove that what he or she says is true is really genuine. <Refers to poker, the card game>.

board
- **go by the board** to be abandoned. <The board here is a ship's board or side, and to go by the board literally was to vanish overboard>.
- **sweep the board** to win all the prizes. <The board referred to is the surface on which card games are played and on which the bets are placed>.

boat
- **burn one's boats** to do something that makes it impossible to go back to one's previous position.
- **in the same boat** in the same situation.
- **miss the boat** to fail to take advantage of a opportunity.
- **push the boat out** to spend money in an extravagant way in order to celebrate something in a lavish way.
- **rock the boat** to do something to endanger or spoil a comfortable or happy situation.

bolt
- **a bolt from the blue** something very sudden and unexpected.
- **shoot one's bolt** to make one's final effort, have no other possible course of action.

bone

- **a bone of contention** a cause of dispute. <Dogs fight over bones>.
- **have a bone to pick with (someone)** to have a matter to disagree about with (someone). <From dogs fighting over a bone>.
- **make no bones about (something)** to have no hesitation or restraint about (saying or doing something openly). <Originally a reference to finding no bones in one's soup, which was therefore easier to eat>.
- **near the bone** 1 referring too closely to something that should not be mentioned; tactless. 2 slightly indecent or crude.

boo

- **would not say boo to a goose** to be extremely timid.

book

- **bring (someone) to book** to make (someone) explain or be punished for his or her actions. <Perhaps referring to a book where a police officer keeps a note of crimes>.
- **by the book** strictly according to the rules.
- **cook the books** illegally to alter accounts or financial records.
- **throw the book at (someone)** to criticize or punish (someone) severely, to charge (someone) with several crimes at once. <Literally, to charge someone with every crime listed in a book>.

boot

- **get the boot** to be dismissed or discharged from one's job.
- **hang up one's boots** to retire from work, to cease doing an activity. <From hanging up football boots after a game>.
- **lick (someone's) boots** to flatter (someone) and do everything he or she wants.
- **pull oneself up by one's bootstraps** to become successful through one's own efforts.
- **put the boot in (someone)** 1 to kick (someone) when he or she is already lying on the ground injured. 2 to treat (someone) cruelly or harshly after he or she has suffered already.
- **the boot is on the other foot** the situation has been completely turned round.
- **too big for one's boots** too conceited.

bottle

- **lose one's bottle** not to have the courage to do something or to go on with something

bottom

- **bottom drawer** a collection of articles for the home, which a young woman gathered together before her marriage.
- **hit rock bottom** to reach the lowest possible level.
- **the bottom line** 1 the most important point or part of something. 2 the result or outcome. <Refers to the bottom line in a financial statement which indicates the extent of the profit or loss>.

bow¹

- **bow and scrape** to behave in a very humble and respectful way.
- **take a bow** to accept acknowledgement of one's achievements. <As above>.

bow²

- **draw the long bow** to exaggerate. <An archer carries a spare bow in case one breaks>.
- **have another/more than one string to one's bow** to have another possibility, plan, etc, available to one.

brain

- **cudgel** or **rack one's brains** to think very hard.
- **pick (someone's) brains** to find out (someone's) ideas and knowledge about a subject so that one can put them to one's own use.

brass

- **get down to brass tacks** to consider the basic facts or issues of something.

bread

- **know which side one's bread is buttered** to know the course of action that is to one's greatest advantage.
- **on the breadline** with scarcely enough money to live on.
- **the greatest thing since sliced bread** a person or thing that is greatly admired.

breath

- **hold one's breath** to wait anxiously for something.
- **take (someone's) breath away** to surprise (someone) greatly.

- **waste one's breath** to say something that is not taken heed of.

breathe

- **breathe down (someone's) neck 1** to be very close behind (someone). **2** to be waiting impatiently for something from (someone).

brick

- **like a cat on hot bricks** very nervous or restless.
- **try to make bricks without straw** to try to do something without the necessary materials or equipment. <A biblical reference, from Pharaoh's command concerning the Israelites in Exodus 5:7>.

bridge

- **build bridges** to do something to help people who are in some kind of opposition to each other to understand each other so that they ar eable to establish a relationship or co-operate with each other.
- **cross a bridge when one comes to it** to worry about or deal with a problem only when it actually arises.

bright

- **bright-eyed and bushy-tailed** very cheerful and lively.
- **look on the bright side** to be optimistic, to see the advantages of one's situation.

broad

- **have broad shoulders** to be able to accept a great deal of responsibility, criticism, etc.
- **in broad daylight** during the day.

brother

- **am I my brother's keeper?** the actions or affairs of other people are not my responsibility. <From the biblical story of Cain and Abel, Genesis 4:9>.
- **Big Brother** a powerful person or organization thought to be constantly monitoring and controlling people's actions. <From the dictator in George Orwell's novel *1984*>.

brown

- **in a brown study** deep in thought.

bucket

- **a drop in the bucket** a very small part of what is needed.
- **kick the bucket** to die. <Bucket here is

perhaps a beam from which pigs were hung after being killed>.

- **weep buckets** to cry a great deal.

bull

- **hit the bull's eye** to do or say something that is very appropriate or relevant. <Refers to the exact centre of a dart board>.
- **like a bull at a gate** in a very unsubtle, unthinking way.
- **like a bull in a china shop** in a very clumsy way.
- **take the bull by the horns** to tackle (something) boldly.

bullet

- **get the bullet** to be dismissed or discharged.

burn

- **the burning question** a question of great interest to many people.

Burton

- **gone for a Burton** dead, ruined, broken, etc. <Originally a military term from Burton, a kind of ale>.

bus

- **busman's holiday** a holiday spent doing much the same as one does when one is at work. <Refers to a bus driver who drives a bus on holiday>.

bush

- **bush telegraph** the fast spreading of information by word of mouth. <A reference to the Australian bush>.

business

- **mean business** to be determined (to do something), to be serious.
- **mind one's own business** to concern oneself with one's own affairs and not interfere in those of other people.

butter

- **butterfingers** a person who often drops things.
- **look as though butter would not melt in one's mouth** to appear very innocent, respectable, etc.

butterfly

- **have butterflies in one's stomach** to have a fluttering sensation in one's stomach as a sign of nervousness.

cake

- **a piece of cake** something easy to do.
- **a slice** *or* **share of the cake** a share of something desirable or valuable.
- **have one's cake and eat it** *or* **eat one's cake and have it** to have the advantages of two things or situations when doing, possessing, etc, one of them would normally make the other one impossible.
- **sell** *or* **go like hot cakes** to sell very quickly.

cage

- **rattle (someone's) cage** to annoy or agitate (someone). <From visitors to a zoo rattling the cages of the animals to get them to react>.

calf

- **kill the fatted calf** to provide a lavish meal, especially to mark a celebration of someone's arrival or return. <From the parable of the prodigal son in the Bible, Luke 15:23>.

can

- **carry the can** to accept blame or responsibility, usually for something that someone else has done.

candle

- **burn the candle at both ends** to work and/ or to play during too many hours of the day.
- **cannot hold a candle to (someone)** to be not nearly as good or as talented as (someone). <Literally, someone who is not good enough even to hold a light while someone else does the work>.
- **the game is not worth the candle** something that is not worth the effort that has to be spent on it. <From the translation of the French phrase *le jeu n'en vaut la chandelle*, referring to a gambling session in which the amount of money at stake was not enough to pay for the candles required to give light at the game>.

canoe

- **paddle one's own canoe** to control one's own affairs without help from anyone else.

cap

- **cap in hand** humbly. <Removing one's cap in someone's presence is a sign of respect>.
- **if the cap fits, wear it** if what has been said

applies to you, then you should take note of it.
- **set one's cap at (someone)** to try to attract (someone of the opposite sex). <Perhaps a mistranslation of French *metter le cap*, to head towards>.

card

- **have a card up one's sleeve** to have an idea, plan of action, etc, in reserve to be used if necessary. <From cheating at cards>.
- **on the cards** likely. <From reading the cards in fortune-telling>.
- **play one's cards close to one's chest** to be secretive or non-communicative about one's plans or intentions. <From holding one's cards close to one in card-playing so that one's opponents will not see them>.
- **play one's cards right** to act in such a way as to take advantage of a situation.
- **put one's cards on the table** to make known one's plans or intentions. <In card-playing, to show one's opponent one's cards>.

carpet

- **sweep (something) under the carpet** to try to hide or forget about (something unpleasant).
- **the red carpet** special, respectful treatment. <Refers to the red carpet put down for a royal person to walk on during official visits>.

carrot

- **carrot and stick** reward as a method of persuasion.

carry

- **carry a torch for (someone)** to be in love with someone, especially with someone who does not return it. <A torch or a flame was regarded as symbolic of love>.

cart

- **put the cart before the horse** to do or say things in the wrong order.

Casanova

- **Casanova** a man who has relationships with many women. <From Giacomo Casanova, a famous 18th-century Italian lover and adventurer>.

Cassandra

- **Cassandra** a person who makes predictions about unpleasant future events but who is never believed. <In Greek legend, Cassandra, who was the daughter of Priam, king of Troy, had the gift of prophecy but was destined never to be believed. She predicted the fall of Troy>.

cast

- **cast pearls before swine** to offer something valuable or desirable to someone who does not appreciate it. <A biblical reference to Matthew 7:6>.

castle

- **castles in the air** *or* **castles in Spain** dreams or hopes that are unlikely ever to be realized.

cat

- **curiosity killed the cat** said as a warning not to pry into other people's affairs.
- **let the cat out of a bag** to reveal something secret or confidential, especially accidentally or at an inappropriate time. <Supposedly referring to a fairground trick in which a customer was offered a cat in a bag when he or she thought it was a piglet in the bag>.
- **like a scalded cat** in a rapid, excited way.
- **like something the cat brought** *or* **dragged in** very untidy or bedraggled.
- **not enough room to swing a cat** very little space.
- **not to have a cat's chance in hell** *or* **a cat's chance in hell** to have no chance at all.
- **play cat and mouse with (someone)** to treat (someone) in such a way that he or she does not know what is going to happen to them at any time. <A cat often plays with its prey, a mouse, before killing it>.
- **put** *or* **set the cat among the pigeons** to cause a disturbance, especially a sudden or unexpected one.
- **rain cats and dogs** to rain very heavily.
- **see which way the cat jumps** to wait and see what other people are going to do and how the situation is developing before deciding on one's course of action.
- **there's more than one way to kill** *or* **skin a cat** there's more than one way or method of doing things.
- **when the cat's away, the mice will play** when the person in charge or in control is not present the people whom he or she is in charge of will work less hard, misbehave, etc.

catch

- **catch (someone) napping** to surprise (someone) when he or she is unprepared or inattentive.
- **Catch 22** a situation in which one can never win or from which one can never escape, being constantly hindered by a rule or restriction that itself changes to block any change in one's plans; a difficulty that prevents one from escaping from an unpleasant or dangerous situation. <From the title of a novel by Joseph Heller>.
- **catch (someone) with his** *or* **her pants** *or* **trousers down** to surprise (someone) when he or she is unprepared or doing something wrong, especially when this causes embarrassment. <Refers to walking in on someone partially dressed>.

caviar

- **caviar to the general** something considered to be too sophisticated to be appreciated by ordinary people. <From Shakespeare's *Hamlet*, Act 2, scene II>.

ceiling

- **go through the ceiling** to rise very high, to soar.
- **hit the ceiling** *or* **roof** to lose one's temper completely.

chalice

- **hand/give (someone) a poisoned chalice** to be given something to do which seems an attractive proposition but which may well lead to failure or extreme difficulties.

chalk

- **as different as chalk and cheese** completely different.
- **chalk it up to experience** accept the inevitability of something.
- **not by a long chalk** not by a long way, by no means. <From the vertical chalk lines drawn to mark scores in a game, the longer lines representing the greater number of points>.

chance

- **have an eye to the main chance** to watch carefully for what will be advantageous or profitable to oneself.
- **not to have the ghost of a chance** not to have the slightest possibility of success.
- **change hands** to pass into different ownership.

change

- **change horses in mid-stream** to change one's opinions, plans, sides, etc, in the middle of something.
- **change one's tune** to change one's attitude or opinion.
- **ring the changes** to add variety by doing or arranging things in different ways.

chapter

- **chapter and verse** detailed sources for a piece of information. <From the method of referring to biblical texts>.

charity

- **charity begins at home** one must take care of oneself and one's family before concerning oneself with others.
- **cold as charity** extremely cold. <Charity is referred to as cold since it tends to be given to the poor and disadvantaged by organizations rather than by individual people and so lacks human feeling or warmth>.

charm

- **lead a charmed life** regularly to have good fortune and avoid misfortune, harm or danger.
- **work like a charm** to be very effective, to work very well.

chase

- **chase after rainbows** to spend time and effort in thinking about, or in trying to obtain, things that it is impossible for one to achieve.
- **cut to the chase** to start discussing or dealing with the most important part of something instead of wasting time on minor points. <Refers to the fact that in certain kinds of film a car chase is the most exciting part>.

cheek

- **cheek by jowl** side by side, very close together. ·

- **turn the other cheek** to take no action against someone who has harmed one, thereby giving him or her the opportunity to harm one again. <A biblical reference to Matthew 5:39, 'Whosoever shall smite thee on thy right cheek, turn to him the left one also'>.

cheese

- **hard cheese** bad luck, a sentiment usually expressed by someone who does not care about the misfortune.

Cheshire

- **grin like a Cheshire cat** to smile broadly so as to show one's teeth. <Refers to *Alice's Adventures in Wonderland* by Lewis Carroll, in which the Cheshire cat gradually disappears except for its smile>.

chest

- **get (something) off one's chest** to tell (someone) about something that is upsetting, worrying or annoying one.
- **old chestnut** an old joke, usually one no longer funny.
- **pull (someone's) chestnuts out of the fire** to rescue (someone) from a difficult or dangerous situation, often by putting oneself in difficulty or danger. <From a story by the 17th-century French writer La Fontaine, in which a monkey use a cat's paw to get hot nuts from a fire>.

chew

- **chew the cud** to think deeply about something.
- **chew the fat** to have a discussion or conversation.

chicken

- **chickens come home to roost** misdeeds, mistakes, etc, that come back with an unpleasant effect on the person who performed the misdeed, especially after a considerable time.
- **count one's chickens before they are hatched** to make plans which depend on something that is still uncertain.

child

- **child's play** something that is very easy to do.

chin

- **keep one's chin up** not to show feelings of depression, worry or fear.

- **take it on the chin** to accept or to suffer (something) with courage.

chip

- **a chip off the old block** a person who is very like one of his or her parents.

- **cash in one's chips** to die. <Refers to a gambler cashing in his or her chips or tokens in exchange for money at the end of a session>.

- **have a chip on one's shoulder** to have an aggressive attitude and act as if everyone is going to insult or ill-treat one, often because one feels inferior. <Refers to a former American custom by which a young man who wished to provoke a fight would place a piece of wood on his shoulder and dare someone to knock it off>.

- **have had one's chips** to have had, and failed at, all the chances of success one is likely to get. <Refers to gambling tokens>.

- **when the chips are down** when a situation has reached a critical stage. <A gambling terms indicating that the bets have been placed>.

choice

- **Hobson's choice** no choice at all; a choice between accepting what is offered or having nothing at all. <Refers to the practice of Tobias Hobson, an English stable-owner in the 17th century, of offering customers only the horse nearest the stable door>.

chop

- **chop and change** to keep altering (something), to keep changing (something).

- **get the chop 1** to be dismissed or discontinued. **2** to be killed.

chord

- **strike a chord** to be familiar in some way.

- **touch a chord** to arouse emotion or sympathy.

circle

- **come full circle** to return to the position or situation from which one started.

- **go round in circles** to keep going over the same ideas without reaching a satisfactory decision or answer.

- **run round in circles** to dash about and appear to be very busy without accomplishing anything.

- **vicious circle** an unfortunate or bad situation, the result of which produces the original cause of the situation or something similar. <In logic, the term for the fallacy of proving one statement by the evidence of another which is itself only valid if the first statement is valid>.

circus

- **a three-ring circus** a place where there is a lot of noise and a lot of confused activity going on.

clean

- **a clean slate** a record free of any discredit; an opportunity to make a fresh start. <Slates were formerly used for writing on in schools>.

- **come clean** to tell the truth about something, especially after lying about it.

- **keep one's nose clean** to keep out of trouble, to behave well or legally.

- **make a clean breast of (something)** to admit to (something), especially after having denied it.

- **make a clean sweep** to get rid of everything which is unnecessary or unwanted.

- **show a clean pair of heels** to run away very quickly.

- **squeaky clean** free of all guilt or blame. <Clean surfaces tend to squeak when wiped>.

- **take (someone) to the cleaners** to cause (someone) to spend or lose a great deal of money.

clear

- **clear as a bell** very easy to hear. <Bells, such as church bells, are very audible>.

- **clear as crystal** very easy to understand or grasp.

- **clear as mud** not at all easy to understand or grasp.

- **clear the decks** to tidy up, especially as a preparation for some activity or project. <Refers to getting a ship ready for battle>.

- **steer clear of (someone _or_ something)** to keep away from or avoid (someone or something).

- **the coast is clear** the danger or difficulty has now passed. <Probably a military term indicating that there were no enemy forces

near the coast and so an invasion was pos-
sible>.

cleft

- **in a cleft stick** unable to decide between
two equally important or difficult courses
of action.

clip

- **clip (someone's) wings** to limit the freedom, power or influence of (someone).
<From the practice of clipping the wings
of a bird to prevent it flying away>.

cloak

- **cloak-and-dagger** involving or relating to
a great deal of plotting and scheming.
<The combination of a cloak and a dag-
ger suggests conspiracy>.

clock

- **like clockwork** very smoothly, without
problems.
- **put back the clock** or **turn the clock back**
to return to the conditions or situation of
a former time.
- **round the clock** all the time; for twenty-
four hours a day.

close¹

- **behind closed doors** in secret.

close²

- **a close shave** something that was only just
avoided, especially an escape from danger,
failure, etc.

cloud

- **cloud cuckoo land** an imaginary place,
where everything is perfect; an unreal world.
- **every cloud has a silver lining** something
good happens for every bad or unpleasant
thing.
- **have one's head in the clouds** to be day-
dreaming and not paying attention to what
is going on around one.
- **on cloud nine** extremely happy.
- **under a cloud** under suspicion, in trouble.

coach

- **drive a coach and horses through (something)** to destroy (an argument etc) completely by detecting and making use of the
weak points in it. <Refers to the fact that
the defects (or holes) in the argument are
so large as to let a coach and horses through
them>.

coal

- **carry** or **take coals to Newcastle** to do
something that is completely unnecessary,
especially to take something to a place
where there is already a great deal of it.
<Refers to Newcastle in England which
was a large coal-mining centre>.
- **haul (someone) over the coals** to scold
(someone) very severely.

coat

- **cut one's coat according to one's cloth**
to organize one's ideas and aims, particularly one's financial aims, so that they are
within the limits of what one has or possesses.

cobweb

- **blow away the cobwebs** to make (someone) feel more energetic and alert after
feeling rather tired and dull.

cock

- **a cock-and-bull story** an absurd story that
is unlikely to be believed.
- **cock a snook at (someone)** to express
one's defiance or contempt of (someone). <Originally referring to a rude gesture of contempt made by putting the end
of one's thumb on the end of one's nose
and spreading out and moving one's fin-
gers>.
- **go off at half cock** to be unsuccessful
because of lack of preparation or because
of a premature start. <Refers to a gun that
fires too soon>.

coffee

- **wake up and smell the coffee** to become
more aware of and more realistic about
what is going on around one.

coin

- **pay (someone) back in his** or **her own
coin** to get one's revenge on someone who
has done harm to one by treating him or
her in the same way.
- **the other side of the coin** the opposite
argument, point of view, etc.

cold

- **get cold feet** to become nervous and
change one's mind about being involved in
(something).
- **give (someone) the cold shoulder** to act

in an unfriendly way to (someone) by ignoring him or her.

- **in a cold sweat** in a state of great fear or anxiety. <From the fact that the skin tends to become cold and damp when one is very frightened>.
- **make (someone's) blood run cold** to cause terror or great distress in (someone).
- **pour** *or* **throw cold water on (something)** to discourage enthusiasm for (something).

colour
- **change colour** to become either very pale or else very red in the face through fear, distress, embarrassment, anger, guilt, etc.
- **nail one's colours to the mast** to commit oneself to a point of view or course of action in a very obvious and final way. <Refers to a ship's colours or flag. If this was nailed to the mast it could not be lowered, lowering the flag being a sign of surrender>.
- **show oneself in one's true colours** to reveal what one is really like after pretending to be otherwise. <Refers to a ship raising its colours or flag to indicate which country or side it was supporting>.
- **with flying colours** with great success. <Refers to a ship leaving a battle with its colours or flag still flying as opposed to lowering them in surrender>.

common
- **common-or-garden** completely ordinary.

conjure
- **a name to conjure with** the name of someone very important, influential or well known. <The suggestion is that such people have magical powers>.

contradiction
- **a contradiction in terms** a statement, idea, etc, that contains a contradiction.

convert
- **preach to the converted** to speak enthusiastically in favour of something to people who already admire it or are in favour of it.

cook
- **too many cooks spoil the broth** if there are a great many people involved in a project they are more likely to hinder it than help it.

cookie
- **that's the way the cookie crumbles** that is the situation and one must just accept it. <Cookie is American English for biscuit>.

cool
- **cool as a cucumber** very calm and unexcited.
- **cool** *or* **kick one's heels** to be kept waiting.
- **keep one's cool** to remain calm.
- **lose one's cool** to become angry, excited etc.

copy
- **blot one's copybook** to spoil a previously good record of behaviour, achievement, etc, by doing something wrong.

corn
- **tread on (someone's) corns** to offend (someone).

corner
- **cut corners** to use less money, materials, effort, time, etc, than is usually required or than is required to give a good result.
- **from all (four) corners of the earth** from every part of the world, from everywhere.
- **in a tight corner** in an awkward, difficult or dangerous situation.
- **paint oneself into a corner** to get oneself into a difficult situation from which there is only one method of escape or action.
- **turn the corner** to begin to get better or improve.

cost
- **cost a bomb** *or* **a packet** to cost a very great deal of money.
- **cost an arm and a leg** to cost an excessive amount of money.
- **cost the earth** to cost a very great deal of money.

cotton
- **wrap (someone) in cotton wool** to be overprotective of (someone).

count
- **out for the count** unconscious or deeply asleep. <Refers to boxing where a boxer who has been knocked down by his opponent has to get up again before the referee counts to ten in order to stay in the match>.

courage

- **have the courage of one's convictions** to be brave enough to do what one thinks one should.
- **pluck up** *or* **screw up courage** to force oneself to be brave.

court

- **laugh (someone** *or* **something) out of court** not to give serious consideration to (someone or something). <Refers to a trivial legal case>.
- **pay court to (someone)** to try to gain the love of (someone).
- **the ball is in (someone's) court** it is (someone's) turn to take action.
- **rule (something) out of court** to prevent (something) from being considered for (something). <Refers to a court of law where evidence, etc, ruled out of court has no effect on the case>.

Coventry

- **send (someone) to Coventry** collectively to refuse to associate with (someone). <Perhaps from an incident in the English Civil War when Royalists captured in Birmingham were sent to the stronghold of Coventry>.

cow

- **a sacred cow** something that is regarded with too much respect for people to be allowed to criticize it freely. <The cow is considered sacred by Hindus>.
- **till** *or* **until the cows come home** for an extremely long time. <Cows walk very slowly from the field to the milking sheds unless someone hurries them along>.

crack

- **a fair crack of the whip** a fair share, a fair chance of doing (something).
- **at (the) crack of dawn** very early in the morning.
- **crack the whip** to treat sternly or severely those under one's control or charge. <From the use of a whip to punish people>.
- **take a sledgehammer to crack a nut** to spend a great deal of effort on a small task or problem.

crest

- **be (riding) on the crest of a wave** to be going through a very successful period.

cricket

- **not cricket** not fair or honourable, unsportsmanlike. <The game of cricket is regarded as being played in a gentlemanly way>.

crocodile

- **crocodile tears** a pretended show of grief or sorrow. <Refers to an old belief that crocodiles weep while eating their prey>.

cross

- **cross the Rubicon** to do something that commits one completely to a course of action that cannot be undone. <Julius Caesar's crossing of the River Rubicon in 49BC committed him to war with the Senate>.
- **have a cross to bear** to have to suffer or tolerate a responsibility, inconvenience or source of distress. <Refers to the fact that in the days of crucifixions, those being crucified had to carry their own crosses>.
- **talk at cross purposes** to be involved in a misunderstanding because of talking or thinking about different things without realizing it.

crow

- **eat crow** to have to admit or accept that one was wrong.

crunch

- **when it comes to the crunch** when a time of testing comes, when a decision has to be made.

cry

- **a far cry from (something)** a long way from (something), very different from (something).
- **cry over spilt milk** to waste time regretting a misfortune or accident that cannot be undone.
- **in full cry** enthusiastically and excitedly pursuing something. <Refers to the cry made by hunting dogs>.

cuckoo

- **a cuckoo in the nest** a person who gains some kind of advantage from a situation without contributing anything useful. <From the cuckoo's habit of laying their eggs in other birds' nests>.

cudgel

- **take up the cudgels on behalf of (someone** *or* **something)** to fight strongly on behalf of (someone or something), to support (someone or something) vigorously.

cue

• **take one's cue from (someone)** to use the actions or reactions of (someone) as a guide to one's own, to copy (someone's) actions. <A theatrical term, literally meaning to use the words of another actor as a signal for one to speak or move>.

cuff

• **off the cuff** without preparation. <Refers to the habit of some after-dinner speakers of making brief headings on the celluloid cuffs of their evening shirts as a reminder of what he or she wanted to say rather than preparing a formal speech>.

cup

• **not be one's cup of tea** not to be something which one likes or appreciates.

cupboard

• **cupboard love** pretended affection shown for a person because of the things he or she gives one. <From people and animals liking those who feed them, food being kept in cupboards>.

• **curry favour with (someone)** to try to gain the approval or favour of (someone) by insincere flattery or by being extremely nice to him or her all the time. <Originally curry favel, from Old French *estriller fauvel*, *fauvel* being a chestnut horse>.

curtain

• **be curtains for (someone** or **something)** to be the end of (someone or something). <Refers to curtains falling at the end of a stage performance>.

• **bring down the curtain on (something)** to cause (something) to come to an end. <See above>.

• **curtain lecture** a private scolding, especially one given by a wife to a husband. <From the curtains that formerly were hung round a bed>.

cut

• **a cut above (someone** or **something)** rather better than (someone or something).

• **cut a long story short** to give a brief account of something quite complicated or lengthy.

• **cut and dried** settled and definite. <Refers to wood that has been cut and dried and made ready for use>.

• **cut and thrust** methods and techniques of rivalry, argument or debate. <Refers to sword fighting>.

• **cut both ways** to have an equal or the same effect on both parts of a question or on both people involved in something.

• **cut it fine** to allow hardly enough time to do or get something.

• **not cut out for (something)** not naturally suited to.

cylinder

• **firing on all cylinders** working or operating at full strength. <Literally used of an internal combustion engine>.

dagger

• **at daggers drawn** feeling or showing great hostility towards each other.

• **look daggers at (someone)** to look with great dislike or hostility at (someone).

daisy

• **be pushing up the daisies** to be dead.

• **fresh as a daisy** not at all tired, lively.

damp

• **a damp squib** something which is expected to be exciting, effective, etc, but which fails to live up to its expectations. <Refers to a wet firework that fails to go off>.

• **put a damper on (something)** to reduce the enjoyment, optimism, happiness of (something).

dance

• **lead (someone) a (merry) dance** to cause (someone) a series of great, usually unnecessary, problems or irritations.

Darby

• **Darby and Joan** a devoted elderly couple. <From the names of such a couple in an 18th-century English ballad>.

dark

• **a shot in the dark** an attempt or guess based on very little information.

• **be whistling in the dark** to try to give the impression that one is more confident of, or less worried about, a situation than one actually is.

• **dark horse** a person or thing whose abilities, worth, etc, is unknown.

dash

- **in the dark** lacking knowledge or awareness.
- **keep it** *or* **something dark** to keep it or something secret.

dash

- **cut a dash** to wear very smart or unusual clothes and so impress others.

Davy Jones

- **Davy Jones's locker** the bottom of the sea. <Davy Jones was a name given in the 18th century to the ruler of the evil spirits of the sea>.

dawn

- **a false dawn** an event which makes a situation look as though it is improving when it is not.

day

- **all in a day's work** all part of one's normal routine, not requiring extra or unusual effort.
- **any day of the week** whatever the circumstances.
- **call it a day** to put an end to (something); to stop doing (something), especially to stop working.
- **carry** *or* **win the day** to be successful, to gain a victory. <Originally a military term meaning to win a battle>.
- **daylight robbery** the charging of prices that are far too high.
- **(your, etc) days are numbered** you are about to be dismissed, be killed, etc.
- **every dog has his day** everyone will get an opportunity at some time.
- **have had one's** *or* **its day** to be past the most successful part of one's or its life.
- **live from day to day** to think only about the present without making any plans for the future.
- **make (someone's) day** to make (someone) very pleased or happy.
- **name the day** to announce the date of one's wedding.
- **not to be one's day** to be a day when nothing seems to go right for one.
- **one of these days** at some time in the future.
- **one of those days** a day when nothing seems to go right.

deaf

- **see daylight** to be coming to the end of a long task.
- **seize the day** to take advantage of any opportunities which occur now, rather than worry about the future.

dead

- **a dead duck** a person or thing that is very unlikely to survive or continue.
- **a dead loss** a person or thing that is completely useless or unprofitable.
- **cut (someone) dead** to ignore (someone) completely.
- **dead and buried** completely dead or extinct with no chance of being revived.
- **dead as a dodo** completely dead or out of fashion. <Refers to a flightless bird that has been extinct since 1700>.
- **dead beat** exhausted.
- **dead from the neck up** extremely stupid.
- **dead in the water** with no hope of success. <Refers to a dead fish which is no use to fishermen or anglers.>
- **Dead Sea fruit** a thing that appears to be, or is expected to be, of great value but proves to be valueless. <Refers to a fruit, the apple of Sodom, that was thought to grow on trees beside the shores of the Dead Sea. It was beautiful to look at but fell to ashes when touched or tasted>.
- **dead to the world** in a very deep sleep.
- **dead wood** a person or thing that is no longer necessary or useful.
- **enough to waken the dead** extremely loud.
- **let the dead bury their dead** past problems, quarrels, etc, are best forgotten. <A biblical reference to Matthew 8:22, in which Jesus said, 'Follow me and let the dead bury their dead'.>
- **over my dead body** in the face of my fierce opposition.
- **step into** *or* **fill dead men's shoes** to take over the position of someone who has died or left under unfortunate circumstances.
- **would not be seen dead in** *or* **with, etc,** extremely unlikely to be seen wearing something, accompanying someone, etc, because of an extreme dislike or aversion.

deaf

- **deaf as a post** completely deaf.

deal

diamond

- **fall on deaf ears** not to be listened to, to go unnoticed or disregarded.
- **stone deaf** completely deaf.
- **turn a deaf ear to (something)** to refuse to listen to (something), to take no notice of (something).

deal

- **a raw deal** unfair treatment.

death

- **at death's door** extremely ill, dying.
- **be in at the death** to be present at the end or final stages of something. <Refers originally to being present at the death of the prey in a hunt>.
- **catch one's death (of cold)** to become infected with a very bad cold.
- **dice with death** to do something extremely risky and dangerous.
- **die the death** to be badly received. <Refers originally to an actor or performer getting a poor reception from the audience>.
- **sick** *or* **tired to death of (someone** *or* **something)** extremely weary or bored with (someone or something).
- **sign one's own death warrant** to bring about one's own downfall, ruin, etc.
- **will be the death of (someone) 1** to cause the death of (someone). **2** to make (someone) laugh a great deal.

deck

- **hit the deck** to fall to the ground.

deep

- **be thrown in at the deep end** to be put suddenly into a difficult situation of which one has no experience. <Refers to the deep end of a swimming pool>.
- **go off at the deep end** to lose one's temper. (See above).

degree

- **give (someone) the third degree** to subject (someone) to intense questioning, especially by using severe methods.
- **to the nth degree** to the greatest possible degree, extent or amount. <Refers to the use of n as a symbol to represent a number, especially a large number>.

dent

- **make a dent in (something)** to reduce (something) by a considerable amount.

depth

- **out of one's depth** in a situation which one cannot cope with. <Refers literally to being in water deeper than one can stand up in>.
- **plumb the depths of (something)** to reach the lowest level of unhappiness, misfortune, etc.

deserts

- **get one's just deserts** to be treated as one deserves, especially to receive deserved punishment.

design

- **have designs upon (someone** *or* **something)** to wish to possess (someone or something), usually belonging to someone else.

device

- **leave (someone) to his** *or* **her own devices** to leave (someone) to look after himself or herself, often after having tried unsuccessfully to help him or her.

devil

- **better the devil you know** it is preferable to have someone or something that one knows to be bad than take a chance with someone or something that might turn out even worse.
- **between the devil and the deep blue sea** faced with two possible courses of action each of which is as unacceptable as the other.
- **needs must when the devil drives** if it is absolutely necessary that something must be done then one must do it.
- **play the devil's advocate** to put forward objections to a plan, idea, etc, simply in order to test the strength of the arguments in its favour.
- **speak of the devil** here is the very person whom we have just been referring to. <Short for 'speak of the devil and he will appear' which refers to a superstition by which it was thought that talking about evil gave it the power to appear>.

diamond

- **rough diamond** a person who behaves in a rough manner but who has good or valuable qualities.

dice

- **load the dice against (someone)** to arrange things so that (someone) has no chance of success. <Refers to a method of cheating in gambling by putting lead or similar heavy material into a dice so that only certain numbers will come up>.

die¹

- **be dying for (something)** to be longing for (something).
- **die with one's boots on** to die while still working. <Refers to soldiers dying in active service>.
- **never say die** never give up hope.

die²

- **the die is cast** a step has been taken which makes the course of future events inevitable. <A translation of the Latin *iacta alea est*, supposedly said by Julius Caesar when he crossed the Rubicon in 49 BC and so committed himself to a war with the Senate>.

differ

- **agree to differ** to agree not to argue about something any more since neither party is likely to change his or her opinion.
- **sink one's differences** to forget about past disagreements.
- **split the difference** to agree on an amount of money halfway between two amounts, especially between the amount that one person is charging for something and the amount that someone else is willing to pay for it.

dig

- **dig one's heels in** to show great determination, especially in order to get one's own wishes carried out.
- **dig one's own grave** to be the cause of one's own misfortune.

dilemma

- **on the horns of a dilemma** in a position where it is necessary to choose between two courses of action. <In medieval rhetoric a dilemma was likened to a two-horned animal on one of whose horns the person making the decision had to throw himself or herself>.

dim

- **take a dim view of (something)** to look with disapproval on (something)

dine

- **dine out on (something)** to be given social invitations because of information, gossip, etc, one can pass on.

dinner

- **like a dog's dinner** an untidy mess.
- **more of (something) than you have had hot dinners** a very great deal of (something).

dirt

- **dirty old man** an elderly man who shows a sexual interest in young girls or young boys.
- **(someone's) name is dirt** *or* **mud** (someone) is in great disfavour.

discretion

- **discretion is the better part of valour** it is wise not to take any unnecessary risks. <Refers to Shakespeare's *Henry IV Part 1*, Act 5, scene IV>.

distance

- **go the distance** to complete something successfully, to last until the end of something.
- **keep one's distance** not to come too close, not to be too friendly.
- **within striking distance** reasonably close.

dividend

- **pay dividends** to bring advantages at a later time. <Refers to dividends paid on money invested, as on stocks and shares>.

do

- **do one's bit** to do one's share of the work, etc.
- **do (someone) in** to kill (someone).
- **done for** without any hope of rescue, help or recovery.
- **do or die** to make the greatest effort possible at the risk of killing, injuring, ruining, etc, oneself.
- **do the honours** to act as host, to serve food or drink to one's guests.
- **do time** to serve a prison sentence.
- **not the done thing** not acceptable behaviour.
- **the do's and don'ts** what one should or should not do in a particular situation.

doctor

- **just what the doctor ordered** exactly what is required.

dog

- **a dog in the manger** a person who stops someone else from doing or having something which he himself or she herself does not want. <From one of Aesop's fables in which a dog prevents the horses from eating the hay in the feeding rack although he himself did not want to eat the hay>.
- **a dog's life** a miserable life.
- **dog eat dog** a ruthless struggle against one's rivals to survive or be successful.
- **go to the dogs** to be no longer good, moral, successful, etc.
- **give a dog a bad name** if bad things are said about a person's character they will stay with him or her for the rest of his or her life.
- **in the doghouse** in disfavour.
- **keep a dog and bark oneself** to employ someone to do a job and then do it oneself.
- **let sleeping dogs lie** do not look for trouble; if there is no trouble, do not cause any.
- **you can't teach an old dog new tricks** the older you get the more difficult it is to learn new skills or accept ideas or new fashions.

doggo

- **lie doggo** to remain in hiding, not to do anything that will draw attention to oneself.

donkey

- **donkey's ages** or **years** a very long time. <Perhaps from a pun on donkey's ears, which are very long>.
- **donkey work** the hard, often tiring or physical, part of any job.
- **talk the hind legs off a donkey** to talk too much or to talk for a very long time.

door

- **darken (someone's) door** to come or go into (someone's) house.
- **have a** or **one foot in the door** to start to gain entrance to somewhere or something when entrance is difficult. <Refers to someone putting a foot in a door to wedge it open in order to gain entrance>.
- **lay (something) at (someone's) door** to blame (someone) for (something).

- **open doors** to give someone an opportunity to improve his or her position, to improve someone's chances of success.
- **show (someone) the door** to make (someone) leave.

dose

- **a dose** or **taste of one's own medicine** something unpleasant done to a person who is in the habit of doing similar things to other people.

dot

- **dot the i's and cross the t's** to attend to details.
- **on the dot 1** exactly on time. **2** exactly at the time stated. <Refers to the dots on the face of a clock>.

double

- **at the double** very quickly. <A military term, literally at twice the normal marching speed>.
- **do a double take** to look at or think about (someone or something) a second time because one has not taken it in or understood it the first time.
- **double Dutch** unintelligible words or language. <Refers to the fact that Dutch sounds a very difficult language to those who are not native speakers of it>.

doubt

- **a doubting Thomas** a person who will not believe something without strong proof. <Refers to the biblical story Thomas, the disciple who doubted Christ, John 21:24–29>.

down

- **down in the dumps** or **down in the mouth** depressed, in low spirits.
- **down the drain** completely wasted.
- **down under** Australia.
- **get down to (something)** to begin to work at (something) in earnest.
- **go downhill** to get worse and worse, to deteriorate.
- **have a down on (someone** or **something)** to be very hostile or opposed to (someone or something).

drawer

- **out of the top drawer** from the upper classes or aristocracy.

dream

- **a dream ticket** used of two people who are expected to work very successfully together. <Originally used to refer to political elections>.

dress

- **dressed to kill** *or* **dressed to the nines** dressed in one's smartest clothes so as to attract attention.

drift

- **get the drift** to understand the general meaning of something.

drink

- **drink like a fish** to drink a great deal of alcoholic drinks.

drop

- **at the drop of a hat** immediately, requiring only the slightest excuse.
- **drop into (someone's) lap** to happen to (someone) without any effort.
- **let (something) drop** to let (something) be known accidentally.

drown

- **drown one's sorrows** to take alcoholic drink in order to forget one's unhappiness.

drum

- **drum (someone) out** to send (someone) away, to ask (someone) to leave. <Refers to the use of drums when an officer was being publicly dismissed from his regiment>.

dry

- **a dry run** a practice attempt, a rehearsal.
- **dry as a bone** extremely dry.
- **dry as dust** extremely dull or boring.
- **dry up** to forget what one was going to say.
- **keep one's powder dry** to remain calm and prepared for immediate action. <Refers to the fact that gunpowder must be kept dry to be effective>.

duck

- **a lame duck** a weak or inefficient person or organization.
- **a sitting duck** a person or thing that is very easy to attack. <Refers to the fact that a sitting duck is easier to shoot at than one flying in the air>.
- **be water off a duck's back** be totally ineffective. <Refers to the fact that water runs straight off the oily feathers on a duck's back>.
- **break one's duck** to have one's first success. <A cricketing term. No score in cricket is known as a duck>.
- **take to (something) like a duck to water** to be able to do (something) right from the beginning naturally and without difficulty
- **ugly duckling** an unattractive or uninteresting person or thing that develops in time into someone or something very attractive, interesting or successful. <Refers to the story by Hans Andersen about a baby swan that is brought up by ducks who consider it ugly by their standards until it grows into a beautiful swan>.

dust

- **let the dust settle** to give things time to calm down.
- **not see (someone) for dust** not to see (someone) again because he has run away. <Refers to clouds of dust left behind by horses or vehicles when they are moving fast>.
- **shake the dust from one's feet** to leave somewhere, usually gladly
- **throw dust in (someone's eyes)** to attempt to confuse or deceive (someone). <Dust temporarily blinds people if it gets into their eyes>.

Dutch

- **Dutch auction** an auction in which the auctioneer starts with a high price and reduces it until someone puts in a bid.
- **Dutch courage** courage that is not real courage but induced by drinking alcohol. <Perhaps from a Dutch military custom of drinking alcohol before going into battle, perhaps from the fact that gin was introduced into England by the Dutch followers of William III>.
- **Dutch treat** a kind of entertainment or celebration where everyone concerned pays for himself or herself. <From Dutch lunch to which all of the guests were expected to contribute some of the food>.
- **go Dutch** to share expenses.
- **talk to (someone) like a Dutch uncle** to scold (someone) or talk to (someone) for

what is supposedly his or her own good.
<Perhaps from the Dutch's reputation for
strict family discipline>.

ear

- **go in one ear and out the other** not to
make any lasting impression.
- **grin from ear to ear** to have a wide smile
on your face.
- **have** *or* **keep one's ear to the ground** to
keep oneself informed about what is happening around one. <Perhaps from a
North American Indian method of track-
ing prey>.
- **(my, etc) ears are burning** someone somewhere is talking about (me, etc). <The
belief that one's ears grow hot when someone is talking about one is mentioned by
Pliny, the Roman writer>.
- **up to one's ears in (something)** deeply
involved in (something). <A comparison
with someone who is almost submerged by
very deep water>.

earth

- **bring (someone) (back) down to earth** to
make (someone) aware of the practicalities of life or of a situation.
- **run (someone** *or* **something) to earth** to
find (someone or something) after a long
search. <Refers to a hunting term for chas-
ing a fox into its earth or hole>.

easy

- **easy as falling off a log** *or* **easy as pie**
extremely easy.
- **easy on the eye** very attractive.

eat

- **have (someone) eating out of one's hand**
to have (someone) doing everything that
one wishes, because he or she likes or admires one. <Refers to an animal that is so
tame that it will eat out of someone's
hand>.

ebb

- **at a low ebb** in a poor or depressed state.
<Refers to the tide when it has flowed
away from the land>.

edge

- **be at the cutting edge of (something)** to
be involved in the most modern, advanced
development or stage of (something).

- **be on the edge of your seat** to be very
excited and eager to know what happens
next.
- **have the edge on (someone** *or* **something)** to have the advantage of (someone
or something).
- **lose one's edge** to become less
effective or less good at what you do. <Re-
fers to a knife becoming blunt>.
- **push (someone) over the edge** to make
someone unable to cope, mentally ill, etc.

egg

- **be left with egg on one's face** to be left
looking foolish.
- **put all one's eggs in one basket** to rely
entirely on the success of one project, etc.
- **teach one's grandmother to suck eggs**
to try to tell someone how to do something
when he or she is much more experienced
than oneself at it.

eight

- **be** *or* **have one over the eight** to be or to
have had too much to drink. <Refers to a
former belief that one could have eight
drinks before one is drunk>.

elbow

- **give (someone) the elbow** to get rid of
(someone), to end a relationship with
(someone).

element

- **in one's element** in a situation in which
one is happy or at one's best. <Refers to
the four elements of medieval science of
fire, earth, air and water>.

elephant

- **a white elephant** something which is useless and troublesome to look after.
<White elephants were given by the Kings
of Siam followers who had displeased
them since the cost of keeping such an
elephant was such that it would ruin the
follower>.
- **have a memory like an elephant** never to
forget things.

eleventh

- **at the eleventh hour** at the last possible
minute. <A biblical reference to the parable of the labourers in the vineyard in
Matthew 20>.

empty

- **empty vessels make most noise** the most foolish or least informed people are most likely to voice their opinions.

end

- **at a loose end** with nothing to do, with no plans.
- **at the end of one's tether** at the end of one's patience, tolerance, etc. <Refers to a rope that will only extend a certain distance to let the animal attached to it graze>.
- **make ends meet** to live within the limits of one's income. <The ends referred to are the start and finish of one's annual accounts>.

enough

- **enough is as good as a feast** if you have enough of something you should be satisfied with that; you do not need any more.

eternal

- **eternal triangle** a sexual relationship between two men and one woman or between two women and one man.

even

- **get** or **keep on an even keel** to be or keep steady or calm with no sudden changes.

event

- **be wise after the event** to realize how a situation should have been dealt with after it is over.

evidence

- **turn Queen's** or **King's evidence** to give evidence against a fellow criminal in order to have one's own sentence reduced.

evil

- **the lesser of two evils** the less unpleasant of two fairly unpleasant choices.
- **put off the evil hour** or **day** to keep postponing something unpleasant.

ewe

- **(someone's) ewe lamb** (someone's) favourite. <A biblical reference to Samuel 12:3>.

exception

- **the exception that proves the rule** the fact that an exception has to be made for a particular example of something proves that the general rule is valid.

eye

- **an eye for an eye (and a tooth for a tooth)** a punishment to match the offence committed. <A biblical reference to Exodus 21:23>.
- **a sight for sore eyes** a pleasant or welcome sight.
- **be one in the eye for (someone)** to be something unpleasant that happens to someone who deserves it.
- **keep an eagle eye on (someone or something)** to watch (someone or something) extremely closely. <Refers to the fact that eagles are thought to have particularly keen vision>.
- **keep a weather eye open** or **keep one's eyes peeled** or **skinned** to keep a close watch, to be alert. <A nautical term for watching for changes in the weather>.
- **make eyes at (someone)** to look at (someone) with sexual interest.
- **not to bat an eyelid** not to show any surprise, distress, etc.
- **raise some/a few eyebrows** to surprise or shock some people.
- **see eye to eye with (someone)** to be in agreement with (someone).
- **there's more to (someone** or **something) than meets the eye** the true worth or state of (someone or something) is not immediately obvious.

face

- **be staring one in the face 1** to be very obvious, although one may not realize this at first. **2** to be likely to happen or to be about to happen.
- **face the music** to face and deal with a situation caused by one's actions. <Perhaps from a performer facing the musicians below the front of the stage as he or she makes an entrance on stage>.
- **fly in the face of (something)** to oppose or defy (something). <Refers to a dog attacking>.
- **get out of (someone's) face** to go away and stop annoying (someone).
- **have a long face** to look unhappy.
- **keep a straight face** to stop oneself from smiling or laughing.

faint **feather**

- **lose face** to suffer a loss of respect or reputation.
- **make** *or* **pull a face** to twist one's face into a strange or funny expression.
- **put a brave face on it** to try to appear brave when one is feeling afraid, distressed, etc.
- **save (someone's) face** to prevent (someone) from appearing stupid or wrong.
- **show one's face** to put in an appearance, especially when one will not be welcome or when one will be embarrassed.

faint

- **faint heart never won fair lady** boldness is necessary to achieve what one desires.
- **not to have the faintest** not to have the slightest idea.

fair

- **by fair means or foul** by any method whatsoever.
- **fair game** a person or thing that it is considered quite reasonable to attack, make fun of, etc.
- **fair play** fairness and justice.
- **fairweather friends** people who are friendly towards one only when one is not in trouble.

fall

- **fall back on (someone** *or* **something)** to rely on (someone or something) if all else fails.
- **fall flat** to fail, to have no effect.
- **fall foul of (something** *or* **something)** to do something that arouses someone's anger or hostility.
- **fall from grace** to lose (someone's) favour.
- **fall over oneself to** to set about doing something with great willingness and eagerness.

false

- **under false pretences** by using deceit.

family

- **run in the family** to be a characteristic found in many members of the same family.

fancy

- **(footloose and) fancy free** not in love with anyone, not romantically attached.
- **take** *or* **tickle one's fancy** to attract one, to arouse a liking in one.

far

- **go far** to be very successful.
- **go too far** to do or say something that is beyond the limits of what is acceptable.

fast

- **play fast and loose with (something)** to act irresponsibly with (something).
- **pull a fast one on (someone)** to deceive (someone). <Refers to bowling a fast ball in cricket>.

fat

- **it isn't over till the fat lady sings** used to remind people that the result of a competition, etc . is not established until the end of the game, match, etc.
- **live off the fat of the land** to live in a luxurious fashion.
- **the fat is in the fire** trouble has been started and it cannot be stopped. <Fat causes a fire to flare up>.

fate

- **a fate worse than death** something terrible that happens to one, often rape.
- **seal (someone's) fate** to ensure that something, usually unpleasant, happens to (someone).
- **tempt fate** to act in a way that is likely to bring one ill luck or misfortune.

fear

- **there is no fear of (something)** it is not likely that (something) will happen.

feast

- **be feast or famine** to be a situation in which there is too much of something or too little.

feat

- **be no mean feat** used to emphasize the difficulty of a task or venture.

feather

- **a feather in one's cap** something of which one can be proud.
- **feather one's (own) nest** to make a profit for oneself, often at the expense of someone else.
- **make the feathers** *or* **fur fly** to cause trouble or a quarrel. <Refers to birds or animals fighting>.
- **ruffle (someone's) feathers** to annoy or upset (someone).

- **show the white feather** to show signs of cowardice. <A white feather in the tail of a fighting cock was a sign of inferior breeding>.

feel

- **feel in one's bones** to know (something) by instinct.
- **feel one's feet** to be becoming used to a situation.

feet

- **at (someone's) feet** 1 easily within (someone's) reach or power. 2 greatly admiring of (someone).
- **drag one's feet** to take a long time to do something.
- **fall** or **land on one's feet** to be fortunate or successful, especially after a period of uncertainty or misfortune.
- **find one's feet** to become capable of coping with a situation.
- **have feet of clay** to have a surprising weakness, despite having been thought to be perfect. <A biblical reference to Daniel 2:31–34>.
- **have both feet on the ground** or **have one's feet on the ground** to be practical and sensible.
- **get under (someone's) feet** to hinder or get in (someone's) way.
- **put one's feet up** to take a rest.
- **stand on one's own feet** to be independent.
- **sweep (someone) off his** or **her feet** to affect (someone) with great enthusiasm or emotion; to influence (someone) to do as one wishes.

fence

- **mend fences** to put things right after a quarrel, etc.
- **sit on the fence** to refuse to take sides in a dispute, etc.

fiddle

- **fit as a fiddle** extremely fit.
- **play second fiddle to (someone)** to be in a subordinate or inferior position to (someone).

field

- **have a field day** to have a very busy, successful or enjoyable day.
- **play the field** to take advantage of many chances offered to one, especially to go

out with several members of the opposite sex.

fight

- **fighting fit** extremely healthy and in good condition.
- **fight shy of (something)** to avoid (something).

fill

- **have had one's fill** to have had enough, to be unable to tolerate any more.

fine

- **get (something) down to a fine art** to have learned to do (something) extremely well.
- **go through (something) with a fine-tooth comb** to search (something) very carefully. <A fine-tooth comb is used to remove the nits (eggs) of head lice from hair>.

finger

- **be all fingers and thumbs** to be clumsy or awkward when using one's hands.
- **burn one's fingers** or **get one's fingers burnt** to suffer because of something that one has been involved in.
- **cross one's fingers** to hope for good fortune.
- **get** or **pull one's finger out** to stop wasting time and get on with something.
- **have a finger in every pie** to be involved in a large number of projects, organizations, etc.
- **have (something) at one's fingertips** to know all the information about (something).
- **let (something) slip through one's fingers** to lose (an advantage, opportunity, etc), often by one's inaction.
- **not to lift a finger** not to do anything at all.
- **point the finger at (someone)** to indicate who is to blame.
- **put one's finger on (something)** to identify (something) exactly.
- **twist** or **wrap (someone) round one's little finger** to be able to get (someone) to do exactly as one wishes.
- **work your fingers to the bone** to work extremely hard.

fire

- **get on like a house on fire** to get on very well.

first

- **hang fire** to wait or be delayed. <Refers to a gun in which there is a delay between the trigger being pulled and the gun being fired>.
- **in the firing line** in a situation in which you are likely to be blamed or criticized. <Refers to people who have been lined up in order to be shot dead.>
- **play with fire** to take tasks, to do something dangerous.
- **set the Thames** or **world on fire** to do something remarkable. <Refers to the River Thames, which it would be impossible to set alight>.
- **under fire** being attacked. <Refers literally to being shot at>.

first

- **first thing** early in the morning or in the working day.
- **in the first flush of (something)** in the early and vigorous stages of (something).

fish

- **have other fish to fry** to have something else to do, especially something that is more important or more profitable.
- **like a fish out of water** ill at ease and unaccustomed to a situation.
- **there are plenty more fish in the sea** many more opportunities will arise; many more members of the opposite sex are around.

fit

- **by fits and starts** irregularly, often stopping and starting.

fix

- **in a fix** in an awkward or difficult situation.

flag

- **hang** or **put the flags out** to celebrate something (a rare event).
- **run (something) up the flagpole** to put forward (a plan or idea) in order to gauge reactions to it.

flame

- **an old flame** a former boyfriend or girlfriend.
- **fan the flames** to make a difficult situation worse.

flash

- **a flash in the pan** a sudden, brief success.

<Refers to a flintlock gun in which the spark from the flint ignited the gunpowder in the priming pan, the flash then travelling to the main barrel. If this failed to go off there was only a flash in the pan>.

flat

- **in a flat spin** in a state of confused excitement.

flavour

- **flavour of the month** a person or thing that is particularly popular at a particular time, although this is likely to be temporary.

flea

- **a flea in one's ear** a sharp scolding.

flesh

- **a thorn in (someone's) flesh** a permanent source of annoyance or irritation. <A biblical reference to II Corinthians 12:7>.
- **get** or **have one's pound of flesh** to obtain everything that one is entitled to, especially if this causes difficulties or suffering to those who have to give it. <Refers to Shakespeare's play *The Merchant of Venice*, in which Shylock tries to enforce an agreement by which he can cut a pound of flesh from Antonio>.

floodgates

- **open the floodgates** to make it possible for a great many people to do something, usually something considered undesirable, or make it likely that this will happen, perhaps by removing some kind of restriction.

floor

- **take the floor** **1** to rise to make a public speech. **2** to begin to dance.
- **wipe the floor with (someone)** to defeat (someone) thoroughly.

fly¹

- **a fly in the ointment** something that spoils something.
- **there are no flies on (someone)** there is no possibility of deceiving or cheating (someone), there is no lack of sense in (someone).
- **would like to be a fly on the wall** would like to be present and able to hear what is going on without being seen.

fly²

- **get off to a flying start** to have a very successful beginning.

foam gab

foam

- **foam at the mouth** to be very angry. <Mad dogs foam at the mouth>.

follow

- **follow suit** to do just as someone else has done. <A reference to card-playing when a player plays the same suit as the previous player>.

fool

- **a fool's paradise** a state of happiness that is based on something that is not true or realistic.
- **be nobody's fool** to have a good deal of common sense.
- **fools rush in (where angels fear to tread)** an ignorant person can sometimes achieve what a warier person cannot. <From Alexander Pope's *An Essay on Criticism*>.
- **make a fool of (someone)** to make (someone) appear ridiculous or stupid.
- **not to suffer fools gladly** not to have any patience with foolish or stupid people.

foot

- **follow in (someone's) footsteps** to do the same as someone else has done before, particularly a relative.
- **get off on the wrong foot** to get off to a bad or unfortunate start.
- **have one foot in the grave** to be very old.
- **put one's foot down** to be firm about something, to forbid someone to do something.
- **put one's foot in it** to do or say something tactless.
- **shoot oneself in the foot** to make a mistake or do something stupid which causes problems for oneself or harms one's chances of success.

form

- **on form** in good condition, fit and in a good humour. <Form refers to the condition of a horse>.

fort

- **hold the fort** to take temporary charge of something.

forty

- **forty winks** a short nap.

frame

- **be in the frame 1** to be likely to get or win

something. **2** to be suspected of being guilty of a crime.

free

- **free and easy** informal, casual.
- **give (someone) a free hand** give (someone) permission to do as he or she wishes.

French

- **take French leave** to stay away from work, etc, without permission. <Refers to an 18th-century French custom of leaving a party without saying goodbye to one's host or hostess>.

Freudian

- **a Freudian slip** the use of a wrong word while speaking that is supposed to indicate an unconscious thought. <Refers to the theories of the psychologist Sigmund Freud>.

Friday

- **man** or **girl Friday** an invaluable assistant. <Refers to Friday, a character in *Robinson Crusoe* by Daniel Defoe>.

friend

- **a friend in need is a friend indeed** a friend who helps when one is in trouble is truly a friend.

frog

- **have a frog in one's throat** to be hoarse.

fruit

- **forbidden fruit** something desirable that is made even more so because one is forbidden for some reason to obtain it. <Refers to the biblical tree in the Garden of Eden whose fruit Adam was forbidden by God to eat, Genesis 3>.

fry

- **out of the frying pan into the fire** free of a difficult or dangerous situation only to get into a worse one.

full

- **be full of oneself** to be very conceited.
- **in the fullness of time** when the proper time has arrived, eventually.

fuss

- **make a fuss of (someone)** to pay a lot of attention to (someone), to show (someone) a lot of affection.

gab

- **the gift of the gab** the ability to talk readily and easily.

gain

- **gain ground** to make progress, to become more generally acceptable or popular.

gallery

- **play to the gallery** to act in an amusing or showy way to the ordinary people in an organization, etc, in order to gain popularity or their support.

game

- **beat (someone) at his** *or* **her own game** to do better than (someone) at his or her activity, especially a cunning or dishonest one.
- **give the game away** to reveal a secret plan, trick, etc, usually accidentally.
- **play the game** to behave fairly and honourably.
- **the game is up** the plan, trick, crime, etc, has been discovered and so has failed.

garden

- **everything in the garden is lovely** everything is fine.
- **lead (someone) up the garden path** to mislead or deceive (someone).

gauntlet

- **run the gauntlet** to be exposed or subjected to blame, criticism or risk. <Gauntlet is a mistaken form of Swedish *gatlopp*. Running the *gatlopp* was a Swedish military punishment in which the culprit had to run between two lines of men with whips who struck him as he passed>.
- **take/pick up the gauntlet** to accept a challenge.
- **throw down the gauntlet** to issue a challenge. <Throwing down a gauntlet, a protective glove, was the traditional method of challenging someone to a fight in medieval times>.

ghost

- **give up the ghost** to die, stop working, etc. <Ghost refers to a person's spirit—a biblical reference to Job 14:10>.

gift

- **look a gift horse in the mouth** to criticize something that has been given to one. <Looking at a horse's teeth is a way of telling its age and so estimating its value>.

gild

- **gild the lily** to add unnecessary decoration or detail. <An adaptation of a speech from Shakespeare's *King John*, Act 4, scene II>.

gilt

- **take the gilt off the gingerbread** to take away what makes something attractive. <Gingerbread used to be sold in fancy shapes and decorated with gold leaf>.

gird

- **gird up one's loins** to prepare oneself for action. <A biblical phrase from the fact that robes had to be tied up with a girdle before men began work or they got in the way, Acts 12:8>.

give

- **give and take** willingness to compromise.

glad

- **glad rags** best clothes worn for special occasions.

glass

- **glass ceiling** an invisible barrier, established by tradition, personal discrimination, etc, which prevents women from achieving the top jobs in their companies, professions, etc.
- **people who live in glass houses should not throw stones** people with faults themselves should not criticize faults in others.

glove

- **fit like a glove** to fit perfectly.
- **take the gloves off** to begin to fight, argue, etc, in earnest. <Refers to boxers who wear protective gloves to soften their blows>.

gold

- **be sitting on a goldmine** to posses something very valuable or potentially profitable, often without realizing this.
- **like living in a goldfish bowl** in a situation where one has very little privacy.
- **strike gold** to do or find something that makes one very rich or very successful.

gnat

- **strain at a gnat (and swallow a camel)** to trouble oneself over a matter of no importance, something only slightly wrong, etc, (but be unconcerned about a matter of great importance, something very wrong, etc). <A biblical reference to Matthew 23:23–24>.

go

- **from the word go** right from the very start of something.
- **make a go of it** *or* **something** to make a success of something.
- **no go** impossible, not given approval.
- **on the go** continually active, busy.

goal

- **score an own goal** to do something which fails to achieve what you set out to do and, instead, harms your own interests.

goalpost

- **move the goalposts** to change the conditions, rules or aims applying to a project, etc, after it is under way so that it is disadvantageous to others but advantageous to oneself.

goat

- **act the goat** to behave in an intentionally silly way.
- **get (someone's) goat** to irritate (someone).

God, god

- **in the lap of the gods** uncertain, left to chance or fate.
- **there but for the grace of God go I** if I had not been fortunate the circumstances of another person could easily also have been mine.

gold

- **a gold mine** a source of wealth or profit.
- **be like gold dust** be very scarce.
- **golden boy** a young man who is popular or successful.
- **golden handshake** a large amount of money given to someone who is leaving a job, usually because he or she has been declared redundant.
- **good as gold** very well-behaved.
- **the crock** *or* **pot of gold at the end of the rainbow** wealth or good fortune that one will never achieve.
- **the golden rule** a principle or practice that it is vital to remember. <Originally the golden rule was that one should do to others as one would wish them to do to oneself>.
- **worth its** *or* **one's weight in gold** extremely valuable or useful.

good

- **be as good as one's word** to do what one has promised do.
- **be on to a good thing** *or* **have a good thing going** to be in a desirable or profitable situation.
- **be up to no good** to be planning something wrong or illegal.
- **give as good as one gets** to be as successful as one's opponent in an argument, contest, fight, etc.
- **good for nothing** worthless.
- **in (someone's) good books** in favour with (someone).
- **make good** to be successful in one's career or business.
- **take (something) in good part** to accept (something) without being offended or angry.

goods

- **deliver the goods** to do what one is required or expected to do.
- **goods and chattels** movable property. <An old legal term>.

goose

- **cook (someone's) goose** to ruin (someone's) chances of success.
- **kill the goose that lays the golden egg** to destroy something that is a source of profit. <Refers to one of Aesop's fables in which the owner of a goose that laid golden eggs killed it thinking to get all the eggs at once, only to discover that there were none>.
- **what's sauce for the goose is sauce for the gander** what applies to one person should apply to another, usually to a member of the opposite sex.

gooseberry

- **play gooseberry** to be the third person present with a couple who wish to be alone.

Gordian

- **cut the Gordian knot** to solve a problem or end a great difficulty by a vigorous or drastic method. <Refers to a legend in which whoever could untie a knot in a rope belonging to King Gordius of Phrygia, would be made ruler of all Asia. Alexander the Great severed the knot by cutting through it with a sword>.

gospel

- **take (something) as gospel** to accept (something) as absolutely true. <The gospel refers to the books of the Bible dealing with the life and teachings of Christ>.

grab

- **up for grabs** ready to be taken, bought, etc.

grace

- **saving grace** a good quality which prevents someone or something from being completely bad or worthless.
- **with a bad** *or* **good grace** in an unpleasant or pleasant and unwilling or willing way.

grade

- **make the grade** to succeed in what you are trying to achieve, often by reaching a required standard. <Originally referred to a train which succeeded in climbing a steep section of track>.

grain

- **go against the grain** to be against someone's inclinations, feelings or wishes. <Refers to the direction of the grain in wood, it being easier to cut or smooth wood with the grain rather than across or against it>.

grape

- **sour grapes** saying that something that one cannot have is not worth having. <Refers to one of Aesop's fables in which a fox that failed to reach a bunch of grapes growing above his head said that they were sour anyhow>.
- **the grapevine** an informal and unofficial way of passing news and information from person to person, gossip.

grass

- **grass widow** a woman whose husband is away from home for a short time for reasons of business or sport. <Originally the term referred to an unmarried woman who had sexual relations with a man or men, the origin being that such relations usually took place out of doors>.
- **let the grass grow under one's feet** to delay or waste time.
- **put** *or* **turn (someone) out to grass** to cause (someone) to retire. <Refers to turning out a horse into a field at the end of its working life>.
- **the grass is always greener on the other side of the fence** another set of circumstances or lifestyle always seems preferable to one's own. <Refers to the habit of grazing animals of grazing through the fence separating them from the next field>.
- **the grass roots** the ordinary people in an organization, etc.

grave

- **(someone) would turn in his** *or* **her grave** (someone) would be very annoyed or upset.

Greek

- **be all Greek to me, etc,** I, etc, don't understand any of it. <Refers to the fact that ancient Greek was considered a difficult language to learn>.

green

- **give the green light to (something)** give one's permission for (something).
- **have green fingers** to be good at growing plants.
- **the green-eyed monster** jealousy.

grief

- **come to grief** to suffer misfortune or failure.
- **give (someone) grief** to criticize or nag (someone).

grim

- **hang on** *or* **hold on like grim death** to take a firm, determined hold of something in difficult or dangerous circumstances.

grin

- **grin and bear it** to tolerate something without complaining.
- **wipe the grin off (someone's face)** to make (someone) stop feeling pleased or satisfied.

grind

- **grind to a halt** slowly begin to stop or cease working.

grip

- **get a grip (of** *or* **on something** *or* **oneself)** to take firm control (of something or oneself).
- **get** *or* **come to grips with (something)** to begin to deal with (something).

ground

- **cut the ground from under (someone's) feet** to cause (someone's) actions, arguments, etc, to be ineffective, often by acting before he or she does.
- **fall on stony ground** to have no attention paid to it. <Refers to seed falling on stony, infertile ground and so not being able to grow>.
- **get in on the ground floor** to be in at the very start of a project, business, etc.
- **get (something) off the ground** to get (a project) started. <Refers literally to a plane>.
- **hit the ground running** to start a new activity immediately with a great deal of energy and enthusiasm.
- **on one's own ground** dealing with a subject, situation, etc, with which one is familiar.
- **run oneself into the ground** to become exhausted from working too hard or trying to do too many things.
- **shift one's ground** to change one's opinions, attitude, etc.
- **stand one's ground** to remain firm, not to yield.
- **suit (someone) down to the ground** to suit someone perfectly.
- **thin** or **thick on the ground** scarce or plentiful.

guard

- **let your guard down/lower your guard/ drop your guard** to stop being careful or alert.
- **on** or **off one's guard** prepared or unprepared for any situation, especially a dangerous or difficult one. <Refers to fencing>.

gum

- **gum up the works** to cause a machine, system, etc, to break down.

gun

- **be gunning for (someone)** to plan to harm (someone).
- **jump the gun** to start before the proper time. <Refers to athletes starting a race before the starting gun goes>.
- **spike (someone's) guns** to cause (someone's) plans or actions to be ineffective. <Refers historically to driving a metal

spike into the touch-hole of a captured enemy gun which could not be moved away in order to render it useless>.
- **stick to one's guns** to remain firm in one's opinions, etc. <Refers to a soldier who keeps shooting at the enemy and does not run away>.

hackles

- **make (someone's) hackles rise** to make (someone) angry. <Hackles are the feathers on the necks of male birds which rise when the bird is angry>.

hair

- **a hair of the dog (that bit one)** an alcoholic drink taken as a supposed cure for having consumed too much alcohol the night before. <From an old belief that if you were bitten by a mad dog and got rabies you could be cured by having hairs of the dog laid on the wound>.
- **get in (someone's) hair** to irritate (someone).
- **keep one's hair on** to remain calm and not get angry.
- **let one's hair down** to behave in an informal, relaxed manner.
- **make (someone's) hair stand on end** to terrify or horrify (someone).
- **not to turn a hair** not to show any sign of fear, distress, etc.
- **split hairs** to argue about small unimportant details, to quibble.
- **tear one's hair (out)** to show frustration or irritation.

half

- **(someone's) better half** (someone's) wife or husband.
- **half a loaf is better than no bread** a little of something desirable is better than nothing.
- **meet (someone) halfway** to reach a compromise agreement with (someone).
- **not half** very much so.

hammer

- **go at it hammer and tongs** to fight or quarrel loudly and fiercely. <Refers to a blacksmith holding a piece of heated iron in his tongs and striking it loudly with his hammer>.

hand

- **be hand in glove with (someone)** to be closely associated with (someone) for a bad or illegal purpose.
- **force (someone's) hand** to force (someone) to do something that he or she may not want to do or be ready to do.
- **give** or **lend (someone) a (helping) hand** to help (someone).
- **go hand in hand** to be closely connected.
- **hand over fist** in large amounts, very rapidly. <Originally a nautical term meaning rapid progress such as can be made by hauling on a rope putting one hand after the other>.
- **have a hand in (something)** to be involved in (something), to have contributed to the cause of (something).
- **have one's hands full** to be very busy.
- **in good hands** well looked after.
- **keep one's hand in** to retain one's skill at something by doing it occasionally.
- **lend (someone) a hand** to help (someone).
- **live from hand to mouth** to have enough money only to pay for one's present needs without having any to save. <Whatever money comes into one's hand is used to put food in one's mouth>.
- **many hands make light work** a job is easier to do if there are several people doing it.
- **my, etc, hands are tied** something prevents me, etc, from acting as I, etc, might wish to.
- **not to do a hand's turn** to do nothing.
- **play into (someone's) hands** to do exactly what someone wants one to do because it is to his or her advantage. <Refers to playing one's hand at cards so as to benefit another player>.
- **show one's hand** to reveal to others one's plans or intentions, previously kept secret. <Refers to showing one's hand to other players in a card game>.
- **take (someone) in hand** to train or discipline (someone).
- **turn one's hand to (something)** to do, to be able to do.
- **wait on (someone) hand and foot** to look after (someone) to such an extent that he or she does not have to do anything for himself or herself.
- **wash one's hands of (someone** or **something)** to refuse to be involved any longer in (something) or to be responsible for (someone or something). <A biblical reference to the action of Pontius Pilate after the crucifixion of Jesus in Matthew 27:24>.
- **with one hand tied behind one's back** very easily.

handle

- **fly off the handle** to lose one's temper. <Refers to an axehead which flies off the handle when it is being used>.

hang

- **get the hang of (something)** to learn how to do (something) or begin to understand (something).
- **hung up on (someone** or **something)** obsessed with (someone or something).

happy

- **happy as a lark** or **sand-boy** extremely happy.
- **happy hunting ground** a place where someone finds what he or she desires or where he or she is successful.
- **the** or **a happy medium** a sensible middle course between two extremes.

hard

- **between a rock and a hard place** see **rock**.
- **hard as nails** lacking in pity, sympathy, softer feelings, etc.
- **hard cash** coins and bank-notes as opposed to cheques, etc.
- **hard facts** facts that cannot be disputed.
- **hard lines** bad luck. <Perhaps a reference to a ship's ropes being made hard by ice>.
- **hard of hearing** rather deaf.
- **hard up** not having much money.
- **take a hard line** to take strong, stern or unyielding action or have strong opinions about something.
- **the hard stuff** strong alcoholic drink, spirits.

hare

- **run with the hare and hunt with the hounds** to try to give one's support to two opposing sides at once.

hash

- **settle (someone's) hash** to deal with

hat

(someone) in such a way that he or she causes no more trouble or is prevented from doing what was intended.

hat

- **hats off to (someone)** (someone) should be praised and congratulated.
- **hat trick** any action done three times in a row. <Refers originally to a cricketer receiving a hat from his club for putting out three batsmen with three balls in a row>.
- **I'll eat my hat** an expression used to express total disbelief in a fact, statement, etc.
- **keep (something) under one's hat** to keep (something) secret.
- **knock (someone *or* something) into a cocked hat** to defeat or surpass (someone or something) completely. <A cocked hat was a three-cornered hat in the 18th-century made by folding the edges of a round hat into corners>.
- **pass the hat round** to ask for contributions of money.
- **take one's hat off to (someone)** to express or show one's admiration for someone).
- **talk through one's hat** to talk about something without any knowledge about it, to talk nonsense.
- **throw one's hat in the ring** to declare oneself a contender or candidate for something. <Refers to a method of making a challenge in prize boxing matches at fairgrounds, etc>.
- **wear a different *or* another hat** to speak as the holder of a different position.

hatch

- **batten down the hatches** to prepare for trouble. <Refers to preparations for a storm on a ship at sea>.
- **hatches, matches and despatches** the announcement of births, marriages and deaths in a newspaper.

hatchet

- **bury the hatchet** to agree to be friends again after a quarrel. <Refers to an American Indian custom of burying tomahawks when peace was made>.

have

- **have had it** to have no hope of survival, success, etc.

head

- **have it in for (someone)** to try to cause trouble for (someone).
- **have it out with (someone)** to discuss areas of disagreement or discontent with someone in order to settle them.
- **let (someone) have it** suddenly to attack (someone) either physically or verbally.

havoc

- **play havoc with (something)** to cause serious damage to (something).

hawk

- **watch (someone) like a hawk** to watch (someone) very carefully.

hay

- **go haywire** to go completely wrong, to go out of control. <Refers to wire that was used to bind hay. It very easily became twisted and therefore came to symbolize confusion>.
- **hit the hay *or* sack** to go to bed. <Beds were formerly filled with hay or made from the same material as sacks>.
- **like looking for a needle in a haystack** *see* **needle**.
- **make hay (while the sun shines)** to profit or take advantage of an opportunity while one has the chance. <Haymaking is only possible in fine weather>.

head

- **bite *or* eat *or* snap (someone's) head off** to speak very sharply and angrily to (someone).
- **bring (something) to a head** to bring something to a state where something must be done about it. <Refers to bringing a boil, etc, to a head>.
- **bury one's head in the sand** to deliberately ignore a situation so that one does not have to deal with it. <Refers to the old belief that ostriches hide their heads in the sand when they are in danger because they think that then they cannot be seen>.
- **cannot make head nor tail of (something)** cannot understand (something) at all.
- **give (someone) his or her head** to allow (someone) to do as he or she wishes. <Refers literally to slackening one's hold on the reins of a horse>.
- **go to (someone's) head I)** to make (some-

heart   **heaven**

one) arrogant or conceited. **2** to make (someone) slightly drunk.

- **have a head for (something)** to have an ability or aptitude for (something).
- **have a (good) head on one's shoulders** to be clever or sensible.
- **have one's head screwed on the right way** to be sensible.
- **head over heels** completely.
- **hold one's head up (high)** not to feel ashamed or guilty, to remain dignified.
- **keep a level head** or **keep one's head** to remain calm and sensible, especially in a difficult situation.
- **keep one's head above water** to have enough money to keep out of debt.
- **knock (something) on the head** to put an end to (something).
- **laugh one's head off** to laugh very loudly.
- **lose one's head** to cease to remain calm, to act foolishly.
- **make headway** to make progress. <Refers originally to ships>.
- **off one's head** insane, not rational.
- **on (someone's) (own) head be it** (someone) must take responsibility or blame.
- **over (someone's) head** (l) too difficult for (someone) to understand. **2** when (someone) seems to have a better right. **3** beyond (someone) to a person of higher rank.
- **put** or **lay one's head on the block** to leave oneself open to blame, punishment, danger, etc. <Refers to laying one's head on the block before being beheaded>.
- **put our, etc, heads together** to discuss something together, to share thoughts on something.
- **rear its ugly head** to appear or happen.
- **scratch one's head** to be puzzled.
- **soft** or **weak in the head** not very intelligent, mentally retarded.
- **talk one's head off** to talk a great deal.
- **turn (someone's) head** to make (someone) conceited.

heart

- **cross one's heart (and hope to die)** this is said to emphasize the truth of what one is saying.

- **do (someone's) heart good** to give (someone) pleasure.
- **eat one's heart out** to be distressed because one cannot have someone or something which one is longing for.
- **from the bottom of one's heart** most sincerely, very much.
- **have one's heart in one's mouth** to feel afraid or anxious.
- **heart and soul** completely, with all one's energy.
- **(someone's) heart goes out to (someone)** (someone) feels sympathy or pity for (someone).
- **(someone's) heart is in the right place** (someone) is basically kind, sympathetic, etc, although not appearing to be so.
- **(someone's) heart is not in it** (someone) is not enthusiastic about something.
- **(someone's) heart sinks** (someone) feels depressed, disappointed, etc.
- **in good heart** cheerful and confident.
- **in (someone's) heart of hearts** in the deepest part of one's mind or feelings.
- **learn something by heart** to memorize (something) thoroughly.
- **lose heart** to grow discouraged.
- **not to have the heart (to do something)** not to be unkind, unsympathetic, etc, enough (to do something).
- **put new heart into (someone)** to make (someone) feel encouraged and more hopeful.
- **set one's heart on** or **have one's heart set on (something)** to desire (something) very much.
- **take heart** to become encouraged.
- **take (something) to heart 1** to be upset by (something). **2** to be influenced by and take notice of (something).
- **wear one's heart on one's sleeve** to let one's feelings be obvious.
- **with all one's heart** most sincerely.

heat

- **in the heat of the moment** while influenced by the excitement or emotion of the occasion.

heaven

- **in seventh heaven** extremely happy. <In Jewish literature the seventh heaven is the

highest of all heavens and the one where God lives>.

- **manna from heaven** something advantageous which happens unexpectedly, especially in a time of trouble. <A biblical reference to Exodus 16:15>.
- **move heaven and earth** to make every effort possible.
- **smell** *or* **stink to high heaven** to have a strong and nasty smell.

heavy

- **make heavy weather of (something)** to make more effort to do something than should be required. <Refers originally to a ship which does not handle well in difficult conditions>.

hedge

- **look as though one has been dragged through a hedge backwards** to look very untidy.

heel

- **bring (someone) to heel** to bring (someone) under one's control. <Refers to making a dog walk to heel>.
- **take to one's heels** to run away.

helm

- **at the helm** in charge. <Refers to the helm of a ship>.

hen

- **like a hen on a hot girdle** very nervous and restless.

here

- **neither here nor there** of no importance.
- **the hereafter** life after death.

herring

- **a red herring** a piece of information which misleads (someone) or draws (someone's) attention away from the truth, often introduced deliberately. <A red herring is a strong-smelling fish whose scent could mislead hunting dogs if it were dragged across the path they were pursuing>.
- **neither fish nor fowl nor good red herring** neither one thing nor the other.
- **packed like herring in a barrel** very tightly packed.

hide¹

- **neither hide nor hair of (someone** *or* **something)** no trace at all of (someone or

something). <Hide is used in the sense of skin>.

hide²

- **on a hiding to nothing** in a situation where one cannot possibly win. <Perhaps a reference to boxing>.

high

- **a high flier** a person who is bound to be very successful or who has achieved great success.
- **be for the high jump** to be about to be punished or scolded.
- **be high time** be time something was done without delay.
- **be** *or* **get on one's high horse** to be or become offended in a haughty manner.
- **high and mighty** arrogant.
- **hunt** *or* **search high and low for (someone** *or* **something)** to search absolutely everywhere for (someone or something).
- **leave (someone) high and dry** to leave (someone) in a difficult or helpless state.
- **riding high** very successful. <Used literally of the moon being high in the sky>.
- **run high** of feelings, tempers, etc, to be extremely angry, agitated, etc. <Refers to the sea when there is a strong current and high waves>.

hill

- **over the hill** past one's youth or one's best.

history

- **the rest is history** used to indicate that no more need be said about something because the details of it are well known.

hit

- **be a hit with (someone)** to be popular with (someone).
- **hit-and-run accident** an accident involving a vehicle where the driver who caused it does not stop or report the accident.
- **hit it off** to get on well, to become friendly.

hog

- **go the whole hog** to do something completely and thoroughly. <Perhaps referring to buying a whole pig for meat rather than just parts of it>.

hold

- **have a hold over (someone)** to have power or influence over (someone).

hole

- **hold good** to be valid or applicable.
- **no holds barred** no restrictions on what is permitted.

hole

- **hole-and-corner** secret and often dishonourable.
- **in a hole** in an awkward or difficult situation.
- **make a hole in (something)** to use a large part of (something).
- **need (something) like (someone) needs a hole in the head** to regard (something) as being completely unwelcome or undesirable.
- **pick holes in (something)** to find faults in (a theory, plan, etc).

holy

- **holier-than-thou** acting as though one is more moral, more pious, etc, than other people. <A biblical reference to Isaiah 65:5>.
- **the holy of holies** a private or special place inside a building. <A literal translation of the Hebrew name of the inner sanctuary in the Jewish Temple where the Ark of the Covenant was kept>.

home

- **a home from home** a place where one feels comfortable and relaxed.
- **bring** or **drive (something) home to (someone)** to cause someone fully to understand or believe (something).
- **do one's homework** to prepare thoroughly for a meeting, etc, by getting all the necessary information.
- **home and dry** having successfully completed an objective.
- **home truth** a plain, direct statement of something that is true but unpleasant or difficult for someone to accept.
- **make oneself at home** to make oneself comfortable and relaxed.
- **nothing to write home about** not very special, not remarkable.

hook

- **by hook or by crook** by any means possible.
- **off the hook** free from some difficulty, problem, etc, or something one does not want to do. <A reference to angling>.

- **sling one's hook** to go away.
- **swallow (something) hook, line and sinker** to believe (something) completely. <Refers to a fish that swallows not only the hook but the whole of the end section of the fishing line>.
- **the home stretch** or **straight** the last part of something, especially when this has been a particularly long or difficult process.

hoop

- **put (someone) through the hoop** to cause (someone) to experience something unpleasant or difficult. <Refers to circus performers who jump through hoops set on fire>.

hop

- **hopping mad** extremely angry.

hope

- **hope against hope** to continue to hope although there is little reason to be hopeful.
- **hope springs eternal (in the human breast)** it is in the nature of human beings to hope. <A quotation from Alexander Pope's *An Essay on Criticism*>.
- **pin one's hopes on (someone** or **something)** to rely on (someone or something) helping one in some way.

horn

- **draw in one's horns** to restrain one's actions, particularly the spending of money. <Refers to a snail drawing in its horns if it is in danger>.
- **lock horns** to argue or fight. <Refers to horned male animals who sometimes get their horns caught together when fighting>.

hornet

- **stir up a hornet's nest** to cause a great deal of trouble.

horse

- **eat like a horse** to eat a great deal.
- **flog a dead horse** to continue to try to arouse interest, enthusiasm, etc, in something which is obviously not, or no longer, of interest.
- **hold one's horses** not to move so fast.
- **horses for courses** certain people are better suited to certain tasks or situations.

<Some horses run better on certain types of ground>.

- **straight from the horse's mouth** from someone closely connected with a situation and therefore knowledgeable about it. <It is as though a horse is giving a tip about a race in which it is running>.

- **wild horses would not drag (someone) to something** *or* **somewhere** nothing would persuade (someone) to attend something or go somewhere.

- **you can take a horse to the water but you cannot make it drink** you can encourage someone to do something but you cannot force him or her to do it.

hot

- **hot on (someone's) heels** close behind someone.

hour

- **the (wee) small hours** the hours immediately following midnight (1am, 2am, etc).

- **the witching hour** midnight. <Witches traditionally are supposed to be active at midnight>.

house

- **bring the house down** to cause great amusement or applause.

- **eat (someone) out of house and home**. to eat a great deal and so be expensive to feed.

- **keep open house** always to be ready and willing to welcome guests.

- **on the house** paid by the owner of shop, pub, etc.

- **safe as houses** completely safe.

hue

- **a hue and cry** a loud protest. <An old legal term meaning a summons for people to join in a hunt for a criminal>.

huff

- **in a** *or* **the huff** upset, offended or sulking.

humble

- **eat humble pie** to have to admit that one has been wrong. <Refers originally to a dish made from the umble or offal of a deer eaten by the lower classes>.

ice

- **break the ice** to ease the shyness or formality of a social occasion.

- **cut no ice** to have no effect.

- **icing on the cake** a desirable but unnecessary addition.

- **on ice** put aside for future use or attention.

- **(skate) on thin ice** (to be) in a risky or dangerous position.

- **the tip of the iceberg** a small sign of a much larger problem. <Refers to the fact that the bulk of an iceberg is hidden underwater>.

ill

- **it's an ill wind (that blows nobody any good)** in almost every misfortune there is something of benefit to someone.

imagination

- **a figment of one's imagination** something which has no reality.

immemorial

- **from time immemorial** from a time beyond anyone's memory, written records, etc; for an extremely long time. <In legal phraseology the expression means 'before the beginning of legal memory'>.

in

- **the ins and outs of (something)** the details of (something).

inch

- **be** *or* **come within an inch of (something)** to be or come very close to.

- **every inch a** *or* **the (something)** exactly the type of (something).

- **give (someone) an inch (and he** *or* **she will take a mile** *or* **an ell)** if one yields in any way to someone then the person in question will make even greater demands. <An ell is an old form of measurement>.

Indian

- **an Indian summer** a time of fine, warm weather in autumn. <Perhaps from a feature of the climate of North America whose original inhabitants were Indians>.

innings

- **have a good innings** to enjoy a considerable period of life, success etc. <Refers to cricket>.

interest

- **a vested interest in (something)** a personal and biased interest in (something).

- **with interest** to an even greater extent than something has been done, etc, to someone.

iron

- **have many** *or* **several irons in the fire** to be involved in several projects, etc, at the same time. < Refers to a blacksmith who heats pieces of iron before shaping them>.
- **rule (someone** *or* **something) with a rod of iron** to rule with sternness or ruthlessness.
- **strike while the iron is hot** to act at a point at which things are favourable to one. <Refers to a blacksmith's work>.
- **the iron hand in the velvet glove** sternness or ruthlessness hidden under an appearance of gentleness.

item

- **be an item** to be regarded as having a romantic relationship.

itch

- **be itching to (do something)** to want very much to (do something).
- **have an itching palm** to be greedy for money.

ivory

- **live in an ivory tower** to have a way of life protected from difficulty or unpleasantness. <*La toure d'ivoire*, French for 'ivory tower', was coined by the poet Charles Augustin Saint-Beuve in 1837>.
- **tickle the ivories** to play the piano. <The keys of a piano are made of ivory>.

jack, Jack

- **a jack of all trades (and master of none)** someone who can do several different kinds of job (but does not do any of them very well).
- **before you can say Jack Robinson** extremely rapidly.
- **every man jack** absolutely everyone. <Perhaps from the fact that Jack is a very common first name>.
- **I'm all right, Jack** my situation is satisfactory, the implication being that it does not matter about anyone else.

jackpot

- **hit the jackpot** to have a great success, often involving a large sum of money. <Refers to the pool of money in poker>.

jam

- **jam tomorrow** the promise of better things in the future. <From a statement by the Red Queen in *Alice Through the Looking-Glass* by Lewis Carroll>.
- **want jam on it** to want an even better situation, etc, than one has already. <Refers to asking for jam on bread when bread is quite sufficient>.

Jekyll

- **a Jekyll and Hyde** someone with two completely different sides to his or her personality <Refers to the character in *The Strange Case of Dr Jekyll and Mr Hyde*, a novel by Robert Louis Stevenson>.

Jeremiah

- **a Jeremiah** a pessimist. <A biblical reference to the Lamentations of Jeremiah>.

jet

- **the jet set** wealthy people who can afford to travel a great deal. <Refers to jet planes>.

jewel

- **the jewel in the crown** the must valuable or successful thing associated with someone or something.

job

- **a job lot** a mixed collection. <Refers to auctioneering>.
- **just the job** exactly what is required.
- **jobs for the boys** used to suggest that jobs are being given to friends and relatives of people in power or of authority, rather than to people who are qualified to get them. Sometimes such jobs are unnecessary and created especially for the friend or relative.
- **make the best of a bad job** to obtain the best results possible from something unsatisfactory.

Job

- **a Job's comforter** someone who brings no comfort at all but makes one feel worse. <A biblical reference to the friends of Job>.
- **enough to try the patience of Job** so irritating as to make the most patient of people angry. <A biblical reference to Job who had to suffer many misfortunes patiently>.

Joe

kiss

Joe
- **Joe Bloggs** or **Public** or **Soap** the ordinary, average person.

joint
- **case the joint** to inspect premises carefully, especially with a view to later burglary.

joker
- **the joker in the pack** someone in a group who is different from the rest in some way and may cause problems or have an effect on a situation. <Refers to a pack of playing cards>.

Jonah
- **a Jonah** someone who brings bad luck. <a biblical reference to the book of Jonah, Jonah 1:4–7>.

Jones
- **keep up with the Joneses** to make an effort to remain on the same social level as one's neighbours by buying what they have, etc.

joy
- **no joy** no success, no luck.

judge
- **sober as a judge** to be extremely sober, not to be at all drunk.

jury
- **the jury is still out** people have not yet reached a conclusion or made a decision about something.

justice
- **do (someone** or **something) justice 1** to show the true value of (someone or something). **2** to eat (a meal, etc) with a good appetite.

keep
- **for keeps** permanently.
- **keep one's own counsel** to keep one's opinions, problems, etc, secret.
- **keep oneself to oneself** not to seek the company of others much, to tell others very little about oneself.
- **keep (something) to oneself** to keep (something) secret.

ken
- **beyond one's ken** outside the range of one's knowledge or understanding. <Literally, ken used to mean range of vision>.

kettle
- **a different kettle of fish** a completely different set of circumstances.
- **a pretty kettle of fish** an awkward or difficult situation.

kibosh
- **put the kibosh on (something)** to spoil or ruin (something's) chances of success.

kick
- **for kicks** for thrills or fun.
- **get a kick out of** to get fun or a thrill out of something.
- **kick oneself** to be annoyed with oneself.
- **kick over the traces** to defy rules that control one's behaviour. <Refers to a horse drawing a cart which gets out of control of the driver>.
- **kick (someone) upstairs** to appoint (someone) to a job which is more senior than the present one but which has less power.

kid[1]
- **handle (someone** or **something) with kid gloves** to deal with (someone or something) very tactfully or delicately.

kid[2]
- **the new kid on the block** the newest person in a place, activity, etc.

kill
- **be in at the kill** to be present when something important or decisive happens, often something that is unpleasant for someone. <Referring to the death of the fox in a foxhunt>.
- **kill (someone) with kindness** to spoil (someone) to the extent that it is a disadvantage to him or her.
- **make a killing** to make a large profit.
- **move in for the kill** to act decisively with a view to defeating one's opponent.

king
- **a king's ransom** a vast sum of money.

kingdom
- **till kingdom come** for a very long time. <Refers to the Lord's Prayer>.
- **to kingdom come** to death. <See above>.

kiss
- **kiss goodbye to (something)** to have to accept that you have lost (something)

or that you are not going to get (something).

- **kiss of death** something which causes the end, ruin or death of something. <A biblical reference to the kiss by which Judas betrayed Jesus>.

kitchen

- **everything but the kitchen sink** used to emphasize how much luggage someone is taking, etc.

kite

- **fly a kite** to start a rumour about a new project to see how people would react if the project were put into operation. <Refers to the use of kites to discover the direction and strength of the wind>.
- **high as a kite** very excited.

kitten

- **have kittens** to get very agitated or angry.

knee

- **bring (someone) to his** *or* **her knees** to humble or ruin (someone). <Refers to going on one's knees to beg for something>.

knickers

- **get one's knickers in a twist** to become agitated.

knife

- **have one's knife in (someone)** to wish to harm (someone).
- **like a (hot) knife through butter** used to emphasize how easily someone has dealt with a difficult situation.
- **on a knife edge** in a very uncertain or risky state.
- **stick the knife in (someone)** to do something that will harm, upset or cause problems for (someone).
- **the knives are out for (someone)** used to describe a situation in which several people are planning to harm or cause problems for (someone).
- **the night of the long knives** a time when an act of great disloyalty is carried out, usually by the sudden removal of several people from power or employment. <Refers to 19 June 1934, when Adolf Hitler had a number of his Nazi colleagues imprisoned or killed>.

knot¹

- **at a rate of knots** extremely rapidly. <Refers to a method of measuring the speed of ships>.

knot²

- **tie the knot** to get married.

know

- **in the know** knowing facts, etc, that are known only to a small group of people.
- **know (something) inside out** to know and understand (something) very well indeed.
- **not to know one is born** to lead a trouble-free, protected life.
- **not to know whether one is coming or going** to be very confused, often because one is very busy.

knuckle

- **rap (someone) over the knuckles** to scold or criticize (someone).

labour

- **a labour of love** a long or difficult job done for one's own satisfaction or from affection for someone rather than for reward.

lamb

- **like a lamb to the slaughter** meekly, without arguing or resisting, often because unaware of danger or difficulty. <A biblical reference to Isaiah 53:7>.

land

- **a land of milk and honey** a place where life is pleasant, with plenty of food and possibilities of success. <A biblical reference to the Promised Land of the Israelites described in Exodus 3:8>.
- **see how the land lies** to look carefully at a situation before taking any action or decision. <Refers literally to sailors looking at the shore before landing>.

lane

- **it's a long lane that has no turning** every period of misfortune, unhappiness, etc, comes to an end or changes to happier circumstances eventually.
- **life in the fast lane** a life which is very busy and active and usually contains a lot of stress and pressure.

language

- **speak the same language** to have similar tastes and views.

lap
- **in the lap of luxury** in luxurious conditions.

large
- **large as life** in person, actually present. <From works of art, particularly sculptural, which are life-size>.
- **larger than life** extraordinary, behaving, etc, in an extravagant way.

last
- **on one's** *or* **its last legs** near to collapse.
- **the last word** the most fashionable or up-to-date example of something.

late
- **better late than never** better for something to arrive, happen, etc, late than never to do so at all.

laugh
- **have the last laugh** to be victorious or proved right in the end, especially after being scorned, criticized, etc. <From the saying he who laughs last laughs longest>.
- **laugh and the world laughs with you (weep and you weep alone)** when someone is cheerful or happy, other people share in his or her joy (but when he or she is sad or miserable, people tend to avoid him or her).
- **laugh on the other side of one's face** to suffer disappointment or misfortune after seeming to be successful or happy.
- **laugh up one's sleeve** to be secretly amused.
- **no laughing matter** a very serious matter.

laurel
- **look to one's laurels** to be careful not to lose one's position or reputation because of better performances by one's rivals. <A reference to the laurel wreath with which the ancient Greeks crowned their poets and victors>.
- **rest on one's laurels** to be content with past successes without trying for any more. <As above>.

law
- **be a law unto oneself** to behave as one wishes rather than obeying the usual rules and conventions.
- **lay down the law** to state one's opinions with great force, to give orders dictatorially.

- **the law of the jungle** the unofficial rules for survival or success in a dangerous or difficult situation where civilized laws are not effective.

lay
- **lay it on thick** *or* **lay it on with a trowel** to exaggerate greatly in one's praise, compliments, etc, to someone.

lead¹
- **a leading question** a question asked in such a way as to suggest the answer the questioner wants to hear.
- **leading light** an important person in a certain group, field, etc.

lead²
- **swing the lead** to avoid doing one's work usually by inventing deceitful excuses. <Originally naval slang>.

leaf
- **take a leaf out of (someone's) book** to use (someone) as an example.
- **turn over a new leaf** to change one's behaviour, etc, for the better.

league
- **not be in the same league as (someone)** not to be as able as (someone). <Refers to the grouping of clubs in soccer, etc, according to ability>.

leap
- **by leaps and bounds** very quickly or successfully.

lease
- **give (someone** *or* **something) a new lease of life** to cause (someone) to have a longer period of active life or usefulness or to have a happier or more interesting life.

least
- **least said soonest mended** the less one says in a difficult situation the less harm will be done.

leave
- **leave (someone) in the lurch** to leave (someone) in a difficult or dangerous situation without any help. <A lurch refers to a position at the end of certain games, such as cribbage, in which the loser has either lost by a huge margin or scored no points at all>.

leeway
- **make up leeway** to take action to recover

from a setback or loss of advantage. <Leeway refers to the distance a sailing ship is blown sideways off its course by the wind>.

left
- **have two left feet** to be clumsy or awkward with one's feet, e.g. when dancing.
- **left, right and centre** everywhere, to an extreme degree.
- **(someone's) left hand does not know what his** *or* **her right hand is doing** (someone's) affairs are extremely complicated.

leg
- **break a leg** used as an interjection to an actor or other stage performer as a means of wishing him or her good luck. <In the theatre it is traditionally considered bad luck to wish an actor good luck in a direct way>.
- **give (someone) a leg up** to give (someone) some assistance to achieve advancement.
- **leg it** to run or go away quickly.
- **not to have a leg to stand on** to have no defence or justification for one's actions.
- **pull (someone's) leg** to try as a joke to make (someone) believe something that is not true.
- **stretch one's legs** to go for a walk.

legend
- **a legend in one's own lifetime** used to indicate that someone has become famous during his/her lifetime.

legion
- **their name is legion** there are a great many of them. <A biblical reference to Mark 5:9>.

length
- **go to great lengths** to take absolutely any action in order to achieve what one wants.

leopard
- **the leopard never changes its spots** a person's basic character does not change.

let
- **let oneself go 1** to enjoy oneself without restraint. **2** to stop taking trouble over one's appearance.

letter
- **the letter of the law** the exact wording of a

law, rule, agreement clause. <A biblical reference to II Corinthians 3:6>.
- **to the letter** in every detail.

level
- **a level playing field** a situation which is completely fair to all involved and in which no one has any particular advantage.
- **find one's** *or* **its (own) level** to find out what situation, position, etc, one is naturally suited to.
- **on the level** honest, trustworthy.

lick
- **a lick and a promise** a quick, not thorough, wash or clean.
- **lick (someone** *or* **something) into shape** to improve (someone or something) greatly to bring up to standard. <Refers to an old belief that bear cubs are born shapeless and have to be licked into shape by their mothers>.

lid
- **blow** *or* **take the lid off (something)** to reveal the truth about (something).
- **keep the lid on (something)** to keep (something) secret or keep (something) under control so that it does not get any worse.
- **put the (tin) lid on (something)** to finish (something) off usually in an unpleasant way.

lie¹
- **give the lie to (something)** to show that (something) is untrue.
- **lie in** *or* **through one's teeth** to tell lies obviously and unashamedly.
- **live a lie** to live a way of life about which there is something dishonest.

lie²
- **take (something) lying down** to accept an unpleasant situation without protesting or taking action against it.
- **the lie of the land** the nature and details of a situation. <Refers to sailors studying the nature of the coastline>.

life
- **breathe new life into (something)** to make (something) more lively, active or successful.

- **come to life** to become active or lively.
- **get a life** used to indicate to someone that you think that he/she has a boring, uninteresting life and should do something to change this.
- **life is just a bowl of cherries** used ironically to indicate that life can be difficult and unpleasant.
- **for dear life** or **for dear life's sake** to a very great extent, very rapidly, hard, etc.
- **lead** or **live the life of Riley** to lead a comfortable and trouble-free life.
- **not on your life** certainly not.
- **risk life and limb** to risk death or physical injury, to take extreme risks.
- **see life** to have wide experience, especially of varying conditions of life.
- **take one's life in one's hands** to take the risk of being killed, injured or harmed.
- **the facts of life** the facts about sex or reproduction.
- **the life and soul of the party** someone who is very lively and amusing on social occasions.
- **while** or **where there's life there's hope** one should not despair of a situation while there is still a possibility of improvement.

light¹

- **bring (something) to light** to reveal or uncover (something).
- **come to light** to be revealed or uncovered.
- **go out like a light** to go to sleep immediately.
- **hide one's light under a bushel** to be modest or silent about one's abilities or talents. <A biblical reference to Matthew 5:15, quoting Christ>.
- **in the cold light of day** when one looks at something practically and calmly.
- **light at the end of the tunnel** possibility of success, happiness, etc, after a long period of suffering, misery etc.
- **see the light** l) to understand something after not doing so. 2 to agree with someone's opinions or beliefs after not doing so. 3 (also **see the light of day**) to come into existence.
- **shed** or **throw light on (something)** to make (something) clearer, e.g. by providing more information about it.

light²

- **be light-fingered** to be likely to steal.
- **light as a feather** extremely light.
- **make light of (something)** to treat (something) as unimportant.

lightning

- **lightning never strikes twice (in the same place)** the same misfortune is unlikely to occur more than once.
- **quick as lightning** or **like greased lightning** extremely rapidly.

lily

- **be lily-livered** to be cowardly. <Refers to an old belief that the liver had no blood in it>.

limb

- **out on a limb** in a risky and often lonely position; having ideas, opinions, etc, different from other people. <Refers to being stuck in an isolated position on the branch of a tree>.
- **tear (someone) from limb to limb** to attack (someone) in a fierce and aggressive way, either in deed or speech.

limbo

- **in limbo** in a forgotten or neglected position.

limelight

- **in the limelight** in a situation where one attracts a great deal of public attention.

limit

- **be the limit** to be as much as, or more than, one can tolerate.
- **off limits** beyond what is allowed.

line

- **all along the line** at every point in an action, process, etc.
- **along** or **on the lines of (something)** similar to (something).
- **be in line for (something)** to be likely to get (something).
- **be** or **come on line** to be ready for use, to be operating. <A computer reference>.
- **be (way) out of line** to behave in a way that is not acceptable.
- **bring (something) into line with (something)** to make (something) the same as or comparable with (something else).
- **down the line** some time in the future.

- **draw a line under (something)** to regard (something unpleasant) as being over and best forgotten so that people can move on.
- **fall into line** to behave according to the relevant rules, regulations or traditions.
- **lay it on the line** to make (something) absolutely clear to someone.
- **not one's line of country** not something which one knows a lot about or is interested in.
- **read between the lines** to understand or deduce something from a statement, situation, etc, although this has not actually been stated. <Refers to a method of writing secret messages by writing in invisible ink between the lines of other messages>.
- **step out of line** to behave differently from what is usually acceptable or expected. <Refers to a line of soldiers on parade>.
- **the line of least resistance** the course of action that will cause one least effort or trouble.
- **toe the line** to obey the rules or orders. <Refers to competitors having to stand with their toes to a line when starting a race, etc>.

lion

- **put one's head in the lion's mouth** to put oneself in a very dangerous or difficult position.
- **the lion's share** having a much larger share than anyone else. <Refers to one of Aesop's fables in which the lion, being a very fierce animal, claimed three quarters of the food which he and other animals had hunted for>.
- **throw (someone) to the lions** deliberately to put (someone) in a dangerous or difficult position, often to protect oneself. <Refers to a form of entertainment in ancient Rome in which prisoners were thrown to wild animals to be attacked and killed>.

lip

- **keep a stiff upper lip** to show no emotion, such as fear or disappointment when danger, trouble, etc, arises.

- **lick one's lips** to look forward to something with pleasure. <A reference to licking one's lips at the thought of appetizing food>.
- **(someone's) lips are sealed** (someone) will not reveal something secret.
- **pay lip-service to (something)** to say that one believes in or agrees with (something) without really doing so and without acting as if one did.
- **read my lips** used by someone to emphasize that people should believe or trust in what he/she is about to say.

litmus

- **a litmus test** something which assesses or demonstrates clearly what something is really like.

live[1]

- **beat** *or* **knock the living daylights out of (someone)** to give (someone) a severe beating.
- **live and let live** to get on with one's own life and let other people get on with theirs without one interfering.
- **live it up** to have an enjoyable and expensive time.

live[2]

- **a live wire** an energetic, enthusiastic person. <Refers to a live electrical wire>.

load

- **a loaded question** a question intended to lead someone into admitting to or agreeing with something when he or she does not wish to do so. <Refers to a dice loaded or weighted so that it tends always to show the same score>.

loaf

- **use one's loaf** to use one's brains, to think clearly.

lock

- **lock, stock and barrel** completely, with everything included. <Refers to the main components of a gun>.
- **under lock and key** in a place which is locked for security.

log

- **sleep like a log** to sleep very soundly.

lone

- **a lone wolf** someone who prefers to be alone.

long

- **in the long run** in the end, after everything has been considered.
- **the long and the short of it** the only thing that need be said, to sum the story up in a few words.

look

- **look askance at (someone or something)** to regard with disapproval or distrust.
- **look before you leap** give careful consideration before you act.
- **not to get a look-in** not to have a chance of winning, succeeding, being noticed, etc.

loose

- **cut loose** to free oneself from the influence of power of (someone or something).
- **on the loose** enjoying freedom and pleasure. <Refers originally to prisoners escaped from jail>.

lord

- **lord it over (someone)** to act in a proud and commanding manner to (someone).

lose

- **lose ground** to lose one's advantage or strong position.
- **play a losing game** to go on with something that is obviously going to be unsuccessful.

loss

- **cut one's losses** not to spend any more time, money or effort on something on which one has already spent a lot to little benefit.

love

- **not for love nor money** not in any way at all.
- **there's no love lost between them** they are hostile to each other.

low

- **keep a low profile** not to draw attention to oneself or one's actions or opinions.
- **lie low** to stay quiet or hidden.

luck

- **down on one's luck** experiencing misfortune.
- **push one's luck** to risk failure by trying to gain too much.
- **strike it lucky** to have good fortune.
- **thank one's lucky stars** to be grateful for one's good fortune.

lull

- **lull (someone) into a false sense of security** to lead (someone) into thinking that all is well in order to attack when he or she is not prepared.

mad

- **mad as a hatter** utterly insane, extremely foolish or eccentric. <Hat-making used to involve the use of nitrate of mercury, exposure to which could cause a nervous illness which people thought was a symptom of insanity>.
- **mad as a March hare** insane, silly, extremely eccentric. <Hares tend to leap around wildly in the fields during March, which is their breeding season>.

make

- **make a day or night of it** to spend a whole day or night enjoying oneself in some way.
- **make do with (something)** to use (something) as a poor or temporary substitute for something.
- **make it up** to become friendly again after a quarrel.
- **make-or-break** bringing either success or failure.
- **on the make** trying to make a profit for oneself.

man

- **a man of his word** someone who always does as he promises.
- **be one's own man** to be independent in one's actions, opinions, etc.
- **man of straw** a man who is considered to be of not much worth or substance.
- **man to man** frankly.
- **the man in the street** the ordinary, average person.
- **to a man** everyone without exception.

manner

- **to the manner born** as if accustomed since birth to a particular way of behaviour etc. <Refers to a quotation from Shakespeare's *Hamlet*>.

map

- **put (somewhere) on the map** to cause (somewhere) to become well known or important.

marble

- **have marbles in one's mouth** to speak with an upper-class accent.
- **lose one's marbles** to become insane or senile.

march

- **get one's marching orders** to be told to leave, to be dismissed. <Refers to a military term>.
- **steal a march on (someone)** to gain an advantage over (someone) by doing something earlier than expected. <Refers literally to moving an army unexpectedly while the enemy is resting>.

mark

- **be a marked man** *or* **woman** to be in danger or trouble because people are trying to harm one. 'Marked' means watched>.
- **beside** *or* **wide of the mark** off the target or subject. <Refers to hitting the target in archery>.
- **be up to the mark** to reach the required or normal standard.
- **get off one's mark** to get started quickly on an undertaking. <Refers to track events in athletics>.
- **hit the mark** to be correct or accurate. <Refers to the target in archery>.
- **leave one's mark on (someone** *or* **something)** to have an important and lasting effect on (someone or something).
- **make one's mark** to make oneself well known, to make a lasting impression.
- **overstep the mark** to do or say something which is unacceptable or offensive.
- **quick off the mark** quick to act. <Refers literally to a runner starting quickly in a race>.

marrow

- **chilled** *or* **frozen to the marrow** extremely cold.

mass

- **the masses** the ordinary people, taken as a whole.

match

- **a shouting match** a loud, angry discussion or argument about something.
- **meet one's match** to find oneself against someone who has the ability to defeat one in a contest, argument or activity.

- **a matter of life or death** something of great urgency, something that might involve loss of life.

meal

- **make a meal of (something)** to treat (something) as if it is more complicated or time-consuming than it is.

measure

- **for good measure** as something in addition to what is necessary.

meat

- **be meat and drink to (someone)** to be very important to (someone).
- **one man's meat is another man's poison** people have different tastes.

Mecca

- **a Mecca** a place that is important to a certain group of people and is visited by them. <Refers to the birthplace of Mohammed to which Muslims make pilgrimages>.

meet

- **meet one's Waterloo** to be finally defeated. <Napoleon was defeated for the last time at Waterloo by Wellington>.

melt

- **be in the melting-pot** to be in the process of changing. <Refers to melting down and reshaping metal>.

mercy

- **at the mercy of (someone** *or* **something)** wholly in the power or control of (someone or something).
- **be thankful for small mercies** to be grateful for minor benefits or advantages in an otherwise difficult situation.

merry

- **make merry** to have an enjoyable, entertaining time, to have a party.

message

- **get the message** to understand.

method

- **there is method in his madness** someone has a good, logical reason for acting as he does, although his actions seem strange or unreasonable. <A reference to Shakespeare's *Hamlet* Act 2, scene ii>.

Midas

- **the Midas touch** the ability to make money or be successful easily. <Refers to a Greek

midnight   **money**

legend about a king of Phrygia whose touch turned everything to gold>.

midnight

- **burn the midnight oil** to work or study until late at night.

mile

- **be miles away** to be thinking about something else and so not concentrating on what is being said to you or what is going on around you.
- **go the extra mile** to make a special effort and do more than you would usually do, more than you have been asked to do, etc in order to achieve something.
- **run a mile** used to indicate the lengths to which someone would go to avoid something.
- **stand** *or* **stick out a mile** to be extremely obvious.

mill

- **a millstone round one's neck** a heavy burden or responsibility.
- **calm as a millpond** extremely calm.
- **go through the mill** to experience a series of difficult or troublesome events, periods or tests. <From the grinding of corn in a mill>.
- **run-of-the-mill** usual, not special.

mince

- **make mincemeat of (someone** *or* **something)** to defeat (someone) soundly, to destroy (something).
- **not to mince matters** to speak completely frankly without trying to be too kind, etc.

mind

- **be** *or* **go out of one's mind** to be or become insane.
- **blow (someone's) mind** to amaze (someone), to excite (someone) greatly.
- **cross one's mind** to enter one's mind briefly.
- **give (someone) a piece of one's mind** to scold or criticize (someone) angrily.
- **great minds think alike** clever people tend to have the same ideas and opinions.
- **in one's right mind** sane, rational.
- **in two minds** undecided.
- **not to know one's own mind** not to know what one really wants to do.

- **put (someone) in mind of (someone** *or* **something)** to remind (someone) of (someone or something).
- **slip one's mind** to be temporarily forgotten.

mint

- **in mint condition** used but in extremely good condition. <Literally the unused condition of a newly minted coin>.

minute

- **up to the minute** modern or fashionable.

misery

- **put (someone) out of his** *or* **her misery** to end a time of worry, anxiety or suspense for (someone). <Originally a term for putting to death a wounded and suffering animal>.

miss

- **a miss is as good as a mile** if one fails at something it does not matter how close one came to succeeding.
- **give (something) a miss** not to go to or attend (something).

moment

- **have one's moments** to have times of success, happiness.
- **not for a moment** not at all.
- **the moment of truth** a crucial time, a time when one has to make an important decision, face up to a crisis, etc.

money

- **have money to burn** to have enough money to be able to spend it in ways considered foolish.
- **money for jam** *or* **old rope** money obtained in exchange for very little work, effort, etc. <Army slang>.
- **money talks** rich people have influence simply because they have money.
- **put one's money where one's mouth is** to give money for a cause or purpose which one claims to support.
- **spend money like water** to spend money very freely.
- **the smart money is on (something)** used to describe an event or situation which is very likely to take place. <Smart money is used to refer to people who know a lot about investment, business deals, etc>.

- **throw good money after bad** to spend money in an unsuccessful attempt to retrieve money which one has already lost.
- **you pays your money and you takes your choice** used to indicate the difficulty or impossibility of deciding which of two choices is the right one.

monkey
- **monkey business** action likely to cause trouble, illegal or unfair activities.
- **not to give a monkey's** not to care at all.
- **speak to the organ grinder, not his monkey** *see* **organ**.

month
- **a month of Sundays** an extremely long time.

Monty
- **the full Monty** used to indicate that something is absolutely complete or comprehensive or that it contains everything that is usually involved in such an activity or situation.

moon
- **ask** *or* **cry for the moon** to ask for something that it is impossible to get.
- **do a moonlight (flit)** to move away suddenly.
- **many moons ago** a very long time ago, sometimes used as a humorous exaggeration.
- **over the moon** extremely happy.
- **promise (someone) the moon** to make promises that have little hope of ever being realized.

more
- **the more the merrier** the more people that are involved the better.

morning
- **the morning after the night before** a morning when one is suffering from a hangover caused by drinking too much alcohol the night before.

moth
- **like a moth to a flame** used to describe someone who finds someone or something irresistibly attractive, even although the person or thing might cause harm or trouble.

motion
- **go through the motions** to make a show of doing something, to pretend to do something.

mould
- **break the mould** to do something in a completely new and better way.
- **cast in the same mould (as someone)** very similar (to someone). <Refers to ironworking>.
- **they broke the mould when they made (someone)** used to emphasize how special or exceptional someone is.

mountain
- **have a mountain to climb** used to emphasize how difficult it is going to be for someone to do or achieve something and how much effort will be needed.
- **if the mountain will not come to Mohammed, then Mohammed must go to the mountain** a saying which indicates that, if someone whom you want to see cannot or is unwilling to come to you, then you should make the effort to go to him or her. <Refers to a story about Mohammed in which he is asked to demonstrate his power by getting Mount Sofa to come to him. When this did not happen, Mohammed is supposed to have said the words which form the saying>.
- **make a mountain out of a molehill** to greatly exaggerate the extent of a problem, etc.
- **move mountains** to achieve something that seems impossible or extremely difficult.

mouse
- **poor as a church mouse** extremely poor.
- **quiet as a mouse** extremely quiet.

mouth
- **be all mouth and trousers** to talk a lot about doing something but never actually do it.
- **have a big mouth** to talk a lot, especially about things, such as secrets, that one should not.
- **out of the mouths of babes and sucklings** used when a child says something that is surprisingly adult, true, wise, etc.
- **shoot one's mouth off** to talk in a loud and often boastful or threatening manner.
- **make one's mouth water** used to emphasize how delicious something smells or looks.

much

- **the movers and shakers** refers to people with power and influence. <Possibly derives from the poem 'Ode' by Arthur O'Shaughnessy (1844–81), 'We are the movers and shakers of the world forever'>.

much

- **much of a muchness** very similar.
- **not much of a (something)** not a very good (something).
- **not up to much** not very good.

mud

- **drag (someone/someone's reputation) through the mud** to damage (someone or someone's reputation) by saying bad things about him or her.
- **mud sticks** used to indicate that, if something bad is said about someone, some people are likely to believe this and to go on believing it, even if it is not at all true or if it has been disproved.
- **(someone's) name is mud** (someone) is in disfavour or is being criticized.
- **sling** *or* **throw mud at (someone** *or* **something)** to say bad or insulting things about (someone or something).

mule

- **stubborn as a mule** extremely stubborn.

multitude

- **cover a multitude of sins** to be able to apply or refer to a large number of different things. <A misquotation from the Bible, I Peter 4:8, 'Charity shall cover the multitude of sins'>.

mum

- **mum's the word** do not say anything.

murder

- **get away with murder** to do something bad, irresponsible, etc, without suffering punishment.
- **I could murder (something)** used to indicate that you would very much like to have (something) to eat or drink.
- **scream blue murder** to scream extremely loudly.

music

- **be music to one's ears** used to indicate that one is very pleased to hear something.

mustard

- **keen as mustard** very eager and enthusiastic.

- **not cut the mustard** not to be able to do or achieve something; not be good enough.

muster

- **pass muster** to be considered good enough. <Refers to the calling together of people in the armed services in order to make sure that their dress and equipment are in good order>.

mutton

- **mutton dressed as lamb** an older person, usually a woman, dressed in clothes suitable for young people.

nail

- **a nail in (someone's) coffin** something which helps to bring about (someone's) downfall or destruction.
- **hit the nail on the head** to be extremely accurate in one's description, judgement, etc, of someone or something.

name

- **be (someone's) middle name** used to emphasize how typical of someone something is.
- **call (someone) names** to apply insulting or rude names to (someone).
- **give (someone** *or* **something) a bad name** to damage the reputation of (someone or something).
- **make a name for oneself** to become famous or well known.
- **name names** to give the names of people, especially people who are guilty or accused of wrong-doing.
- **no names, no pack-drill** no names will be mentioned and so no one will get into trouble. <'Pack-drill' refers to a form of army punishment in which the soldiers being punished were forced to march up and down carrying all their equipment>.
- **the name of the game** the important or central thing.
- **to one's name** in one's possession or ownership.

nasty

- **a nasty piece of work** someone who is very unpleasant or behaves very unpleasantly.

navel

- **contemplate one's navel** to be too much concerned with oneself and one's own activities and problems rather than with other, often more important, problems,

near
- **a near miss** something unpleasant that very nearly happened, often the near collision of two planes in the sky.
- **a near thing** the act of just avoiding an accident, misfortune, etc.
- **one's nearest and dearest** one's close family.

neck
- **be in (something) up to one's neck** to be very much involved in something bad or illegal.
- **get it in the neck** to be severely scolded or punished.
- **have the brass neck to (do something)** to have the impertinence or brazenness to (do something).
- **neck and neck** exactly equal.
- **risk one's neck** to put one's life, job, etc, in danger.
- **stick one's neck out** to take a risk or do something that may cause trouble.
- **this** *or* **that, etc, neck of the woods** this or that, etc, part of the country. <Originally a term for a remote community in the woods of the early 19th-century American frontier>.

needle
- **like looking for a needle in a haystack** an impossible search.

nerve
- **get on (someone's) nerves** to irritate (someone).
- **have a nerve** to be impertinent or brazen.
- **live on one's nerves** to be worried and anxious all the time.
- **lose one's nerve** to become scared, and so be unable to continue with an activity or course of action.
- **touch a nerve** to refer to something about which someone feels particularly sensitive.
- **war of nerves** a situation in which two opponents or enemies use psychological means against each other, for example by frightening or threatening the other side, rather than direct action.

nest
- **a nest-egg** savings for the future.
- **fly the nest** to leave one's parent home and go and live elsewhere.
- **foul your own nest** to do something which could have a bad effect on your own interests, activities or relationships.

net
- **cast one's net wide** to involve a large number of people or things or a large area.
- **slip through the net** not to be found or identified.

nettle
- **grasp the nettle** to set about an unpleasant or difficult task in a firm and determined manner.

never
- **never-never land** an imaginary land where conditions are ideal. <Refers to the idealized land in J.M. Barrie's play *Peter Pan*>.
- **on the never-never** by hire purchase.

new
- **new broom** someone who has just been appointed to a post and who is eager to be efficient, make changes, etc. <From the saying a new broom sweeps clean, a new broom being more effective than the old one>.

news
- **break the news to (someone)** to tell (someone) about something, usually something unpleasant or sad, that has happened.
- **no news is good news** if one has not received any information about someone or something then all is likely to be well since if something bad, such as an accident, had happened one would have heard.

next
- **next door to (something)** very nearly (something).
- **next to nothing** almost nothing, very little.

niche
- **carve a niche for oneself** to succeed in creating a secure job or position for oneself or for something.

nick
- **in good** *or* **poor nick** in good or poor condition.
- **in the nick of time** just in time, at the last possible minute.

nine

- **a nine days' wonder** something that arouses surprise and interest for a short time only. <Refers to a saying quoted by Chaucer—'where is no wonder so great that it lasts more than nine days'>.

ninepins

- **go down like ninepins** to become ill or damaged, or to be killed or destroyed rapidly, one after the other.

nip

- **nip (something) in the bud** to put a stop or end to (something) as soon as it develops.

nit

- **get down to the nitty-gritty** to begin to deal with the basic practical details, problems, etc.
- **nit-picking** the act of finding very minor faults in something, quibbling. <Refers to picking nits out of hair>.

no

- **no end of (something)** a great deal of (something).
- **no go** unsuccessful, in vain.
- **no way** under no circumstances.

nod

- **a nod is as good as a wink to a blind horse** a hint is often all that is necessary to communicate thoughts or feelings.
- **give/get the nod** to give/be given permission or approval for something.
- **have a nodding acquaintance with (someone or something)** to know (someone or something) slightly. <Refers to knowing someone well enough to nod in greeting to him or her>.
- **nod off** to fall asleep, sometimes accidentally.

noise

- **big noise** an important person.
- **make all the right noises** to say things which are considered the right response to a particular situation or the things which someone wants to hear.

nook

- **every nook and cranny** absolutely everywhere. <Literally, in all the corners and cracks>.

nose

- **cut off one's nose to spite one's face** to do something that harms oneself, usually in order to harm someone else.
- **follow one's nose** to go straight forward.
- **get up (someone's) nose** to annoy or irritate (someone).
- **have a nose around** to have a good look round a place, usually out of curiosity and when one is not supposed to be doing so.
- **have a nose for (something)** to have a talent or ability for finding or noticing something.
- **keep (one's or someone's) nose to the grindstone** to keep (someone) working hard without stopping.
- **lead (someone) by the nose** to get (someone) to do whatever one wants. <Refers to the ring on a bull's nose>.
- **look down one's nose at (someone or something)** to regard or treat (someone or something) with disdain or contempt.
- **on the nose** exactly.
- **pay through the nose** to pay a great deal of money for something.
- **poke one's nose into (something)** to pry into or interfere in other people's affairs. <Refers literally to a dog>.
- **powder one's nose** a euphemism, sometimes used by women, meaning to go to the toilet.
- **put (someone's) nose out of joint** to make (someone) jealous or offended by taking a place usually held by him or her, e.g. in the affections of a person whom he or she loves. <Refers to a person whose nose has been broken by being hit in the face>.
- **rub (someone's) nose in it** to keep on reminding (someone) about something he or she has done wrong. <Refers literally to rubbing a dog's nose in its faeces with the intention of house-training it>.
- **see further than the end of one's nose** to be concerned with more than just what is happening in the immediate present and in the immediate vicinity.
- **thumb one's nose at (someone or something)** see **thumb**.

note

- **turn up one's nose at (something)** to treat (something) with dislike or disgust.
- **under (someone's) (very) nose 1** right in front of (someone) and so easily seen. **2** while (someone) is actually present.

note

- **strike the right note** to say or do something suitable for the occasion. <Refers to playing a musical instrument>.

nothing

- **come to nothing** to fail.
- **go for nothing** to be wasted or unsuccessful.
- **have nothing on (someone) 1** not to be nearly as good, skilful, bad, etc, as (someone). **2** to have no proof or evidence of (someone's) wrongdoing.
- **have nothing to do with (someone *or* something)** to avoid contact with (someone or something).
- **nothing ventured, nothing gained** one cannot achieve anything if one does not make an attempt or take a risk.
- **there is nothing to choose between (two people *or* things)** there is hardly any difference in quality, ability, etc, between (two people or things).
- **there's nothing to it** it is very easy.
- **think nothing of (something)** not to regard (something) as out of the ordinary, difficult, etc.

nowhere

- **be in the middle of nowhere** be in a place which is a long way away from a town or city, a lot of people, etc, often carrying the suggestion that the place is boring.
- **get nowhere** to make no progress, to have no success.

nudge

- **nudge, nudge, wink, wink** used to indicate that there is some form of sexual innuendo or hidden reference in something that has been said. <Came into common use influenced by a sketch by Eric Idle in the TV series *Monty Python's Flying Circus*>.

number

- **get *or* have (someone's) number** to find out or know what kind of person (someone) is and what he or she is likely to do.

- **(someone's) number is up** (someone) is about to suffer something unpleasant, such as dying, failing, being punished, being caught, etc.
- **number one** oneself.

nut[1]

- **a hard nut to crack** a difficult problem or person to deal with.
- **in a nutshell** briefly, to sum up.
- **the nuts and bolts of (something)** the basic details or practicalities of (something).

nut[2]

- **be nuts about (someone *or* something)** to like (someone or something) a very great deal, to be wildly enthusiastic about (someone or something).
- **do one's nut** to get very angry.
- **go nuts** to become extremely angry.

oak

- **great oaks from little acorns grow** a saying used to emphasize that even large and important things often begin a small way.

oar

- **put *or* stick one's oar in** to interfere in another's affairs, conversation, e.g. by offering unwanted opinions. <Perhaps refers to someone who is being rowed in a boat by others and who suddenly decides to take part in the rowing unasked>.
- **rest on one's oars** to take a rest after working very hard. <Refers literally to rowing>.

object

- **money, distance, etc, is no object** it does not matter how much money, distance, etc, is involved in the particular situation. <Originally 'money is no object' meant money or profits were not the main aim but it came to be misapplied>.

occasion

- **rise to the occasion** to be able to carry out whatever action is required in an important or urgent situation.

odd

- **against all the odds** in spite of major difficulties.
- **be at odds with (someone *or* something)** to be in disagreement with (someone or something), not to be in accordance with (something).

- **lay odds** to bet. <Refers to betting on horses>.
- **make no odds** to be of no importance, to make no difference.
- **odd man out** someone or something that is different from others. <Refers literally to someone left out of a game when the teams have been chosen>.
- **odds and ends** small objects of different kinds.
- **over the odds** more than one would usually expect to pay. <Refers originally to a horse-racing term>.

off

- **in the offing** about to or likely to happen, appear, etc. <A nautical term. Offing refers to the whole area of sea that can be seen from a particular point on shore>.
- **off and on** *or* **on and off** occasionally.

oil

- **be no oil painting** to be not at all attractive.
- **oil and water** used to emphasize how different two people or things are.
- **oil the wheels** to make something easier to do or obtain. <Wheels turn more easily if oil is applied to them>.
- **pour oil on troubled waters** to attempt to bring a state of calm and peace to a situation of disagreement or dispute. <Since oil floats on water it has the effect of making waves flat>.
- **strike oil** to obtain exactly what one wants, to be successful.

old

- **an old hand** someone who is very experienced (at doing something).
- **old as the hills** extremely old.
- **old hat** old-fashioned, no longer popular.
- **old master** (a work by) any great painter before the 19th century, especially of the 15th and 16th centuries.
- **the old-boy network** a system in which jobs and other advantages are obtained on the basis of knowing the right people rather than on ability. <The connection with such people is often that one was at school with them>.
- **the old country** the country from which an immigrant or his or her parents or grandparents originally came.
- **the old guard** the older members of a group who are old-fashioned in their opinions and tastes. <The translation of the name applied to the most experienced section of Napoleon's army>.

olive

- **olive branch** a sign of a wish for peace. <The olive branch was an ancient symbol of peace>.

omelette

- **you can't make an omelette without breaking eggs** a saying indicating that it is impossible to achieve something worthwhile without causing a few problems or difficulties.

on

- **be not on** used to indicate emphatic disapproval of or lack of acceptance of something.
- **be on to (someone)** having discovered some previously secret or unknown information about (someone) or his or her activities.

once

- **give (someone) the once-over** to look at or study (someone or something) quickly.

one

- **a one-horse race** a competition, contest, etc, in which one person or side is certain to win.
- **a one-night stand** a relationship, arrangement, etc, that lasts for one evening or night only. <Literally a single performance in one place given by a pop group, etc, on tour>.
- **get one over on (someone)** to gain a victory or advantage over (someone).
- **have a one-track mind** to think only of one subject all the time.
- **have had one too many** to have had too much to drink.
- **it takes one to know one** used to indicate that people who have faults of their own find it easy to spot such faults in others.
- **not be oneself** to be feeling slightly unwell, to be more depressed, etc, than usual.

onion

- **know one's onions** to know a subject, one's job, etc.

open

- **an open-and-shut case** free from uncertainty, having an obvious outcome.
- **an open secret** a supposed secret that is known to many people.
- **keep an open mind** to be willing to listen to other people's suggestions, ideas, etc, instead of just concentrating on one's own point of view.
- **lay oneself (wide) open to (something)** to put oneself in a position in which one is liable to be in receipt of (blame, criticism, accusations, attack, etc).

opposite

- **(someone's) opposite number** the person in another company, country, etc, whose job or role corresponds to someone's.

option

- **keep one's options open** to delay making a definite decision so that all choices are available as long as possible.

oracle

- **work the oracle** to produce the desired result, to obtain what one wants, especially by using cunning, influence or bribery. <Refers to the oracle at Delphi in Greek legend>.

order

- **the order of the day** something that should be done, worn, etc, because conventional, common, fashionable, etc. <Refers originally to a list of items to be discussed in the British parliament on a particular day>.

organ

- **speak to the organ grinder, not his monkey** used to emphasize that one wants to deal with someone in authority, not with someone associated with him or her who has no power. <An organ grinder was a person who played a kind of musical instrument on wheels, known as a barrel organ, in the street and he often had a monkey on the barrel organ to attract people or to collect gifts of money>.

other

- **look the other way** to ignore or disregard something wrong, illegal, etc.

out

- **come out** to make public the fact that one is a homosexual.
- **get (something) out of your system** see **system**.
- **out and about** going around outside, e.g. after an illness.

outside

- **at the outside** at the most.

over

- **be all over (someone)** to be extremely friendly and attentive to (someone).
- **over and done with** completely finished, at an end.

overboard

- **go overboard (about** or **for someone** or **something)** to be extremely enthusiastic about (someone or something).

overdrive

- **go into overdrive** to start to work extremely hard or to become extremely active.

owe

- **I owe you one** used to indicate that someone has done one some kind of favour and that one must return this some time.

own

- **come into one's own** to have the opportunity to show one's good qualities, talent, skill, etc.
- **hold one's own 1** to perform as well as one's opponents in a contest, an argument, etc. **2** to be surviving, to be holding on to life.

p

- **mind one's p's and q's** to be very careful, to be polite and well behaved. <Perhaps refers to a warning to a printer to be careful of the letters p and q so as not to confuse them>.

pace

- **put (someone** or **something) through its** or **his** or **her paces** to test the ability of (someone or something) by getting them to demonstrate what it, he or she is capable of. <Refers originally to assessing horses>.
- **show one's paces** to demonstrate one's abilities.
- **stay the pace** to maintain progress in an activity at the same rate as others.

pack   patch

pack

- **send (someone) packing** to send (someone) away firmly and frankly.

pain

- **a pain in the neck** someone or something that constantly irritates one.
- **no pain, no gain** a saying used to emphasize the fact that the acquiring of something advantageous or desirable often involves something difficult or unpleasant, but it is worth it.

paint

- **like watching paint dry** used to describe something extremely boring.
- **paint the town red** to go out and celebrate in a lively, noisy manner.

palm

- **grease (someone's) palm** to give (someone) money, to bribe (someone).
- **have (someone) in the palm of one's hand** to have (someone) in one's power and ready to do as one wishes.

paper

- **paper over the cracks** to try to hide faults, mistakes, difficulties, etc, in a hasty or careless way in order to pretend that there were no faults, mistakes, etc.
- **paper tiger** someone or something that has the outward appearance of being powerful and threatening but is in fact ineffective.

par

- **below** _or_ **not up to par** **1** not up to the usual or required standard. **2** not completely well.
- **on a par with (something)** of the same standard as (something), as good as (something).
- **par for the course** what might be expected, what usually happens. <Originally a golfing term meaning the number of strokes that would be made in a perfect round on the course>.

part

- **look the part** to have the appropriate appearance of a particular kind of person.
- **part and parcel (of something)** something that is naturally or basically part (of something).

- **take (something) in good part** to accept (something) without being angry or offended.
- **take (someone's) part** to support (someone) in an argument, debate, etc.
- **the parting of the ways** the point at which people must go different ways, take different courses of action, make different decisions, etc. <A biblical reference to Ezekiel 21:21>.

party

- **the party line** the official opinions, ideas, attitudes, etc, as set down by the leaders of a particular group.
- **the party's over** a pleasant or happy time has come to an end.

pass

- **make a pass at (someone)** to try to start a romantic or sexual relationship with (someone). <Originally a fencing term, meaning to thrust with a foil>.
- **pass away** to die.
- **pass by on the other side** to ignore someone in trouble and not help him or her. <A biblical reference to the parable of the Samaritan, Luke 10>.

past

- **I, etc, would not put it past (someone) to (do something)** I, etc, think (someone) is quite capable of (doing something bad).
- **past it** less good, etc, than when one or it was not so old.
- **past master** someone extremely talented or skilful.

pasture

- **pastures new** _or_ **fresh fields and pastures new** used to indicate a new and different place or situation. <The longer version of the phrase is a misquotation of 'fresh woods and pastures new' from John Milton's poem 'Lycidas'.

pat

- **a pat on the back** an indication of praise or approval.

patch

- **not to be a patch on (someone** _or_ **something)** not to be nearly as good as (someone or something).
- **patch it** _or_ **things up** to become friends again after a quarrel.

path   **pie**

path
- **beat a path to (someone's) door** to visit (someone) very frequently or in large numbers.

pave
- **pave the way for (something)** to make it possible or easier for (something to happen).

pay
- **put paid to (something)** to prevent (an action, plan, etc) from being carried out.

peace
- **keep the peace** to prevent disturbances, fighting, quarrelling, etc.
- **make one's peace with (someone)** to become, or try to become, friendly with (someone) again after a period of disagreement.

peacock
- **proud as a peacock** extremely proud.

pearl
- **pearls of wisdom** something wise or helpful, often used ironically.

pedestal
- **put (someone) on a pedestal** to treat (someone) with great respect and admiration. <Refers to the practice of putting statues of famous people on pedestals>.

peg
- **bring (someone) down a peg or two** to make (someone) more humble. <Refers to tuning musical instruments>.
- **off the peg** of clothes, ready to wear, not made for one specially.
- **a square peg in a round hole** used to describe someone who does not fit into a particular situation or environment and feels uncomfortable in it.

penny
- **a penny for them** *or* **your thoughts** what are you thinking about?
- **in for a penny, in for a pound** if one is going to do something one might as well do it boldly and thoroughly.
- **not to have a penny to one's name** to have no money at all.
- **penny wise and pound foolish** being careful with small items of expenditure and extravagant with large ones.

- **spend a penny** to urinate. <From the former price of admission to the cubicle of a public toilet>.
- **the penny drops** I, etc, suddenly understand. <Refers to a coin in a slot machine>.
- **turn up like a bad penny** to reappear or keep reappearing although not wanted or welcome.
- **two a penny** of little value because very common.

petard
- **hoist with one's own petard** to be the victim of one's own action which was intended to harm someone else. <Refers to Shakespeare's *Hamlet*, Act 3, scene IV. A petard was a device containing explosives used by military engineers>.

philistine
- **a philistine** someone who is not interested in artistic or intellectual pursuits. <The Philistines were a fierce race of people who fought against the Israelites in biblical times. The present meaning was influenced by German>.

phrase
- **to coin a phrase** literally, to say something new and inventive, but used usually to introduce a cliché or a common saying or expression.

pick
- **pick and choose** to choose very carefully from a range of things.

picnic
- **be no picnic** used to emphasize how difficult or unpleasant something is.

picture
- **be out of the picture** to be no longer involved in something.
- **the big picture** the whole situation, not just some details.
- **get the picture** to understand what is being explained or described.
- **put (someone) in the picture** to give (someone) all the information and detail about a situation.

pie
- **nice as a pie** exceptionally pleasant or friendly, often unexpectedly.

piece   **plain**

- **pie in the sky** something good expected or promised in the future which is unlikely to come about. <Refers to a quotation from a poem by the American poet Joe Hill>.

piece

- **go to pieces** to be unable to continue coping with a situation, life, etc.

pig

- **buy a pig in a poke** to buy (something) without examining it carefully or without knowing its worth. <Supposedly referring to a fairground trick in which a prospective customer was sold a cat in a bag thinking that it was a piglet>.
- **make a pig of oneself** to eat greedily, to eat a great deal.
- **make a pig's ear of (something)** to make a mess of (something), to do (something) very badly or clumsily.
- **pigs might fly** it is extremely unlikely that that will happen.

pikestaff

- **plain as a pikestaff** very obvious. <Pikestaff was originally packstaff, a staff for holding a traveller's pack and lacking any ornamentation. This sense of plain has been confused with that of plain meaning clear>.

pillar

- **from pillar to post** from one place to another, often repeatedly. <Refers originally to the game of real tennis>.

pilot

- **be on automatic pilot** to do something without thinking about what you are doing, because of tiredness, distress, etc., usually succeeding in doing it correctly because you have done it before.

pin

- **for two pins** given the least encouragement or reason.
- **on pins and needles** in a state of anxiety or suspense.
- **you could have heard a pin drop** there was silence.

pinch

- **at a pinch** if it is absolutely necessary.
- **feel the pinch** to have financial problems.

pink

- **in the pink** in good health. <Refers to the pink complexion of some healthy people>.
- **the pink of perfection** absolute perfection. <Refers to a quotation from Oliver Goldsmith's play, *She Stoops to Conquer*>.

pip

- **pipped at the post** beaten at the last minute. <Refers originally to horse-racing. A horse is pipped at the post if another horse passes it at the end of the race>.

pipe

- **in the pipeline** in preparation, happening soon. <Refers to crude oil being piped from the well to the refineries>.

piper

- **pay the piper** to provide the money for something and therefore be entitled to have a say in the organization of it. <Refers to the saying 'He who pays the piper calls the tune'>.
- **pipe dream** a wish or idea that can never be realized. <Refers to visions experienced by opium smokers>.

pistol

- **hold a pistol to (someone's) head** to use force or threats to get (someone) to do as one wishes.

place

- **fall into place** to become understood when seen in terms of its relationship to other things.
- **go places** to be successful in one's career.
- **know one's place** to accept the lowliness of one's position and act accordingly.
- **a place in the sun** a situation in which one will be happy, successful, well of, etc..
- **put (someone) in his** *or* **her place** to remind (someone) angrily of the lowliness of his or her position or of his or her lack of experience, knowledge, etc.

plague

- **avoid (someone** *or* **something) like the plague** used to emphasize how keen one is to keep away (from someone or something).

plain

- **plain sailing** easy progress. <Perhaps confused with plane sailing, a method of making navigational calculations at sea in which

the earth's surface is treated as though it were flat>.

plate

• **have (something) handed to one on a plate** to get (something) without having to put any effort into it.

play

• **make a play for (someone or something)** to try to obtain (someone or something).

• **play hard to get** to make it difficult for someone to get to know one in order to make him or her more keen to do so.

plot

• **the plot thickens** the situation is getting more complicated and more interesting. <Refers to a quotation from George Villiers' play *The Rehearsal*>.

plug

• **pull the plug on (something)** to stop supporting (something), to stop (something) from continuing.

plum

• **have a plum in one's mouth** to speak with what is regarded as an upper-class accent.

plunge

• **take the plunge** to go ahead and do something, especially something difficult or risky, especially after having spent some considerable time thinking about it.

poacher

• **poacher turned gamekeeper** used to describe someone who has changed their job, attitude, opinion, etc, and now holds completely opposite views.

pocket

• **in (someone's) pocket** under the control or influence of (someone).

• **line one's pocket** to make money for oneself dishonestly.

• **out of pocket** having made a loss.

poetic

• **poetic justice** deserved but accidental punishment or reward.

• **poetic licence** the disregarding of established rules of form, grammar, fact, etc, by writers to achieve a desired effect.

point

• **the point of no return** the stage in a process, etc, when it becomes impossible either to stop or change one's mind. <Originally referred to the point in the flight of an aircraft after which it did not have enough fuel to return to its place of departure>.

• **up to a point** to some extent but not completely.

poison

• **poison-pen letter** an anonymous letter saying bad things about someone.

port

• **any port in a storm** any solution to a problem or difficulty will suffice.

possum

• **play possum** to pretend to be asleep, unconscious or dead. <The possum pretends to be dead when it is under threat of attack from another animal>.

post[1]

• **from pillar to post** from one place to another, often repeatedly.

post[2]

• **keep (someone) posted** to keep (someone) informed about developments in a situation.

pot

• **go to pot** to get into a bad or worse state. <Refers to meat being cut up and stewed in a pot).

• **keep the pot boiling** to keep something going or operating.

• **take pot-luck** to have a meal at someone's house, etc, without having anything specially prepared for one. <Literally to take whatever happens to be in the cooking-pot at the time>.

• **the pot calling the kettle black** someone criticizing (someone) for doing (something) that he or she does himself or herself.

• **the *or* a watched pot never boils** when one is waiting for something to happen, etc, the time taken seems longer if one is constantly thinking about it.

pour

• **it never rains but it pours** when something goes wrong it goes wrong very badly or other things go wrong too.

powder

• **be sitting on a powder keg** to be in a very

risky or dangerous situation in which something could easily go wrong quite suddenly.

power

- **more power to (someone's) elbow** may (someone) be successful.
- **the power behind the throne** the person who is really in charge of or in control of an organization, etc, while giving the impression that it is someone else.
- **the powers that be** the people in charge, the authorities.

practice

- **practice makes perfect** if one practises doing something one will eventually be good at it.

practise

- **practise what one preaches** to act in the way that one recommends to others.

praise

- **sing (someone's _or_ something's) praises** to praise (someone or something) with great enthusiasm.

premium

- **be at a premium** to be much in demand and, therefore, difficult to obtain. <A financial term meaning literally 'sold at more than the nominal value'>.

press

- **press-gang (someone) into (doing something)** to force (someone) or persuade (someone) against his or her will to (do something). <The press gang was a group of sailors in the 18th century who seized men and forced them to join the navy>.

pretty

- **come to a pretty pass** to get into a bad state.
- **cost a pretty penny** to cost a large amount of money.
- **sitting pretty** in a very comfortable or advantageous position.

prey

- **be a prey to (something)** regularly to suffer from (something).
- **prey on (someone's) mind** to cause constant worry or anxiety to (someone).

price

- **at a price** at a very high price.
- **a price on (someone's) head** a reward

offered for the capture or killing of (someone).

pride

- **pride goes before a fall** being too conceited often leads to misfortune.
- **pride of place** the most important or privileged position.
- **swallow one's pride** to behave in a more humble way than one usually does or than one would wish to do.

prime

- **prime mover** someone or something that gets something started.

pro

- **the pros and cons** the arguments for and against. <Latin _pro_, 'for', and _contra_, 'against'>.

production

- **make a production of (something)** to make (something) appear to be much more complicated than it actually is.

proof

- **the proof of the pudding is in the eating** the real worth of something is only found out when it has been into practice or use.

proud

- **do (someone) proud** to treat (someone) exceptionally well or lavishly.

pull

- **pull the other one!** used to emphasize to someone that you do not believe him or her. Sometimes the phrase is extended to **pull the other one; it's got bells on!** <A reference to the phrase: pull (someone's) leg>.

pulse

- **keep one's finger on the pulse** to keep oneself informed about recent developments in a situation, organization, etc, or in the world. <Refers to a doctor checking the rate of someone's pulse for health reasons>.

Punch

- **pleased as Punch** extremely pleased or happy. <Refers to the puppet show character who is usually portrayed smiling gleefully>.

punch

- **pull one's punches** to be less forceful or harsh in one's attack or criticism than one is capable of. <Refers to striking blows in boxing without using one's full strength>.

- **roll with the punches** not to let difficulties or problems discourage one or have a bad or upsetting effect on one.

pup

- **sell (someone) a pup** to deceive (someone), often to sell or recommend something that turns out not to be as good as he or she thought.

purpose

- **at cross purposes** involved in a misunderstanding because of talking or thinking about different things without realizing it.

purse

- **hold the purse strings** to be in charge of financial matters.
- **you can't make a silk purse out of a sow's ear** *see* silk.

push

- **at a push** used to indicate that something can be done if it is absolutely necessary, but it will not be easy.
- **give (someone) the push** to dismiss (someone).

put

- **put it on** to feign, to pretend.
- **put-up job** something done to deceive or trick (someone).

putty

- **putty in (someone's) hands** easily influenced or manipulated by (someone). <Putty is a malleable substance>.

Pyrrhic

- **Pyrrhic victory** a success of some kind in which what it takes to achieve is not worth it. <From the costly victory of King Pyrrhus of Epirus, over the Romans at Heraclea in 280 BC>.

QT

- **on the QT** secretly. <An abbreviation of quiet>.

quantity

- **an unknown quantity** someone or something of which very little is known. <Refers literally to a mathematical term>.

queer

- **in Queer Street** in financial difficulties. <Perhaps changed from Carey Street in

London where the bankruptcy courts were>.

- **queer (someone's) pitch** to upset (someone's) plans or arrangements. <Pitch here refers to the site of a market stall. Originally to queer someone's pitch was to set up a stall beside it selling the same kind of goods>.

question

- **a question mark over (something)** doubt or uncertainty in relation to (something).
- **out of the question** not possible.
- **pop the question** to ask (someone) to marry one.

queue

- **jump the queue** to go ahead of others in a queue without waiting for one's proper turn.

qui

- **on the qui vive** very alert. <From the challenge of a French sentry *Qui vive?* 'Long live who, whose side are you on?'>.

quick

- **cut (someone) to the quick** to hurt (someone's) feelings very badly. <The quick is the sensitive skin under the nail>.

quid

- **quids in** a fortunate position.

quit

- **call it quits** to agree that neither person owes the other one anything and that neither one has any kind of advantage over the other.

R

- **the three R's** reading, writing and arithmetic, thought of as the essential basics of education. <From *r*eading, *w*riting and a*r*ithmetic>.

rack

- **go to rack and ruin** to fall into a state of disrepair or into a worthless condition. <Rack means destruction>.

rage

- **all the rage** very fashionable or popular.

rail

- **off the rails** not sensible, disorganized, deranged. <Refers to a train leaving the track>.

rain

- **keep** *or* **put away** *or* **save (something)**

for a rainy day to keep (something, especially money) until one really needs it. <Formerly most jobs, such as farm jobs, were dependent on the weather. Since they could not be carried out in rainy weather no money was earned then>.

• **rain or shine** whatever the weather.

• **take a rain check on (something)** used to indicate that you are unable to accept an invitation but would like to postpone it until a later date. <American in origin and a reference to the part of a ticket that you keep when a sports fixture cannot take place because of bad weather so that you can use it for entry to the fixture when it does take place>.

rake

• **thin as a rake** extremely thin.

rampage

• **be** *or* **go on the rampage** to rush about wildly or violently.

rank

• **close ranks** to act together and support each other as a defensive measure.

• **pull rank** to make unfair use of a position of authority to make someone else do as one wishes or to give one some kind of advantage.

rap

• **take the rap for (something)** to take the blame or punishment for (something).

rat

• **like a drowned rat** soaking wet.

• **smell a rat** to have a suspicion that something is wrong or that one is being deceived. <Refers to a terrier hunting>.

• **the rat race** the fierce competitive struggle for success in business, etc. <A nautical phrase for a fierce tidal current>.

raw

• **touch (someone) on the raw** to hurt or anger (someone).

razor

• **sharp as a razor** quick-witted and very intelligent.

read

• **take (something) as read** to assume (something).

real

• **the real McCoy** something genuine and very good as opposed to others like it which are not. <Perhaps from Kid McCoy, an American boxer who was called The Real McCoy to distinguish him from other boxers of the same name>.

reason

• **see reason** to be persuaded by someone's advice, etc, to act or think sensibly.

• **within reason** within sensible limits.

rebound

• **on the rebound** to start a new relationship while still suffering from the disappointment experienced at the end of the previous relationship.

record

• **for the record** so that it will be noted.

• **set the record straight** to put right a mistake or misunderstanding.

red

• **a red-letter day** a day remembered because something particularly pleasant or important happened or happens on it. <From the fact that important dates in the year are sometimes shown in red on calendars>.

• **catch (someone) red-handed** to find (someone) in the act of doing something wrong or unlawful. <Refers to finding a murderer with the blood of a victim on his or her hands>.

• **in the red** in debt, overdrawn. <From the use of red ink to make entries on the debit side of an account>.

• **like a red rag to a bull** certain to make (someone) angry. <From the widespread belief that bulls are angered by the sight of the colour red although they are in fact colour-blind>.

• **on red alert** ready for an an immediate danger. <Originally a military term for mobilizing civilians during an air-raid>.

• **red tape** the rules and regulations, official papers, etc, that are thought to characterize government departments. <From the reddish tape used by government offices to tie bundles of papers>.

• **see red** to get very angry.

reed

- **a broken reed** someone who is too weak or unreliable to be depended upon.

rest

- **lay (someone) to rest** to bury (someone).
- **rest assured** you can be quite certain.

return

- **return to the fold** to come or back to one's family, an organization, a set of principles or beliefs, etc, which one has previously left. <Refers to a sheep returning to the sheep-pen>.

rhetorical

- **rhetorical question** a question which does not require an answer.

rhyme

- **without rhyme or reason** without any logical or sensible reason or explanation.

rich

- **rich as Croesus** extremely rich. <Croesus was a ruler of the kingdom of Lydia who was very wealthy>.
- **strike it rich** to obtain wealth, often suddenly or unexpectedly.

riddance

- **good riddance to (someone *or* something)** I am glad to have got rid of (someone or something).

ride

- **be riding for a fall** to be on a course of action that is likely to lead to unpleasant results or disaster for oneself. <Refers originally to hunting>.
- **take (someone) for a ride** to deceive or trick (someone). <Originally American gangsters' slang for killing someone, from the practice of killing someone in a moving vehicle so as not to attract attention>.

rift

- **a rift in the lute** a slight disagreement or difficulty that might develop into a major one and ruin a project or relationship. <Refers to a quotation from Tennyson's *Idylls*>.

right

- **get *or* keep on the right side of (someone)** to act in such a way that (someone) feels or continues to feel friendly and well disposed towards one.

- **Mr *or* Miss Right** the perfect man or woman for one to marry.
- **right-hand man *or* woman** someone's most valuable and helpful assistant.
- **serve (someone) right** to be something unpleasant that (someone) deserves.
- **set (something) to rights** to bring (something) into a correct, organized, desired, etc, state.

ring

- **a dead ringer** someone who looks extremely like someone else. <Perhaps from the use of the phrase to mean a horse, similar to the original, illegally substituted in a race>.
- **have a ringside seat** to be in a position to observe clearly what is happening. <Originally refers to boxing>.

riot

- **read the riot act to (someone)** to scold (someone) severely and warn him or her to behave better. <The Riot Act of 1715 was read to unlawful gatherings of people to break the gathering up. If the people refused to disperse action could be taken against them>.

rise

- **rise and shine** to get out of bed and be lively and cheerful.
- **take a rise out of (someone)** to tease or make fun of (someone) so that he or she gets annoyed.

river

- **sell (someone) down the river** to betray or be disloyal to (someone). <Refers historically to selling slaves from the upper Mississippi states to buyers in Louisiana where working and living conditions were much harsher>.

road

- **hit the road** start out on a journey.
- **one for the road** one last drink before leaving.

roaring

- **do a roaring trade in (something)** to be selling a lot of (something).

rob

- **rob Peter to pay Paul** to pay (someone) with the money that should go to pay a debt owed to (someone else). <Refers to Saints

Peter and Paul who share the same feast day, 29 July>.

rock

* **between a rock and a hard place** to be in a situation in which one is faced with a choice between two equally unpleasant or unacceptable alternatives.
* **steady as a rock** extremely steady, motionless.

rocket

* **not rocket science** used to indicate that something is quite easy and does not require much intellect or skill.

rod

* **make a rod for one's own back** to do something which is going to cause harm or problems for oneself in the future.
* **spare the rod and spoil the child** if a child is not punished for being naughty it will have a bad effect on his or her character.

rogue

* **a rogue's gallery** a police collection of photographs of known criminals.

roll

* **a rolling stone (gathers no moss)** a person who does not stay very long in one place (does not acquire very much in the way of possessions or responsibilities).
* **a roll in the hay** an informal way of describing having sex, especially when this is not part of a serious relationship.
* **be on a roll** used to indicate that things are going well and that good progress is being made.
* **be rolling in it** *or* **in money** to have a great deal of money.
* **be rolling in the aisles** to be laughing very heartily.

Rome

* **all roads lead to Rome** all ways of fulfilling an aim or intention end in the same result and so it does not does not matter which way one uses.
* **fiddle while Rome burns** to do nothing while something important is being ruined or destroyed. <The Emperor Nero was said to have played on a lyre while Rome was burning>.
* **Rome was not built in a day** a difficult task cannot be completed satisfactorily quickly.
* **when in Rome do as the Romans do** one should follow the customs, behaviour, etc, of the people one is visiting or living with. <A saying of St Ambrose>.

rooftop

* **shout (something) from the rooftops** to tell a great many people about (something).

roost

* **rule the roost** to be the person in charge whose wishes or orders are obeyed.

rope

* **give (someone) enough rope (and he will hang himself)** let (someone foolish) act as he or she pleases and he or she will bring about his or her own ruin, downfall, misfortune, etc.
* **know the ropes** to know the details and methods associated with a business, procedure, activity, etc.
* **on the ropes** used to describe a situation which is very close to failure or defeat.
* **rope (someone) in** to include (someone), to ask (someone) to join in, often against his or her will. <Refers to lassoing cattle in the American West>.
* **show (someone) the ropes** to teach (someone) the details and methods involved (in something).

rose

* **come up smelling of roses** to come out of a situation with some kind of advantage when it was expected to result in blame or harm for one.
* **everything's coming up roses** everything is turning out to be successful or happy.
* **look at (someone** *or* **something) through rose-coloured** *or* **rose-tinted spectacles** *or* **glasses** to view (someone or something) in an extremely optimistic light.

rough

* **give (someone) the rough edge of one's tongue** to scold or criticize (someone) severely.
* **ride roughshod over (someone)** to treat (someone) without any respect and without

any regard for his or her views or feelings. <Horses are roughshod to give a better grip on icy, etc, roads>.

- **take the rough with the smooth** to accept the disadvantages as well as the advantages and benefits of a situation.

round

- **go the rounds** to be passed from person to person.
- **in round figures** *or* **numbers** to the nearest whole number, especially one that can be divided by ten.
- **round trip** the journey to somewhere plus the journey back.

rub

- **rub (something) in** to keep reminding someone about (something which he or she would rather forget).
- **rub off on (to) (someone)** to be passed to (someone), to affect (someone).
- **rub (someone) up the wrong way** to irritate (someone). <Refers to rubbing an animal's coat up the wrong way>.
- **there's the rub** that's the problem. <Refers to a quotation from Shakespeare's *Hamlet*, Act 3, scene I>.

rug

- **pull the rug (out) from under (someone)** suddenly to stop giving important help or support to (someone), to leave (someone) in a weak position.

rule

- **rule of thumb** a rough or inexact guide used for calculations of some kind.

run

- **a run for (someone's) money** a creditable or worthy performance or opposition. <A racing term indicating that the horse one has backed has actually raced although it has not won>.
- **(someone's) cup runneth over** someone feels very happy. <A biblical reference to Psalm 23:5>.
- **in the running** with a chance of success.
- **run its course** to continue to its natural end, to develop naturally.
- **run out on (someone** *or* **something)** to abandon (someone or something).
- **take a running jump** to go away.

rut

- **in a rut** in a routine, monotonous way of life. <Refers to the rut made by a cartwheel, etc>.

sabre

- **rattle one's sabre** to put on a show of anger or fierceness without resorting to physical force in order to frighten someone.

sack

- **sackcloth and ashes** sorrow or apology for what one has done or failed to do. <People in mourning used to wear sackcloth and throw ashes over their heads. The phrase has several biblical references, e.g. Matthew 11:21>.

safe

- **safe and sound** totally unharmed.
- **there's safety in numbers** it is safer to undertake a risky venture if there are several people involved.

sail

- **sail close to the wind** to come close to breaking the law or a rule.
- **sail under false colours** to pretend to be different in character, beliefs, status, work, etc, than is really the case. <Refers to a ship flying a flag other than its own, as pirate ships sometimes did>.

salad

- **(someone's) salad days** (someone's) carefree and inexperienced youth.

salt

- **below the salt** in a humble, lowly or despised position. <Formerly the salt container marked the division at a dinner table between the rich and important people and the more lowly people, the important people being near the top and so above the salt>.
- **rub salt in the wound** to make someone feel worse. <Salt used to be used as an antiseptic but it was painful on raw wounds>.
- **take (something) with a grain** *or* **pinch of salt** to treat (something) with some disbelief.
- **the salt of the earth** someone very worthy or good. <A biblical reference to Matthew 5:13>.
- **worth one's salt** worth the money one is

paid, of any worth. <Salt was once a valuable commodity and the reference is to that given to servants or workers>.

Samaritan

- **a good Samaritan** someone who helps people when they are in need. <A biblical reference to the parable in Luke 10>.

sand

- **build (something) on sand** to establish (something) without having enough support, money, likelihood of survival, etc, to make it secure or practicable. <A biblical reference to Matthew 7:26>.

sardine

- **packed like sardines** crowded very close together. <Sardines are sold tightly packed in tins>.

scarlet

- **scarlet woman** an immoral or promiscuous woman. <A biblical reference to the woman in scarlet in Revelation 17>.

scene

- **behind the scenes** out of sight of the public, etc. <Refers literally to people in a theatrical production who work behind the scenery offstage>.
- **come on the scene** to arrive or appear.
- **not (someone's) scene** not the kind of thing that (someone) likes.
- **set the scene for (something)** to prepare the way for (something), to be the forerunner of (something). <Refers originally to the preparation of the stage for theatrical action>.

scent

- **throw (someone) off the scent** to distract (someone) from a search for someone or something, e.g. by giving him or her wrong information. <Refers literally to dogs>.

scheme

- **the best-laid schemes of mice and men (gang aft agley)** the most carefully arranged plans (often go wrong). <Refers to a quotation from Robert Burns's poem, 'To a Mouse'>.

science

- **blind (someone) with science** to talk about something in such a complicated

technical way that it is difficult for a layperson to understand.

score

- **know the score** to know exactly what is involved, to know all the facts of a situation. <Literally to know from the score in a game who is likely to win or lose>.
- **settle old scores** to get revenge for wrongs committed in the past.

scratch

- **start from scratch** to start from the very beginning, without any advantages. <Refers to the starting line (formerly scratched on the ground), from which runners start unless their handicap allows them to start further down the track>.
- **up to scratch** up to the required standard. <Refers originally to a scratch in the centre of a boxing ring to which boxers had to make their way unaided after being knocked down to prove that they were fit to continue>.

screw

- **have a screw loose** to be deranged, to be very foolish. <Refers literally to malfunctioning machinery>.

Scrooge

- **Scrooge** an extremely mean person. <Refers to a character in Charles Dickens's *A Christmas Carol*>.

Scylla

- **between Scylla and Charybdis** faced with having to choose between two equally undesirable choices. <Refers to Homer's *Odyssey* in which Odysseus had to sail down a narrow strait between Scylla, a monster on a rock, and Charybdis, an extremely dangerous whirlpool>.

sea

- **a sea change** a complete change in a situation, someone's opinion, attitude, etc.
- **all at sea** puzzled, bewildered.

seam

- **be bursting at the seams** to be extremely full.
- **come** *or* **fall apart at the seams** to be in a state of collapse or ruin. <From clothes coming to pieces>.

second

- **second nature** a firmly established habit.

- **second sight** the supposed power of seeing into the future.
- **second thoughts** a change of opinion, decision, etc.

seed
- **go to seed** to become shabby and uncared-for. <Refers literally to plants seeding after flowering and being no longer attractive or useful>.

separate
- **separate the sheep from the goats** see **sheep**.

sewn
- **(all) sewn up** completely settled or arranged.

shade
- **put (someone** or **something) in the shade** to be much better, etc, than (someone or something). <Refers to making someone seem dark by being so much brighter oneself>.
- **shades of (someone** or **something)** that reminds me of (someone or something). <It is as though the shade or ghost of someone or something were present>.

shadow
- **worn to a shadow** made exhausted and thin by over working.

shakes
- **in two shakes of a lamb's tail** in a very short time.

shape
- **knock (someone** or **something) into shape** to get (something) into the desired or good condition.
- **shape up or ship out** used to tell someone that he or she should start acting in a more responsible or appropriate way or get out.

sheep
- **might as well be hanged for a sheep as a lamb** if one is going to do something slightly wrong and have to pay a penalty one might as well do something really wrong and get more benefit. <Refers to the fact that stealing a lamb or a sheep used to be punishable by death>.
- **separate the sheep from the goats** to distinguish in some way the good, useful, talented, etc, people from the bad, useless or stupid, etc, ones. <A biblical reference to Matthew 25:32>.

shelf
- **on the shelf** unmarried and unlikely to get married because of being unattractive, old, etc. <Refers to goods that are not sold>.

shell
- **come out of one's shell** to become less shy. <Refers to a tortoise or crab, etc>.

ship
- **shipshape and Bristol fashion** neat, in good order. <Originally applied to ships. Bristol was formerly the largest port in Britain>.
- **ships that pass in the night** people who meet by chance and only on one occasion. <Refers to a quotation from 'Tales of a Wayside Inn' poem by Henry Wadsworth Longfellow>.
- **spoil the ship for a ha'porth of tar** to spoil something of value by not buying or doing something which would improve it but not cost very much. <Ship is dialect here for sheep—tar used to be used to prevent infections in sheep or to treat wounds>.
- **when (someone's) ship comes in** when (someone) becomes rich or successful. <Refers to merchants waiting for their ships to return with goods to sell>.

shoe
- **in (someone's) shoes** in (someone else's) place.
- **on a shoestring** using very little money.

shoot
- **shoot (something) down in flames** to destroy. <Refers literally to destroying aircraft by shooting at them>.

shop
- **talk shop** to talk about one's work.

short
- **by a short head** by a very small amount. <Refers to horse-racing>.
- **caught** or **taken short** having a sudden, urgent need to go to the toilet.
- **give (someone** or **something) short shrift** to spend very little time or thought on (someone or something). <Short shrift was the short time given to a criminal for confession before execution>.

- **make short work of (something)** to deal with or get rid of (something) very quickly.
- **sell (someone** *or* **something) short** not to do justice to, to belittle (someone or something). <Literally to give a customer less than the correct amount of something>.
- **short and sweet** short and to the point.

shot

- **a long shot** a guess or attempt unlikely to be accurate or successful, but worth trying.
- **a shot across the bows** something given as a warning. <From naval warfare>.
- **a shot in the arm** something that helps to revive (something). <Literally, an injection in the arm>.
- **big shot** an important person.
- **call the shots** to be in charge of events or a situation.
- **like a shot** very quickly or willingly.
- **shotgun wedding** a forced wedding, usually because the bride is pregnant. <From the idea that the groom was forced into the wedding by shotgun>.

shoulder

- **a shoulder to cry on** a sympathetic listener.
- **put one's shoulder to the wheel** to begin to work hard. <Refers to putting one's shoulder to the wheel of a cart, etc, to push it out of muddy ground, etc>.
- **rub shoulders with (someone)** to associate closely with (someone).
- **shoulder to shoulder** side by side.

shout

- **shout (something) from the rooftops** *see* **rooftop.**

show

- **get the show on the road** to get something started or put into operation. <Used originally of a theatre company going on tour>.
- **steal the show** to attract the most attention at an event. <Refers to someone getting most of the applause at a theatrical performance>.

sick

- **sick as a parrot** very disappointed.

side

- **let the side down** to hinder one's colleagues by not performing, etc, as well as they have.

- **on the side** in a way other than by means of one's ordinary occupation.
- **take sides** to support a particular person, group, etc, against another.

sieve

- **have a memory like a sieve** to be extremely forgetful.

sign

- **sign on the dotted line** to make a firm commitment to do something, often one that is legally binding. <Refers to the signing of a formal agreement or contract>.

sight

- **out of sight, out of mind** one ceases to think about someone who has gone away or about something which is no longer in front of one.

silence

- **silence is golden** it is better to say nothing in a particular situation.

silent

- **the silent majority** the people who make up most of the population but who rarely make their views known although these are thought to be moderate and reasonable.

silk

- **you can't make a silk purse out of a sow's ear** one cannot make something good or special out of poor materials.

silver

- **born with a silver spoon in one's mouth** to be born into an aristocratic or wealthy family. <Perhaps from the custom of giving a christening present of a silver teaspoon>.

sin

- **ugly as sin** extremely ugly.

sing

- **sing from the same hymn** *or* **song sheet** to be in agreement about something, often to show this agreement publicly.

six

- **a sixth sense** intuition, an ability to feel or realize something not perceived by the five senses.
- **at sixes and sevens** in a state of confusion and chaos.
- **knock (someone) for six** to take (someone) completely by surprise. <Refers to

cricket—literally to score six runs off a bowl>.

- **six of one and half a dozen of another** so similar as to make no difference. <Half a dozen is six>.

sixty

- **the sixty-four (thousand) dollar question** the most important and/or difficult question. <From an American quiz game in which the contestant won one dollar for the first question, two for the second, four for the third, up to the last when he or she won sixty-four dollars or lost it all>.

size

- **cut (someone) down to size** to humble (someone), to reduce (someone's) sense of his or her own importance.

skeleton

- **have a skeleton in the cupboard** to have a closely kept secret about some cause of shame.

skin

- **by the skin of one's teeth** only just, very narrowly.
- **no skin off my, etc, nose** no difference to me, etc, of no concern to me, etc.
- **save one's skin** to save one's life or one's career.
- **skin and bone** extremely thin.

sky

- **praise (someone *or* something) to the skies** to praise (someone) extremely highly.
- **the sky's the limit** there is no upper limit.

slap

- **a slap in the face** a rebuff.
- **a slap on the wrist** a reprimand.

sleeve

- **have *or* keep (something) up one's sleeve** to keep (a plan, etc) in reserve or secret for possible use at a later time. <Refers to cheating at cards by having a card up one's sleeve>.

slip

- **a slip of the tongue** a word or phrase said in mistake for another.
- **give (someone) the slip** to succeed in escaping from or evading (someone).
- **let (something) slip** to say or reveal (something) accidentally.

- **there's many a slip 'twixt cup and lip** something can easily go wrong with a project, etc, before it is completed.

small

- **it's a small world** an expression used when one meets someone one knows somewhere unexpected.
- **small talk** light conversation about trivial matters.
- **the small print** the parts of a document where important information is given without being easily noticed.

smash

- **a smash-and-grab** a robbery in which a shop window is smashed and goods grabbed from behind it.
- **a smash hit** a great success. <Originally referred to a very successful popular song>.

smear

- **smear campaign** an attempt to blacken or damage someone's reputation by making accusations or spreading rumours about him or her.

smoke

- **go up in smoke** to end in nothing.
- **there's no smoke without fire** there is always some kind of basis to a rumour, however untrue it appears to be.

snail

- **at a snail's pace** extremely slowly.

snake

- **a snake in the grass** a treacherous person. <From Virgil's *Aeneid*>.

sneeze

- **not to be sneezed at** not to be ignored or disregarded.

sock

- **pull one's socks up** to make an effort to improve.
- **put a sock in it** to be quiet.

soft

- **have a soft spot for (someone)** to have a weakness, affection or exceptional liking for (someone).
- **a soft touch *or* mark** someone who is easily taken advantage of, deceived etc.

song

- **for a song** for very little money.

soon

- **make a song and dance about (something)** to cause an unnecessary fuss about (something).

soon

- **speak too soon** to say something that takes for granted something not yet accomplished.

sore

- **a sore point** a subject which annoys or offends someone.
- **stick out like a sore thumb** to be very noticeable.

sort

- **it takes all sorts (to make a world)** one should be tolerant of everyone whatever they are like.
- **out of sorts** not feeling quite well, rather bad-tempered.

soul

- **the soul of (something)** a perfect example of (something).

soup

- **in the soup** in serious trouble.

spade

- **call a spade a spade** to speak bluntly and forthrightly.
- **do the spadework** to do the hard preparatory work at the beginning of a project. <Digging is the first stage of building houses, etc>.
- **in spades** used to emphasize the large amount of something.

spanner

- **throw a spanner in the works** to hinder or spoil (a project, plan, etc).

spar

- **sparring partner** someone with whom one often enjoys a lively argument. <Literally refers to someone with whom a boxer practises>.

spare

- **go spare** to become very angry or distressed.

speak

- **be on speaking terms** to be friendly towards someone and communicate with him or her.
- **speak for itself** to need no explanation.

spick

- **spick and span** clean and tidy.

spirit

- **the spirit is willing (but the flesh is weak)** one is not always physically able to do the things that one wishes do. <A biblical quotation, Matthew 26:40–41>.

spit

- **be the spitting image** or **the spit and image** or **the dead spit of (someone or something)** to be extremely like (someone or something).

spleen

- **vent one's spleen** to express one's anger and frustration. <The spleen was thought to be the source of spite and melancholy>.

split

- **a split second** a fraction of a second.

spoil

- **be spoiling for (something)** to be eager for (a fight, etc).

spoke

- **put a spoke in (someone's) wheel** to hinder (someone's) activity. <Spoke is from Dutch spoak, a bar formerly jammed under a cartwheel to act as a brake when going downhill>.

sponge

- **throw up the sponge** to give up a contest, struggle, argument, etc. <Refers originally to a method of conceding defeat in boxing>.

spot

- **hit the spot** used to indicate that something is just what is required or is completely satisfactory.
- **in a spot** in trouble, in difficulties.
- **knock spots off (someone)** to beat or surpass (someone) thoroughly.
- **put (someone) on the spot** to place (someone) in a difficult or awkward situation.
- **rooted to the spot** unable to move from fear, horror, etc.

sprat

- **a sprat to catch a mackerel** something minor or trivial given or conceded in order to obtain some major gain or advantage.

square

- **back to square one** back at the beginning. <Refers to an instruction in board games>.

squeak
- **a narrow squeak** a narrow escape.

stab
- **have a stab at (something)** to have a try at (something).
- **stab (someone) in the back** to behave treacherously towards (someone), to betray (someone).

stable
- **lock the stable door after the horse has bolted** to take precautions against something happening after it has already happened.

stage
- **a stage whisper** a loud whisper that is intended to be heard by people other than the person to whom it is directed. <From the fact that whispers on stage have to be audible to the audience>.
- **stage fright** the nervousness, sometimes leading to him or her forgetting words, felt by an actor when in front of an audience; often extended to that felt by anyone making a public appearance.

stamp
- **(someone's) stamping ground** a place where (someone) goes regularly. <Refers literally to animals>.

stand
- **know where one stands** to know the exact nature of one's position or situation.
- **make a stand against (something)** to oppose or resist (something one believes to be wrong, etc).
- **stand corrected** to accept that one has been wrong.
- **stand on ceremony** to be very formal.
- **stand up and be counted** to declare one's opinions publicly.

start
- **a false start** an unsuccessful beginning, resulting in one in having to start again. <From a start in a race which has to be repeated, e.g. because a runner has left the starting line before the signal has been given>.
- **be under starter's orders** to be ready to start doing something.
- **for starters** to begin with. <Starter refers literally to the first course of a meal>.

status
- **status quo** the situation as it is, or was, before a change. <Latin, literally 'the state in which'>.
- **status symbol** a possession which supposedly demonstrates high social position.

stay
- **stay the course** to continue to the end or completion of (something).

steady
- **go steady** to go out together regularly, to have a romantic attachment to each other.

steam
- **get all steamed up** to get angry or agitated.
- **get up steam** to gather energy and impetus to do (something). <Literally used of increasing the pressure of steam in an engine before it goes into operation>.
- **let off steam** to give free expression to one's feelings or energies. <Literally to release steam from a steam engine to in order to reduce pressure>.
- **run out of steam** to become exhausted, to lose enthusiasm. <Refers literally to the steam engine>.
- **under one's own steam** entirely through one's own efforts.

step
- **take steps** to take action of some kind.

stick
- **a stick to beat (someone) with** something which can be used to criticize or damage (someone).
- **get hold of the wrong end of the stick** to misunderstand a situation or something said or done.
- **give (someone) stick** to scold or criticize (someone). <Refers literally to beating someone with a stick>.

sticky
- **be on a sticky wicket** to be in a difficult or awkward situation that is difficult to defend. <Refers to cricket when the state of the ground or the weather make it difficult for the batsman to hit the ball>.
- **come to a sticky end** to meet some misfortune or an unpleasant death.

still
- **still waters run deep** quiet people often think very deeply or have strong emotions.

stitch
- **a stitch in time saves nine** prompt action at the first sign of trouble saves a lot of time and effort later.
- **have (someone) in stitches** to make (someone) laugh a great deal.
- **without a stitch on** completely naked.

stock
- **on the stocks** in preparation, in the process of being made or arranged. <Refers to the fact that a ship is supported on stocks, a wooden frame, while being built>.
- **take stock (of something)** to assess (a situation).

stomach
- **turn (someone's) stomach** to make (someone) feel sick, to disgust (someone).

stone
- **a stone's throw** a very short distance.
- **be set in stone** to be something that cannot be changed.
- **leave no stone unturned** to try every means possible.

stool
- **fall between two stools** to try to gain two aims and fail with regard to both of them, usually because of indecision.

stop
- **pull out all the stops** to put as much effort and energy into something as possible. <Refers to pulling out the stops of an organ so that it plays at full volume>.
- **stop dead** to stop suddenly and abruptly.
- **stop short of (something or doing something)** not to go as far as (something or doing something).

store
- **in cold storage** in reserve.
- **set great store by (something)** to consider (something) to be of great importance or value.

storm
- **a storm in a teacup** a great fuss made over a trivial matter. <Refers to the title of a farce written by William Bernard in 1854>.
- **take (someone or something) by storm** to make a very great and immediate impression (on someone or something). <Literally to capture a fort, etc, by a sudden violent military attack>.
- **weather the storm** to survive a difficult or troublesome situation or period of time. <Refers originally to ships>.

story
- **the same old story** a situation, etc, that occurs frequently.

straight
- **go straight** to start leading an honest life.
- **straight as a die** completely honest and fair.
- **straight talking** frank and honest statement or conversation.
- **the straight and narrow (path)** a good, virtuous way of life. <A variation on a biblical reference, 'Straight is the gate and narrow is the way which leadeth unto life', Matthew 7:4>.

stranger
- **be a stranger to (something)** to have no experience of (something).

straw
- **a straw in the wind** a small or minor incident, etc, that indicates what may happen in the future.
- **clutch at straws** to hope that something may happen to get one out of a difficulty or danger when this is extremely unlikely. <From the saying, 'A drowning man will clutch at a straw'>.
- **draw the short straw** to be the one in a group who has to perform an unpleasant or undesirable task. <Pulling out a straw from a collection of different lengths is a kind of lottery to decide who is to do something>.
- **the last straw or the straw that breaks the camel's back** an event, etc, which, added to everything that has already happened, makes a situation impossible. <From the saying that it is the last straw added to its burden that breaks the camel's back>.

stream
- **come on stream** to begin to be used or to operate.

street
- **be right up one's street** to be exactly what one likes or what is suitable for one.

strength

- **go from strength to strength** to progress successfully from one achievement to another.
- **on the strength of (something)** relying on (something).

stretch

- **at full stretch** using all one's energy, abilities, powers, etc, as much as possible.
- **stretch a point** to go further than the rules or regulations allow in giving permission, etc, for something.

stride

- **get into one's stride** to become accustomed to doing something and so do it well and effectively. <A reference to running>.
- **make great strides** to make very good progress.
- **take (something) in one's stride** to cope with (something) without worrying about it. <Refers to a horse jumping an obstacle without altering its stride>.

string

- **have (someone) on a string** to have (someone) in one's control. <Refers to someone manipulating a puppet>.
- **how long is a piece of string?** used to emphasize how difficult or impossible it is to give a definite answer to a question.
- **pull strings** to use influence to gain an advantage or benefit of some kind. <As above>.
- **with no strings attached** without any conditions or provisos.

stroke

- **put (someone) off his _or_ her stroke** to hinder or prevent (someone) from proceeding smoothly with an activity. <Refers to upsetting the rhythm of someone's rowing>.

strong

- **be (someone's) strong suit** be something at which (someone) is very good. <Refers to card-playing>.

stuff

- **a stuffed shirt** a pompous, over-formal person.
- **knock the stuffing out of (someone) 1** to beat (someone) severely. **2** to discourage (someone) completely, to deprive (some-

one) of vitality. <Refers to stuffed animals>.
- **strut one's stuff** to do something which you know you do well, usually in a proud and confident way.

stumbling

- **a stumbling block** something that hinders or prevents progress. <A biblical reference to Romans 14:13>.

stump

- **stir one's stumps** to hurry up. <Stumps here means legs>.

style

- **cramp (someone's) style** to hinder (someone) from acting in the way that he or she would like or is accustomed to.

sugar

- **sugar daddy** an elderly man who has a young girlfriend or mistress to whom he gives expensive presents.
- **sugar the pill** to make something unpleasant more pleasant.

suit

- **men in (grey) suits** used to describe the powerful men who are in control of an organization, government, etc.
- **one's birthday suit** nakedness.

Sunday

- **(someone's) Sunday best** (someone's) smartest, formal clothes, of the kind worn to church on Sundays.

sure

- **sure as eggs is eggs** used to emphasize the certainty of something.

surface

- **scratch the surface of (something)** to deal with only a very small part of (something).

swallow

- **one swallow does not make a summer** a single success, etc, does not mean that a generally successful, etc, time is about to come. <Refers to the fact that swallows begin to come to Britain at the start of summer>.

swan

- **(someone's) swan song** the last work or performance by a musician, poet, playwright, actor, etc, before his or her death or retirement; by extension also applied to

sweat
talk

anyone who does anything for the last time. <Refers to an ancient legend that the swan sings as it is dying although it is otherwise silent>.

sweat
• **the sweat of one's brow** one's hard work.

sweet
• **be all sweetness and light** to seem to be pleasant and good-tempered.
• **have a sweet tooth** to like sweets, cakes and deserts.
• **sweet nothings** affectionate things said to someone with whom one is in love, endearments.

swim
• **be in the swim** be actively involved in social or business activities.

swing
• **get into the swing of things** to become accustomed to (something) and begin to understand and enjoy it. <Refers to the swing of a pendulum>.
• **go with a swing** to be very successful.
• **in full swing** at the most lively or busy part of something.
• **not enough room to swing a cat** see **cat**.
• **what you lose on the swings you gain on the roundabouts** disadvantages in one area of life are usually cancelled out by advantages in another.

swoop
• **at** or **in one fell swoop** in one single action or attempt, at the same time. <Refers to a quotation from Shakespeare's *Macbeth*, Act 4, scene III, the reference being to a hawk swooping on poultry>.

sword
• **a double-edged** or **two-edged sword** used to indicate that something has a bad and a good side.
• **cross swords with (someone)** to enter into a dispute with (someone).
• **the sword of Damocles** a threat of something bad that is likely to happen at any time. <Refers to a legend in which Damocles was forced by Dionysius of Syria to sit through a banquet with a sword hanging by a single hair over his head>.

T
• **to a T** exactly, very well. <Perhaps T stands for tittle, a small dot or point>.

tab
• **keep tabs on (someone** or **something)** to keep a check on (someone or something).
• **pick up the tab for (something)** to pay for (something). <Tab is an American term for bill>.

table
• **turn the tables on (someone)** to change a situation so that one gains the advantage (over someone) after having been at a disadvantage. <From the medieval game of tables, of which backgammon is a form, in which turning the board round would exactly reverse the position of the players>.

tail
• **chase one's tail** to spend a great deal of time and effort trying to do something but achieving very little.
• **have one's tail up** to be confident of success.
• **turn tail** to turn round and leave a difficult or dangerous situation.
• **with one's tail between one's legs** in an ashamed, miserable or defeated state. <From the behaviour of an unhappy dog>.

take
• **take after (someone)** to resemble.
• **take it out on (someone)** to treat (someone) in an angry or nasty way because one is disappointed, angry, etc, about something.

tale
• **live to tell the tale** to survive a dangerous or threatening situation, often used humorously.
• **tell tales** to report someone's wrong-doing.
• **thereby hangs a tale** there is a story associated with that. <A pun on tail, used by Shakespeare>.

talk
• **talk down to (someone)** to speak to (someone) in a condescending way as if he or she were inferior.
• **talk nineteen to the dozen** to talk a great deal and usually very rapidly.

tall
- **the talk of the town** someone or something that is the subject of general conversation or gossip.

tall
- **a tall order** a difficult task.
- **a tall story** a story which is extremely unlikely.

tangent
- **go** *or* **fly off at a tangent** suddenly to leave the subject being discussed or the task being undertaken and move to a completely different subject or task.

tango
- **it takes two to tango** used to indicate a particular situation has to involve two people and that, therefore, both bear some responsibility.

tape
- **have** *or* **get (someone** *or* **something) taped** to have a full knowledge or understanding of (someone or something). <As if measured with a tape>.

tar
- **be tarred with the same brush** to have the same faults.

taste
- **leave a nasty taste in the mouth** to leave someone with unpleasant memories or associations.

tea
- **not for all the tea in China** not for anything at all, certainly not. <For a long time, China was the source of the world's tea>.

tear
- **tear a strip off (someone)** to scold (someone) severely.

teeth
- **by the skin of one's teeth** *see* **skin**.
- **cut one's teeth on (something)** to practise on or get early experience from (something). <Refers to children being given something to chew on to help their teeth come through>.
- **draw the teeth of (someone** *or* **something)** to make (someone or something) no longer dangerous. <Refers to pulling out an animal's teeth.>
- **get one's teeth into (something)** to tackle (something) vigorously.

like pulling teeth used to indicate how difficult something is to do.
- **kick (someone) in the teeth** to refuse to help or support (someone) when he or she is in need of it.
- **set one's teeth on edge** to irritate one.
- **teething troubles** problems occurring at the very beginning of a new project, etc. <From the pain experienced by babies when teeth are just coming through>.

tell
- **I told you so** I warned you and I was right to do so.

tender
- **leave (someone** *or* **something) to (someone's) tender mercies** to leave (someone or something) in the care of (someone nasty, inefficient, etc).

tenterhooks
- **be on tenterhooks** be very anxious or agitated waiting for something to happen. <Tenterhooks were hooks for stretching newly woven cloth>.

territory
- **it goes with the territory** used to indicate that something, usually some kind of problem or difficulty, usually occurs in connection with a particular, job, activity or situation and should be expected.

test
- **stand the test of time** to survive or still be in use or popular after a considerable period of time.

that
- **that's that** there is no more to be said or done.

thick
- **give (someone) a thick ear** to slap (someone) across the ear, to box (someone's) ears.
- **thick and fast** in great quantities and at a fast rate.
- **thick as thieves** extremely friendly.
- **thick as two short planks** extremely stupid.
- **through thick and thin** whatever difficulties arise.

thief
- **set a thief to catch a thief** the best way to

catch or outwit a dishonest or deceitful person is to use the help of another who is dishonest as he or she knows the technique.

thin

- **be thin on top** to be balding.
- **spread oneself too thin** to try to do several different things at once, often with the result that none of them are done very well or properly.
- **thin as a rake** extremely thin.

thing

- **do one's (own) thing** to do what one likes to do or what one is good at doing.
- **have a thing about (someone** or **something) 1** to be very fond of or be particularly attracted to (someone or something). **2** to be scared of, to have a phobia about (someone or something).
- **one of those things** something that must be accepted.
- **see things** to see someone or something that is not there.
- **the thing is** the most important point or question is.

think

- **have another think coming** to be quite mistaken.

thread

- **hang by a thread** to be in a very precarious or uncertain state. <Probably a reference to the sword of Damocles>.
- **lose the thread** to cease to follow the course or development of an argument, conversation, etc.

throat

- **at each other's throats** quarrelling fiercely.
- **jump down (someone's) throat** to attack (someone) verbally or in an angry or violent manner.
- **ram (something) down (someone's) throat** to try forcefully to make (someone) accept ideas, opinions, etc.
- **stick in one's throat** or **gullet** to be difficult for one to accept or tolerate.

throw

- **throw up** to vomit.

thumb

- **thumb a lift** to ask for (and get) a lift in

someone's vehicle by signalling with one's thumb.
- **thumb one's nose at (someone or something)** to express defiance or contempt at (someone or something), originally by making the rude gesture of putting one's thumb to one's nose.
- **thumbs down** rejection or disapproval. <From the method employed by the crowds in ancient Rome to indicate whether they thought the defeated gladiator should live or die after a fight between two gladiators. If the crowds turned their thumbs down the gladiator died. If they turned them up the gladiator lived.>
- **thumbs up** acceptance or approval. <See **thumbs down** above>.
- **twiddle one's thumbs** to do nothing, to be idle. <Literally to rotate one's thumbs round each other, indicating a state of boredom>.
- **under (someone's) thumb** under one's control or domination.

thunder

- **steal (someone's) thunder** to spoil (someone's) attempt at impressing people by doing what he or she intended to do before him or her. <John Dennis, a 17th/18th century playwright, invented a machine for simulating thunder in plays. When someone else used a similar device in a rival play Dennis said that he had stolen his thunder>.

ticket

- **just the ticket** exactly what is required.
- **meal ticket** someone who can be relied upon to support one, providing food and so on.

tickle

- **be tickled pink** to be delighted.

tide

- **swim against the tide** to do, say or believe things which are the opposite of what the majority of people are doing, saying or believing.
- **the tide is turning** used to indicate that a changing is occurring in people's attitudes, tastes, beliefs, etc.

tie

- **be tied up** to be busy or engaged.

tight

- **in a tight corner** *or* **spot** in a difficult or dangerous situation.
- **run a tight ship** to run an efficient, well-organized firm etc.
- **sit tight** to be unwilling to move or take action.

tightrope

- **walk a tightrope** to be in a very difficult situation, often one which involves opposing groups, which requires one to act with great caution and delicacy.

tile

- **a night on the tiles** a celebratory evening spent in a wild and unrestrained manner. <Refers to roof tiles and to cats sitting on them at night>.

tilt

- **at full tilt** at maximum speed. <Refers to knights tilting or jousting>.

time

- **ahead of one's time** with ideas in advance of one's contemporaries, often not understood.
- **all in good time** soon, when it is the right time.
- **behind the times** not up-to-date, old-fashioned.
- **do time** to be in prison.
- **have no time for (someone** *or* **something)** to have a very low opinion of someone or something and to wish not to associate with him, her or it.
- **have the time of one's life** to have a very enjoyable time.
- **have time on one's hands** to have more free time than one can usefully fill with work, etc.
- **in (someone's) own good time** when it is convenient for (someone), at whatever time or speed he or she chooses.
- **keep time 1** of a clock to show the time accurately. **2** to perform an action in the same rhythm as someone else.
- **kill time** to find something to do to pass some idle time, especially time spent waiting for someone or something.
- **mark time** to remain in one's present position without progressing or taking any action. <Refers to soldiers moving their feet as if marching but not actually moving forwards>.
- **not before time** not too soon, rather late.
- **no time at all** a very short time.
- **pass the time of day with (someone)** to greet (someone) and have a brief conversation, e.g. about the weather.
- **play for time** to act so as to delay an action, event, etc, until the time that conditions are better for oneself. <In games such as cricket it means to play in such a way as to avoid defeat by playing defensively until the close of the game>.
- **take time by the forelock** to act quickly and without delay. <Refers to the fact that time was often represented by an old man with no hair except for a forelock, a length of hair over his forehead>.
- **time and tide wait for no man** time moves on without regard for human beings and therefore opportunities should be grasped as they arise as they may not be there for very long.
- **time and time again** repeatedly.
- **time flies** time passes very quickly.

tip

- **be on the tip of one's tongue** to be about to be said.

tit

- **tit for tat** repayment of injury or harm for injury or harm. <Perhaps a variation on tip for tap, blow for blow>.

to

- **toing and froing** repeatedly going backwards and forwards.

toast

- **warm as toast** very warm and cosy.

tod

- **on one's tod** alone. <From Cockney rhyming slang 'on one's Tod Sloan', meaning 'on one's own', Tod Sloan having been a famous American jockey>.

toe

- **be on one's toes** to be alert and prepared for action.
- **make one's toes curl** to make one feel very uncomfortable or embarrassed.

Tom

- **put a toe in the water** to start doing something very slowly or gradually to see if one likes it, whether it will be successful, whether people will approve, etc.
- **tread on (someone's) toes** to offend (someone) by doing or saying (something) that is against his or her beliefs or opinions.

Tom

- **a peeping Tom** a man who gets sexual enjoyment from secretly watching women undress or women who are naked, especially by looking through the windows of their houses. <From the story of Lady Godiva who is said to have ridden naked through the streets of Coventry as part of a bargain made with her husband, Leofric, Earl of Mercia, to persuade him to lift a tax he had placed on his tenants. Everyone was to stay indoors so as not to see her but a character, later called Peeping Tom, looked out to see her and was struck blind>.
- **every** *or* **any Tom, Dick and Harry** absolutely everyone or anyone, every ordinary person. <From the fact that all three are common English Christian names>.

tongue

- **have one's tongue in one's cheek** to say something that one does not mean seriously or literally, sometimes to say the opposite of what one means for a joke.
- **hold one's tongue** to remain silent or to stop talking.
- **set tongues wagging** to start people gossiping.

tooth

- **be** *or* **get long in the tooth** to be or become old.
- **fight tooth and nail** to fight, struggle or argue fiercely and determinedly.

top[1]

- **blow one's top** to lose one's temper.
- **get on top of one** used to indicate that someone is not coping with all the things that require to be done.
- **off the top of one's head** without much thought, without research or preparation.
- **over the top** too much, to too great an extent.

- **the top of the ladder** *or* **tree** the highest point in a profession, etc.

top[2]

- **sleep like a top** to sleep very soundly. <A pun on the fact that sleep used of a top means 'to spin steadily without wobbling'>.

toss

- **argue the toss** to dispute a decision. <Refers to arguing about the result of tossing a coin>.

touch

- **it's touch and go** it's very uncertain or precarious. <Perhaps refers to a ship that touches rocks or the ground but goes on past the danger without being damaged>.
- **lose one's touch** to lose one's usual skill or knack. <Probably refers to someone's touch on piano keys>.
- **the common touch** the ability to understand and get on with ordinary people.
- **the finishing touches** the final details which complete something.

tow

- **have (someone) in tow** to have someone following closely behind one.

towel

- **throw in the towel** to give up, to admit defeat. <From a method of conceding defeat in boxing>.

tower

- **a tower of strength** someone who is very helpful and supportive.

town

- **go to town** to act or behave without restraint, with great enthusiasm or with great expense.

track

- **cover one's tracks** to hide one's activities or movements.
- **from the wrong side of the tracks** used of someone who comes from a poor or less desirable area of town. <American in origin and refers to the fact that, when railways were built, they often divided an area into two sharply divided districts>.
- **keep** *or* **lose track of (someone** *or* **something)** to keep or fail to keep oneself informed about the whereabouts or progress of (someone or something).

trail

* **make tracks (for)** to leave or set out (for).
* **on the right** *or* **wrong track** on the right or wrong course to get the correct answer or desired result.

trail

* **blaze a trail** to show or lead the way in some new activity or area of knowledge. <Refers to explorers going along a path and marking the way for those coming after them by stripping sections of bark from trees (blazing)>.

trial

* **trials and tribulations** difficulties and hardships.

trick

* **do the trick** to have the desired effect, to achieve the desired result.
* **never to miss a trick** never to fail to take advantage of a favourable situation or opportunity to bring advantage to oneself.
* **up to one's (old) tricks** acting in one's usual (wrong, dishonest or deceitful) way.

trooper

* **swear like a trooper** to swear very frequently or very strongly. <A trooper was an ordinary cavalry soldier>.

trot

* **on the trot** **1** one after the other. **2** very active and busy.

trousers

* **wear the trousers** to make all the important decisions in a household.

trump

* **play one's trump card** to use something very advantageous to oneself that one has had in reserve for use when really necessary. <In card games a trump is a card of whichever suit has been declared to be higher-ranking than the others>.
* **turn up trumps** to do the right or required thing in a difficult situation, especially unexpectedly. <*See* above, refers to drawing a card from the trump suit>.

tune

* **call the tune** to be the person in control who gives the orders. <Refers to the saying 'He who pays the piper calls the tune'>.
* **in tune with (something)** in agreement with (something), compatible with (something).
* **to the tune of (something)** to the stated sum of money, usually high or higher than is expected or is reasonable.

turkey

* **cold turkey** a form of treatment for drug or alcohol abuse involving sudden and complete withdrawal as opposed to gradual withdrawal.
* **talk turkey** to talk plainly and honestly.

turn

* **a turn-up for the books** something favourable which happens unexpectedly. <Referred originally to a horse that unexpectedly won a race, the book meaning the total number of bets on a race>.
* **do (someone) a good turn** to help (someone) in some way.
* **done to a turn** cooked exactly right, cooked to perfection.
* **give (someone) quite a turn** to give (someone) a sudden shock or surprise.
* **turn turtle** to turn upside down, to capsize. <A turtle is helpless and easy to kill if it is turned over on its back>.

twice

* **think twice** to give careful consideration.

two

* **in two ticks** in a very short time. <Refers to the ticking of a cloak>.
* **put two and two together** to come to a (correct) conclusion from what one sees and hears.
* **two of a kind** two people of a very similar type or character.
* **two's company, (three's a crowd)** a third person who is with a couple is often unwanted as they want to be alone.

umbrage

* **take umbrage** to show that one is offended. <Originally meant to feel overshadowed, from Latin *umbra*, 'shade'>.

uncle

* **Uncle Sam** the United States of America. <Probably from the initials US which were stamped on government supplies, possibly because someone called Uncle Sam was employed in handling such supplies>.

under

- **under the influence** under the influence of alcohol, drunk.

up

- **be on the up-and-up** to be making successful progress.
- **be (well) up in** *or* **on (something)** to have an extensive knowledge of (something).
- **be up and running** to have started and be operating well.
- **be up to (someone)** it is (someone's) responsibility or duty.
- **be up to (something)** **1** to be occupied with or in (something, often something dishonest, etc). **2** to be good enough, strong enough, etc, to do (something).
- **up and about** out of bed, after an illness.
- **up and doing** active and busy.
- **ups and downs** good fortune and bad fortune, successful periods and unsuccessful periods.
- **upstage (someone** *or* **something)** to take attention or interest away from (someone or something).

upshot

- **the upshot** the result or outcome. <Literally the last shot in an archery competition>.

upper

- **have** *or* **get the upper hand (of** *or* **over) (someone)** have or get an advantage or control (over someone).
- **on one's uppers** very poor. <Literally with no soles on one's shoes>.
- **upper-crust** of the upper class or aristocracy. <Refers literally to the upper part of the pastry of a pie above the filling>.

uptake

- **quick** *or* **slow on the uptake** quick or slow to understand.

Uriah

- **Uriah Heep** a sycophant, someone who always fawns over and toadies to others. <Refers to a character in Charles Dickens's novel *David Copperfield*>.

U-turn

- **do a U-turn** to change one's opinion, policy, etc, completely. <Refers originally to vehicle drivers making a turn in the shape of the letter U to reverse direction>.

vain

- **take (someone's) name in vain** to use (someone's) name disrespectfully, especially to swear using God's name. <A biblical reference to Exodus 20:7>.

variety

- **variety is the spice of life** the opportunity to do different things, experience different situations, etc, is what makes life interesting. <A quotation from a poem by William Cowper>.

veil

- **draw a veil over (something)** not to discuss (something), to keep (something) hidden or secret.

vengeance

- **with a vengeance** very strongly, much, etc.

vex

- **a vexed question** a difficult issue or problem that is much discussed without being resolved.

victory

- **landslide victory** a victory in an election by a very large number of votes.

view

- **a bird's-eye view of (something)** **1** a view of (something) seen from high above. **2** a brief description, etc, of (something).

villain

- **the villain of the piece** the person responsible for an act of evil or wrongdoing. <Refers originally to the villain in a play>.

vine

- **a clinging vine** a possessive person, someone who likes always to be with someone else.
- **wither on the vine** to die to come to an end without being used, finished, etc. <Literally of grapes withering on the vine instead of being picked and eaten or made into wine>.

violet

- **a shrinking violet** a very timid, shy person.

voice

- **a voice crying in the wilderness** (someone) expressing an opinion or warning that no one takes any notice of. <A biblical reference to John the Baptist in Matthew 3:3>.
- **the still, small voice (of reason)** the

volume

expression of a calm, sensible point of view. <A biblical reference to I Kings 19:12>.

volume

• **speak volumes** to express a great deal of meaning without putting it into words.

vote

• **a vote of confidence** a vote taken to establish whether or not the government, a group of people, a person, etc, is still trusted and supported.

• **vote with one's feet** to leave.

wagon

• **circle the wagons** of a group of people, to work together to protect themselves against possible harm or danger. <In the American West pioneers used to form their wagons into a circle if they were under attack>.

• **on the wagon** not drinking alcohol. <Refers to a water wagon>.

wake

• **in the wake of (something)** immediately following, and often caused by (something). <Refers literally to the strip of water left by the passing of a ship>.

wall

• **be climbing the wall(s)** to feel frustrated, bored or impatient.

• **go to the wall** to suffer ruin. <Origin uncertain>.

• **off the wall** unconventional, strange.

• **up the wall** very annoyed, irritated, harassed, etc.

• **walls have ears** someone may be listening (to a secret conversation.

Walter

• **a Walter Mitty** someone who invents stories about himself to make his life seem more exciting. <Refers to a character in a James Thurber short story>.

war

• **have been in the wars** to have a slight injury.

• **on the warpath** very angry. <An American Indian expression>.

wart

• **warts and all** including all the faults, disadvantages. <Refers to the fact that Oliver Cromwell instructed his portrait painter, Sir Peter Lely, to paint him as he really was,

including his warts, rather than try to make him look more handsome>.

wash

• **come out in the wash** to come to a satisfactory end. <Used literally of a stain on clothes, etc, that comes out when the article is washed>.

• **(something) won't wash** to be regarded as unacceptable or incredible.

water

• **blow (someone or something) out of the water** to destroy or defeat (someone or something) utterly.

• **hold water** to be accurate, to be able to be proved true. <From a vessel that is not broken>.

• **muddy the waters** to confuse a situation.

• **test the water/waters** to try to find out what the reaction is likely to be to a plan before one puts this into effect.

• **tread water** to take very little action. <Literally to keep oneself afloat in water by moving the legs (and arms)>.

• **water under the bridge** something that is past and cannot be changed and should be forgotten.

wave

• **make waves** to cause trouble.

• **on the same wavelength as (someone)** having the same opinions, attitudes, tastes, etc, as (someone).

way

• **be set in one's ways** to have a set routine in your life and to dislike having this disrupted.

• **get into the way of (something *or* doing something)** to become accustomed to (something or doing something).

• **get *or* have one's own way** to do or get what one wants.

• **go back a long way** used to indicate that people have known each other for a long time.

• **go out of one's way** to do more than is really necessary, to make a special effort.

• **go the way of all flesh** to die or come to an end.

• **have a way with (someone *or* something)** to have a special knack with (someone or something), to be good at handling (some-one or something).

- **have everything one's own way** to get everything done according to one's wishes.

- **have it both ways** to have the advantages of two sets of situations, each of which usually excludes the possibility of the other.

- **lead the way** to go first, to be in front.

- **lose one's way** to cease to know where one is or which direction one is going in.

- **make way for (someone** or **something)** to stand aside to leave room for (someone or something).

- **mend one's ways** to improve one's behaviour.

- **not to know which way to turn** to be in trouble and to be too confused to be able to decide what to do for the best.

- **pay one's way** to pay one's expenses or one's share of expenses.

- **see one's way to (doing something)** to be able and willing to (do something).

- **there are no two ways about it** no other opinion, attitude, etc, is possible.

- **under way** in progress.

- **ways and means** methods, especially unofficial ones.

- **where's there's a will there's a way** a saying used to indicate that if one is determined to do something, then one will find a way to succeed in doing so.

wayside

- **fall by the wayside** to fail to continue to the end of something; to give up in the course of doing something. <A biblical reference to the parable of the sower in Luke 8:5>.

wear

- **be the worse for wear 1** to be in a bad state, looking tired, ill, untidy, etc. **2** to be drunk.

weather

- **under the weather** unwell.

web

- **a tangled web** used to describe a very complicate, confused situation.

wedge

- **drive a wedge between** to cause disagreement or ill will between two people or two groups, especially when they were formerly friendly.

- **the thin end of the wedge** a minor event or action which could be the first stage of something major and serious or harmful.

weight

- **a weight off one's mind** used to indicate that one no longer has to worry about something which has been worrying one for some time.

- **carry weight** to have influence, to be considered important.

- **pull one's weight** to do one's fair share of work, etc.

- **punch above one's weight** to try to do something which is thought to be beyond one's abilities.

- **take the weight off one's feet** to sit down.

- **throw one's weight about** or **around** to use one's power and influence in a bullying way.

- **throw one's weight behind (someone** or **something)** to support (someone or something).

west

- **go west** to be ruined, to be finished. <Airmen's slang from World War I>.

wet

- **wet behind the ears** to be young, inexperienced and naive.

- **have a whale of a time** to have an extremely enjoyable time.

what

- **give (someone) what for** to scold or punish (someone).

- **know what's what** to know the details of a situation, to know what is going on.

- **what have you** and similar things.

wheel

- **a fifth wheel** a person or thing that is not needed or is not wanted. <Refers to the fact that a vehicle needs only four wheels to keep running>.

- **reinvent the wheel** to do something which one considers new or innovative, but which is, in fact, very similar to something which has been done by someone else; to start a project from scratch without taking advantage of available information, research, etc.

- **set the wheels in motion** to start a process off.

- **wheeling and dealing** acting in an astute but sometimes dishonest or immoral way, especially in business.
- **wheels within wheels** used to indicate a very complicated situation with many different things involved, all influencing each other.

whip

- **have the whip hand** to have control or an advantage. <Refers to coach-driving>.
- **a whipping boy** someone who is blamed and punished for someone else's mistakes. <Refers literally to a boy who was punished for any misdeeds a royal prince made, since the tutor was not allowed to strike a member of the royal family>.

whisker

- **win by a whisker** to win by a very short amount.

whistle

- **wet one's whistle** to have a drink.
- **whistle for (something)** to ask for (something) with no hope of getting it. <Perhaps from an old sailors' superstition that when a ship is becalmed whistling can summon up a wind>.

white

- **a whited sepulchre** someone who pretends to be moral and virtuous but is in fact bad. <A biblical reference to Matthew 23:27>.
- **white lie** a not very serious lie.
- **whiter than white** extremely honest and moral.

wick

- **get on (someone's) wick** to annoy or irritate (someone) greatly.

wide

- **be wide open** used of a competition of some kind to indicate that it is very difficult to predict the winner as the competitors seem equally good.

wild

- **a wild goose chase** a search or hunt that cannot end in success.
- **sow one's wild oats** to enjoy oneself in a wild and sometimes promiscuous way when one is young.
- **spread like wildfire** to spread extremely rapidly. <Wildfire was probably a kind of fire started by lightning>.

will

- **with a will** enthusiastically and energetically.

wind

- **get one's second wind** to find renewed energy to go on doing something after a period of feeling tired and weak.
- **get wind of (something)** to receive information about (something) <Referring to the scent of an animal carried by the wind>.
- **in the wind** about to happen, being placed or prepared.
- **get the wind up** to become frightened or nervous.
- **raise the wind** to get enough money to do (something).
- **spit in the wind** to try to do something impossible and so waste time and effort.
- **take the wind out of (someone's) sails** to reduce (someone's) pride in his or her cleverness, abilities, etc. <Refers to the fact that a ship takes the wind out of another ship's sails if it passes close to it on the windward side>.
- **throw caution to the (four) winds** to begin to behave recklessly.
- **whistle in the wind** to make a statement or promise which is pointless since it is very unlikely to have any effect or produce any results.

windmill

- **tilt at windmills** to struggle against imaginary opposition. <Refers to an episode in Cervantes' novel *Don Quixote* in which the hero mistakes a row of windmills for giants and attacks them>.

window

- **go out the window** to disappear completely; to be ignore or forgotten about.
- **window-dressing** the presentation of something to show the most favourable parts and hide the rest. <Refers literally to the arranging of goods in a shop window to attract customers>.

wing

- **on a wing and a prayer** used to indicate that you hope to do something successfully even although you do not have the resources to do so.

wink

- **spread one's wings 1** to leave home. **2** to try to put into practice one's own ideas, to make use of one's abilities. <Refers to young birds ready to try to fly and leave the nest for the first time>.
- **take (someone) under one's wing** to take (someone) under one's protection and guidance. <Refers to the practice of some birds of covering their young with their wings>.
- **try one's wings** to try to do something which one has never done before in order to see if one will be successful at it.
- **waiting in the wings** in a state of readiness to do something, especially to take over someone else's job. <Literally waiting in the wings of a theatre stage ready to go on>.
- **wing it** to do something without planning or preparation, to improvise.

wink

- **not sleep a wink** not to be able to sleep at all.
- **tip (someone) the wink** to give (someone) information secretly or privately.

wire

- **down to the wire** to the last possible minute.
- **get** *or* **have one's wires crossed** to be involved in a misunderstanding. <Refers to telephone wires>.

wise

- **none the wiser** knowing no more than one did before.
- **put (someone) wise to (something)** to give (someone) information about (something), make (someone) aware of (something).

wish

- **wishful thinking** believing that, or hoping that, something unlikely is true or will happen just because one wishes that it would.
- **wish (someone) joy of (something)** to wish that something will be a pleasure or benefit to someone (although one doesn't think it will).

wit

- **at one's wits' end** worried and desperate.
- **keep one's wits about one** to be alert and watchful.

word

- **live by one's wits** to live by cunning schemes rather than by working.
- **pit one's wits against (someone)** to use one's intelligence to try to defeat (someone).
- **scare (someone) out of his** *or* **her wits** to frighten (someone) very much.

witch

- **witch-hunt** a search for and persecution of people who are thought to have done something wrong or hold opinions which are thought to be dangerous etc. <Refers historically to organized hunts for people thought to be witches>.

wolf

- **a wolf in sheep's clothing** someone evil and dangerous who seems to be gentle and harmless. <A biblical reference to Matthew 7:15>.
- **cry wolf** to give a false warning of danger, to call unnecessarily for help. <Refers to one of Aesop's fables in which a shepherd boy used to amuse himself by calling out that a wolf was coming to attack his sheep and did this so many times when it was not true that no one believed when it was true, and all his sheep were killed>.
- **keep the wolf from the door** to prevent poverty and hunger.

wood

- **not to be able to see the wood for the trees** not to be able to consider the general nature of a situation, etc, because one is concentrating too much on details.
- **out of the woods** out of danger or difficulties.
- **touch wood** to touch something made of wood supposedly to keep away bad luck. <Refers to a well-known superstition>.

wool

- **pull the wool over (someone's) eyes** to deceive (someone).
- **wool-gathering** day-dreaming. <Refers to someone wandering around hedges gathering wool left by sheep>.

word

- **eat one's words** to admit that one was wrong in what one said.
- **get a word in edgeways** *or* **edgewise** to

have difficulty in breaking into a conversation.

- **hang on (someone's) words** to listen carefully and eagerly to everything that someone says.
- **have a word in (someone's) ear** to tell (someone) something in private.
- **have words** to argue or quarrel.
- **keep one's word** to do as one promised to do.
- **put in a good word for (someone)** to say something favourable about (someone), to recommend (someone).
- **put words into (someone's) mouth** to say that someone has said something when he/she did not; to suggest that someone is going to say something when he/she has no intention of doing so.
- **say the word** say what you want and your wishes will be carried out.
- **take (someone's) word for it** to believe what someone says without question and without proof.
- **take the words out of (someone's) mouth** to say what (someone) was just about to say.

work

- **all work and no play makes Jack a dull boy** people should take some leisure time and not work all the time.
- **give (someone) the works** to give (someone) the complete treatment. <Originally slang for to kill someone>.
- **have one's work cut out** to face a very difficult task. <Literally to have a lot of work ready for one>.
- **worked up** agitated, annoyed.

world

- **a man of the world** a sophisticated and worldly man.
- **come down in the world** to be less well off, less successful etc. than formerly.
- **come up in the world** to be better off, more successful, etc. than formerly.
- **do (someone) the world of good** to have a very good effect on (someone); to be of great benefit or advantage to (someone).
- **for all the world like (someone or something)** exactly like (someone or something).
- **not the end of the world** used to make

someone realize that things are not as bad as they think they are.

- **not to have long for this world** to be about to die.
- **on top of the world** very cheerful and happy.
- **out of this world** remarkably good.
- **think the world of (someone)** to be extremely fond of (someone).
- **the world is (someone's) oyster** (someone) has a great many possible opportunities or chances. <Refers to a quotation from Shakespeare's *The Merry Wives of Windsor*, Act 2, scene II>.

worm

- **a can of worms** an extremely complicated and difficult situation. <Refers to the fact that worms wriggle around a lot>.
- **(even) the worm turns** even the most humble or meek person will protest if treated badly enough.

worth

- **for all one is worth** using maximum effort.

wound

- **lick one's wounds** to try to recover from a situation in which one has been badly defeated or humiliated.
- **reopen old wounds** to remind people of past unpleasant experiences which they would prefer to forget about.

wrap

- **keep (something) under wraps** to keep (something) secret or hidden.
- **take the wraps off (something)** to reveal, or give details about, something that has been secret up till now.
- **wrapped up in (someone *or* something)** absorbed in, giving all one's attention to (someone or something).
- **wrap (something) up** to finish (something) completely.

writ

- **writ large** used to indicate that something is in its most extreme form.

write

- **the writing on the wall** something which indicates that something unpleasant, such as failure, unhappiness, disaster, etc, will happen. <A biblical reference to Daniel

5:5–31, in which the coming destruction of the Babylonian empire is made known to Belshazzar at a feast through mysterious writing on a wall>.

wrong

- **get on the wrong side of (someone)** to cause (someone) to dislike or be hostile to one.
- **not to put a foot wrong** not to make a mistake of any kind.

yarn

- **spin a yarn** to tell a long story, especially an untrue one that is given as an excuse. <Telling a story is compared to spinning a long thread>.

year

- **the year dot** a long time ago, the beginning of time.

yesterday

- **not born yesterday** not easily fooled.

young

- **you're only young once** one should take advantage of the opportunities that arise when one is young and has the energy, freedom, etc, to enjoy or exploit them.

zero

- **zero hour** the time at which something is due to begin. <Originally a military term>.

Clichés

Clichés are an established feature of the English language, being particularly common in spoken English language and in informal written contexts. Some of them are hundreds of years old; others have taken only a short time to become popular.

People tend to use them unconsciously and most of us are unaware of quite how often we use them. There are many who claim to dislike clichés and regard them as somehow spoiling the language, but even they would find that they use quite a lot of them, if they stopped to analyse what they say and write.

People dislike clichés because they are overused. Many clichés start out as a particularly imaginative or neat way of saying something, but they become used so often by so many people that they lose their freshness and originality.

It would be almost impossible to rid our speech and writing entirely of clichés and, in any case, they often add a bit of colour to the language. Since they are such an established feature of English, it is important for learners of English to learn how to use them correctly. However, particularly in fairly formal speech or writing, it is essential to try to avoid using them too frequently

Some clichés are used in contexts in which they are virtually meaningless and act simply as conversational fillers. For example, there are people who use the expression **at this moment in time** regularly when the word 'now' would be more appropriate. Likewise, many people use clichés such as **the thing is**, **at the end of the day** or **you know what I mean** in this way.

Below is a selection of common clichés which are particularly overused and so should be used sparingly. Some of these are more thoroughly explained in the English Idioms section.

accidents will happen	things go wrong at some time in everyone's life
across the board	applying to everyone or to all cases
actions speak louder than words	how a person acts is more important than what they say
to add insult to injury	to make matters worse
after due consideration	after some thought
all things considered	after some thought
an accident waiting to happen	a dangerous situation
any port in a storm	a welcome solution in a bad situation
as a matter of fact	the following statement is true
at death's door	an exaggeration to say someone is ill
at the drop of a hat	without much of a reason at all
at the end of the day	ultimately
at this juncture	now
at this moment in time	now
avoid like the plague	to strenuously avoid
back to the drawing board	back to the beginning
bag and baggage	all your possessions
bag of tricks	the equipment necessary to do something
batten down the hatches	there's going to be trouble
beggars can't be choosers	one needs a favour and has no other choice
be that as it may	that may be so
better late than never	an ironic way of saying something or someone is late
bite the bullet	to get on with something despite unpleasantness
a blessing in disguise	a bad situation from which may come good

blissful ignorance

blissful ignorance	to be in the happy state of not knowing of an unpleasant situation
a blot on the landscape	an ugly thing (usually a building) in a beautiful place
blushing bride	an ironic description of a bride
bone of contention	a cause of dispute
the bottom line	the outcome or conclusion; most important factor
bright-eyed and bushy-tailed	alert and awake
by the same token	using the same reasoning, or on the other side of the argument
call it a day	give up and stop a venture
the calm before the storm	a time before an unpleasant situation where everything seems fine
Catch 22	a situation in which one can never win or from which one can never escape
categorical denial	strong denial
caught napping	unprepared for a situation
chalk and cheese	opposites
champing at the bit	enthusiastic to get started at something
chapter and verse	every detail
cheek by jowl	very close together
chop and change	alternate
a close shave	an escape which was very nearly disastrous
to coin a phrase	ironically, this is said when one is using a cliché
come full circle	to return to the beginning of something
a commanding lead	emphasis of in the lead
common or garden	everyday
conspicuous by one's absence	to deliberately boycott something
cool, calm and collected	emphasis of calm
cover a multitude of sins	a flattering surface on something, usually refers to clothing
at crack of dawn	very early
cross that bridge when you come to it	deal with matters in hand and think of other problems when they arise
to cut a long story short	to summarise
cut and dried	settled and definite
the cutting edge	the latest technology
damn with faint praise	to praise in a patronising or deliberately ironic way
a damp squib	something which promises excitement but disappoints
a dark horse	someone with a secret, usually an exciting or exotic one
day in, day out	every day
dead as a dodo	actually dead, or more metaphorically, out of favour
dead in the water	has no chance of working
dead to the world	fast asleep
a deafening silence	a silence which is very prominent and embarrassing
dig one's own grave	to be the cause of one's own misfortune
a dirty tricks campaign	a campaign, usually political, uncovering, or possibly creating rumours of, a scandal regarding one's opponent
dog eat dog	a ruthless struggle against one's rivals to survive or be successful.
donkey's years ago	many years ago

don't count your chickens before they are hatched	don't presume anything before it happens
doom and gloom	pessimism
draw a blank	no result
drown one's sorrows	to get drunk to get over a disappointment
Dutch courage	to get drunk to have the confidence to do something
each and every one of you	everyone
eager for the fray	looking for a fight
easier said than done	more difficult than it appears to be
eat humble pie	to admit that you are wrong
economical with the truth	to leave out important facts
the end of an era	the end of an important phase
enough is enough	no more can be tolerated
the envy of the world	enviable
every cloud has a silver lining	bad situations can sometimes have consolations
every dog has his day	everyone has their individual triumphs
every little helps	a little help from a lot of different sources will eventually add up to create something more substantial
every man jack	everyone
everything but the kitchen sink	almost all your belongings
explore every avenue	to look for all possibilities
face facts	be honest with yourself
face the music	face up to difficulties
the fact of the matter	the truth of the situation
fair and square	honestly
fall between two stools	to try to gain two things at once and fail with regard to both of them
fall on deaf ears	an explanation given to someone who doesn't want to listen
famous last words	making a statement about an event directly before the exact opposite happens
far and wide	a great area
far be it for me	this is something I would never do (usually said ironically)
a fate worse than death	an exaggeration meaning death would be preferable
a feeding frenzy	where many people are desperately after the same information (usually of the press)
few and far between	very rare
a fighting chance	a good chance of succeeding, or surviving
fighting fit	in good health
the finishing touches	in the final stages
first and foremost	first and most importantly
first things first	most important things first
a flash in the pan	a passing fashion or idea that will not last
the flavour of the month	a person or fashion that is popular at the moment but may not last
flog a dead horse	to pursue something that is not worth pursuing
the fly in the ointment	an unpleasant feature that spoils something
food for thought	something that makes you think
footloose and fancy free	single and looking for fun
forewarned is forearmed	to be prepared so that you are able to cope with a possible event

a forlorn hope

a forlorn hope	no hope
fraught with danger	dangerous
fresh fields and pastures new	a new and different place or situation
from the sublime to the ridiculous	from a state of greatness to one of ridiculouness
from the word go	from the start
from time immemorial	since a long time ago
gainful employment	in work
gather ye rosebuds while ye may	make the most of your youth
a general exodus	everyone has left at once
generous to a fault	extremely generous
a gentleman's agreement	an agreement in word alone
get down to brass tacks	to consider the basic facts
get more than one bargained for	to encounter more difficulties than expected
the gift of the gab	the ability to talk readily and easily
gild the lily	to add unnecessary decoration
give up the ghost	to die (person); to stop working (object)
a glowing tribute	a flattering tribute
a glutton for punishment	someone who has suffered but who goes back for more
go against the grain	to act against your better judgement or wishes
go from strength to strength	to get better and better
it goes without saying	you should know what I'm talking about
a golden opportunity	a great and unexpected opportunity that should be grasped
good as gold	perfectly behaved
the gory details	a description of the details of a situation (not necessarily a bad one)
grasp the nettle	to set about a difficult task in a determined way
the greatest thing since sliced bread	a very popular admired thing or person
green with envy	very jealous
grin and bear it	to suffer a bad situation without complaint
grind to a halt	to stop suddenly
a guiding light	someone who guides the way in a particular field
halcyon days	a nostalgic (and idealistic) reference to a perfect time in one's life
hale and hearty	healthy
half the battle	the most difficult part of a situation is over with
hand over fist	in large amounts; very rapidly
the happy couple	newly married people
a hard act to follow	someone who has previously been very successful at something
a helping hand	help
high and dry	left in a helpless state
hit the nail on the head	to be extremely accurate in one's description
a hive of activity	a very busy area
Hobson's choice	no choice at all
the honest truth	emphasis of the truth of a statement
hope against hope	to continue to hope although there is little reason to be hopeful
horses for courses	certain people are better suited to certain tasks than others

kill with kindness

how time flies	time passes very quickly
if you can't beat 'em, join 'em	if the majority disagree with you then why not just go along with them
if you can't stand the heat, get out of the kitchen	if you can't cope with the job in hand then leave
ill-gotten gains	possessions acquired dishonestly
in all conscience	being completely fair and honest
in a nutshell	briefly; to sum up
in any shape or form	in any way at all
in less than no time	in a very short time
in no uncertain terms	in a very direct way
in splendid isolation	standing out in a unique way
in the cold light of day	when one looks at something rationally and calmly
in the dim and distant past	something happened a long time ago (and should be forgotten)
in the fullness of time	when the proper time has elapsed
in the nick of time	just in time
in the pipeline	in preparation
in the present climate	in the present situation
in this day and age	in these times
it'll all come out in the wash	things will turn out for the best in the end
it never rains but it pours	when something goes wrong other things go wrong too
it's a long story	it is complicated
it's a small world	said when coincidental meetings occur
it's early days	it's too early to come to a conclusion
it takes two to tango	it's not the fault of one person
jack of all trades	someone who knows a little about a lot of things
jam tomorrow	the (possibly false) promise of better things in the future
the jewel in the crown	the most valuable or successful thing associated with someone or something
jobs for the boys	jobs given to friends rather than to those most worthy of them
jump on the bandwagon	to show interest because it's fashionable
just between you and me (and the gatepost)	this is a secret
just deserts	to get the punishment that is due to you
just for the record	so that it will be noted
just one of those things	something that has to be accepted
just what the doctor ordered	just what is required
keep a low profile	not to draw attention to oneself
keep oneself to oneself	not to tell others very much about oneself or to mix with others very much
keep one's head above water	to be just coping with a situation
keep one's nose to the grindstone	to keep working hard
keep the wolf from the door	to make just enough money to survive
kickstart	to encourage something or to give, e.g., a project, an extra push
kill the fatted calf	to provide a lavish meal for a celebration
kill two birds with one stone	to complete two tasks at once
kill with kindness	to be generous in some way to someone when it's not in his or her best interest

the kiss of death

the kiss of death	something which will cause the ruin of something
knee-jerk reaction	an immediate (reflex) response to something
know all the answers	to have all the information
know for a fact	emphasising that ones knows something
know where one stands	to know the nature of one's position
know which side one's bread is buttered on	to know when one is in a fortunate position
a labour of love	a difficult job done for the satisfaction of it
the lap of luxury	in luxurious surroundings
large as life	in person, actually present
last but not least	although someone or something is last, it is not the least important thing
the last straw	an event which makes a situation impossible
a leading light	a leader, longstanding, in a certain area
leave in the lurch	to abandon
leave no stone unturned	to search everywhere
leave to someone's tender mercies	to be left in the care of someone inefficient or dangerous
let bygones be bygones	forget about past grievances
let's face it	face the truth
level playing field	a fair basis for something
the life and soul of the party	a lively entertaining person
light at the end of the tunnel	fortunate outcome following times of trouble
a little bird told me	I can't tell you my sources
lock, stock and barrel	everything included
a lone wolf	a loner
the long arm of the law	the police
make an honest woman of	marry
make ends meet	to survive on little money
make the supreme sacrifice	to die
make someone an offer they can't refuse	an irresistible offer
make waves	to get yourself noticed; to cause trouble.
man and boy	as a child and an adult
the man in the street	ordinary person
manna from heaven	something unexpectedly advantageous
man to man	as equals, regardless of background etc.
many hands make light work	the more helpers there are the quicker a job will be done
mark my words	take note of what I'm saying
a matter of life or death	a very grave situation
method in one's madness	actions seem to be foolish but actually have a motive behind them
a millstone round one's neck	a hindrance
the moment of truth	when the result of something becomes apparent
a moot point	a point of argument
more in sorrow than in anger	more disappointed in someone's actions than angry
the more the merrier	the more people involved the better
move heaven and earth	to go to great lengths to achieve something
move the goalposts	to change the aims of a project so that it is disadvantageous to others but advantageous to oneself
the movers and shakers	those with power

pale into insignificance

much of a muchness	ordinary, indistinguishable from others
mutton dressed as lamb	an older person (usually female) dressed in a way that is unflatteringly young
my lips are sealed	it's a secret and I won't tell
name names	be specific as to whom it is that you are talking about
the name of the game	the important or central thing behind something
nearest and dearest	close family and close friends
needless to say	something that it should be unnecessary to state
a new dawn	a new opportunity or era
the nitty gritty	basic practical details
no expense spared	lots of money has been spent
no gain without pain (no pain, no gain)	you have to experience bad things in order to progress
nothing to write home about	not very interesting
no news is good news	if you haven't heard anything then it's possible that nothing bad has happened
no rest for the wicked	ironic way of saying that a person is extremely busy and has to get on with their work
no show without Punch	this person always seems to turn up (but is not really wanted)
no smoke without fire	there's always some basis to a rumour
nothing ventured, nothing gained	if you don't at least try to do something you'll never know if you'll succeed
not just a pretty face	intelligent as well as beautiful (often said in an ironic way by someone who knows that he or she is not beautiful)
not to put too fine a point on it	not to get too detailed
nuts and bolts	the basic details or practicalities of something
odds and ends	objects of different kinds, perhaps that are left over and don't match
older and wiser	to have got more wise with age
once bitten, twice shy	to have experienced an unfortunate situation and have learned from it
once in a blue moon	very rarely
one in a million	very rare
one of life's little ironies	a situation that is the opposite of what one hoped would happen
one of those days	a bad day
only time will tell	you'll just have to wait and see what happens
on the back burner	put to one side to be worked on later
on the dot	exactly
opening gambit	an opening move
an open secret	information not publicly discussed but which is not a secret
or words to that effect	something of the same meaning but said in a different way
out of sight, out of mind	that which you don't see you are less likely to think about
over and done with	finished
over my dead body	I'll die before I let that happen
over the hill	too old
pale into insignificance	overshadowed by something else

par for the course

par for the course	an expected experience in a certain situation
part and parcel	an expected experience in a certain situation
the patter of tiny feet	a pregnancy
the picture of health	very healthy
pie in the sky	unrealistic expectations
plain sailing	easy
pleased as Punch	very pleased
the plot thickens	a revelation makes a story more intriguing or complicated
the point of no return	you've gone so far that going back is not a possible option
a poisoned chalice	a seemingly attractive proposition that is actually dangerous
pound of flesh	revenge
the powers that be	people in charge
practice makes perfect	to keep practising will achieve perfection in a certain area
pride and joy	something that makes one very proud
pride of place	in a very prominent position
prime of life	at an age where one is fit, healthy and mentally sharp
pull out all the stops	to do everything possible
put one's best foot forward	to make the best attempt possible
put two and two together	to come to a conclusion about something
quality of life	an enjoyable fulfilling life
quality time	time spent giving an individual lots of attention
quantum leap	a sudden breakthrough
quite the reverse	the opposite
a race against time	time is running out
rain or shine	whatever the weather
a rainy day	an unspecified time in the future
the rat race	the capitalist way of life
read my lips	listen carefully to what I'm saying
red tape	the rules and regulations of government office
reinvent the wheel	wasting time doing work that's already been done
a reliable source	a trustworthy basis for something
a resounding silence	a meaningful silence
right as rain	in full health
rings a bell	sounds familiar
rising tide	events that are about to take over
risk life and limb	to put your life in danger
a rolling stone	a person who never stays very long in one place
a rose between two thorns	a beautiful or good person who has to decide between two unattractive choices
a rose by any other name	whatever a beautiful thing happens to be named it remains beautiful
Rome wasn't built in a day	a difficult task cannot be finished quickly
a rough diamond	a person with a rough manner but who has great qualities
rule with a rod of iron	to discipline in a strict manner
rumour has it	I have heard rumours telling me this
safe and sound	totally unharmed
a safe haven	a place of safety

the salt of the earth	a down to earth reliable person
saved by the bell	saved from a bad situation by another event coming along
to say the least	relates that the reaction or emotion which is being described is being understated
search high and low	to look everywhere
second to none	the best
sell like hot cakes	to be very popular
separate the sheep from the goats	to distinguish the talented people from the stupid ones
a shadow of one's former self	to be in some way diminished, either in physical size or in emotions
the shape of things to come	how the future might be
share and share alike	to be fair in one's dealings
ships that pass in the night	strangers who meet once and never again
shoot oneself in the foot	to say or do something that is to one's own detriment
short and sweet	short and to the point
the show must go on	despite misfortune an event will go ahead
signed, sealed and delivered	finalised
a sign of the times	something which indicates what society is like now
the silent majority	the people who do not make their opinions known publicly
six of one and half-a-dozen of the other	the same outcome
the sixty four thousand dollar question	a key question that sums up a situation
slave over a hot stove	to cook
slowly but surely	to work in a slow but careful way
smell a rat	to suspect something is wrong
the social whirl	hectic social life
so far, so good	at this point in the proceedings everything is fine
son and heir	first-born son
so near and yet so far	to have nearly accomplished something but near accomplishment is simply not good enough to get acclaim
sour grapes	saying that something one cannot have is not worth having
spick and span	very tidy
the spirit is willing	not physically able to do something that one wishes to do
stand up and be counted	make your opinions known publicly
a storm in a teacup	a fuss over nothing
strange as it may seem	this may look strange but it is actually true
suffer a sea change	to have a complete change in attitude or opinion
suffer in silence	to put up with something and not complain
the survival of the fittest	to survive or flourish at the expense of those who are weaker
sweetness and light	kind and friendly (usually just on the surface)
swings and roundabouts	the same outcome
take the bull by the horns	to tackle something boldly
take the rough with the smooth	to accept that bad things can happen as well as good
talk of the devil	said when someone or something you've just been talking about suddenly appears

tall, dark and handsome

tall, dark and handsome	the clichéd idea of the perfect man
a tall order	an unreasonable or very trying request
a (slight) technical hitch	a mistake or hold up
teething troubles	problems at the beginning of a project
tender loving care (TLC)	to be looked after
terra firma	to have one's feet safely on the ground
thankful for small mercies	to be grateful for some small benefits in an otherwise unfortunate situation
that'll be the day	that's not going to happen
that's for me to know and for you to find out	it's a secret
that's life	unexpected or difficult things can happen, you can't stop them
that's the way the cookie crumbles	unexpected or difficult things can happen, you can't stop them
there but for the grace of God go I	I could be in that situation
there's no fool like an old fool	foolish behaviour in an older person always seems even more foolish than if a young person acted that way
these things happen	unexpected or difficult things can happen, you can't stop them
through thick and thin	through good times and bad
throw in the towel	to give up
tie the knot	to get married
tighten one's belt	to be careful with your money
time flies	time passes quickly
the tip of the iceberg	there's a bigger problem that has still to surface or be dealt with
tired and emotional	drunk
a tissue of lies	a statement that is entirely dishonest in every way
tomorrow is another day	you can try again another time
too good to be true	so good that you can't believe it to be so
too little, too late	not enough to solve a problem and too late in any case
too many chiefs and not enough Indians	too many people want to be in charge and no one wants to do the real work
too numerous to mention	it would take too long to mention all the things I want to mention
touch and go	a precarious situation
a tower of strength	strong and reliable
trials and tribulations	difficulties
turn over a new leaf	to completely start over again in a new way
'twas ever thus	it has always been like this
unaccustomed as I am to public speaking	(usually said ironically) I'm not used to speaking in public
unavoidable delay	a delay caused by something you have no control over
under a cloud	depressed
under the sun	in the whole world
under the weather	feeling run down
the university of life	learning from real life experience

unsung hero	someone who has not received the credit they deserve
an untimely end	the death of someone who was very young and expected to make much of their life
untold wealth	wealth of uncertain but probably very large amounts
the unvarnished truth	a response that doesn't cover up any unpleasant facts
up in arms .	furious
up to the hilt	thoroughly prepared
vanish into thin air	to disappear without trace
variety is the spice of life	lots of different things in your life make it more exciting
vested interest	a motive (usually financial) for having an interest in something
a vexed question	a difficult situation that is much discussed but still not solved
a vicious circle	a bad situation, the result of which produces the original cause of the situation
vote with one's feet	to show displeasure by leaving a situation
wait on hand and foot	to do everything for someone
walls have ears	people might be eavesdropping
warts and all	good and bad
water under the bridge	a situation that has passed and should be forgotten about
wedded bliss	a (possibly ironic) way of describing marriage
the wee small hours	after midnight
a well-earned rest	a rest following hard work
what with one thing and another	considering all the other things that have happened
wheels within wheels	a complicated situation that has other things involved
when all is said and done	when all things have been considered and the argument is over
when in Rome	join in with the customs of the people you are with
who/which shall remain nameless	who need not be mentioned because we know who I am talking about
the whys and wherefores	the reasoning behind an argument
without more ado	without waiting any longer
the witching hour	midnight
with bated breath	excitedly
wonders will never cease	something has happened that has been long awaited but was not really expected to come about
a word to the wise	a piece of advice
the world's your oyster	the world is there for you to explore
the writing is on the wall	something is indicating that something bad is going to happen
you can say that again	what you've said is true and I agree
you can't make a silk purse out of a sow's ear	you can't make something attractive out of something worthless/unattractive
you can't teach an old dog new tricks .	there's no point in trying to make people change
you can't win 'em all	bad things inevitably happen and you can't do anything about it
you know what I mean	(added as emphasis to find out if listener empathises)
you must be joking	I find what you've said ridiculous or unbelievable

your chariot awaits

your chariot awaits	(ironic) said when someone is about to get into a vehicle
you're only young once	make the most of your life
your guess is as good as mine	neither of us know anything about this subject

Similes

A simile is a figure of speech in which a thing or person is, for the sake of comparison, said to be like another. The word *simile* is derived from *similis*, the Latin word for like. The words *like* or *as* usually appear in the simile, as in: *the rumour spread like wildfire, she was as slim as a wand*. Some similes are extremely common. A list of these is given below.

agile as a monkey
alike as (like) two peas in a pod
bald as a coot
black as ebony
blind as a bat
bold as brass
brave as a lion
brown as a berry
calm as a millpond
changeable as the moon
cheerful as the day is long
clear as daylight
clear as mud (=not at all clear)
common as muck
cool as a cucumber
cunning as a fox
dead as a doornail
deaf as a post
drunk as a lord
dry as a bone
dry as dust (boring)
dull as ditchwater
easy as pie
easy as falling off a log
fit as a fiddle
flat as a pancake
frisky as a colt
good as gold
green as grass
happy as a pig in muck
happy as a sandboy
hard as nails
helpless as a babe in arms
hollow as a drum
hot as hell
innocent as a new-born babe
keen as mustard
light as a feather
lively as a cricket
mad as a hatter

merry as a lark
neat as a pin
old as the hills/Methuselah
patient as Job
plain as a pikestaff
playful as a kitten
pleased as Punch
poor as a church mouse
pretty as a picture
proud as a peacock
quick as a flash
quiet as a mouse
rare as hen's teeth
rich as Croesus
safe as houses
sharp as a razor
sick as a dog
sick as a parrot (disappointed)
silent as the grave
simple as ABC
slow as a snail
sly as a fox
smart as paint
smooth as silk
sober as a judge
straight as a die
stubborn as a mule
sure as death
swift as an arrow
tall as a steeple
thick as thieves (friendly)
thick as two short planks (stupid)
thin as a rake
tight as a drum
tough as old boots
uncertain as the weather
weak as water
white as snow/a ghost
wily as a fox
wise as Solomon

Proverbs

action
Actions speak louder than words
It is the first step that is the most difficult
One good turn deserves another
Sooner begun, sooner done
The early bird catches the worm

age
A creaking door hangs long on its hinges
All would live long, but none would be old
An old fox is not easily snared
Crabbed age and youth cannot live together
Don't teach your grandmother to suck eggs
Life begins at forty
The best wine comes out of an old bottle
There's many a good tune played on an old fiddle
There's no fool like an old fool
There's none so old that he hopes not for another year of life
They who live longest will see most
Years know more than books
You are never too old to learn
You are only as old as you feel
You can't teach an old dog new tricks
Youth and age will never agree

anticipation
Don't count your chickens until they are hatched
It is better to travel hopefully than to arrive
It isn't over until the fat lady sings
There's many a slip 'twixt cup and lip

appearance
A fair face may hide a foul heart
All cats are grey in the dark
All that glitters is not gold
Appearances are deceptive
Beauty is but skin deep
Beauty is in the eye of the beholder
Beware the wolf in sheep's clothing
Be what you appear to be
Clothes make the man
Fine feathers make fine birds
First impressions are the most lasting
Handsome is as handsome does
Never judge from appearances
The eyes are the window of the soul

The fairest rose at last is withered
There is no making a good cloak of bad cloth
Things are not always what they seem
You can't judge a book by its cover
You must not hang a man by his looks

caution
A stitch in time saves nine
Better safe than sorry
Better the devil you know than the devil you don't know
Curiosity killed the cat
Cut your coat according to the cloth
Don't count your chickens before they are hatched
Don't put all your eggs in one basket
Don't throw out the baby with the bathwater
Haste makes waste
Least said is soonest mended
Let sleeping dogs lie
Look before you leap
Make haste slowly
Marry in haste, repent at leisure
More haste, less speed
Once bitten, twice shy
One step at a time
Second thoughts are best
Slow and steady wins the race
The burnt child fears the fire
The less said the better
Think first and then speak
You must learn to walk before you can run

change
A change is as good as a rest
A new broom sweeps clean
A rolling stone gathers no moss
Better the devil you know
Don't change horses in mid-stream
There is nothing new under the sun
You can't put back the clock
You can't put new wine in old bottles
Variety is the spice of life

character
Blood will tell
Cut off a dog's tail and he will be a dog still
The apple never falls far from the tree

choice

The leopard cannot change its spots
What's bred in the bone comes out in the flesh
You cannot make a silk purse out of a sow's ear

choice

You cannot have it both ways
You cannot have your cake and eat it
You cannot serve god and Mammon
You cannot serve two masters
You pays your money, you takes your choice

conduct

Ask no questions and you will be told no lies
Civility costs nothing
Cleanliness is next to godliness
Do as I say, not as I do
Do as you would be done by
Do not bite the hand that feeds you
Don't cut off your nose to spite your face
Don't hide your light under a bushel
If the cap fits, wear it
It is better to give than to receive
Least said soonest mended
Let sleeping dogs lie
Live and let live
Moderation in all thing
Never look a gift horse in the mouth
One good turn deserves another
People in glass houses should not throw stones
Practise what you preach
Pride goes before a fall
See no evil, hear no evil, speak no evil
Spare the rod and spoil the child
There is no use flogging a dead horse
The rolling stone gathers no moss
Travel broadens the mind
When in Rome do as the Romans do
When the cat's away the mice will play
You cannot have your cake and eat it

courage and cowardice

A bully is always a coward
Attack is the best form of defence
Conscience makes cowards of us all
Discretion is the better part of valour
Faint heart never won fair lady
Fortune favours the bold
He that fights and runs away may live to fight another day
It is better to be a coward for a minute than

dead for the rest of your life
Nothing ventured, nothing gained

crime

All are not thieves whom the dogs bark at
An old poacher makes the best gamekeeper
Better to do nothing than to do ill
Caesar's wife must be above suspicion
Crime never pays
It's an ill bird that fouls its own nest
One rotten apple in the barrel infects all the rest
Poverty is the mother of crime
Set a thief to catch a thief
There are more thieves than are hanged
There is honour among thieves
To err is human, to forgive divine
Two wrongs do not make a right
You might as well be hanged for a sheep as a lamb

death

All men must die
As a man lives so shall he die
Dead men tell no tales
Death is a remedy for all ills
Death is the great leveller
Death spares neither men nor beast
Fear of death is worse than death itself
It is as natural to die as to be born
Nothing is certain but death and taxes
One funeral makes many orphans
Shrouds have no pockets
The dead are soon forgotten
The good die young
We die as we live
When one is dead it is for a long time
Whom the gods love die young
You can only die once

delay

Better late than never
He who hesitates is lost
Never put off till tomorrow what you can do today
Procrastination is the thief of time
Time lost cannot be recalled
Tomorrow never comes

eating and drinking

Adam's ale is the best brew
An apple a day keeps the doctor away
An army marches on its stomach

folly

Drink little that you may drink long
Eat to live, not live to eat
Good wine makes good blood
Hunger is the best sauce
In vino veritas (There is truth in wine)
Man cannot live by bread alone
The way to a man's heart is through his stomach
Thirst makes wine out of water
When the wine is in the wit is out

folly

A fool and his money are soon parted
A fool's bolt is soon shot
Empty vessels make the most sound
Fools rush in where angels fear to tread
Fortune favours fools
He that is born a fool is never cured
Little things please little minds
There's no fool like an old fool
The world is full of fools
We have all been fools in our time

friendship

A fair-weather friend changes with the wind
A favourite has no friends
A friend in need is a friend indeed
A man is known by the company he keeps
A trouble shared is a trouble halved
Birds of a feather flock together
Fish and guests stink after three days
He that lies down with dogs will get up with fleas
It is good to have friends in high places
One good turn deserves another
Save us from our friends
The best of friends must apart

happiness

A blithe heart makes a blooming visage
A happy heart is better than a full purse
All happiness is in the mind
Be happy when you can for you are a long
   time dead
Content is happiness
Happy is the country which has no history
It is a poor heart that never rejoices
Joy and sorrow are next-door neighbours
Laughter is the best medicine
No pleasure without pain

health

A creaking gate lasts longest
An apple a day keeps the doctor away

law

Early to bed and early to rise makes a man
   healthy, wealthy and wise
Feed a cold and starve a fever
God heals, and the physician has the thanks
Health is better than wealth
The doctor is often more to be feared than
   the disease

home

Dry bread at home is better than roast meat
   abroad
East west, home's best
Home is where the heart is
The hare always returns to her form
There's no place like home

honesty

An honest man's word is as good as his bond
Better beg than steal
Confession is good for the soul
Honesty is the best policy
No honest man ever repented of his honesty
Plain dealing is best
Tell the truth and shame the devil
The truth will out

hope and optimism

A drowning man clutches at straws
Every cloud has a silver lining
He that lives on hope has but a slender diet
Hope for the best and prepare for the worst
Hope keeps man alive
Hope springs eternal
It's an ill wind that blows nobody any good
Look on the bright side
The darkest hour is that before the dawn
The longest night will have an end
Tomorrow is another day
Too much hope deceives
Where there's life, there's hope

law

Better no law than law not enforced
Every land has its own law
Every man is held to be innocent until he is
   proved guilty
Ignorance of the law excuses no man
Possession is nine tenths of the law
The law is an ass
The more laws, the more offenders
There's one law for the rich and another for
   the poor

You cannot make people honest by an act of parliament

learning and knowledge
A little knowledge is a dangerous thing
A little learning is a dangerous thing
Experience is the best teacher
It is easy to be wise after the event
Knowledge is power
Much learning makes men mad
to know all is to forgive all
We must learn from our mistakes
What you don't know can't hurt you
Where ignorance is bliss, 'tis folly to be wise

love
Absence makes the heart grow fonder
All's fair in love and war
All the world loves a lover
Better be an old man's darling than a young man's slave
Faint heart never won fair lady
It is best to be off with the old love before you are on with the new
Love begets love
Love comes in at the window and out at the door
Love conquers all
Love is blind
Love makes the world go round
Love sees no faults
Love will find a way
Lucky at cards, unlucky in love
Out of sight, out of mind
Pity is akin to love
The course of true love never did run smooth
The way to a man's heart is through his stomach
'Tis better to have loved and lost than never to have loved at all
Who would be loved, must love

marriage
Marriage is a lottery
Marriages are made in heaven
Marry in haste, repent at leisure
Marry in Lent and you'll live to repent
Marry your son when you will, your daughter when you can
Men are April when they woo, December when they wed
Wedlock is a padlock

miserliness
Don't spoil the ship for a hap'orth of tar
Grasp all, lose all
Greedy folks have long arms
Kill not the goose that lays the golden egg
The more you get, the more you want

opportunity
A bird in the hand is worth two in the bush
Gather ye rosebuds while ye may
Make hay while the sun shines
Nothing venture, nothing gain
Opportunity seldom knocks twice
Strike while the iron is hot
Take time by the forelock
There's no time like the present
The tide must be taken when it comes
Time and tide wait for no man

patience
An oak is not felled at one stroke
A watched pot never boils
Everything comes to him who waits
Patience is a virtue
Rome was not built in a day
They also serve who only stand and wait
We must learn to walk before we can run

power
A cat may look at a king
A house divided against itself cannot stand
All men cannot be masters
Attack is the best form of defence
Little is done where many command
Might is right
Money is power
No man can serve two masters
Power corrupts
The ballot is stronger than the bullet
The mightier they are, the harder they fall
The weakest go to the wall
United we stand, divided we fall
When Greek meets Greek then comes the tug of war
When two play one must lose
Why keep a dog and bark yourself?

regret
It is easy to be wise after the event
It is too late to shut the stable door after the horse has bolted
Past cure, past care

responsibility

There's no use in crying over spilt milk
Things past cannot be recalled
We never know the worth of the water till
the well runs dry
What's done cannot be undone
You cannot make omelettes without breaking eggs

responsibility

A bad workman blames his tools
As you make your bed, so you must lie on it
As you reap, so shall you sow
Every man is the architect of his own fortune
Paddle your own canoe
The absent party is always to blame

silence

A closed mouth catches no flies
Silence is golden
Speech is silver, silence is golden
Still waters run deep
There is a time to speak and a time to be silent
When in doubt say nothing

sleep

One hour's sleep before midnight is worth
two after
Sleep is better than medicine
Sleep is the brother of death
There will be sleeping enough in the grave

talking

Barking dogs seldom bite
Fine words butter no parsnips
The tongue is more venomous than a serpent's sting

time

History repeats itself
There is a time and place for everything
Time and tide wait for no man
Time cures all things
Time flies
Time is a great healer
Time is money
Time lost cannot be recalled

wealth and poverty

A fool and his money are soon parted
Born with a silver spoon in one's mouth
Enough is as good as a feast
God helps those who help themselves

Half a loaf is better than no bread
He that goes a-borrowing goes a-sorrowing
He who has nothing fears nothing
He who pays the piper may call the tune
It is better to be born lucky than rich
It is better to be poor and well than rich and ill
Lend your money and lose your friend
Money is a good servant but a bad master
Money is not everything
Money is power
Money makes money
Money talks
Neither a borrower nor a lender be
Penny wise and pound foolish
Poverty is no disgrace but it is a great inconvenience
Poverty is not a crime
Take care of the pennies and the pounds will
take care of themselves
The art is not in making money but in keeping it
Time is money
What you've never had, you never miss
When poverty comes in at the door, love flies
out of the window

weather

A cold April the barn will fill
After the storm comes a calm
A green Yule means a fat churchyard
April and May are the key to the year
April showers bring forth May flowers
Lightning never strikes twice
Rain before seven, fine before eleven
Red sky at night, shepherd's delight, red sky
in the morning, shepherd's morning
St Swithin's Day, if thou dost rain, for forty
days it will remain

work

A good beginning is half the work
A work done ill must be done twice
Business before pleasure
From small beginnings come great things
If a thing is worth doing it is worth doing well
Many hands make light work
No gain without pain
The devil finds work for idle hands to do
The labourer is worthy of his hire
The work praises the workman
Too many cooks spoil the broth
You cannot make bricks without straw

WORDFINDER

Wordfinder

This section aims to help the reader to locate words associated with particular subjects and themes. Each entry either has an equivalent one-word derivation or has a short definition to aid usage.

Although space here does not permit every term associated with each subject to be included, it is hoped that this section will be of especial use to help point the user to areas for further study.

The first lists give the common term first, arranged alphabetically and by theme and the technical term follows. The second section has the technical terms, arranged alphabetically by subject.

Nouns and adjectives

The words in bold below are nouns and the words opposite are the adjectives that are derived from them.

air	aerial (= in the air)	**god**	divine
ant	formic	**goose**	anserine
bear	ursine	**Greek**	Hellenic
bee	apian	**hand**	manual
bird	avian	**head**	cephalic
birth	natal	**heart**	cardiac
blood	haemal/haematic	**heat**	thermal
brain	cerebral	**horse**	equine
breast	mammary/pectoral	**island**	insular
brother	fraternal/brotherly	**judge**	judicial
cat	feline	**kidney**	renal
chest	pectoral/thoracic	**kitchen**	culinary
church	ecclesiastical	**king/queen**	royal/regal
city	urban/civic	**land**	terrestrial
cookery	culinary	**language**	linguistic
country	rural/rustic	**law**	legal
cow	bovine	**letter**	epistolary
day	diurnal	**lion**	leonine
death	fatal/lethal/mortal	**liver**	hepatic
deer	cervine	**lung**	pulmonary
dog	canine	**machine**	mechanical
drawing	graphic	**man**	male/masculine/virile
ear	aural	**marriage**	marital/matrimonial
earth	terrestrial	**money**	monetary
eye	optic/ocular/ophthalmic	**monkey**	simian
face	facial	**moon**	lunar
father	paternal/fatherly	**mother**	maternal/motherly
film	cinematic	**mouth**	oral
finger	digital	**night**	nocturnal
fish	piscine	**nose**	nasal
fox	vulpine	**number**	numerical
gas	gaseous	**parrot**	psittacine
goat	caprine/hircine	**pig**	porcine

pope   seals

pope	papal	teaching	pedagogic
punishment	penal/punitive	uncle	avuncular
rat	murine	voice	vocal
river	fluvial	war	martial
sea	marine/maritime	water	aquatic/aqueous
sheep	ovine	wine	vinous
ship	marine/maritime	wolf	lupine
star	astral/stellar	woman	female, feminine
sun	solar	womb	uterine
stomach	gastric		

Collective nouns

A collective noun is one which refers to a group of people, animals or things considered as a whole. A selection of these is given below.

acrobats	troupe	gulls	colony
actors	company	hare	husk/down
angels	host	hartebeest	herd
antelopes	herd	hawks	cast
apes	shrewdness	herring	shoal
artistes	troupe	horses	herd/stable/harras
asses	drove/pace	hounds	pack
baboons	troop	kangaroos	troop
badgers	cete/colony	kittens	kindle/litter
bears	sloth	lapwings	desert
bees	swarm/hive	larks	exaltation
bells	carillon	leopards	leap
birds	flock	lions	pride
bishops	bench	listeners	audience
boars	sounder	locusts	swarm
buffaloes	herd	magpies	tittering
caterpillars	army	moles	labour
churchgoers	congregation	monkeys	troop
cows	herd	moose	herd
crows	murder	mourners	cortege
dancers	troupe	mules	pack/barren
directors	board	musicians	orchestra
dogs	pack/kennel	nightingales	watch
ducks	paddling	owls	parliament/stare
eagles	convocation	partridges	covey
elephants	herd	peacocks	pride/muster
elks	gang	pigeons	flock/flight
falcons	cast	pigs	herd/sounder
ferrets	business	poems	anthology
fish	school/shoal	ponies	drove
flies	swarm	pups	litter
flowers	bouquet/bunch	rabbits	colony/bury/nest (young)
foxes	skulk	ravens	unkindness
geese	gaggle	rhinoceroses	crash
giraffes	herd	rooks	building
goats	flock/herd/tribe	sailors	crew
goldfinches	charm	seals	pod/colony

sheep			death, heaven and hell

sheep	flock	vipers	nest
ships	fleet	walruses	pod
singers	choir	whales	school/gam/pod
soldiers	battalion/regiment/army	whiting	pod
stars	constellation	wild geese	skein
thrushes	mutation	witches	coven
tigers	ambush	wolves	pack
turkeys	rafter	zebra	herd

Animal homes

ants	anthill	horses	stable/paddock
birds	aviary	insects	insectarium
bees	apiary/hive	lions	den
cats	cattery	moles	tunnel/burrow
cows	byre/cowshed/pasture	otters	holt/lodge
dogs	kennel	pigeons	pigeon loft
eagles	eyrie	pigs	sty/pen
doves	dovecote	rabbits	warren/burrow/hutch
fish	aquarium	rooks	rookery
foxes	earth/lair	squirrels	drey
hares	form	swans	swannery
hens	henhouse/coop	wolves	den/lair
heronry	heron		

Studies

ageing	gerontology
agriculture	geoponics
air in motion	aerodynamics
air, mechanical properties	pneumatics
algae	phycology
altitude, measuring	hypsometry
anaesthetics	anaesthesiology
muscles	kinesiology
ancient remains to study past societies	archaeology
ancient manuscripts	palaeography
animal behaviour	ethology
animals	zoology
bacteria	bacteriology
Bible interpretation	hermeneutics
birds	ornithology
birds' eggs	oology
blood vessels	angiology
books	bibliography
buildings, designing	architecture
bullfighting	tauromachy
carbon compounds	organic chemistry
carving shells, bone, etc	scrimshaw
caves	speleology
cell structure	cytology
chaos theory	chaology
chemistry of biological processes	biochemistry
children	paedology
China, culture, language, etc.	Sinology
Christian Church	ecclesiology
chromosomes	cytogenetics
Church services/orders	liturgics
classification of organisms	taxonomy
climate	climatology
climate, influence of	phenology
coats of arms	heraldry
coins, medals, etc	numismatics
colour	chromatics
combining tones into a composition with structure	music
computers	information technology
computers, shrinking of	nanotechnology
construction of buildings	tectonics
crime	criminology
crystals	crystallography
dating by rings in tree trunks	dendrochronology
death	thanatology
death, heaven and hell	eschatology

debate   **living organisms**

debate	polemics
demons, superstitions	demonology
dental science	odontology
dialects	dialectology
diet and nutrient intake	nutrition
diet and food intake	dietetics
disease	aetiology
dreams	oneirology
drugs	pharmacology
drug dispensing	pharmaceutics
Earth's crust, features	plate tectonics
Earth's crust, history and structure of	geology
Earth's geological structure, forces of	tectonics
Earth's magnetic field	geomagnetism
Earth's natural features, physical geography	physiography
Earth's physical nature	geography
Earth's surface	geomorphology
earthquakes	seismology
eating well	gastronomy
ecology	bionomics
Egypt, ancient	Egyptology
electrical charges at rest	electrostatics
embryos	embryology
endocrine glands	endocrinology
energy	energetics
environments	ecology
excrement	scatology
family descent	genealogy
ferns	pteridology
fingerprints	dactylography
firearms	ballistics
fireworks	pyrotechnics
fish	ichthyology
flight	aeronautics
flower arranging, Japanese	ikebana
flowers, fruits and vegetables, cultivating	horticulture
fluids in motion	hydrokinetics
fluids, mechanical properties of	hydrodynamics
flying aircraft	aviation
forces, the effects of in producing or changing motion	kinetics
forests	forestry
fossil animals	palaeozoology
fossil plants	palaeobotany
fossilisation	taphonomy
fossils	palaeontology
friction, lubrication	tribology

fruit growing	pomology
fungi or mushrooms	mycology
gas, measuring	gasometry
genetics/selective breeding	eugenics
geographical distribution of plants and animals	chorology
geologic timescale	geochronology
God, religious doctrine	theology
government systems	political science
government	politics
government, the art of	statecraft
grapes and grape-growing	viticulture
hair diseases	trichology
handwriting	graphology
Holy Spirit	pneumatology
home management	home economics
human and animal social behaviour	sociobiology
human behaviour	psychology
human beings	anthropology
human social organization and relationships	social science
humour	humorology
hygienic conditions	sanitation
icons	iconology
immunity to disease	immunology
inscriptions	epigraphy
intellect	noetimics
judging character from facial features	physiognomy
judging character from the shape of the skull	phrenology
knowledge, processes and grounds of	epistemology
lakes and ponds	limnology
land cultivation	agronomy
language	linguistics
language, social and cultural context of	sociolinguistics
language, history and structure	philology
larynx	laryngology
law, philosophy of	jurisprudence
laws of the mind	nomology
laws, drawing up of	nomography
life development	biogenesis
light on living organisms	photobiology
light	optics
liquids, mechanical properties	hydraulics
literature and the arts	humanities
living organisms and mechanical systems	cybernetics
living organisms	biology

living organisms, processes of   **serums**

living organisms, processes of	physiology
low temperatures	cryogenics
magnetism	magnetics
manoeuvring troops	tactics
map drawing	cartography
mapping surface features	topography
marine mammals	cetology
material things	natural science
matter and energy	physics
meaning derived from context	pragmatics
measurement	mensuration
measuring time	horology
mechanical systems that function like living organisms	bionics
medicine, substances used in	materia medica
mental disorders	psychopathology
mental powers	psychometrics
metals and alloys	metallography
metals and ores	metallurgy
microfossils (e.g. pollen)	palynology
microscopic single cell animals (protozoans)	protozoology
microscopic structure of animal and plant tissues	histology
military forces, organization	logistics
miracles	thaumatology
molluscs	malacology
moon, geology of	selenology
moon, mapping of	selenography
mosses	bryology
motion and the action of forces on bodies	mechanics
motion-picture photography	cinematography
motives in individuals	psychodynamics
music, for orchestra	orchestration
musical sounds	harmonics
mythical creatures	cryptozoology
navigating	navigation
number, quantities, forms, space, etc, and their relationships	mathematics
numbers, their supposed meanings	numerology
oceans	oceanography
origins and culture	ethnology
paper folding, Japanese	origami
papyri	papyrology
paranormal mental phenomena	parapsychology
parasites	parasitology
past events, analysis of	history
pharynx	pharyngology
photographs	photography
physical geography at periods in the past	palaeogeography
physical structure of plants and animals	anatomy
physical therapy	physiotherapy
physics applied to biology	biophysics
planetary positions	astrology
plant evolution	phytogenesis
plants	botany
plants, chemistry of	phytochemistry
plants, geography of	phytogeography
poetry, theory or study of	poetics
poetry, writing	poesy, poetry
points, lines, planes and solids	geometry
poisons	toxicology
populations	demography
prehistoric events	prehistory
print or prints	printmaking
printing from wood blocks	xylography
pronunciation and the representation of speech sounds	phonetics
pronunciation, correct	orthoepy
proper names	onomastics
properties of substances	chemistry
psalms or hymns, singing	psalmody
psychological and physiological processes	psychophysiology
public speaking	oratory
punishment and prevention of crime	penology
pure motion	kinematics
radio waves given out by bodies in space	radio astronomy
radioactive materials, purification of	radiochemistry
reading in words, numbers expressed by symbols	numeration
reasoning	logic
religious dogmas	dogmatics
reporting on current events	reportage
robots	robotics
rock strata	stratigraphy
rockets	rocketry
rocks, physical characteristics	lithology
rocks, structure	petrology
sea depths	bathymetry
selling	salesmanship
senility or ageing	nostology
sermons	homiletics
serums	serology

sexuality   feet, treatment of

sexuality	sexology
signs and symbols, use	pragmatics
signs and symbols in language	
	semiology, semiotics
skeletal system, joints, muscles, etc	
	orthopedics
skin and its diseases	dermatology
skulls	craniology
snakes and amphibians	herpetology
social relations, small groups	sociometry
society, social relationships	sociology
soils	pedology
space flight	astronautics
speaking and writing	rhetoric
speech sounds, sound systems of	
language	phonology
spelling	orthography
stamps	philately
stars and the universe	astronomy
stomach, diseases of the	
	gastrology, gastroenterology
stuffing the skins of animals	taxidermy
teaching	pedagogy
theatrical representation	histrionics
thought, reasoning, conduct and the	
nature of the universe	philosophy
three-dimensional art from	
wood, clay, stone, etc.	sculpture

trees and bushes, trimming into	
ornamental shapes	topiary
trees	dendrology
tumours	oncology
types of objects, etc, for	
classification purposes	typology
UFOs	ufology
universe, nature, origins, and	
development of the	cosmology
urogenital diseases	urology
verse form, metrical structure	metrics
verse forms	prosody
viruses	virology
volcanoes	volcanology
waste disposal	garbology
water, properties of	hydrology
weights and measures or	
units of measurement	metrology
winds	anemology
wines	enology
wood engravings	xylography
words, forms of and their	
arrangement in sentences	grammar
words, meanings	semantics
words, sources	etymology
workers' environments	ergonomics

Occupations

Area of work	Title
accepting goods in exchange for money	
	pawnbroker
ageing, effects of	gerontologist
ancient artefacts and remains	
	archaeologist
animals, medical treatment of	veterinarian
barrels	cooper
bell ringing	campanologist
bones, medical manipulation of	osteopath
brass	brazier
building design	architect
cancer, medical treatment	oncologist
caretaker of a building	janitor
caricatures	cartoonist
casino	croupier
cattle driving	drover
children, medical conditions of	
	paediatrician
church caretaker	sexton

clay receptacles	potter
coal miner	collier
computer systems	systems analyst
dental assistance	hygienist
dictionary compilation	lexicographer
drives the car of another	chauffeur
drug dispensing	pharmacist, chemist
earth, structure and composition	geologist
edits and corrects text	editor
essential oils	aromatherapist
eye diseases, medical treatment of	
	ophthalmologist
eye glasses, selling and fitting	
	optician (dispensing)
eyes, examining and prescription of	
corrective lenses	optician
	(ophthalmic), optometrist
fabrics and sewing material	draper
feet, beauty treatment of	pedicurist
feet, treatment of	chiropodist

female reproductive organs, medicine of **writing life stories**

female reproductive organs, medicine of	gynaecologist
finances of a school	bursar
fish	fishmonger
flying planes	pilot, aviator
flowers	florist
fortune telling from the stars	astrologer
fossils and bones	palaeotologist
fruit and vegetables	greengrocer
fruit	fruiterer
funerals	undertaker
fur clothing, sells or makes	furrier
furniture coverings	upholsterer
glass, doors and windows	glazier
graphical artwork	graphic designer
hair and scalp disorders	trichologist
hats	milliner
herbal remedies	herbalist
hired to fight for a foreign army	mercenary
homeopathy	homeopath
horse-riding in races	jockey
horses, fits shoes of	farrier
hospital attendant, male	orderly
human and animal behaviour	psychologist
human development	anthropologist
hypnosis to treat conditions	hypnotherapist
hypnosis to produce an artificial state of relaxation	hypnotist
iron working	blacksmith
language, historical development	philologist
languages	linguist
leather	tanner
libraries	librarian
livestock	stockbreeder
living organisms	biologist
machinery	mechanic
machines design, construction, or maintenance	engineer
magic tricks	conjuror, illusionisst, magician
maps	cartographer
massage	masseur, masseuse
medical diagnosis and treatment	doctor, physician
metal utensils, selling	ironmonger
metal working	smith
muscles, workings of	kinesiologist
nails and hands, beauty treatments	manicurist

needles, insertion of to stimulate energy points	acupuncturist
news, reports on, photographs or edits	journalist
novels, writes	novelist
numbers, quantities, shapes, angles, equations, etc	mathematician
payments in a shop	cashier, teller
physical therapies	physiotherapist
physician who does not specialize	general practitioner
physics, i.e. the properties of matter and energy	physicist
plants, cultivation	horticulturalist
plants, study of	botanist
play writing	playwright
poetry writing	poet
poultry	poulterer, poultryman
pressure points on the hands and feet	reflexologist
prison guarding	warder
races and cultures	ethnologist
selling on behalf of someone	broker
sewing items	haberdasher
ship's accounts, and attending to passengers	purser
shorthand typing	stenographer
skin, treatment of	dermatologist
space, stars and planets	astronomer
speaking many languages	polyglot
spine and joints	chiropractor
stamps	philatelist
stocks, buying and selling	stockbroker
stuffing dead animals	taxidermist
supervision of exams	invigilator
supportive role to another profession, e.g., nurses	auxiliary
surgical treatment	surgeon
teacher who travels from one school to another	peripatetic
teaching	pedagogue
technical drawing	draughtsman
teeth, treatment of	dentist
telephone switchboard	telephonist
textiles and cloth	mercer
water pipes, installation	plumber
wheels	wheelwright
wine	vintner
women before and after childbirth, medical treatment of	obstetrician
writing life stories	biographer

Phobias

abandonment	athagoraphobia	dogs	cynophobia
accidents	dystychiphobia	dolls	pediophobia
anger	angrophobia	dreams	oneirophobia
animals	zoophobia	drinking	dipsophobia
ants	myrmecophobia	dust	amathophobia
asymmetry	asymmetriphobia	eating	phagophobia
bathing	ablutophobia	eight	octophobia
beards	pogonophobia	enclosed spaces	claustrophobia
bees	apiphobia	eyes	ommetaphobia
being seen	ophthalmophobia	faeces	coprophobia
being stared at	scopophobia	failure	kakorrhaphiophobi
birds	ornithophobia	falling	basiphobia
black	melanophobia	falsehood	mythophobia
blood	haemophobia	feathers	pteronophobia
blushing	erythrophobia	fire	pyrophobia
books	bibliophobia	fish	ichthyophobia
bridges	gephyrophobia	flood	antlophobia
buried alive	taphophobia	flowers	anthophobia
butterflies, moths	mottephobia	flying	aerophobia
cancer	cancerophobia	forgetting	athazagoraphobia
car journeys or cars	amaxophobia	Friday 13th	paraskavedekatriaphobia
cats	ailurophobia	frogs	ranidaphobia
cemeteries	coimetophobia,	garlic	alliumphobia
	kosmikophobia	ghosts	phantasmophobia
ceremonies	teleophobia	glass	hyalophobia
chickens and poultry	alektorophobia	going out alone	isolophobia,
childbirth	lockiophobia		agoraphobia
children	pedophobia	hair	chaetophobia
chocolate	xocolatophobia	heat	thermophobia
choking	anginophobia	heights	illyngophobia
churches	ecclesiophobia	heights	acrophobia
clothing	vestiphobia	hell	hadephobia
clowns	coulrophobia	homosexuality	homophobia
cold	psychrophobia	horses	equinophobia
computers	cyberphobia	hospitals	nosocomephobia
constipation	coprastasophobia	ice and frost	pagophobia
cooking	mageirocophobia	illness	nosophobia
corpses/death	necrophobia	immobility of a joint	anleylophobia
crawling	entomophbia	imperfection	atelophobia
criticism	allodoxaphobia	injections	trypanophobia
crowds	demophobia, agoraphobia	insanity	dementophobia
dark	nyctphobia	insects	entomophobia
death	thanatophobia	isolation	isolophobia
defeat	kakorrhaphiophobia	kissing or being kissed	philemaphobia
deformity	dysmorphophobia	knees	genuphobia
dentists, dental treatment	dentophobia	knives or sharp objects	aichmophobia
depths	bathophobia	lakes	limnophobia
dining out, dinner parties	deipnophobia	laughter	geliophobia
dirt	mysophobia	lice	pediculophobia
doctors	iatrophobia	liquids	hygrophobia

loneliness or being alone   wrinkles

loneliness or being alone	autophobia	**red**	ereuthophobia
long words	sequipedalophobia	**responsibility**	hypegiaphobia
love – being in love	philophobia	**ridicule**	catagelophobia
maggots	scoleciphobia	**school**	didaskaleinophobia
marriage	gamophobia	**sea**	thalassophobia
meat	carnophobia	**sexual intercourse**	coitophobia
medicines	pharmacophobia	**sexual matters**	erotophobia
men	androphobia	**shadows**	sciaphobia
menstruation	menophobia	**sharks**	galeophobia
mice	musophobia	**shellfish**	ostraconophobia
mirrors and seeing oneself reflected		**sin – fear of committing a**	enissophobia
	catoptrophobia	**single – fear of being**	anuptaphobia
money	chrematophobia	**sleep**	somniphobia
monsters	teratophobia	**smothering**	pnigerophobia
mushrooms and fungi	mycophobia	**snakes**	ophidiophobia
music	melophobia	**snow**	chionophobia
narrow objects and places	anginophobia	**solitude**	autophobia
needles and pins	aichmophobia	**sourness**	acerophobia
newspapers	graphophobia	**spiders**	arachnophobia
noise	phonophobia	**stings**	cnidophobia
nosebleeds	epistaxiophobia	**storm**	ceraunophobia
nuclear weapons	nucleomituphobia	**stuttering**	psellismophobia
nudity	gymnophobia	**sunlight**	heliophobia
numbers in general	arithmophobia	**symmetry**	symmetrophobia
obesity	obesophobia	**technology**	technophobia
odours	olfactophobia	**teeth, dental treatment**	odontophobia
old age and growing old	gerascophobia	**telephones**	telephonophobia
old people	gerontophobia	**termites**	isopterophobia
open spaces	agoraphobia	**thirteen**	triskaidekaphobia
opposite sex	heterophobia	**thunder and lightning**	astraphobia
otters	lutraphobia	**tombs and tombstones**	placophobia
pain	algophobia	**touch (being touched)**	haptephobia
parasites	parasitophobia	**trees**	dendrophobia
penis	icthyphallophobia	**ugliness**	cacophobia
people or society	anthropophobia,	**undressing**	dishabiliophobia
	sociophobia	**untidiness**	ataxophobia
phobia	phobophobia	**urine and urination**	urophobia
plants	batonophobia	**vaccination**	vaccinophobia
pleasurable feelings	hedonophobia	**vegetables**	lachanophobia
pointed objects	aichmophobia	**voids**	kenophobia
poison	toxicophobia	**vomiting**	emetophobia
politicians	politicophobia	**walking**	ambulophobia
poverty	peniaphobia	**wasps**	spheksophobia
precipices	cremnophobia	**water**	hydrophobia
pregnancy (and childbirth)	tocophobia	**weight gain**	obesophobia
priests	hierophobia	**white**	leukophobia
public speaking	glossophobia	**wild animals**	agrizoophobia
rabies	cynophobia	**wine**	oenophobia
radiation	radiophobia	**women**	gynaecophobia/gynophobia
rain	ombrophobia	**work**	ergophobia
rape	virginitiphobia	**worms**	scoleciphobia
rats	zemmiphobia	**wrinkles**	rhytiphobia

States and emotions

affectation the state of taking on a way of dress or mannerism intended to impress.

affection fondness for someone.

agitation a feeling of excitable worry.

altruism selfless concern for the welfare of others.

amazement a feeling of extreme surprise.

anger a feeling of great annoyance.

apathy the absence of interest in something.

arrogance the act of behaving in an unpleasant way with an inflated sense of one's own importance.

astonishment a feeling of extreme surprise.

audacity a bold or cheeky way of engaging in something.

beauty the quality of being very pleasing to look at.

bombasticness the quality of using pompous language.

boredom a feeling of weariness resulting from very dull surroundings.

bravery the quality of being able to overcome fear in order to deal with difficulties.

brusqueness the quality of being curt or blunt in one's speech.

caution the state of showing great care.

charisma the quality of being influential in a charming way.

charm the quality of having a pleasing personality that is attractive to others

clumsiness the quality of lacking bodily co-ordination.

concern care or worry about something.

confusion the feeling of being mixed up or unsure about something.

consolation comfort in the face of difficulties.

contentedness the feeling of being happy with what one has.

courage the quality of being able to overcome fear in order to deal with difficulties.

cowardice the quality of being unable to overcome one's fear in the face of danger.

cynicism belief in the worst of people and situations.

dejection a feeling of disappointment and unhappiness.

delectation pleasure or enjoyment.

depression the feeling of being extremely unhappy and weary.

discontent the feeling of being unhappy with what one has.

discretion the quality of being able to treat situations with care so as to avoid embarrassments.

disgrace the state resulting from being shamed by something.

displeasure unhappiness over something.

disquiet a feeling of anxiousness or unease.

domination the quality of being controlling.

ecstasy a state of rapturous happiness.

effeminacy the quality of having feminine characteristics.

egotism a belief in one's own importance far above others.

empathy the feeling of having a common bond with someone.

enmity the quality of being unfriendly.

exasperation the state of being annoyed possibly by a repeated mistake or irritation.

excitement the state of having strong feelings aroused, either into agitation or into happiness

extravagance the act of being overly generous with something, usually money.

fanaticism excessive devotion to something.

fear the feeling of alarm that ensues when faced with danger.

garrulousness the quality of constantly talking in a wordy or frivolous way.

gratification the state of being pleased with something.

gratitude the feeling of being thankful for something.

gregariousness the quality of enjoying the company of others.

happiness joy or gladness.

hatred a strong emotional displeasure.

hope the feeling of wanting something to happen and also having some conviction that it might actually happen.

honesty the quality of being truthful.

humiliation the state of feeling ashamed after having been embarrassed.

humility to be conscious of one's inadequacies.

hypocrisy when one's actions are at odds with what one says.

hysteria the state of behaving in an unreasonably excited state to the point of frenzy.

impatience a lack of tolerance for things which take time.

incisiveness observant, intelligent and probably witty.

indifference the absence of interest in something.

indiscretion the quality of being unable to take care that one avoids causing the embarrassment of others

infatuation a passionate, but ultimately short, interest in something.

intolerance to give no respect to the wants of beliefs of others.

irritation a feeling of annoyance or anger.

joy deep, heartfelt happiness.

liveliness the state of appearing to be full of life.

loquaciousness the quality of being very talkative.

love deep affection for and feeling of connection with another person.

masochism the love of experiencing pain.

misanthropism hatred of mankind.

misery extreme, deeply felt unhappiness.

misogamy hatred of marriage.

misogyny hatred of women.

modesty the quality of being understated and unpretentious about one's talents.

optimism looking on the bright side.

paroxysmic to make an uncontrollable outburst.

passion intense enthusiasm, either erotic or generally.

patriotism love for one's country.

pedantry the quality of giving too much importance to correctness, or to showing off one's learning.

penitence the quality of being sorry for one's actions and seeking forgiveness for them.

pessimism looking on the dark side.

philanthropism service to the good of mankind.

pleasure the feeling of the enjoyment of something agreeable.

polyandry the state of being married to more than one husband at the same time.

polygamy the state of having more than one wife or husband at the same time.

polygyny the state of having more than one wife at the same time.

predilection the state of having a preference for something.

presumption the state of believing something to be true before you have any evidence of the fact.

pretension the quality of pretending to be, like, etc, something you are not.

pride a high sense of self worth.

profligacy the quality of being shamelessly debauched.

regret the state of feeling sorry that something has happened.

relief the great release of tension felt when the cause of worry or fear is removed.

repentance the act of being sorry for one's past actions.

repression the state of restraining certain emotions or beliefs.

sadism the love of causing pain to others.

satisfaction the feeling that one is happy and totally fulfilled with something.

sesquipedalianism the quality of using long and ponderous expressions.

sensitivity the quality of being easily hurt either emotionally or physically.

stoicism the quality of showing no interest in either pleasure or pain.

submission the quality of allowing others to take charge to the detriment of oneself.

sybaritism a love of indulgence and luxury.

sycophancy the quality of being overly flattering to win favour.

sympathy to feel pity for what someone is suffering.

tolerance the quality of showing consideration for the beliefs of others.

ugliness the quality of being unpleasant to look at.

unease the feeling that all is not well.

vanity the quality of being overly concerned with one's appearance.

vulgarity the quality of lacking taste and manners.

wariness the feeling of feeling cautious about something.

wit the quality of having intelligence and humour.

worry the feeling of anxiety and fear associated with danger or stress.

Specialist Subjects

Art

abstract art art which intentionally avoids recognizable, lifelike representation of the observed world.

abstract expressionism art that is based on freedom of expression, spontaneity and random composition, characterized by loose, unrestrained brushwork and often indistinct forms.

acanthus a plant motif widely used in Greek and Roman ornament and later in **baroque** design.

acrylic paint a versatile synthetic paint that is quick-drying and can be used in thick, heavy layers or thin washes on almost all surfaces.

action painting a form of **abstract expressionism** in which the paint is applied to the canvas in the course of a series of movements (dancing, cycling or rolling about on canvas) by the artist.

Aesthetic Movement an informal group of British artists who wished to break away from the rigidity of Victorian design.

aesthetics an area of philosophy that is concerned with the ideals of taste and beauty and which provides criteria for the critical study of the arts.

altarpiece a decorated wall, screen or sectional painting set behind the altar of a Christian church, a feature of church décor dating from the 11th century.

alto rilievo *see* **relief**.

amaretto *or* **amorino** (*plural* **amaretti** *or* **amorini**) a small, plump naked boy used in painting and sculpting to represent Cupid or children.

American Designers' Gallery founded in 1928 in New York, this was one of the first attempts to accord design its rightful status as a creative art.

American Society of Interior Designers American professional association founded in 1975.

applied arts art that serves a useful purpose or that adds decoration to functional objects. The term can include architecture, interior design, ceramics, furniture design, graphics, etc. It is usually contrasted with the term fine arts which includes painting, drawing, sculpture, print-making, etc.

appliqué a style of art characterized by the application of materials over other materials to form a design.

aquarelle a French term for watercolour painting, where a water-based paint is applied to dampened paper in thin glazes which are gradually built up into areas of varying tone.

Arabesque an elegant flourish used in design, deriving from Moresque patterns of the 16th century.

Art Deco the decorative art of the 1920s and 1930s in Europe and north America, originally called **Jazz Modern.** It was classical in style with slender, symmetrical, geometric or rectilinear forms, a simple style.

Art Nouveau a style of decorative art popular between 1890 and World War I in Europe and North America. Its main effects were seen in the applied arts, graphics, furniture and fabric design and architecture. Its design is characterized by flowing organic forms and asymmetric linear structures.

Arts and Crafts Movement a movement of the late 19th century which reacted against factory-produced goods.

ascription *same* as **attribution**.

assemblage a style of art characterized by the putting together of various objects, such as pieces of painted wood, old shoes, etc, to form a meaningful or decorative integrated whole.

attribution the assigning of an unsigned picture to an artist on the basis of similarity of style or subject.

autograph a term used to describe a painting by one artist only who has not been assisted by pupils or assistants.

Baroque a highly ornamental, flamboyant style of European art and architecture which lasted from the mid-16th century until the early 18th century.

bas relief *see* **relief**.

basso rilievo *see* **relief**.

Bauhaus a German school of applied arts and architecture founded by the architect Walter Gropius at Weimar in 1919. One of its aims was to narrow the gap between fine art and the applied arts, while the other was to focus on architecture as the environment of art.

Biedermeyer term first coined in 1890s to refer to the simple design style of the 1820s and 1830s in a derogatory way.

bistre *or* **bister** a warm brown pigment prepared from the soot of wood, especially from beech wood.

body paint *see* **gouache**.

brushwork the distinctive way in which an artist applies paint, being equivalent to the individual nature of handwriting.

burin an instrument for engraving on copper, steel, etc. Made of tempered steel, it is prismatic in shape with one end attached to a short wooden handle and the other ground off obliquely so as to produce a sharp triangular point.

caricature a drawing of a person in which his or her most prominent features are exaggerated or distorted in order to produce a recognizable but ridiculous portrait.

cartoon 1 a drawing, or series of drawings, intended to convey humour, satire or wit. **2** a full-size drawing for a painting, mural or fresco. The drawing was fully worked on paper and then mapped out onto the surface to be painted.

cartridge paper a thick sort of paper originally manufactured for soldiers' cartridges, but now extensively used in art, its rough surface being exceptionally suitable for drawing on.

casting the art of working metals by pouring them while in a fluid condition into moulds in which they solidify and harden into the form of the mould which they fill.

cave paintings *see* **Lascaux**.

chalk a soft stone, similar to a very soft limestone, used for drawing. **Crayon** is powdered chalk mixed with oil or wax.

charcoal the carbon residue from wood which has been partially burned and will make easily erasable black marks. Used mainly to make preliminary drawings.

classicism a style of art based on order, serenity and emotional restraint, with reference to the classical art of the ancient Greeks and Romans. It followed strict ideals of beauty and figures drawn in this style were usually symmetrical and lacked the normal irregularities of nature.

collage a piece of art created by adhering pieces of paper, fabric, wood, etc. on to a flat surface.

colour an effect caused in the eye by light of various wavelengths, the colour seen depending on the specific wavelengths of light reflected by an object. Most objects contain pigments which absorb certain light frequencies and reflect others. A white surface is one in which all light frequencies are reflected, while a black surface absorbs all frequencies. Colours used by artists are made by combining pigments of vegetable or mineral extraction with a suitable medium, e.g. linseed oil.

colourist a term used in art criticism to refer to an artist who places more importance and emphasis on colour than on line and form.

composition the arrangement of elements in a drawing, painting or sculpture in proper proportion to each other and to the painting as a whole.

concrete art a term used to describe severely geometrical **abstract art**.

constructivism a movement in **abstract expressionism** concerned with forms and movement in sculpture and aesthetics of the industrial age. Works in this style, which were deliberately non-representational, made use of plastics, glass and wood.

crayon *see* **chalk**.

Cubism an art movement started by Pablo Picasso and Georges Braque. This style moved towards a more intellectual representation of objects. The result was a series of multi-viewpoint images, often broken up into geometric shapes.

Dada an art movement that began in Zurich in 1915 and whose name was chosen at random. Its aim was to reject accepted aesthetic and cultural values and to promote an irrational form of non-art or anti-art.

De Stijl Dutch art and design movement founded in 1917, which was strongly influenced by Cubism.

decoupage a style of art consisting of cutout paper figures or designs covering a surface

diptych a pair of paintings or carvings on two panels hinged together so that they can be opened or closed.

distemper a non-permanent paint made by mixing colours with eggs or glue instead of oil.

eclecticism the act of borrowing from other styles to create a new art style.

emboss to mould or carve in relief

encaustic painting a method of painting **murals,** practised in ancient times, using a medium composed principally of wax dissolved by heat.

engraving a technique of cutting an image into a metal or wood plate using special tools. The term is also used for a print produced in this way.

etching a technique of making an engraving in a metal plate using acid to bite out the image, rather than tools. The term is also used for a print produced in this way.

figurative art *or* **representational art** art that recognizably represents figures, objects or animals from real life, as opposed to **abstract art**.

fine arts *see* **applied arts**

foxing spotting and staining on paintings done on paper caused by mould.

fresco the art of painting on fresh plaster, from the Italian word for 'fresh'. The term can also refer to a mural painted in this way.

functionalism an architectural theory developed from the idiom that form should reflect function. It evolved into a style in the 1920s, and formed the basis for Modernism.

genre painting a painting that has for its subject a scene from everyday life, as opposed to a historical event, a mythological scene, etc.

gesso a white, absorbent prepared ground of plaster to be painted on using oil paint or tempera.

Glasgow School a group of architect designers, including Charles Rennie Mackintosh, Frances and Margaret MacDonald and George MacNair who developed a version of art nouveau.

Gothic the predominant architectural style of Western Europe from the mid-12th century to the early 16th century.

gouache an opaque mixture of watercolour paint and white paint, also called **poster paint** or **body paint**.

graphic art a linear visual art, such as drawing, painting, engraving, etching, etc.

graver *same as* **burin**.

grisaille a monochrome painting made using only shades of grey, often used as a sketch for oil paintings.

grotesque a style of ornamental painting or sculpture characterized by a motif of flowers or leaves, often with strange or imaginary animals or human figures.

ground the first layer of colour in a painting on which the other colours are worked, the primary or predominating colour.

High-Tech architectural and design style developed in the 1970s and '80s in which conventional furnishings were replaced by industrial artefacts and floors were left uncovered.

history painting a genre of painting that has as its subject a scene from history, a scene from mythology or a scene from great works of literature.

icon *or* **ikon** a religious image, often that of a saint, painted on a wooden panel. The word comes from the Greek word *eikon* meaning likeness.

impasto an Italian word used to describe the thickness and textures that can be achieved with acrylic or oil paint.

Impressionism an art movement originating in France in the 1860s, the main artists concerned being Cezanne, Degas, Manet, Monet, Morisot, Camille Pissaro, Renoir and Sisley. They were concerned with representing day-to-day existence in a realistic way, recording the fleeting effects of light and movement. Their usual subjects were landscapes or social scenes.

Indian ink a black ink, originally from China and Japan, consisting of finely divided carbon suspended in a solution of gum, glue or varnish.

intaglio the cutting into a stone or other material or the etching or engraving on a metal plate of an image, the opposite of **relief.** Intaglio printing techniques include engraving and etching.

Jazz Modern *see* **Art Deco**.

kinetic art an art form in which light or balance are used to create a work that moves or appears to move. More complicated kinetic art objects are made to move by electric motors.

Lascaux the site in the Dordogne district of France of some outstanding Palaeolithic cave paintings, painted in a bold, direct style, and rock engravings. Dating from around 15,000 BC, they depict local animals on a large scale.

lithography the art of drawing with special pigments on a flat stone or metal plate, parts of which have been made receptive to ink, and of producing impressions from it on paper.

maesta the Italian word for 'majesty' used in art to refer to a depiction of the Virgin and Child on a throne surrounded by angels and saints.

mahlstick *or* **maulstick** a stick used by painters to steady and support the hand while working

Mannerism an exaggerated, artificial art style found in Italy between around 1520 and 1600, representing a reaction against the balanced forms and perspectives of Renaissance art and characterized by elongated figures, harsh colours and unusual perspectives.

medium a material used in art, e.g. oil in painting, pencil in drawing, or bronze in sculpture. The term is also used to refer to a method, e.g. painting as opposed to sculpture.

mezzo rilievo *see* **relief.**

mezzotint a method of engraving on copper or steel in imitation of drawing in Indian ink, the light areas being scraped and burnished out of a prepared dark ground.

miniature a painting, usually a portrait, of very small dimensions, generally executed in watercolours on vellum and later on porcelain.

modernism a reaction against the florid excesses of art nouveau, it sought to strip away unnecessary ornament and decoration in architecture and design.

monochrome a drawing or painting executed in one colour only.

montage a technique similar to collage, where the images are photographic.

mosaic small cubes of variously coloured marbles, glass or other substances set together so as to produce a geometrical or artistic design.

motif a repeated theme, subject or figure, e.g. in a design.

mural a picture or design painted directly onto a wall, a practice that began in very early times.

Naïve Art the name given to a style of untrained artists noted for its simplicity. Often there is little attention to formal perspective and an intuitive use of space, composition and colour.

nature morte the French term for still life, which translates literally as 'dead nature'.

Neo-Classicism a movement in art and architecture in the late 18th and early 19th centuries which was essentially a reaction against, Baroque and Rococo. Classical forms and principles of order were used.

Neo-Impressionism a development of Impressionism resulting in a system of dots of pure colour applied according to scientific principles to create an image of great purity and luminosity.

niello a method of decorating metal plates by cutting lines in the metal and filling them up with a black or coloured composition, a technique used by goldsmiths.

nocturne a painting showing some of the characteristic features of night life.

Novembergruppe an informal association of radical artists which was founded in Berlin in 1918 and promoted new expressive forms of communication.

objet d'art a small, valuable artistic article.

oil paint a paint made by mixing colour pigment with oil (generally linseed oil) to produce a slow-drying malleable sticky substance.

op art *or* **optical art** an **abstract art** that uses precise, hard-edged patterns in strong colours and makes the images appear to move.

pastel a paint medium of powdered colour mixed with gum Arabic to form a hard stick.

pastiche 1 an artistic work that contains elements borrowed from other sources. **2** an artistic work in imitation of another's style.

patina the fine green rust or verdigris with which ancient bronze statues, etc. became covered as a result of exposure.

pencil a mixture of graphite and clay in the form of a stick and covered with a hard casing.

pentimento a part of a painting that has been painted over by the artist but later reappears.

perspective in art, the representation of a three-dimensional view in a two-dimensional space.

pieta the Italian word for 'pity', used in art to refer to a painting or sculpture of the body of the dead Christ being supported by the Virgin.

plaster cast in art, a sculptor's model in plaster of Paris.

plaster of Paris a composition of several kinds of gypsum and water made into a quick-setting paste.

pointillism in painting, the practice of applying small strokes or dots of colour to a surface so that from a distance they blend together.

polyptych a painting, usually an **altarpiece,** consisting of two or more paintings within a decorative frame.

pop art a realistic art style that uses techniques and subject from commercial art, comic strips, posters, etc.

portraiture the art of painting, drawing or sculpting the likeness of someone, either the face, the figure to the waist or the whole person.

poster paint *see* **gouache**.

Post-Impressionism a blanket term used to describe the works of artists in the late 19th century who rejected **Impressionism**.

potto *same as* **amoretto**.

Pre-Raphaellite Brotherhood a movement founded in 1848 by Holman Hunt, John Millais and Dante Gabriel Rossetti, who wanted to recreate the innocence of Italian painting before Raphael. They drew their imagery from medieval legends and literature.

primary colours the colours red, blue and yellow which, in painting, cannot be produced by mixing other colours. Colours which can be produced in this way are known as secondary colours.

priming an undercoat or size used to prepare a surface for painting.

primitive 1 belonging to the pre-Renaissance period in art. **2** characteristic of often deliberately unsophisticated modern works of art or of artists working in that genre.

provenance the date, origin and subsequent history of a work of art.

red chalk *see* **sanguine**.

relief a sculptural form that is not freestanding. The three-dimensional shape is either carved or built up. Relief sculpture can be *low relief (basso rilievo* or *bas-relief)*, where the depth of the pattern is less than half; *medium relief (mezzo-rilievo)*, where the depth of the pattern is roughly half; or *high relief (alto rilievo)*, where practically all the medium has been removed.

Renaissance meaning literally 'rebirth', a term referring to developments in art, philosophy and culture during the 14th, 15th and 16th centuries. The movement reached a peak between 1500 and 1520 with the works of Leonardo da Vinci and Michelangelo.

replica a copy of a painting or a piece of sculpture made by the person who executed the original.

representational art *same as* **figurative art**.

reredos a relatively small altarpiece that can stand on the floor itself or on a pedestal behind it.

retable a fairly large and complex altarpiece that rises from floor level.

rilievo the Italian term for relief.

Rococo a style in art, established around the beginning of the 18th century, following on from Baroque and even more exaggerated in terms of embellishments and flourishes.

Romanticism an art movement dating from the late 18th until the mid-19th century. A reaction to the order and restraint of classicism and identified with the attitudes of Romantic writers such as Wordsworth, Byron, Goethe and Rousseau. Romantic painters tended to imbue landscapes with powerful emotions.

sanguine a reddish-brown chalk that includes ferric oxide, used in drawing.

school in art, a group of artists who hold similar principles and work in a similar style.

screen painting *same as* **silk-screen painting**.

sculpture the art of carving, cutting or hewing stone, wood or other materials, or of forming or modelling clay or wax, to create images in three-dimensional form or in relief.

scumble a thin coating of semi-opaque colour applied to a painting or drawing to soften the lines and colours and create a hazy effect.

secondary colours *see* **primary colours**.

sepia a brown pigment used in drawing, originally prepared from a black juice secreted by certain glands of the cuttlefish.

sfumato the gradual blending of one area of colour into another without a sharp outline, as shown in the works of Leonardo da Vinci.

sgraffito a technique for creating a design by cutting lines into pottery, plaster or

stucco to reveal a different layer of colour below.

Shaker an austere style of furniture design, produced by the Shaker sect on the east coast of America.

silk-screen painting a method of printing similar to stencilling, in which a fine mesh of silk is covered with an impermeable coating for areas where colour is not to be allowed through and without a coating where colour is to show.

size a kind of weak glue used by painters to mix with colours.

sketch a preliminary drawing made by an artist to establish points of composition, scale, etc.

still life a drawing or painting which depicts inanimate objects, such as a bowl of fruit or a vase of flowers.

stippling the technique of painting, drawing or engraving using dots rather than lines.

Surrealism a style of painting and drawing characterized by a dreamy or fantastic quality. The surrealist movement began in France in the 1920s and 1930s and was inspired by the dream theories of Sigmund Freud and by the literature and poetry of Rimbaud and Baudelaire.

tempera a paint medium made by mixing colour pigments with egg, much used until the development of oil paint.

terracotta a mixture of fine clay and fine-grained white sand with crushed pottery, first slowly air-dried and then baked in a kiln to the hardness of stone; much used in statues, figures, etc.

tondo a circular painting or sculpture, from the Italian word for 'round'.

torso the trunk of a statue deprived of head and limbs.

triptych a painting, usually an **altarpiece**, consisting of three hinged parts, the outer two folding over the middle section.

underpainting a preliminary layer of colour in a painting showing the design and areas of light and shade.

vanitas still life a **still life** containing objects which are symbolic of the transience of life, e.g. skulls, hour-glasses, etc.

vehicle in art, a medium in which paints, gums, varnishes, etc. are dissolved and prepared for use.

wall painting *same as* **mural**.

watercolour a paint medium of colour pigments mixed with water-soluble gum Arabic. When moistened with water, a watercolour paint produces a transparent colour that is applied to paper.

woodcut the art of engraving on wood or of producing, by means of special cutting tools, a design or picture in relief on the surface of a block of wood from which impressions can be taken by means of ink or pigment.

Biology

acellular without any cells; not made up of cells.

adaptation the change that occurs in an organism in response to its environment.

agamic produced without sexual action, asexual.

alga (*pl* **algae**) any of a group of chiefly aquatic lower plants without root, stem or leaves, classified according to colour.

amino acid any of the 20 standard organic compounds from which all the protein components of the body are built up.

amoeba (*pl* **amoebae, amoebas**) a microscopic invertebrate found in fresh water, damp soil and the digestive tracts of animals that consists of a gelatinous mass which constantly alters its state.

anaerobe, anaerobium (*pl* **anaerobes, anaerobia**) a microbe that can live without air.

androgen one of a group of hormones that is responsible for the development of the sex organs and also the secondary sexual characteristics in the male.

androgenous having only male offspring.

androgynous combining both sexes or bearing both male and female organs; hermaphroditical.

anoestrus the period of sexual inactivity in mammals between periods of oestrus.

antibody (*pl* **antibodies**) a protein produced by an organism in response to the action of a foreign body, such as the toxin of a parasite, that neutralizes its effects.

bacteria (*sing* **bacterium**) single-celled organisms that underpin all life-sustaining processes, identified by shape.

biology the study of living organisms.

biosynthesis (*pl* **biosyntheses**) the formation of chemical compounds by living organisms.

carnivore any animal that eats the flesh of other animals.

carpel a simple pistil, or one of the parts of a compound pistil or ovary of a flower.

cell a microscopic unit of living matter.

cellular made up of cells.

chorion the exterior membrane of a seed or foetus.

chromosome any of the microscopic rodshaped bodies bearing genes.

coagulate to change from a liquid to partially solid state, to clot.

colony (*pl* **colonies**) a collection of organisms in close association.

cytogenesis, cytogeny cell formation in plants and animals.

cytoplasm the substance of a cell as opposed to its nucleus.

daughter a cell produced by the division of another.

decomposition the breakdown of a substance from a more complicated form into a simpler one.

dehydration the loss of water from the body through diuresis, sweating, etc.

deoxyribonucleic acid *see* DNA.

differentiation specialization.

DNA *abbr* = deoxyribonucleic acid, the main component of chromosomes that stores genetic information.

embryo (*pl* **embryos**) an animal during the period of its growth from a fertilized egg up to the third month; a human product of conception up to about the second month of growth; a thing in a rudimentary state.

endocrine glands glands that secrete hormones directly into the bloodstream (e.g. pituitary, pineal, thyroid, parathyroid adrenal, testicles, ovaries and pancreas), also called ductless glands.

endoplasm the inner layer of protoplasm.

endosmosis osmosis inwards through the porous membrane of a cell, etc, by a surrounding liquid.

enzyme any protein molecule that acts as a natural catalyst and is found in the bodies of all bacteria, plants and animals.

erectile able to become enlarged and rigid through sexual stimulation.

erythrocyte a red blood cell.

eukaryote any member of a class of living organisms (except viruses) that has in each of its cells a nucleus within a membrane.

excrete to eliminate or discharge wastes from the body.

exocrine gland a gland that discharges its secretions through a duct (e.g. salivary glands and sweat glands).

exocrine secreting though a duct; of or relating to exocrine glands or their secretions.

Fallopian tube either of the two tubes through which the egg cells pass from the ovary to the uterus.

fertilization the fusion of sperm and ovum to form a zygote, which then undergoes cell division to become an embryo.

fission a split or cleavage; the reproductive division of biological cells.

flagellum (*pl* **flagella, flagellums**) a whiplike appendage.

foetus *n* (*pl* **foetuses**) the unborn young of an animal, especially in its later stages; in humans, the offspring in the womb after the eighth week of development until birth.

fruit the seed-bearing part of any plant.

gamete a reproductive cell that unites with another to form the cell that develops into a new individual.

gene any of the complex chemical units in the chromosomes by which hereditary characteristics are transmitted.

genome the total genetic information stored in the chromosomes of an organism.

genus (*pl* **genera**) a taxonomic division of plants and animals below a family and above a species; a class of objects divided into several subordinate species.

gestation period the period from conception to birth in mammals.

granulocyte any of the phagocytic (amoeboid) leucocytes (white blood cells).

habitat the normal environment of an animal or plant, specified by particular features, e.g. rivers, ponds, sea shore.

haemocyte a blood cell, especially a red blood cell

haemoglobin a protein consisting of haem and globin that gives red blood cells their colour and is important in the transportation of oxygen to the body's tissues.

herbivore a plant-eating animal.

heterogenous originating outside of the body; foreign.

heterologous abnormal in type or structure; derived from a different species; consisting of the same elements in varying proportions.

heteromorphism deviation from the natural form or structure.

homologous having evolved from a common ancestor, regardless of present-day function.

immotile not motile.

immune system the natural defence system in the body of a vertebrate animal that helps to protect it against diseases caused by micro-organisms and parasites.

immunoglobulin a protein, called an antibody, that is produced by special cells in the blood called B-cells.

in vitro occurring outside the living body and in an artificial environment.

in vivo occurring inside the living body.

incept to ingest.

insulin a hormone that controls absorption of sugar by the body, secreted by islets of tissue in the pancreas.

integument a natural covering as skin, a rind, a husk, etc.

intussusception the expansion of a cell.

isomorphism similarity in form.

karyotype the number, shapes and sizes of the chromosomes within the cells of an organism.

keratin a fibrous sulphur-rich protein consisting of coiled polypeptide chains, which occur in hair, hooves, horn and feathers.

kinesis the response of an organism to a particular stimulus in which the response is proportional to the intensity of the stimulation.

leucocyte a white blood cell.

lipase any enzyme capable of breaking down fat to form fatty acids and glycerol.

lipoprotein any protein that has a fatty acid as a side chain.

loculus, locule *n* (*pl* **loculi, locules**) a small cavity or cell.

lymphocyte a type of white blood cell. There are T-lymphocytes (T-cells) which coordinate the immune system's attack and B-lymphocytes (B-cells) which produce proteins called antibodies which attach themselves to pathogens and destroy them.

macrocyte a red blood cell (erythrocyte) that is abnormally large.

macrophage a large scavenger cell (phagocyte), numbers of which are found in various tissues and organs of the body including the liver, spleen, bone marrow, lymph nodes, and connective tissue. It forms part of the immune system of vertebrates.

mamma *n* (*pl* **mammae**) the milk-secreting organ of female mammals, such as the udder of a cow, or breast of a woman.

mammal any member of a class of warm-blooded vertebrates that suckle their young with milk.

mammary gland the gland in female mammals that produces milk.

mammilla (*pl* **mamillae**) a nipple.

mandible the lower jaw of a vertebrate; the mouth parts of an insect; either jaw of a beaked animal.

marsupial of an order of mammals that carry their young in a pouch.

mast cell a large, blood-borne cell that has a fast-acting role in the body's immune system in fighting inflammation.

maturation the progressive generation of cells already present in the ovary and testis, mitosis.

meiosis (*pl* **meioses**) the process of cell division where a nucleus splits into four, each new nucleus having half the number of chromosomes that the original one had.

membrane a thin, pliable, composite, layer of lipoprotein surrounding an individual cell, or of fibrous tissue surrounding an organ, lining a cavity or tube or separating tissues and organs within the body.

meninges (*sing* **meninx**) the three membranes covering and protecting the brain and the spinal cord.

mesoblast the middle germinal layer of an ovum, the basis of muscles, bones, blood, etc.

metabolism all the chemical and physical processes which occur in living organisms and that maintain life and growth.

metaphase a stage of cell division in mitosis or meiosis.

metaplasm that part of the contents of a cell consisting of inert matter.

microbiology the biology of bacteria and other microorganisms and their effects.

microcyte an unusually small red blood corpuscle, often present in disease.

microorganism an organism visible only through a microscope.

microphyte a microscopic vegetable growth, especially a parasitic one.

migration the seasonal movement of animals, especially birds, fish and some mammals (e.g. porpoises).

milk a white nutritious liquid secreted by female mammals for feeding their young.

milt the sperm of a male fish; its reproductive glands when filled with this; the spleen of some animals. To fertilize (the roe of female fish), especially artificially.

mimesis mimicry.

mitochondrion (*pl* **mitochondria**) a tiny rod-like structure, numbers of which are present in the cytoplasm of every cell.

mitosis (*pl* **mitoses**) the type of cell division undergone by most body cells by means of which the growth and repair of tissues can take place. *Compare* **meiosis**.

modification a change in an organism caused by environmental factors but not passed on.

mollusc an invertebrate animal usually enclosed in a shell, as oysters, etc.

monad a single-celled organism.

monocyte the largest type of white blood cell (leucocyte) that is capable of motion and ingests foreign bodies such as bacteria and tissue particles.

monotreme one of a primitive order of Australian egg-laying mammals, with a single vent for digestive, urinary and genital organs.

morphosis (*pl* **morphoses**) a development in an organism or its parts marked by structural change.

morula (*pl* **morulas, morulae**) the spherical mass of cells produced by the splitting of the ovum in its primary stage.

motile the ability to move without outside aid.

motor nerve a nerve, containing motor neuron fibres, that carries electrical impulses outwards from the central nervous system to a muscle or gland to bring about a response there.

motor neuron one of the units or fibres of a motor nerve. An upper motor neuron is contained within the central nervous system, a lower motor neuron has its cell body in the spinal cord or brain stem.

mutation a sudden change in some inheritable characteristic of a species due to a change that takes place in the DNA (the genetic material) of the chromosomes of a cell, caused by faulty replication of the cell's genetic material at cell division.

myelin sheath a fatty substance that surrounds axons in the central nervous system of vertebrates and functions as an insulating layer.

myelocyte a cell that is an immature type of granulocyte responsible for the production of white blood cells.

neurotransmitter a chemical by which nerve cells communicate with each other or with muscles.

neuter having no sex organs; a neuter person, word, plant or animal.

nitrogen cycle the regular circulation of nitrogen due to the activity of organisms.

nucleic acid a linear molecule composed of four nucleotides that occurs in two forms: DNA (deoxyribonucleic acid) and RNA (ribonucleic acid).

nucleus (*pl* **nuclei, nucleuses**) the central part or core around which something may develop, or be grouped or concentrated; the part of an animal or plant cell containing genetic material.

oestrogen one of a group of steroid hormones secreted mainly by the ovaries and, to a lesser extent, by the adrenal cortex and placenta. The testicles also produce small amounts.

oestrus, oestrum the period of ovulation of mammals, when they are said to be on heat.

omnivore any organism that eats both plant and animal tissue.

ontogeny the complete development of an individual to maturity.

oocyte a cell in the ovary that undergoes meiosis to produce an ovum, the female reproductive cell.

oogenesis the formation of an ovum.

oosperm a fertilized ovum.

ooze a deep sea mud made up of clays and the calcareous or siliceous remains of certain organisms, e.g., diatoms.

organ a part of an animal or plant consisting of two or more types of tissue that performs a vital or natural function, such as the liver, kidney, heart and brain.

organelle any structure that is bound by a membrane to separate it from the other cell constituents and which has a particular function within the cell, e.g. a mitochondrion.

organism any living creature, including micro-organisms, plants, and animals; any living thing; an organized body.

osmosis (*pl* **osmoses**) the process in which solvent molecules move through a semi-permeable membrane to the more concentrated solution.

ovary (*pl* **ovaries**) one of the two female reproductive organs producing eggs (ova) and hormones (mainly oestrogen and progesterone).

oviduct the tube which conducts the ovum from the ovary to the uterus.

oviferous egg-carrying.

oviform egg-shaped.

ovine pertaining to sheep.

oviparous producing young by eggs.

ovisac the cavity in the ovary which contains the ovum.

ovoviviparous producing eggs containing the young in a living state, as certain animals; relating to the development of offspring within the body of the female where there is no development of a placenta.

ovulation the release of an egg from an ovary which then moves down the Fallopian tube to the uterus.

ovule the germ borne by the placenta of a plant which develops into a seed after fertilization.

ovum (*pl* **ova**) *n* the mature, unfertilized female egg cell, which is roughly spherical with an outer membrane and a single nucleus.

penis (*pl* **penises, penes**) the male copulative and urinary organ in mammals.

perspiration exuding sweat created by the exocrine glands.

phagocyte an amoeboid cell that engulfs invading particles.

phenotype the detectable characteristics of an organism, i.e. its appearance which is determined by the interaction between its genotype and the environment in which the organism develops.

pheromone a molecule that functions as a chemical communication signal between individuals of the same species.

photosynthesis the process by which a green plant manufactures sugar from carbon dioxide and water in the presence of light.

phototaxis the movement or reaction of an organism in response to light.

phototropism a growth movement shown by parts of plants in response to the effect of light.

plasmodium (*pl* **plasmodia**) a mass of protoplasm formed by the union of single-cell organisms.

plumule a down feather; the embryonic stem of a plant.

porphyrin a naturally occurring pigment, such as chlorophyll.

prepotency a dominant hereditary influence.

progesterone a steroid hormone that is vital in pregnancy. It is produced by the corpus luteum of the ovary when the lining of the uterus is prepared for the implanting of an egg cell.

prokaryote, procaryote any organism that lacks a true-membrane nucleus and is either a bacterium or a blue-green alga.

prophase the first stage of meiosis or mitosis in cells of eukaryotes.

protein a complex organic compound containing nitrogen that is an essential constituent of food.

protoplasm a semi-fluid viscous colloid, the essential living matter of all plant and animal cells.

radicle the part of a seed that develops into a root; a root-like subdivision of a nerve or vein.

regeneration the repair or regrowth of the bodily parts of an organism that have been damaged and have been subsequently lost.

regression the tendency to an average state from an extreme one.

replication the duplication of genetic material, generally before cell division.

reproduction the production of new individuals of the same species either by asexual or sexual means.

respiration the process by which living cells of an organism release energy by breaking down complex organic compounds into simpler ones using enzymes.

revert to return to a former or primitive type.

ribonucleic acid (RNA) a complex nucleic acid, present mainly in the cytoplasm of cells but also in the nucleus, essential to protein development.

ribosome any of the tiny particles containing RNA and protein in cells where protein synthesis takes place; the structure within the cell that is the site of protein synthesis in all eukaryotic and prokaryotic cells.

RNA *see* **ribonucleic acid**.

sac a bag-like part or cavity in a plant or animal.

scrotum (*pl* **scrota** *or* **scrotums**) the pouch of skin containing the testicles.

seed the small, hard part (ovule) of a plant from which a new plant grows; the source of anything; sperm or semen; to produce or shed seed.

selection the process by which certain animals or plants survive while others are eliminated, natural selection.

seminiferous producing or containing semen; (*plants*) bearing seeds.

seta (*pl* **setae**) a bristle or similar appendage of an animal or plant.

sexual reproduction the production of progeny that have initially arisen from the fusion of male and female gametes in a process called fertilization.

skeleton the bony framework of the body of a human, an animal, or a plant.

species (*pl* **species**) a class of plants or animals with the same main characteristics, enabling interbreeding.

sperm semen; the male reproductive cell.

sporangium (*pl* **sporangia**) (*in fungi, etc*) an organ or part in which asexual spores are produced.

spore an asexual reproductive body produced by algae, fungi and ferns, capable of giving rise to new individuals.

sporogenesis the formation of spores in plants and animals.

squama (*pl* **squamae**) (something resembling) a scale.

sting a sharp, pointed organ of a bee, wasp, etc, or hair on a plant, used for injecting poison.

strain a plant or animal within a species having a common characteristic.

symbiosis a mutually advantageous partnership between two interdependent plant or animal species.

taxonomy the classification of living things into groups based on similarities of biological origin, design, function, etc.

T-cell a type of white blood cell that forms in the bone marrow and moves to the thymus gland, situated in the thorax.—*also* **T-lymphocyte**.

telophase the last and fourth stage of meiosis or mitosis in eukaryotic cells.

testicle, testis (*pl* **testes**) one of the pair of male sex organs that are situated within the scrotum. They produce sperm and secrete the hormone testosterone.

testosterone a steroid hormone secreted by the testes that promotes the development of male characteristics. *See also* **androgen**.

thrombin an enzyme that contributes to blood clotting.

tissue a mass of organic cells of a similar structure and function; one of the primary layers composing any of the parts of the body, consisting of a large number of cells with a similar structure and function, e.g. connective tissue; a group of cells with a similar function that aggregate to form an organ.

umbilicus (*pl* **umbilici**) the navel; a navel-shaped depression on a plant or animal.

uncinate having a hook-shaped part.

ungulate (an animal) having hooves.

uniparous producing a single egg or a single offspring at birth.

unisexual of one sex only; having male or female sex organs but not both.

uterus (*pl* **uteri**) the female organ in which offspring are developed until birth, the womb.

vagina ((*pl* **vaginas, vaginae**) in female mammals and humans, the canal connecting the uterus and the external sex organs.

vascular of, consisting of, or containing vessels as part of a structure of animal and vegetable organisms for conveying blood, sap, etc.

velum (*pl* **vela**) the soft palate; a membranous covering or organ, such as the membranous covering of certain molluscs or that covering a developing mushroom.

ventricle a small cavity; one of the lower chambers of the heart, which pumps blood; one of the four cavities of the brain.

vesicle a bladder-like vessel or cavity, especially one filled with serous fluid; a small sac found in some seaweeds and aquatic plants.

villus (*pl* **villi**) the velvety fibre of the mucous membrane of the intestine; the soft hair covering a fruit or flower.

vulva (*pl* **vulvae, vulvas**) the external female genitalia, comprising two pairs of fleshy folds (labia) surrounding the opening of the vagina.

womb the female organ in which offspring are developed until birth, the uterus.

X-chromosome one of the pair (with the Y-chromosome) of sex chromosomes that occur in females.

Y-chromosome one of the pair (with the X-chromosome) of sex chromosomes that occur in males.

zooid resembling but not completely being an animal or plant. A zooid organism; an animal organism produced by fission; (*corals, etc*) a member of a compound organism.

zygospore a spore formed from the fusion of gametes.

zygote the cell formed by the union of an ovum and a sperm; the developing organism from such a cell.

Botany

abscission the shedding of parts.

acarpous not producing fruit; sterile or barren.

acaulescent stemless or with a very short stem.

accrescent increasing; growing.

accrete grown into one.

acrocarpous having (like the mosses) the fruit at the end of the primary axis.

acrospire the sprout of a seed.

aculeate having aculei or sharp prickles.

anemophilus fertilized by pollen carried by the wind, wind-pollinated.

angiosperm a plant having its seeds protected by a covering.

anther the part of a flower's stamen containing pollen.—antheral *adj.*

apheliotropic turning from the sun.

aphyllous without leaves.

apocarpous having the carpels of the ovary separate or distinct.

arista (*pl* aristae) the awn or beard of grasses; a bristle.

axil the angle formed by the upper side of an organ or branch with the stem or trunk to which it is attached.

axillary pertaining to, springing from, or situated in, the axil.

axis the main central part of a plant, usually consisting of the stem and root.

botanical, botanic pertaining to plants and botany.

botany (*pl* botanies) the study of plants.

brachiate having branches in pairs, each pair at right angles to the next.

bract a modified leaf growing from a flower stem or enveloping a head of flowers.

bulb the underground bud of plants such as the onion and daffodil.

bulbil a small bulb formed at the side of an old one; a small solid or scaly bud, which detaches itself from the stem, becoming an independent plant.

calyx (*pl* calyxes, calyces) the outer series of leaves that form the cup from which the petals of a flower spring.

capreolate furnished with tendrils.

capsule a seed case.

carpel a simple pistil, or one of the parts of a compound pistil or ovary of a flower.

chlorophyl, chlorophyll the green photosynthetic colouring matter in plants.

chloroplast an organelle found within the cells of green plants and algae, where photosynthesis takes place.

cleistogamy self-fertilization without opening of the flower.

colloid a viscid inorganic transparent substance.

coma the silky hairs at the end of a seed.

comate hairy.

composite having many flowers in the guise of one, as the daisy.

cone the scaly fruit of the pine, fir, etc.

coniferous bearing fruit cones.

corolla the inner envelope of a flower composed of two or more petals.

cotyledon a seed lobe or rudimentary leaf or leaves of an embryo; kinds of plant, chiefly evergreens.

cupule a cup-shaped part, as of the acorn.

deciduous shedding all leaves annually, at the end of the growing season.

decumbent resting on the ground, trailing.

dioecious, diecious having male and female organs respectively in separate individuals.

emersed rising out of water.

endosperm

endosperm the albumen of a seed.

epiphyte a plant which grows on another plant but is not fed by it.

evergreen having foliage that remains green all year.

excurrent (*leaf*) having a midrib running beyond the edge.

extine the outer coat of the pollen grain.

fascicle a cluster of leaves, roots, etc.

filament the anther-bearing stalk of a stamen.

foliage leaves.

foliose having many leaves.

footstalk the supporting stem of a plant or flower.

frondescence the act of producing leaves; foliage.

fructiferous (*plant etc*) bearing fruit.

fruit the seed-bearing part of any plant.

fugacious (*petals, etc*) falling off very early.

gamogenesis sexual reproduction.

geotropism a tendency in the roots of certain plants to turn in the direction of the earth.

gynoecium the female organs of a flower.

heterogamous bearing two kinds of flowers that differ sexually.

hypogeal *or* **hypogean** *or* **hypogeous** underground.

indeciduous not deciduous; evergreen.

indusium (*pl* **indusia**) the covering of the growing spores in many ferns.

jugate having leaflets in pairs.

leguminous belonging to a family of flowering and pod-bearing plants.

leucoplast a colourless object that contains reserves of starch and is found in some plant cells.

marcescent withering without falling off.

medulla (*pl* **medullas, medullae**) the pith of plants.

megaspore the protective covering containing the embryo in flowering plants (*also* **macrospore**).

mesocarp the middle layer of the seed vessel of a fruit.

mesophyll the internal tissues of a leaf that are between the upper and lower epidermal layers and contain chlorophyll.

mesophyte a plant requiring an average water supply.

monandrous having one stamen only.

monospermous, monospermal one-seeded.

motile exhibiting movement.

nervate ribbed.

nervation the arrangement of veins, venation.

node the joint of a stem and leaf or leaves.

nodule a small swelling or structure on a plant, especially the root, which is due to nitrogen-fixing bacteria.

nutation the turning of flowers towards the sun.

nyctitropism the so-called sleep of plants, turning in a certain direction at night.

ovule the germ borne by the placenta of a plant which develops into a seed after fertilization.

palaeobotany the study of fossil plants.

pappus (*pl* **pappi**) the feathery substance on the seeds of some plants, e.g., dandelion, thistle.

parenchyma the soft cellular tissue or pith of plants.

paroicous, paroecious with the two sexes developing in close proximity.

parthenocarpy the formation of fruit without seeds having been formed or fertilized.

perennial a plant lasting more than two years.

petiolate growing on a petiole.

petiole a leaf stalk.

phanerogam a flowering plant.

phloem the tissue which carries food around a plant.

photosynthesis the process by which a green plant manufactures sugar from carbon dioxide and water in the presence of light.

phyllode a flattened petiole with the functions of a leaf.

phyllotaxy, phyllotaxis the arrangement of leaves on a stem.

phyton the smallest unit of a plant capable of growing into a new plant.

pistil the seed-bearing part of a flower.

pistillate having a pistil; with a pistil but no stamens.

plumule the embryonic stem of a plant.

pollen the yellow dust, containing male spores, that is formed in the anthers of flowers.

pollinate to fertilize by uniting pollen with seed.

polygamy the condition of having staminate, pistillate, and hermaphrodite flowers on one plant.

protoplasm a semi-fluid viscous colloid, the essential living matter of all plant and animal cells.

pseudocarp a fruit formed from parts other than the ovary.

pulvinate, pulvinated having a cushionlike pad or swelling.

pyxis (*pl* **pyxides**) a seed capsule with a lid that falls off to release the seeds.

quinate with five leaflets on a petiole.

raceme an arrangement of flowers directly on a main stem, as in the lily of the valley.

radicle the part of a seed that develops into a root; a root-like subdivision of a nerve or vein.

rhizome a stem on or below ground that produces roots below and shoots above; a rootstock.

sap the vital juice of plants; energy and health.

saprophyte a plant or fungus that grows on dead organic matter.

sclerenchyma a tissue forming the hard fibrous parts of plants.

scutellum (*pl* **scutella**) any of the small horny scales or plates on a plant.

seed the small, hard part (ovule) of a plant from which a new plant grows.

sepal any of the individual parts of the calyx of a flower.

sericeous covered in fine hairs.

set a rooted cutting of a plant ready for transplanting.

shrub a woody plant smaller than a tree with several stems rising from the same root.

spermatophyte a plant that produces seeds.

spinose spiny.

sporangium (*pl* **sporangia**) an organ or part in which asexual spores are produced.

spore an asexual reproductive body produced by algae, fungi and ferns.

stalk the stem of a plant.

stamen (*pl* **stamens** *or* **stamina**) the pollen-bearing part of a flower.

stele (*pl* **stelae** *or* **steles**) the vascular tissue in the stems and roots of plants.

stem a plant stalk.

stigma the part of a flower that receives pollen.

stipe a short stalk or stem of a plant, especially of a mushroom.

stoma (*pl* **stomata**) a minute aperture in the epidermis of a plant for the passage of gases.

stroma (*pl* **stromata**) any tissue that functions as a framework in plant cells.

strophism the twisting of a stalk as it grows in response to a stimulus from a particular direction, e.g., light.

succulent having fleshy tissue.

systemic (*insecticide, etc*) designed to be taken up into the plant tissues.

tap root a main root that grows vertically downwards and has small lateral roots.

tendril a thread-like shoot of a climbing plant by which it attaches itself for support.

thermotropism the growth of a plant in the direction of a heat source.

thorn a sharp point or prickle on the stem of a plant or the branch of a tree.

transpiration the loss of water vapour from pores in the leaves of plants.

tree a tall, woody, perennial plant having a single trunk, branches, and leaves.

tropism growth of a plant organ in a particular direction due to an external stimulus, e.g. touch, light.

tuber the swollen, fleshy root of a plant where reserves of food are stored up, as a potato.

uniparous producing one axis.

vegetable a herbaceous plant grown for food; of, relating to or derived from plants.

vegetative propagation a type of reproduction in which the non-sexual organs of the plant are capable of producing progeny.

vein a branching rib in a leaf.

velamen a thick, moisture-absorbing aerial root, consisting of dead cells, found on some plants.

velum a membranous covering or organ, such as that covering a developing mushroom.

venter the swollen base of that part of some plants containing the egg cell.

ventral of, pertaining to, or located on that part of a plant facing towards the stem, especially a leaf.

ventricle a small cavity.

vernation the arrangement of leaves within a bud.

vesicle a small sac found in some seaweeds and aquatic plants.

vespertine, vespertinal opening in the evening.

villous, villose covered with long, thin, soft hairs.

villus (*pl* **villi**) the soft hair covering a fruit or flower.

xanthophyll an orange or yellow pigment in autumn leaves.

Business

above-the-line those entries that appear above a horizontal line in a profit and loss account, which divides the entries that establish the profit or loss from the entries that indicate the distribution of profit.

accounts the financial statements of a company prepared from a system of recorded financial transactions. They consist at least of a profit and loss account and the balance sheet of the company.

accrual an expense that is outstanding at the end of an accounting period and requires to be included in the accounts for the period.

actuals commodities that can be bought and used rather than goods that are traded on the basis of a futures contract.

actuary a trained statistician.

agent a person appointed by someone, called the principal, to act on his or her behalf in some capacity.

amalgamation the combination of two or more companies.

arbitration a procedure for settling an industrial dispute in which a third party is called in to settle the dispute.

arrears a debt that has not been settled by the due date.

asset an article or property that is owned by a company or individual and has a monetary value.

audit an independent examination of a company's financial statements by a qualified auditor.

auditor a professional accountant who is trained to conduct an independent assessment of the accuracy and fairness of a company's financial statements, called an audit.

bankruptcy the state of individuals who are unable to pay their debts.

base rate the interest rate used as a basis by banks when setting the interest rates that they charge their customers.

bear market a situation on the stock exchange or currency market in which there is persistent selling and limited buying, thereby causing prices to fall.

below-the-line referring to entries that occur below the horizontal line in a company's profit and loss account.

black economy a form of economic activity that is undisclosed, unrecorded and thus not liable for taxation.

black knight an individual or company that makes an unwelcome or hostile takeover bid for a company. *See* **white knight**.

black market an illegal market for a commodity or service, either because these are rationed by government, as in wartime, or forbidden, as with drugs.

blue-chip company a company with considerable assets and a well-established reputation.

blue-collar worker a manual worker, so called because of the blue overalls worn by manual workers in factories, etc. *See* **white-collar worker**.

board of directors a group of directors responsible for running a company.

bond a financial security that is issued by a borrower to a lender.

book-keeping the keeping of the account books of a company. *See* **accounts**.

bottom line a term used in accounting to denote the net profit from a business after all costs have been paid.

brown goods goods such as television sets,

hi-fi equipment, etc, so called because they are often brown in colour.

budget a financial statement containing a company's plans and policies for a specified accounting period.

bull market a situation on the stock exchange or currency market in which there is persistent buying and limited selling, thereby causing prices to rise.

capital the funds that are invested in a business; the total value of the assets that a person holds minus any liabilities; plant or machinery that is used by a company in the production of goods or services.

capitalism an economic and political system in which individuals are free to dispose of their capital without major interference from the government.

cartel an association of suppliers formed to regulate prices and sales conditions of the goods or services that they provide.

cash legal tender in the form of coins and banknotes.

cheque a preprinted form on which instructions are given to an account holder or a bank to pay a stated sum to a named recipient.

collateral an asset, such as a life-assurance policy, shares or the title deeds to a house, that a borrower is required to pledge as security against a loan.

commission a payment that is made to an intermediary, such and a salesperson, the commission usually being calculated as a percentage of the value of the goods or services sold.

commodity a raw material, such as grain, coffee, tea, wool, etc, that is traded in; any economic good.

conglomerate a group of related companies, often active in diverse and unrelated fields, usually controlled by a holding company.

consignment an arrangement between an exporter and an importer by which the exporter receives payment for goods only when they have been transported and sold by the importer.

consortium a combination of two or more large companies formed for a specific and limited purpose, such as the submitting of a quotation for an exceptionally large project.

consumer a person who purchases and uses goods and services to satisfy his or her needs.

contract an agreement between two or more parties that is legally enforceable.

cost expenditure on the purchasing of goods or services; expenditure of a company's resources, usually money, involved in producing and selling its products or in achieving its goals.

crash a rapid and serious fall of prices on the stock market; a breakdown of a computer system.

credit the sum of money that a trader will allow a customer to owe him or her before payment is asked for.

creditor a person or company to whom another person or company owes money, for example in respect of goods or services supplied.

currency the money of a particular country; any kind of money that is in general use as cash, being passed from person to person as coins and banknotes.

dealer[1] a trader of any kind; a person who deals for himself or herself as a principal on the Stock Exchange rather than as an agent or broker.

dealer[2] *or* **broker** a member of the Stock Exchange.

debit an entry on the left-hand or debtor side of a double-entry company accounts.

debtor a company or individual that owes money to another.

deed a document that has been signed, sealed and delivered.

default failure to carry out the terms of a contract.

deflation a fall in the level of the general prices in an economy, the opposite of inflation.

depreciation the reduction in value of an asset during the course of its operative life; the reduction in value of the currency of one country against another.

depression a severe form of recession.

devaluation a reduction in the exchange rate of one currency against another.

direct debit an order given to a bank by an account-holder to pay regular amounts from his or her account to an organization or individual.

discount a reduction in the list price of goods; the amount by which the market price of a financial security is below its par value; a deduction from a bill of exchange when it is purchased before its maturity date.

distribution the process of storing products and delivering them to customers; the division of property and assets according to a legal procedure.

e-commerce financial and business transactions that take place over the worldwide web.

econometrics the employment of statistical techniques in the analysis of economic data.

embargo a ban on trade with a country or group of countries or on particular products.

emoluments the total amount of financial benefit from an employment or office, including salary, fee or wage, expenses and perquisites.

ergonomics the study of the relation of workers to their working environment with a view to maximizing efficiency and providing safe, comfortable working conditions.

estate the total of a person's assets minus his or her liabilities as valued on death.

executor a person who is named in a will to carry out the task of gathering in any assets relating to the estate of the deceased, discharging any liabilities and distributing any remaining assets to the beneficiaries named in the will.

expense a sum spent for goods or services in a company that is normally set against profit in the profit and loss account; money spent by an employee in the course of his or her work for a company and subject to refund by the company.

exports goods or services that are sold to buyers in foreign countries.

fiscal year the government's accounting year, which is used for assessing personal income tax.

fixed asset or **capital asset** an asset, such as buildings, land, plant and machinery, that is used long-term in the trade or business of a company rather than for resale.

flotation the process by which a new company is launched as a public limited company for the first time and offers shares for sale to the public.

franchise a license granted to a manufacturer, distributor, trader, etc, that allows him or her to manufacture or sell a product or service in a particular area for a specified period of time.

free trade the export and import of goods and services from one country to another without the imposition of restrictions such as tariffs or quotas.

fraud the acquiring of a financial advantage by means of deliberate deception or false representation.

futures contract or **futures** an agreement to buy or sell a specified quantity of a fixed security, currency or commodity at a specified price at a specified date in the future.

futures market or **forward market** a market that deals in futures contracts.

gainsharing a system of paying workers by which a proportion of pay is linked to gains in the level of productivity or to a reduction in the level of costs.

globalization or **internationalization** the investment in financial markets on an international basis.

grey knight in a situation involving a company takeover bid, a potential bidder whose intentions are undeclared and thus unknown. *See* **white knight**.

grey market legal trading in goods of which there is a scarcity at a particular time; a market in shares that have not been issued, although they are due to be issued within a short time.

gross domestic product (often abbreviated to **GDP**) the total monetary value of the goods and services produced by an economy over a specified period.

gross income income earned by a person or organization that is subject to tax but from which tax has not yet been deducted.

gross national product (often abbreviated to **GNP**) the total monetary value of all the goods and services produced in an economy over a specified period (gross domestic product) plus the net income received from abroad in the form of interest, profits, rents and dividends.

import duty a tax that is levied by a government on imported products.

imports goods or services that are purchased from another country.

imprest a system used in the control of petty cash expenditure in which an opening balance is made available at the beginning of an accounting period. At the end of the accounting period vouchers are collected in respect of any money spent and the balance restored to the original amount.

income money received in recompense for work done, as a return on investment, by way of rent received when renting out property, etc.

income tax a form of direct taxation that is imposed by the government on income, such as wages, interest, rents, etc.

index-linked the term used to describe economic variables such as wages, social security benefits, etc, when these are related to a price index in some predetermined way.

industrial action organized action that is undertaken by employees in order to bring pressure to bear on employers to get them to agree to their demands.

industry the branch of commercial enterprise that is concerned with the manufacture of goods, as in heavy industry, or concerned with the creation of related goods or services, as in the soft drinks industry.

inflation an increase in the general level of prices in an economy with a resultant fall in the purchasing power of money.

insider dealing the dealing in financial securities by someone who has access to information that is not yet generally available and would affect the price of the securities, the aim being to exploit this knowledge to make a profit or avoid a loss.

insolvency the inability to meet one's debts when these become due.

insurance a system that provides a person or company with protection against financial loss that may result from damage to or theft of property, loss of property or against death or injury in return for the payment of an insurance premium.

interest the charge that is made for borrowing money in the form of a loan.

invoice a document that shows the amount that is due to the issuer of the invoice for goods or services supplied, itemizes the products and individual prices and is issued as a request for payment.

job an identifiable piece of work or unit of service carried out by a company.

job description a detailed statement of the tasks and responsibilities that an employee is expected by the employer to carry out as part of his or her employment.

junk bond a high-interest, high-risk bond issued as a means of financing a takeover bid.

ledger a collection of company accounting records of a similar type, such as the purchase, or creditors', ledger or the sales, or debtors', ledger.

lessee a person or company that is granted a lease.

lessor a person or company that grants a lease.

liability a claim in respect of money borrowed on the resources of an individual or company.

licence a document giving official permission to do something.

lien the right of an individual to retain possession of the goods of another, who is in debt to him or her, until the debt has been settled.

limited company a company in which the liability of its members with reference to the debts of the company is limited.

limited liability an arrangement that limits the maximum loss that a shareholder sustains in the event of the company in which he or she holds shares being wound up.

liquidation the process that brings about the dissolution of a company.

margin the difference between the selling price and the cost price of goods or services.

market the trading or selling opportunities from a particular sector.

marketing the process relating to the various steps involved in identifying and satisfying customers' needs.

mediation the intervention in an industrial dispute of a neutral third party who acts as a go-between to the parties in the dispute with the object of getting the parties to reach a compromise solution.

merchandizing the in-store promotion by a retailer of selected products.

merchant bank a bank that originally specialized in the provision of finance for merchants, often being involved in foreign trade.

merger the combination of two or more firms into a single business on a basis that is given mutual agreement by the management of the relevant firms and is given the approval of the relevant shareholders.

monopoly a market structure in which there is only one supplier or producer.

monopsony a market in which there is only a single buyer.

mortgage the advance of a loan to a person or firm, called the mortgagor or borrower, by another person or organization, usually a financial institution such as a bank, called the mortgagee or lender, the loan being used to acquire an asset, usually a piece of property.

national debt the money that is owed by a government to domestic and overseas lenders.

nationalization the process of bringing the assets of a company under the control of the state instead of private ownership.

net profit the profit that a company makes after all running costs and expenses have been taken into account; the final profit that a company makes after all relevant taxes have been deducted from net profit above.

net receipts the total amount of money received by a company or in a business transaction after the deduction of costs, raw materials, relevant taxation, etc.

net the term used to refer to an amount that remains after certain deductions have been made.

oligopoly a kind of market structure in which relatively few sellers supply the needs of a large number of buyers.

open-market operations the buying or selling of government bonds and treasury bills as a means of controlling the money supply.

overdraught a form of credit facility that allows the holder of a bank checking account to let the account go into debit up to an agreed limit, interest being charged on the daily debit balance.

overhead *or* **overhead cost** a cost that is not directly related to the materials or labour directly concerned with a product.

pension a payment received by people who have retired from employment or who have reached a certain age.

portfolio a collection of financial securities that is held by an investor; a list of the loans made by an organization; a collection of products that are marketed by a firm.

premium[1] the payment made to an insurance company by a person or firm taking out insurance protection. *See* **insurance**.

premium[2] an amount that is in excess of the nominal value of a share, bond or other financial security.

president the usual American term for the person who in the UK would be called managing director.

privatization the transference of a publicly owned company or industry from the state to the private sector.

product a name applied to both goods and services that are purchased by consumers; an item that is manufactured by a company.

production the process that transforms materials, labour and capital into goods and services.

productivity a measure of the output of a company per unit of input, often measured in terms of output per man hour.

profit the difference that occurs when a company's sales revenue is greater than its total costs in providing the relevant goods or services.

promissory note a document that contains a promise to pay a certain sum of money to a specified named person or to the bearer and must be delivered to the payee or bearer.

prospectus a document that sets out details about a new issue of shares and invites the public to subscribe for the shares.

public limited company (usually abbreviated to **plc** or **PLC**) a company that is registered as a public company and that may offer shares and securities to the public.

purchase ledger the ledger in which are recorded the personal accounts of a company's suppliers.

quality control the process of ascertaining that the quality of a product or service meets specified performance criteria that will ensure a high standard of the product or service.

raider an individual or organization that makes a habit of initiating hostile takeover bids.

rally a rise in stock market prices after a fall.

rationalization the reorganization of an organization or industry with the intention of increasing efficiency and profitability.

receivership a situation in which a company defaults on a debt or debts and a **receiver** is appointed to realize the company's assets in order to pay off any creditors.

recession a fall or marked slowing-down in the rate of growth of the gross domestic product.

redundancy the termination of a person's employment when his or her employment ceases to be required by the employer, whether because of rationalization, downsizing, etc.

registered office the official address of a company in the United Kingdom to which all official correspondence must be sent.

remuneration money paid in the form of wages, salary or fees for work done or services rendered.

repossession the process of taking back something that is being paid for by instal-

ments or by a mortgage system when the contracted regular payments have not been met.

retailer an individual or company that stocks a particular type of product or a range of products for sale to consumers, as opposed to a wholesaler.

risk capital any business capital that is invested in a project when there is a significant element of risk of loss in the event of the project failing.

royalties payments paid for the right to make use of property belonging to someone else for one's own gain.

running costs the costs that are incurred in the operation of a company or fixed asset, such as expenditure on power in a factory.

salary payment, usually paid monthly and usually expressed as an annual amount, made by employers to employees in return for work done.

security an asset or group of assets to which a lender of money has recourse if the borrower of the money defaults on the agreed loan repayments; a financial asset such as a share, bond or stock.

seed capital a small amount of capital that is needed to pay for any research and development that has to be carried out before the setting up of a new business.

sequestration the confiscation of the property of a person or organization because of failure to comply with a court order.

service an economic activity that is carried out to meet a personal or business demand. Unlike the provision of goods, the provision of services does not result in the transfer of ownership of any tangible object.

service industry the section of industry that is concerned with the provision of a service rather than goods.

settlement[1] the payment of an outstanding debt or loan.

settlement[2] the conclusion of an industrial dispute or civil litigation as a result of a voluntary agreement between the parties involved.

share a financial security that is issued by a company as a means of raising long-term capital, and conferring on the holder a legal right to part of the profits of a company.

share capital the part of the capital of a company that derives from the issue of shares.

shop steward an employee of a company who represents the interests of his or her colleagues in negotiations with management.

single market an association of countries trading without restrictions, especially the countries of the European Union.

sleeping partner a person who has capital in a business partnership and shares in the profits but who does not take any part in the business activity of the partnership.

sponsor the issuing house that handles a new issue of shares for a company.

stakeholder a person who has an interest in the operation and performance of a company.

standing order an instruction to a bank by a customer to pay from his or her account a regular fixed sum of money on a specified date into the account of a person or company.

stock in the UK, a fixed-interest security that is issued in fixed units by a company, local authority or the government and that is traded on the stock market ; any collection of assets.

stockbroker an agent who acts as a market intermediary and buys and sells securities on a stock exchange on behalf of clients in return for remuneration in the form of commission.

strike a form of industrial action in which there is an organized refusal to work on the part of a workforce or on the part of some of the members of the workforce in order to force the employers to agree to the workers' demands.

subrogation the right of an insurer to take over any other methods that the insured person may have recourse to for acquiring compensation for the same occurrence, after the insured person has received any compensation due by the insurer.

subscriber a person who is a signatory of a memorandum of association of a new company, who pays for a specified quantity of shares and who is involved in appointing the first directors of the company.

subsidy a payment paid by a government or organization to enable a certain business activity to take place or to take place more effectively or cheaply.

superannuation an occupational pension scheme in which contributions to the scheme are deducted from an employee's pay and passed by the employer to the trustees of a pension fund or to an insurance company.

surety a sum of money held as a guarantee of something.

takeover bid an attempt by a company or individual to take over a company by making an offer to shareholders to buy their shares at a specified price in order to gain a majority of the shares and so take control of the company.

tax return a form on which a taxpayer makes an annual statement of income and related circumstances so that the appropriate tax liability can be assessed.

tender[1] an invitation from a prospective buyer of goods or services to prospective suppliers so that the latter may submit competing bids.

tender[2] a method of selling shares by offering them to members of the general public who are invited to make a bid for shares, subject to a minimum bid price.

trade price the price that is paid to a wholesaler or manufacturer by a retailer for goods that will then be sold on for a higher price, taking account of the retailer's costs.

trade union the UK name for labour union.

trust fund a fund that consists of the assets belonging to a trust.

turnover the total sales figure recorded by a company for a specified period.

underwriting the acceptance by a financial organization of the financial risks involved in an enterprise on receipt of an agreed fee.

unit cost the cost of a unit of production or sales in the expenditure of a company, arrived at by dividing the total production cost by the number of units involved.

unit price the price paid per unit of product or article purchased or the price charged per unit of article or product sold.

unit trust a form of trust established in the UK to administrate a portfolio of securities on the stock exchange in which small investors can purchase units.

value-added tax (often abbreviated to **VAT**) an indirect tax levied by the UK government on value added to goods or services.

white goods consumer goods, such as washing machines, which were so named because they were originally finished in white enamel paint.

white knight in a situation involving a takeover bid, a person or company that makes a bid that is more welcome than a previous bid that was seen as unacceptable or unwelcome in some way.

white-collar worker a worker who is not a manual worker but works in the clerical, administrative or personnel departments of a company or works in one of the professions.

zero-based budgeting a system of budgeting that involves the preparation of a budget from a zero base, i.e. starting from the initial assumption that there is no commitment to spend on any activity and that every item of expenditure on every activity has to be justified.

Z-score a statistic that has been devised to try to summarize the susceptibility of a business to failure.

Chemistry

acid a substance that releases hydrogen ions during a chemical reaction, one that with certain other substances forms salts.

alcohol an organic compound with an oxygen/hydrogen group (hydroxyl) attached to the molecule.

alkali (*pl* **alkalis, alkalies**) any salt or mixture that neutralizes acids and with a pH value greater than 7.

alkaloid a body or substance containing alkaline properties.

alkane a saturated compound containing hydrogen and carbon with single bonds between each carbon atom.

alkene an unsaturated compound containing hydrogen and carbon with double bonds between the carbon atoms.

alkyne an unsaturated compound containing hydrogen and carbon with triple bonds between the carbon atoms.

allomorphism property in certain substances of assuming a different form while remaining the same in constitution.

allotropy, allotropism the capability shown by certain chemical elements to assume different forms, each characterized by peculiar qualities, as the occurrence of carbon in the form of the diamond, charcoal and plumbago.

amine any of several organic compounds formed by replacing hydrogen atoms of ammonia by one or more univalent hydrocarbon radicals.

amino acid any of the 20 standard organic compounds from which all the protein components of the body are built up.

amorphous non-crystalline.

anhydrous without water, applied to minerals in which the water of crystallization is not present.

anion a negatively charged ion; the element in a body decomposed by voltaic action, which is evolved at the positive pole or anode.

atom the smallest particle that makes up all matter and still retains the chemical properties of the element.

atomic number the number of protons in the nucleus of an atom.

base any substance that dissociates in water to produce hydroxide ions.

biochemistry the study of the chemistry of biological processes and substances in living organisms.

bivalent having a valency of two.

bond the force that holds atoms together to form a molecule.

Boyle's law a law that at a constant temperature the volume of a gas lessens in proportion to an increase in the pressure of the gas.

Bunsen burner a burner that mixes gas and air to produce a smokeless flame of great heat.

burette, buret a narrow, graduated glass tube, usually with a tap, for measuring the volume of liquids.

carbide a compound of carbon with another element, especially calcium carbide.

carbon a nonmetallic element, a constituent of all organic matter.

carbonate a salt of carbonic acid.

catabolism a downward series of changes by which complex bodies are broken down into simpler forms.

catalysis the acceleration or retardation of a chemical reaction by the action of a catalyst.

catalyst a substance which accelerates or retards a chemical reaction without itself undergoing any permanent chemical change; a person or thing which produces change.

chemical a substance used in, or arising from, a chemical process.

chemist a person skilled in chemistry.

chemistry science of the properties of substances and their combinations and reactions; chemical structure.

cleavage the tendency of minerals and rocks to shear and split along particular planes.

combine to form a compound with.

compound two or more elements combined in a substance in definite proportions, in the form of molecules held together by chemical bonds.

concentrate to increase the strength of by diminishing bulk, to condense.

concentration the quantity of a substance dissolved in a fixed amount of liquid to form a solution.

covalent bond the joining of two atoms due to the equal sharing of their electrons.

cracking an industrial process in which large complicated molecules are broken down into smaller ones.

crystal a solid substance, geometrically shaped owing to the regular arrangement of its molecules.

dehydration the removal of a water molecule from a compound or a more complex molecule by the action of heat.

desiccant a substance that absorbs water, used as a drying agent.

dialysis a method for separating small molecules from larger ones in a solution.

diffusion the natural process by which molecules will disperse evenly throughout a particular substance.

disintegration the process by which one or more particles is given off from the nucleus of an atom.

dissociation decomposition of a molecule into single atoms.

dissolution the dissolving of a substance in a liquid to form a solution in which all the material is evenly distributed.

divalent having a valence of two.

ductility the property of metals that allows them to be drawn out into a wire.

dyad a bivalent atom, element, or radical.

effloresce to crystallize; to become encrusted with crystals as a result of loss of water.

electrolysis chemical decomposition achieved by passing an electric current through a substance in solution or molten form; the passage of an electric current through an electrolyte to effect chemical change.

electron an indivisible particle that is negatively charged and free to orbit the positively charged nucleus of every atom.

electrophoresis a method for separating the molecules within a solution using an electric field.

element any of the 105 known substances composed of atoms with the same number of protons in their nuclei. *See* **Appendix**.

empirical formula a chemical formula of a compound that shows the simplest ratio of atoms present in the compound.

endothermic reaction a chemical reaction in which heat energy is absorbed.

enzyme any protein molecule that acts as a natural catalyst and is found in the bodies of all bacteria, plants and animals.

epoxy of or containing an oxygen atom and two other groups, usually carbon, which are themselves linked with other groups.

equilibrium a condition in which the proportion of the chemicals reacting together and the products being formed is constant.

equivalence, equivalency (*pl* **equivalences, equivalencies**) the property of having equal valency.

ester an organic hydrocarbon compound formed from organic acids.

evaporation the process by which a substance changes from a liquid to a vapour (gas).

exothermic reaction a chemical reaction in which heat energy is released to the surrounding environment.

Fahrenheit a temperature scale with a freezing point of 32° and boiling point at 212°.

faraday a quantity of charge carried by one mole of electrons.

fats a group of organic compounds that occur widely in plants and animals and serve as long-term energy stores.

fatty acids a class of organic compounds containing a long hydrophobic hydrocarbon chain and a terminal carboxylic acid group which is extremely hydrophilic.

filtrate the liquid remaining after filtration, having been separated from a solid/liquid mixture.

filtration separation of a solid from a liquid by passing the mixture through a suitable separation medium.

fractional distillation *or* **fractionation** the process used for separating a mixture of liquids into component parts by distillation.

free energy *or* **Gibb's free energy** a thermodynamic quantity that gives a direct measure of spontaneity of reaction in a reversible process.

functional group an arrangement of atoms joined to a carbon skeleton, which gives an organic compound its particular chemical properties.

galvanizing the industrial process by which one type of metal is coated with a thin layer of another, more reactive metal.

galvanometer an instrument for detecting or measuring small electric currents.

gas an air-like substance with the capacity to expand indefinitely and not liquefy or solidify at ordinary temperatures.

group the vertical columns of elements in the periodic table.

halide a compound consisting of a halogen and another element.

halogen any of the five chemical elements, found in group 7 of the periodic table, that are the extreme form of the non-metals, i.e. fluorine, chlorine, bromine, iodine and astatine.

homologous series chemical compounds that are related by having the same functional groups but formulae that differ by a specific group of atoms.

hydrate a chemical compound of water with some other substance.

hydrolysis the chemical breakdown of organic compounds by interaction with water.

hydroxide a compound derived from water through the replacement of one of the hydrogen atoms by another atom or group.

hydroxyl the OH group comprising an oxygen and a hydrogen atom bonded together.

incalescent increasing in heat.

indicator a chemical substance, usually a large organic molecule, that is used to detect the presence of other chemicals in a solution.

inert gas any of the unreactive gases that include helium, neon, argon, krypton, xenon and radon. *Also* **noble gas**.

inhibitor a substance that stops or slows down a chemical reaction.

initiator a substance that starts a chemical reaction.

inorganic chemistry the chemistry of all substances except those containing carbon.

isomer any of two or more chemical compounds whose molecules contain the same atoms but in different arrangements.

isomorphism the quality of having the same crystalline form despite being formed of different elements.

isotonic having the same tone or tension; having the same osmotic pressure.

isotope any of two or more forms of an element having the same atomic number but different atomic weights.

ketone an organic compound that contains a carbonyl group within the compound rather than at either end of the compound.

kinetics the science of the effects of forces in producing or changing motion; the study of the mechanisms and rates of chemical reactions.

labile unstable.

Lassaigne's test a chemical test for the presence of nitrogen and also sulphur or halogens.

ligand any molecule or atom capable of forming a bond with another molecule by donating an electron pair to form a complex ion.

metal any of a class of chemical elements which are often lustrous, ductile solids, and are good conductors of heat, electricity, etc, such as gold, iron, copper, etc.

metalloid a nonmetallic element that possesses some of the chemical properties associated with metals and some associated with non-metals.

metameric having the same elements and molecular weight but different properties.

metathesis (*pl* **metatheses**) a reaction between two compounds in which the first and second parts of one unite with the second and first parts of the other.

mineral a substance with a definite and characteristic chemical composition and usually with a crystalline structure and certain physical properties, including hardness, lustre, cleavage, colour, fracture and relative density.

mineralogy the study of any chemical element or compound extracted from the earth.

molarity the number of moles of a substance dissolved in one litre of solution.

mole the amount of substance that contains the same number of elementary particles as there are in 12g of carbon.

molecular formula the chemical formula that indicates both the number and type of any atom present in a molecular substance.

molecular weight the total of the atomic weights of all the atoms present in a molecule; the average mass per molecule of any substance relative to one-twelfth the mass of an atom of carbon-12.

molecule the smallest chemical unit of an element or compound that can exist independently; a small particle.

monad a radical or atom with a valency of one.

monobasic having one base or atom of a base.

monomer a simple molecule that is the basic unit of polymers.

monosaccharide a sugar that cannot be further broken down into simpler sugars by hydrolysis.

monovalent with a valency of one; univalent.

neutral neither acid nor alkaline.

neutralization a reaction that either increases the pH of an acidic solution, or decreases the pH of an alkaline solution, to neutral seven.

neutron a subatomic elementary particle with no electric charge and the same mass approximately as a proton.

neutron number the number of neutrons in the nucleus of an atom.

nitrate a salt of nitric acid.

nitration the addition of the nitro group to organic compounds.

nitride a compound of nitrogen with a metal, also with phosphorus, silicon or boron.

nitrite a salt of nitrous acid.

nitrogen a colourless, odourless gas that exists as a molecule containing two atoms and forms almost 80% of the atmosphere by volume.

noble gases the elements comprising group 8 of the periodic table: helium, neon, argon, krypton, xenon and radon.

noble metals metals, e.g. platinum, silver and gold, that are highly resistant to corrosion.

non-metal a chemical element, e.g. carbon, that is not a metal.

nuclear chemistry the study of reactions involving the changes from one type of atom to another due to a nuclear reaction.

nucleon either a proton or a neutron, the ordinary components of a nucleus.

nucleus (*pl* **nuclei**, **nucleuses**) the centrally positively charged portion of an atom.

octad an element or radical with a valence of eight.

open chain an organic compound with an open chain, not a ring structure, as in aliphatic compounds, e.g. alkanes, alkenes and alkynes, and compounds formed from them.

organic chemistry the branch of chemistry that is concerned with the study of carbon compounds.

organic of the class of compounds that are formed from carbon; (of vegetables, etc) grown without the use of artificial fertilizers or pesticides.

osmosis the process in which solvent molecules move through a semi-permeable membrane to the more concentrated solution.

oxidation any chemical reaction that is characterized by the gain of oxygen or the loss of electrons from the reactant; the operation of converting into an oxide.

oxide a compound formed by the combination of oxygen with another element, with the exception of the inert gases.

oxidize to cause to undergo a chemical reaction with oxygen; to rust.

oxygen highly reactive gas which occurs as the molecule made up of two atoms. The most abundant of all the elements.

ozone a condensed form of oxygen that exists not with the usual two atoms of oxygen, but with three atoms per molecule.

pentavalent with a valency of five.

peptide bond a covalent linkage formed when two amino acids join together.

period a horizontal row in the periodic table, e.g. those elements between an alkali metal and the next inert gas.

periodic table a list of chemical elements tabulated by their atomic number. *See* **Appendix**.

phase a part of a system that is chemically uniform but that occurs in a different form.

phospholipids biological compounds that resemble fats.

photochromics materials which are sensitive to light.

photolysis chemical decomposition caused by light or other electromagnetic radiation.

physical chemistry the branch of chemistry concerned with the effect of chemical structure on physical properties and of physical changes brought about by chemical reactions.

pi bond the covalent bond formed when two atoms join to form a molecule.

platinum metals a block of six transition elements with similar properties: ruthenium, rhodium, palladium, osmium, iridium and platinum.

polar having positive and negative electricity.

polarity the condition of being polar; attraction towards a particular object or in a specific direction; the state, positive or negative, of a body.

polyatomic with more than two atoms in the molecule.

polybasic having more than two bases or atoms of a base.

polymer a compound that has large molecules composed of many simpler molecules.

polypeptide a single linear molecule that is formed from many amino acids joined by peptide bonds.

positron a particle of the same size as an electron, but with a positive charge.

precipitation the formation of an insoluble substance (precipitate) in a reaction between two solutions.

principle a chemical constituent with a characteristic quality.

proton an elementary particle in the nucleus of all atoms, carrying a unit positive charge of electricity.

quadrivalent with four valences; with a valence of four, tetravalent.

quaternary an atom bound to four other atoms or groups, or containing such an atom.

quinquevalent having a valence of five, pentavalent.

radical a group of atoms within a compound, which are not able to exist on their own and are not changed when the substance is involved in chemical reactions.

radiochemistry the scientific study and purification of radioactive materials.

radioelement a radioactive chemical element.

react to undergo a chemical reaction.

reaction an action set up by one substance in another.

reactor a vessel in which a reaction occurs; a nuclear reactor.

reagent a chemical substance or solution that is used to detect, measure, or react with other substances.

redox reaction a chemical reaction in which both reduction and oxidation are involved.

reducing agent any substance that will lose electrons during a chemical reaction.

reduction any chemical reaction that is characterized by the loss of oxygen or by the gain of electrons from one of the reactants.

relative molecular mass the total of the atomic weights of all the atoms present in a molecule; the average mass per molecule of any substance relative to one-twelfth the mass of an atom of carbon-12. *Also* **molecular weight**.

retardant a substance that slows down a chemical reaction.

salt a compound of an acid and a base.

saturated absorbing the maximum amount possible of a substance.

spontaneous combustion the self-igniting of a substance through internal chemical processes such as oxidation.

steroid any of a large number of compounds sharing the same chemical structure, including sterols and many hormones; any of a group of lipids with a characteristic structure comprising four carbon rings fused together.

structural formula a formula providing information on the atoms present in a molecule and the way that they are bound together, i.e., an indication of the structure.

sublimation the formation of a vapour directly from a solid, without going through the liquid phase.

substitution a reaction in which an atom or group in a molecule is replaced by another atom or group, often hydrogen by a halogen, hydroxyl, etc.

substrate a substance in a reaction that is catalyzed by an enzyme.

surfactant *or* **surface-active agent** a compound that reduces the surface tension of its solvent, e.g., a detergent in water.

synthesis the production of a compound by a chemical reaction.

tetravalent having a valency of four.

thermochemistry the branch of chemistry dealing with the heat changes of chemical reactions.

thermolysis breakdown of a compound or molecule by heat.

titration a method of determining the amount of a constituent in a solution by adding a known quantity of a reagent.

transition element one of the elements in the periodic table that is characterized by an incomplete inner electron shell and a variable valency.

transition point the point at which a substance may exist in more than one solid form, in equilibrium.

triatomic having three atoms in the molecule.

trivalent having a valency of three.

universal indicator a mixture of certain substances, which will change colour to show the changing pH of a solution.

unsaturated having double or triple bonds and therefore able to form products by chemical addition; (*vegetable fats*) containing fatty acids with double bonds.

valence electron, valency electron one of the electrons present in the outermost shell of an atom of a corresponding element.

valence, valency the power of elements to combine; the number of atoms of hydrogen that an atom or group can combine with to form a compound.

volatile denoting any substance that can easily change from the solid or liquid state to its vapour.

voltaic pertaining to electricity generated by chemical action or galvanism; galvanic.

zymogen a form of an enzyme that is inactive.

zymurgy the chemistry of fermentation in brewing, etc.

Computer terms

acronym the abbreviation of words to their initial letters to enable more rapid communication.

address a location in a computer system that is identified by a name or code.

alias a representation of an original document or file that can be used as if it was the original.

application program a computer program that performs specific tasks.

archive a store of files (either program or data) that is kept as a backup.

artificial intelligence (AI) the ability of an artificial mechanism to exhibit intelligent behaviour by learning from experience.

attachment a file attached to an email.

backup a copy of a program or data file that is kept for archive purposes.

bells and whistles the advanced features that an application program contains.

binary the language of all computers in which all numbers, letters and special characters are represented by 1 and 0.

bitmap a method of storing graphics information in memory in which a bit is devoted to each pixel (picture element) on screen.

bookmark a bookmark, added to the Favorites list in the browser, enables a website to be re-accessed at a later date.

bootstrapping a program routine designed to make a computer ready for use.

broad band an analogue communications method using high bandwidth.

browse to display records in a format suitable for quick on-screen review and editing.

browser a software program that enables the web to be searched.

bug a hardware or software error.

bulletin board a computer service set up by organizations to provide or exchange information.

byte a combination of bits used by the computer to represent a character. Units that are used most often are the kilobyte and megabyte, representing 1,024 bytes and 1,048,576 bytes.

cache an area of the random access memory (*see* **RAM**) in a computer that is used as a temporary storage for frequently used data.

CD ROM (Compact Disk Read Only Memory).

A storage media which has a capacity of 650 megabytes, which is equivalent to a quarter of a million pages of text.

character a single letter, number, space, special character or symbol.

chat forum a conference area which allows two or more users to type messages and converse in real time.

check box a small box that is used to choose between different options in a dialog box. When the box has a cross in it the option is selected; when empty the option is deselected.

chip a tiny chip or wafer of silicon that contains minute electronic circuitry and forms the core of a microprocessor or computer.

client a personal computer or workstation in a local area network that is used to request information from a network's file server.

code a list of instructions written to solve a particular problem.

command an instruction or set of instructions that will start or stop an operation in a computer program.

community the population of an online information service or bulletin board.

compact disc *see* CD ROM.

computer an electronic data processing device, capable of accepting data, applying a prescribed set of instructions to the data, and displaying the result in some manner or form.

console the terminal that is used to control the computer system.

cookie a file created by a web server which is transmitted to, and stored on, the hard disk of the computer making the connection. When the same site is visited again, it matches the data and 'recognizes' the individual browser.

coprocessor a secondary or support chip that is used alongside the main chip to provide added power for specific operations such as graphics display or mathematical calculations.

copy to create a duplicate of a file, graphic or program without changing the original version.

corrupted file a file or part of a file that has become unreadable.

crash an unexpected termination of an application.

cross-platform applies to the use of software and files on computer with a different hardware system.

cursor an indicator on the screen of a VDU, used by a computer to direct a user to the point at which data is entered.

cyber café a café where customers can browse the Internet, play computer games or look at CDs.

cybernetics the study of computer control systems and the relationship between these artificial systems and biological systems.

cyberspace a user connects with cyberspace when he or she logs on to an online service or connects with another computer.

data bits the elements of a character sent during asynchronous communications that contain the actual data.

data jargon for information.

database a file of information (data) that is stored in a structured manner and used by a program such as a database management system. Information is usually subdivided into particular data fields.

desktop in an operating system environment that uses a graphical user interface the desktop is the computer representation of a physical desk top onto which files and folders can be placed.

desktop publishing (DTP) the software and hardware that makes possible the composition of text and graphics.

dialog box a window that is an integral part of a program and is used to convey information or request information from the user about the operations of the program.

digispeak the use of acronyms in online communication.

digital a term used to describe the use of two states, on or off, in order to represent all data. A computer is digital since it represents all data in a series of 1s and 0s.

digital video/versatile disk (DVD) a storage/reply medium which is very versatile and commonly used for audio/video usage.

directory the table of contents of a computer file system that allows convenient access to specific files. A directory is an area of the disk that stores files.

disk drive the piece of hardware and elec-

tronics that enables information to be read from, and written to, a disk. The recording and erasing is performed by the read/write head. The circuitry controlling the drive is called the *disk drive controller.*

document traditionally, a piece of work created in a word processing program such as a letter, memo or report.

domain name most commonly used to mean the name referring to an Internet site, service or computer and in the main representing a business or an organization.

domain type another part of an address which indicates what sort of organization is involved.

DOS (Disk Operating System) the program responsible for communications between a computer and its peripheral devices such as the disk drive, printer or the VDU.

dots per inch (DPI) a measure of the resolution of a screen or printer. The more dots per inch that the computer can display or print the higher the resolution.

download to copy a file from an online information service or from another computer to your computer.

drop down menu a list of command options that appears only when the main command is selected.

dump the process of transferring the contents of memory in one storage device to another storage device or item of hardware.

echo to show on screen the commands being executed by a computer as they are being performed.

e-commerce (or electronic commerce) making online business transactions, or buying products or services online.

edutainment the growing selection of computer software that educates the user while being entertaining.

e-journal an online publication which can be accessed on the web, commonly used in the academic world.

email *or* **e-mail** the use of a network of computers to send and receive messages. Files sent with emails are known as attachments.

emoticon an icon representing emotion (hence the name) made up of standard keyboard characters.

Ethernet a local area network (LAN) hardware standard capable of linking up to 1,024 computers in a network.

export to create a data file in one program that can be transferred to another computer and be read by another program.

extension a set of three characters after the file name which helps in recognizing the file type.

Favorites enables the user to build up a list of frequently visited sites. By selecting 'Add to Favorites' a chosen site can be accessed from the Favorites list.

fax or **fax machine** or **facsimile** a device capable of transmitting or receiving an exact copy of a page of printed or pictorial matter over telephone lines.

field a defined group of characters or numbers within a specific space in a database program.

file a collection of data that is given a distinct name and is stored on the computer's secondary storage. Files are stored within directories, analogous to the old system of filing cabinet, drawers and folders.

filter to select certain files from a database by setting up a set of criteria.

floppy disk a removable secondary medium of storage for computers. The disks are made of a plastic that is coated with magnetic material. The whole thing is protected by a rigid plastic cover.

folder the directory in which files are located or stored.

font a complete set of letters, numbers, special characters and punctuation marks of a particular size and for one identifiable typeface whether roman or bold (the weight), italic or upright (the posture).

format the preparation of a hard disk or floppy disk for use by laying down clearly defined recording areas. The format is the way in which the magnetic pattern is laid down on the disk.

fragmentation the process of saving and deleting files will result in a particular file being located in many sectors on the disk.

freeware copyrighted programs that are provided by the author free of charge.

function any single operation of a computer or word processor.

fuzzy logic a description of the development away from strict logical arguments to take account of human or non-logical behaviour.

gateway a device that converts communications from one protocol or bandwidth to another. This function allows two different types of network to communicate with each other.

geek a person with an obsession with computers, programming and the Internet.

glitch a malfunction caused by a hardware fault.

gopher a means of searching for files using a particular set of menus. Outdated by search engines such as AltaVista, Google and Yahoo.

goto a programming phrase that directs the program logic to a part of the program in order to accomplish a specific function.

grandparent the oldest file in a grandparent, parent, son backup system.

grey scale the shades of grey from white to black that a computer can display.

groupware software that caters for sharing of documents, management of documents, scheduling facilities, and conferencing.

hacker the term usually refers to someone who accesses other people's computers, with the aid of communications technology, and without permission.

handshaking a greeting between two devices, such as a modem to modem or computer to printer, that signals that data transmission between the devices can proceed.

hard copy a document or file that is printed as opposed to one that is stored in a computer's memory or stored on disk.

hard disk a fixed disk that forms a storage medium within the computer. It includes the storage medium, the read/write head and the electronics to connect it to the computer.

head the device used by a disk drive to read a disk. As each side of a disk can be read by a separate head the number of heads is often used as shorthand for the number of sides (e.g. double-sided disk).

history the history on a web browser is a listing of all recently-visited sites on the Internet.

home page this now usually means the opening page of a website, which is like the title and contents page introducing the viewer to the company/service, etc, and showing what is contained on the site.

housekeeping activities that are performed to reduce clutter on the computer desktop and disks and generally make for efficient use of the computer.

hub a device at the centre of a computing system to which all the computers in a network are connected, allowing intercommunication.

hyperlink a link between objects. The link can be text, as icon, or graphic. Pages on the web have links that may connect with other pages on that site, another site completely or may enable an email to be sent.

hypertext a link from one word in a document to another area of a document.

icon a symbol on screen that represents something or some process or function in the computer.

import to open a file that has been created in one application in another application.

interface the term for the ports and the correct electronic configuration between two or more devices.

Internet a worldwide system of linked computer networks.

Internet Relay Chat (IRC) a type of 'meeting to chat' facility on the Internet which runs in real time, and can lead to discussions between a large group of people across the world.

Internet Service Provider (ISP) a company that allows people to connect up to the Internet through their own computer system.

joystick an input device controlling the cursor of a computer, normally used for computer games.

key a button on a keyboard.

keyboard a set of alphabetic, numeric, symbol and control keys that relays the character or command to a computer, which then displays the character on the screen.

kilobyte (K, KB, kbyte) the basic unit of measurement for computer memory equal to 1024 bytes.

laptop a small portable computer that can operate from its own power supply and can be used almost anywhere.

libraries stores of prewritten programming routines for use in generating applications.

log off to end a session working at a computer terminal or system.

log on to begin working at a computer terminal or system.

macro a record of commands used regularly in an application that can be activated by a keystroke.

mail merge the process of merging two files (one letter and one database of addresses) for the purpose of creating a mail shot.

mailbox within the electronic mail system, a disk file or memory area in which messages for a particular destination (or person) are placed.

mainframe a computing system that serves the needs of a whole organization.

megabyte (MB, mbyte) one million bytes (characters) of information. The common storage measurement for memory and hard disks, e.g. 4 megabytes of RAM, with a 210-megabyte hard disk drive.

megahertz (MHz) a measurement of one million hertz, i.e. cycles per second. This is the unit used for computers and refers to the speed of the central processing unit.

memory the circuitry and devices that are capable of storing data as well as programs. Memory is the computer's primary storage area, e.g. RAM as distinguished from the secondary storage of disks.

menu a list of commands, applications, or other options that are available to the computer user on a monitor or VDU.

microprocessor or **microchip** an electronic device (integrated circuit) that has been programmed to follow a set of logic-driven rules. It is essentially the heart of any computer system.

MIME (multipurpose Internet mail extensions) the commonest form in which attachments are sent with emails. MIME encodes the file for transmission and then decodes it at the receiving end.

monitor another name for display, screen or VDU.

morphing a technique that appears to melt one image into another image to create a special.

motherboard the main printed circuit board in a computer.

mouse an input device that controls the on-screen cursor. Movement of the mouse causes a similar movement of the cursor on the computer screen.

multimedia the process of combining computer data, sound and video images to create an environment similar to television. The market for multimedia on compact disks is now expanding rapidly.

nanotechnology the study of how to make computers, materials and components smaller and more efficient.

net short for the Internet.

netizen literally 'net citizen', someone who uses the Internet.

network the interconnection of a number of terminals or computer systems by data communication lines.

newsgroup an interactive discussion group online.

offline equipment that is not under the direct control of the central processing unit.

online when a computer is connected via a modem to an online service or Internet service provider.

output computer output comes in the form of printed reports, letters, information sent to a storage device and the image on screen. Output devices are peripherals that will accept information from the computer.

parent file in a series of three backups of a file the parent file is the second oldest file.

partition a section of a hard disk that is created for a particular purpose.

password a key word that is selected by a user to protect files from unauthorized access.

patch an addition to a computer software program that is released after the launch of the main product and which corrects a fault (bug) or enhances the running of the program.

path the means of pointing to the exact location of a file on a computer disk. It uses a hierarchical structure of directories in which files are stored.

PC (Personal Computer) a microcomputer that can be programmed to perform a variety of tasks for home and office.

port a plug or socket through which data may be passed into and out of a computer.

printer the device that produces hard copy.

processor a device in computing that can perform arithmetical and logical operations.

program a set of instructions arranged for directing a computer to perform a desired operation.

prompt a symbol or message that informs the user that the computer is ready to accept data.

protocol the conventions or rules that govern how and when messages are exchanged in a communications network.

query in a database management program, a query is when the user asks the program to find a particular reference or type of data that is in the records of the database.

queue when two or more files are waiting for an action to take place.

quit to exit from a program.

RAM (Random Access Memory) *or* **main memory** *or* **internal memory** the memory that can be, and is, altered in normal computer operations.

reboot to restart the computer without turning off the power.

record to store data on a disk.

recover to restore lost or damaged files.

reformat to repeat a formatting operation on a disk or to proceed with a formatting operation on a disk that has already been formatted. In a word processing, page layout or spreadsheet program, it means to change the style of the text.

refresh to update the image on the computer screen.

restore to recreate the conditions or state of a disk, file or program before an error or event occurred to destroy or corrupt the data.

retrieve to obtain data previously stored on file in order that work can be done on the data.

return a command key on the keyboard that is used to initiate a chosen command.

robot an electromechanical device that may perform programmed tasks.

ROM (Read Only Memory) the part of a computer's internal memory that can be read but not altered. It contains the essential programs (system programs).

run to initiate or execute a program. The computer reads the code from the disk and stores all or part of the code in the RAM. The computer can then perform tasks.

save to transfer the contents of a computer's RAM to a hard disk or floppy disk.

screen another name for the VDU, display or monitor.

screen saver a utility program designed to prolong the life of a screen by switching off the image after a period of non-use.

script a list of instructions that automatically perform a task within an application program.

scroll to move the active window over a document so that a different part of the document is visible in the window. Scrolling can be vertical or horizontal.

search engine a tool used to look for and retrieve information on the web.

sector a storage area on a disk.

select to chose a portion of a document in which to perform a particular task.

server a computer used in a local area network that is the main source of programs or shared data.

set up to install a piece of hardware or software into a computer system so that it works with the system.

shareware software that can be obtained on a trial basis but to continue to use the program a fee must be paid to the author.

snail mail the term sometimes used to describe the postal service as opposed to electronic mail.

sort a command that organizes data into a particular order.

source the file or disk from which information or data is taken by the processor.

spam the term given to junk mail in email transmissions.

spike a surge of electricity that at best causes a system crash or at worst can burn out components inside the computer.

spooler a utility program that is used to facilitate printing.

spreadsheet a program that creates an on-screen worksheet, which is a series of rows and columns of cells into which values, text and formulae can be placed.

storage the retention of programs and data in a computer in such a way as to allow the computer processor to access the information when required.

stylesheet a file that has been saved with all the formatting required for a particular task.

syntax the set of rules that govern the way in which a command or statement is given to

a computer so that it recognizes the command and proceeds accordingly.

telecommunications the use of the telephone systems, either land lines or satellite, to transmit information.

template a document that is prewritten and formatted and ready for final adjustment before printing.

terabyte (TB, tbyte) a measurement of memory capacity that is approximately equal to one trillion bytes. The actual number is 1,099,511,627,776 bytes.

terminal an input/output device consisting of a monitor, keyboard and connection to a central server.

tile to set windows in a side-by-side fashion on the desktop.

title bar a shaded bar containing the name of the file that is found at the top of an on-screen window.

toolbar a strip of buttons that appears at the top of the screen that are used to select commands without using menus.

toolbox a set of prewritten programs or routines used by programmers for incorporation into larger programs.

trackball an input device that is similar to a mouse but instead of moving over the desk, the ball is moved within a static unit that may be embedded in the case of a laptop computer.

trackpad an input device that is a development of the trackball. It consists of a square pad embedded in the case of a laptop computer, and movement of the finger over the pad moves the cursor on the screen.

transfer to move information from disk to memory and vice versa.

translate to change a file that has been saved in one file format to another so that the file can be opened in a different program.

Trojan horse a program that appears to perform a valid function but, in fact, contains hidden codes that can cause damage to the system that runs the program.

troubleshoot to investigate the reason for a particular occurrence or malfunction in a computer system.

typeface a set of characters sharing a unique design, such as Courier or Times. Typefaces can be serif or sans serif.

undo a command available in programs that

unformatted   **azimuthal projection**

reverses the effect of the previous command given.

unformatted a term indicating that an item of magnetic media requires formatting prior to being put into operation.

upgrade to purchase the most recent version of software released by the author or to purchase a new hardware update, such as a new computer system.

upload to copy a file from your computer to another computer connected through the telecommunication system. (*See also* **download**.)

utility program a program that helps the user to obtain the most benefit from a computer system by performing routine tasks, e.g. copying data from one file to another.

vaccine a utility program designed to prevent a computer virus from attacking a system.

vaporware software under development that is marketed in advance of its release.

virtual drive part of a computer's internal memory that is defined to act like a disk drive.

virtual memory (**VM**) the use of disk drive storage to extend the ram of a computer.

virtual reality a computer-generated environment that allows the user to experience various aspects of life.

virus a program that is designed to cause damage to systems that the virus infects. A virus program can copy itself from file to file and disk to disk and spread quickly.

voice mail a system that stores voice communication on disk and can replay the message on command.

voice recognition the ability of a computer to recognize a voice, translate it into a digital pattern and reproduce the pattern as text or as computer generated speech.

wallpaper an on-screen design that acts as a backdrop to the icons, windows, etc.

Graphical user interface computer operating systems have facilities to change the patterns through control panels.

what if analysis a procedure using a spreadsheet to explore the effect of changes in one input into a calculation.

wild card a special character that is substituted for another character or range of characters in a search of filenames.

window an on-screen frame, usually rectangular in shape, that contains the display of a file.

wizard a computerized expert system that leads the user through the sometimes complex process of creating a document such as an advertising flyer or a newsletter.

word processing a method of document preparation, storage and editing using a personal computer.

word wrap a feature of word processing programs that automatically moves words down to the next line if they go beyond the right-hand margin.

worksheet a matrix of rows and columns in a spreadsheet program into which are entered headings, numbers and formulae.

worldwide web a hypertext-based document retrieval system linked to the internet.

worm a virus in the form of a program that makes copies of itself from one disk drive to another, or through email.

wrap around type type that is contoured so that it surrounds a graphic item in a document. This is a feature of desktop publishing programs such as PageMaker, where it is called text wrap.

write an operation of the central processing unit that records information on to a computer's RAM. It more commonly refers to the recording of information onto secondary storage media such as disk drives.

zap to delete or get rid of a program or file from a computer memory.

Geography

absolute humidity is the actual mass of water vapour in each cubic metre of air while

anticyclone moving air of higher pressure that the surrounding air. *See* **cyclone** .

atmosphere the layer of gases and dust

surrounding the Earth. *See* **troposphere**, **stratosphere** and **ozone layer**.

atmospheric pressure the downward force of the atmosphere on the surface of the Earth.

azimuthal projection also called a zenithal

projection. A map where part of the Earth's surface is projected onto a plane at a tangent, either at one of the poles, at the equator or in between.

Beaufort scale a system for indicating wind strength, developed in 1805 by the British Admiral Sir Francis Beaufort.

cirrus of clouds, resembling fibres.

climate characteristic weather conditions produced by a combination of factors, such as rainfall and temperature. The major climatic zones are, from the Equator:

humid tropical climate: hot and wet

subtropical, arid and semi-arid climate: desert conditions, extremes of daily temperature

humid temperate climate: warm and moist with mild winters

boreal (Northern Hemisphere) climate: long, cold winters; short summers.

sub-arctic (or sub-Antarctic) climate: generally cold with low rainfall

polar climate: always cold.

cloud a mass of droplets of water or ice formed by the condensation of moisture in a mass of rising air. There are three major groups.

cold front the leading edge of a cold air mass, which moves under warm air, forcing the latter to rise. The result is a fall in temperature, with rainfall passing behind the front.

conical projection map a map of conic type, used for maps of a small continent.

connate water groundwater which is water trapped in a sedimentary rock since its formation.

continent any one of the several large landmasses that cover 29 per cent of the Earth's surface. There are seven continents making up the Earth: Asia, Africa, North and Central America, South America, Antarctica, Europe, Oceania.

Coriolis force a major factor that influences tides. Air or water is pushed to the side because of the Earth's rotation. In the Northern Hemisphere, water moving across the Earth's surface is pushed to the right (and conversely to the left in the Southern Hemisphere).

cumulus of clouds, resembling 'heaps'.

currents fast-moving large-scale flows (the slower movements are called *drifts*). The rotation of the Earth, prevailing winds, temperature and seawater densities contribute to the formation of currents. Major currents move clockwise in the Northern Hemisphere and anticlockwise in the Southern Hemisphere.

cyclone an area of low atmospheric pressure with closely packed isobars producing a steep pressure gradient and therefore very strong winds. Because of the Earth's rotation, the winds circulate clockwise in the Southern Hemisphere and anticlockwise in the Northern Hemisphere.

desert an arid or semi-arid (that is, dry and parched with under 25 centimetres of rainfall annually) region in which there is little or no vegetation.

dew the condensation of water vapour in the air caused by a cooling of the air.

doldrums a zone of calm, or light, winds around the Equator, applied particularly to the oceans, with obvious links to the time when sailing ships were becalmed.

drainage basin the area from which a river's water is derived.

Equator the line encircling the earth with a latitude of 0°, of equal distance from both north and south poles, dividing the north and south hemispheres.

flood where land not normally covered by water is temporarily underwater.

floodplain the area in a river valley that may be covered by water when a river is in flood.

front the surface at which two air masses with different meteorological properties meet.

geography the study of the Earth's surface, including all the landforms their formation and associated processes, which comprises *physical geography*. Such aspects as climate, topography and oceanography are covered.

gnomonic projection map a map of azimuthal type, used for seismic survey.

grassland one of the four major types of vegetation, the others being forest, savanna and desert. Grasslands are characterized by seasonal drought, limited precipitation and occasional fires.

hail a small pellet of frozen water that forms by raindrops being taken higher into colder parts of the atmosphere.

hygrometer the instrument used to measure relative humidity.

humidity the amount of moisture in the Earth's atmosphere.

hurricane a wind that on the beaufort scale exceeds 120 kilometres per hour (75 miles per hour).

International date line to compensate for the accumulated time change across time zones, the *International Date Line* was introduced. It runs roughly on the 180-degree meridian. To cross it going east means repeating a day, while crossing it going west means losing a day.

irrigation the process by which water is taken to dry land to encourage or facilitate plant growth.

isobar a line on a weather map that joins points of equal pressure connected for the varying heights of recording.

jet stream westerly winds at high altitudes (above 12 kilometres/8 miles), found mainly between the poles and the tropics that form narrow jet-like streams.

latitude the angular distance north or south of the **Equator** used to measure points on the Earth's surface. *See* **longitude**.

lightning the discharge of high voltage electricity between a cloud and its base and between the base of the cloud and the Earth. There are various forms of lightning, including *sheet*, *fork* and *ball*, and it may carry a charge of around 10,000 amps. *See* **thunder**.

longitude the angular distance of a point measured on the Earth's surface to the east or west of a 'central' reference point. *See* **latitude**.

map a flat, two-dimensional representation of a three-dimensional subject, e.g. an area of land, that contains a variety of data that will differ depending upon the type of map.

meanders the wide loops formed in a river which swings from side to side.

Mercator projection a map of cylindrical type, used for navigation.

meridian an imaginary line circling the earth joining the north and south poles at right angles to the Equator.

meteorology the scientific study of the conditions and processes within the Earth's atmosphere. This includes the pressure, temperature, wind speed, cloud formations, etc, that, over a period of time, enable meteorologists to predict likely future weather patterns. Information is generated by weather stations and also by satellites in orbit around the Earth.

monsoon in general, winds that blow in opposite directions during different seasons. Monsoons are related to temperature changes in the subtropics and pressure alterations associated with changing **jet streams**.

natural gas hydrocarbons in a gaseous state which when found are often associated with liquid petroleum. The gas is a mixture of methane and ethane, with propane and small quantities of butane, nitrogen, carbon dioxide and sulphur compounds.

neap tide when the Sun is at right angles to the Moon, the effect is minimised, resulting in a low neap tide.

ocean a body of water that occupies an ocean basin, the latter beginning at the edge of the continental shelf. A more general definition is all the water on the Earth's surface, excluding lakes and inland seas. The oceans are the North and South Atlantic Oceans, the North and South Pacific Oceans, the Indian Ocean and the Arctic Ocean.

oceanography the study of all aspects of the oceans, from their structure and composition to the life within and the movements of the water.

ox-bow lake a narrow neck of land may develop from a meandering river. Thus the river alters and shortens its course, leaving a horseshoe-shaped remnant, or ox-bow lake.

ozone layer a part of the Earth's atmosphere, at a height of approximately 16–32 kilometres (10–20 miles), that contains ozone. Ozone is present in very small amounts

(1 to 10 parts per million), but it fulfils a very important role by absorbing much of the Sun's ultraviolet radiation, which in excess has harmful effects.

Peter's projection map a map of modified cylindrical type, used to depict the Earth's densely populated areas in proportion.

rain one form of precipitation in which drops of water condense from the water vapour in the atmosphere to form rain drops. Other types of precipitation, all water in some liquid or solid form, include snow, hail, sleet, drizzle and also dew.

relative humidity varies with temperature, with cold air holding little moisture, warm air much more

remote sensing the collection of a variety of information without contact with the object of study, e.g. aerial photography from both aircraft and satellites and the use of infrared, ultraviolet and microwave radiation emitted from the object.

river a stream of water that flows into the sea or in some cases into lakes or swamps.

river system a river with its tributaries

savanna is similar to grassland but with scattered trees. There are usually well-defined seasons: cool and dry, hot and dry, followed by warm and wet, and during the latter there is a rich growth of grasses and small plants.

savanna *see also* **grasslands**.

snow a form of precipitation which forms below freezing (0°C or 32°F) and, depending upon the temperature, occurs in different shapes.

spicules ice crystals which form well below freezing. They are small and needle-like.

spring tide when the Sun, Moon and Earth are aligned, the effects are combined and result in a maximum tide, the high *spring tide* (when the Moon is new or full).

stereographic projection map a map of azimuthal type, used widely in structural geology, crystallography.

stratosphere one of the layers of the atmosphere, lying above the troposphere. It lies at a height of between 10 and 50 kilometres (6 and 30 miles) and shows an increase

in temperature from bottom to top where it is at freezing point (0°C or 32°F).

stratus of clouds, with a sheet-like appearance.

thunder is the rumbling noise that accompanies lightning. It is caused by the sudden heating and expansion of the air by the discharge, causing sound waves. *See* **lightning**.

tide the regular rise and fall of the water levels in the Earth's oceans and seas, which is caused by the gravitational effect of the Moon and Sun. The Moon exerts a stronger pull than the Sun (roughly twice the effect).

time zones zones that run north-south, with some variations, across the Earth and represent different times. Each zone is one hour earlier or later than the adjacent zone and is 15 degrees of *longitude*.

tornado a narrow column of air that rotates rapidly and leaves total devastation in its path. It develops around a centre of very low pressure with high velocity winds (well over 300 kilometres/185 miles per hour) blowing anticlockwise and with a violent down draught.

trade winds play an important part in the atmospheric circulation of the Earth, and they are mainly easterly winds that blow from the subtropics to the Equator.

tropical a tropical climate does not have a cool season, and the mean temperature never falls below 20°C (68°F). Rainfall can be very high indeed.

tropics two lines of latitude that lie 23.5 degrees north and south of the Equator. The northern line is the *Tropic of Cancer* and the southern the *Tropic of Capricorn*, and the region between them is called the tropics.

tropopause in the Earth's atmosphere, the point at which the change in temperature with height (the lapse rate) stops and the temperature remains constant for several miles.

troposphere the part of the Earth's atmosphere between the surface and the tropopause (the boundary with the stratosphere).

tsunami (*plural* **tsunami**) an enormous sea wave caused by the sudden large-scale movement of the sea floor, resulting in the displacement of large volumes of water.

tundra the treeless region between the snow and ice of the Arctic and the northern extent of tree growth. The ground is subject to permafrost, but the surface layer melts in the summer. The surface therefore can support little plant life. There is also *alpine tundra*, found on the highest mountain tops.

warm front occurs in a depression, between warm air moving over cold air, and it heralds drizzle followed by heavy rain that then gives way to rising temperatures.

weather the combined effect of atmospheric pressure, temperature, sunshine, cloud, humidity, wind and the amount of precipitation that together make up the weather for a certain place over a particular (usually short) time period.

weathering a combination of chemical and physical processes on the surface of the Earth that breaks down rocks and minerals. Weathering can be divided into mechanical, chemical and organic.

westerlies one of the strongest wind flows which flow from the high pressure of the subtropics to the low pressure of the Temperate Zone. Depressions are most common in this wind system.

wind a generally horizontal or near horizontal movement of air caused by changes in atmospheric pressure in which air normally moves from areas of high to low pressure.

wind chill is the effect that the wind has in lowering apparent temperatures by increasing heat loss from the body.

Geology

abrasion wearing away through grinding, rubbing and polishing.

active layer the top layer of perma frost which thaws in the summer,

active volcano a volcano that is erupting, whether clouds of ash and steam or lava.

alluvium deposits produced as a result of the action of streams or rivers.

annular drainage formation of streams in circular patterns around a structure of the same shape (e.g. an igneous intrusion).

aquifer a layer of rock, sand or gravel that is porous and therefore allows the passage and collection of water.

artesian well a well in which water rises to the surface by internal pressure. *See also* **aquifer**.

attrition the reduction in size of particles by friction and impact.

barbed drainage a drainage pattern where the tributaries imply a direction of flow contrary to what actually happens.

boulder clay a deposit that is glacial in origin and made up of boulders of varying sizes in finer grained material, mainly clay.

cavitation characteristic of high-energy river waters where air bubbles collapse, sending out shock waves that impact on the walls of the river bed.

central type volcano a volcano where the lava supply comes from a central vent.

centripetal drainage the flow of streams into a central depression where there may be a lake or river.

chalk a soft, fine-grained sedimentary rock made of calcium carbonate formed mainly from the skeletons and shells of very small marine organisms.

coal a mineral deposit that contains a very high carbon content and occurs in banded layers (*seams*) resembling rock.

composite volcano a *central type* volcano – the lava supply comes from a central vent – shows steep angles of slope because of a build-up of lava and pyroclastic material.

corrasion the use of boulders, pebbles, sand, etc, carried by a river to wear away the floor and sides of a river bed.

corrosion all erosion achieved through solution and chemical reaction with materials encountered in the water.

crystal a solid, the arrangement of the atoms

in which create a specific framework that gives it a characteristic shape.

deflation the removal of loose sand and silt by the wind.

dendritic drainage a random branching unaffected

dormant volcano a volcano which is neither extinct nor active, which may have the potential for eruption.

drainage the movement of water derived from rain, snowfall and the melting of ice and snow on land that results eventually in its discharge into the sea.

earthquake movement of the earth caused by the sudden release of stress that may have accumulated over a long period

erosion the destructive breakdown of rock and soil by a variety of agents that, together with weathering, form denudation, or a wearing away of the land surface.

evaporite a sedimentary rock formed by the evaporation of water containing various salts, resulting in their deposition.

extinct volcano a volcano where the activity ceased a long time ago.

fissure volcano a volcano which erupts through splits where the Earth's crust is under tension.

folds and **faults** geological features that develop through tectonic activity.

fossil fuels fuels that are created by the fossilization of plant and animal remains.

fossils the remains of once living plants and animals that have been preserved (usually) in the rock layers of the Earth.

geochemistry the study of the chemical make-up of the Earth, has also been taken to include other planets and moons within the solar system.

geochronology the study of time on a geological scale.

geological timescale a division of time since the formation of the Earth (4600 million years ago) into units, during which rock sequences were deposited, deformed and eroded. The following table shows the various subdivisions, many of the names owing their derivation to particular locations, rock sequences and so on:

Era	Epoch	Life form
Cenozoic	Recent	modern man.
	Pleistocene	Stone Age man.
	Pliocene	many mammals, elephants.
	Oligocene	pig and ape ancestors.
	Eocene	modern flora and fauna.
	Palaeocene	horse and cattle ancestors.
Mesozoic	Cretaceous	end of the dinosaurs and the ammonites.
	Jurassic	appearance of birds and mammals.
	Triassic	dinosaurs appear; corals of modern type.
Palaeozoic	Permian	amphibians and reptiles more common; conifer trees appear.
	Carboniferous	coal forests reptiles appear, winged insects.
	Devonian	amphibians appear; fishes more common; ammonites appear; early trees; spiders.
	Silurian	first coral reefs; spore-bearing land. plants appear
	Ordovician	first fish-like vertebrates: trilobites and graptolites common.
	Cambrian	first fossils period; trilobites, graptolites, molluscs, crinoids, radiolaria, etc.
	Precambrian	sponges, worms, algae, bacteria; all primitive. forms.

geology the scientific study of the Earth, its origins, structure, processes and composition. It includes a number of topics that have developed into subjects in their own right: geochemistry, mineralogy, petrology (study of rocks), structural geology, geophysics, palaeontology, stratigraphy, economic and physical geology.

geomagnetism the study of the Earth's magnetic (*geomagnetic*) field.

geomorphology the study of *landforms*, their origin and change, that is, the study of the Earth's surface.

geophysics the study of all processes *within* the Earth (that is, the crust and the interior) and concerned with the physical properties of the Earth.

geothermal energy the temperature within the Earth increases with depth. At the edges of some tectonic plates the gradient increases dramatically, and it is sometimes possible to harness this heat as geothermal energy.

glaciation the term meaning an ice age or a part of an ice age when glaciers and ice sheets are enlarged significantly.

glacier an enormous mass of ice, on land, that moves very slowly. They act as powerful agents of erosion on the underlying rocks.

groundwater water that is contained in the voids within rocks, i.e. in pores, cracks and other cavities and spaces.

humus in soil, humus is decomposing (breaking down) organic material that is produced from dead organisms, leaves, and other organic material by the action of bacteria and fungi.

hydrology the study of water and its cycle, which covers bodies of water and how they change.

hypabyssal rocks are small igneous rocks forming from magma at shallow depths.

ice age a period in the history of the Earth when ice sheets expanded over areas that were normally ice-free.

igneous rocks crystallize from magma and formed at the surface as lava flows (*extrusive*) or beneath the surface as *intrusions*, pushing their way into existing rocks.

island arcs an example of volcanic activity associated with subduction at an ocean trench.

juvenile water groundwater generated during and coming from deep magmatic processes.

lava molten rock at about 1100 or 1200°C (2012 or 2192°F) erupted from a volcano or a similar fissure.

limestone a sedimentary rock that is made up mainly of calcite (calcium carbonate, $CaCO_3$) with dolomite ($CaMg(CO_3)_2$).

lithosphere the crust and uppermost part of the mantle of the earth.

loam soil which contains mixtures of sand, silt and clay with organic material. In addition to plant roots, soil contains an enormous number of organisms, including fungi, algae, insects, earthworms, nematodes (roundworms) and several billion bacteria.

magma the fluid, molten rock beneath the surface of the Earth. Magma may undergo many stages of change and movement before being extruded at the surface as *lava*.

marl a lime-rich clay.

metamorphic rocks rocks that are formed by the alteration or recrystallisation of existing rocks by the application of heat, pressure, change in volatiles (gases and liquids), or a combination of these. There are several categories of *metamorphism* based upon the conditions of origin: *regional*—high pressure and temperature as found in *orogenic* (mountain-building) areas; *contact*—where the rocks are adjacent to an igneous body and have been altered by the heat (with little or no pressure); *dynamic*—very high, confined pressure with some heat, as generated in an area of faulting or thrusting, that is, where rock masses slide against each other; *burial*—which involves high pressure and low temperature, e.g. as found at great depth in sequences of sedimentary rocks. The key feature of all metamorphic rocks is that the existing *assemblage* (group) of minerals is changed by the pressure and/ or heat and the presence of volatiles. New minerals grow that are characteristic of the new conditions. Typical metamorphic rocks are schist, slate, gneiss, marble, quartzite and hornfels. Depending on the type of metamorphism, there are systems of classification into *zones* or *grades* where specific minerals appear in response to increasing pressure and/or temperature.

meteoric water groundwater which percolates through the soil.

mineral a naturally occurring inorganic substance that has a definite and characteristic chemical composition and crystal structure. Minerals have particular features and properties

mineralogy the scientific study of minerals, i.e. any chemical element or compound extracted from the Earth. It involves the following properties: colour, crystal form and cleavage, hardness, specific gravity, lustre (how the mineral reflects light) and streak (the colour created by scratching the mineral on a special porcelain plate). Together, these properties help to identify and classify minerals. One of the most important features is the *cleavage*, which is the tendency for minerals to split along particular, characteristic planes that reflect and are controlled by the internal structure of the crystal. The plane of splitting is that which is weakest, because of the atomic structure of the crystal.

Mohs scale a test introduced in 1822 by a German mineralogist, Friedrich Mohs, measures the hardness of minerals,

1 talc	**6** orthoclase (feldspar)
2 gypsum	**7** quartz
3 calcite	**8** topaz
4 fluorite	**9** corundum
5 apatite	**10** diamond

mounds a distinctive feature of permafrost caused simply by the increase in volume that accompanies the freezing of water, which pushes up surface layers of soil.

mountains the upward projection of the earth's surface through the process of *orogeny* or *orogenesis*, involves the accumulation of enormous thicknesses of sediments that are subsequently folded,

faulted and thrusted, with igneous intrusions at depth (plutons of granite), producing rock complexes involving sedimentary, igneous and metamorphic rocks.

ocean ridges in the Earth's crust, a plate boundary where plates are moving apart (constructive).

ocean trenches in the Earth's crust, a plate boundary where plates are moving together (also for young mountain ranges) (destructive).

ore a naturally occurring substance that contains metals or other compounds that are commercially useful and which it is economically feasible to mine for profit.

parallel drainage streams running parallel to each other because of folded rocks or steep slopes with little vegetation.

peat an organic deposit formed from plant debris that is laid down with little or no alteration or decomposition (breakdown) in a waterlogged environment. Peat is produced in bogs, fens, swamps, moors and wetlands, with some variation in peat structure depending upon the acidity of the conditions.

permafrost ground that is permanently frozen except for surface melting in the summer. It is technically defined as being when the temperature is below freezing point for two consecutive years, and it can extend to depths of several hundred feet.

petroleum *or* **crude oil** a mixture of naturally occurring hydrocarbons, formed by the decay of organic matter that, under pressure and increased temperatures, forms oil.

pingo distinctive feature of permafrost which is a large mound, up to 40–50 metres (130–165 feet) high.

plate tectonics a concept that brings together the variety of features and processes of the Earth's crust and accounts for continental drift, sea-floor spreading, volcanic and earthquake activity and crustal structure.

plutonic rocks large igneous bodies forming from magama solidifying at some depth;

polygonal cracks a distinctive feature of permafrost, and the result of contraction caused by cooling in winter.

radial drainage streams flowing outwards from a higher area.

rectangular drainage controlled by faults and joints, the latter often in igneous rocks.

rocks aggregates of minerals or organic matter. They can be divided into three types, based upon the way they are formed: igneous rocks, sedimentary rocks, and metamorphic rocks.

sedimentary rocks rocks that are formed from existing rock sources by the processes of erosion and weathering. They include rocks of organic or chemical origin and can be divided into *clastic* rocks, that is, made of fragments, *organic* or *chemical*. Many sedimentary rocks contain fossils.

seismograph an instrument that is used in the study of earthquakes (*seismology*) to record the shock waves (*seismic waves*) as they spread out from the source.

shield volcano a *central type* volcano. The lava supply comes from a central vent, the sides of which are almost flat because of the rapid flow of the lava.

soil the thin layer of uncompacted material comprising organic matter and minute mineral grains that overlies rock and provides the means by which plants can grow. Soil is formed by the breakdown of rock in a number of ways. The texture of the soil affects its ability to support plants.

stalactites in areas of limestone, created by calcium rich waters trickling through rocks and caves. This deposit builds up very slowly into a stalactite, which projects down from the roof.

stalagmites if water continues to drop on to the ground from a stalactite, a complementary upward growth develops into a stalagmite

stratigraphy the study of stratified rocks, that

is, rocks that were originally laid down in layers. It deals with the position of rocks in geological time and space, their classification and correlation between different areas.

subduction a process at destructive plate boundaries where one tectonic plate dips beneath the other at an oceanic.

talik a zone of unfrozen ground between the active layer (top layer) of permafrost and the permafrost itself.

topsoil soil made up of mosses, lichens and fungi, a mixture of organisms (including bacteria, decayed organic material, weathered rock and *humus*).

transform faults in the Earth's crust, a plate boundary where plates move sideways past each other (conservative).

trap a particular geological configuration where oil is confined by impermeable rocks.

trellis drainage by surface rocks; streams aligned with the trend of underlying rocks.

unconformity a break in the deposition of sedimentary rocks, representing a gap in the geological record.

vadose water water which occurs between the water table and the surface of the Earth

volcanic rocks igneous rocks forming from magma erupted at the surface as lava.

volcano a natural vent or opening in the Earth's crust that is connected by a pipe, or *conduit*, to a chamber at a depth that contains magma. Through this pipe (usually called a *vent*) lava, volcanic gases, steam and ash may be ejected.

water table the level below which water saturates the spaces in the ground; the top of the zone where groundwater saturates permeable rocks. It is where atmospheric pressure is equalled by the pressure in the groundwater.

Legal terms

acquittal the decision by a court that a person prosecuted for a criminal offence is not guilty.

ad valorem in proportion to the value of something.

adjournment the postponing of the hearing of a case

affidavit a written statement that may be presented as evidence.

alibi a defence that a person charged with a

criminal offence was elsewhere when the offence was committed and therefore cannot be responsible for it.

allegation a statement of fact that must be supported by evidence at a trial.

annulment 1 a court ruling that a marriage was never legally valid. **2** the cancellation of a bankruptcy order.

bail the releasing from custody of a person awaiting trial or appealing against conviction.

barrister a member of The Bar and of one of the Inns of Court. A barrister acts upon the instructions of a solicitor. A barrister is also known as counsel.

caveat emptor literally 'let the buyer beware'.

codicil a document that amends a will and must be drawn up in the same way as a will.

constitutional law the law relating to the relationship between a citizen and the state.

contract an agreement that is legally binding, provided a number of conditions are met.

conveyancing the process by which the ownership of property is transferred.

co-respondent a person who is accused of having sexual intercourse with the married partner of someone else.

corroboration evidence that confirms the accuracy of other evidence.

counsel another term for an advocate or a barrister.

criminal law the law of a nation that deals with the definition of offences and the punishment of offenders.

cross-examination the questioning of a witness by someone other than the person who called the witness.

custody 1 holding a person in imprisonment. **2** legal possession or control.

defamation publishing in words or pictures a statement about a person which diminishes his or her reputation.

defence 1 the plea made by a defendant in court. **2** a legal or factual issue that, if given in favour of the defendant, absolves him or her. **3** the colloquial name for the counsel acting for the defendant.

defendant a person against whom court proceedings are brought.

double jeopardy the rule that a person may not be prosecuted twice for the same crime.

duress pressure exerted on a person to act in a particular way.

entrapment encouraging a person to commit an offence with the aim of securing a conviction

ex gratia as a favour and without legal obligation, as in an *ex gratia* payment.

ex officio by virtue of an office held. The Lord Chancellor is, *ex officio*, a member of the government.

ex parte on behalf of.

examination the questioning of a witness under oath.

exhibit an object or document, identified by letter or number, and shown in court.

felony an obsolete term for an offence that is more serious than a misdemeanour.

flagrante delicto in the course of committing an offence. The term is most frequently used in relation to an accusation of adultery.

forbearance deliberate failure to exercise a legal right.

foresight an awareness that an act will have certain consequences.

grand larceny *see* **petty larceny**.

habeas corpus a writ that means literally 'that you have the body', used to challenge the holding of a person in custody.

in flagrante delicto *see* **flagrante delicto**.

in loco parentis literally, 'in the place of a parent'.

in re literally 'in the matter of'.

in rem literally 'against the thing'.

incitement the offence of persuading or attempting to persuade another person to commit an offence.

incommunicado without the ability or means to communicate.

injunction a court order that prohibits a person from doing something (*prohibitory injunction*) or requires a person to do something (*mandatory injunction*).

instrument a written legal document, such as a will or deed.

international law laws that address the rights and obligations of states in the ways they deal with each other.

intra vires literally 'within the power'.

judge an official who is empowered to adjudicate on matters brought before the courts.

judgment the court's decision on a matter that has come before it.

jurisdiction 1 the power of a court to hear a case and make an order. 2 the territorial area within which the court's power may be exercised.

jurisprudence 1 the study of law as a philosophy, as opposed to individual laws or legal systems. 2 the decisions of courts.

juror a member of a jury.

jury a group of jurors who are required to hear a case and reach a verdict.

justice the protection of rights and the punishment of wrongs, which, ideally, a legal system is designed to achieve.

law 1 a rule that is part of a body of law. 2 the rules governing a society that may be enforced.

lease a contract that grants the use of land for a specified period often in return for rent.

legislation 1 the written law of a country, in the UK effectively Acts of Parliament. 2 the making of written law.

legislature the body that makes legislation; in the UK the Crown, the House of Commons and the House of Lords.

liability 1 a legal obligation or duty. 2 an amount owed.

libel a form of defamation made in writing or in images, or in radio or television broadcasts. Unlike slander, libel must be in some permanent form.

licence 1 formal permission to do something which would otherwise be unlawful. 2 permission granted by one person to another to do something, e.g. enter land for a specified purpose.

lien a person's right to hold property belonging to another until such time as any claim against the owner has been settled.

litigation 1 taking legal action. 2 the area of law concerned with contentious matters.

locus standi literally 'the right to stand'. It is the right to bring an action or to challenge a decision.

magistrates voluntary part-time justices of the peace appointed by the Crown and usually have no formal legal training.

malfeasance committing an unlawful act.

malice the attitude of a person who intentionally commits a wrong without just cause.

manslaughter unlawful killing that does not constitute murder and often represents a reduced charge on a number of grounds, including mitigation, gross negligence, and being drunk.

martial law government by the military when civilian rule has broken down or is unable to function for whatever reason.

mens rea literally 'guilty mind'.

misfeasance the improper performance of an otherwise lawful act.

mitigation the lessening or 'softening' of a penalty.

nisi literally 'not final'.

non compos mentis literally 'not of sound mind'.

nonfeasance failure to perform an act that one is lawfully bound to do.

notary or **notary public** a legal official, usually a solicitor, who attests deeds and protests dishonoured bills.

notice knowledge of a fact.

null and void invalid, without force.

objection 1 in court proceedings, an intervention by counsel that asserts that a question put by opposing counsel is improper and should be disallowed, or that a document or exhibit should not be received. 2 in planning law, opposition to an application to build, alter, etc, a building, which plans have had to be advertised so that objections can be raised.

offence the term usually employed to refer to a crime.

offender a person who is guilty of committing a crime.

omnia praesumuntur contra spoliatorem literally 'all things are presumed against a wrongdoer'.

ordinance 1 legislation under the Royal prerogative. 2 a Parliamentary decree that does not have the consent of the House of Lords.

overrule to set aside an earlier court decision, done by statute or by a higher court. The overruling of a judgment on appeal is called reversal of judgment.

pardon the extinguishing of a punishment through exercise of the prerogative of mercy or by Act of Parliament. A pardon excuses a misdemeanour but does not quash a conviction.

parole, also known as **release on licence**, the

early, conditional release of a prisoner following assessment by the Parole Board. Prisoners given specific sentences are automatically eligible for parole after a certain period of time. A prisoner can be recalled to prison during his or her period of parole; a prisoner who commits an offence during the parole period may have to serve the outstanding part of the original sentence.

parties 1 persons who are involved together in litigation. 2 persons who join together in a transaction, such as a contract or deed.

penalty a clearly stated punishment for a crime.

per capita literally 'by heads', distribution of property among all persons entitled to a share of it.

per curiam literally 'by the court', usually abbreviated to *per cur*. The term is used to describe a decision made by the court as a whole rather than the opinion of an individual judge.

per incuriam literally 'through want of care'. A court decision that constitutes a mistake of law, e.g. because it does not apply a statute or ignores a binding precedent.

perjury the offence of knowingly making a false statement when sworn as a witness. Perjury is punishable by a fine or imprisonment.

persona non grata literally 'unacceptable person', the term used to describe a diplomat whose presence is unacceptable to the country to which he or she is accredited.

petty larceny the offence of stealing property worth less than 12 pence. Stealing goods worth more than 12 pence was *grand larceny*. The distinction was abolished in 1827.

plaint a written statement of the cause of an action.

plaintiff a person who brings an action in court to seek redress from another, called the defendant.

plea 1 a response, by or on behalf of an accused person, in the form of a formal statement in court, to the charges made against him or her. 2 in a common-law action, a defendant's answer to a plaintiff's declaration.

plead to put forward a plea.

pleadings in civil actions, formal written statements in which one party to an action states the facts of the allegation against his or her opponent.

precedent a court decision or judgment that is used as the basis for subsequent decisions and judgments. They are usually binding on lower courts when made in higher courts. The principles of the decision, known as *ratio decidendi*, are binding; other parts may not be.

preferment 1 bringing a bill of indictment before a court. 2 bringing a charge against a person.

prima facie case a case in which there is enough evidence in favour of a party to prove his or her case.

prima facie evidence, also known as **presumptive evidence**, evidence that, although not conclusive, offers sufficient proof of a fact; evidence that is sufficient to relieve a party of the burden of proof.

principal 1 the person who actually commits a crime. A person who aids or abets is known as the *secondary party*. 2 the person on whose behalf an agent acts. 3 a sum of money lent or invested.

probation the placing of an offender over the age of 16 under the supervision of a probation officer for a period of six months to three years. The offender must be willing to be bound by the probation order, to be of good behaviour during the probation period, and not to commit other offences.

propositus 1 that person immediately concerned. 2 an ancestor from whom descent is traced. 3 a testator.

prosecution 1 the instituting of legal proceedings, especially criminal proceedings, in the courts. 2 the term used to refer to the party pursuing such proceedings.

prosecutor the person who institutes criminal proceedings, usually in the name of the Crown.

quango an acronym from **qu**asi-**a**utonomous **n**on-**g**overnmental **o**rganization to describe a body appointed by the government but not a government department. It usually has regulatory and operational functions.

Queen's Counsel (QC) a senior barrister who appears for or against the Crown. He or she is appointed on the recommendation of the Lord Chancellor and wears a silk gown.

Queen's evidence evidence given for the Crown by a co-accused person who 'turns Queen's evidence', i.e. confesses guilt and gives testimony against his or her co-accused.

real estate interests in land held by the deceased at the time of his or her death.

real evidence the form of evidence constituted by physical objects that can be shown to a jury.

real property, also known as **realty**, **1** freehold land. **2** property that it would be possible to recover in a real action.

rejoinder the answer of a defendant to the reply of a plaintiff, which can only be served by leave of the court.

release 1 the discharge of a person from custody. **2** renunciation of a claim against another person; a document by which a person discharges another from any claim.

remand holding in custody or releasing on bail a person charged with a crime during an adjournment.

remission prior to 1991, the cancellation of part of a prisoner's sentence, typically one third, for good behaviour.

renvoi literally 'sending back'. In private international law, the application by the courts of one country of the law of another country.

repeal the abrogation of a statute by a later statute. Any transaction completed before repeal is unaffected.

reprieve the formal suspending of the carrying out of a sentence.

repudiation refusal to be bound by the terms of a contract. A person repudiating would usually be in breach of contract.

requisition 1 a demand by an intending purchaser of land for a search for encumbrances. **2** the compulsory taking of property.

rescission a remedy in cases of breach of contract, whereby an injured party may bring the contract to an end by performing no further part of it, recovering any part performed and seeking damages.

respondent a person against whom a petition is presented or an appeal brought.

sans recours literally 'without recourse [to

me]', words used on a bill of exchange to indicate that an endorser is not liable.

satisfaction 1 the fulfilling of a claim. **2** the doctrine that payment, performance or some other act discharges an obligation.

schedule 1 a formal list. **2** an appendix to an Act of Parliament listing supplementary details.

sedition the speaking or writing of words intended to bring into contempt, or incite disaffection against, the Sovereign, the government and the administration of justice of the UK.

sentence the punishment imposed by the court on a person who pleads guilty to an offence or who has been found guilty by a jury. It is usually within the court's discretion to recommend an appropriate sentence.

settlement a disposition of land made by deed or will. Trusts are created and designate the beneficiaries and the terms under which they are to take the property.

sine die literally 'without a day', indefinitely.

slander spoken words that constitute defamation.

solicitor a person qualified to conduct legal proceedings and to give advice on legal matters.

sub judice under judicial consideration, not yet decided. The *sub judice* rule makes it an offence of contempt of court to publish comments that might prejudice a fair trial.

subpoena an order to a person to appear on a certain date in court to give evidence. A person who fails to obey a subpoena is in contempt of court.

sue to make a claim for a remedy through proceedings in the civil courts.

suit 1 a claim in court. **2** also used of litigation in general.

summons in both civil and criminal cases, a court order to a person to appear in court at a specified place on a specified date.

suspended sentence a sentence that the court orders should not take place immediately. A sentence of more than two years cannot be suspended.

tenure the relationship between landlord and tenant that determined the terms on which land was held. The feudal forms of tenure were mostly abolished in the 1920s.

test case an action that determines the legal

position of people who are not party to the action.

testament a will that disposes of a person's personal property but not land; usually refers to a will without that distinction.

testate on death, having left a valid will.

third party any person other than the principals in proceedings, or other than the parties to a contract.

title 1 a person's right of ownership of property, or evidence of that right. **2** the heading of an Act of Parliament.

title deeds documents that show evidence of the rightful ownership of land.

treason a breach of allegiance to the Crown, first defined in 1351. Modern forms of treason include waging war against the sovereign and giving aid and comfort to the sovereign's enemies in times of war.

treaty a written and signed agreement between states and governed by international law.

trespass an unlawful interference with a person or with a person's possession of land or goods. It is an actionable tort and it is not necessary to show that actual damage has been caused.

trial a formal investigation and determination of matters between parties in court. Most trials are conducted in public.

tribunal a body with administrative or judicial powers but outside the court system. Tribunals are usually made up of lawyers and lay people with specialist knowledge and experience. They are convened to hear and judge, for example, industrial disputes.

ultra vires literally 'beyond the powers', a term describing the exceeding of legal powers and authority, especially by a corporation, of those conferred on it.

verdict the decision of a jury as to the guilt or innocence of an accused, and considered in secret after all the evidence has been heard and the judge has summed-up.

void without force, having no legal effect.

waiver abandonment or non-assertion of a legal right.

ward a person who is under the protection and care of another person or the court.

warrant 1 a document authorizing action. **2** a document issued by a magistrate ordering that someone be arrested and brought before the court.

warranty in contract law, a term or promise that, if breached, entitles the innocent party to damages. The term is used colloquially to describe a manufacturer's promise to repair or replace defective goods.

will a declaration of the intentions of a person regarding the disposal of his or her property on death. A will must be in writing and be signed and witnessed by two or more witnesses. A person making a will is called a testator.

witness 1 a person who gives formal or sworn evidence at a hearing. **2** to give evidence or proof.

writ a court order commanding some action or forbearance.

Literary terms

Absurd, Theatre of *see* **Theatre of the Absurd.**

acrostic a type of poem in which the initial letters of each line form a word reading downwards in order.

act a division of a play, the acts often being divided into **scenes**.

allegory a form of narrative in which the characters and events symbolize an underlying moral or spiritual quality, or represents a hidden meaning beneath the literal one.

alliteration a figure of speech in which a sequence of words begin with the same letter or sound.

anagram a kind of literary game in which a word is disguised by changing the order of its letters so as to make a different word.

analogy a figure of speech rather like the **simile** in which there is an inference of a resemblance between two items that are being compared.

Angry Young Men a term used in mid-1950s Britain to refer to a group of English writers who had left-wing sympathies, a dislike of English provincialism and intellectual pretentiousness. John Osborne's play *Look Back in Anger* epitomized this mood.

anthology a collection of short works in either verse or prose by various authors. The term is also used to refer to selected passages from longer works.

anticlimax a figure of speech in which there is a sudden descent from the lofty to the ridiculous or the trivial, as in 'She went home in a flood of tears and a taxi'.

antithesis a figure of speech in which contrasting ideas are balanced for effect, as in 'We need money, not advice', 'More haste, less speed'.

assonance a figure of speech in which vowel sounds are repeated to give a half-rhyme effect, as in 'with gun, drum, trumpet, blunderbuss and thunder'.

autobiography the story of one's own life.

ballad a narrative poem or song in brief stanzas, often with a repeated refrain, and frequently featuring a dramatic incident. Ballads were originally very much part of an oral tradition.

bathos a figure of speech consisting of sudden descent from the lofty or noble to the ridiculous or trivial.

Beat Generation a group of American writers, artists and musicians who were anti-Western in their values and experimented with communal living and communal ownership, Eastern philosophies and the taking of illegal drugs. They were also interested in modern jazz.

Bildungsroman a novel which describes the development of the central character from youth to maturity. The term, which is German for 'education novel' derives from Goethe's *Wilhelm Meister's Apprenticeship*.

black comedy a comedy which contains rather bitter jokes about unpleasant or tragic aspects of life.

blank verse verse which is unrhymed and is usually made up of lines which contain ten syllables and have the stress on every second syllable.

border ballads were based on the violent world of the English/Scottish border area from the late Middle Ages to the 17th cen-

tury. Examples of these include *Sir Patrick Spens* and *Thomas the Rhymer*. *See* **ballad**.

broadside ballads were popular from Elizabethan times in England, dealt with a wide range of subjects of current interest and were printed on a single side of a broadsheet. *See* **ballad**.

canto a term in Italian literature, and literally meaning 'song' used to indicate a division of a long poem. The term has been borrowed into English with the same meaning.

carol a hymn of praise which is especially associated with Christmas.

comedy a form of drama , usually of a light and humorous kind and frequently involving misunderstandings that are resolved in a happy ending.

comedy of humours a form of comedy especially associated with Ben Jonson as in his play *Every Man in his Humour* (1598) in which the characters have names and behaviour appropriate to their dominant humour. This is based on the premise popular in medieval medical theory that there were four principal humours in the body: blood, phlegm, choler or yellow bile and melancholy or black bile. Whichever one of these predominated was thought to determine temperament.

comedy of manners a form of comedy which features intrigues, invariably involving sex and/or money, among an upper section of society. The central characters are usually witty and sophisticated and there is often much mockery of characters from inferior walks of life who try to imitate the behaviour of those who are socially superior to them.

commedia dell'arte a form of Italian **comedy,** popular from the Renaissance until the eighteenth century, which used stock farcical characters and plots as a basis for improvisation.

couplet a pair of rhymed lines of verse of equal length. The most common form is the so-called **heroic couplet** which has ten syllables and five stresses in each line.

deus ex machina a Latin term meaning 'god

from the machine', i.e. a god introduced into the action of a play to resolve a seemingly insoluble situation. The term has come to mean any twist in a plot which resolves or develops the action of a play in an unexpected way.

doggerel a kind of carelessly written, irregular verse, often of a light-hearted or frivolous nature.

dramatic irony a situation in which a character in a play, novel, etc, says or does something that has a meaning for the audience or reader, other than the obvious meaning, that he/she does not understand. Its use is common in both comedy and tragedy.

dramatic monologue a poetic form which invents a character or takes one from history or legend and then makes comments on life, art, etc through the character.

elegy a serious and reflective poem, especially one written as a lament for someone who has died. e.g. *Lycidas* (1637) written by John Milton on the death of his friend Edward King.

end-rhyme end rhymes occur at the end of a line, the most common position.

enjambment the continuing of the sense from line to line in a poem so that it is not appropriate to pause at the end of a line.

epic a word that originally referred to a very long narrative poem dealing with heroic deeds and adventures on a grand scale, as Homer's *Iliad*.

epigram a figure of speech consisting of a brief, pointed and witty saying.

epistolary novel a novel in the form of a series of letters written to and from the main characters, sometimes presented by the author in the anonymous role of 'editor'.

epitaph an inscription on a tomb or a short verse or piece of prose which might serve as this.

euphemism *see* section on **Euphemism**.

existentialism a modern school of philosophy based on a perception of life in which a person is an actor forced to make choices in an essentially meaningless universe that functions as a colossal and cruel **Theatre of the Absurd**. Its main writers are French,

notably Jean-Paul Sartre and Albert Camus.

fable a story that is intended to convey a moral lesson. Fables frequently feature animals that speak and act like human beings. Most famous are those of Aesop.

figure of speech a form of expression used to heighten the effect of a statement. The most commonly known are **similes** and **metaphors**, but there are many more, such as personification.

foot a basic unit of rhythm in poetry composed of a fixed combination of stressed and unstressed, or long and short, syllables.

free verse any form of verse without traditional metrical or stanzaic form. It is usually characterized by 'natural speech' cadences, is dependent on alliteration and the subtle placing of syllabic stresses. It is often unrhymed, although it can be rhymed.

figure of speech a form of expression used to heighten the effect of a statement. The most commonly known are **similes** and **metaphors**, but there are many more, such as **personification**.

Gothic novel a type of novel which was extremely popular in the late 18th century, combining elements of the supernatural and the macabre, often in settings such as ruined abbeys or ancient castles.

haiku a short Japanese poem in three unrhymed lines with an exact number of syllables per line, the syllable pattern being 5-7-5. The traditional subject matter is usually something to do with nature.

heroic couplet *see* **couplet**.

heroic tragedy a form of **tragedy** which became very popular during the **Restoration**. Such tragedies were usually written in bombastic rhymed couplets and featured the adventures in love and war of improbably noble characters in exotic locations, past and present.

humours *see* **comedy of humours**.

hyperbole a figure of speech consisting of exaggeration or over-statement, used for emphasis, as in 'I could eat a horse' and in 'I am boiling in this heat'.

iambic foot the classical verse foot which

consisted of a short syllable followed by a long syllable.

imagism a poetry movement of the early 20th century which advocated using everyday language and precise representation of the image of the subject discussed. The poems were short and to the point and could be of any subject. One of the most prominent imagist poets was Ezra Pound.

internal rhymes internal rhymes occur in the middle of a line rather than at the end of a line. *See* **end-rhyme**.

irony the use of a word or words to convey something that is completely different from the literal meaning, being the direct opposite of one's thoughts, as in 'This is a fine state of affairs' when in fact things have gone wrong.

Jacobean period a term used to indicate the period of the reign of James I (1603–25). The Jacobean period was the first period that was rich in prose. Francis Bacon being one of the best known of the prose writers of the time.

journalese a derogatory name for the style of writing and choice of vocabulary supposedly found in newspapers, such as widespread use of clichés, sensational language and short sentences.

lampoon a personal satirical attack in the form of verse, common in the late 17th and 18th centuries.

lay a term, first used in the medieval period, to refer to a lyrical or narrative work, especially one recited or sung to music.

limerick a humorous five-lined piece of light verse, with the first two lines rhyming with each other, the third and fourth lines rhyming with each other, and the fifth line rhyming with the first line. Usually there are three stressed beats in the first, second and fifth lines and two stressed beats on the third and fourth lines.

literary criticism the formal study, discussion and evaluation of a literary work.

litotes a kind of understatement in which a statement is conveyed by contradicting or denying its opposite, as in 'She's not exactly communicative' (meaning she is silent or reserved).

lyric in ancient Greece the name given to a verse sung to a lyre. In modern English the word is used to refer to most forms of short poetry, especially to those poems which are personal in tone and theme or those which are of a non-narrative kind.

malapropism the incorrect use of a word, often through confusion with a similar-sounding word. Malapropism is called after Mrs Malaprop, a character in a play called *The Rivals* (1775), a comedy by R. B. Sheridan.

masque a form of dramatic entertainment which combined verse, music, dancing and scenic effect and was popular in England between 1580 and 1630, especially at the royal court and among aristocrats.

meiosis a figure of speech using understatement to emphasize the size or importance of something, as in 'He's a decent enough bloke' and 'He's rather a decent tennis player'.

melodrama a form of drama which seems to have first arisen in France in the 18th and which contained elements of music, spectacle, sensational incidents and sentimentalism. The form reached its peak in the popular theatre of 19th century England.

metaphor a figure of speech that compares two things by saying that one thing is another, as in 'He was a lion in the fight' (meaning that he was as brave as a lion). By extension, metaphor refers to a word or phrase used in a sentence where it does not have a literal meaning, as in 'a butter mountain', 'They walked home with leaden feet'.

metaphysical poetry a poetry movement of the 17th century noted for the intense feeling, extended metaphor and striking, elaborate imagery, often with a mystical element. Donne is regarded as the first important metaphysical poet.

metonym a figure of speech in which a word or expression is used to as a substitute for something with which it has a close relationship, as in 'The White House has yet to comment on the proposal' (meaning that the President of the United States has yet to comment on the proposal).

metre the measure of the rhythm of a line of verse when the line can be divided into units of metrical feet. *See* **foot**.

mixed metaphor the situation that occurs when unrelated **metaphors** are put in the same sentence. Examples include 'She sailed into the room with both guns blazing'.

mystery plays *or* **cycle plays** a type of drama performed in England from later 14th century until the later half of the 16th century. The plays consisted of a sequence of episodes or pageants based on events in Christian history and they were often performed on wagons at fixed points in the streets of a town

naturalism a late 19th-century French literary movement denoting fiction characterized by a close observation and documentation of everyday life, and with a strong emphasis on the influence of the material world on individual behaviour. The leading exponent of this school was French novelist Emile Zola.

neoclassicism a term denoting any movement which emphasized the virtues of imitating the style and teachings of the great classical writers and artists. The hallmarks of neoclassicism are traditionally defined as balance, moderation, attention to formal rules, avoidance of emotional display and the assumption that human nature has changed little, if at all, since classical times.

nihilism a philosophical movement originating in mid-19th century Russia which rejected all established authority and values

No *see* **Noh**

Noh a form of highly stylized drama in 14th-century Japan. The typical Noh play is short, slow-paced, draws heavily on classical Japanese symbolism and usually involves song, dance, mime and intricately detailed costume.

novel a sustained fictional prose narrative. The novel, as the term is generally understood, with complex characterization and multi-layered stands of plot and character development, is essentially a creation of 18th-century writers in English.

novella a short version of the novel.

nursery rhyme a, usually traditional, short verse or song sung for children. Many nursery rhymes have their roots in ancient, and sometimes unpleasant, events. An example is 'Ring a Ring o' Roses' which refers to the Great Plague.

ode in ancient Greece, originally a poem intended to be sung, a lyric poem written in an elaborate form and usually dignified in subject and style. The word is now loosely applied to any elaborate lyric poem.

onomatopoeia a figure of speech that uses words whose sound suggests their meaning, as in 'The sausages sizzled in the pan'.

oxymoron a figure of speech that is based on the linking of incongruous or contradictory words, as in 'and honour rooted in dishonour stood' (Tennyson) and 'the wisest fool in Christendom'.

pastoral any piece of literature celebrating the country way of life.

pathetic fallacy a term invented by the critic John Ruskin to refer to the tendency of poets to attribute human emotions or qualities to inanimate objects.

personification a form of **metaphor** that represents an inanimate object or abstract notion as possessing the attributes of a person. For example, Uncle Sam is a personification of the United States of America, while John Bull is a personification of England.

picaresque novel a type of novel in which the hero undergoes an episodic series of adventures, the term being derived from the Spanish word *picaro*, a rogue.

poet laureate a poet appointed to a court or other formal institution. In Britain, the post of poet laureate is held for life and the poet is expected, although not forced, to write a poem to commemorate important events.

pun a play on words based on the use of a word with more than one meaning, or of two words which sound the same. Examples include 'Whether life is worth living or not depends on the liver.'

realism in literature, a true and faithful representation of reality in works of fiction.

Renaissance in literature, the revival which occurred in Europe in the 14th–16th century as a result of the rediscovery of the great writers, notably the works of Plato and Aristotle.

Restoration period the period of the reign of Charles II (1660–85), following the restoration of the British monarchy in 1660.

revenge tragedy a form of **tragedy** which appeared in the late **Elizabethan period**, heavily influenced by bloodthirsty language and the plots of the plays of the Roman poet Seneca, in which revenge, often for the death of a son or father, is the prime motive. The earliest example is *The Spanish Tragedy* (1588–89) by Thomas Kyd, while Shakespeare's *Hamlet* is the greatest example.

rhyme the effect produced by using words that end with the same or similar sounds.

Romanticism a term denoting any movement in the arts which emphasizes feeling and content, as opposed to form and order. The Romantic movement can be roughly dated from the late 18th century to the early 19th century.

semiotics *see* **structuralism**.

sentimental comedy a form of English comedy which arose in the early 18th century and which focused on the problems of middle-class characters. The plays always end happily and feature strongly contrasting good and bad characters and high emotional peaks. The form was developed by Richard Steele in a conscious reaction to the excesses of the comedy of the **Restoration** period (*see* **comedy of manners**).

simile a figure of speech in which something is compared with another and said to be like it. Examples of similes include 'She is like an angel', 'Her hair is like silk'.

sonnet a short poem consisting of 14 lines and a rhyme scheme which conforms to one or other of a variety of patterns. Originally, the subject matter was usually love, although it became more varied after the 16th century.

stream of consciousness the narrative technique in which characters voice their feelings, thoughts, and impressions directly with no authorial comment and no orthodox dialogue or description. Two well-known writers in this genre are James Joyce and Virginia Woolf.

structuralism in literary criticism, a critical approach to literature in which the text being studied is viewed as a cultural product which cannot be read in isolation, the text being held to absorb its meaning from the interconnected pattern of linguistic codes and symbols of which it is but a part. The process of studying the codes, etc. and their relation to each other is known as **semiotics**.

syllepsis *same as* **zeugma**.

symbolism a French poetry movement of the late 19th century which rejected the philosophy of both **realism** and **naturalism** by seeking to express a state of mind by a process of suggestion, rather than by attempting to portray objective reality.

synecdoche a figure of speech in which the part is put for the whole. For example, in 'The power of the sceptre is fading', 'sceptre' is used for 'monarch'; in 'The country has a fleet of a hundred sail', 'sail' is used for 'ship'.

Theatre of the Absurd a form of theatre developed in the 1960s which characterized the human condition as one of helplessness in the face of an irrational, absurd universe. The characters in such plays, of which the best known are by Samuel Beckett and Harold Pinter, tend to communicate in disjointed, inconsequential language.

tragedy a form of drama in which a hero or heroine comes to a bad end. The cause of this unfortunate state of affairs can either be a personal flaw in the hero or heroine, circumstances beyond his or her control, or a combination of these two factors.

tragicomedy a term usually reserved to describe plays in which all of the action seems to be leading inevitably towards a tragic ending, but resolves itself more or less happily at the end.

zeugma or **syllepsis** a figure of speech that uses a single word to apply to two words that are not appropriate to each other, as in 'We collected our coats and our baby', 'She left the building and her job' and 'She left in a taxi and a fit of hysterics'. Zeugma is similar to **bathos**.

Mathematics

acute angle an angle between 0° and 90°.

addition the act or result of adding.

algebra the branch of mathematics dealing with the properties and relations of numbers; the generalization and extension of arithmetic.

aliquant being a part of a number that does not divide it without a remainder, as eight is the aliquant part of 25.

aliquot being a part of a number of quantity that will divide it without a remainder, as eight is the aliquot part of 24.

arithmetic computation (addition, subtraction, etc) using real numbers; calculation.

arithmetic series the sum of the terms in a sequence of quantities.

associative having elements whose result is the same despite the grouping.

base a base is the number raised to a certain power, which will produce a fixed number.

binary system a type of code in arithmetic that uses a combination of the two digits 0 and 1, expressed to the base 2.

binomial an expression or quantity consisting of two terms connected by the sign plus (+) or minus (−).

binomial theorem the general algebraic formula, discovered by Newton, by which any power of a binomial quantity may be found with performing the progressive multiplication.

biquadratic pertaining to the fourth power. The fourth power, arising from the multiplication of a square number or quantity by itself.

bisect to divide into two equal parts.

Boolean algebra a system of symbolic logic used in the manipulation of sets and other mathematical entities, and in computing science.

bow compass a compass with jointed legs.

calculate to reckon or compute by mathematics.

calculus a system of mathematical rules which considers small increments of a variable x.

coefficient a numerical or constant factor in an algebraic term.

commutative having a result that is independent of the order in which the elements are combined.

complement the quantity by which an angle falls short of 90°.

complementary angles two angles totalling 90°.

complex fraction a fraction with fractions for the numerator or denominator or both.

complex number a number having both real and imaginary parts.

cos *abbr* = cosine.

cosine in a right-angled triangle, the sine of a complement of an angle.

covers *abbr* = coversed sine.

coversine the versed sine of the complement of an angle or arc.

cube root the number that gives the stated number when cubed.

decimal numbers a structured system of numbers based on ten.

decrement a negative increment of a variable.

denominator the number below the line in a vulgar fraction.

dependent variable in a mathematical expression, the quantity with a value that depends on the other independent variables.

derivative the rate of change of one quantity with respect to another; differential coefficient

determinant an algebraic term expressing the sum of certain products arranged in a square or matrix.

difference the result of the subtraction of one number from another.

differential relating to increments in given functions; relating to, or using, a difference.

differential calculus a system of mathematical rules which considers the values of ratios of differentials and the corresponding changes in a function, to find the rate at which a function in changing.

differential coefficient derivative.

differentiate to calculate the derivative of.

differentiation a procedure used in calculus for finding the derivative of a function. The calculation of a differential.

discontinuity a function that is discontinuous.

discontinuous of a function that varies discontinuously and whose differential coefficient may therefore become infinite.

disjoint having no elements in common.

distance the length of a line needed to join particular points.

divide to ascertain how many times one quantity contains another.

division the process of dividing one number by another.

ellipse a closed plane figure formed by the plane section of a right-angled cone; a flattened circle.

ellipsoid an elliptical spheroid; an oval.

ellipticity the extent of deviation of an oval from a circle or sphere.

epicycle a small circle, the centre of which is situated on the circumference of a larger circle.

epicycloid a curve described by a point in the circumference of one circle which rolls round the circumference of another circle.

equation a formal statement of equivalence (as in logical and mathematical expressions) with the relations denoted by the sign $=$.

Euclidean pertaining to or accordant with the geometrical principles of Euclid, the Greek mathematician (fl 3rd century BC).

exponent a symbol, usually a number, that appears as a superscript to the right of a mathematical expression and indicates the power to which an expression is raised.

exponential function a mathematical function in which the constant quantity of the expression is raised to the power of a variable quantity, i.e. the exponent.

exponential having a variable in an exponent; expressed by an exponential function.

expression a collection of symbols serving to express something.

factor any of two or more numbers that, when multiplied together, form a product; a person who acts for another.

factorial an integer multiplied by all lower integers, e.g. $4 \times 3 \times 2 \times 1$.

figure a geometrical form.

flexure the curving of a line or surface.

fluxion differential calculus.

fraction a quantity less than a whole, expressed as a decimal or with a numerator and denominator.

frustum (pl **frustums, frusta**) the part of a cone, pyramid, etc, left after the top is cut off.

function a quantity whose value depends on the varying value of another.

geodesic the shortest distance between two points on a curved surface, determined by triangulation.

geometric progression a sequence in which the terms differ by a constant ratio (e.g. 1, 2, 4, 8, 16…).

geometry the branch of mathematics dealing with the properties, measurement, and relationships of points, lines, planes, and solids.

googol the figure 1 followed by 100 zeroes (expressed as 10^{100}).

googolplex the figure 1 followed by a googol of zeroes (expressed as 10googol or $10^{10^{100}}$).

helicoid resembling a flattened spiral; a spirally curved geometrical figure.

helix (pl **helices, helixes**) a curve in the form of a spiral, which encircles the surface of a cone or cylinder at a constant angle.

horizontal being at right-angles with the vertical and parallel to the horizon.

hyperbola (pl **hyperbolas, hyperbolae**) a curve formed by a plane intersecting a cone at a greater angle to its base than its side.

hypocycloid a curve traced by the point on the circumference of a circle, which rolls on to the inside of another circle.

hypotenuse the side of a right-angled triangle opposite the right angle.

icosahedron (pl **icosahedrons, icosahedra**) a solid bounded by 20 plane faces.

independent variable a variable that may have any value, which does not depend upon the value of the other quantities present.

infinity (∞) an unlimited number, quantity, or time period.

information theory statistical analysis of information communication systems.

integer any member of the set consisting of the positive and negative whole numbers and zero, such as -5, 0, 5.

integral calculus the determination of definite and indefinite integrals and their use in the solution of differential equations.

integral the value of the function of a variable whose differential coefficient is known.

integrate to find the integral of.

integration a branch of calculus using various types of formulae.

intercept a point of intersection of two geometric figures; interception by an interceptor.

interpolate to estimate a value between two known values.

involution the process of raising an arithmetical or algebraic quantity to a given power.

irrational number a real number (e.g. π) that cannot be expressed as the result of dividing one integer by another.

isogon a figure with equal angles.

linear equation any equation containing two variables and of the general form $y = mx + c$, where x and y are the variables, m is the slope of the line and c is the intercept or the point where the curve crosses the y-axis.

locus (*pl* **loci**) the path of a point or curve, moving according to some specific rule; the aggregate of all possible positions of a moving or generating element.

logarithm the exponent of the power to which a fixed number (the base) is to be raised to produce a given number, used to avoid multiplying and dividing when solving problems.

lune a figure formed on a plane or sphere by two intersecting arcs of circles.

magnitude the absolute value or length of a physical or mathematical quantity.

mantissa the decimal part of a logarithm.

mathematics the science dealing with quantities, forms, space, etc and their relationships by the use of numbers and symbols.

matrix (*pl* **matrices, matrixes**) an array of elements, i.e. numbers or algebraic symbols, set out in rows and columns.

maximal in an ordered set, the member last in order.

medial of or in the middle; mean; average; pertaining to or denoting an average; median.

minuend the number from which another number is to be subtracted.

mixed number a number that is a combination of an integer and a fraction.

modulus (*pl* **moduli**) the measure of the value quantity regardless of its sign.

multinomial an expression that consists of the sum of several terms, a polynomial.

multiple a number exactly divisible by another.

multiplication table a list of multiples of a particular number.

n *abbr* = indefinite number.

natural numbers the whole numbers..

negative denoting a quantity less than zero, or one to be subtracted.

node the point at which a curve crosses itself; the point of rest in a vibrating body.

nth of or having an unspecified number.

numerator the number or quantity to be divided by the denominator of a fraction.

numerical value the absolute value of a number.

oblique angle any angle that does not equal 90° (right angle) or any multiple of 90°.

obtuse angle any angle that lies between but does not equal 90° and 180°.

octahedron a geometrical solid that consists of eight equilateral triangular faces.

order of magnitude the approximate size of an object or quantity usually expressed in powers of 10.

ordinal number 1st, 2nd etc., rather than 1, 2 etc (cardinal numbers).

ordinate one of the coordinates of a point; a straight line in a curve terminated on both sides by the curve and bisected by the diameter; the vertical or y-axis in a geometrical diagram for Cartesian co-ordinates.

origin in a graph, the point of intersection of the horizontal (x) and the vertical (y) axes.

osculate to make contact (with).

parabola the curve formed by the cutting of a cone by a plane parallel to its side.

parameter an arbitrary constant, the value of which influences the content but not the structure of an expression.

parentheses the curved brackets ( ) used to group terms or as a sign of aggregation in a mathematical or logical expression.

partial fractions the simple fractions into which a larger fraction may be separated so that the sum of the simpler fractions equals the original fraction.

Pascal's triangle an array of numbers in the shape of a pyramid starting with 1, such that each number is the sum of the two numbers in the row directly above it.

perimeter the curve or line bounding a closed figure; the length of this.

pi the Greek letter (π) used as a symbol for the ratio of the circumference to the diameter of a circle, approx. 3.14159.

polar axis the diameter of a sphere which passes through both poles.

polynomial an expression consisting of a sum of terms each of which is a product of a constant and one or more variables raised to a positive or zero integral power.

positive greater than zero, plus.

postulate an unproved assumption taken as basic; an axiom.

power notation the use of a small number (an exponent) placed next to an ordinary number to show how many times the ordinary number is multiplied by itself.

power the result of continued multiplication of a quantity by itself a specified number of times.

prime of a number, divisible only by itself and 1.

probability the ratio of the chances in favour of an event to the total number.

problem a proposition stating something to be done; an intricate unsettled question.

product the number obtained by multiplying two or more numbers together.

progression a series of numbers, each differing from the succeeding according to a fixed law.

proportion the equality of two ratios; a share or quota.

proposition a problem to be solved.

quadrangle a plane figure with four sides and four angles, a rectangle; a court enclosed by buildings.

quadrant a quarter of the circumference of a circle; an arc of 90 degrees; an instrument with such an arc for measuring angles, altitudes, or elevations; a curved street.

quadratic square; involving the square but no higher power.

quadratic equation an equation involving the square and no higher power of the unknown quantity.

quadrature the finding of a square with an area exactly equal to a circle or other figure or a surface.

quadrilateral any geometric shape that has four sides, e.g. a rectangle, square, kite, parallelogram, or rhombus; a combination or group that involves four parts or individuals.

quartic pertaining to the fourth power, biquadratic; the fourth power, arising from the multiplication of a square number or quantity by itself.

quaternary with four variables.

quaternion the number 4; a set of 4; a calculus or method of investigation using a generalized complex number with four components.

quotient the result arrived at when a quantity is divided by another quantity.

quotient rule a mathematical method used in calculus.

radius (*pl* **radii**) a straight line joining the centre of a circle or sphere to its circumference; a thing like this, a spoke; a sphere of activity.

radix (*pl* **radices, radixes**) a number that is the base of a number system or for computation of logarithms.

rational number a number expressed as the ratio of two integers.

real number any rational or irrational number.

reciprocal an expression so related to another that their product is 1; the inverse of a fraction.

reduction the conversion of a fraction into decimal form.

reflex (of an angle) of more than 180°.

regression the connection between the expected value of a random variable and the values of one or more possibly related variables.

remainder the result of subtraction; the quantity left over after division.

result an outcome; a value obtained by mathematical calculation.

right angle an angle of 90°.

root the factor of a quantity which multiplied by itself gives the quantity.

round circular, spherical, or cylindrical in form; expressed to the nearest ten, hundred, etc, not fractional; to express as a round number; to complete; to go or pass around.

scalar having magnitude but not direction.

scale a graduated measure; an instrument so marked; the basis for a numerical system, 10 being that in general use.

scalene having three sides of unequal length.

section the cutting of a solid by a plane; a plane figure formed by this.

sector a space enclosed by two radii of a circle and the arc they cut off.

series (*pl* **series**) a progression of numbers or quantities according to a certain law.

set the totality of points, numbers, or objects that satisfy a given condition.

set theory the branch of mathematics concerned with the relations and properties of sets.

sigma the 18th letter of the Greek alphabet (Σ), related to S and used as a symbol indicating summation.

sign a conventional mark used to indicate an operation to be performed.

significant figures the digits in a number that contribute to its value.

similar corresponding exactly in shape if not size.

simple fraction a fraction in which both the numerator and denominator are whole numbers.

simultaneous equations two or more equations with two or more unknown variables, which may have a unique solution.

sine in a right-angled triangle, the ratio of the side opposite an angle to the hypotenuse.

solid geometry geometry of three-dimensional figures.

square root ($\sqrt{}$) a number that when multiplied by itself produces a given number (*2 is the square root of 4*).

statistics the branch of mathematics dealing with the collection, analysis and presentation of numerical data.

sum the result of an addition.

superpose to place (a geometric figure) on top of another so that their outlines coincide; to lay (something) on top of something else.

surd a number containing an irrational root; an irrational number.

take to subtract (from).

tangent a straight line that just touches the circumference of a circle; a function of an angle in a right-angled triangle, defined as the ratio of the side opposite the angle to the length of the side adjacent to it.

topology the study of the properties of geometric figures that are unaffected by distortion.

torus (*pl* **tori**) a donut-shaped ring that is generated by rotating a circle about an axis.

triangle a plane figure with three angles and three sides.

trigonometric function any of various functions (e.g. sine, cosine, tangent) expressed as ratios of the sides of a right-angled triangle.

trigonometry the branch of mathematics concerned with calculating the angles of triangles or the lengths of their sides.

trinomial a polynomial consisting of three terms.

unit the smallest whole number, 1.

unity the number or numeral 1; a quantity assuming the value of 1.

V *abbr* = vector; velocity.

vanish to become zero.

variable a changing quantity that can have different values, as opposed to a constant.

vertex (*pl* **vertexes, vertices**) the point at which two sides of a polygon or the planes of a solid intersect.

vinculum a horizontal line over quantities having the effect of a parenthesis.

vulgar fraction an ordinary fraction with one number (numerator) over the other (denominator). *Also* **simple fraction**.

whole number an integer or natural number.

x an algebraic variable; the x-axis or a coordinate along the x-axis.

x-axis the axis of a graph of the Cartesian coordinate system that lies on a horizontal plane.

x-coordinate a coordinate along the x-axis.

y an algebraic variable; the y-axis or a coordinate along the y-axis.

y-axis the axis of a graph of the Cartesian coordinate system that lies on the vertical plane.

y-coordinate a coordinate along the y-axis.

z an algebraic variable; the z-axis.

z, Z the third unknown quantity.

Music

a cappella *or* **alla capella** (*Italian*) literally 'in the chapel style'; unaccompanied choral singing.

accent the emphasis given to specific notes to indicate rhythm.

answer the second entry of the main subject (theme) of a fugue which is played a fifth higher or lower than the first entry.

anticipation the sounding of a note (or notes) of a chord before the rest of the chord is played.

archi (*Italian*) literally 'bows'. A term that refers to all stringed instruments played with a bow.

aria (*Italian*) a song or air. Originally the term was used for any song for one or more voices but it has come to be used exclusively for a long, solo song as found in oratorio and opera.

arioso (*Italian*) literally 'like an aria'.

arrangement an adaptation of a piece of music for a medium different from that for which it was originally composed.

atonal music music that is not in any key. Atonal music is particularly associated with the works of Schoenberg.

augmentation the lengthening of the time values of notes in melodic parts with the result that they sound more impressive and grand. The opposite of augmentation is diminution.

bass the lowest adult male voice; an addition to the instrument name to indicate the largest member of a family of instruments (except where contrabass instruments are built).

beat a unit of rhythmic measure in music, indicated to a choir or orchestra by the movement of a conductor's baton.

bel a unit used in the measurement of the intensity of sound, named after its inventor, Alexander Graham Bell (1847–1922).

brace the vertical line, usually with a bracket, which joins two staves of music to indicate that they are played together.

break in jazz, a short, improvised, solo passage; the point in a vocal or instrumental range where the register changes.

breve originally the short note of music (*c*.13th century), but as other notes have been introduced, it is now the longest note and is only occasionally used. Also **double whole note**.

broken octaves a term used to describe a passage of notes that are played alternately an octave apart; they frequently occur in piano music.

cadence literally a 'falling', a term used to describe the concluding phrase at the end of a section of music.

cadenza (*Italian*) literally 'cadence', but it has come to have two specific meanings: **1** an elaborate ending to an operatic aria. **2** a flourish at the end of a passage of solo music in a concerto.

cancel a note which is neither sharpened nor flattened. Also **natural**.

changing note *or* **cambiatta** a dissonant passing note which is a third away from the preceding note, before being resolved.

choir the place, defined by special seats or 'choir stalls', in a large church or cathedral where singers are positioned; a body of singers, such as a male-voice choir, church choir; a section of the orchestra, e.g. 'brass choir'.

choral pertaining to music that involves a chorus, e.g. choral symphony.

chord a combination of notes played simultaneously, usually not less than three.

chorus a body of singers. *See* **choir**; music written for a body of singers (usually to follow an introductory piece); a refrain that follows a solo verse.

chromatic *adj* (from Greek *chromatikos,* 'coloured') pertaining to notes which do not belong to a prevailing scale, e.g. in C major all sharps and flats are chromatic notes. The *chromatic scale* is a scale of twelve ascending or descending half steps (semitones); and a *chromatic chord* is a chord that contains chromatic notes. *See also* **twelve-note music**.

classical pertaining to a certain form of music which adheres to basic conventions and forms that are more concerned with carefully controlled expression rather than unrestrained emotion; a term used to describe 'serious' music as opposed to popular music.

clef a symbol positioned on a line of a stave which indicates the pitch of the line and consequently all the notes on the stave. Three clefs are commonly used: alto (tenor), treble and bass.

coda (*Italian*) literally a 'tail', meaning a passage at the end of a piece of music which rounds it off.

codetta (*Italian*) a 'little tail', i.e. a shorter version of a coda.

combination tone a faint (third) note that is heard when two notes are sounded simultaneously; it is also called a 'resultant tone.'

common chord a major or minor chord, usually consisting of a keynote and its third and fifth.

compass the musical range of a voice or instrument.

composer an author of music.

composition a work of music; the putting together of sounds in a creative manner; the art of writing music.

compound interval an interval which is greater than an octave.

compound time musical time in which each beat **1** in a bar is divisible by three, e.g. 6/8, 9/8 and 12/8 time.

concert pitch the internationally agreed pitch, according to which A above middle C (in the middle of the treble clef) is fixed at 440 hertz (cycles per second).

concord a combination of sounds (such as a chord) that are satisfactory and sound agreeable. The opposite of dissonance.

conducting the art of directing and controlling an orchestra or choir (or operatic performance) by means of gestures.

conjunct a succession of notes of different pitch.

contralto the lowest female voice, which usually has a range of about two octaves.

counterpoint the combination of two or more independent melodic lines that fit together to create a coherent sound texture.

counter-subject a melody, found in a fugue, that is contrapuntal to the main theme (subject), i.e. after singing the subject, a voice carries on to sing the counter-subject while the answer is sung.

counter-tenor the highest natural male voice (not to be confused with falsetto).

couplet the same as duplet; a two-note slur; a song in which the same music is repeated for every stanza.

croche (*French*) an eighth note (quaver).

cross rhythms rhythms that appear to have conflicting patterns and are performed at the same time as one another.

crotchet (quarter note) a note with a quarter of the time value of a whole note (semibreve).

decibel one tenth of a bel, a unit for measuring sound. A decibel represents the smallest change in loudness that can be detected by the average human ear.

degree a step of a scale; the position of each note on a scale is identified by its degree.

diatonic belonging to a scale. The diatonic notes of a major scale consist of five tones **1** (T) and two half steps (semitones) (S), arranged ttsttts. *Compare* **chromatic**.

diminished interval a perfect or major interval reduced by one half step (semitone) by flattening the upper note or sharpening the lower one.

diminution the shortening of note time-values, so that a melody is played more quickly, usually at double speed.

direct a sign placed at the end of a line or page of old music that indicates the pitch of the following note or notes.

discord a chord or combination of notes which creates an unpleasant or jarring sound that needs to be resolved.

dissonance the creation of an unpleasant sound or discord.

dodecaphonic relating to dodecaphony, the twelve-note system of composition.

doh the spoken name for the first note of a major scale in tonic sol-fa.

dominant 1 the fifth note above the tonic of a major or minor scale. **2** the name given to the reciting note of Gregorian chants.

Dorian mode a term applied to the ascending scale which is played on the white keys of a piano beginning at D.

dot a mark used in musical notation. When it is placed after a note, it makes the note half as long again; when it is placed above a note it indicates staccato.

double 1 a word used to describe certain instruments that are built an octave lower

double whole note   **half note**

than normal, e.g. a double bassoon (also called a 'contrabassoon') is built an octave lower than a standard bassoon. **2** a term used to describe a type of variation found in 17th-century French instrumental music in which melody notes are embellished with ornamentation.

double whole note *see* **breve**.

duet a combination of two performers or a composition for such a pair, e.g. piano duet.

duple time a form of musical time in which the number of beats in a bar is a multiple of two, e.g. 2/4 (two quarter notes) and 6/8 (six eighth notes in two groups of three).

duplet a group of two notes of equal value which are played in the time normally taken by three.

dynamic accents accents which correspond to the regular rhythm of a piece of music, as indicated by the time signature.

eighth-note a note which is half the length of a quarter note and the eighth of a semibreve (whole note). Known in British notation as a **quaver**.

enharmonic intervals intervals that are so small that they do not exist on keyboard instruments; an example is the interval from A sharp to B flat.

episode **1** in a fugue, a passage that connects entries of the subject. **2** in a rondo, a contrasting section that separates entries of the principal theme.

eurhythmics a system of teaching musical rhythm by graceful physical movements. It was invented in 1905 by Émile Jaques-Dalcroze, whose training institute was founded in Dresden in 1910 .

expressionism a term borrowed from the visual arts which implies the expression of inner emotions.

fa in the tonic sol-fa, the fourth degree in any major scale.

faburden literally 'false bass' or 'drone', the lowest of three voices in the English 15th-century improvised harmonization of plainsong melody.

false relation in harmony, the occurrence of a note bearing an accidental, which is immediately followed, in another part, by the same note which does not bear an accidental, or vice versa.

falsetto (*Italian*) an adult male voice, used in the register above its normal range. It has often been used, to comic effect, in operas.

fanfare a flourish of trumpets, or other instruments (e.g. the organ) that imitate the sound of trumpets.

fifth an interval of five notes (the first and last notes are counted) or seven semitones (half steps), e.g., from C to G.

figure a short musical phrase that is repeated in the course of a composition.

figured bass the bass part of a composition which has numerical figures written below the notes to indicate how the harmony above should be played.

fingering a type of notation that indicates which fingers should be used to play a piece of music.

flat 1 a note which is lowered by one semitone (half step) as indicated by the flat sign. **2** a note (or notes) produced at too low a pitch and hence 'out of tune.'

form the structure of a composition. The basic elements of musical composition which define a given piece's form are repetition, variation and contrast. Examples of recognized forms include fugue, rondo, sonata form, etc.

fourth an interval of four notes (including the first and last) or five semitones (half step), e.g. C to F.

fugue a contrapuntal composition for two or more parts (commonly called 'voices') which enter successively in imitation of each other.

G string the fourth on the violin; third on viola, 'cello, and guitar; first on doublebass.

gamut **1** the note G on the bottom line of the bass clef. **2** an alternative (now obsolete) word for the key of G. **3** the whole range of musical sounds, from the lowest to the highest, hence the common phrase 'to run the gamut'.

grace note an ornamental, extra note, usually written in small type, used to embellish a melody.

gradation by degrees of the scale.

half note a note, formerly the shortest in time-value, with half the value of a whole note (semibreve); the equivalent to a minim in British terminology.

half step, half tone a pitch interval halfway between two whole tones; the smallest interval regularly used in modern Western music.—also known as a **semitone**.

harmonics the sounds that can be produced on stringed instruments by lightly touching a string at one of its harmonic nodes, i.e. at a half-length of a string, quarter-length and so on.

harmony 1 the simultaneous sounding of two or more notes, i.e chords. A harmonious sound is an agreeable or pleasant sound (concord); but harmonization may also produce sounds, which to some ears at least, are unpleasant (discord). **2** the structure and relationship of chords.

heterophony (*Greek*) literally 'difference of sounds', i.e. two or more performers playing different versions of the same melody simultaneously.

hexachord a scale of six notes which was used in medieval times.

homophony a term applied to music in which the parts move 'in step' and do not have independent rhythms. *Compare* **polyphony**.

hook the black line attached to the stem of all notes of less value than a quarter note.

improvisation the art of playing or 'inventing' music that has not already been composed, i.e. spontaneous composition. Some forms of music (especially jazz) often rely heavily on the ability of performers to improvise certain sections.

indeterminacy a term used by John Cage to describe music that does not follow a rigid notation but leaves certain events to chance or allows performers to make their own decisions when performing it.

inflected note a note with an accidental placed before it, i.e. it is sharpened or flattened.

interlude a title sometimes used for a short part of a complete composition; e.g. a piece of music performed between the acts of an opera.

intermezzo (*Italian*) **1** a short piece of piano music. **2** a short comic opera performed between the acts of a serious opera, especially in the 16th and 17th centuries.

interpretation the way in which a performer plays a piece of composed music. No composer can possibly indicate exactly how a piece should be played and, to some degree, it is up to the performer to play it as he or she thinks fit.

interval the gap or 'sound distance', expressed numerically, between any two notes, i.e. the difference in pitch between two notes. For example, the interval between C and G is called a fifth because G is the fifth note from C. *Perfect intervals* are intervals that remain the same in major and minor keys (i.e. fourths, fifths, octaves.)

intonation a term used to describe the judgement of pitch by a performer.

inversion a term which literally means turning upside down. It can refer to a chord, interval, theme, melody or counterpoint.

Ionian mode a mode which, on the piano, uses the white notes from C to C.

isorhythm a term used to describe a short, rhythm pattern that is repeatedly applied to an existing melody which already has an distinct rhythm.

key signature the sign (or signs) placed at the beginning of a composition to define its key. A key signature indicates all the notes that are to be sharpened or flattened in the piece; should a piece move temporarily into another key, the relevant notes can be identified with accidentals.

la (lah) 1 the note A. **2** in the tonic sol-fa, the sixth note (or submediant of the major scale).

leger lines, ledger lines short lines added above or below a stave to indicate the pitch of notes that are too high or low to be written on the stave itself.

ligature 1 a 12th-century form of notation for a group of notes. **2** a slur indicating that a group of notes must be sung to one syllable. **3** the tie used to link two notes over a bar line. **4** the metal band fixing the reed to the mouthpiece of a clarinet etc.

Lydian mode 1 a scale used in ancient Greek music, the equivalent of the white notes on a piano from C to C. **2** from the Middle Ages onwards, the equivalent of a scale on the white notes on a piano from F to F.

lyric a short poem, or sequence of words, for a song. The term has a particular application to 20th-century musicals and pop songs.

manual   **opus**

manual a keyboard on an organ or harpsi-
chord; organs may have four manuals,
named Solo, Swell, Great, and Choir.

measure a bar.

mediant the third note in a major or minor
scale above the tonic (lowest note), e.g. E
in the scale of C major.

melody a succession of notes, of varying
pitch, that create a distinct and identifiable
musical form. Melody, harmony and
rhythm are the three essential ingredients
of music. The criteria of what constitutes a
melody change over time.

mezzo (*Italian*) literally 'half', so *mezzo-soprano* means a voice between soprano and
contralto.

microtones intervals that are smaller than a
semitone in length, e.g. the quarter-tone.

middle C the note C which occupies the first
ledger line below the treble staff, the first
ledger line above the bass staff, and is indicated by the C clef.

minim a note, formerly the shortest in time-
value, with half the value of a whole note
(semibreve); the equivalent of a half-note
in US terminology.

minor (*Latin*) 'less' or 'smaller'. Minor intervals contain one semitone less than major.
The minor third is characteristic of scales
in the minor mode.

Mixolydian mode 1 The set of notes, in ancient Greek music, which are the equivalent of the white notes on a piano from B
to B. 2 in church music of the Middle Ages
onwards, the equivalent of the white notes
on a piano from G to G.

modes the various sets of notes or scales
which were used by musicians until the concept of the key was accepted (*c*.1650).
Modes were based on what are now the
white notes of the piano.

modulation the gradual changing of key during the course of a part of a composition by
means of a series of harmonic progressions.

monody a type of accompanied solo song
which was developed during the late-16th
and early 17th centuries. It contained dramatic and expressive embellishments and
devices, and consequently had an influence
on opera.

mordent a musical ornament whereby one
note rapidly alternates with another one

degree below it; this is indicated by a sign
over the note.

motif (motive) a small group of notes which
create a melody or rhythm, e.g. the first
four notes of Beethoven's 5th symphony
form a motif.

movement a self-contained section of a larger
instrumental composition, such as a symphony.

musicology the scientific study of music.

mutation stops organ stops that produce
sound, usually a harmonic, which is different from the normal or octave pitch corresponding to the key which is depressed.

mute any device used to soften to reduce the
normal volume, or alter the tone, of an instrument.

natural *see* **cancel.**

ninth an interval of nine notes, in which both
the first and last notes are counted.

nonet a group of nine instruments, or a piece
of music for such a group.

note 1 a sound which has a defined pitch
and duration. 2 a symbol for such a sound.
3 the key of a piano or other keyboard instrument.

nuance a subtle change of speed, tone, etc.

o when placed over a note in a musical score
for strings, indicates that the note must be
played on an open string or as a harmonic.

oblique motion two parallel melody lines, or
parts: one moves up or down the scale while
the other stays on a consistent note.

octave an interval of eight notes, inclusive
of the top and bottom notes, e.g. C to C.

octet a group of eight instruments, or a piece
for such a group.

open string any string on an instrument that
is allowed to vibrate along its entire length
without being stopped.

opera a dramatic work in which all, or most,
of the text is sung to orchestral accompani-
ment. The word stands for *opera in
musica* (*Italian*), meaning a 'musical work'.

operetta a short opera or a term taken to
mean an opera with some spoken dialogue,
and a romantic plot with a happy ending.

opus (*Latin*) 'work'; a term used by composers (or their cataloguers) to indicate the
chronological order of their works. It is
usually abbreviated to Opus and is followed
by the catalogued number of the work.

oratorio the musical setting of a religious or epic libretto for soloists, chorus and orchestra, performed without the theatrical effects of stage and costumes, etc.

orchestra a group of instruments and their players. A standard orchestra contains four families of instruments: strings, woodwind, brass and percussion.

orchestration the art of writing and arranging music for an orchestra.

ornaments and graces embellishments to the notes of a melody, indicated by symbols or small notes.

overture a piece of music that introduces an an opera, oratorio, ballet or other major work. However, a concert overture is often an independent piece, written for performance in a concert hall.

parameter a 20th-century term used to describe aspects of sound that can be varied but which nevertheless impose a limit. It is particularly applied to electronic music with regard to volume, etc.

part a voice or instrument in a group of performers, or a piece of music for it.

passing note a note that is dissonant with the prevailing harmony but which is nevertheless useful in making the transition from one chord or key to another.

pause a symbol over a note or rest to indicate that this should be held for longer than its written value.

pentatonic scale a scale composed of five notes in an octave. It is found in various types of folk music from Scottish to Chinese.

perfect interval *see* **interval**.

philharmonic (*Greek*) literally, 'music loving'; an adjective used in the titles of many orchestras, societies, etc.

phrase a short melodic section of a composition, of no fixed length, although it is often four bars long.

polyphony (*Greek*) literally, 'many sounds', i.e. a type of music in which two or more parts have independent melodic lines, arranged in counterpoint.

polytonality the use of two or more keys at the same time.

position a term used in the playing of stringed instruments for where the left hand should be placed so that the fingers can play different sets of notes; e.g. first position has the hand near the end of the strings, second position is slightly further along the finger-board.

prelude an introductory piece of music or a self-contained piano piece in one movement.

prima donna (*Italian*) the 'first lady', i.e. the most important female singer in an opera.

principal 1 the leader of a section of an orchestra (e.g. principal horn). **2** a singer who takes leading parts in an opera company, but not the main ones (e.g. a principal tenor).

quadruple time (common time) the time of four quarter notes (crotchets) in a bar; it is indicated by the time-signature 4/4 or C.

quadruplet a group of four notes of equal value played in the time of three.

quarter note (crotchet) a note with a quarter of the time value of a whole note (semibreve).

quarter tone half a semitone, which is the smallest interval traditionally used in Western music.

quartet a group of four performers or a composition for such a group.

quaver eighth note; a note which is half the length of a quarter note (crotchet) and the eighth of a whole note (semibreve).

quintet a group of five performers, or a piece of music for such a group.

quintuple time five beats, usually quarter notes, in a bar, i.e. 5/4 time.

ray in the tonic sol-fa, the second note of the major scale.

recitative a way of singing (usually on a fixed note) in which the rhythm and lilt is taken from the words and there is no tune as such. It is commonly used in opera and oratorio.

register a part of a singer's vocal compass, e.g. chest register, head register, etc. The term is also applied to certain instruments, e.g. the Chalumeau register of the clarinet.

relative major, relative minor terms used to describe the connection between a major key and a minor key that share the same key signature, e.g. A minor is the relative key of C major.

reprise a musical repetition; it is often found in musical comedies when songs heard in one act are repeated in another.

resolution a term for a process in harmony by which a piece moves from discord to concord.

retardation a suspension in which a discordant note is resolved upwards by one step rather than downwards.

retrograde motion a term for music that is played backwards.

rhythm the aspect of music that is concerned with time. In notation, rhythm is determined by the way in which notes are grouped together into bars, the number and type of beats in a bar (as governed by the time signature), and the type of emphasis (accent) that is given to the beats. Along with melody and harmony, it is one of the essential characteristics of music.

scales an ordered sequence of notes that ascend or descend in pitch. The most frequently used scales in European music are the 'major' and 'minor' scales, which use tones (whole notes) and semitones (halfnotes) as steps of progression.

score music written down in such a way that it indicates all the parts for all the performers, i.e. the whole composition.

scoring the writing of a score.

semibreve a 'half of a breve' (a breve is a double whole note); the note with the longest time-value normally used in modern Western notation. In US notation, this is called a whole note.

Semidemisemiquaver sixty-fourth note.

semiquaver a note with half the time-value of an eighth note (quaver), and a sixteenth the time-value of a whole note (semibreve). In US notation, this is called a sixteenth-note.

Semiquaver Rest stop rest the length of a semiquaver (sixteenth note).

semitone half step; the smallest interval regularly used in modern Western music.

septet a group of seven performers or a piece of music written for such a group.

septuplet a group of seven notes of equal time-value to be played in the time of four or six.

sequence 1 the repetition of a short passage of music in a different pitch. 2 a form of hymn in Latin used in the Roman Catholic Mass, such as *dies irae* and *stabat mater*.

seventh an interval in which two notes are seven steps apart (including the first and last), e.g. F to E.

sextet a group of six performers or a piece of music written for such a group.

sextolet *see* **sextuplet**.

sextuplet a group of six notes to be performed in the time of four notes.

sharp the sign which raises the pitch of the line or space on which it stands on a stave by a semitone.

signature *see* **key signature**; **time signature**.

simple interval any interval which is an octave or less. Compare compound interval.

simple time *see* **compound time**.

sine tone an electronically produced note that is entirely 'pure'.

sixteenth-note a note with half the time-value of an eighth note (quaver), and a sixteenth the time-value of a semibreve. In British notation, this is called a semiquaver.

slur a curved line that is placed over or under a group of notes to indicate that they are to be played, or sung, smoothly, that is, with one stroke of the bow (violin music) or in one breath (singing).

song musical setting of poetry or prose; poem that can be sung; name used to designate the second subject of a sonata.

soprano the highest pitch of human voice, with a range of about two octaves above approximately middle C. The term is also applied to some instruments, such as soprano saxophone (the highest pitched saxophone).

sound a term in acoustics for tones resulting from regular vibrations as opposed to noise.

stave (staff) a set of horizontal lines (usually five) on which music is written. Each line, and the gaps between them, represent a different pitch.

stem the line, or 'tail', attached to the head of all notes smaller than a whole note (semibreve).

stopping on stringed instruments, the placing of fingers on a string to shorten its effective length and raise its pitch.

strings a general term for the stringed instruments of the violin family.

subdominant the fourth note of the major or minor scale.

subject a musical theme (a substantial group

of notes) on which a composition (or part of a composition) is constructed, e.g. the first and second subjects in the exposition in sonata form; the subject in a fugue; also the leading voice (first part) of a fugue.

submediant the sixth note of the major or minor scale.

suspension a device used in harmony in which a note sounded in one chord is sustained while a subsequent chord is played (or sung), producing a dissonance which is then resolved.

syncopation an alteration to the normal arrangement of accented beats in a bar. This is usually done by placing accents on beats or parts of a beat that do not normally carry an accent.

tail the stem attached to the head of a minim (half note), or a smaller note.

temperament the way in which intervals between notes have been 'tempered', or slightly altered, in Western music so that the slight discrepancy in seven octaves is distributed evenly over the range. In 'equal temperament' an octave is divided into twelve semitones, which means that, e.g. D sharp is also E flat; this is a compromise, for strictly there is a marginal difference between D sharp and E flat.

tempo (*Italian*) 'time'. The time taken by a composition, therefore the speed at which it is performed, hence the pace of the beat. A *tempo* means 'in time'. Tempo can also mean a movement of a sonata or symphony, as in *il secondo tempo,* 'the second movement'.

tenor 1 the highest adult male voice with a range an octave to either side of middle C. **2** as a prefix to the name of an instrument, it indicates the size between an alto member of the family and a bass, e.g. tenor saxophone. **3** the reciting note in psalm singing. **4** an obsolete term for a viola (tenor violin).

tetrachord a group of four notes.

theme the melody, or other musical material, that forms the basis of a work or a movement and which may be varied or developed. It may return in one form or another throughout a composition.

thirty-second note a demisemiquaver.

tie a curved line that joins two notes of the

same pitch together, indicating that they should be played as one long note.

timbre (*French*) the quality of a tone, or the characteristic sound of an instrument.

time signature a sign placed at the beginning of a piece of music that indicates the number and value of beats in a bar. A time signature usually consists of two numbers, one placed above the other. The lower number defines the unit of measurement in relation to the semibreve (whole note); the top figure indicates the number of those units in a bar, e.g., 3/4 indicates that there are three quarter notes (crotchets) in a bar.

time the rhythmic pattern (number of beats in a bar) of a piece of music, as indicated by the time signature. Duple time has two beats in a bar, triple time has three beats in a bar, and so on.

time-names (rhythm-names) a French method of teaching time and rhythm in which beats are given names, such as 'ta', 'ta-te' etc.

tonality the use of a key in a composition.

tone 1 an interval comprising two semitones, e.g. the interval between C and D. **2** (*US*) a musical note. **3** the quality of sound, e.g. good tone, sharp tone etc. **4** in plainsong, a melody.

tonic sol-fa a system of notation and sight-singing used in training, in which notes are sung to syllables. The notes of the major scale are: doh, re, me, fah, soh, la, te, doh (doh is always the tonic, whatever the key). The system was pioneered in England by John Curwen in the mid-19th century.

tonic the first note of a major or minor scale.

transcription *see* **arrangement**.

transition 1 the changing from one key to another during the course of a composition. **2** a passage linking two sections of a piece, which often involves a change of key.

transposing instruments instruments which sound notes different from those actually written down, e.g. a piece of music in E flat for the B flat clarinet would actually be written in F.

transposition the changing of the pitch of a composition. Singers sometimes ask accompanists to transpose a song higher or lower so that it is better suited to their voice range.

treble the highest boy's voice.

triad a chord of three notes which includes a third and a fifth.

trill an ornament in which a note is rapidly alternated with the note above. It is used in both vocal and instrumental pieces.

trio 1 a group of three performers, or a piece of music written for such a group. **2** the middle section of a minuet, as found in sonatas, symphonies, etc. It was originally a section scored for three parts.

triplet a group of three notes played in the time of two notes.

tritone an interval consisting of three whole tones.

tuning the adjusting of the pitch of an instrument so that it corresponds to an agreed note, e.g. an orchestra will usually have all its instruments tuned to the note of A.

twelve-note music (twelve-tone system) a method of composition formulated and advanced by Schoenberg. In the system, the twelve chromatic notes of an octave can only be used in specific orders called 'note rows'; no note can be repeated twice within a note row, and the rows must be used complete. In all, there are 48 ways in which a note row can be arranged (using inversion, retrograde motion and inverted retrograde motion) and it is with note rows that compositions are constructed.

unison the sounding of the same note or its octave by two or more voices or instruments.

up beat the upward movement of a conductor's baton or hand, indicating the unstressed (usually the last) beat in a bar.

vibration a term in acoustics, for the wavelike motion by which a musical tone is produced. Sound vibrations are mechanical; radio vibrations are electro-magnetic and inaudible.

vibrato (*Italian*) literally, 'shaking', i.e. a small but rapid variation in the pitch of a note.

virtuoso (*Italian*) a skilled performer on the violin or some other instrument. The word was formerly synonymous with 'amateur'.

vocalization control of the voice and vocal sounds, and the method of producing and phrasing notes with the voice.

voice 1 to regulate so as to give the correct tone; sound produced by speaking or singing; the quality of this; the power of speech. The three categories of adult male voice (bass, baritone and tenor); the three female categories (contralto, mezzo-soprano and soprano); and the two boy categories (treble and alto). **2** parts in contrapuntal compositions are traditionally termed 'voices'.

whole note, whole tone the note with the longest time-value normally used in modern Western notation; an interval of two half steps (two semitones); (*Brit*) a semibreve ('half of a breve': a breve is a double whole note);

whole-tone scale a scale in which all the intervals are whole-tones, i.e. two half steps (semitones).

woodwind a term for a group of blown instruments that were traditionally made of wood (some of which are now made of metal), e.g. flutes, oboes, clarinets and bassoons, etc.

Physics

absorption decrease in the intensity of radiation by interaction with matter.

absorptivity the rate of absorption of radiation by a material.

acceleration an increase in the speed at which an object is travelling.

acoustics a branch of physics that is concerned with sound.

adiabatic change a change that occurs with no alteration in the heat content of the system.

aerodynamics the study of the forces exerted by air or other gases in motion, especially around solid bodies such as aircraft.

alpha particle (α) a helium nucleus with a short straight range from the source of emission, one of the earliest particles recognized in radioactivity.

alpha ray radiation of alpha particles.

alternating current an electric current that reverses the direction of its flow regularly.

alternator an electric generator that produces alternating current.

amp *abbr* = ampere, a unit of electric current.

amplitude the intensity of a sound wave, the maximum deviation of an oscillation from the mean or zero.

angström the unit of measurement, one hundred millionth of a centimetre, formerly used for optical wavelengths, now largely displaced by the nanometer.

angular momentum a vector property characteristic of the rotatory motion of a body around an axis: the product of the angular velocity and moment of inertia.

angular velocity the rate of rotation of a body measured in radians/second.

aplanatic free from, or correcting, spherical or chromatic aberration.

Archimedean screw an instrument for raising water, consisting of a flexible tube wound spirally around or within a cylinder in the form of a screw. When placed in an inclined position, with the lower end immersed in water, by the revolution of the screw the water is raised to the upper end.

Archimedes' principle a law that when a body is immersed in a liquid, the weight it appears to have lost equals the weight of the displaced liquid.

astrophysics the branch of astronomy that deals with the physical and chemical constitution of the stars.

atmospheric pressure the pressure exerted by the atmosphere, 1.01325 x 105 newtons at sea level.

atomic energy the energy derived from nuclear fission.

attraction the mutual action by which bodies tend to be drawn together.

Avogadro's constant *or* **Avogadro's number** the number of particles present in one mole of a substance. It is given the symbol N or L and has the value of 6.023 x 10^{23}.

Avogadro's law the principle formulated by the Italian scientist Amedeo Avogadro (1776–1856) which states that equal volumes of all gases contain the same number of molecules when under the same temperature and pressure. For the purpose of calculation, one mole of gas will occupy a volume of 22.4 litres at standard conditions, i.e. 273.15K and 1 atmosphere.

battery an electric cell that supplies current.

becquerel a unit of radioactivity in the SI scheme.

beta particle (β) an electron or positron ejected from the nucleus of an atom during radioactive disintegration.

beta ray a stream of penetrating rays emitted by radioactive substances.

biophysics the application of physics to biology.

Boyle's law a law devised by the Irish scientist Robert Boyle (1627–1691) which states that at a constant temperature, the volume of a gas lessens in proportion to an increase in the pressure of the gas. Hence at a constant temperature, if the pressure is doubled the volume is halved.

buoyancy ability to float or rise; cheerfulness; resilience.

capacitance the property of a system that enables it to store an electrical charge.

capacitor a device for storing electric charge.

capacity the former name for capacitance.

centrifugal force a force that acts in direct and equal opposition to a body that is spinning fast around a central point.

centripetal force a force that pulls a spinning body in towards the centre.

cgs units a metric system of units based on centimetre, gram and second. Replaced by SI units.

chaos theory the theory that the behaviour of dynamic systems is haphazard rather than mathematical.

charge a build-up of electricity.

collision an interaction or meeting between particles in which momentum is maintained.

condensation the process by which a substance changes from gas to liquid.

condense to change from a gas into a liquid.

conduction the conducting or transmission of heat or electricity through a medium.

conductor a substance that conducts heat or electricity.

convection the transmission of heat through a liquid by currents; the process whereby warmer air rises while cooler air drops.

coulomb an SI unit of electric charge; the quantity of electricity conveyed by a current of one ampere in one second.

current the transmission of electricity through a conductor.

decay the decrease in amplitude or intensity with time.

density the degree of denseness or concentration; stupidity; the ratio of mass to volume.

diffraction the breaking up of a ray of light into coloured bands of the spectrum, or into a series of light and dark bands.

diode a semiconductor device for converting alternating to direct current; a basic thermionic valve with two electrodes.

direct current an electric current that flows in one direction only.

dispersion the separation of light into colours by diffraction or refraction.

distance the measurement of how far an object has travelled along a particular path.

Doppler effect a change in the apparent frequency of a wave experienced if the source of the wave is moving.

drag a force of friction that retards the movement of an object through the air.

dynamics the branch of physics that deals with forces and their effect on the motion of bodies.

elasticity a property of any material that will stretch when forces are applied to it and recover when the forces are relaxed.

electricity a form of energy comprising certain charged particles, such as electrons and protons.

electrodynamics the area of physics dealing with electric currents.

electrokinetics the area of physics dealing with electricity in motion.

electromotive force a source of energy producing an electric current; the amount of energy drawn from such a source per unit current of electricity passing through it, measured in volts.

emf *abbr* = electromotive force.

endothermic reaction a chemical reaction in which heat energy is absorbed.

energy capacity to do work.

equilibrium a state of balance of weight, power, force, etc.

evaporation the process by which a substance changes from a liquid to a vapour (gas).

exothermic reaction a chemical reaction in which heat energy is released to the surrounding environment.

fission a split or cleavage; the reproductive division of biological cells; the splitting of the atomic nucleus resulting in the release of energy, nuclear fission.

fluidics the investigation and application of flowing liquid or gas in tubes to simulate the flow of electrons in conductors.

focal length the distance between the focal point and optical centre of a lens or mirror.

focal point the point on the axis of a lens or mirror at which rays meet after reflection or refraction.

force (the intensity of) an influence that causes movement of a body or other effects.

frequency (*f*) the number of complete wavelengths passing any given reference point on the line of zero disturbance in one second.

friction the force that opposes motion and always acts parallel to the surface across which the motion is taking place.

fulcrum the fixed point on which a lever turns.

fusion a nuclear reaction in which unstable nuclei combine to create larger, more stable nuclei with the release of vast amounts of energy.

gamma radiation, gamma rays (γ) shortwave electromagnetic radiation from a radioactive substance.

gas a substance with the capacity to expand indefinitely and not liquefy or solidify at ordinary temperatures.

Geiger tube *or* **Geiger-Müller tube** an instrument that can detect and measure radiation.

geophysics the physics of the Earth.

geothermal, geothermic of, relating to, or using the heat of the Earth's interior.

gravitation a natural force of attraction that tends to draw bodies together.

gravity the attraction of bodies toward the centre of the earth, the moon, or a planet.

half-life the time taken for a radioactive isotope to lose exactly half of its radioactivity.

heat energy produced by molecular agitation.

Hooke's law the physical relationship between the size of the applied force on an elastic material and the resulting extension.

hydrokinetics the branch of physics concerned with the study of fluids in motion.

hydrostatics the branch of physics concerned with the study of fluids at rest.

inertia the tendency of matter to remain at rest (or continue in a fixed direction) unless acted on by an outside force; disinclination to act.

infrared radiation electromagnetic radiation lying in the electromagnetic spectrum between visible light and microwaves, most often generated by hot objects (black body radiation).

insulation the act of insulating; the material used for insulating.

insulator something which insulates; a nonconductor of electricity, heat, or sound.

interference the meeting or interaction of two or more waves (water, electromagnetic or sound).

joule a unit of energy equal to work done when a force of one newton acts over a distance of one metre.

K *abbr* = Kelvin(s).

kilocalorie *or* **calorie** a unit of heat used to express the energy value of food, equal to 1000 calories.

kinetic energy the energy possessed by a moving body by virtue of its mass and velocity.

kinetics the science of the effects of forces in producing or changing motion; the study of the mechanisms and rates of chemical reactions.

L *abbr* = Avogadro number.

latent heat the measurement of heat energy involved when a substance changes state.

lattice the particular arrangement of atoms in a crystal structure.

lepton any of various elementary particles, such as electrons and muons, that participate in weak interactions with other elementary particles.

lever a simple machine consisting of a bar turning about a fixed point called a fulcrum.

liquid a substance that, unlike a gas, does not expand indefinitely and, unlike a solid, flows readily.

longitudinal wave the classification for a wave that is produced when the vibrations occur in the same direction as the direction of travel for that wave.

lx *abbr* = lux.

magnetic flux a measure of the strength of a magnetic field over a given area.

magnetism the effective force that originates within the earth and that behaves as if there were a powerful magnet at the centre of the earth, producing a magnetic field.

magnitude the absolute value or length of a physical or mathematical quantity.

mass the measure of the quantity of matter that a substance possesses.

mass number the total number of protons and neutrons in the nucleus of any atom.

matter any substance that occupies space and has mass: the material of which the universe is made.

mechanics the science of motion and the action of forces on bodies; knowledge of machinery.

melting point the temperature at which a substance is in a state of equilibrium between the solid and liquid states, e.g. ice/water.

meniscus the crescent-shaped surface of a liquid contained in a tube; a lens convex on one side and concave on the other.

microphysics the physics of elementary particles.

moment a measure of the turning effect of a force about a point and the force multiplied by the perpendicular distance from the point.

momentum the impetus of a moving object, equal to the product of its mass and its velocity.

motion the change in the physical position of an object.

N *abbr* = newton.

NA *abbr* = (Avogadro) number (*also* **L**).

neutral having zero charge.

neutrino a stable elementary particle with almost zero mass and spin 1/2.

newton the SI unit of force that imparts acceleration of 1 metre per second per second to a mass of 1 kg.

nuclear energy energy released as a result of nuclear fission or fusion.

nuclear fission the splitting of a nucleus of an atom either spontaneously or by bombarding it with particles.

nuclear fusion the combining of two nuclei into a heavier nucleus, releasing energy in the process.

nuclear of or relating to a nucleus; using nuclear energy.

ohm (Ω) the unit of electrical resistance. Between two points of an electrical conductor, one volt (V) is needed to force a current (I) of one ampere through a resistance (R) of one ohm, i.e. $V = IR$. This is known as **Ohm's law** (after German physicist Georg Simon Ohm) which can be rewritten: $R = V/I$.

optics the branch of physics dealing with the study of light.

orbit the path of an electron around the nucleus of an atom.

oscillate to swing back and forth as a pendulum.

oscillation the regular fluctuation of an object whether by means of a cycle, vibration or rotation.

period the time taken for a body to complete one full oscillation, which can involve a vibration, rotation, or harmonic motion.

photometry the area of physics concerned with the measurement of light.

photon a quantum or packet of energy that is a basic part of all electromagnetic waves.

physics the branch of science concerned with matter and energy and their interactions in the fields of mechanics, acoustics, optics, heat, electricity, magnetism, radiation, atomic structure, and nuclear phenomena.

plane any level or flat surface.

polychromatic, polychromic, polychromous having a mixture of wavelengths.

potential difference the work done in driving a unit of electric charge (one coulomb) from one point to another in a current-carrying circuit.

potential energy a body has potential energy if and when it has been moved to a position from which it can do work when released. When it is released the body has the energy of motion, i.e. kinetic energy.

power a source of energy, a measure of the rate of doing work expresses as the work done per unit time. It is measures in watts.

precession the westward motion of the equinoxes caused mainly by the attraction of the Sun and Moon on the equatorial bulge of the Earth.

precessional motion the type of motion shown by a gyroscope.

pressure force per unit of area.

propagation to move through, cause to move through or transmit. The transmission of light in straight lines.

pulley a wheel with a grooved rim for a cord, etc, used to raise weights by downward pull or change of direction of the pull.

quantum a small amount or unit of electromagnetic radiation that can be thought of as a particle of energy.

quark a hypothetical elementary particle; any of the theoretical building blocks that participate in the strong interactive forces between elementary particles.

radio astronomy the recording and study of radio waves given out by many bodies in space including the sun, stars and quasars.

radioactivity the giving out of particles (known as α or β particles and γ rays) by unstable substances that are disintegrating.

radiography the method or process of making an image of an object on photographic film (or on a fluorescent screen), using X-rays (or similar rays such as gamma rays); the diagnostic technique used to examine the body using X-rays; the production of X-ray photographs for use in medicine, industry, etc.

recombination the process whereby a free electron combines with an ion in an ionized gas and energy is released as electromagnetic radiation.

reflection the property of certain surfaces whereby rays of light (or other wave motion) striking the surface are returned (reflected) in accordance with definite laws.

refraction the bending of, most commonly, a light ray when it travels from one medium to another, e.g., air to water.

relativity the theory of the relative, rather than absolute, character of motion, velocity, mass, etc, and the interdependence of time, matter, and space derived by Albert Einstein. Establishes the concept of a four-dimensional space–time continuum where there is no clear line between three-dimensional space and independent time, hence space and time are considered to be bound together. The *special theory of relativity* states that the speed of light is the same for all observers, whatever their speed. The *general theory of relativity* states that matter in space causes space to curve so as to set up a gravitational field and gravitation becomes a property of space.

repulsion the tendency of bodies to repel each other.

resistance non-conductivity, opposition to a steady current.

resistivity resistance to the passage of an electrical current; the reciprocal of a material's conductivity, giving the resistance in terms of its dimensions.

resistor a component of electric circuits, used to provide a known resistance.

scattering the dispersal of waves or particles upon impact with matter.

Schrödinger equation the basic equation used in wave mechanics, which describes the behaviour of a particle in a force field.

secondary emission the emission of secondary electrons from a solid surface due to bombardment by a beam of primary electrons or other elementary particles.

semisolid having the properties between that of a liquid and that of a solid.

sensitivity the smallest signal that can be detected above background noise in recording equipment.

SI unit an internationally recognized system of units, Système International d'Unités, employed for all scientific and technical purposes. Includes, metre, kilometre, second, ampere, kelvin, candela, mole, radian and steradian.

simple harmonic motion motion that is characteristic of many systems that vibrate or oscillate.

simple machine the lever, the inclined plane and the wheel.

singularity a point or region where time and space become absolutely distorted and ordinary laws of physics no longer apply.

solar cell a cell that converts the Sun's rays into electricity.

solar constant the quantity of the Sun's energy radiated onto a given area of the Earth's surface in a prescribed period; the energy received on the Earth's surface, allowing for any losses due to the atmosphere.

solar energy energy of any form that is derived from the Sun.

solid neither liquid nor gaseous. A substance where the molecules move so slowly that they bond to one another.

sound the effect upon the ear created by air vibrations with a frequency between 20 Hz (hertz) and 20 kHz (20,000 Hz).

specific gravity the ratio of the density of a substance to that of the same volume of water.

specific heat capacity the heat required to raise the temperature of a unit of mass of a given substance by one degree.

speed the ratio of distance covered by a body moving in a straight line or continuous curve to the time required to cover that distance.

standing wave a disturbance produced when two similar wave motions are transmitted in opposite directions at the same time.

static electricity electricity which is stationary as opposed to flowing in a current.

statics the branch of mechanics dealing with the forces that produce a state of equilibrium.

strain distortion produced by forces acting on a material.

stress a system of forces producing or sustaining a strain. To exert pressure on.

stroboscope a device for observing motion by making the subject visible at prescribed intervals using a synchronized flashing light.

substrate the single crystal or semiconductor used as the base on which an integrated circuit or transistor is printed.

superconductivity the complete loss of electrical resistance exhibited by certain materials at very low temperatures.

superfluidity the flowing of a fluid without friction.

supersaturation the state of a solution when it contains more dissolved solute than is required to produce a saturated solution.

surface tension the tension created by forces of attraction between molecules in a liquid, resulting in an apparent elastic membrane over the surface of the liquid.

tachyon a theoretical elementary particle that can travel faster than light.

temperature degree of heat or cold against a standard scale. The average kinetic energy of the atoms or molecules of a substance.

terminal velocity the greatest speed reached by a projected or falling object; the speed of a projectile when it reaches its target.

thermal conductivity a measure of the rate of heat flow along a body by conduction.

thermodynamics the branch of physics concerned with the relationship between heat and other forms of energy.

thermoelectric, thermoelectrical of or derived from electricity generated by difference of temperature.

thermonuclear of or relating to nuclear fusion or nuclear weapons that utilize fusion reactions.

torque a force that causes rotation around a central point, such as an axle.

torsion a twisting effect on an object when equal forces are applied at both ends but in opposite directions.

transducer a device that converts one form of energy into another, often a physical quantity into an electrical signal, as in microphones and photocells.

transformer a device for changing the voltage of an alternating current.

transistor a semiconductor device that is used in three main ways: as a switch, as a rectifier, and as an amplifier creating strong signals from weak ones.

transmission the act of transmitting; something transmitted; a system using gears, etc, to transfer power from an engine to a moving part, especially wheels of a vehicle; a radio or television broadcast.

transverse wave a wave in which the vibration occurs at right angles to the direction of wave propagation.

tribology the study of friction, lubrication, and wear, as occurs when two surfaces are in contact in relative motion.

ultraviolet radiation a form of radiation that occurs beyond the violet end of the visible light spectrum of electromagnetic waves.

Van Allen radiation belts two belts of radiation consisting of charged particles (electrons and protons) trapped in the Earth's magnetic field and forming two belts around the earth.

vapour pressure the pressure exerted by a vapour whether in a mixture of gases or by itself; the part of the atmospheric pressure that is due to water molecules contained in the atmosphere.

vector a physical quantity having both direction and magnitude, e.g. displacement, acceleration, etc; an aircraft's or missile's course.

velocity of light the vector quantity for light travelling through a given medium, approximately $3.0 \times 10^8 \text{ms}^{-1}$ through air or a vacuum.

velocity the rate of change of position of any object; speed.

vibration the rapid alternating of particles caused by the disturbance of equilibrium.

viscosity a property of fluids that indicates their resistance to flow.

voltage electrical energy that moves a charge around a circuit, measured in volts.

volume the amount of space occupied by an object or substance; quantity, amount; intensity of sound; a book; one book of a series.

w *abbr* = work.

W = watt.

watt a unit of power equal to 1 joule per second, symbol W.

wattage power, measured in watts.

wave a mechanism of energy transfer through a medium. The origin of the wave is vibrating particles, which store and release energy while their mean position remains constant as it is only the wave that travels. Waves can be classified as being either longitudinal waves, e.g. sound, or transverse waves, e.g. light, depending on the direction of their vibrations.

wave mechanics the theory in quantum mechanics that describes the behaviour of elementary particles in terms of their wave properties.

wavelength (λ) the distance between two similar and consecutive points on a wave, which have exactly the same displacement value from the rest position (that is, the same amplitude). An example would be the distance between two crests (maximum displacement) or two troughs (maximum displacement).

Wb *abbr* = weber.

weak interaction an interaction between elementary particles that is responsible for certain particle decay processes.

weber a unit of magnetic flux.

weight the vertical force experienced by a mass as a result of the force of gravity upon it. Weight equals mass multiplied by acceleration. It is measured in units of force (newtons) but also often units of mass (kilograms).

work the transfer of energy (i.e. the changing of energy into a different form) as in potential energy into kinetic energy or chemical energy into heat energy.

APPENDIX

APPENDIX

World Facts

Afghanistan
Area: 251,773 sq mi (652,225 sq km)
Population: 20,833,000
Capital: Kabul
Other cities: Herat, Kandahar, Mazar-e-Sharif
Form of government: Republic
Religions: Sunni Islam, Shia Islam
Currency: Afghani

Albania
Area: 11,009 sq mi (28,748 sq km)
Population: 3,670,000
Capital: Tirana (Tiranè)
Other cities: Durrès, Shkodèr, Vlorë
Form of government: Socialist Republic
Religion: Constitutionally atheist but mainly Sunni Islam
Currency: Lek

Algeria
Area: 919,595 sq mi (2,381,741 sq km)
Population: 29,168,000
Capital: Algiers (Alger)
Other cities: Oran, Constantine, Annaba
Form of government: Republic
Religion: Sunni Islam
Currency: Algerian dinar

American Samoa *see* SAMOA, AMERICAN.

Andorra
Area: 175 sq mi (453 sq km)
Population: 65,900
Capital: Andorra la Vella
Form of government: Republic
Religion: Roman Catholicism
Currency: Euro

Angola
Area: 481,354 sq mi (1,246,700 sq km)
Population: 11,185,000
Capital: Luanda
Other cities: Huambo, Lobito, Benguela, Lubango
Form of government: People's Republic
Religions: Roman Catholicism, African traditional religions
Currency: Kwanza

Anguilla
Area: 37 sq mi (96 sq km)
Population: 12,400
Capital: The Valley
Form of government: British Overseas Territory
Religion: Christianity
Currency: East Caribbean dollar

Antigua and Barbuda
Area: 171 sq mi (442 sq km)
Population: 66,000
Capital: St John's
Form of government: Constitutional monarchy
Religion: Christianity (mainly Anglican)
Currency: East Caribbean dollar

Argentina
Area: 1,073,518 sq mi (2,780,400 sq km)
Population: 35,220,000
Capital: Buenos Aires
Other cities: Cordoba, Rosario, Mar del Plata, Mendoza, La Plata, Salta
Form of government: Federal republic
Religion: Roman Catholicism
Currency: Peso

Armenia
Area: 11,506 sq mi (29,800 sq km)
Population: 3,893,000
Capital: Yerevan
Other major city: Kunmayr (Gyumri)
Form of government: Republic
Religion: Armenian Orthodox
Currency: Dram

Aruba
Area: 75 sq mi (193 sq km)
Population: 87,000
Capital: Oranjestad
Form of government: Self-governing Dutch territory
Religion: Christianity
Currency: Aruban florin

Australia
Area: 2,988,902 sq mi (7,741,220 sq km)
Population: 18,871,800
Capital: Canberra
Other cities: Adelaide, Brisbane, Melbourne, Perth, Sydney
Form of government: Federal parliamentary state
Religion: Christianity
Currency: Australian dollar

Austria
Area: 32,378 sq mi (83,859 sq km)
Population: 8,106,000
Capital: Vienna (Wien)
Other cities: Graz, Linz, Salzburg, Innsbruck
Form of government: Federal republic
Religion: Roman Catholicism
Currency: Euro

Azerbaijan
Area: 33,436 sq mi (86,600 sq km)
Population: 7,625,000
Capital: Baku
Other major city: Sumqayit
Form of government: Republic
Religions: Shia Islam, Sunni Islam, Russian Orthodox
Currency: Manat (= 100 gopik)

Azores
Area: 901 sq mi (2,335 sq km)
Population: 336,100
Capital: Ponta Delgada

Bahamas, The
Area: 5,358 sq mi (13,878 sq km)
Population: 284,000
Capital: Nassau
Other important city: Freeport
Form of government: Constitutional Monarchy
Religion: Christianity
Currency: Bahamian Dollar

Bahrain
Area: 268 sq mi (694 sq km)
Population: 599,000
Capital: Manama (Al Manamah)
Form of government: Hereditary Monarchy
Religions: Shia Islam, Sunni Islam
Currency: Bahrain Dinar

Bangladesh
Area: 55,598 sq mi (143,998 sq km)
Population: 120,073,000
Capital: Dhaka
Other cities: Chittagong, Khulna, Narayanganj, Saidpur
Form of government: Republic
Religion: Sunni Islam
Currency: Taka

Barbados
Area: 166 sq mi (430 sq km)
Population: 265,000
Capital: Bridgetown
Form of government: Constitutional Monarchy
Religions: Anglicanism, Methodism
Currency: Barbados Dollar

Belarus (Belorussia, Byelorussia)
Area: 80,155 sq mi (207,600 sq km)
Population: 10,203,000
Capital: Minsk
Other cities: Homyel (Gomel), Vitsyebsk, Mahilyov
Form of government: Republic
Religions: Russian Orthodox, Roman Catholicism
Currency: Rouble

Belau *see* PALAU.

Belgium
Area: 11,783 sq mi (30,519 sq km)
Population: 10,159,000
Capital: Brussels
Other cities: Antwerp, Charleroi, Ghent, Liège, Oostende
Form of government: Constitutional monarchy
Religion: Roman Catholicism
Currency: Euro

Belize
Area: 8,763 sq mi (22,696 sq km)
Population: 222,000
Capital: Belmopan
Other major city: Belize City
Form of government: Constitutional monarchy
Religions: Roman Catholicism, Protestantism
Currency: Belize Dollar

Belorussia   **Burkina Faso**

Belorussia *see* BELARUS.

Benin
Area: 43,484 sq mi (112,622 sq km)
Population: 5,563,000
Capital: Porto-Novo
Form of government: Republic
Religions: African traditional religions,
    Roman Catholicism, Sunni Islam, Christian
Currency: CFA Franc

Bermuda
Area: 20 sq mi (53 sq km)
Population: 64,000
Capital: Hamilton
Form of government: British Overseas
    Territory
Religions: Protestantism, Roman Catholi-
    cism
Currency: Bermuda dollar
Area: 18,147 sq mi (47,000 sq km)
Population: 1,812,000
Capital: Thimphu
Form of government: Constitutional
    Monarchy
Religions: Buddhism, Hinduism
Currency: Ngultrum

Bolivia
Area: 424,165 sq mi (1,098,581 sq km)
Population: 8,140,000
Capital: La Paz (administrative), Sucre
    (legal)
Other cities: Cochabamba, Santa Cruz,
    Oruro, Potosi
Form of government: Republic
Religion: Roman Catholicism
Currency: Boliviano

Bosnia-Herzegovina
Area: 19,735 sq mi (51,129 sq km)
Population: 4,510,000
Capital: Sarajevo
Other cities: Banja Luka, Mostar, Tuzla
Form of government: Republic
Religions: Eastern Orthodox, Sunni Islam,
    Roman Catholicism
Currency: Dinar (unofficially the Euro)

Botswana
Area: 224,607 sq mi (581,730 sq km)
Population: 1,490,000

Capital: Gaborone
Other cities: Francistown, Molepolole,
    Mahalapye
Form of government: Republic
Religions: African traditional religions,
    Christian
Currency: Pula

Brazil
Area: 3,300,171 sq mi (8,547,403 sq km)
Population: 157,872,000
Capital: Brasília
Other cities: Balem, Belo Horizonte,
    Curitiba, Porto Alegre, Recife, Rio de
    Janeiro, Salvador, São Paulo
Form of government: Federal Republic
Religion: Roman Catholicism
Currency: Cruzeiro

British Indian Ocean Territory
The Chagos Archipelago, a group of five
    coral atolls in the middle of the Indian
    Ocean. A British colony.
Area: 20 square miles/52 square kilometres.)

Brunei
Area: 2,226 sq mi (5,765 sq km)
Population: 300,000
Capital: Bandar Seri Begawan
Other cities: Kuala Belait, Seria
Form of government: Monarchy (sultanate)
Religion: Sunni Islam
Currency: Brunei dollar

Bulgaria
Area: 42,823 sq mi (110,912 sq km)
Population: 8,356,000
Capital: Sofiya
Other cities: Burgas, Plovdiv, Ruse, Varna
Form of government: Republic
Religion: Eastern Orthodox
Currency: Lev

Burkina Faso (Burkina)
Area: 105,792 sq mi (274,000 sq km)
Population: 10,780,000
Capital: Ouagadougou
Other cities: Bobo-Dioulasso, Koudougou
Form of government: Republic
Religions: African traditional religions,
    Sunni Islam
Currency: CFA franc

Burma

Burma *see* MYANMAR.

Burundi
Area: 10,747 sq mi (27,834 sq km)
Population: 6,088,000
Capital: Bujumbura
Form of government: Republic
Religion: Roman Catholicism
Currency: Burundi franc

Byelorussia *see* BELARUS.

Cambodia
Area: 69,898 sq mi (181,035 sq km)
Population: 10,273,000
Capital: Phnom-Penh
Other cities: Battambang, Kampong Cham
Form of government: People's Republic
Religion: Buddhism
Currency: Riel

Cameroon
Area: 183,569 sq mi (475,442 sq km)
Population: 13,560,000
Capital: Yaoundé
Other major city: Douala
Form of government: Republic
Religions: African traditional religions,
    Roman Catholicism, Sunni Islam
Currency: CFA franc

Canada
Area: 3,849,674 sq mi (9,970,610 sq km)
Population: 29,964,000
Capital: Ottawa
Other cities: Calgary, Toronto, Montréal,
    Vancouver, Québec City, Winnipeg
Form of government: Federal Parliamentary
    State
Religions: Roman Catholicism, United
    Church of Canada, Anglicanism
Currency: Canadian dollar

Canary Islands
Area: 2,808 sq mi (7,273 sq km)
Population: 1,493,000
Capital: Las Palmas, on Gran Canaria
Currency: Euro

Cape Verde
Area: 1,557 sq mi (4,033 sq km)
Population: 396,000

Capital: Praia
Form of government: Republic
Religion: Roman Catholicism
Currency: Cape Verde Escudo

Cayman Islands
Area: 102 sq mi (264 sq km)
Population: 38,000
Capital: George Town, on Grand Cayman
Form of government: British overseas territory
Religion: Christianity
Currency: Cayman Islands dollar

Central African Republic
Area: 240,535 sq mi (622,984 sq km)
Population: 3,344,000
Capital: Bangui
Other cities: Bambari, Bangassou
Form of government: Republic
Religions: African traditional religions,
    Roman Catholicism
Currency: CFA Franc

Chad
Area: 495,755 sq mi (1,284,000 sq km)
Population: 6,515,000
Capital: N'Djamena
Other cities: Sarh, Moundou, Abéché
Form of government: Republic
Religions: Sunni Islam, African traditional
    religions
Currency: CFA Franc

Channel Islands
Area: 75 square miles/194 square kilometres
Population: 143,000
Main islands: Jersey and Guernsey, also
    includes Alderney, Sark, Herm and Brechou.
Government:British Crown dependencies.
Religions: Anglicanism, Roman Catholi-
    cism, Presbyterianism, Methodism
Currency: Pound sterling

Chile
Area: 292,135 sq mi (756,626 sq km)
Population: 14,419,000
Capital: Santiago
Other cities: Arica, Concepcion, Valparaiso,
    Viña del Mar
Form of government: Republic
Religion: Roman Catholicism
Currency: Chilean Peso

China
Area: 3,705,408 sq mi (9,596,961 sq km)
Population: 1,246,872,000
Capital: Beijing (Peking)
Other cities: Chengdu, Guangzhou, Harbin, Shanghai, Tianjin, Wuhan
Form of government: People's Republic
Religions: Buddhism, Confucianism, Taoism
Currency: Yuan

Colombia
Area: 439,737 sq mi (1,138,914 sq km)
Population: 35,626,000
Capital: Bogotá
Other cities: Barranquilla, Cali, Cartagena, Medellin
Form of government: Republic
Religion: Roman Catholicism
Currency: Colombian peso

Comoros, The
Area: 720 sq mi (1,865 sq km) excluding Mayotte
Population: 538,000
Capital: Moroni
Other cities: Dornoni, Fomboni, Mutsamudu, Mitsamiouli
Form of government: Federal Islamic Republic
Religion: Sunni Islam
Currency: Comorian franc

Congo
Area: 132,047 sq mi (342,000 sq km)
Population: 2,668,000
Capital: Brazzaville
Other major city: Pointe-Noire
Form of government: Republic
Religions: Christian, African traditional religions
Currency: CFA franc

Congo, Democratic Republic of
Area: 905,355 sq mi (2,344,858 sq km)
Population: 46,812,000
Capital: Kinshasa
Other cities: Bukavu, Lubumbashi, Matadi, Mbuji-Mayi, Kananga, Kisangani
Form of government: Republic
Religions: Roman Catholicism, Protestantism, Islam
Currency: Congolese Franc

Cook Islands
Area: 93 sq mi (240 sq km)
Population: 18,500
Capital: Avarua, on Rarotonga
Form of government: Self-governing in association with New Zealand
Religion: Christianity
Currency: Cook Islands Dollar/New Zealand dollar.

Costa Rica
Area: 19,730 sq mi (51,100 sq km)
Population: 3,398,000
Capital: San José
Other cities: Alajuela, Límon, Puntarenas
Form of government: Republic
Religion: Roman Catholicism
Currency: Colon

Côte d'Ivoire
Area: 124,504 sq mi (322,463 sq km)
Population: 14,781,000
Capital: Yamoussoukro
Other cities: Abidjan, Bouaké, Daloa
Form of government: Republic
Religions: African traditional religions, Sunni Islam, Roman Catholicism
Currency: CFA franc

Croatia (Hrvatska)
Area: 21,824 sq mi (56,538 sq km)
Population: 4,501,000
Capital: Zagreb
Other cities: Osijek, Rijeka, Split
Form of government: Republic
Religions: Roman Catholicism, Eastern Orthodox
Currency: Kuna (unofficially the euro)

Cuba
Area: 42,804 sq mi (110,861 sq km)
Population: 11,019,000
Capital: Havana (La Habana)
Other cities: Camaguey, Holguin, Santa Clara, Santiago de Cuba
Form of government: Socialist Republic
Religion: Roman Catholicism
Currency: Cuban peso

Cyprus
Area: 3,572 sq mi (9,251 sq km)
Population: 756,000

Czech Republic

Eritrea

Capital: Nicosia
Other cities: Famagusta, Limassol, Larnaca
Form of government: Republic
Religions: Greek Orthodox, Sunni Islam
Currency: Cyprus pound

Czech Republic, The

Area: 30,450 sq mi (78,864 sq km)
Population: 10,315,000
Capital: Prague (Praha)
Other cities: Brno, Olomouc, Ostrava, Plzen
Form of government: Republic
Religions: Roman Catholicism, Protestant-ism
Currency: Koruna

Denmark

Area: 16,639 sq mi (43,094 sq km)
Population: 5,262,000 (excluding the FAEROE ISLANDS)
Capital: Copenhagen (København)
Other cities: Ålborg, Århus, Odense
Form of government: Constitutional Monarchy
Religion: Lutheranism
Currency: Danish krone

Djibouti

Area: 8,958 sq mi (23,200 sq km)
Population: 617,000
Capital: Djibouti
Form of government: Republic
Religion: Sunni Islam
Currency: Djibouti franc

Dominica

Area: 290 sq mi (751 sq km)
Population: 74,000
Capital: Roseau
Form of government: Republic
Religion: Roman Catholicism
Currency: East Caribbean dollar

Dominican Republic

Area: 18,816 sq mi (48,734 sq km)
Population: 8,052,000
Capital: Santo Domingo
Other cities: Barahona, Santiago, San Pedro de Macoris
Form of government: Republic
Religion: Roman Catholicism
Currency: Dominican Republic peso

East Timor

Area: 5,743 sq mi (14,874 sq km)
Population: 857,000
Capital: Dili
Form of government: Under UN transitional administration
Religions: Roman Catholism
Currency: US dollar

Ecuador

Area: 109,484 sq mi (283,561 sq km)
Population: 11,698,000
Capital: Quito
Other cities: Ambato, Guayaquil, Cuenca, Machala
Form of government: Republic
Religion: Roman Catholicism
Currency: Sucre

Egypt

Area: 386,662 sq mi (1,001,449 sq km)
Population: 60,603,000
Capital: Cairo (El Qâhira)
Other cities: Alexandria, Giza, Port Said, Suez
Form of government: republic
Religions: Sunni Islam, Christianity
Currency: Egyptian pound

El Salvador

Area: 8,124 sq mi (21,041 sq km)
Population: 5,796,000
Capital: San Salvador
Other cities: Santa Ana, San Miguel
Form of government: Republic
Religion: Roman Catholicism
Currency: Colón

Equatorial Guinea

Area: 10,830 sq mi (28,051 sq km)
Population: 410,000
Capital: Malabo
Other major city: Bata
Form of government: Republic
Religion: Roman Catholicism
Currency: CFA franc

Eritrea

Area: 45,406 sq mi (117,600 sq km)
Population: 3,280,000
Capital: Asmara
Other cities: Mitsiwa, Keren, Nak'fa, Ak'ordat

Estonia

Form of government: Republic
Religions: Sunni Islam, Christianity
Currency: Ethiopian birr

Estonia
Area: 17,413 sq mi (45,227 sq km)
Population: 1,453,800
Capital: Tallinn
Other cities: Tartu, Narva, Pärnu
Form of government: Republic
Religions: Eastern Orthodox, Lutheranism
Currency: Kroon

Ethiopia
Area: 426,373 sq mi (1,104,300 sq km)
Population: 58,506,000
Capital: Addis Ababa (Adis Abeba)
Other cities: Dire Dawa, Gonder, Jima
Form of government: Federation
Religions: Ethiopian Orthodox, Sunni Islam
Currency: Ethiopian Birr

Faeroe (Faroe) Islands (Føroyar)
Area: 540 sq mi (1,399 sq km)
Population: 47,000
Capital: Tørshavn
Form of government: Self-governing Region of Denmark
Religion: Lutheranism
Currency: Danish Krone

Falkland Islands
Area: 4,700 sq mi (12,173 sq km)
Population: 2,200
Capital: Stanley
Form of government: British Crown Colony
Religion: Christianity
Currency: Falkland Islands Pound

Fiji
Area: 7,056 sq mi (18,274 sq km)
Population: 797,000
Capital: Suva
Form of government: Republic
Religions: Christianity, Hinduism
Currency: Fijian dollar

Finland
Area: 130,559 sq mi (338,145 sq km)
Population: 5,125,000
Capital: Helsinki (Helsingfors)
Other cities: Turku, Tampere

Georgia

Form of government: Republic
Religion: Lutheranism
Currency: Euro

France
Area: 212,935 sq mi (551,500 sq km)
Population: 58,375,000
Capital: Paris
Other cities: Lyon, Marseille, Nantes, Nice
Form of government: Republic
Religion: Roman Catholicism
Currency: Euro

French Guiana *see* GUIANA.

French Polynesia
Area: 1,544 sq mi (4,000 sq km)
Population: 223,000
Capital: Papeete
Form of government: Overseas Territory of France
Religions: Protestantism, Roman Catholicism
Currency: CFP franc

French Southern and Antarctic Territories
Territories in Antarctica and the Antarctic Ocean administered by FRANCE. They include the Crozet Islands and Kerguelen.

Gabon
Area: 103,347 sq mi (267,668 sq km)
Population: 1,106,000
Capital: Libreville
Other major city: Port Gentile
Form of government: Republic
Religions: Roman Catholicism, African traditional religions
Currency: CFA Franc

Gambia
Area: 4,361 sq mi (11,295 sq km)
Population: 1,141,000
Capital: Banjul
Form of government: Republic
Religions: Sunni Islam, Christianity
Currency: Dalasi

Georgia
Area: 26,911 sq mi (69,700 sq km)
Population: 5,411,000
Capital: T'bilisi
Other cities: Kutaisi, Rustavi, Batumi

Germany

Guinea

Form of government: Republic
Religions: Georgian and Russian Orthodox, Islam
Currency: Lari

Germany
Area: 137,735 sq mi (356,733 sq km)
Population: 81,912,000
Capital: Berlin
Other cities: Bonn, Cologne,, Düsseldorf , Frankfurt, Hamburg, Munich, Stuttgart
Form of government: Republic
Religions: Lutheranism, Roman Catholicism
Currency: Euro

Ghana
Area: 92,100 sq mi (238,537 sq km)
Population: 17,459,350
Capital: Accra
Other cities: Sekondi-Takoradi, Kumasi, Tamale
Form of government: Republic
Religions: Christianity, Islam, African traditional religions
Currency: Cedi

Gibraltar
Area: 2.5 sq mi (6.5 sq km)
Population: 27,100
Capital: Gibraltar
Form of government: Self-governing British colony
Religion: Christianity
Currency: Gibraltar pound

Greece
Area: 50,949 sq mi (131,957 sq km)
Population: 10,475,000
Capital: Athens (Athínai)
Other cities: Iráklian, Lárisa, Patras, Piraeus, Thessaloníki
Form of government: Republic
Religion: Greek Orthodox
Currency: Euro

Greenland (Kalaallit Nunaat)
Area: 840,000 sq mi (2,175,600 sq km)
Population: 58,200
Capital: Gothåb (Nuuk)
Form of government: Self-governing region of Denmark
Religion: Lutheranism
Currency: Danish krone

Grenada
Area: 133 sq mi (344 sq km)
Population: 92,000
Capital: St George's
Form of government: Independent state within the Commonwealth
Religions: Roman Catholicism, Anglicanism, Methodism
Currency: East Caribbean dollar

Guadeloupe
Area: 658 sq mi (1,705 sq km)
Population: 431,000
Capital: Basse Terre
Other main town: Pointe-à-Pitre
Form of government: French overseas department
Religion: Roman Catholicism
Currency: Euro

Guam
Area: 212 sq mi (549 sq km)
Population: 153,000
Capital: Agana
Form of government: Unincorporated territory of the USA
Religion: Roman Catholicism
Currency: US dollar

Guatemala
Area: 42,042 sq mi (108,889 sq km)
Population: 10,928,000
Capital: Guatemala City
Other cities: Cobán, Puerto Barrios, Quezaltenango
Form of government: Republic
Religion: Roman Catholicism
Currency: Quetza

Guiana (French) *or* Guyane
Area: 34,749 sq mi (90,000 sq km)
Population: 153,000
Capital: Cayenne
Form of government: French Overseas Department
Religion: Roman Catholicism
Currency: Euro

Guinea
Area: 94,926 sq mi (245,857 sq km)
Population: 7,518,000
Capital: Conakry

Guinea-Bissau Iran

Other cities: Kankan, Kindia, Labé
Form of government: Republic
Religion: Sunni Islam
Currency: Guinea franc

Guinea-Bissau
Area: 13,948 sq mi (36,125 sq km)
Population: 1,091,000
Capital: Bissau
Form of government: Republic
Religions: African traditional religions,
  Sunni Islam
Currency: Peso

Guyana
Area: 83,000 sq mi (214,969 sq km)
Population: 838,000
Capital: Georgetown
Other cities: Linden, New Amsterdam
Form of government: Cooperative republic
Religions: Hinduism, Protestantism, Roman
  Catholicism
Currency: Guyana dollar

Guyane *see* GUIANA.

Haiti
Area: 10,714 sq mi (27,750 sq km)
Population: 7,336,000
Capital: Port-au-Prince
Other towns: Cap-Haïtien, Les Cayes, Gonaïves
Form of government: Republic
Religions: Roman Catholicism, Voodooism
Currency: Gourde

Honduras
Area: 43,277 sq mi (112,088 sq km)
Population: 6,140,000
Capital: Tegucigalpa
Other cities: San Pedro Sula, La Ceiba,
  Puerto Cortès
Form of government: Republic
Religion: Roman Catholicism
Currency: Lempira

Hong Kong
Area: 415 sq mi (1,075 sq km)
Population: 6,687,200
Form of government: Special Autonomous
  Province of China
Religions: Buddhism, Taoism, Christianity
Currency: Hong Kong dollar

Hungary
Area: 35,920 sq mi (93,032 sq km)
Population: 10,193,000
Capital: Budapest
Other cities: Debrecen, Miskolc, Pécs,
  Szeged
Form of government: Republic
Religions: Roman Catholicism, Calvinism,
  Lutheranism
Currency: Forint

Iceland.
Area: 39,769 sq mi (103,000 sq km)
Population: 275,300
Capital: Reykjavík
Other cities: Akureyri, Kópavogur
Form of government: Republic
Religion: Lutheranism
Currency: Icelandic króna

India
Area: 1,269,346 sq mi (3,287,590 sq km)
Population: 970,930,000
Capital: New Delhi
Other cities: Ahmadabad, Bangalore,
  Bombay, Calcutta, Delhi, Madras,
  Hyderabad, Kanpur
Form of government: Federal Republic,
  Secular Democracy
Religions: Hinduism, Islam, Sikkism,
  Christianity, Jainism, Buddhism
Currency: Rupee

Indonesia
Area: 735,358 sq mi (1,904,569 sq km)
Population: 196,813,000
Capital: Jakarta
Other cities: Bandung, Medan, Palembang,
  Semarang, Surabaya
Form of government: Republic
Religions: Sunni Islam, Christianity,
  Hinduism
Currency: Rupiah

Iran, Islamic Republic of
Area: 634,293 sq mi (1,648,195 sq km)
Population: 61,128,000
Capital: Tehran
Other cities: Esfahan, Mashhad, Tabriz
Form of government: Islamic Republic
Religion: Shia Islam
Currency: Rial

Iraq

Iraq
Area: 169,235 sq mi (438,317 sq km)
Population: 20,607,000
Capital: Baghdad
Other cities: Al-Basrah, Al Mawsil
Form of government: Republic
Religions: Shia Islam, Sunni Islam
Currency: Iraqi dinar

Ireland, Republic of
Area: 27,137 sq mi (70,284 sq km)
Population: 3,626,000
Capital: Dublin (Baile Atha Cliath)
Other cities: Cork, Galway, Limerick,
  Waterford
Form of government: Republic
Religion: Roman Catholicism
Currency: Euro

Israel
Area: 8,130 sq mi (21,056 sq km)
Population: 6,100,000
Capital: Tel Aviv (Tel Aviv-Yafo)
Other cities: Jerusalem, Haifa
Form of government: Republic
Religions: Judaism, Sunni Islam, Christianity
Currency: New Israeli shekel

Italy
Area: 116,320 sq mi (301,268 sq km)
Population: 57,339,000
Capital: Rome (Roma)
Other cities: Milan, Naples, Turin, Genoa,
  Palermo, Florence
Form of government: Republic
Religion: Roman Catholicism
Currency: Euro

Jamaica
Area: 4,243 sq mi (10,990 sq km)
Population: 2,491,000
Capital: Kingston
Other town: Montego Bay
Form of government: Constitutional monarchy
Religions: Anglicanism, Roman Catholi-
  cism, Protestantism
Currency: Jamaican dollar

Japan
Area: 145,870 sq mi (377,801 sq km)
Population: 125,761,000
Capital: Tokyo

Korea, Democratic People's Republic of

Other cities: Osaka, Nagoya, Sapporo,
  Kobe, Kyoto, Yokohama
Form of government: Constitutional Monarchy
Religions: Shintoism, Buddhism, Christianity
Currency: Yen

Jordan
Area: 37,738 sq mi (97,740 sq km)
Population: 5,581,000
Capital: Amman
Other cities: Aqaba, Irbid, Zarqa
Form of government: Constitutional monarchy
Religion: Sunni Islam
Currency: Jordanian dinar

Kazakhstan
Population: 15,671,000
Capital: Astana
Other major city: Almaty
Form of government: Republic
Religion: Sunni Islam
Currency: Tenge

Kenya
Area: 224,081 sq mi (580,367 sq km)
Population: 31,806,000
Capital: Nairobi
Other towns: Mombasa, Eldoret, Nakuru
Form of government: Republic
Religions: Roman Catholicism, Protestant-
  ism, other Christianity, African tradi-
  tional religions
Currency: Kenya shilling

Kiribati
Area: 280 sq mi (726 sq km)
Population: 80,000
Capital: Tarawa
Government: Republic
Religions: Roman Catholicism, Protestantism
Currency: Australian dollar

Korea, Democratic People's Republic of
Area: 46,540 sq mi (120,538 sq km)
Population: 22,466,000
Capital: Pyongyang
Other cities: Chongjin, Wonsan, Hamhung
Form of government: Socialist Republic
Religions: Buddhism, Confucianism,
  Chondogyo (a combination of Taoism
  and Confucianism)
Currency: Won

Korea, Republic of

Area: 38,368 sq mi (99,373 sq km)
Population: 46,430,000
Capital: Seoul (Soul)
Other cities: Pusan, Taegu
Form of government: Republic
Religions: Buddhism, Christianity, Confucianism, Chondogyo (a combination of Taoism and Confucianism), Unification Church
Currency: Won

Kuwait

Area: 6,880 sq mi (17,818 sq km)
Population: 1,866,100
Capital: Kuwait City (Al Kuwayt)
Government: Constitutional Monarchy
Religions: Sunni Islam, Shia Islam
Currency: Kuwaiti dinar

Kyrgyzstan

Area: 76,641 sq mi (198,500 sq km)
Population: 4,575,000
Capital: Bishkek
Other major city: Osh
Form of government: Republic
Religion: Sunni Islam
Currency: Som

Laos

Area: 91,429 sq mi (236,800 sq km)
Population: 5,035,000
Capital: Vientiane
Other cities: Luang Prabang, Savannakhét, Paksé
Form of government: People's Republic
Religion: Buddhism
Currency: New Kip

Latvia

Area: 24,942 sq mi (64,600 sq km)
Population: 2,491,000
Capital: Riga
Other cities: Liepaja, Daugavpils
Form of government: Republic
Religion: Lutheranism
Currency: Lat

Lebanon

Area: 4,015 sq mi (10,400 sq km)
Population: 3,084,900
Capital: Beirut (Beyrouth)

Other important cities: Tripoli, Sidon
Form of government: Republic
Religions: Shia Islam, Sunni Islam, Christianity
Currency: Lebanese pound

Lesotho

Area: 11,720 sq mi (30,355 sq km)
Population: 2,078,000
Capital: Maseru
Form of government: Constitutional monarchy
Religions: Roman Catholicism, other Christianity
Currency: Loti

Liberia

Area: 43,000 sq mi (111,369 sq km)
Population: 2,820,000
Capital: Monrovia
Other major city: Buchanan
Form of government: Republic
Religions: African traditional religions, Sunni Islam, Christianity
Currency: Liberian dollar

Libya

Area: 679,362 sq mi (1,759,540 sq km)
Population: 4,389,739
Capital: Tripoli (Tarabulus)
Other cities: Benghazi, Misrăta
Form of government: Socialist People's Republic
Religion: Sunni Islam
Currency: Libyan dinar

Liechtenstein

Area: 62 sq mi (160 sq km)
Population: 31,320
Capital: Vaduz
Form of government: Constitutional monarchy (principality)
Religion: Roman Catholicism
Currency: Swiss franc

Lithuania

Population: 3,701,300
Capital: Vilnius
Other cities: Kaunas, Klaipeda, Siauliai
Form of government: Republic
Religion: Roman Catholicism
Currency: Litas

Luxembourg

Luxembourg, Grand Duchy of
Population: 412,000
Capital: Luxembourg City
Other cities: Esch-sur-Algette, Differdange, Dudelange
Form of government: Constitutional Monarchy (Duchy)
Religion: Roman Catholicism
Currency: Euro

Macao *or* Macau
Area: 7 sq mi (18 sq km)
Population: 440,000
Capital: Macao
Form of government: Special Administrative Region under Chinese Sovereignty
Religions: Buddhism, Roman Catholicism
Currency: Pataca

Macedonia, The Former Yugoslav Republic of (FYROM)
Area: 9,928 sq mi (25,713 sq km)
Population: 2,174,000
Capital: Skopje
Other cities: Kumanovo, Ohrid
Form of government: Republic
Religions: Eastern Orthodox, Islam
Currency: Dinar

Madagascar
Area: 226,658 sq mi (587,041 sq km)
Population: 15,353,000
Capital: Antananarivo
Other cities: Fianarantsoa, Mahajanga, Toamasina, Toliara
Form of government: Republic
Religions: African traditional religions, Roman Catholicism, Protestantism
Currency: Franc Malgache

Malawi
Area: 45,747 sq mi (118,484 sq km)
Population: 10,114,000
Capital: Lilongwe
Other cities: Blantyre, Zomba
Form of government: Republic
Religions: African traditional religions, Roman Catholicism, Presbyterianism
Currency: Kwacha

Malaysia, The Federation of
Area: 127,320 sq mi (329,758 sq km)
Population: 20,581,000
Capital: Kuala Lumpur
Other cities: Ipoh, George Town, Johor Baharu
Form of government: Federal Constitutional Monarchy
Religion: Islam
Currency: Ringgit or Malaysian dollar

Maldives, Republic of
Area: 115 sq mi (298 sq km)
Population: 263,000
Capital: Malé
Form of government: Republic
Religion: Sunni Islam
Currency: Rufiyaa

Mali
Area: 478,841 sq mi (1,240,192 sq km)
Population: 11,134,000
Capital: Bamako
Other towns: Gao, Kayes, Ségou, Mopti, Sikasso
Form of government: Republic
Religions: Sunni Islam, African traditional religions
Currency: CFA franc

Malta
Area: 122 sq mi (316 sq km)
Population: 376,500
Capital: Valletta
Form of government: Republic
Religion: Roman Catholicism
Currency: Maltese pound

Marshall Islands
Area: 70 sq mi (181 sq km)
Population: 58,000
Capital: Dalag-Uliga-Darrit (on Majuro atoll)
Form of government: Republic in free association with the USA
Religion: Protestantism
Currency: US dollar

Martinique
Area: 425 sq mi (1,102 sq km)
Population: 384,000
Capital: Fort-de-France
Form of government: Overseas Department of France
Religion: Roman Catholicism
Currency: Euro

Mauritania

Namibia

Mauritania or the **Islamic Republic of Mauritania**
Area: 395,956 sq mi (1,025,520 sq km)
Population: 2,351,000
Capital: Nouakchott
Other cities: Kaédi, Nouadhibou
Form of government: Republic
Religion: Sunni Islam
Currency: Ouguiya

Mauritius
Area: 788 sq mi (2,040 sq km)
Population: 1,160,000
Capital: Port Louis
Form of government: Republic
Religions: Hinduism, Roman Catholicism, Sunni Islam
Currency: Mauritian rupee

Mexico
Area: 756,066 sq mi (1,958,201 sq km)
Population: 96,578,000
Capital: México City
Other cities: Guadalajara, León, Monterrey, Puebla, Tijuana
Form of government: Federal Republic
Religion: Roman Catholicism
Currency: Mexican peso

Micronesia, Federated States of
Area: 271 sq mi (702 sq km)
Population: 109,000
Capital: Palikir
Form of government: Republic
Religion: Christianity
Currency: US dollar

Moldova (Moldavia)
Area: 13,012 sq mi (33,700 sq km)
Population: 4,327,000
Capital: Chisinau
Other cities: Tiraspol, Tighina, Bel'tsy
Form of government: Republic
Religion: Russian Orthodox
Currency: Leu

Monaco
Area: 0.4 sq mile (1 sq kilometre)
Population: 32,000
Capital: Monaco
Form of government: Constitutional Monarchy

Religion: Roman Catholicism
Currency: Euro

Mongolia
Area: 604,829 sq mi (1,566,500 sq km)
Population: 2,354,000
Capital: Ulaanbaatar
Other cities: Altay, Saynshand, Hovd, Choybalsan, Tsetserleg
Form of government: Republic
Religions: Buddhism, Shamanism, Islam
Currency: Tughrik

Montenegro *see* Yugoslavia.

Morocco
Area: 172,414 sq mi (446,550 sq km)
Population: 27,623,000
Capital: Rabat
Other cities: Casablanca, Fès, Marrakech, Tangier
Form of government: Constitutional Monarchy
Religion: Sunni Islam
Currency: Dirham

Mozambique
Area: 309,496 sq mi (799,380 sq km)
Population: 16,916,000
Capital: Maputo
Other towns: Beira, Nampula
Form of government: Republic
Religions: African traditional religions, Roman Catholicism, Sunni Islam
Currency: Metical

Myanmar, Union of
Area: 261,228 sq mi (676,578 sq km)
Population: 45,922,000
Capital: Rangoon (Yangon)
Other cities: Mandalay, Moulmein, Pegu
Form of government: Republic
Religion: Buddhism
Currency: Kyat

Namibia
Area: 318,261 sq mi (824,292 sq km)
Population: 1,575,000
Capital: Windhoek
Form of government: Republic
Religions: Lutheranism, Roman Catholicism, other Christianity
Currency: Namibian dollar

Nauru
Area: 8 sq mi (21 sq km)
Population: 11,000
Capital: Nauru
Form of government: Republic
Religions: Protestantism, Roman Catholicism
Currency: Australian dollar

Nepal, Kingdom of
Area: 56,827 sq mi (147,181 sq km)
Population: 21,127,000
Capital: Kathmandu
Other city: Biratnagar
Form of government: Constitutional
  monarchy
Religion: Hinduism, Buddhism
Currency: Nepalese rupee

Netherlands, The
Area: 15,770 sq mi (40,844 sq km)
Population: 15,517,000
Capital: Amsterdam
Seat of government: The Hague
  (s'Gravenhage)
Other cities: Rotterdam, Eindhoven
Form of government: Constitutional
  Monarchy
Religions: Roman Catholicism, Dutch
  Reformed, Calvinism
Currency: Euro

Netherlands Antilles
Area: 309 sq mi (800 sq km)
Population: 207,300
Capital: Willemstad
Form of government: Self-governing Dutch
  Territory
Religion: Roman Catholicism
Currency: Netherlands Antilles guilder

New Caledonia or Nouvelle Calédonie
Area: 7,172 sq mi (18,575 sq km)
Population: 189,000
Capital: Noumea
Form of government: French Overseas
  Territory
Religion: Roman Catholicism
Currency: CFP franc

New Zealand
Area: 104,454 sq mi (270,534 sq km)
Population: 3,681,546

Capital: Wellington
Other cities: Auckland, Christchurch,
  Dunedin, Hamilton
Form of government: Constitutional
  monarchy
Religions: Anglicanism, Roman Catholi-
  cism, Presbyterianism
Currency: New Zealand dollar

Nicaragua
Area: 50,193 sq mi (130,668 sq km)
Population: 4,663,000
Capital: Managua
Form of government: Republic
Religion: Roman Catholicism
Currency: Córdoba oro

Niger
Area: 489,191 sq mi (1,267,000 sq km)
Population: 9,465,000
Capital: Niamey
Other cities: Agadez, Maradi, Tahoua, Zinder
Form of government: Republic
Religion: Sunni Islam
Currency: CFA franc

Nigeria
Area: 356,669 sq mi (923,768 sq km)
Population: 115,120,000
Capital: Abuja
Other cities: Lagos, Onitsha, Enugu,
  Ibadan, Kano, Ogbomosho
Form of government: Federal Republic
Religions: Islam, Christianity, African
  traditional religions
Currency: Naira

Northern Mariana Islands
Area: 179 sq mi (464 sq km)
Population: 49,000
Capital: Saipan
Form of government: Commonwealth in
  union with the USA
Religion: Roman Catholicism
Currency: US dollar

Norway
Area: 125,050 sq mi (323,877 sq km)
Population: 4,445,500
Capital: Oslo
Other cities: Bergen, Trondheim, Stavanger,
  Kristiansand, Tromsö

Form of government: Constitutional
  monarchy
Religion: Lutheranism
Currency: Norwegian krone

Oman or the Sultanate of Oman
Area: 119,498 sq mi (309,500 sq km)
Population: 2,302,000
Capital: Mascat (Musqat)
Other towns: Salalah, Al Khaburah,
  Matrah
Form of government: Monarchy
Religions: Ibadi Islam, Sunni Islam
Currency: Rial Omani

Pakistan or the Islamic Republic of Pakistan
Area: 307,374 sq mi (796,095 sq km)
Population: 134,146,000
Capital: Islamabad
Other cities: Faisalabad, Hyderabad,
  Karachi, Lahore, Rawalpindi
Form of government: Federal Islamic
  Republic
Religions: Sunni Islam, Shia Islam
Currency: Pakistan rupee

Palau
Area: 177 sq mi (459 sq km)
Population: 17,000
Capital: Koror
Form of government: Free Associated
  Republic (USA)
Religions: Roman Catholicism and
  Modekngei
Currency: US dollar

Palestine
Area: Gaza 146 sq mi (360 sq km); Jericho
  27 sq mi (70 sq km); West Bank 2,269 sq
  mi (5,860 sq km)
Population: Gaza 924,200; Jericho 20,600;
  West Bank 2,050,000
Form of government: Republic, with limited
  powers
Religions: Sunni Islam, Shia Islam, Eastern
  Catholicism
Currency: None (Israeli and Jordanian
  currency used)

Panama
Area: 29,157 sq mi (75,517 sq km)
Population: 2,674,000

Capital: Panama City
Other cities: Colón, Puerto Armuelles,
  David
Form of government: Republic
Religion: Roman Catholicism
Currency: Balboa

Papua New Guinea
Area: 178,704 sq mi (462,840 sq km)
Population: 4,400,000
Capital: Port Moresby
Form of government: Republic
Religions: Protestantism, Roman Catholi-
  cism
Currency: Kina

Paraguay
Area: 157,048 sq mi (406,752 sq km)
Population: 4,955,000
Capital: Asunción
Other cities: Concepción, Ciudad del Este,
  Encarnación
Form of government: Republic
Religion: Roman Catholicism
Currency: Guaraní

Peru
Area: 496,225 sq mi (1,285,216 sq km)
Population: 25,015,000
Capital: Lima
Other cities: Arequipa, Callao, Chiclayo,
  Cuzco, Trujillo
Form of government: Republic
Religion: Roman Catholicism
Currency: Nuevo sol

Philippines
Area: 115,813 sq mi (300,000 sq km)
Population: 71,899,000
Capital: Manila
Other cities: Cebu, Davao, Quezon City,
  Zamboanga
Form of government: Republic
Religions: Sunni Islam, Roman Catholicism,
  Protestantism
Currency: Philippine peso

Pitcairn Islands
Area: 2 sq mi (5 sq km)
Population: 50
Form of government: British Overseas
  Territory

Religion: Seventh Day Adventism
Currency: New Zealand dollar

Poland
Area: 124,808 sq mi (323,250 sq km)
Population: 38,628,000
Capital: Warsaw (Warszawa)
Other cities: Gdansk, Kraków, Lódz,
Poznan, Wroclaw
Form of government: Republic
Religion: Roman Catholicism
Currency: Zloty

Portugal
Area: 35,514 sq mi (91,982 sq km)
Population: 9,920,800
Capital: Lisbon (Lisboa)
Other cities: Braga, Coimbra, Faro, Oporto,
Setúbal
Form of government: Republic
Religion: Roman Catholicism
Currency: Euro

Puerto Rico
Area: 3,427 sq mi (8,875 sq km)
Population: 3,736,000
Capital: San Juan
Form of government: Self-governing common-
wealth (in association with the USA)
Religions: Roman Catholicism, Protestantism
Currency: US dollar

Qatar
Area: 4,247 sq mi (11,000 sq km)
Population: 558,000
Capital: Doha (Ad Dawhah)
Form of government: Absolute Monarchy
Religion: Wahhabi Sunni Islam
Currency: Qatar riyal

Réunion
Area: 969 sq mi (2,510 sq km)
Population: 664,000
Capital: St Denis
Form of government: French overseas
department
Religion: Roman Catholicism
Currency: Euro

Romania
Area: 92,043 sq mi (238,391 sq km)
Population 22,520,000

Capital: Bucharest (Bucuresti)
Other cities: Brasov, Constanta, Galati, Iasi,
Timisoara, Craiova, Brâila, Arad, Ploiesti
Form of government: Republic
Religions: Romanian Orthodox, Roman
Catholicism
Currency: Leu

Russia or the **Russian Federation**
Area: 6,592,850 sq mi (17,075,400 sq km)
Population: 146,100,000
Capital: Moscow (Moskva)
Other cities: St Petersburg, Nizhniy
Novgorod, Novosibirsk, Samara
Form of government: Republic
Religions: Russian Orthodox, Sunni Islam,
Shia Islam, Roman Catholicism
Currency: Rouble

Rwanda
Area: 10,169 sq mi (26,338 sq km)
Population: 5,397,000
Capital: Kigali
Other major city: Butare
Form of government: Republic
Religions: Roman Catholicism, African
traditional religions
Currency: Rwandan franc

St Christopher (St Kitts) and Nevis
Area: 101 sq mi (261 sq km)
Population: 41,000
Capital: Basseterre
Other major city: Charlestown
Form of government: Constitutional monarchy
Religions: Anglicanism, Methodism
Currency: East Caribbean Dollar

St Helena
Area: 47 sq mi (122 sq km)
Population: 5,200
Capital: Jamestown
Form of government: British Overseas
Territory
Currency: St Helena pound

St Lucia
Area: 240 sq mi (622 sq km)
Population: 144,000
Capital: Castries
Form of government: Constitutional
Monarchy

St Pierre and Miquelon

Singapore

Religion: Roman Catholicism
Currency: East Caribbean Dollar

St Pierre and Miquelon
Area: 93 sq mi (240 sq km)
Population: 6,300
Capital: Saint Pierre
Form of government: French overseas territory
Religion: Roman Catholicism
Currency: Euro

St Vincent and the Grenadines
Area: 150 sq mi (388 sq km)
Population: 113,000
Capital: Kingstown
Form of government: Constitutional
  monarchy
Religions: Anglicanism, Methodism, Roman
  Catholicism
Currency: East Caribbean dollar

Samoa (Western)
Area: 1,093 sq mi (2,831 sq km)
Population: 166,000
Capital: Apia
Form of government: Constitutional
  Monarchy
Religion: Protestantism
Currency: Tala

Samoa, American
Area: 77 sq mi (199 sq km)
Population: 56,000
Capital: Pago Pago
Form of government: Unincorporated
  Territory of the USA
Religion: Christianity
Currency: US dollar

San Marino
Area: 24 sq mi (61 sq km)
Population: 25,000
Capital: San Marino
Other cities: Borgo Maggiore, Serravalle
Form of government: Republic
Religion: Roman Catholicism
Currency: Euro

São Tomé and Príncipe
Area: 372 sq mi (964 sq km)
Population: 135,000
Capital: São Tomé

Form of government: Republic
Religion: Roman Catholicism
Currency: Dobra

Saudi Arabia
Area: 830,000 sq mi (2,149,690 sq km)
Population: 18,836,000
Capital: Riyadh (Ar Riyãd)
Other cities: Ad Dammam, Mecca, Jeddah,
  Medina
Form of government: Monarchy
Religions: Sunni Islam, Shia Islam
Currency: Riyal

Senegal
Area: 75,955 sq mi (196,722 sq km)
Population: 8,572,000
Capital: Dakar
Other cities: Kaolack, Thiès, St Louis
Form of government: Republic
Religions: Sunni Islam, Roman Catholicism
Currency: CFA franc

Serbia *see* Yugoslavia.

Seychelles
Area: 175 sq mi (455 sq km)
Population: 76,000
Capital: Victoria
Form of government: Republic
Religion: Roman Catholicism
Currency: Seychelles rupee

Sierra Leone
Area: 27,699 sq mi (71,740 sq km)
Population: 4,297,000
Capital: Freetown
Other city: Bo
Form of government: Republic
Religions: African traditional religions,
  Sunni Islam, Christianity
Currency: Leone

Singapore
Area: 239 sq mi (618 sq km)
Population: 3,044,000
Capital: Singapore
Form of government: Parliamentary
  Democracy
Religions: Buddhism, Sunni Islam,
  Christianity, Hinduism
Currency: Singapore dollar

Slovakia

Sweden

Slovakia (Slovak Republic)
Area: 18,928 sq mi (49,035 sq km)
Population: 5,374,000
Capital: Bratislava
Other cities: Kosice, Zilina, Nitra
Form of government: Republic
Religion: Roman Catholicism
Currency: Slovak koruna

Slovenia
Area: 7,821 sq mi (20,256 sq km)
Population: 1,991,000
Capital: Ljubljana
Other cities: Maribor, Kranj
Form of government: Republic
Religion: Roman Catholicism
Currency: Tolar

Solomon Islands
Area: 11,157 sq mi (28,896 sq km)
Population: 391,000
Capital: Honiara
Form of government: Parliamentary
  Democracy within the Commonwealth
Religion: Christianity
Currency: Solomon Islands dollar

Somalia
Area: 246,201 sq mi (637,657 sq km)
Population: 9,822,000
Capital: Mogadishu (Muqdisho)
Other major towns: Hargeysa, Burco
Form of government: Republic
Religion: Sunni Islam
Currency: Somali shilling

South Africa
Area: 471,445 sq mi (1,221,037 sq km)
Population: 42,393,000
Capital: Pretoria (administrative), Cape
  Town (legislative)
Other cities: Johannesburg, Durban, Port
  Elizabeth, Soweto
Form of government: Republic
Religions: Christianity, Hinduism, Islam
Currency: Rand

Spain
Area: 195,365 sq mi (505,992 sq km)
Population: 39,270,400
Capital: Madrid
Other cities: Barcelona, Valencia, Seville,

Zaragoza, Malaga, Bilbao
Form of government: Constitutional
  Monarchy
Religion: Roman Catholicism
Currency: Euro

Sri Lanka
Area: 25,332 sq mi (65,610 sq km)
Population: 18,354,000
Capital: Colombo
Other cities: Trincomalee, Jaffna, Kandy,
  Moratuwa
Form of government: Republic
Religions: Buddhism, Hinduism, Christian-
  ity, Sunni Islam
Currency: Sri Lankan rupee

Sudan
Area: 967,500 sq mi (2,505,813 sq km)
Population: 27,291,000
Capital: Khartoum (El Khartum)
Other cities: Omdurman, Khartoum North,
  Port Sudan
Form of government: Republic
Religions: Sunni Islam, African traditional
  religions, Christianity
Currency: Sudanese dinar (of 10 pounds)

Suriname
Area: 63,037 sq mi (163,265 sq km)
Population: 423,000
Capital: Paramaribo
Form of government: Republic
Religions: Hinduism, Roman Catholicism,
  Sunni Islam
Currency: Suriname guilder

Swaziland
Area: 6,704 sq mi (17,364 sq km)
Population: 938,700
Capital: Mbabane
Other towns: Big Bend, Manzini,
  Mankayane, Lobamba
Form of government: Monarchy
Religions: Christianity, African traditional
  religions
Currency: Lilangeni

Sweden
Area: 173,732 sq mi (449,964 sq km)
Population: 8,843,000
Capital: Stockholm

Switzerland

Other cities: Göteborg, Malmö, Uppsala, Örebro, Linköping
Form of government: Constitutional Monarchy
Religion: Lutheranism
Currency: Krona

Switzerland

Area: 15,940 sq mi (41,284 sq km)
Population: 7,076,000
Capital: Bern
Other cities: Zürich, Basle, Geneva, Lausanne
Form of government: Federal Republic
Religions: Roman Catholicism, Protestantism
Currency: Swiss franc

Syria or the Syrian Arab Republic

Area: 71,498 sq mi (185,180 sq km)
Population: 14,619,000
Capital: Damascus (Dimashq)
Other cities: Halab, Hims, Dar'a
Form of government: Republic
Religion: Sunni Islam
Currency: Syrian pound

Taiwan

Area: 13,800 sq mi (35,742 sq km)
Population: 21,854,270
Capital: T'ai-pei
Other cities: Kao-hsiung, T'ai-nan, Chang-hua, Chi-lung
Form of government: Republic
Religions: Taoism, Buddhism, Christianity
Currency: New Taiwan dollar

Tajikistan

Area: 55,250 sq mi (143,100 sq km)
Population: 5,919,000
Capital: Dushanbe
Other major city: Khujand
Form of government: Republic
Religion: Shia Islam
Currency: Tajik rouble

Tanzania

Area: 362,162 sq mi (938,000 sq km)
Population: 30,799,100
Capital: Dodoma
Other towns: Dar es Salaam, Zanzibar, Mwanza, Tanga
Form of government: Republic

Religions: Sunni Islam, Roman Catholicism, Anglicanism, Hinduism
Currency: Tanzanian shilling

Thailand

Area: 198,115 sq mi (513,115 sq km)
Population: 60,206,000
Capital: Bangkok (Krung Thep)
Other cities: Chiang Mai, Nakhon Ratchasima, Ubon Ratchathani
Form of government: Constitutional monarchy
Religions: Buddhism, Sunni Islam
Currency: Baht

Togo

Area: 21,925 sq mi (56,785 sq km)
Population: 4,201,000
Capital: Lomé
Other major city: Sokodé
Form of government: Republic
Religions: African traditional religions, Roman Catholicism, Sunni Islam
Currency: CFA franc

Tonga

Area: 288 sq mi (747 sq km)
Population: 99,000
Capital: Nuku'alofa
Form of government: Constitutional monarchy
Religions: Methodism, Roman Catholicism
Currency: Pa'anga

Trinidad and Tobago

Area: 1,981 sq mi (5,130 sq km)
Population: 1,297,000
Capital: Port of Spain
Other towns: San Fernando, Arima
Form of government: Republic
Religions: Roman Catholicism, Hinduism, Anglicanism, Sunni Islam
Currency: Trinidad and Tobago dollar

Tunisia

Area: 62,592 sq mi (162,155 sq km)
Population: 9,092,000
Capital: Tunis
Other cities: Sfax, Bizerte, Sousse
Form of government: Republic
Religion: Sunni Islam
Currency: Dinar

Turkey
Area: 299,158 sq mi (774,815 sq km)
Population: 62,697,000
Capital: Ankara
Other cities: Istanbul, Izmir, Adana, Bursa
Form of government: Republic
Religion: Sunni Islam
Currency: Turkish lira

Turkmenistan
Area: 188,456 sq mi (488,100 sq km)
Population: 4,569,000
Capital: Ashkhabad (Ashgabat)
Other cities: Chardzhou, Mary, Turkmen-
bashi
Form of government: Republic
Religion: Sunni Islam
Currency: Manat

Turks and Caicos Islands
Area: 166 sq mi (430 sq km)
Population: 23,000
Capital: Grand Turk
Form of government: British Crown Colony
Religion: Christianity
Currency: US dollar

Tuvalu
Area: 10 sq mi (24 sq km)
Population: 10,000
Capital: Funafuti
Form of government: Constitutional
Monarchy
Religion: Protestantism
Currency: Tuvalu dollar/Australian dollar

Uganda
Area: 93,065 sq mi (241,038 sq km)
Population: 19,848,000
Capital: Kampala
Other cities: Entebbe, Jinja, Soroti, Mbale
Form of government: Republic
Religions: Roman Catholicism, Protestant-
ism, African traditional religions, Sunni
Islam
Currency: Uganda shilling

Ukraine
Area: 233,090 sq mi (603,700 sq km)
Population: 51,094,000
Capital: Kiev (Kiyev)
Other cities: Dnepropetrovsk, Donetsk,

Khar'kov, Odessa, Lugansk, Sevastopol
Form of government: Republic
Religions: Russian Orthodox, Roman
Catholicism
Currency: Rouble

United Arab Emirates (UAE)
Area: 32,278 sq mi (83,600 sq km)
Population: 2,260,000
Capital: Abu Zabi (Abu Dhabi)
Other cities: Dubai, Sharjh, Ras al Khaymah
Form of government: Monarchy
Religion: Sunni Islam
Currency: Dirham

United Kingdom of Great Britain and Northern Ireland (UK)
Area: 94,248 sq mi (244,101 sq km)
Population: 58,784,000
Capital: London
Other cities: Manchester, Glasgow,
Liverpool, Edinburgh, Cardiff, Belfast
Form of government: Constitutional
Monarchy
Religions: Protestantism, Roman Catholi-
cism, Islam, Judaism
Currency: Pound sterling

United States of America (USA)
Area: 3,536,278 sq mi (9,158,960 sq km)
Population: 270,299,000
Capital: Washington DC
Other cities: New York, Chicago, Detroit,
Houston, Los Angeles, Philadelphia, San
Diego, San Francisco
Form of government: Federal republic
Religions: Protestantism, Roman Catholicism,
Judaism, Eastern Orthodox, Sunni Islam
Currency: US dollar

Uruguay
Area: 68,500 sq mi (177,414 sq km)
Population: 3,203,000
Capital: Montevideo
Form of government: Republic
Religions: Roman Catholicism, Protestantism
Currency: Peso Uruguayos

Uzbekistan
Area: 172,742 sq mi (447,400 sq km)
Population: 24,000,000
Capital: Tashkent

Vanuatu

Zambia

Other cities: Urgench, Nukus, Bukhara,
 Samarkand
Form of government: Republic
Religion: Sunni Islam
Currency: Soum

Vanuatu
Area: 4,706 sq mi (12,189 sq km)
Population: 169,000
Capital: Vila
Form of government: Republic
Religion: Roman Catholicism
Currency: Vatu

Vatican City State
Area: 0.2 sq mile (0.44 sq kilometre)
Population: 1,000
Capital: Vatican City
Form of government: Papal
 commission
Religion: Roman Catholicism
Currency: Euro

Venezuela
Area: 352,145 sq mi (912,050 sq km)
Population: 21,710,000
Capital: Caracas
Other cities: Maracaibo, Valencia,
 Barquisimeto
Form of government: Federal republic
Religion: Roman Catholicism
Currency: Bolívar

Vietnam
Area: 128,066 sq mi (331,689 sq km)
Population: 75,181,000
Capital: Hanoi
Other cities: Ho Chi Minh City, Haiphong,
 Hué, Dà Nang
Form of government: Socialist Republic
Religions: Buddhism, Taoism, Roman
 Catholicism
Currency: New dong

Virgin Islands, British
Area: 58 sq mi (151 sq km)
Population: 19,000
Capital: Road Town
Form of government: British overseas
 territory
Religion: Protestantism
Currency: US dollar

Virgin Islands, US
Area: 134 sq mi (347 sq km)
Population: 106,000
Capital: Charlotte Amalie
Form of government: Self-governing US
 Territory
Religion: Protestantism
Currency: US dollar

Wallis and Futuna Islands
Area: 77 sq mi (200 sq km)
Population: 15,000
Capital: Mata-Uru
Form of government: French overseas
 territory
Religion: Roman Catholicism
Currency: CFP franc

Western Sahara
Area: 102,703 sq mi (266,000 sq km)
Population: 266,000
Capital: Laâyoune (El Aaiún)
Form of government: Republic (*de facto*
 controlled by Morocco)
Religion: Sunni Islam
Currency: Moroccan dirham

Western Samoa *see* Samoa.

Yemen
Area: 203,850 sq mi (527,978 sq km)
Population: 15,919,000
Capital: San'a
Commercial Capital: Aden (Adan)
Other cities: Al Hudaydah, Ta'izz
Form of government: Republic
Religions: Zaidism, Shia Islam,
 Sunni Islam
Currency: Riyal

Yugoslavia (FRY)
Area: 39,449 sq mi (102,173 sq km)
Population: 10,574,000
Capital: Belgrade (Beograd)
Other cities: Nis, Novi Sad, Pristina
Form of government: Federal Republic
Religions: Eastern Orthodox, Islam
Currency: New dinar (Kosovo and
 Montenegro have adopted the euro).

Zambia
Area: 290,587 sq mi (752,618 sq km)

Zaire   **Zimbabwe**

Population: 8,275,000
Capital: Lusaka
Other cities: Kitwe, Ndola,
  Mufulira
Form of government: Republic
Religions: Christianity, African traditional
  religions
Currency: Kwacha

Zaire *see* CONGO, DEMOCRATIC REPUBLIC OF THE.

Zimbabwe
Area: 150,872 sq mi (390,757 sq km)
Population: 11,908,000
Capital: Harare
Other cities: Bulawayo, Mutare, Gweru
Form of government: Republic
Religions: African traditional religions,
  Anglicanism, Roman Catholicism
Currency: Zimbabwe dollar

Chemical Elements

Element	Symbol	Atomic No	Relative Atomic Mass*	Element	Symbol	Atomic No	Relative Atomic Mass*
Actinium	Ac	89	{227}	Indium	In	49	1114.82
Aluminium	Al	13	26.9815	Iodine	I	53	126.9044
Americium	Am	95	{243}	Iridium	Ir	77	192.2
Antimony	Sb	51	121.75	Iron	Fe	26	55.847
Argon	Ar	18	39.948	Krypton	Kr	36	83.80
Arsenic	As	33	74.9216	Lanthanum	La	57	138.91
Astatine	At	85	{210}	Lawrencium	Lr	103	{257}
Barium	Ba	56	137.34	Lead	Pb	82	207.19
Berkelium	Bk	97	{247}	Lithium	Li	3	6.939
Beryllium	Be	4	9.0122	Lutetium	Lu	71	174.97
Bismuth	Bi	83	208.98	Magnesium	Mg	12	24.305
Bohrium	Bh	107		Manganese	Mn	25	54.938
Boron	B	5	10.81	Meitnerium	Mt	109	
Bromine	Br	35	79.904	Mendelevium	Md	101	{259}
Cadmium	Cd	48	112.40	Mercury	Hg	80	200.59
Caesium	Cs	55	132.905	Molybdenum	Mo	42	95.94
Calcium	Ca	20	40.08	Neodymium	Nd	60	144.24
Californium	Cf	98	{251}	Neon	Ne	10	20.179
Carbon	C	6	12.011	Neptunium	Np	93	{237}
Cerium	Ce	58	140.12	Nickel	Ni	28	58.71
Chlorine	Cl	17	35.453	Niobium	Nb	41	92.906
Chromium	Cr	24	51.996	Nitrogen	N	7	14.0067
Cobalt	Co	27	58.9332	Nobelium	No	102	{255}
Copper	Cu	29	63.546	Osmium	Os	76	190.2
Curium	Cm	96	{247}	Oxygen	O	8	15.9994
Dubnium	Db	105		Palladium	Pd	46	106.4
Dysprosium	Dy	66	162.50	Phosphorus	P	15	30.9738
Einsteinium	Es	99	{254}	Platinum	Pt	78	195.09
Erbium	Er	68	167.26	Plutonium	Pu	94	{244}
Europium	Eu	63	151.96	Polonium	Po	84	{209}
Fermium	Fm	100	{257}	Potassium	K	19	39.102
Fluorine	F	9	18.9984	Praseodymium	Pr	59	140.907
Francium	Fr	87	{223}	Promethium	Pm	61	{145}
Gadolinium	Gd	64	157.25	Protactinium	Pa	91	{231}
Gallium	Ga	31	69.72	Radium	Ra	88	{226}
Germanium	Ge	32	72.59	Radon	Rn	86	{222}
Gold	Au	79	196.967	Rhenium	Re	75	186.20
Hafnium	Hf	72	178.49	Rhodium	Rh	45	102.905
Hassium	Hs	108		Rubidium	Rb	37	85.47
Helium	He	2	4.0026	Ruthenium	Ru	44	101.07
Holmium	Ho	67	164.930	Rutherfordium	Rf	104	
Hydrogen	H	1	1.00797	Samarium	Sm	62	150.35

Element	Symbol	Atomic No	Relative Atomic Mass*	Element	Symbol	Atomic No	Relative Atomic Mass*
Scandium	Sc	21	44.956	Tin	Sn	50	118.69
Seaborgium	Sg	106		Titanium	Ti	22	47.90
Selenium	Se	34	78.96	Tungsten	W	74	183.85
Silicon	Si	14	28.086	Ununbium	Uub	112	
Silver	Ag	47	107.868	Ununnilium	Uun	110	
Sodium	Na	11	22.9898	Unununium	Uuu	111	
Strontium	Sr	38	87.62	Uranium	U	92	238.03
Sulphur	S	16	32.064	Vanadium	V	23	50.942
Tantalum	Ta	73	180.948	Xenon	Xe	54	131.30
Technetium	Tc	43	{97}	Ytterbium	Yb	70	173.04
Tellurium	Te	52	127.60	Yttrium	Y	39	88.905
Terbium	Tb	65	158.924	Zinc	Zn	30	65.37
Thallium	Tl	81	204.37	Zirconium	Zr	40	91.22
Thorium	Th	90	232.038				
Thulium	Tm	69	168.934				

* Values of the *Relative Atomic Mass* in brackets refer to the most stable, known, isotope.

Elements listed by symbol

Symbol	Element	Symbol	Element	Symbol	Element	Symbol	Element
Ac	Actinium	Er	Erbium	N	Nitrogen	S	Sulphur
Al	Aluminium	Es	Einsteinium	Na	Sodium	Sb	Antimony
Am	Americium	Eu	Europium	Nb	Niobium	Sc	Scandium
Ar	Argon	F	Fluorine	Nd	Neodymium	Se	Selenium
As	Arsenic	Fe	Iron	Ne	Neon	Si	Silicon
At	Astatine	Fm	Fermium	Ni	Nickel	Sm	Samarium
Au	Gold	Fr	Francium	No	Nobelium	Sn	Tin
B	Boron	Ga	Gallium	Np	Neptunium	Sr	Strontium
Ba	Barium	Gd	Gadolinium	O	Oxygen	Ta	Tantalum
Be	Beryllium	Ge	Germanium	Os	Osmium	Tn	Terbium
Bi	Bismuth	H	Hydrogen	P	Phosphorous	Tc	Technetium
Bk	Berkelium	He	Helium	Pa	Protactinium	Te	Tellerium
Br	Bromine	Hf	Hafnium	Pb	Lead	Th	Thorium
C	Carbon	Ho	Holmium	Pd	Palladium	Ti	Titanium
Ca	Calcium	I	Iodine	Pm	Promethium	Tl	Thallium
Cd	Cadmium	In	Indium	Po	Polonium	Tm	Thulium
Ce	Cerium	Ir	Iridium	Pr	Praseodymium	U	Uranium
Cf	Californium	Kr	Krypton	Pt	Platinum	V	Vanadium
Cl	Chlorine	La	Lanthanum	Pu	Plutonium	W	Tungsten
Cm	Curium	Li	Lithium	Ra	Radium	Xe	Xenon
Co	Cobalt	Lu	Lutetium	Rb	Rubidium	Y	Yttrium
Cr	Chromium	Md	Mendelevium	Rh	Rhodium	Yb	Ytterbium
Cs	Caesium	Mg	Magnesium	Rn	Radon	Zn	Zinc
Cu	Copper	Mn	Manganese	Ru	Ruthenium	Zr	Zirconium
Dy	Dysprosium	Mo	Molybdenum				

The periodic table

Group	1A	2A	3B	4B	5B	6B	7B	8B	8B	8B	1B	2B	3A	4A	5A	6A	7A	8A
	H 1																	He 2
	Li 3	Be 4											B 5	C 6	N 7	O 8	F 9	Ne 10
	Na 11	Mg 12					*Transition Elements*						Al 13	Si 14	P 15	S 16	Cl 17	Ar 18
	K 19	Ca 20	Sc 21	Ti 22	V 23	Cr 24	Mn 25	Fe 26	Co 27	Ni 28	Cu 29	Zn 30	Ga 31	Ge 32	As 33	Se 34	Br 35	Kr 36
	Rb 37	Sr 38	Y 39	Zr 40	Nb 41	Mo 42	Tc 43	Ru 44	Rh 45	Pd 46	Ag 47	Cd 48	In 49	Sn 50	Sb 51	Te 52	I 53	Xe 54
	Cs 55	Ba 56	La 57 *	Hf 72	Ta 73	W 74	Re 75	Os 76	Ir 77	Pt 78	Au 79	Hg 80	Tl 81	Pb 82	Bi 83	Po 84	At 85	Rn 86
	Fr 87	Ra 88	Ac 89 °	Rf 104	Db 105	Sg 106	Bh 107	Hs 108	Mt 109	Uun 110	Uuu 111	Uub 112	Uut† 113	Uuq† 114	Uup† 115	Uuh† 116	Uus† 117	Uuo† 118
* Lanthanides				Ce 58	Pr 59	Nd 60	Pm 61	Sm 62	Eu 63	Gd 64	Tb 65	Dy 66	Ho 67	Er 68	Tm 69	Yb 70	Lu 71	
° Actinides				Th 90	Pa 91	U 92	Np 93	Pu 94	Am 95	Cm 96	Bk 97	Cf 98	Es 99	Fm 100	Md 101	No 102	Lr 103	

The names and symbols of elements 104 to 112 in this table have been approved by the international Union of Pure and Applied Chemistry (IUPAC).

†There are a further six symbols for elements that can reliably be predicted but have not, as yet, been discovered. All these elements exist for a very short time in laboratory experiments and decay radioactively.

SI Units

The International System of Units (SI units)

Quantity	Symbol	Unit	Symbols
acceleration	a	metres per second squared	ms^{-2} or m/s^2
area	A	square metre	m^2
capacitance	C	farad	$F(1F = 1\ AsV^{-1})$
charge	Q	coulomb	$C(1C = 1\ As)$
current	I	ampere	A
density	ρ	kilograms per cubic metre	kgm^{-3} or $kg/m3$
force	F	newton	$N(1N = 1\ kg\ ms^{-2})$
frequency	f	hertz	$Hz(1Hz = 1s^{-1})$
length	l	metre	m
mass	m	kilogram	kg
potential difference	V	volt	$V(1V = 1JC^{-1}\ or\ WA^{-1})$
power	P	watt	$W(1W = 1Js^{-1})$
resistance	R	ohm	$(1\ = 1V\ A^{-1})$
specific heat capacity	c	joules per kilogram kelvin	$Jkg^{-1}\ K^{-1}$
temperature	T	kelvin	L
time	t	second	s
volume	V	cubic metre	m^3
velocity	v	metres per second	m^{s-1} or m/s
wavelength	λ	metre	m
work, energy	W, E	joule	$J(1J = 1Nm)$

Useful prefixes adopted with SI units

Prefix	Symbol	Factor
tera	T	10^{12}
giga	G	10^9
mega	M	10^6
kelo	k	10^3
hecto	h	10^2
deda	da	10^1
deci	d	10^{-1}
centi	c	10^{-2}
milli	m	10^{-3}
micro	μ	10^{-6}
nano	n	10^{-9}
pico	p	10^{-12}
femto	f	10^{-15}
atto	a	10^{-18}

The Greek Alphabet

Name	Capital	Lower Case	English Sound
alpha	Α	α	a
beta	Β	β	b
gamma	Γ	γ	g
delta	Δ	δ	d
epsilon	Ε	ε	e
zeta	Ζ	ζ	z
eta	Η	η	e
theta	Θ	θ	th
iota	Ι	ι	i
kappa	Κ	κ	k
lambda	Λ	λ	l
mu	Μ	μ	m
nu	Ν	ν	n
xi	Ξ	ξ	x
omicron	Ο	ο	o
pi	Π	π	p
rho	Ρ	ρ	r
sigma	Σ	σ	s
tau	Τ	τ	t
upsilon	Υ	υ	u
phi	Φ	φ	ph
chi	Χ	χ	kh
psi	Ψ	ψ	ps
omega	Ω	ω	o

Musical Notation

♯	sharp
♭	flat
♮	natural
𝄪	double sharp
♭♭	double flat
♮♯	a single sharp used after a double sharp
♮♭	a single flat used after a double flat
𝄎, ▐●▌	breve, double whole note

𝅝	whole note; semibreve
𝅗𝅥	half note; minim
𝅘𝅥	quarter note; crochet
𝅘𝅥𝅮	eighth note; quaver
𝅘𝅥𝅯	sixteenth note; semiquaver
𝅘𝅥𝅰	thirty-second note; demisemiquaver
𝅘𝅥𝅱	sixty-fourth note; hemisemidemiquaver

357

Scientific Classification

Scientific classification

Scientific classification of organisms into groups based on similarities of structure and origin is called **taxonomy**.

In descending order:

kingdom one of the five biological divisions into which living organisms can be divided: Prokaryotae (bacteria), Prototistae (algae, Protozoans), Fungi, Plantae and Animalae. Also, in general usage, refers to the divisions animal, vegetable, or mineral.

phylum (*plural* **phyla**) one of the major divisions of the animal or vegetable kingdoms containing one or more classes.

class a group or groups into which a phylum is divided, made up of one or more orders.

order any of the groups into which a class is divided, made up of one or more families.

family in scientific classifications, a group of individuals more comprehensive than a genus and less so than an order.

genus (*plural* **genera**) a division of plants and animals below a family and above a species.

species (*plural* **species**) a group of animals or plants that bear a close resemblance to each other in the more essential features of their organisation and produce similar progeny, several species uniting to form a genus.

race a group of individuals that is different in one or more ways from other members of the same species. They may be different because they occupy another geographical area, perhaps showing a variation in colour, or they may exhibit behavioural, physiological or even genetic differences. The term is sometimes used in the same way as subspecies. Animals from different races are able to interbreed.

variety a race that is not distinct enough to be counted as a separate species.

Actinozoa *or* **Anthozoa** a class of small marine animals belonging to the phylum Coelenterata (Cnidaria), which includes sea pens, sea pansies, sea feathers, sea fans, sea anemones and corals and also includes jellyfish and hydras.

Agnatha a vertebrate class that contains lampreys and hagfishes (order Cyclostomata). These are aquatic, eel-like animals.

Amphibia a vertebrate class of which salamanders, newts, frogs and toads are members. Amphibians were the first vertebrates to colonise land, about 370 million years ago.

Angiospermae a class of flowering plants. These are the most complex and highly developed plants, and this enables them to live in a great many different habitats.

Animalae the kingdom which includes the animal

Annelida an invertebrate phylum to which ragworms (class Polychaeta), earthworms (class Oligochaeta), and leeches (class Hirudinea) belong.

Arachnida an invertebrate class to which spiders, scorpions, mites, ticks, king crabs, harvestmen, etc, all belong.

Arthropoda the largest phylum of invertebrate animals containing over one million known species. They include such classes as the Crustacea (lobsters, crabs, shrimps), Insecta (insects), Arachnida (spiders, mites, scorpions) and Myriapoda (millipedes and centipedes).

Arthropoidea the suborder of the order Primate which includes monkeys, apes and humans.

Artiodactyla a mammalian order that includes cattle, camels, hippopotamuses, pigs, deer, antelope, goats, sheep and llamas. One of the two orders that make up the group called the Ungulates, the other being the Perissodactyla.

Aves (birds) a class of vertebrates that evolved from flying reptiles and still show features of their ancestry, e.g. laying eggs and having scales on the legs.

Bacillariophyta the division to which *diatoms*,

a type of algae, belong. They are simple, single-celled plants that sometimes form chains or colonies and live in both marine and freshwater environments.

Bivalvia a class of the phylum Molluska to which many species of shellfish, called bivalves, belong e.g. mussels, oysters, scallops and clams.

Brachiopoda a phylum of ancient marine invertebrate animals. Brachiopods, or lampshells, possess a special structure, called a *lophophore*, that is used for feeding and respiration.

Bryophyta the division of the plant kingdom to which mosses belong.

Carnivora an order of mammals that include flesh-eating predators and carrion-eaters. Two suborders are Fissipedia (toe-footed), e.g. wolves, dogs, cats and badgers, and Pinnepedia (fin-footed), e.g. walruses, sea lions and seals.

Cephalopoda a class of marine molluscs to which the nautilus, squid, cuttlefish, octopus and the (extinct) fossil ammonite belong.

Cestoda a class of the phylum Platyhelminthes. Cestodes are the parasitic tapeworms that live inside the gut of a vertebrate.

Cetacea an order of marine mammals comprising the dolphins and whales.

Chelonia an order of the class Reptilia comprising turtles, terrapins and tortoises. The body of these animals is encased in a bony shell.

Chiroptera the mammalian order to which bats belong, the main characteristic of which is flight.

Chlorophyta the division of organisms to which green algae, the largest and most varied group of algae, belong.

Chondrichthyes (cartilaginous fishes) a class of fishes which have a skeleton composed entirely of cartilage, e.g. rays, sharks and skates.

Cnidaria *or* **Coelenterata** the phylum of aquatic invertebrates to which hydras, jellyfish, sea anemones and corals belong.

Coleoptera a vast order (the largest in the animal kingdom) of the class Insecta to which beetles and weevils belong. There are about 500,000 known species.

Copepoda a large subclass of the class

Crustacea to which tiny marine and freshwater invertebrate animals belong.

Crustacea a class of the phylum Arthropoda to which lobsters, crayfish, crabs, shrimps, prawns, barnacles and water fleas belong.

Decapoda the order of the class Crustacea to which prawns, shrimps, lobsters and crabs belong.

Diptera a large insect order that contains about 80,000 species including flies.

Echinodermata a phylum of marine invertebrates to which starfish, brittle stars, sea urchins, sea cucumbers, sea lilies and sea daisies belong.

Foraminifer a phylum of small marine animals (Protozoans) that have hard shells made of calcium carbonate or silica.

Fungi the kingdom which includes organisms that lack chlorophyl, leaves and stems and reproduce by spores, such as moulds, mildew, yeasts, mushrooms and toadstools.

Gastropoda a class of the phylum Molluska to which invertebrate animals with a shell, such as limpets, whelks, conches, and snails belong.

Gymnospermae the class (or subdivision) of the division Spermatophyta, seed plants, to which conifers, cycads and ginkgos belong.

Hemiptera the order of the class Insecta to which bugs belong, e.g. leaf hoppers, scale insects, bed bugs, aphids, cicadas and water boatmen.

Hominidae a family of the order Primate; includes modern man as well as fossil hominids. All belong to the genus *Homo*. Their main characteristic is the ability to walk upright.

Hydrozoa the class of the phylum Cnidaria to which corals known as millepore corals, hydras and such animals as the Portuguese man-of-war (*Physalia*) and *Vellela* belong.

Hymenoptera the order of the class Insecta to which bees, wasps, ants, sawflies and ichneumon flies belong.

Insecta a class of invertebrate animals belonging to the phylum Arthropoda, with over 750 million species. There are 26 orders, e.g. beetles (Coleoptera), flies (Diptera), bees and ants (Hymenoptera), butterflies (Lepidoptera), and grasshoppers (Orthoptera).

Insectivora the order of small mammals to

which moles, shrews and hedgehogs belong. Their diet is mainly insects.

Isopoda the order of the class Crustacea to which woodlice, fish lice and pill bugs belong. Isopods inhabit marine, freshwater and terrestrial environments.

Lepidoptera the order of the class insecta to which moths and butterflies belong.

Malacostraca the subclass of the class Crustacea to which prawns and other similar marine and freshwater animals belong.

Mammalia the vertebrate class that contains approximately 4500 species that feeds its young with milk from the female mammary glands and, except monotremes (Monotremata), bring forth living young rather than eggs. Includes humans, apes, whales and marsupials,

Metatheria the subclass of the class Mammalia to which marsupial mammals belong, such as kangaroos, koala bears and opossums. The female has a pouch on the abdomen where her young complete their development.

Molluska the phylum of invertebrate animals to which many with shells, such as slugs and snails (class Gastropoda), mussels and oysters (class Bivalvia) and cuttlefish, squids and octopuses (class Cephalopoda) all belong. It includes over 50,000 species.

Monotremata the lowest order of the mammals comprising only the monotremes: the duckbill platypus and the echidna of Australia.

Myriapoda the class of the phylum Arthropoda to which centipedes (subclass Chilopoda) and millipedes (subclass Diplopoda) belong.

Mysticetti a suborder of Cetacea, including the plankton-feeding whales.

Nematoda the phylum of invertebrate animals to which roundworms belong.

Odonata the order of the class insecta to which dragonflies and damselflies belong.

Odontocetti a suborder of Cetacea including the marine predators: dolphins, killer whales and toothed whales.

Oligochaeta the class of the phylum Annelida to which earthworms and some other worm species belong.

Orthoptera the order of the class Insecta to which grasshoppers, crickets, locusts, preying mantises and cockroaches belong.

Perissodactyla the order of the class Mammalia to which herbivorous grazing mammals such as horses, zebras, rhinoceroses and tapirs belong. These animals characteristically have hoofed feet and an odd number of toes.

Plantae the kingdom which includes all plants.

Platyhelminthes the phylum to which flatworms, of which there are about 20,000 species, belong. There are four classes in this group: the Turbellaria (free-living worms), Cestoda (tapeworms), Trematoda (parasitic flukes) and Monogenea (flukes).

Polychaeta the class of the phylum Annelida to which worms such as the ragworm (*Nereis*), lugworm (*Arenicola*) and fan worm (*Sabella*) belong.

Porifera the phylum of invertebrate animals to which sponges, of which there are about 9000 species, belong.

Primate the mammalian order that includes monkeys, lemurs, apes and human beings. Characteristic features are manual dexterity, good binocular vision and eye-to-hand coordination. The brain is large and the primates are highly intelligent. There are two suborders, the Prosimii (lemurs) and Anthropoidea (monkeys, apes and humans).

Proboscidea the order of placental mammals to which elephants belong, characterised by having a trunk (proboscis) and tusks that are modified incisor teeth.

Prokaryotae the kingdom which includes bacteria.

Prosimii the suborder of the order Primate that includes lemurs.

Prototheria the subclass to which two groups of mammals, the monotremes, that is, the platypuses and spiny anteaters (echidnas), belong. These are the only living mammals that lay eggs.

Prototistae the kingdom, distinct from plants and animals which includes algae and Protozoans.

Pteridophyta a division of the plant kingdom

which includes the ferns. There are about 12,000 species.

Radiolaria the order to which the tiny, marine protozoan animals present in plankton belong.

Reptilia (reptiles) a class of vertebrates that were the first animals to exist entirely independently of water. Reptiles usually lay eggs, are cold-blooded and have a dry skin covered with horny scales. Modern reptiles include snakes, lizards, turtles, tortoises and crocodiles.

Rodentia an order of mammals containing rats, mice, squirrels, capybaras and beavers.

Rodents are herbivorous or omnivorous and tend to breed rapidly.

Sporozoa a class of protozoan organisms that are parasites of higher animals. An example is *Plasmodium*, which causes malaria.

Squamata the order of the class Reptilia to which lizards and snakes belong.

Turbellaria the class of the phylum Platyhelminthes to which flatworms such as *Planaria* belong.

Vertebrata a major subphylum that includes all the animals with backbones: fishes, amphibians, reptiles, birds and mammals.

Animals

amoeba phylum Protozoans.

anaconda order Squamata, class Reptilia.

ant order Hymenoptera, class Insecta, phylum Arthropoda.

apes order Primate, class Mammalia.

bat order Chiroptera, class Mammalia.

beaver order Rodentia, class Mammalia.

bee order Hymenoptera, class Insecta, phylum Arthropoda.

beetle order Coleoptera, class Insecta, phylum Arthropoda.

birds class Aves.

boa order Squamata, class Reptilia.

butterfly order Lepidoptera, class Insecta, phylum Arthropoda.

camels order Artiodactyla, class Mammalia.

capybara order Rodentia, class Mammalia.

cat suborder Fissipedia, order Carnivora, class Mammalia.

caterpillar order Lepidoptera, class Insecta, phylum Arthropoda.

cattle order Artiodactyla, class Mammalia.

centipede subclass Chilopoda, class Myriapoda, phylum Arthropoda.

chameleon order Squamata, class Reptilia.

cobra order Squamata, class Reptilia.

cockroach order Orthoptera, class Insecta, phylum Arthropoda.

conch class Gastropoda, phylum Molluska.

corals class Actinozoa, phylum Cnidaria.

sea anemone class Actinozoa, phylum Cnidaria.

cricket order Orthoptera, class Insecta, phylum Arthropoda.

deer order Artiodactyla, class Mammalia.

dog order Carnivora, class Mammalia.

dolphin order Cetacea, class Mammalia.

dragonfly order Odonata, class Insecta, phylum Arthropoda.

earthworm class Oligochaeta, phylum Annelida.

leech class Hirudinea, phylum Annelida .

elephant order Proboscidea, class Mammalia.

fanworm class Polychaeta, phylum Annelida.

fish (bony) class Osteichthyes.

fish (cartilaginous) class Chondrichthytes.

fly order Diptera class Insecta, phylum Arthropoda.

frog class Amphibia.

gila monster order Squamata, class Reptilia.

goat order Artiodactyla, class Mammalia.

grasshopper order Orthoptera, class Insecta phylum Arthropoda.

hagfish order Cyclostomata, class Agnatha.

hedgehog order Insectivora, class Mammalia.

hippopotamus order Artiodactyla, class Mammalia.

horse order Perissodactyla, class Mammalia.

human species Homo sapiens, genus Homo, family Hominidae, order Primate, class Mammalia.

ichneumon fly order Hymenoptera, class Insecta, phylum Arthropoda.

iguana order Squamata, class Reptilia.

jellyfish class Hydrozoa, phylum Cnidaria.

kangaroo order Metatheria, class Mammalia.

killer whale order Cetacea, class Mammalia.

king crab class Arachnida, phylum Arthropoda.

koala order Metatheria, class Mammalia.

lamprey order Cyclostomata, class Agnatha.

lampshell class Bivalvia, phylum Brachiopoda.

leaf hopper order Hemiptera, class Insecta, phylum Arthropoda.

leech class Hirudinea, phylum Annelida .

limpet class Gastropoda, phylum Molluska.

llama order Artiodactyla, class Mammalia.

lobster order Decapoda, class Crustacea, phylum Arthropoda.

crab order Decapoda, class Crustacea, phylum Arthropoda.

locust order Orthoptera, class Insecta, phylum Arthropoda.

lugworm class Polychaeta, phylum Annelida.

mamba order Squamata, class Reptilia.

mammoth order Proboscidea, class Mammalia.

marsupial subclass Metatheria, class Mammalia.

mice order Rodentia, class Mammalia.

millipede subclass Diplopoda, class Myriapoda, phylum Arthropoda .

mites class Arachnida, phylum Arthropoda.

mole order Insectivora, class Mammalia.

monitor lizard order Squamata, class Reptilia.

monkey order Primate, class Mammalia.

mosquito order Diptera, class Insecta, phylum Arthropoda.

moths order Lepidoptera, class Insecta, phylum Arthropoda.

nautilus class of Cephalopoda, the phylum Molluska .

newt class Amphibia.

octopus class Cephalopoda, phylum Molluska.

opossum order Metatheria, class Mammalia.

pig order Artiodactyla, class Mammalia.

platypus order Prototheria, class Mammalia.

polyp class Actinozoa, phylum Coelenterata.

prawn subclass Malacostraca, class Crustacea, phylum Arthropoda.

praying mantis order Orthoptera, class Insecta, phylum Arthropoda.

racoon order Carnivora, class Mammalia.

ragworm class Polychaeta, phylum Annelida.

rat class Rodentia, order Mammalia.

rattlesnake class Squamata, order Reptilia.

ray class Chondrichthyes.

rhinoceros order Perissodactyla, class Mammalia.

roundworm phylum Nematoda.

salamander class Amphibia.

sawfly order Hymenoptera, class Insecta, phylum Arthropoda.

scale insect order Hemiptera class Insecta phylum Arthropoda.

scorpion class Arachnida, phylum Arthropoda.

sea cucumber, **sea daisy**, .

sea lily, **sea urchin** phylum Echinodermata.

sea lion and **seal** order Carnivora, class Mammalia.

sea snake order Squamata, class Reptilia.

shark class Chondrichthyes.

sheep order Artiodactyla, class Mammalia.

shrimp subclass Malacostraca, class Crustacea phylum Arthropoda.

skate class Chondrichthyes .

slug, **snail** class Gastropoda, phylum Molluska.

snake order Squamata, class Reptilia.

spider class Arachnida, phylum Arthropoda.

spiny anteater order Prototheria, class Mammalia.

squid class Cephalopoda, phylum Molluska.

squirrel order Rodentia, class Mammalia.

starfish phylum Echinodermata.

tapeworm class Cestoda, phylum Platyhelminthes.

tapir order Perissodactyla, class Mammalia.

terrapin order Chelonia, class Reptilia.

tick class Arachnida, phylum Arthropoda.

toad *class* Amphibia.

tortoise order Chelonia, class Reptilia.

turtle order Chelonia, class Reptilia.

vampire bat order Chiroptera, class Mammalia.

viper order Squamata, class Reptilia.

walrus suborder Pinnepedia, order Carnivora, class Mammalia.

wasp order Hymenoptera, class Insecta, phylum Arthropoda.

water boatman order Hemiptera, class Insecta, phylum Arthropoda.

weevil order Coleoptera, class Insecta, phylum Arthropoda.

whale order Cetacea, class Mammalia.

whelk class Gastropoda, phylum Molluska.

zebra order Perissodactyla, class Mammalia.

Letter Writing

Presentation and Layout

Address of the sender

There are certain conventions to be observed when considering the layout of a letter. One of these concerns the address of the sender. This, including the postcode, should be placed in the top right -hand corner of the sheet of paper. Formerly it was standard practice to indent each line of the address and this is still common today, as:

> 23 Park Drive,
> Seafield,
> Blackshire,
> RA14 2TY

However, it is now becoming customary not to indent the lines of the sender's address but simply to have the first letter of the second line placed immediately under the first letter of the first line and so on, as:

> 23 Park Drive,
> Seafield,
> Blackshire,
> RA14 2TY

It was formerly the practice to place a comma at the end of each line of the address of the sender. Now, however, there is a general tendency to use less punctuation than was formerly the case, and it is now common to dispense with punctuation in addresses, whether or not they are indented.

Abbreviations in addresses

Abbreviations are common in some parts of addresses, although the full forms are also frequently used in some cases. When abbreviations are used, the question of whether or not to put a full stop arises. Abbreviations that are formed from the first and last letters of words and are in fact contractions and should not be given full stops. Thus you would use *Rd* (or *Road*), *St* (or *Street*), *Mt* (or *Mount*), *Mr* (*Mister* is rarely used), and so on.

In the case of abbreviations that are not contractions but abbreviations that are simply the beginning letters of words, full stops were formerly required, as *ref.* for *reference*, and *Esq.* (*Esquire* is rarely used). Nowadays, however, there has been a general decline in the amount of punctuation used and such abbreviations are now frequently found without full stops, *ref* and *Esq*, for example.

The names of counties are frequently abbreviated in addresses. Since these are not abbreviations that are contractions but abbreviations in the same category as *ref.* for *reference* described above, abbreviations of counties would formerly always have ended with a full stop, as *Lancs.* for *Lancashire*, but nowadays, following a general decrease in punctuation, they are frequently found without a full stop, as *Yorks* for *Yorkshire*.

Postcode

The postcode is often placed on a separate line after the county, as opposite. Alternatively, it can be placed on the same line as the county, although this sometimes makes for rather a long line, and is discouraged by the post office.

Telephone number

Telephone number

Some people choose to put their telephone number on letters, and certainly it can often be useful to the recipient of a letter, if not entirely necessary. The positioning of a telephone number, and, if appropriate, the fax number, is to some extent a matter of taste. The telephone number can be placed under the postcode, usually leaving a blank line between the postcode and the telephone number, in line with the first line of the address where this has been indented, as:

```
                                    23 Park Drive,
                                       Seafield,
                                         Blackshire,
                                            RA14 2TY

                                    Tel: 01X1 222444
```

Since the date also has to be placed somewhere with the address, the right-hand corner of your sheet of paper can become quite crowded, and some people choose to place the telephone number somewhere at the top of the left-hand side of the paper. It is sometimes positioned on the same line as the first line of the address, as:

```
  Tel: 01X1 222444                 23 Park Drive,
                                    Seafield,
                                    Blackshire,
                                    RA14 2TY
```

Alternatively, the telephone number can be placed on the same line as another line of the address, often that of the postcode, as:

```
                                    23 Park Drive,
                                    Seafield,
                                    Blackshire,
  Tel: 01X1 222444                 RA14 2TY
```

Pre-printed letterheads

Some people choose to take some of the trouble out of the layout of letters by having their addresses pre-printed on their writing paper. Of course this is standard practice on business stationery and the majority of larger companies spend quite a lot of time, effort and money on acquiring an eye-catching design that will reflect what they wish to project as their corporate image. It will normally include their name, address, telephone number and fax number, often along the top of the page. However, many private individuals now have pre-printed letterheads for both personal and business stationery. In the case of personal stationery, some people choose to have their pre-printed letterhead centred at the top of the page instead of having it in the more traditional place at the top right-hand corner of the page. Others choose to have their telephone number included, but others choose simply to have their addresses printed and to write their telephone numbers on those letters that they wish to carry it.

Date

The date should be placed under the postcode. There is often a line left blank between the postcode and the date. In cases where the lines of the address are indented the date is usually aligned with the first line of the address, as:

Address of recipient

```
                                    23 Park Drive,
                                    Seafield,
                                       Blackshire,
                                         RA14 2TY.

                                    24 May 2002
```

Various forms of the date are possible. Some people opt for the style given above, i.e. *24 May* 2002 but some prefer to use *24th May* 2002. Others again adopt the style that is more common in North America, i.e. *May 24,* 2002. Putting the date in numbers only is also a possibility, i.e. *24/5/02* or *24:5:0*. People who prefer to use numbers in dates should be aware that in North America the month is placed first, rather than the day of the month. Thus *24 May 2002* would be *5/24/02*.

Address of recipient

If you are writing a personal letter there is no need to include the address of the person to whom the letter is being sent, but if you are sending a business letter you should include this. It should be placed on the left-hand side of the paper starting on the line after the date. Unlike the address of the sender, the address of the person to whom the letter is being sent is not usually indented. If the name of the person to whom your business letter is addressed is known to you, this should be included as well, as:

```
Tel: 01X1 222444               23 Park Drive,
                               Seafield,
                                  Blackshire,
                                    RA14 2TY
24 May 1966

Mr James Black
The Manager,
Cosmo Furniture Store,
12–15 King Street,
Seafield,
Blackshire,
RA11 6DR
```

Often in a business communication the date is put at the right-hand corner, not immediately under the address of the sender, but aligned with the postcode of the address of the intended recipient, as:

```
Tel: 01X1 222444               23 Park Drive,
                               Seafield,
                                  Blackshire,
                                    RA14 2TY
Mr James Black
The Manager,
Cosmo Furniture Store,
12–15 King Street,
Seafield,
Blackshire,
RA11 6DR                               24 May 1966
```

Companies in addresses

Nowadays it is quite common to omit the *Mr*. Only the name is used, as *James Black,* but this is considered by some people to be a little informal.

If a first name is reduced to an initial this was formerly always followed by a full stop, as *Mr J. Black.* It is best to follow this convention but nowadays it is quite common to find initials without full stops as the general level of punctuation has decreased.

Companies in addresses

The name of some companies is followed by *Ltd*, indicating that they are limited companies. Others are followed by *plc* or *PLC*, indicating that they are public limited companies:

The Manager,
The World Book Company plc,
43 Potter Row,
Lindon,
W1P 6DKW

The Managing Director,
Smithfield Properties Ltd,
34 Station Road,
Birchingham,
B2P 6RPJ

Reference numbers

If you are replying to a business letter you should quote any reference number that is on it as this will speed up the process of dealing with the contents of your letter. If you have a reference you should also include it, although this is less likely if you are a private individual who is writing a business letter rather than an employee of a firm writing on its behalf.

The word 'reference' is usually abbreviated and formerly was always spelt with a full stop, although the full stop is now frequently omitted. The reference number is usually placed under the date and on the same line as the first line of the recipient's address, as:

Tel: 01X1 222444

23 Park Drive,
Seafield,
Blackshire,
RA14 2TY

24 May 1966
Ref. JM/Dk19

The Manager
Cosmo Furniture Store,
12–15 King Street,
Seafield,
Blackshire,
RA11 6DR

Opening greeting

The opening greeting should begin at the edge of the page and be placed under the last line of the recipient's address, where this has been included, often with a line left blank, as:

The Manager,
Cosmo Furniture Store,
12–15 King Street,
Seafield,
RA11 6DR.

Dear Sir,

Opening greeting

In the case of personal letters where there is no recipient's address the opening greeting should go at the left-hand side after the date, usually with a line left blank, as:

> 23 Park Drive,
> Seafield,
> Blackshire,
> RA14 2TY.
> 24 May 1966
>
> Dear Mary,

How you address the intended recipient of your letter in your opening greeting depends on who the person is and on your relationship to the person. If you know it is a man to whom you are writing but you do not know his name, it is still standard practice to write *Dear Sir*. This sounds very formal in these rather informal days and there are people who are in favour of using the title or job of the person addressed in your opening greeting, as:

Dear Manager,

Dear Personnel Officer,

If you are comfortable with this form of address and you are confident that the person to whom you are writing will find it perfectly acceptable then that is fine. Of course the problem is that you might not be in a position to know that such a greeting will be acceptable to the intended recipient.

This approach does at least have the advantage that a greeting that denotes the job of the recipient of your letter is likely to be unisex. This gets around the problem of not knowing whether the person to whom your letter is addressed is a man or a woman.

If you know that the person to whom your letter is addressed is a woman and do not know her name, then the standard conventional greeting is *Dear Madam*. This sounds even more formal than *Dear Sir*, but at the moment the only way around this is to adopt the style mentioned above of greeting the person in terms of the person's job.

The situation is even worse if you do not know the sex of the person to whom you are writing. The conventional standard letter greeting in such a situation is *Dear Sir or Madam*, which sounds extremely formal indeed. It is in this situation that even *Dear Manager*, for example, might seem more acceptable to some.

If you are writing to a firm and you know very little about the set-up, it is still quite common practice to use the opening greeting *Dear Sirs*. This is used formally if you are writing to more than one man, as to the partners in a firm, without specifying who they are. *Messrs.* can also be used if you are writing to more than one man by name. This is now considered a bit old-fashioned. However, it is still used in business letters:

Dear Messrs. Brown, Green and Black,

Even if you do know the name of the person to whom you are writing, your problems are not over. Not so long ago there would have been no problem. You would either have been on first name terms with someone or you would not have been. Friends and family members were addressed at the beginning of a letter by their first names, such as *Dear James* or *Dear Jane* or by their relationship to you, as *Dear Mother* or *Dear Father*. Business correspondents who were known to you were addressed in such terms as *Dear Mr Brown* or *Dear Miss James*.

Closing greeting

Nowadays things have changed a bit. If you know someone's name but do not know him or her well enough to use just a first name you can opt for such letter greetings as *Dear Peter Smith* or *Dear Anne Jones*, this being considered less formal than *Dear Mr Smith* or *Dear Miss Jones* and a kind of halfway house between these and the familiar *Dear Peter* or *Dear Anne*. It is a convention that was much disliked by some people at first but is now becoming widespread.

This new convention gets around the problem of how to address women, whether to call them *Miss*, *Mrs* or *Ms*, it being very difficult to establish the marital status of all the women to whom one might write. *Ms*, which can refer to all women, removes the need to know whether a woman is married or not.

Closing greeting

This is placed under the last paragraph—there is often a blank line between the two—and above the signature. Some choice is possible as to the positioning of the closing greeting. There are some people who prefer to place it towards the right, as:

I hope that you will attend to this matter as soon as possible.
Yours sincerely,

Others prefer to place the closing greeting towards the left, as:

I hope that you will attend to this matter as soon as possible.
Yours sincerely,

Others again prefer to place the closing greeting in the centre, as;

I hope that you will attend to this matter as soon as possible.
Yours sincerely,

The closing greeting can take various forms. It was formerly the strict convention that letters that began with the opening greeting *Dear Sir* or *Dear Madam* should end with the closing greeting *Yours faithfully*. Many people still adhere to this convention but others feel that it is peculiar and inappropriate to bring the concept of faithfulness into a letter to someone whom one does not know, it not really being a situation where the concept of fidelity is relevant. On the whole it sounds rather stuffy in what is an age that is much less formal than previous ages.

People who dislike *Yours faithfully* or feel that it is inappropriate opt for *Yours sincerely*, even when they use the opening greeting *Dear Sir* or *Dear Madam*. Formerly this was used only when the opening greeting was more personal. Thus, if you began a letter *Dear Mr Jones* or *Dear Mrs Smith* you would close it with *Yours sincerely*. If it was even more personal and you began your letter with *Dear John* or *Dear Mary* you would still close it with *Yours sincerely*, unless the person was a close friend or relative, in which case you might opt for something more affectionate. The *Yours sincerely* convention still applies, except that its use has been extended in some cases to more formal letters.

If your correspondent is a close personal friend you might choose to close the letter with something even less formal than *Yours sincerely* such as *Yours affectionately*, *Yours ever*, or just *Yours*. The closing greetings *love* or *With Love* should be kept for those correspondents for whom you have a really deep affection and with whom you have a really close relationship, although nowadays many people use the greeting very lavishly and very loosely, particularly on postcards or greetings cards.

It is sometimes useful to put a closing greeting that is warmer than *Yours sincerely* but more formal and less affectionate than those suggested for close friends or relative. In such a situation *Best wishes* or *With all best wishes* is usually quite suitable.

Signature

As has been mentioned above, the signature is placed under the closing greeting, usually with a blank line between them. Since not everyone's signature is legible—indeed some people seem to pride themselves on the very illegibility of their signatures—it is important to place your name underneath your signature so that people are in no doubt about the identity of the writer of the letter and in no doubt about the exact name of the person to whom they should address a reply, as:

> I hope that you will attend to this matter as soon as possible.
>
> Yours sincerely,
>
> *John Burns*
>
> John Burns

In business letters it is also a good idea to include your position in an organization or firm where this is relevant, as:

> I hope that you will attend to this matter as soon as possible.
>
> Yours sincerely,
>
> *John Burns*
>
> John Burns
> Club Secretary

Sometimes people sign letters on behalf of someone else. This is particularly common in the case of a secretary or assistant who signs a letter for a boss who has written a letter, or who is at least responsible for it, but is unable to sign it because of absence from the office, for example. This often appears as follows:

> I hope that you will attend to this matter as soon as possible.
>
> Yours sincerely,
>
> *Lorraine Green*
>
> Lorraine Green
> p.p. John Burns

However, *p.p.* does not stand for *on behalf of*, as is generally assumed, but is an abbreviation of the Latin phrase *per procurationem*, meaning *by proxy*. Thus, *p.p.* should really precede the name of the person signing the letter rather than the name of the

Addressing envelopes

person on whose behalf the letter is being signed, but modern practice does not follow this.

The practice of getting someone else to sign one's letters is a practice disliked by many people, and they are offended when they receive one, particularly if it is not a circular. The theory behind the practice is that letters might get unduly delayed if the person who had written was going to be out of the office for some time.

It is important to remember to sign your letters. If you are in a hurry it is all to easy to type a letter on the word processor, print it out and put it in an envelope without signing it. Since you will have typed your name on it there will be no problem for the recipient in identifying the sender, but unsigned letters can cause offence.

Addressing envelopes

When you are addressing envelopes you should ideally start writing about halfway down the envelope but legibilty is the most important thing about addressing an envelope.

The conventions relating to addressing envelopes are similar to those relating to writing addresses in letters. The person's name goes on the first line and the address follows. The house number, not forgetting flat number where relevant, and street comes first in the address, followed by the town, county and postcode.

As is the case with addresses in letters, the address on envelopes is frequently indented. However, it is now common for the lines of the address to be placed one under the other with no indentation, as:

> Mr John Burns
> Flat 3
> 23 Whitehill Street
> SEAFIELD
> Blackshire
> RA9 5JX

As is the case with addresses in letters, there is often minimal punctuation on envelope addresses nowadays, so commas are not necessary.

Some people choose to print addresses in block capital letters for clarity. Others write most of the address in ordinary handwriting but print the town in block capital letters, especially if this is a large town to make it more prominent, a feature appreciated by those involved in the postal service

Main text

Much of the information relating to the main text of the letter will relate either to the actual content or to the language and style, which is dealt with in the next chapter, but there are some features of it that are connected with how the letter looks, and so should be dealt with under presentation.

Headings

If you are writing a business letter, and particularly if there is likely to be a series of letters on a specific subject, it is useful to put a heading at the top of your letter so that your recipient can see immediately what the letter is about. If such a heading is

Paragraphs

used it should be underlined and be placed after the opening greeting, often with a line left blank between them. The heading can be centred or placed at the left-hand side according to choice and according to the layout of the rest of the letter. For example if you intend placing your closing greeting at the left-hand side you might also decide to place the heading of the letter at the left-hand side, as:

> Dear Mr Hunt,
>
> <u>Repairs to 24 Seaview Terrace</u>

If you intend placing your closing greeting either in the centre or at the right-hand side of the page then you might well choose to position the heading in the centre of the page, particularly if you have indented the paragraphs (see below). The first paragraph begins immediately after the heading, often with a blank line between the heading and opening paragraph, as:

> Dear Mr Smith,
>
> <u>Repairs to 24 Seaview Terrace</u>
>
> I am once again writing to draw your attention to the fact that the repairs to my garage undertaken by your firm are still not complete.

Paragraphs

Information on paragraphs is given in the next chapter on style and language. However, paragraphs must also be mentioned in respect to the layout and presentation of letters.

Formerly it was the standard convention to indent the start of each new paragraph, including the first one after the opening greeting. Nowadays it is very common for paragraphs not to be indented. This also applies to the opening paragraph, as:

> Dear Mary,
>
> Thank you very much for the generous book token that you sent for my birthday. I have already exchanged it for a copy of the new biography of Dickens.
>
> I hope that you will be able to come and visit us in the summer. June would be the best month for us but let us know what suits you.

Summary

These then are some of the conventions relating to the layout and presentation of letters and envelopes. As you will have seen, there is some scope for choice in some cases, such as in the positioning of telephone and reference numbers. In addition, the general layout of a letter must be decided according to the size of the paper that you use and according to the length of your letter.

Style

As far as possible it is best to write in a style that seems natural to you as you are writing it. People who are nervous of writing are quite frequently advised to try and write as they speak, and it is particularly true of personal letters to close friends and family that the letters will be more appreciated if you write in this way. The letter will then reflect your personality and make them feel that it has brought you almost physically closer to them.

Writing as you speak, however, may not be such good advice if you are writing a formal business letter, especially if you have a very informal style of speaking.

On the other hand, you should not try to adopt an extremely formal, rather stuffy style with which you do not feel comfortable and which you really do not understand. Such a style often involves rather difficult or even old-fashioned words that you would find difficult to use with any degree of expertise.

The best advice is to try and be yourself as much as possible without being too conversational. Try reading the letter aloud to make sure that it sounds natural to you and is a true record of what you want to say and how you want to say it.

You should aim for simplicity and clarity. This often means aiming for brevity. Complicated, convoluted ways of saying something should be avoided in favour of the straightforward. Very long, complex sentences should also be avoided.

As has just been mentioned, brevity should be one of your major aims when writing business letters. People may not have the time or the inclination to read great screeds. A page and a half of A4 paper is about the extent that will be tolerated.

Overall brevity is to be praised, as long as you get in everything that absolutely has to be said. However, it is worth trying to avoid having all your sentences very short. Although this makes for clarity it also makes for rather a staccato style, which can sound rather sharp. Such a style is undoubtedly better in a business letter than a convoluted one involving very long sentences but it is better to aim for a middle way with some short sentences and some rather longer ones. This will help to create a feeling of continuity.

Another feature of letter-writing that makes for smoother flowing prose is the avoidance of sentences that all begin with the same word. If the sentences are also short this can emphasize the staccato style created by a series of short sentences. This avoidance of sentences beginning with the same word is very difficult to achieve, particularly if that word is 'I'. It is sometimes almost impossible to avoid this and one just has to live with it.

When you are writing a business letter you are not writing a literary work and so its content is more important than the style. However, you may as well aim to be as stylish as possible, which may enhance the impression that your letter will create.

Punctuation and Grammar

If you wish to create a favourable impression on the recipient of your letter, it is important to make sure that your letter is grammatical and that it is correctly punctuated. For help with these areas of language see the section in this book on **Usage and Grammar**.

Spelling

It is extremely important that business letters and more formal personal letters are spelt correctly. A list of some words that are frequently misspelt is given in the Section on **Spelling**, but you should also make sure that you have a reliable dictionary to hand so that you can check those words about which you are unsure.

Word processors and home computers often have a spelling check so that you can make sure that your piece of typing is correctly spelt. The spelling list on some of these machines, however, is not very comprehensive, and the word you wish to check may not be on it. Furthermore, you can end up with the wrong spelling even if you have checked it. A simple word processor system will accept a word if it is a correctly spelt word even if it is not the right word in the context. For example, it would accept *there shoes* when the phrase should be *their shoes* because *there* is a word, although not the correct word in the context.

Language and vocabulary

In writing letters, especially business letters or formal personal letters, you should avoid slang words and words that are exceptionally colloquial. Contracted forms, *can't, won't, isn't, we'll, I'm*, and so on, should be avoided in written formal English. Also to be avoided are jargon words, words that are technical or specialized and used by a particular group of people, such as scientists or doctors.

On the other hand, you should not try to use very formal words or very formal constructions. There used to be a number of very formal conventions used in the writing of business letters, as in *Re your letter of the 17th ult.*, but these are now considered unnecessarily stuffy. Try to keep your English as natural as possible.

Try to avoid using too many clichés, although this can be difficult, especially when you are writing personal letters in which it is not easy to find the right thing to say, such as letters of sympathy to the bereaved. See the section on **Clichés** in this book.

When writing formal letters it is always useful to keep a dictionary near to hand. If you have any doubts about the meaning of a word you should always look it up.

Content

The content of your letter, of course, depends on what message you want to get across and on the circumstances in which you find yourself. Some sample letters have been included in this chapter as guidelines only rather than to be copied. They will give you a general indication as to what is appropriate in certain situations.

For the most part they are business letters or formal personal letters from private individuals. People working for organizations, or representing them, should have guidelines already set down and may have to follow company policy over certain matters relating to correspondence.

For example, there may be an established procedure for dealing with complaints. One piece of advice is relevant to them, that is, reply promptly and be polite. Nothing annoys someone who is already annoyed more than receiving a very much delayed reply to a letter of complaint, receiving an offhand or aggressive letter or, worse, receiving no reply at all. Remember the old adage about the customer always being right—whether or not this is in fact the case.

Informal personal letters have not been dealt with here simply because they are so personal.

Letters relating to property and goods

One area of life that tends to lead us to write letters is that of possessions, whether it is property or goods that we have bought or that we are buying.

We often write to complain or to ask for damaged things to be fixed. In order to be most effective they should be brief and to the point. There is no point in going into great detail. In the case of letters of complaint they should be factual rather than emotional, and calm and restrained rather than abusive. Examples of such letters are given below.

Letters relating to property

Tel:

Address
Date

Abbeyhill Roofing Ltd
46 Abbeyhill,
Norwood
Whiteshire
NW2 4XY

Dear Sirs,

The roof of my house was damaged in the recent gales and the ceiling of one of the bedrooms is now leaking. I have contacted my insurance company and they have asked me to get three written estimates before selecting a contractor to carry out the work.

I would be glad if you could inspect the property as soon as possible and give me an estimate. Please telephone to arrange a suitable time if you are interested in submitting an estimate.

It is important that the work is carried out urgently.

Yours sincerely,

Tom Henderson

Tom Henderson

Tel:

Address
Date

Mr Mark Garden
Central Construction Ltd
Craigpark
Whiteshire
CP12 8TY.

Dear Mr Garden,

I am writing to confirm in writing my telephone acceptance of your estimate dated 5th March for work to the stonework of my garage.

I understand that work will begin on 19th March and will take about two days.

I look forward to seeing you on the 19th.

Yours sincerely,

Ann Blackridge

Ann Blackridge

Tel: Address
                                                            Date

Michael Little
Greenfingers
Landscape Gardeners
46 Station Road
Craigpark
Whiteshire
CP12 P34

Dear Michael Little,

   Thank you for submitting an estimate for landscaping the garden at the above address and for doing so promptly.

   Unfortunately I am writing to say that I am not accepting your estimate. It was a good deal higher than those that were submitted by other firms.

Yours sincerely,

Phillip Smith

Philip Smith

Tel: Address
                                                            Date

Mr Frank Smith
Manager
Slating and Roofing Contractors
16 Scott Street
Craigpark
Whiteshire
CP19 6KM

Dear Mr Smith,

Repairs to Roof at 56 Wood Road

   Your firm recently completed some repairs to the roof of my house. I have to tell that you that I am not at all satisfied with the work.

   The first time that it rained, the ceiling in one of the upstairs bedrooms leaked.

   I have tried without success to contact you by telephone and left several messages with your secretary. I have been forced to write since you have not returned any of my calls.

   The faulty work must be put right as soon as possible. Please get in touch either by telephone or by letter to make an appointment to come and inspect the roof and to arrange a date for it to be put right.

   I chose your firm on the personal recommendation of a

Presentation and layout

friend and I am extremely disappointed to have been let down.

I look forward to hearing from you right away.

Yours sincerely,

Sarah Jones

Sarah Jones

Tel: Address

Date

Dimble's Fashion Catalogue
65 Kingsway
Brownpool
Longshire
BP5 5TY

Dear Sirs,

Catalogue No. HT 2398

I have just received the dress that I ordered for my grand-daughter from your catalogue on 4th May. It has not reached the standard that I have come to expect from your company.

My granddaughter tried the dress on when it arrived and I was angry and disappointed to find that the sewing on both the hem and the seam on the left-hand side was undone. In addition there is a dark stain on the white collar of the dress, suggesting that the dress has either been worn before or tried on without due care being taken.

As you can imagine my granddaughter was very upset, particularly since she had planned to wear the dress to her birthday party. There is really nothing that can compensate her for this disappointment.

I have not enclosed the dress referred to since I see no reason why I should go to any further expense by paying for packaging and postage. However, I will be glad to receive either a full refund or an undamaged dress together with instructions about returning the damaged one at your expense.

I would hope that any further orders that I place with your company will be dealt with in a more satisfactory way. Meanwhile I look forward to hearing your comments on the present situation.

Yours sincerely,

Robert Atkinson

Robert Atkinson

Tel: Address
                                    Date

Mr Pierre Bouleau,
Bon Appetit,
60 Princes Street
Brownwich
Broadshire
BR13 8FY.

Dear Pierre,

As you know my family and I have been regular clients of your restaurant since it opened two years ago. Until our visit last Saturday we had always been extremely satisfied and had recommended it to several of our friends.

Unfortunately we will not be recommending it to anyone else unless things improve greatly since we were disappointed by both the food and the service on our last visit. The food we were served was not up to anything like your previous standard and was served cold by sullen waitresses who could not have cared less.

We gather from friends that you have opened another restaurant in the area and are spending some time concentrating on that. However, the clients of your original restaurant deserve attention as well – otherwise we will go elsewhere.

I look forward to hearing your views on the subject.

Yours sincerely,

John Burns

John Burns

Letters relating to employment

Many of the letters that we find we have to write relate to employment. A letter of resignation is one kind of letter that we may have to write at some point in our working life, although because of the high unemployment ratio now these are much less common than they once were. Not very long ago people could resign before they found another job, safe in the knowledge that they would do so easily.

Of course, people still do resign from their jobs and when they do, many of them have to formalize this by putting the fact in writing. Here, as in the case of many business letters, you should aim for brevity. However much you hated the job or however badly you think you have been treated, you should not be abusive.

There is no point in trying to settle old scores in your letter of resignation. You may feel that it would do you a lot of good to tell your employers what they can do with their job, but you should think of the future. Even if you did not need a reference from your employers for the job that you have just obtained, you may need one in the future. Since you will have to indicate your employment record on your CV, the employers you are now leaving may be contacted in the future by prospective employers.

Letters relating to unemployment

Then there is another point to be considered. In the case of large companies, bosses move around as well as employees. Who knows? The boss to whom you are now being abusive in writing may well one day end up as your boss again.

There is much to be said, therefore, for writing a letter of resignation that will keep relations with your ex-employers as warm as possible. If you can possibly bring your-self to do it, you should include something positive about how you feel about your years of employment with them. It may even be true.

Letters of application are much more common than letters of resignation. These take two forms—letters applying for advertised posts and letters written to investigate possible job opportunities.

The latter are mostly written by young people who are just leaving school or further education and seeking their first job. Since finding a first job is an extremely difficult task, job-seekers so doing should be prepared to bombard firms that operate in the areas in which they are most interested.

They should be prepared to be disappointed on two counts. Obviously there may be no job available and they may get a letter of rejection. Often more discouraging is the fact that they may receive no acknowledgement of their letters at all.

If you are writing a letter that is not a reply to an advertisement you may well not know to whom you should send your letter. In the case of reasonably large firms you should address letters of application to the personnel manager. If the firm does not have an employee of this title the letters will be passed to the person in the company who deals with employment. Your letter should contain a CV and a brief typed letter trying to sell yourself and your skills to the firm.

If the letter is a reply to an advertisement you should obviously comply with the requests made by it. Sometimes a CV is asked for, in which case you should send a brief letter accompanying it in which you state why you are right for the job.

CVs often look remarkably similar to each other and so it is a good idea to try and personalize your letter to bring favourable attention to your application.

Both the CV and the letter should be typed unless otherwise stated. It is becoming increasingly common for firms to ask for letters of application to be handwritten. Many firms and organizations send out application forms. These can be quite challenging, especially if they ask such questions as 'Why do you want this post?' or 'What qualities do you feel you could bring to this post?' and can take considerable time to complete.

The CV has become a central part of most job applications. Given the difficulty of finding a job and the importance of presenting yourself in as positive a way as possible, many people get their CVs compiled by one of the professional agencies that have been set up to provide such a service. The CV is very important and must be correctly spelt, neatly set out and give a general air of professionalism.

There has been a recent change in attitudes to CVs. Until relatively recently it was the preferred practise to put just about everything the applicant had ever done or was ever interested in on the CV. This often made for a very long and crowded document and took a long time for prospective employers to digest. Furthermore, particularly in the case of school leavers or new graduates, many of the CVs are remarkably similar.

For these reasons there is now a tendency to keep the CV fairly brief and to treat it more as record of qualifications and employment. Employers have grown to rely more on the letter accompanying the CV than on the CV itself. Such letters are an opportunity for applicants to sell themselves to prospective employers and should be a brief account of all the features, qualifications and experience that make you ideal for the advertised post.

Resignation

Tel: Address
                                                                        Date

Mr Frank Brown
Personnel Manager
Lomond Financial Services
35 Milton Street
Neathing
Whiteshire
NT12 8DR

Dear Mr Brown,

I am writing to inform you of my decision to resign from the company. As is required by the conditions of my contract I am giving you four weeks' notice, which begins today.

My reason for leaving is that I have obtained a more senior post with Carlton Investment Services.

I have very much enjoyed working with Lomond Financial Services and I shall be sorry to leave. However, at the moment there is little opportunity for promotion at my level and so I feel that I must move on.

Yours sincerely,

Richard Todd

Richard Todd

Job application

Tel: Address
                                                                        Date

Ms Diane Brand,
Personnel Manager
Moneywise Insurance Ltd
47 Castle Road
Laddington
Redshire
LD3 9 RT

Dear Ms Brand,

I am writing in reply to your advertisement in 'The Chronicle' of 5th August for a nursery assistant in the crèche run by your firm for children of employees.

As you will see from my CV, I have just left school and am taking a year out before taking up a place at Neath Teachers' Training College. When I graduate I would like to find a post teaching younger children in the primary school and I am therefore looking for a job working with young children during my year out to gain some experience.

Job application

I am extremely interested in the advertised post and think that I have the right experience and personality for the job. Since I have three sisters who are much younger than me and several young cousins, I am used to dealing with young children. I frequently baby-sit for my own family and also for several of our neighbours.

I like working with children, which is why I am making primary teaching my career. However, I do appreciate that working with them requires great energy, enthusiasm, initiative and patience and I would bring all these qualities to the post of nursery assistant.

As to leisure activities, I play the piano and the guitar and like dancing and painting. All these activities are useful to people who are working with children.

References can be obtained from the head teacher of my school, Mr Peter Sharp, and from Ms Jean Peden, a neighbour for whom I baby-sit frequently. Their addresses and telephone numbers are given in my CV.

I look forward to hearing from you.

Yours sincerely,

Joanna Smart

Joanna Smart

Tel: **Address**
                                                    Date

Ms Esther Martin
Editorial Director
Paragon Publishing Ltd
30 Blandford Lane,
Kingsferry
Whiteshire
KF15 7KL

Dear Ms Martin

I am about to graduate from Glasburgh University with an Honours Degree in English Language and am interested in obtaining a post in the publishing industry. Although I would welcome the opportunity to work in any of the areas of publishing I would prefer the editorial area.

Most of my family are engaged in the publishing industry in some form and I have wanted to be in publishing since before I left school. With that in mind I have had various temporary jobs and periods of work experience involving books, as you will see from my CV, which I enclose.

Since these jobs have included work as an assistant editor on an encyclopedia, work in the design department of a publishing house, work as a production assistant on a magazine and a regular Saturday job at my local bookseller's, I feel that I have the right background to enter publishing. In addition, I have been the assistant editor of our student newspaper for two years.

My hobbies include photography and writing. I have had several articles published in 'The Forth Review', our local weekly newspaper, mostly in the form of theatre reviews.

I am a good communicator and work well under pressure. I am used to working with computers and took a word processing course before going to university.

I look forward to hearing from you.

Yours sincerely,

Sarah Brown

Sarah Brown

CV (Curriculum Vitae)

NB It is important that these are set out neatly and attractively. Some people choose to take advantage of the potential of home computers and word processors to use a selection of type sizes and typefaces, but too much variety can be rather distracting and even ugly. The suggested CV below relates only to the content.

CV	
Name	John Smith
Address	65 Queen's Road
	Blackford
	Whiteshire
	BD14 7 RT
Telephone	01X1 666888
Date of birth	24 February 1951
Nationality	British
Marital status	divorced
Secondary education	
1962–68	Raxworth Grammar School
	25 Beach Road
	High Raxworth
	Braxshire
	RX4 8DG
O' levels	
	English, French, Maths, Spanish, History, German, Geography, Art
'A' levels	
	English Grade A, French Grade B, Spanish Grade B

References

Further Education
1968–1971 Glasburgh University
     Dean Square
     Glasburgh
     Blackshire
     GB3 9RF

Degree BA (Honours) French and German
    Upper Second class

Employment
1971–1978 Translator Publications Dept
     Unitech Ltd Newridge

1978–1987 Head of Translation
     Publications Dept
     Chemec plc
     Birchingham

1987–2001 Chief Translator
     Chemec plc
     New York

Leisure Activities Golf, hill-walking, photography, cinema, theatre-going.

Referees

Robert Adams	Peter Schwartz
Editorial Director	Head of Publications
Publications	Unitech Ltd
Chemec plc	Newridge
37 Sea Way	Newshire
Brownpool	NR4 8RT
Newshire	
BL5 9KL	

References

Tel: Address
               Date

Ms Jane White
Head Teacher
St Mark's Secondary School
5 School Lane
Stonyburn
Blackshire
SB12 7TY

Dear Ms White,

Letters of condolence

I am writing to ask if I may use you as one of my referees for a job for which I am applying. The job is clerical assistant with Global Insurance.

I left school at the end of the summer term and passed 6 GCSEs. Since then I have been working as an au pair in France.

I was a pupil at St Mark's from 1986–1992. In my last year I was in Ms Peter's form class.

I hope that you will be able to help.

Yours sincerely

Joan Rogers

Joan Rogers

Letters of condolence

Unless we are away from home for some time it is unusual for many of us to write personal letters as the telephone is more convenient. However, there a few situations where a reasonably formal letter is required. One of these situations occurs with the death of someone we know reasonably well but who is not a close friend. In the case of close friends we would probably visit the bereaved person and send an informal note. In cases such as the death of a work colleague, it is more appropriate to send a short, reasonably formal letter. It is often hard to think of anything to write that will bring comfort, but many recipients of such letters find comfort just in the fact that people have thought highly enough of their relative to write.

It is difficult to avoid clichés in letters of sympathy and condolence, but bereavement is not an area in which striving for originality is particularly appropriate. In the circumstances a few clichés are probably quite acceptable. Unless your handwriting is completely illegible it is better to write, rather than type, letters of sympathy as it seems much more personal.

Tel: Address
                                                                                                  Date

Dear Mrs Hughes,

I was so sorry to hear of the sudden death of your husband. Please accept my deepest sympathy.

It is some time since I saw Peter but we were good friends when I worked with him at G & H Law's. I particularly enjoyed his good sense of humour. He could cheer us all up when we were feeling low.

He will be much missed by his colleagues at Law's and also by the community in general. He gave so much of his time to raising funds for charity.

I know that your family will be round you at this time but if there is anything I can do please do not hesitate to get in touch.

With kind regards,
Yours sincerely,

Maureen Brown

Letters of thanks

Letters of thanks

The other situation in which it is often better to write a personal letter rather than telephone is with letters giving thanks for gifts or for some act of kindness. Some people feel insulted if no written message of thanks is sent.

Just as letters of bereavement require a marked degree of sensitivity, so to do letters of thanks, especially those in response to presents. Often they require a degree of tact as totally unsuitable presents often have to be acknowledged as well as acceptable ones. It is often difficult also to decide how to fill the space. You can keep the message brief, but you have to do better than two lines. However much or little you choose to write you should write the letter by hand.

Tel: Address
Date

Dear Margaret,

Thank you very much for having me to stay over Easter. It was very kind of you to invite me and I really appreciated being part of a family again. As you know both my children are working abroad this year and I miss them.

It was very pleasant to get out of the bustle of London for a few days. I must say that you live in a very beautiful part of the world and it was good to have time to explore it. I could not believe that the weather was so warm at this time of year.

I would love to return your hospitality. If ever any of you, or preferably all of you, feel like a few days in London, just get in touch. You will be very welcome. I know you were glad to leave London for the country but it has its compensations.

With very many thanks,

Yours sincerely,

Lorraine Green

Tel: Address
Date

Dear Great-Aunt Gertrude,

I am writing to thank you very much for the birthday present that you sent me. It was kind of you to remember, although I feel that I am reaching the age when I would be better forgetting birthdays.

The silk scarf was absolutely lovely. The purple colour will go really well with my new winter coat. It needs a bright colour to cheer it up a bit.

I hope that you are well and are getting out a bit despite this depressing winter weather. When the weather improves you must think of coming up to London. Do let me know if you would like to come. We would all love to see you.

With many thanks and best wishes,

Love,

Jill